GURPS

Fourth Edition

Basic Set: Characters

GURPS Game Design by STEVE JACKSON
GURPS Fourth Edition Revision by DAVID L. PULVER and SEAN M. PUNCH
Cover Design by VICTOR R. FERNANDES
Cover Art by JOHN ZELEZNIK
Edited by ANDREW HACKARD and STEVE JACKSON

Illustrated by ABRAR AJMAL, ALEX FERNANDEZ, TED GALADAY, ERIC LOFGREN,
JOHN MORIARTY, TORSTEIN NORDSTRAND, GLEN OSTERBERGER, V. SHANE,
BOB STEVLIC, ERIC WILKERSON, and JIM ZUBKAVICH

ISBN 978-1-55634-729-0

6 7 8 9 10

STEVE JACKSON GAMES

President/Editor-in-Chief/*GURPS* System Design ▌ STEVE JACKSON

Chief Executive Officer ▌ PHILIP REED

Chief Operating Officer ▌ SAMUEL MITSCHKE

Managing Editor ▌ MIRANDA HORNER

GURPS Line Editor ▌ SEAN PUNCH

Production Manager ▌ SAMUEL MITSCHKE

Art Director/Page Design ▌ PHILIP REED

Production Artists ▌ JUSTIN DE WITT, ALEX FERNANDEZ, and PHILIP REED

Production Assistant ▌ BRIDGET WESTERMAN

Production Administrator ▌ DARRYLL SILVA

Prepress Checkers ▌ MIRANDA HORNER and LEONARD BALSERA

Print Buyer ▌ MARYLAND FALKENBERG

Marketing Director ▌ BRIAN ENGARD

Sales Manager ▌ ROSS JEPSON

Errata Coordinator ▌ JENNIFER ATKINSON

GURPS FAQ Maintainer ▌ VICKY "MOLOKH" KOLENKO

Infinite Worlds Concept by John M. Ford and Steve Jackson
Iconic Characters Created by Kenneth Hite
Editorial Assistance by Jeff Rose
Proofreading by Steve Jackson and Sean M. Punch

Additional Material: Kenneth Hite, Robert M. Schroeck, William H. Stoddard

Fourth Edition Testing and Rules Refinement: James Cambias, Paul Chapman, Mark Cogan, Peter V. Dell'Orto, John M. Ford, Devin L. Ganger, Robert Gilson, Kenneth Hite, Roberto Hoyle, Steven Marsh, Phil Masters, Elizabeth McCoy, Walter Milliken, Bill Oliver, Kenneth Peters, Giles Schildt, Gene Seabolt, William H. Stoddard, Michael Suileabhain-Wilson, William Toporek, Brian J. Underhill, Andy Vetromile, Hans-Christian Vortisch, Jeff Wilson, Jonathan Woodward

Helpful Comments: Michelle Barrett, Kim Bernard, T. Bone, C. Lee Davis, Shawn Fisher, Bob Portnell, Lisa Steele, Stéphane Thériault, Chad Underkoffler

Credits for earlier editions:

Additional Material: Steve Beeman, Craig Brown, Jerry Epperson, Jeff George, Scott Haring, Mike Hurst, Stefan Jones, Jim Kennedy, David Ladyman, Jeff Lease, Walter Milliken, Steffan O'Sullivan, Ravi Rai, W. Dow Rieder, Art Samuels, Scorpia, Curtis Scott

Playtest: Norman Banduch, Jeb Boyt, Keith Carter, Caroline Chase, James Crouchet, Jim Gould, Scott Haring, Rob Kirk, David Ladyman, Martha Ladyman, Creede Lambard, Sharleen Lambard, C. Mara Lee, Mike Lopez, Michael Moe, David Noel, Susan Poelma, Warren Spector, Gerald Swick, Allen Varney, Dan Willems

Blindtest: Aaron Allston, Mark Babik, Sean Barrett, Bill Barton, Vicki Barton, James D. Bergman, David Castro, Bruce Coleman, Jerry Epperson, Jeff Flowers, Dave Franz, Cheryl Freedman, Jeff George, Kevin Gona, Kevin Heacox, Carl Leatherman, Guy McLimore, Alexis Mirsky, Joseph G. Paul, Greg Poehlein, Greg Porter, Randy Porter, Mark Redigan, Glenn Spicer, John Sullivan, Rick Swan, Kirk Tate, David Tepool, Bob Traynor, Alexander von Thorn, and many others

Reality Checking: Warren Spector, Monica Stephens, Allen Varney, Jim Gould, David Noel, Rob Kirk

Research Assistance: Mike Hurst, Jeffrey K. Greason, Walter Milliken

Helpful Comments: Many of the above, plus Tim Carroll, Nick Christenson, Jim Duncan, David Dyche, Ron Findling, Mike Ford, Steve Maurer, John Meyer, Ken Rolston, Dave Seagraves, Bill Seurer, Brett Slocum, Gus Smedstad, Karl Wu, and Phil Yanov

Many thanks to everyone above – and for all the others we couldn't list.
And special thanks to everyone who enjoyed the first three editions and said so!

CONTENTS

INTRODUCTION 5
  About the Authors 6
WHAT IS ROLEPLAYING? 7
  Mini-Glossary 7
  Materials Needed for Play 8
QUICK START 8
  Metric Conversions 9

1. CREATING A
   CHARACTER 10
  Character Points 10
  Character Concept. 11
  How GURPS Works: Realism
    and Game Balance 11
  Character Types 12
  Example of Character
    Creation: Dai Blackthorn 12
  Character Creation
    Checklist 13
SAMPLE CHARACTER SHEET 13
  Things Not Shown on the
    Character Sheets 13
BASIC ATTRIBUTES 14
  How to Select
    Basic Attributes. 14
  Handedness 14
  How GURPS Works: IQ,
    Sentience, and Sapience 15
SECONDARY CHARACTERISTICS 15
DAMAGE TABLE 16
  Machines and Fatigue 16
BASIC LIFT AND
    ENCUMBRANCE TABLE 17
  Example of Character
    Creation (cont'd) 18
BUILD 18
  Size Modifier (SM) 19
  How GURPS Works:
    ST, Mass, and Move 19
  Shopping for the Big, Tall,
    Thin, and Small 20
AGE AND BEAUTY 20
  Age. 20
  Physical Appearance 21

Other Physical Features 21
  Example of Character
    Creation (cont'd) 22
SOCIAL BACKGROUND 22
  Technology Level (TL) 22
  Culture 23
  Language 23
  Sapience and Language 23
  Accents 24
  Broken to Broken 24
  Example of Character
    Creation (cont'd) 25
WEALTH AND INFLUENCE 25
  Wealth. 25
  Starting Wealth. 26
  Reputation 26
  Tech Level and Starting Wealth . . . 27
  Importance. 28
  Classless Meritocracies. 28
  Special Rules for Rank. 29
  Example of Character
    Creation (cont'd) 30
  Privilege. 30
  Social Restraints. 30
FRIENDS AND FOES 31
  Associated NPCs 31
  Contacts 31
IDENTITIES 31
  Alternate Identity vs.
    Secret Identity 31

2. ADVANTAGES 32
  Types of Advantages 32
  Advantage Origins 33
  Potential Advantages 33
  What's Allowed 34
  Turning Advantages
    Off and On 34
ADVANTAGE LIST. 34
  Frequency of Appearance 36
  Limited Defenses 46
  Alternative Attacks 61
  Perks 100
MODIFIERS 101
  Enhancements 102
  Attack Enhancements
    and Limitations 102
  Turning Enhancements
    Off and On 102
  Limitations. 110
  Optional Rule:
    Limited Enhancements. 111
  Examples of Modified
    Attacks 114
  Gadget Limitations 116
  Example of Character
    Creation (cont'd) 116
NEW ADVANTAGES 117

Modifying Existing
    Advantages 117
  Designing Entirely
    New Advantages 118

3. DISADVANTAGES. 119
  Disadvantages for Heroes 119
  Restrictions on Disadvantages. . 120
  Types of Disadvantages. 120
  Secret Disadvantages 120
  Self-Control for Mental
    Disadvantages. 120
  Self-Imposed Mental
    Disadvantages 121
  "Buying Off" Disadvantages. . . . 121
DISADVANTAGE LIST 122
  Example of Character
    Creation (cont'd) 162
QUIRKS 162
  Mental Quirks 162
  Example of Character
    Creation (cont'd) 164
  Physical Quirks 165
NEW DISADVANTAGES 165
  Modifying Existing
    Disadvantages. 165
  Brand-New Problems 166

4. SKILLS 167
  Controlling Attribute. 167
  Choosing Your
    Beginning Skills 167
  Difficulty Level. 168
  Technological Skills 168
  Tech-Level Modifiers. 168
  Prerequisites. 169
  Specialties. 169
  Grouped Skills 169
  Familiarity 169
BUYING SKILLS 170
  Skill Notation 170
  Improving Your Skills. 170

SKILL COST TABLE 170
MEANING OF SKILL LEVELS 171
  Probability of Success. 171
  Relative Skill Level 171
  Choosing Your Skill Levels 172
SKILL DEFAULTS: USING
  SKILLS YOU DON'T KNOW 173
SKILL LIST 174
  Optional Rule: Wildcard Skills . . 175
  Geographical and
    Temporal Scope. 176
  Planet Types 180
  Physiology Modifiers 181
  Skills for Design,
    Repair, and Use 190
  Example of Character
    Creation (concluded) 227
TECHNIQUES 229
  Creating Techniques 229
  Buying and Improving
    Techniques 230
TECHNIQUE COST TABLE 230
  Using Techniques 230
  Sample Combat
    Techniques 230
  Double Defaults and
    Techniques 232
  Sample Noncombat
    Techniques 232

5. MAGIC 234
  Glossary of Magical Terms. 234
LEARNING MAGIC 235
  Prerequistes 235
  Mana 235
CASTING SPELLS 235
  Distraction and Injury. 236
  Caster and Subject 236
  Time Required 236
  Energy Cost 236
  Critical Spell Failure Table 236
  Magic Rituals. 237
  Limits on Effect. 237
  Duration of Spells and
    Maintaining Spells 237
  Canceling Spells 237
  Casting Spells While
    Maintaining Other Spells . . . 238
  Ceremonial Magic 238
DIFFERENT KINDS OF MAGIC 239
  Colleges of Magic. 239
  Spell Classes. 239
  Area Spells on a Battle Map. . . . 239
  Magic Staffs 240
  Dissipating Held Melee
    and Missile Spells 241
  Long-Distance Modifiers 241
  Alternative Magic Systems 242
SPELL LIST 242
  Air Spells 242
  Body Control Spells. 244
  Communication and
    Empathy Spells. 245
  Earth Spells 245
  Enchantment Spells 246
  Fire Spells 246
  Gate Spells 247

  Healing Spells 248
  Knowledge Spells 249
  Light and Darkness Spells 249
  Meta-Spells. 250
  Mind Control Spells 250
  Movement Spells 251
  Necromantic Spells 251
  Protection and
    Warning Spells 252
  Water Spells 253

6. PSIONICS 254
  Glossary of Psi Terminology . . . 254
POWERS, TALENTS, AND ABILITIES . . . 254
  Pside Effects. 255
  Gaining New Psi Abilities. 255
USING PSI ABILITIES 255
PSIONIC POWERS. 255
  Antipsi. 255
  ESP 255
  Psychic Healing. 256
  Psychokinesis (PK) 256
  Psionics and Magic 256
  Telepathy 257
  Teleportation 257
  Examples of Psionic Powers 257
  Other Powers 257

7. TEMPLATES 258
CHARACTER TEMPLATES 258
  How to Use Character
    Templates 258
  Are Character Templates
    "Character Classes"? 259
  Sample Character Templates. . . 259
  Uniqueness 259
RACIAL TEMPLATES 260
  How to Use Racial Templates . . 261
  Sample Racial Templates 261
  Omitting Racial Traits 262
META-TRAITS 262

8. EQUIPMENT 264
  Money 264
COST OF LIVING 265
COST OF LIVING TABLE 265
  What Cost of Living
    Gets You:
    A Modern Example 266
BUYING EQUIPMENT 266
  Legality Class 267

WEAPONS 267
  Choosing Your Weapons 267
  Weapon Statistics 268
  Glossary of Arms and Armor. . . 268
  Optional Rule:
    Modifying Dice + Adds 269
  Melee Weapons 271
  Silver Weapons 275
  Muscle-Powered
    Ranged Weapons 275
  Bodkin Points. 277
  Hand Grenades and
    Incendiaries. 277
  Firearms 278
  "Smartgun" Electronics 278
  Optional Rule: Malfunction 279
  Heavy Weapons 281
ARMOR 282
  Armor Tables 282
  Wearing Armor 286
SHIELDS 287
  Carrying Weapons and
    Other Gear. 287
MISCELLANEOUS EQUIPMENT 288

9. CHARACTER
DEVELOPMENT. 290
IMPROVEMENT THROUGH
  ADVENTURE 290
  Traits Gained in Play 291
  Money. 291
  Quick Learning
    Under Pressure 292
IMPROVEMENT THROUGH STUDY . . . 292
  Jobs. 292
  Finding a Teacher. 293
  Optional Rule:
    Maintaining Skills. 294
  Learnable Advantages. 294
TRANSFORMATIONS 294
  Body Modification. 294
  Mind Transfer 296
  Supernatural Afflictions 296
  Death. 296

TRAIT LISTS 297
ADVANTAGES 297
DISADVANTAGES 299
MODIFIERS. 300
SKILLS 301
TECHNIQUES 304
SPELLS 304

ICONIC CHARACTERS 307

COMBAT LITE 324
COMBAT TURN SEQUENCE. 324
MANEUVERS 324
RANGED ATTACKS 326
ATTACKING 326
DEFENDING. 326
DAMAGE AND INJURY. 327
RECOVERY. 328
FATIGUE 328

INDEX 329

CHARACTER SHEET 335

INTRODUCTION

GURPS stands for "Generic Universal RolePlaying System." It was originally a joke . . . a code word to describe the game while we looked for a "real" name. Years went by – literally! – as the game developed. We never found a better name, and now that the Fourth Edition is in your hands, the name is more appropriate than ever.

"Generic." Some people like quick, fast-moving games, where the referee makes lots of decisions to keep things moving. Others want ultimate detail, with rules for every contingency. Most of us fall somewhere in between. **GURPS** starts with simple rules, and – especially in the combat system – builds up to as much *optional* detail as you like. But it's still the same game. You may all use it differently, but your campaigns will all be compatible.

"Universal." I've always thought it was silly for game companies to publish one set of rules for fantasy, another one for Old West, another one for science fiction, and another one for super powers. **GURPS** is *one* set of rules that's comprehensive enough to let you use *any* background. There are worldbooks and supplements that "fine-tune" the generic system for any game world you want. But they *are* still compatible. If you want to take your Wild West gunslinger and your WWII commando fortune hunting in Renaissance Italy . . . go for it! And because that's exactly the kind of game that so many of our fans play, the Fourth Edition adds an overarching background created to support just such campaigns.

"RolePlaying." This is not just a hack-and-slash game. The rules are written to make true roleplaying possible – and, in fact, to encourage it. **GURPS** is a game in which you take on the persona of another character – and pretend, for a little while, to *be* that character.

"System." It really is. Most other RPGs started out as a simple set of rules, and then were patched and modified, ad infinitum. That makes them hard to play. **GURPS,** more than ever in the Fourth Edition, is a unified whole. We've gone to a great deal of effort to make sure that it all works together, and it all *works*. **GURPS** will let you create any character you can imagine, and do anything you can think of . . . and it all makes sense.

GURPS has been in print now for nearly 20 years. It was not designed in a vacuum; every game builds on the ones that came before. We learn from our successes – and from the successes of others. I think the best games are those that are simple, clear and easy to read, and I've tried hard to make **GURPS** "friendly."

One important influence was Hero Games' **Champions,** for the flexibility of its character-creation system. Another was Flying Buffalo's **Tunnels & Trolls,** for its appeal to solitaire gamers. Finally, M.A.R. Barker's **Empire of the Petal Throne** remains noteworthy, even after decades of competition and imitation, for the detail and richness of its alien game world.

But there's more to **GURPS** than trying to repeat past success. The failures of earlier systems are important, too. In **GURPS,** I've tried to achieve several things I think earlier designs missed.

First and foremost, of course, is the *flexibility* of a "universal" system. Others have tried this, but have fallen into the twin traps of watered-down combat (where a lightning bolt is just like a .45 pistol) or incompatibility (where players have to learn so many alternate rules for each new game and characters don't easily cross over). **GURPS** presents a single, unified system that allows for great diversity without losing its coherence. This Fourth Edition incorporates dozens of rules that originally appeared in supplements published for the Third Edition. They seemed important enough to bring into the **Basic Set** – so here they are.

Second is *organization*. Every gamer has had the experience of hunting frantically through one book after another,

looking for a rule . . . and not finding it. **GURPS** is extensively cross-referenced, with a Table of Contents, an Index, and a Glossary of terms used in the game.

Third is *ease of play*. In **GURPS,** most of the detailed calculations are done before you start play . . . they are entered on the character sheet, and saved until you need them. Once play actually begins, it should not be complex. I've tried to make **GURPS** as fast-moving yet realistic as possible. It's up to you to decide whether I succeeded.

Most roleplaying systems depend for their success on a continual flow of "official" supplements and adventures. **GURPS** is different. True, we've released a lot of material already, and we plan to do much more; a totally universal system offers great leeway, and we've got a supplement list as long as your arm. But **GURPS** is designed to be as compatible as possible with supplements written for *different* games. The reason? Simple. Suppose that you're a **GURPS** player. You're at the hobby shop, and you see a really interesting supplement package. But it's by another publisher, for another game.

No problem. The **GURPS** system breaks everything down into plain English and simple numbers. Distances are given in feet and miles, rather than arbitrary units; times are given in minutes and seconds. That's what makes it generic. That also makes it easy to translate. If you see an interesting supplement for another game, go right ahead and get it. You can use it as a sourcebook for **GURPS.**

Likewise, if your gaming group favors other systems . . . you can still use your **GURPS** adventures. As long as that other game uses units that you can translate into feet, minutes, and other plain-English terms, you can import your **GURPS** adventures.

When **GURPS** was launched, we dreamed of its becoming the "standard" roleplaying system. The hobby has grown hugely since then! There will never be a single standard . . . but **GURPS** is *one* of the standards, and that's fine. We have never tried to drive others out of the market, or even to force them to conform to us. Instead, *we* are conforming to *them* – by producing a system that will work with *any* clearly written adventure.

At any rate, here it is. I'm satisfied that **GURPS** is the most realistic, flexible, and "universal" system ever developed. This Fourth Edition is the culmination of 18 years of continuous development and two years of concerted revision. I hope you like it.

In closing, I want to acknowledge and thank the two revisors of this edition. Sean Punch, the **GURPS** line editor, and David Pulver spent two years collating feedback, experimenting with variant systems, and knitting a decade and a half of rules material into a coherent whole. It would not have happened without them.

– Steve Jackson

Notes on the Fourth Edition

This edition represents a leap forward in more ways than just rules. As the hobby has changed, so have the standards and expectations for role-playing-game supplements. So . . .

● *The **Basic Set** is bigger.* As new trends and genres emerge, a generic game needs to cover more and more ground. This means an ever-growing quantity of rules and advice. Since 1986, **GURPS** has expanded to deliver. A **Basic Set** in two large, comprehensive volumes puts the power of those years of development in your hands.

● *The **Basic Set** is more solid.* Core rulebooks see a great deal of use, while *large* rulebooks put a lot of strain on their bindings. Thus, both volumes of the **Basic Set** are hardbacks, and the material has been divided between them to ensure that they're big enough to be solid without coming apart under their own weight.

● *Regular support will continue.* We plan to issue new releases indefinitely . . . and that's not an empty promise! As of January 2011, more than 100 **GURPS** Fourth Edition supplements are available in either print or PDF.

Holding this book, you might ask, "Why does this edition of the **Basic Set** come in *two* volumes? Why not one *big* book, like the Third Edition and lots of other RPGs?" The answer involves a bit of history . . .

The first two editions of **Basic Set** – released in 1986 and 1987 – were boxed sets containing cardboard figures, combat maps, dice, and *two* rulebooks (sound familiar?). **Book 1: Characters** was aimed mainly at players, while **Book 2: Adventuring** was

more of a GM's guide. This was a logical division of content for a RPG, and quite common in the '80s.

By the time of the third edition (1988), gamers had come to prefer economical all-in-one rulebooks to expensive boxed sets. We decided to dispense with the box and release **Basic Set**, *Third Edition* as a single book. We managed to shoehorn everything into one volume. We continued to call it the **Basic Set** – even though it was not a boxed set – so that retailers and customers would know that it was the same game.

By 1995, we had published over 100 titles for **GURPS**. However, it just wasn't feasible to keep them all in print, so it became progressively harder to find certain supplements. Meanwhile, gamers with large **GURPS** libraries were finding it increasingly difficult to locate specific rules. To solve these problems, we compiled the most frequently used

rules from all of **GURPS** into two expansion volumes: **Compendium I: Character Creation** and **Compendium II: Combat and Campaigns.**

Most **GURPS** supplements written between 1996 and 2003 required one or both of the **Compendia.** The basic rules had effectively spread to *three* books. In the process, several internal inconsistencies became evident – the almost-inevitable result of growth by agglomeration.

Basic Set, *Fourth Edition* addresses the inconsistencies by recasting **Basic Set,** *Third Edition* and the two **Compendia** as a unified system. It occupies two volumes not because we think we will make more money that way, but because condensing three books into one proved impossible – there was too much material! But these two volumes contain the best of *18 years* of **GURPS** development, making *Fourth Edition comprehensive* in a way that few other RPGs are.

About the Authors

Steve Jackson

Steve Jackson has been playing games for entirely too many years, and designing them professionally since 1977. His other game-design credits include **Ogre** and **G.E.V.,** the award-winning **Illuminati,** the best-selling **Car Wars**, the atrocious **Munchkin** and its offshoots, and many others. He has served as an officer and volunteer for various industry associations, and was the youngest person ever inducted into the Origins "Hall of Fame."

He is the founder of Steve Jackson Games, in Austin, Texas.

Steve is an active member of the Science Fiction Writers of America. He is a semi-retired science fiction *fan*, and once spent a great deal of time writing for various zines and helping to run conventions. He now enjoys reading others' writing and attending others' cons. So it goes.

His other hobbies include surfing the net, playing with Lego and rolling-ball toys, gardening (especially water lilies), and tropical fish.

David L. Pulver

David L. Pulver grew up in Canada, England, and New Zealand. He has been a science fiction fan for most of his life, an avid gamer since 1978, and a professional author since 1988. **GURPS Ultra-Tech** was his first book. He has since written over 50 RPGs and supplements, among them **Transhuman Space, GURPS Bio-Tech,** and **Big Eyes, Small Mouth,** *Second Edition.* He lives in Victoria, British Columbia.

Sean M. Punch

Sean "Dr. Kromm" Punch set out to become a particle physicist in 1985, ended up the **GURPS** Line Editor in 1995, and has engineered rules for almost every **GURPS** product since. He developed, edited, or wrote dozens of **GURPS** *Third Edition* projects between 1995 and 2002. In 2004, he produced the **GURPS Basic Set**, *Fourth Edition* with David Pulver. Since then, he has created **GURPS Powers** (with Phil Masters), **GURPS Martial Arts** (with Peter Dell'Orto), **GURPS Zombies**, and the **GURPS Action, GURPS Dungeon Fantasy**, and **GURPS Power-Ups** series . . . among many other things. Sean has been a gamer since 1979. His big non-gaming interests are mixology and Argentine tango. He lives in Montréal, Québec with his wife, Bonnie, and their cat, Zephyra.

And because this edition's **Basic Set** is comprehensive, there is no need to "bolt on" extra rules that will come to be seen as mandatory. This should put the brakes on growth by agglomeration The **Basic Set** is truly all you need to run nearly any kind of game: fantasy, science fiction, supers, horror . . . *anything*. We believe that's a big win, and we think you will agree!

– *Sean Punch*

WHAT IS ROLEPLAYING?

In a roleplaying game (RPG), each player takes the part of a "character" participating in a fictional adventure. A referee, called the Game Master (GM), chooses the adventure. He determines the background and plays the part of the other people the characters meet during their adventure. The adventure may have a fixed objective – save the Princess, find the treasure, stop the invasion – or it may be open-ended, with the characters moving from one escapade to the next. A roleplaying "campaign" can be open ended, lasting for *years*, as characters (and players) come and go. It's all up to the GM and the players.

No game board is necessary for a roleplaying game – although some systems, including **GURPS,** include optional "boardgame" rules for combat situations. Instead, the game is played *verbally*. The GM describes the situation and tells the players what their characters see and hear. The players then describe what they are doing to meet the challenge. The GM describes the results of these actions . . . and so on. Depending on the situation, the GM may determine what happens arbitrarily (for the best possible story), by referring to specific game rules (to decide what is realistically possible), or by rolling dice (to give an interesting random result).

Part of the object of a roleplaying game is to have each player meet the situation as his *character* would. A roleplaying game can let a player take the part of a stern Japanese samurai, a medieval jester, a wise priest, a stowaway gutter kid on her first star-trip . . . or absolutely anyone else. In a given situation, all those characters would react differently. And that's what roleplaying is about! Thus, good roleplaying teaches cooperation among the players, and broadens their viewpoints.

But roleplaying is not purely educational. It's also one of the most creative possible entertainments. Most entertainment is passive: the audience just sits and watches, without taking part in the creative process. In roleplaying, the "audience" joins in the creation. The GM is the chief storyteller, but the players are responsible for portraying their characters. If they want something to happen in the story, they *make* it happen, because they're in the story. Other types of media are mass-produced to please the widest possible audience, but each roleplaying adventure is an individual gem, crafted by those who take part in it. The GM provides the raw material, but the final polish comes from the players themselves.

Mini-Glossary

Below are a few important terms used in this book. The complete glossary appears on pp. 563-565.

advantage: A useful *trait* that gives you an "edge" over another person with comparable *attributes* and *skills*. See Chapter 2.

attributes: Four numbers – *Strength, Dexterity, Intelligence,* and *Health* – that rate a character's most basic abilities. Higher is always better! See pp. 14-15.

cinematic: A style of play where the needs of the story outweigh those of realism, even when that would produce improbable results. See p. 488.

d: Short for "dice." "Roll 3d" means "roll three ordinary six-sided dice and add them up." See p. 9.

Dexterity (DX): An *attribute* that measures agility and coordination. See p. 15.

disadvantage: A problem that renders you less capable than your other *traits* would indicate. See Chapter 3.

enhancement: An extra capability added to a *trait*. This increases the *point* cost of the trait by a percentage. See pp. 102-109.

Fatigue Points (FP): A measure of resistance to exhaustion. See p. 16.

Health (HT): An *attribute* that measures physical grit and vitality. See p. 15.

Hit Points (HP): A measure of ability to absorb punishment. See p. 16.

Intelligence (IQ): An *attribute* that measures brainpower. See p. 15.

limitation: A restriction on the use of a *trait*. This reduces the *point* cost of the trait by a percentage. See pp. 110-117.

point: The unit of "currency" spent to buy *traits* for a character. The more points you have, the more capable you are. Point costs for traits are often written in brackets; e.g., "Combat Reflexes [15]" means the Combat Reflexes trait costs 15 points. See p. 10.

prerequisite: A *trait* you must have to qualify for another trait. If the prerequisite is a *skill*, you must have at least one *point* in it. See p. 169.

skill: A number defining your trained ability in an area of knowledge or broad class of tasks. See Chapter 4.

Strength (ST): An *attribute* that measures physical muscle and bulk. See p. 14.

trait: An *advantage, attribute, disadvantage, skill,* or other character "building block" that affects game play and costs *points* to add, modify, or remove.

The other important thing about roleplaying is that it doesn't have to be competitive. In most roleplaying situations, the party will succeed or fail as a group, depending on how well they cooperate. The greatest rewards of good roleplaying come not in "winning," but in *character development*. The more successfully a player portrays his character (as judged by the GM), the more that character will gain in ability.

When it's all said and done, the GM and the players will have created a story . . . the story of how the characters met, learned to work together, encountered a challenge, and (we hope) triumphed!

HOW TO LEARN GURPS

If you have some experience with roleplaying games already, you should find **GURPS** easy to pick up. But if this is your first RPG, you'll have a little more to learn. Relax – if you got this far, you'll be fine!

Don't be alarmed by the physical size of the game. There's a lot of material here – two thick books – but we've done our best to make it easy to use.

The tables of contents (pp. 3-4 and 339-341) and the index (pp. 329-334 or 570-575) are as detailed as we could manage.

We've also added several features to make the rules easier to learn. The *Quick-Start* (below) and *Conventions* (p. 9) sections cover the most important game concepts. The *Glossary* (pp. 563-565) defines the terms used in the game – and an abridged version (see *Mini-Glossary*, p. 7) appears here so you can understand the *Quick Start* rules without flipping pages.

The best way to learn **GURPS** is to join a group of friends who already play. If you're starting out on your own, here's what we recommend:

1. Quickly skim this book, just to get the flavor of the game. Don't worry about the details yet.

2. Read the *Mini-Glossary* (p. 7) to learn the basic terminology.

3. Read the *Quick-Start* and *Conventions* sections to learn the basic game concepts.

4. Read *Creating a Character* (pp. 10-12) to get an idea of the different things characters can do.

5. Read the rest of the rules in detail, as your time permits.

GURPS Lite may also be useful to you. It's a 32-page distillation of the basic system; you can download it free at **gurps.sjgames.com/lite**.

Once you have absorbed the rules, you can be the GM for your friends, and help *them* learn the game. You can do whatever you want . . . that's the whole point of the system.

Most important: Have fun!

QUICK START

This section is a brief guide to the whole **GURPS** game system. The **Basic Set** spans two thick volumes, but most of that is detail, "color," and special cases. The game system is actually *easy*.

GURPS is designed to be "friendly," both for the player and the Game Master. The rulebooks include a lot of detail, but they're indexed and cross-referenced to make things easy to find. And all the detail is optional – use it only when it makes the game more fun.

There are only three basic "game mechanics" in **GURPS**. Learn these and you can start to play.

(1) *Success Rolls.* A "success roll" is a die roll made when you need to "test" one of your skills or attributes. For instance, you might test, or *roll against*,

your Strength to stop a heavy door from closing, or against your Guns skill to hit an enemy with your pistol.

The only dice used in **GURPS** are six-sided ones. Roll three dice for a success roll. If your roll is *less than* or *equal to* the skill or ability you are testing, you succeeded. Otherwise, you failed. For example, if you are rolling against Strength, and your ST level is 12, a roll of 12 or less succeeds.

Sometimes you will have *modifiers* to a roll. For instance, if you were trying to stop a *very heavy* door from closing, you might have to roll against Strength at -2 (or ST-2, for short). In that case, with a Strength of 12, you would need to roll a 10 or less to succeed. Rolling a 10 or less is harder than rolling a 12 or less, just as stopping a

heavy door is harder than stopping an ordinary one.

For an especially easy task, you would get a *bonus* to your attempt. You might roll "Animal Handling+4" to make friends with a very friendly dog. If your Animal Handling skill were 12, a roll of 16 or less would succeed. Making a roll of 16 or less is easier than making the base skill roll of 12 or less, because a friendly dog is easy to deal with.

For details on success rolls, see pp. 343-361.

(2) *Reaction Rolls.* A "reaction roll" is a roll made by the Game Master (or GM) to determine how his nonplayer characters (NPCs) react to the player characters. This roll is always optional; the GM may predetermine reactions.

But sometimes it's more fun to let the dice control the reactions.

To check reactions, the GM rolls 3 dice and consults the *Reaction Table* (pp. 560-561). The higher his roll, the better the NPCs will react, and the better the treatment they will give the PCs.

Many traits give *reaction modifiers* that add to or subtract from reaction rolls. If you have a +2 reaction due to your good looks, the GM will add 2 to any reaction roll made by someone who can see you. This is likely to improve the way they behave toward you!

For details on reaction rolls, see p. 494.

(3) *Damage Rolls.* A "damage roll" is a roll made in a fight, to see how much harm you did to your foe. Damage rolls use the "dice+adds" system (see *Dice,* below).

Many things can affect the final injury inflicted by your attack. Armor reduces the damage received by the wearer. Certain attacks do extra damage if they get through armor. "Critical hits" can do extra damage. All these things are explained in the combat rules – see Chapters 11-13. But the combat system is "modular"; you can use *all* the rules for a complex, detailed, realistic combat simulation – or just those in Chapter 11 for a quick game.

There's another important system – but you don't need to know it to start with. It's the *character creation* system. The GM will give each player a number of points to spend on his character. High attribute levels cost points, as do advantages and skills. Disadvantages, such as Greed and Berserk, are also available; these give you *extra* points. Details appear in Chapters 1-4.

These rules let you do all your calculations *before* play starts, and enter them on the Character Sheet (p. 13). That way, you don't have to bother with calculations during play!

Got all that? Good. Now you can play **GURPS**. The rest is just detail. Have fun.

CONVENTIONS

GURPS uses the following mathematical conventions.

Dice

GURPS uses six-sided dice only. All "success rolls," and most other rolls, require you to throw three dice ("3d") at once, add up the number of pips, and compare the total to a "target number."

To figure combat damage, and for many other things, **GURPS** uses the "dice+adds" system. If a weapon does "4d+2" damage, this is shorthand for "roll 4 dice and add 2 to the total." Likewise, "3d-3" means "roll 3 dice and subtract 3 from the total."

If you see just "2d," that means "roll two dice." For instance, if an adventure says, "The base is guarded by 5d human soldiers and 2d+1 robots," that's short for, "Roll five dice for the number of human guards at the base. Then roll two dice, and add 1, for the number of robots."

For really huge numbers, dice can be multiplied. For instance, "2d×10" means "roll 2 dice and multiply by 10."

Rounding

A mathematical formula is often the best way to ensure that a rule is fair, realistic, or universal. But formulas sometimes yield inconvenient fractions. Except where instructed otherwise, round off fractions as follows:

Round **up** *for point costs.* When you modify a point cost by a percentage, or multiply it by a factor, round all fractions *up.* For instance, a 25% enhancement to a 15-point ability would result in 18.75 points, which would round to 19 points. For negative numbers, "up" means "in the positive direction"; e.g., if you multiply -7 points by 1/2 to get -3.5 points, round the result to -3 points.

Round **down** *for character feats and combat results.* When you do math to determine what a character can do – how much he can lift, how far he can jump, etc. – or to calculate injury or other combat results, round all fractions *down.* For instance, for an attack that inflicts 3 points of injury with a 50% damage bonus, round down from 4.5 to 4 points.

Exceptions and special cases (such as "round to the nearest whole number" or "do not round off") are noted explicitly with the relevant rule.

Metric Conversions

GURPS uses the old imperial units of measurement, rather than metric, because most of our readers are Americans who use the old system. But not all! Every year, more and more people in the rest of the world start **GURPS** campaigns. And outside the U.S., people think in metric. We can't afford to do two editions of everything, but we *can* provide this conversion table.

Note that there are two conversion columns. The first column is an approximation, easy to do in your head, and good enough for gaming. The second column is the *real* metric equivalent, for those times when you want to be exact.

Imperial	Game Metric	Real Metric
1 inch (in.)	2.5 cm	2.54 cm
1 foot (ft.)	30 cm	30.48 cm
1 yard (yd.)	1 meter	0.914 meters
1 mile (mi.)	1.5 km	1.609 km
1 pound (lb.)	0.5 kg	0.454 kg
1 ton	1 metric ton	0.907 metric tons
1 gallon (gal.)	4 liters	3.785 liters
1 quart (qt.)	1 liter	0.946 liters
1 ounce (oz.)	30 grams	28.349 grams
1 cubic inch (ci)	16 cubic cm	16.387 cu. cm
1 cubic yard (cy)	0.75 cubic m	0.765 cubic m

Temperature: When dealing with changes in temperature, one Fahrenheit degree is 5/9 the size of a degree Celsius. So a change of 45°F is equal to a change of 25°C. To convert actual thermometer readings, subtract 32 from the Fahrenheit temperature and multiply the result by 5/9. So 95°F is 5/9 of (95-32), or 5/9 of 63, or 35°C.

CHAPTER ONE
CREATING A CHARACTER

When you roleplay, you take the part of another person – a "character" that you create. **GURPS** lets you decide exactly what kind of hero you will become. Asteroid miner? Wizard? Professional time-traveler? You can take your inspiration from a fictional hero or heroine, or create your new "self" from the ground up. Once you know what role you want to play, it's time to bring that character to life!

The GM (Game Master – the person "running" the game) will give you a number of *character points* with which to "buy" your abilities. For instance, the stronger you want to be, the more points it will cost. You can also buy advantageous social traits, such as wealth, and special abilities called *advantages* (see Chapter 2).

If you want more abilities than you can afford on the budget given to you by your GM, you can get extra points by accepting below-average strength, appearance, wealth, social status, etc., or by taking *disadvantages* – specific handicaps such as bad vision or fear of heights (see Chapter 3).

Advanced players can fine-tune these traits by adding *enhancements* and *limitations;* see pp. 101-117. Such modifiers will raise or lower the basic point cost of the modified trait.

Start with a character sheet (see p. 13) and fill it in as you go along, keeping track of the points you spend. We have included examples at each stage to illustrate the process.

CHARACTER POINTS

Character points are the "currency" of character creation. Anything that improves your abilities *costs* character points: you must spend points equal to the listed price of an ability to add that ability to your character sheet and use it in play. Anything that reduces your capabilities has a negative cost – that is, it *gives you back* some points. For instance, if you start with 125 points, buy 75 points of advantages, and take -15 points of disadvantages, you have 125 - 75 + 15 = 65 points remaining.

Starting Points

The GM decides how many character points the player characters (PCs) – the heroes – start with. This depends on how capable he wants them to be, and can range from under 25 points (small children) to 1,000 points or more (godlike beings), with 100-200 points being typical for career adventurers.

This beginning point level is sometimes referred to as the *power level* of the campaign (see *Power Level*, p. 487). This is not the same as the "stakes" of the campaign! Heroes with abilities that let them overcome even the toughest opposition in an optimistic fantasy campaign might face mortal danger in a dark horror scenario.

In most campaigns, all the PCs start at the same power level. This is simple and fair. However, not all people are equally capable in real life, and it is common in fiction for one character to be obviously superior. If everyone agrees, some players might play "lead protagonists," worth more points than the other PCs, or "sidekicks," worth fewer points.

Disadvantage Limit

A *disadvantage* is anything with a negative cost, including low attributes, reduced social status, and all the specific disabilities listed in Chapter 3. In theory, you could keep adding disadvantages until you had enough points to buy whatever advantages and skills you wanted. In practice, most GMs will want to set a limit on the disadvantage points a PC may have.

The purpose of a disadvantage limit is to keep the game from becoming a circus, with the PCs' troubles stealing the spotlight from the setting, the adventure, and everything else the GM has created. Most GMs find it difficult to run an *engaging* game if the PCs are completely dysfunctional – e.g., clumsy, one-eyed, alcoholic outlaws who are afraid of the dark.

A disadvantage cap serves another purpose as well: it restricts the abilities available to starting characters, allowing the GM to set an upper limit on the capabilities of the PCs. A good rule of thumb is to hold disadvantages to 50% of starting points – for instance, -75 points in a 150-point game – although this is entirely up to the GM.

However, if the GM rules that all PCs *must* have certain disadvantages (e.g., all the PCs are spies, with a Duty to their agency), these "campaign disadvantages" should not count against the disadvantage limit. Disadvantages that are part of your racial makeup (your "racial template"; see p. 260) are also exempt.

Character Points in Play

Your character's starting point total is only relevant when he first enters play. Shortly thereafter, he will start to change. The GM will sometimes reward you with extra points to spend, or even new abilities . . . but you might *lose* capabilities, too. All of these things will change your point total.

Eventually, your PC will be worth more or fewer points than those of your companions, even though you all started out equal. Don't worry about it! Develop the habit of regarding your point total as a useful measure of your capability *at this time* – not as a gauge of overall campaign power level, or of your personal success or importance relative to the other players or PCs.

For more on character evolution, see Chapter 9.

CHARACTER CONCEPT

The two most important things to know about your character are *who he is* and *what role you want him to play* *in his adventures*. Find out what kind of game the GM plans to run and what kinds of characters he intends to allow. Then start filling in the details. There are several ways to approach this.

You can choose the abilities you want, spend your character points, and work out a character concept that fits the abilities. A good character is much more than a collection of abilities, but "shopping" for abilities can be a great inspiration.

You might instead decide on your character's focal qualities first – the handful of things that *define* him, such as personal history, appearance, behavior, aptitudes, and skills. Think about how he acquired those qualities, then spend your points on features that go with these traits. (You might find it useful to work out a biography first, as described below.)

Finally, you might find it helpful to answer some basic questions about your character, using the answers to develop a biography before you spend *any* points. For instance:

● Where was he born and where did he grow up? Where does he live now?

● Who were his parents? (Does he know?) Are they still alive? If not, what became of them? If so, does he get along with them?

● What training does he have? Was he an apprentice? A student? Or is he self-taught?

● What is his current occupation? What other jobs has he held?

● What social class does he belong to? How wealthy is he?

● Who are his friends? His enemies? His closest professional associates?

● What were the most important moments of his life?

● What are his likes and dislikes? Hobbies and interests? Morals and beliefs?

● What are his motivations? Plans for the future?

You can answer such questions in your head, on paper, or in an interview with the GM. You can even discuss them with the other players (but you will want to keep *some* secrets, even from your friends). Or you might prefer to answer them by writing a life history.

How GURPS Works: Realism and Game Balance

Character design in **GURPS** is intended to give a *balanced* hero, someone whose strengths and weaknesses more or less cancel each other out.

In real life, of course, being super-strong doesn't necessarily mean you have to give up something else. And being weak in body doesn't mean you'll automatically be good at something else. A totally realistic system would be one in which a character's strength (for instance) was determined randomly, with no relationship to his intelligence or social status . . . and so on for all his other capabilities.

But random choices aren't really satisfactory for *heroes*. You might end up with a superman . . . or a weak, stupid, boring clod. You avoid people like that in real life; why would you want to become one, even for a minute, in a game?

In **GURPS,** two characters built on the same number of points start off "equal," but not the *same*. You can design the type of character you want while leaving room for growth and improvement.

Life Histories

To really solidify your character concept, you can write your character's life history, or "character story." You don't *have* to write a character story – but it's recommended. If you do, then you should show this story to the GM, but not necessarily to the other players. This can serve as a great aid to roleplaying, and can help the GM integrate your character into his campaign world.

As your character adventures and gains experience, his "story" will get longer and more detailed. Not only will you have the adventures themselves to remember . . . the more you play your character, the more you'll work out his background, history, and motivations.

Characterization Bonus

Writing a life history amounts to roleplaying a character before the campaign begins. The GM might choose to reward players who write detailed character stories with a few extra character points for good roleplaying (see p. 498) – perhaps 1 to 5 points. The story need not be a literary masterpiece to merit bonus points, but it should be more than just a token effort, and should attempt to answer all of the questions listed under *Character Concept* that are relevant to the character.

CHARACTER TYPES

A character can have any combination of abilities he can afford, provided the GM agrees. (Players of other RPGs take note: this means that **GURPS** does not use character classes.) However, all of his abilities should paint a picture consistent with his character concept. Some inspirations from heroic fiction:

Exotic. An alien, angel, robot, "super" (a comic-book superhuman), or other hero *defined* by his unusual powers or nature. Most of his starting points should go toward high attributes, exotic or supernatural advantages (see p. 32), or a racial template (see p. 260). As a result, he probably has fewer mundane abilities than his fellow adventurers.

Jack-of-All-Trades. A many-skilled hero: mercenary, bush pilot, reporter, etc. DX and IQ are most important. Advantages such as Talent and Versatile can help. Pick one or two skills from those suggested for each of the other character types. A Jack-of-All-Trades isn't as good as a dedicated expert, but he has *some* skill in many areas.

Mouthpiece. A bard, con man, or other person who exploits wit and charm. IQ is crucial. Charisma, Cultural Familiarity, Rapier Wit, Voice, and a good appearance are all useful. Most important are skills that emphasize social interaction: Carousing, Fast-Talk, Merchant, Public Speaking, and so on.

Sage. A "wise man" – priest, professor, scientist, etc. High IQ is essential. Classic advantages are Eidetic Memory, Intuition, Language Talent, and Languages (and, in some campaigns, Illuminated!). He needs several *related* IQ/Hard skills in obscure fields (Expert Skills are especially suitable), as well as Research, Teaching, and Writing.

Scout. A seasoned outdoorsman or "ranger." All attributes are equally important; some extra Basic Move and Perception can be extremely useful. The archetypal scout advantage is Absolute Direction. Valuable skills include Area Knowledge, Camouflage, Naturalist, Navigation, Survival, and Tracking.

Sneak. Thieves and spies need high DX and IQ, as well as good Perception. Helpful advantages include High Manual Dexterity and Night Vision. Many skills are appropriate – Acting, Current Affairs, Disguise, and Savoir-Faire suit a worldly spy, while a fantasy thief should pick Climbing, Lockpicking, Pickpocket, and Traps. Stealth skill is universal!

Specialist. An expert at *one* skill. His knowledge runs deep and narrow; he is

---

Example of Character Creation: Dai Blackthorn

To illustrate character creation, we present Dai Blackthorn, thief extraordinaire! Dai hails from the Infinite Worlds setting in Chapter 20.

Dai's career started on Yrth, a medieval fantasy world populated by descendants of Crusades-era folk pulled from Earth by a dimensional rift. He remembers nothing of his birth or early childhood; he was a street kid. When he was about seven, he was taken in by an old thief who taught him to be a pickpocket and second-story man, and Dai learned well. But the Thieves' Guild didn't like the competition, and when Dai was 15, the Guild set fire to the old man's house, and picked off the fleeing occupants with crossbows. Only Dai escaped.

At the time, he thought that he had made a terror-fueled leap from the burning building's roof to the next one. Later he realized that that jump had been impossible. Something else had happened. In fact, the fear of death had unlocked his psionic gift of teleportation, though it took time before he realized the truth and gained control of his abilities. When he did, he became a master thief indeed, living in quiet comfort and reveling in the marketplace talk of "impossible robberies" that no lock and no wizard could stop.

Then Dai crossed paths, and swords, with an equally formidable rival . . . a world-jumping criminal using stolen technology to loot Yrth's treasures. Matters were complicated further by the arrival of an ISWAT team pursuing the world-jumper. When the dust had settled, two of the agents owed their lives to the little thief . . . but he knew too much. They couldn't just let him go.

So they recruited him. After all, a good teleport is hard to find. As for Dai, he was ready for new challenges . . .

We'll create Dai as a full member of ISWAT. As an established hero, he'll have a base of 250 points.

the opposite of the Jack-of-All-Trades. His skill is *very* high (at least 18), with a good score in the attribute it is based on. Any advantage that gives a skill bonus is helpful – *especially* Talent.

Tinkerer. An engineer, inventor, technician, or other mechanical genius. IQ is vital; DX is useful. Any kind of technological skill fits this sort of character (see *Skills for Design, Repair, and Use,* p. 190), and Scrounging skill is *de rigueur.* Cinematic inventors should also have High TL, Gadgeteer, and Gizmos.

Warrior. A professional fighter needs high ST, DX, and HT, and might wish to buy up Hit Points and Basic Speed. Useful advantages include Combat Reflexes, Hard to Kill, and High Pain Threshold; cinematic warriors should also consider Extra Attack and Weapon Master. Combat skills are a must, and Leadership, Strategy, and Tactics can help. Modern commandos should add skills such as Explosives, Forward Observer, and Parachuting.

Wizard. IQ and Magery are crucial. Extra Fatigue Points are useful for powering magic. Of course, a wizard needs spells – as many as he can afford! Although wizards are most common in magical worlds, the "surprise value" of a mage on a low-magic world can compensate for his reduced effectiveness.

CHARACTER CREATION CHECKLIST

Be sure to visit *all* of the following sections during character creation:

- *Basic Attributes* (p. 14) and *Secondary Characteristics* (p. 15). These affect almost everything else on your character sheet, so pick them first.
- *Build* (p. 18) and *Age and Beauty* (p. 20). These sections describe the in-game effects of height, weight, age, looks, etc.
- *Social Background* (p. 22), *Wealth and Influence* (p. 25), *Friends and Foes* (p. 31), and *Identities* (p. 31). Determine what kind of society you are from, where you stand in the game world, how others regard you, and who you can count on for support – or for a knife in the back!

See pp. 335-336 for a full-sized, two-page character sheet which you may copy for your own use. This and other *GURPS* forms may also be downloaded at **gurps.sjgames.com/resources**.

Things Not Shown on the Character Sheet

There are several things you *might* want to keep track of separately:

Job Details. It can be important to know what you do for a living when you're not adventuring (unless adventuring is your job – lucky you!) and how long you spend doing it. This determines your income and on-the-job training opportunities. Military characters should keep a service record.

Life History. If you write down your character story, keep it in a separate file so you can easily expand it as your adventures unfold.

Spells. Wizards often know *dozens* of spells – more than easily fit on a character sheet. If you wish, you can just note the total point cost of *all* your spells under "Skills" and write out your full spell list on a separate "grimoire" or "spellbook" sheet.

Vital Statistics. If you think your parents' names, your place and date of birth (or zodiacal birth sign), your bloodline (or *race* – in some settings, you might need to specify that you are an ordinary human!), and similar traits are likely to matter, keep a separate "personnel file" on yourself that contains such details.

- *Advantages* (p. 32). Chapter 2 lists dozens of special talents and powers. *Perks* (p. 100) are special "mini-advantages" that can help individualize your character.
- *Disadvantages* (p. 119). Chapter 3 lists a wide variety of negative traits, from inconvenient to crippling.

Mental disadvantages and *Quirks* (p. 162), special mini-disadvantages, can help you define your personality.
- *Skills* (p. 167) and *Techniques* (p. 229). The abilities in Chapter 4 describe what you can actually *do*. Be sure to match your skills to your occupation and character type.

Aside from attributes, which you should normally select first, the order you work through these sections makes little difference . . . start with the one most important to you, and work from there.

BASIC ATTRIBUTES

Four numbers called "attributes" define your basic abilities: Strength (ST), Dexterity (DX), Intelligence (IQ), and Health (HT).

A score of 10 in any attribute is *free*, and represents the human average. Higher scores cost points: 10 points to raise ST or HT by one level, 20 points to raise DX or IQ by one level. Similarly, scores lower than 10 have a negative cost: -10 points per level for ST or HT, -20 points per level for DX or IQ. (Remember – negative point values mean you get those points back to spend on something else!)

Most characters have attributes in the 1-20 range, and most normal humans have scores in the 8-12 range. Scores above 20 are possible but typically reserved for godlike beings – ask the GM before buying such a value. The exception is ST, which can range significantly beyond 20 even for normal humans. At the other end of the scale, a score of 0 is defined in special cases, but 1 is the minimum score for a human. No one may have a *negative* score.

> ## How to Select Basic Attributes
>
> The basic attributes you select will determine your abilities – your strengths and weaknesses – throughout the game. Choose wisely.
>
> **6 or less:** *Crippling.* An attribute this bad severely constrains your lifestyle.
>
> **7:** *Poor.* Your limitations are immediately obvious to anyone who meets you. This is the lowest score you can have and still pass for "able-bodied."
>
> **8 or 9:** *Below average.* Such scores are limiting, but within the human norm. The GM may forbid attributes below 8 to active adventurers.
>
> **10:** *Average.* Most humans get by just fine with a score of 10!
>
> **11 or 12:** *Above average.* These scores are superior, but within the human norm.
>
> **13 or 14:** *Exceptional.* Such an attribute is immediately apparent – as bulging muscles, feline grace, witty dialog, or glowing health – to those who meet you.
>
> **15 or more:** *Amazing.* An attribute this high draws constant comment and probably guides your career choices.
>
> All of the above assumes a *human*. For nonhumans, read each point above or below the human norm of 10 as a 10% deviation from the racial norm instead.

Strength (ST)

±10 points/level

Strength measures physical power and bulk. It is crucial if you are a warrior in a primitive world, as high ST lets you dish out *and absorb* more damage in hand-to-hand combat. Any adventurer will find ST useful for lifting and throwing things, moving quickly with a load, etc. ST directly determines Basic Lift (p. 15), basic damage (p. 15), and Hit Points (p. 16), and affects your character's Build (p. 18).

Lifting capacity is proportional to the *square* of ST. Compared to the average human adult (ST 10 – 10×10 = 100), ST 14 is about twice as strong (14×14 = 196), ST 17 is roughly three times as strong (17×17 = 289), and ST 20 is four times as strong (20×20 = 400 = 4×100). Likewise, ST 7 is about half as strong (7×7 = 49), ST 6 is approximately 1/3 as strong (6×6 = 36), and ST 5 is only 1/4 as strong (5×5 = 25 = 100/4).

> ## Handedness
>
> Decide whether you are right-handed or left-handed. Whenever you try to do anything significant with the other hand, you are at -4 to skill. This does not apply to things you *normally* do with your "off" hand, like using a shield.
>
> **GURPS** assumes you are right-handed unless you decide otherwise or buy Ambidexterity (p. 39). If you choose to be left-handed, any combat result that would damage your right hand affects your left instead, and vice versa. Left-handedness is a feature worth 0 points.

Strength is more "open-ended" than other attributes; scores greater than 20 are common among beings such as large animals, fantasy monsters, and robots. Even a human could have a ST over 20 – record-setting weightlifters can be *very* strong!

Those with nonhuman physiologies may, with the GM's permission, purchase their ST with one or both of the *limitations* below. You may not reduce a point cost by more than 80% through limitations; treat any total over -80% as -80%. (For more on limitations, see p. 110.)

Special Limitations

No Fine Manipulators: If you have either level of the disadvantage No Fine Manipulators (p. 145), you may purchase ST more cheaply. -40%.

Size: Large creatures may purchase ST more cheaply; see p. 19 for details. -10% × Size Modifier, to a maximum limitation of -80% (for Size Modifier +8 or higher).

Dexterity (DX)
±20 points/level

Dexterity measures a combination of agility, coordination, and fine motor ability. It controls your basic ability at most athletic, fighting, and vehicle-operation skills, and at craft skills that call for a delicate touch. DX also helps determine Basic Speed (a measure of reaction time, p. 17) and Basic Move (how fast you run, p. 17).

How GURPS Works:
IQ, Sentience, and Sapience

Sentience is self-awareness. Any being with a **GURPS** IQ of at least 1 is sentient by definition. To create nonsentient beings – plants, brainless clone bodies, etc. – take IQ 0, for -200 points. Nonsentient creatures cannot learn skills or have any purely mental traits.

Sapience is defined as the ability to use tools and language. In **GURPS**, this requires at least IQ 6. Those with IQ 5 or less cannot learn technological skills (see p. 168) or possess Languages (see p. 23) – not even the initial Language that most characters get for free. They can still communicate primitive concepts (such as hunger or danger) through gesture or vocalization, and may be trained to respond to a few commands (see *Pets and Trained Animals*, p. 458).

Those with nonhuman physiologies may, with the GM's permission, purchase their DX with the following limitation.

Special Limitations

No Fine Manipulators: If you have either level of the disadvantage No Fine Manipulators (p. 145), you may purchase DX more cheaply. -40%.

Intelligence (IQ)
±20 points/level

Intelligence broadly measures brainpower, including creativity, intuition, memory, perception, reason, sanity, and willpower. It rules your basic ability with all "mental" skills –

sciences, social interaction, magic, etc. Any wizard, scientist, or gadgeteer needs a high IQ first of all. The secondary characteristics of Will (p. 16) and Perception (p. 16) are based on IQ.

Health (HT)
±10 points/level

Health measures energy and vitality. It represents stamina, resistance (to poison, disease, radiation, etc.), and basic "grit." A high HT is good for anyone – but it is *vital* for low-tech warriors. HT determines Fatigue Points (p. 16), and helps determine Basic Speed (p. 17) and Basic Move (p. 17).

SECONDARY CHARACTERISTICS

"Secondary characteristics" are quantities that depend directly on your attributes. You can raise or lower these scores by adjusting your attributes. You can modify some of them directly: start with the value calculated from your attributes and spend the required points to adjust it away from that base level. This does not affect the related attribute scores.

Damage (Dmg)
see Striking ST (p. 88)

Your ST determines how much damage you do in unarmed combat or with a melee weapon. Two types of damage derive from ST:

Thrusting damage (abbreviated "thrust" or "thr") is your basic damage with a punch, kick, or bite, or an attack with a thrusting weapon such as a spear or a rapier.

Swinging damage (abbreviated "swing" or "sw") is your basic damage with a swung weapon, such as an axe, club, or sword – anything that acts as a lever to multiply your ST.

Consult the *Damage Table* (p. 16) for your basic damage. This is given in "dice+adds" format; see *Dice* (p. 9). Note that specific attack forms and weapons can modify this!

Add 1d to both thrust and swing damage per full 10 points of ST above 100.

Damage is often abbreviated "Dmg." On your character sheet, list thrust followed by swing, separated by a slash; e.g., if you had ST 13, you would list "Dmg 1d/2d-1."

Basic Lift (BL)
see Lifting ST (p. 65)

Basic Lift is the maximum weight you can lift over your head with *one* hand in *one* second. It is equal to (ST×ST)/5 lbs. If BL is 10 lbs. or more, round to the nearest whole number; e.g., 16.2 lbs. becomes 16 lbs. The average human has ST 10 and a BL of 20 lbs.

Doubling the time lets you lift 2×BL overhead in one hand. Quadrupling the time, and using *two* hands, you can lift 8×BL overhead.

Damage Table

ST	Thrust	Swing		ST	Thrust	Swing
1	1d-6	1d-5		27	3d-1	5d+1
2	1d-6	1d-5		28	3d-1	5d+1
3	1d-5	1d-4		29	3d	5d+2
4	1d-5	1d-4		30	3d	5d+2
5	1d-4	1d-3		31	3d+1	6d-1
6	1d-4	1d-3		32	3d+1	6d-1
7	1d-3	1d-2		33	3d+2	6d
8	1d-3	1d-2		34	3d+2	6d
9	1d-2	1d-1		35	4d-1	6d+1
10	1d-2	1d		36	4d-1	6d+1
11	1d-1	1d+1		37	4d	6d+2
12	1d-1	1d+2		38	4d	6d+2
13	1d	2d-1		39	4d+1	7d-1
14	1d	2d		40	4d+1	7d-1
15	1d+1	2d+1		45	5d	7d+1
16	1d+1	2d+2		50	5d+2	8d-1
17	1d+2	3d-1		55	6d	8d+1
18	1d+2	3d		60	7d-1	9d
19	2d-1	3d+1		65	7d+1	9d+2
20	2d-1	3d+2		70	8d	10d
21	2d	4d-1		75	8d+2	10d+2
22	2d	4d		80	9d	11d
23	2d+1	4d+1		85	9d+2	11d+2
24	2d+1	4d+2		90	10d	12d
25	2d+2	5d-1		95	10d+2	12d+2
26	2d+2	5d		100	11d	13d

The amount of equipment you can carry – armor, backpacks, weapons, etc. – is derived from BL. For more on this, as well as a ST-to-BL table, see *Encumbrance and Move* (p. 17).

Hit Points (HP)

±2 points per ±1 HP

Hit Points represent your body's ability to sustain injury. By default, you have HP equal to your ST. For instance, ST 10 gives 10 HP.

You can increase HP at the cost of 2 points per HP, or reduce HP for -2 points per HP. In a realistic campaign, the GM should not allow HP to vary by more than ±30% of ST; e.g., a ST 10 character could have between 7 and 13 HP. Nonhumans and supers are not subject to this limit.

You can temporarily lose HP to physical attacks (such as swords), energy attacks (such as lasers), supernatural attacks, disease, poison, hazards, and anything else that can injure or kill. You can also "burn" HP to power certain supernatural abilities. If you lose enough HP, you will eventually fall unconscious; if you lose too many HP, you will *die*. Lost HP do *not* reduce ST, despite being based on ST.

Injury is often compared to a multiple of your HP; e.g., "2×HP" or "HP/2." Where this is the case, use your *basic* HP score in the formula, not your *current* HP total.

For information on the effects of injury and on recovering lost HP, see pp. 418-425.

Those with nonhuman physiologies may, with the GM's permission, buy additional HP with the following limitation.

Special Limitations

Size: Large creatures may purchase HP more cheaply; see p. 19 for details. -10% × Size Modifier, to a maximum limitation of -80% (for Size Modifier +8 or higher).

Will

±5 points per ±1 Will

Will measures your ability to withstand psychological stress (brainwashing, fear, hypnotism, interrogation, seduction, torture, etc.) and your resistance to supernatural attacks (magic, psionics, etc.). By default, Will is equal to IQ. You can increase it at the cost of 5 points per +1, or reduce it for -5 points per -1. You cannot raise Will past 20, or lower it by more than 4, without GM permission.

Note that Will does not represent *physical* resistance – buy HT for that!

Perception (Per)

±5 points per ±1 Per

Perception represents your general alertness. The GM makes a "Sense roll" against your Per to determine whether you notice something (see *Sense Rolls*, p. 358). By default, Per equals IQ, but you can increase it for 5 points per +1, or reduce it for -5 points per -1. You cannot raise Per past 20, or lower it by more than 4, without GM permission.

Fatigue Points (FP)

±3 points per ±1 FP

Fatigue Points represent your body's "energy supply." By default, you have FP equal to your HT. For instance, HT 10 gives 10 FP.

You can increase FP at the cost of 3 points per FP, or reduce FP for -3 points per FP. In a realistic campaign, the GM should not allow FP to vary by more than ±30% of HT; e.g., a HT 10 character could have between 7 and

---

Machines and Fatigue

Those with the Machine meta-trait (p. 263) should list FP as "N/A," regardless of HT. They can neither buy extra FP nor reduce FP to save points. This is both an advantage and a disadvantage: machines do not fatigue, but they cannot spend FP to use extra effort or fuel special abilities. When a machine operates beyond its normal limits, it risks lasting structural damage. This takes the form of reduced HT, not lost FP. A character with the Machine meta-trait should buy up HT to be more tolerant of being "redlined."

Overall, this is a 0-point feature (see *Features and Taboo Traits*, p. 261).

13 FP. Nonhumans and supers are not subject to this limit. Also, while HT is usually limited to 20, there is no such limit on FP.

You burn FP gradually during strenuous activity. Disease, heat, hunger, missed sleep, and the like can also sap FP. You can deliberately "spend" FP to fuel extra effort (see p. 356) and supernatural powers (e.g., magic spells). As well, some attacks cause FP damage instead of or in addition to HP damage. If you lose enough FP, you will slow down or fall unconscious – and if you lose too many, you risk death from overexertion! Lost FP do *not* reduce HT, despite being based on HT.

Fatigue is often compared to some multiple of your FP; e.g., "2×FP" or "FP/2." Where this is the case, use your *basic* FP score in the formula, not your *current* FP total.

For more on losing and recovering FP, see pp. 426-427.

Basic Speed

±5 points per ±0.25 Speed

Your Basic Speed is a measure of your reflexes and general physical quickness. It helps determine your running speed (see *Basic Move*, below), your chance of dodging an attack, and the order in which you act in combat (a high Basic Speed will let you "out-react" your foes).

To calculate Basic Speed, add your HT and DX together, and then divide the total by 4. *Do not round it off.* A 5.25 is better than a 5!

You can increase Basic Speed for 5 points per +0.25, or reduce it for -5 points per -0.25. In a realistic campaign, the GM should not allow characters to alter Basic Speed by more than 2.00 either way. Nonhumans and supers are not subject to this limit.

Dodge: Your Dodge defense (see *Dodging*, p. 374) equals Basic Speed + 3, dropping all fractions. For instance, if your Basic Speed is 5.25, your Dodge is 8. Encumbrance reduces Dodge; see *Encumbrance and Move* (below). You must roll under your Dodge on 3d to duck or sidestep an attack.

Basic Move

±5 points per ±1 yard/second

Your Basic Move is your ground speed in yards per second. This is how fast you can run – or roll, slither, etc. – *without encumbrance* (although you can go a little faster if you "sprint" in a straight line; see p. 354).

Basic Move starts out equal to Basic Speed, less any fractions; e.g., Basic Speed 5.75 gives Basic Move 5. An average person has Basic Move 5; therefore, he can run about 5 yards per second if unencumbered.

You can increase Basic Move for 5 points per yard/second or reduce it for -5 points per yard/second. For normal humans, training or a sleek build can justify up to 3 yards/second of increased Basic Move, while disability or poor fitness can explain up to 3 yards/second of reduced Basic Move. Nonhumans and supers are not subject to these limits. Races and supers who can move *very* fast should see *Enhanced Move* (p. 52).

Your Move score in combat is your Basic Move modified for your encumbrance level; see *Encumbrance and Move* (below).

Encumbrance and Move

"Encumbrance" is a measure of the total weight you are carrying, *relative to your ST*. The effects of encumbrance are divided into five "encumbrance levels." All but the lowest level will reduce your actual Move to a fraction of your Basic Move and give a penalty to Dodge, as follows:

No Encumbrance (0): Weight up to Basic Lift. Move = Basic Move. Full Dodge.

Light Encumbrance (1): Weight up to 2×BL. Move = Basic Move × 0.8. Dodge -1.

Medium Encumbrance (2): Weight up to 3×BL. Move = Basic Move × 0.6. Dodge -2.

Heavy Encumbrance (3): Weight up to 6×BL. Move = Basic Move × 0.4. Dodge -3.

Extra-Heavy Encumbrance (4): Weight up to 10×BL. Move = Basic Move × 0.2. Dodge -4.

Drop all fractions. Encumbrance can never reduce Move or Dodge below 1.

Note that these levels are numbered from 0 to 4. When a rule tells you to add or subtract your encumbrance level from a die roll, this is the number to use. For instance, encumbrance gives a penalty to Climbing, Stealth, and Swimming skills.

Home Gravity

Gravity is measured in "Gs." Earth's gravity is 1G. Note the gravity of your home world if it differs from 1G; e.g., "1.2G" for a world with 1.2

Basic Lift and Encumbrance Table

This table summarizes Basic Lift and encumbrance levels for ST 1-20.

ST (lbs.)	BL	Encumbrance Levels (lbs.)				
		None (0)	Light (1)	Medium (2)	Heavy (3)	Extra-Heavy (4)
1	0.2	0.2	0.4	0.6	1.2	2
2	0.8	0.8	1.6	2.4	4.8	8
3	1.8	1.8	3.6	5.4	10.8	18
4	3.2	3.2	6.4	9.6	19.2	32
5	5	5	10	15	30	50
6	7.2	7.2	14.4	21.6	43.2	72
7	9.8	9.8	19.6	29.4	58.8	98
8	13	13	26	39	78	130
9	16	16	32	48	96	160
10	20	20	40	60	120	200
11	24	24	48	72	144	240
12	29	29	58	87	174	290
13	34	34	68	102	204	340
14	39	39	78	117	234	390
15	45	45	90	135	270	450
16	51	51	102	153	306	510
17	58	58	116	174	348	580
18	65	65	130	195	390	650
19	72	72	144	216	432	720
20	80	80	160	240	480	800

times Earth's gravity. All weights are multiplied by local gravity, so to function like someone with a given BL on Earth, multiply the desired BL by your home gravity and buy the ST corresponding to the adjusted BL. For instance, to operate in 1.2G as if you were a ST 10 person in 1G, start with BL for ST 10, which is 20 lbs., and multiply by 1.2 for gravity to get a BL of 24 lbs. This BL corresponds to ST 11, so you'd need ST 11 in 1.2G to function as well as a ST 10 person in 1G.

Move in Other Environments

Water Move is normally Basic Move/5, rounded down. You can increase water Move directly for 5 points per yard/second, or reduce it for -5 points per yard/second. Members of land-dwelling races must have Swimming skill (p. 224) to increase water Move, and cannot buy more than +2 yards/second. If you're Amphibious (p. 40), both water and ground Move equal Basic Move, and changes to Basic Move adjust *both* scores. If you're Aquatic (p. 145), water move equals Basic Move and ground Move is 0.

Air Move is 0 without special advantages. If you have Flight (p. 56), air Move equals Basic Speed × 2 (*not* Basic Move × 2). You can increase air Move directly for 2 points per yard/second, or reduce it for -2 points per yard/second. If you have Walk on Air (p. 97), your air Move equals your ground Move, because the air is like solid ground beneath your feet.

Example of Character Creation (cont'd)

Dai is on the small side: ST 8 (-20 points). A "thief extraordinaire" should have catlike grace, so we give him an *amazing* DX 15 (100 points). Dai is also cunning and tough enough to survive on the street; therefore, we take IQ 12 (40 points) and HT 12 (20 points) – above average without being extreme.

Now we look at the secondary characteristics these choices give:

ST 8 gives a thrust damage of 1d-3, a swing damage of 1d-2, a Basic Lift of 13 lbs., and 8 HP. But Dai is tough, and no easier to kill than the average man, so we raise HP to 10 (4 points).

IQ 12 gives Dai a Will and Perception of 12. Since a talented thief must be able to spot traps and pursuers, we increase Per to 15 (15 points) – amazing, and a match for his DX!

HT 12 gives Dai 12 FP, but Dai prefers to *avoid* fatiguing labor in the first place, so we lower FP to 10 (-6 points), which is average.

Dai's Basic Speed is (15 + 12)/4 = 6.75. To get Dodge 10 and Basic Move 7 – useful for evading enemies when his teleportation fails – we raise Basic Speed to an even 7.00 (5 points).

Adding everything up, these traits cost Dai 158 points.

BUILD

You are free to select any height and weight the GM deems reasonable for a member of your race. These choices *do* occasionally matter in play – for instance, when you attempt to impersonate an enemy, wear someone else's armor, cross a rickety bridge, reach a high ledge, or hide behind cover.

If you are lighter or heavier than usual for your ST, you may qualify for a build-related disadvantage. The following table gives the thresholds for these disadvantages for normal humans.

The extremes of each weight range usually match the extremes of the associated height range. Overlaps are *intentional*. Consider two ST 10 men who stand 5'8" and weigh 175 lbs.: one might be big-boned and lean, the other fine-boned and chubby. Depending on muscle tone, a 160-lb. man could have any ST from 9 to 13 and claim "Average" build.

Regardless of weight, you never *have* to take a build-related disadvantage. If you want to be ST 9, 5'1," and

250 lbs. with "Average" build, the GM should allow it.

Build-related disadvantages are described below. In some settings, the GM may require you to take reaction modifiers if you select these traits, but this is not automatic.

Skinny

-5 points

You have approximately 2/3 the average weight for your ST. This gives you -2 to ST when you resist

Build Table

ST	Height Range	Weight Range by Build				
		Skinny	Average	Overweight	Fat	Very Fat
6 or less	4'4"-5'2"	40-80 lbs.	60-120 lbs.	80-160 lbs.	90-180 lbs.	120-240 lbs.
7	4'7"-5'5"	50-90 lbs.	75-135 lbs.	100-175 lbs.	115-205 lbs.	150-270 lbs.
8	4'10"-5'8"	60-100 lbs.	90-150 lbs.	120-195 lbs.	135-225 lbs.	180-300 lbs.
9	5'1"-5'11"	70-110 lbs.	105-165 lbs.	140-215 lbs.	160-250 lbs.	210-330 lbs.
10	5'3"-6'1"	80-120 lbs.	115-175 lbs.	150-230 lbs.	175-265 lbs.	230-350 lbs.
11	5'5"-6'3"	85-130 lbs.	125-195 lbs.	165-255 lbs.	190-295 lbs.	250-390 lbs.
12	5'8"-6'6"	95-150 lbs.	140-220 lbs.	185-290 lbs.	210-330 lbs.	280-440 lbs.
13	5'11"-6'9"	105-165 lbs.	155-245 lbs.	205-320 lbs.	235-370 lbs.	310-490 lbs.
14 or more	6'2"-7'	115-180 lbs.	170-270 lbs.	225-355 lbs.	255-405 lbs.	340-540 lbs.

knockback. You get -2 to Disguise – or to Shadowing, if you are trying to follow someone in a crowd. Your HT may not be above 14.

Overweight

-1 point

You have approximately 130% the average weight for your ST. You get -1 to Disguise – or to Shadowing, if you are trying to follow someone in a crowd. However, your extra fat gives you +1 to Swimming rolls, and +1 to ST when you resist knockback.

Fat

-3 points

You have approximately 150% the average weight for your ST. You get -2 to Disguise – or to Shadowing, if you are trying to follow someone in a crowd. However, your extra fat gives you +3 to Swimming rolls, and +2 to ST when you resist knockback. Your HT may not be above 15.

Very Fat

-5 points

You have approximately *twice* the average weight for your ST. You get -3 to Disguise – or to Shadowing, if you are trying to follow someone in a crowd. However, the extra fat gives you +5 to Swimming rolls, and +3 to ST when you resist knockback. Your HT may not be above 13.

Size Modifier Table

Longest Dimension	Size Modifier		Longest Dimension	Size Modifier
0.05 yard (1.8")	-10		3 yards (9')	+1
0.07 yard (2.5")	-9		5 yards (15')	+2
0.1 yard (3.5")	-8		7 yards (21')	+3
0.15 yard (5")	-7		10 yards (30')	+4
0.2 yard (7")	-6		15 yards (45')	+5
0.3 yard (10")	-5		20 yards (60')	+6
0.5 yard (18")	-4		30 yards (90')	+7
0.7 yard (2')	-3		50 yards (150')	+8
1 yard (3')	-2		70 yards (210')	+9
1.5 yards (4.5')	-1		100 yards (300')	+10
2 yards (6')	0		150 yards (450')	+11

SIZE MODIFIER (SM)

Size Modifier rates a person or object's most significant dimension: length, width, or height. It is a modifier to rolls to hit you in combat and to Vision rolls made to spot you. Thus, it is a bonus for large creatures, a penalty for small ones. Although large creatures are easier targets, a positive SM qualifies them to buy ST and HP more cheaply by taking the "Size" limitation.

Most humans – and humanoids, robots, etc. that can pass for human – have SM 0, and can ignore this rule. Nonhumans use the SM on their racial template. However, your SM may deviate from racial average if you are not full-grown, or if you are a genetic dwarf or giant.

When creating a creature that is larger or smaller than a human, find its SM by looking up its *longest* dimension – height for upright creatures such as giants, length for horizontal creatures such as cats and dragons, diameter for blobs – on the *Size Modifier Table* (above).

If a creature's longest dimension falls between two entries on the table, base its SM on the higher value. Box-, sphere-, or blob-shaped characters add +2 to SM; *elongated* boxes, like most ground vehicles, add +1.

It is neither an advantage nor a disadvantage to have a nonzero SM – the benefits and drawbacks tend to cancel out. The exceptions are genetic dwarfism and gigantism, as these conditions affect bodily proportions (notably relative arm and leg length) and have social ramifications (you stand out in a crowd).

Dwarfism (-1 SM)

-15 points

You are abnormally short for your species. Regardless of ST, your height falls below the lowest value on the Build Table – under 4'4," for a human. This gives you Size Modifier -1. Choose your weight from the first line of the Build Table and reduce it by 15%.

You have -1 to Basic Move (short legs). In combat, your reach is reduced by 1 yard. This is partly because you have short arms and partly because you must use scaled-down weapons (regardless of your ST, your arms lack the leverage to control full-sized weapons).

You get -2 to Disguise – or to Shadowing, if your are trying to follow someone in a crowd. In backward settings, the GM may require you to take a Social Stigma if you suffer from Dwarfism.

How GURPS Works: ST, Mass, and Move

It would be more realistic to calculate Basic Move from ST-to-mass ratio; for instance, a Fat character would move slower than one of Average build. If you want to simulate this, buy +1 Basic Move if your PC is Skinny, -1 if he is Overweight, -2 if he is Fat, or -3 if he is Very Fat, all at the usual point cost.

Women are on average lighter and weaker than men. You can simulate this by buying -1 or -2 to ST for the usual point cost. Choose a weight appropriate to this lower ST.

The GM should never *require* either of the above options. Most players prefer to choose ST, height, weight, and sex without being penalized!

GURPS handles mass considerations descriptively for nonhumans; e.g., a race that stumbles along under excess body weight will have a racial penalty to Basic Move.

A member of *any* race may be a dwarf. Scale down height by a factor of 0.75 from the racial average, and modify racial SM by -1. Otherwise, the rules remain the same.

Gigantism (+1 SM)
0 points
You are abnormally tall for your species. Regardless of ST, your height falls above the highest value on the Build Table – over 7', for a human. This gives you Size Modifier +1 and +1 to Basic Move (long legs), and qualifies you to buy ST and HP at a discount. Choose your weight from the last line of the Build Table and increase it by 10%.

You get -2 to Disguise – or to Shadowing, if you are trying to follow someone in a crowd. On the other hand, height often provides a bonus to Intimidation skill (see p. 202). In backward settings, the GM may require you to take a Social Stigma if you suffer from Gigantism.

A member of *any* race may be a giant. Scale your height up by a factor of 1.25 from the racial average, and modify racial SM by +1. Otherwise, the rules remain the same.

AGE AND BEAUTY

Age and physical appearance play a major role in how others perceive you. Choose carefully! Except in settings with magic or advanced biotechnology, you will be unable to change your mind after the game begins.

AGE

You are free to pick any age the GM agrees is within the usual lifespan for your race. Adventurers usually fall somewhere between "young adult" and "old" – 18 to 70 years, for humans – but fiction is full of heroic youths and sharp 90-year-old veterans.

Children

In many game worlds, especially those based on cartoons and fairytales, children are just small adults. By real-world standards, such children would be exceptional. However, even in a realistic campaign, those who wish to roleplay "heroic" children do not have to play less-capable characters – they can create their characters normally.

Players interested in complete realism are welcome to make children smaller and less capable than adults. To create a believable child, decide what his attributes will be when he is full-grown, reduce them, and purchase the reduced values *instead of* the full values.

A human infant has 30% of his adult ST score, 40% of his adult DX, 50% of his adult IQ, and Size Modifier -3. A 5-year-old has 60% of his adult ST, 70% of his adult DX and IQ, and SM -2. A 10-year-old has 80% of his adult ST, 90% of his adult DX and IQ, and SM -1. A 15-year-old has adult scores. Interpolate between these values for children in other age groups. HT is usually unaffected by age, but young children might be at -1 or so relative to their adult HT. Note that there is no point cost for Size Modifier; this is merely a special effect.

For nonhumans, use the above rules, but adjust the age categories upward or downward in proportion to the race's rate of development. For instance, a race that reaches adulthood at age 36 instead of age 18 doubles the age thresholds given above. Size Modifier is equal to the sum of the SM given for a human child and the racial SM.

In many societies, children are subject to social restrictions. A child generally is Dead Broke (see p. 25), worth -25 points, and has Social Stigma (Minor) (see p. 155), for -5 points. These traits are usually balanced against Patron (Parents; 15 or less), worth 30 points – see *Patrons* (p. 72).

As a child grows up, he should gradually improve his attributes toward their full adult values, reduce the appearance roll for his Patron (and eventually get rid of it altogether), increase his wealth, and buy off his Social Stigma. These changes have their usual point costs.

The Elderly

If you age *in play*, you will eventually have to make HT rolls to avoid attribute loss (see *Age and Aging*, p. 444). These rolls start at the first "aging threshold" for your race, becoming more frequent at the second threshold and again at the third. These thresholds are 50, 70, and 90 years for humans.

If you *start* at an advanced age, you have no special disadvantages. Not everyone ages well, but heroes are exceptional, and you are free to make elderly characters as fit and as capable as you wish. There are plenty of examples of this kind of person in fiction – and in real life!

To create a character who *has* declined with age, first decide what his attributes were before he got old. Reduce his ST, DX, and HT by 10% at the second aging threshold, or reduce ST, DX, and HT by 20% and IQ by 10% at the third aging threshold. Then purchase the reduced values instead of the values he had in his prime.

Note that in many societies, the elderly enjoy great respect. Represent this by taking Social Regard (Venerated) – see p. 86.

PHYSICAL APPEARANCE

Appearance is mostly a "special effect" – you may choose any physical appearance you like. At minimum, note the color of your skin, hair, and eyes (or other features appropriate to your race: scales, feathers, paint job, etc.). However, certain traits count as advantages or disadvantages.

Appearance Levels

Appearance is rated in levels. Most people have "Average" appearance, for 0 points. Good looks give a reaction bonus; this is an advantage and costs points. Unappealing looks give a reaction penalty; this is a disadvantage, and gives you back points. These reaction modifiers only affect those who can see you! Those who cannot see you might have to make a new reaction roll upon first meeting you in person (GM's option).

Reaction modifiers due to appearance only affect members of your own race, a very similar race, or a dissimilar race that finds your race attractive (for whatever reason). In all cases, the GM's word is final; humans are "very similar" to elves, but bug-eyed monsters are unlikely to care about a human's appearance except in a silly campaign.

Horrific: You are indescribably monstrous or unspeakably foul, and cannot interact with normal mortals. This gives -6 on reaction rolls. The GM may decide that this trait is supernatural and unavailable to normal characters. *-24 points.*

Monstrous: You are hideous *and* clearly unnatural. Most people react to you as a monster rather than a sapient being. This gives -5 on reaction rolls. Again, this trait might not be appropriate for normal characters. *-20 points.*

Hideous: You have any sort of disgusting looks you can come up with: a severe skin disease, wall-eye . . . preferably several things at once. This gives -4 on reaction rolls. *-16 points.*

Ugly: As above, but not so bad – maybe only stringy hair and snaggle teeth. This gives -2 on reaction rolls. *-8 points.*

Unattractive: You look vaguely unappealing, but it's nothing anyone can put a finger on. This gives -1 on reaction rolls. *-4 points.*

Average: Your appearance gives you no reaction modifiers either way; you can blend easily into a crowd. A viewer's impression of your looks depends on your behavior. If you smile and act friendly, you will be remembered as pleasant-looking; if you frown and mutter, you will be remembered as unattractive. *0 points.*

Attractive: You don't enter beauty contests, but are definitely good-looking. This gives +1 on reaction rolls. *4 points.*

Handsome (or Beautiful): You *could* enter beauty contests. This gives +4 on reaction rolls made by those attracted to members of your sex, +2 from everyone else. *12 points.*

Very Handsome (or Very Beautiful): You could *win* beauty contests – regularly. This gives +6 on reaction rolls made by those attracted to members of your sex, +2 from others. *Exception:* Members of the same sex with reason to dislike you (more than -4 in reaction penalties, regardless of bonuses) *resent* your good looks, and react at -2 instead. As well, talent scouts, friendly drunks, slave traders, and other nuisances are liable to become a problem for you. *16 points.*

Transcendent: You are an "ideal specimen." This gives +8 (!) on reaction rolls made by those attracted to members of your sex, +2 from others, and all the troublesome side effects of Very Handsome. The GM is free to reserve this trait for angels, deities, and the like. Such entities frequently possess Charisma (p. 41) or Terror (p. 93) as well. *20 points.*

Special Options

The following options are available for above-average appearance, and do not affect point costs:

Androgynous: If your appearance is Handsome (Beautiful) or better, you may specify that your looks appeal equally to both sexes. You get a flat reaction modifier instead of a sex-dependent bonus: +3 for Handsome, +4 for Very Handsome, or +5 for Transcendent.

Impressive: If you are Attractive or better, you can specify that you have exceptional physical presence that doesn't manifest as sexual magnetism. This is typical of tigers and aged royalty. If your appearance is Handsome (Beautiful) or above, use the "flat" reaction bonuses given for Androgynous.

Special Enhancements

Universal: Your reaction modifier applies to *everyone* who can see you, regardless of race. If your appearance is Handsome (Beautiful) or above, use the "flat" reaction bonuses given for Androgynous. This modifier is most common for Hideous or worse monsters and for Attractive or better gods, faeries, and the like. The GM may deem it off-limits to normal mortals. *+25%.*

Special Limitations

Off-the-Shelf Looks: You can apply this to any appearance better than Attractive. Through ultra-tech or magic, your looks are a variation on a standard type or famous person. You're as beautiful as ever, but you get *half* the usual reaction bonus with people from your own culture, because they've seen it all before. ("Oh, look! Another Mr. Universe 2003!") *-50%.*

OTHER PHYSICAL FEATURES

There is more to appearance than good (or not-so-good) looks. You may take any combination of the following traits in conjunction with *any* appearance level.

Fashion Sense

5 points

Your look is always one step ahead of the crowd. You have the ability to create a fashion statement out of the cheapest and most nondescript materials. This gives +1 to reaction rolls in social situations when you have a chance to plan your attire in advance. You can also give *someone else* a +1 reaction bonus when you put together the outfit.

Mistaken Identity

-5 points

You are often mistaken for someone else. Your "double's" allies approach you and tell you things you don't want to know, and his acquaintances will treat you in strange and irritating ways. His enemies are after you, too! You might eventually get things straightened out, but not without some effort.

If *every* member of your race looks the same, your race qualifies for a bizarre feature (see *Features and Taboo Traits*, p. 261), but you do not have Mistaken Identity.

Odious Personal Habits
-5, -10, or -15 points

You usually or always behave in a fashion repugnant to others. An Odious Personal Habit (OPH) is worth -5 points for every -1 to reaction rolls made by people who notice your problem. Specify the behavior when you create your character, and work out the point value with the GM.

Examples: Body odor, constant scratching, or tuneless humming would give -1 to reactions, and are worth -5 points apiece. Constant bad puns or spitting on the floor would give -2 to reactions, worth -10 points apiece. We leave -15-point habits (-3 to reactions) to the imagination of those depraved enough to want them!

The reaction penalty for an OPH applies only to members of your race. It is up to the GM to handle the reactions of other races. A constant drool will irritate other humans, but a Martian might not even notice – and a troll might think it was cute! Of course, an entire *race* can behave in a manner repugnant to most other races. These "Odious Racial Habits" are priced identically to OPHs.

Pitiable
5 points

Something about you makes people pity you and want to take care of you. You get +3 on all reaction rolls from those who consider you to be in a position of helplessness, weakness, or need (which *never* includes those with the Callous disadvantage). Taken in conjunction with above-average looks, Pitiable means you are "cute" instead of "sexy"; in combination with below-average looks, it means you are "appealingly homely," like a basset hound.

Unnatural Features
-1 point/level

You are superficially "normal" but have one or more disturbing cosmetic features. To qualify for points, these must be unnatural *for your race*. Pointed ears and eyes like hot coals would be unnatural for a human, but not for a demon from Hell! You *must* specify the origin of your Unnatural Features: magical curse, ultra-tech surgery, rare disease, etc.

Unnatural Features need not be unattractive (if they are, you can also claim points for below-average appearance), but they make it easy for others to identify you and hard for you to blend into a crowd. Each level, to a maximum of five levels, gives -1 to your Disguise and Shadowing skills and +1 to others' attempts to identify or follow you (including *their* Observation and Shadowing rolls), unless almost everyone else in the crowd happens to share your features.

Example of Character Creation (cont'd)

We want Dai to look *unremarkable* – thieves who stand out don't last long! So we choose an Average build. For ST 8, this suggests a height between 4'10" and 5'8," and a weight of 90 to 150 lbs. We pick 5'6" and 115 lbs. We make Dai's appearance Average as well. Since Dai is average in all respects, he pays 0 points. His point total remains at 158 points.

SOCIAL BACKGROUND

The next few sections discuss your society's level of technological development, cultures, and languages. It is an advantage to be technologically advanced, culturally literate, or linguistically talented. *Inadequacy* in these areas can be a crippling disadvantage.

TECHNOLOGY LEVEL (TL)

"Technology level" (or "tech level") is a number that rates technological development. The more advanced the society, the higher its TL; see *Tech Level and Starting Wealth* (p. 27) for examples from Earth's history. The GM will tell you the TL of his world. Be sure to note this, as it affects your access to certain traits – notably skills – and equipment.

Characters *also* have a TL, equal to that of the technology with which they are most familiar. Unless you are especially primitive or advanced, you should record the TL of your game world as your personal TL and move on.

In some game worlds, your personal TL may differ from the campaign average. A world might be TL8 on average, but the citizens of one advanced nation might be TL9 while those from an underdeveloped region might be TL7. And the TL of a space, time, or dimension traveler might differ radically from that of his current surroundings.

Being from a higher TL than the campaign norm is an advantage; being from a lower TL is a disadvantage.

Low TL
-5 points/TL below campaign TL

Your personal TL is below that of the campaign world. You start with *no* knowledge (or default skill) relating to equipment above your personal TL. You will be able to learn DX-based technological skills (pertaining to vehicles, weapons, etc.) in play, if you can find a teacher, but fundamental differences in thinking prevent you from learning IQ-based technological skills. To overcome this limitation, you must buy off this trait, increasing your personal TL. This usually requires a lengthy period of re-education (see Chapter 9).

High TL

5 points/TL above campaign TL

Your personal TL is above that of the campaign world. You may enter play with skills relating to equipment up to your personal TL. This is most useful if you also have access to high-TL equipment (see *Tech Level and Equipment*, p. 27), but the knowledge of a high-tech doctor or scientist can be very useful in a low-tech setting, even without specialized equipment!

CULTURE

You are automatically familiar with the social peculiarities of one major culture of your choice. You suffer no skill penalties when interacting with people from that culture. The GM will provide a list of cultures to choose from (or let you invent your own – many GMs appreciate players' contributions to the game world!).

When dealing with an *unfamiliar* culture, you have -3 to use any skill with a significant cultural component, including Carousing, Connoisseur, Criminology, Dancing, Detect Lies, Diplomacy, Fast-Talk, Games, Gesture, Heraldry, Intimidation, Leadership, Merchant, Poetry, Politics, Psychology, Public Speaking, Savoir-Faire, Sex Appeal, Sociology, Streetwise, and Teaching. To get rid of this penalty, buy the following advantage:

Cultural Familiarity

1 or 2 points/culture

You are familiar with cultures other than your own, and do not suffer the -3 penalty for unfamiliarity. This costs 1 point per culture of the same (or very similar) race, or 2 points per alien culture.

To prevent point-cost inflation, the GM should use broad definitions of culture: East Asian, Muslim, Western, etc. A single nation would have to be *very* different to merit its own Cultural Familiarity. In fantasy worlds, the GM might wish to have one culture per race; in a futuristic setting, an entire planet or even a galactic empire might have a single, monolithic culture.

See *Cultural Adaptability* (p. 46) for additional options.

LANGUAGE

GURPS assumes that most characters can read and write their "native" language. This ability costs no points, but you should note your native language on your character sheet; e.g., "English (Native) [0]."

The rest of this section is only important if you can communicate in more than one language (an advantage) or have difficulty with your native tongue (a disadvantage).

Sapience and Language

The *Language* rules are for *sapient* characters. You must have at least IQ 6 to receive a native tongue for free and be able to learn new languages. Sapience does not guarantee the physical capacity for speech, though – you might need to rely on sign language.

Those with IQ 5 or less *do not get a native tongue for free* and *cannot learn languages*. They can only communicate basic concepts. They can be taught a few commands, however – see Chapter 16.

Comprehension Levels

The point cost to learn an additional language depends on your "comprehension level": a measure of how well you function in that language overall. There are four comprehension levels:

None: You are *completely* incapable of functioning in the language. If you do not spend points on a non-native language, this comprehension level is assumed – there is no need to note it for *every* language you don't know! *0 points/language.*

Broken: You can recognize important words and understand simple sentences if they are spoken slowly. You have -3 when using skills that depend on language, such as Fast-Talk, Public Speaking, Research, Speed-Reading, Teaching, and Writing. This doubles to -6 for artistic skills that rely on the beauty of the language (Poetry, Singing, etc.). In stressful situations – e.g., encounters involving combat or reaction rolls – you must roll against IQ to understand or make yourself understood in the language. On a failure, you convey no information, but you may try again. Critical failure means you convey the *wrong* information! For hurried speech, bad phone connections, etc., this roll is at -2 to -8! Native speakers who already dislike foreigners (see *Intolerance*, p. 140) react to you at an extra -1. *2 points/language.*

Accented: You can communicate clearly, even under stress. However, your speech and writing are idiosyncratic, and it is obvious that this is not your native language. You have -1 when using skills that depend on language, doubled to -2 for artistic skills. You receive no reaction penalty from native speakers, but you will be unable to pass for a native (this can be a major problem for would-be spies!). *4 points/language.*

Native: You have full mastery of the language, including idioms. You can *think* in the language. You have no penalty to use skills that depend on language. You start with one language at this level for free. If you buy Native comprehension in a foreign tongue, you can pass for a native speaker. *6 points/language.*

Exceptional Competence and Incompetence

Great orators, writers, and other masters of the language should start with Native-level comprehension, then learn skills such as Public Speaking and Writing at very high levels.

Poorly educated individuals who can barely get by in their *native* tongue should take the point difference between their actual level and Native level as a disadvantage. For instance, someone who has his native tongue at Broken level has a -4-point disadvantage.

Spoken vs. Written Language

The point costs above assume that you read/write and speak the language equally well. If your written and spoken ability differ, select separate spoken and written comprehension levels and pay *half* cost for each. For instance, if you learned to write French from a book, you might have "French: Spoken (None)/Written (Native) [3]."

Literacy

Your written comprehension level determines your degree of literacy in that language:

Literacy is a written comprehension of Accented or better. You can read and write competently and at full speed.

Semi-literacy is a written comprehension of Broken. A semi-literate person would require three minutes to read this sentence, and would have to make an IQ roll to understand the full meaning! Many words are always unintelligible to a semi-literate person, including some in this paragraph.

Illiteracy is a written comprehension of None. If this is the case, *you really can't read!* Signs, scrolls, books, and names on maps (though not the maps themselves) are completely incomprehensible to you. The *player* may pass secret notes to the GM (and vice versa), but the *character* cannot read *anything*.

At TL4 and below, it is quite possible to go all your life without *needing* to read. In settings like this, illiteracy or semi-literacy is the norm. Most people have a spoken comprehension level of Native, but their written comprehension is Broken or None.

Illiteracy in your native tongue – Spoken (Native)/Written (None) – is a disadvantage worth -3 points. Semi-literacy – Spoken (Native)/Written

---

Accents

If your spoken comprehension is Broken or better, you can attempt to fake a regional accent. To fool someone, you must *win* a Quick Contest of Acting (p. 174) or Mimicry (Speech) (p. 210) vs. his IQ. You are at -6 for Broken comprehension, or -2 for Accented . . . but a non-Native *listener* has similar penalties to his IQ roll!

Each accent is a separate familiarity (see p. 169) for Acting or Mimicry. To memorize a new accent, you must listen to that accent used in conversation for at least one hour and make a successful roll against the higher of IQ or Linguistics, at +5 for Eidetic Memory or +10 for Photographic Memory (see *Eidetic Memory*, p. 51).

Broken to Broken

If you and the person with whom you are speaking both have a comprehension level of Broken, conversation will be difficult. This is definitely a "stressful situation"! Each of you must roll against IQ once per piece of information; all the usual modifiers apply. If you both succeed, you get the point across. If one of you fails, you just fail to communicate. But if *both* of you fail, the listener gets the wrong idea. This could be embarrassing or dangerous – possibly for both of you. The GM should be creative!

(Broken) – is worth -2 points. The GM should not count these points against the disadvantage limit if illiteracy is the norm in the game world.

Sign Language

A true sign language – e.g., American Sign Language – is complex, stylized, and can communicate almost any concept. Treat it as any other language, with one important difference: a sign language has *one* form (signed) instead of two (spoken and written). As a result, sign languages costs half as much: 1 point for Broken, 2 points for Accented, and 3 points for Native comprehension.

Characters with the Deafness (p. 129) or Mute (p. 125) disadvantages start with one sign language and *written* ability in one regular language – both at Native level – *instead of* spoken and written ability in one language. Those who are illiterate, or incompetent at sign language, can buy down their language abilities using the usual rules.

Learning Languages

To learn a new language, use the rules for learning skills (p. 292): 200 hours of learning gives you one point to spend. Note that language study is *four times as hard* without a teacher!

If you live in another country and speak its language at all times, that is the automatic equivalent of 4 hours/day of training; there is no need to allocate specific study time unless you want to get more than this default. Thus, every 50 days, you get a character point to spend in that language.

WEALTH AND INFLUENCE

Now you need to determine your position in your society: How much money do you have, what privileges do you enjoy, and how do others react to you?

WEALTH

Wealth is relative. A middle-class American lives in more luxury than a medieval king, though he may have fewer gold coins in his basement. It all depends on the game world – see *Tech Level and Starting Wealth* (p. 27). In most worlds, the range of standard starting wealth and income is relatively great, and your skills determine your job and income; see *Economics* (p. 514) for more information.

Personal wealth is rated in "wealth levels." A level of "Average" costs no points, and lets you support an average lifestyle for your game world. The rest of these rules apply if you are unusually poor or wealthy, have a source of income that does not require you to work, or are in debt.

Wealth

Variable

Above-average Wealth is an advantage; it means you start with two or more times the average starting wealth of your game world. Below-average Wealth is a disadvantage; it means you start with only a fraction of average starting wealth. The precise meaning of each wealth level in a particular game world will be defined in the associated worldbook.

Dead Broke: You have no job, no source of income, no money, and no property other than the clothes you are wearing. Either you are unable to work or there are no jobs to be found. *-25 points.*

Poor: Your starting wealth is only 1/5 of the average for your society. Some jobs are not available to you, and no job you find pays very well. *-15 points.*

Struggling: Your starting wealth is only 1/2 of the average for your society. Any job is open to you (you *can* be a Struggling doctor or movie actor), but you don't earn much. This is appropriate if you are, for instance, a 21st-century student. *-10 points.*

Average: The default wealth level, as explained above. *0 points.*

Comfortable: You work for a living, but your lifestyle is better than most. Your starting wealth is twice the average. *10 points.*

Wealthy: Your starting wealth is five times average; you live very well indeed. *20 points.*

Very Wealthy: Your starting wealth is 20 times the average. *30 points.*

Filthy Rich: Your starting wealth is 100 times average. You can buy almost anything you want without considering the cost. *50 points.*

Multimillionaire: "Filthy rich" doesn't even begin to describe your wealth! For every 25 points you spend beyond the 50 points to be Filthy Rich, increase your starting wealth by another factor of 10: Multimillionaire 1 costs 75 points and gives 1,000 times average starting wealth, Multimillionaire 2 costs 100 points and gives 10,000 times starting wealth, and so on, to a maximum level (usually 3 or 4) set by the GM. *50 points + 25 points/level of Multimillionaire.*

Wealth and Status

In some game worlds, Status (see p. 28) is closely tied to Wealth. In a setting like this, if you are Wealthy or better, you get +1 Status for free. This bonus increases to +2 at Multimillionaire 1 and to +3 at Multimillionaire 2. No one may claim more than +3 Status from Wealth.

Independent Income
1 point/level

You have a source of income that does not require you to work: stock portfolio, trust fund, rental property, royalties, pension, etc. Your monthly income is 1% of your starting wealth (adjusted for wealth level) per level of this trait, to a maximum of 20%. If your income derives from investments, you need not specify their value; this trait assumes that you cannot or will not invade your capital.

This trait is unrelated to wealth level. A Filthy Rich heiress has Independent Income . . . but so do an Average pensioner and a Poor welfare recipient.

Independent Income most often means your occupation is something like dilettante, retiree, or welfare recipient – not an actual "job."

However, you can have Independent Income *and* a job; just add the income from both sources. If you are wealthy, this allows you to work less than full time (e.g., 10 hours per week instead of 40, for 1/4 the usual salary) and still make a good living.

Debt
-1 point/level

You owe money. This could represent a loan, back taxes, child support, or alimony . . . or "hush money" paid to blackmailers . . . or "protection money" extorted by gangsters. You must make a monthly payment equal to 1% of your starting wealth (adjusted for wealth level) per level of this trait, to a maximum of 20%. Debt can accompany any wealth level above Dead Broke; plenty of multimillionaires owe significant amounts of money!

Your monthly payment is deducted from your monthly earnings at your job. If your job cannot cover your Debt, you have to pay out of your cash reserves, take a second job, or *steal*.

If you cannot pay – or *choose* not to pay – there will be trouble. For bank loans, this means repossession of your worldly goods. For alimony, child support, fines, or taxes, this means a court date. And if you owe money to the mob, you might end up being strong-armed into criminal activities . . . or staring down the barrel of a shotgun. The GM should be creative!

It is assumed that you cannot easily rid yourself of this obligation. It takes more than money to buy off Debt – you must pay off the points and work out a logical in-game explanation with the GM.

REPUTATION

It is possible to be so well-known that your reputation becomes an advantage or a disadvantage. This affects reaction rolls made by NPCs (see p. 494). A reputation has four elements: *Details, Reaction Modifier, People Affected,* and *Frequency of Recognition.*

Details

The details of your reputation are entirely up to you; you can be known for bravery, ferocity, eating green

---

Starting Wealth

"Starting wealth" covers both money and property. Start with the amount of money your wealth level entitles you to for your game world. Buy the possessions you want to start with (see Chapter 8, or consult the equipment list in the relevant worldbook). Any unspent money is your "bank account."

Realistically, if you have a settled lifestyle, you should put 80% of your starting wealth into home, clothing, etc., which leaves only 20% for "adventuring" gear. If you are a wanderer (pioneer, knight-errant, Free Trader, etc.), or Poor or worse, the GM might allow you to spend *all* your starting wealth on movable possessions.

The GM should not allow wealthy PCs to bankroll their poorer associates. This makes below-average Wealth little more than "free points." The GM might allow rich characters to *hire* poor ones. If so, he should make it obvious – through such means as NPC reactions ("Oh, so you're the hired help?") – that the poorer PC is earning his disadvantage points by giving up some of his independence.

Trading Points for Money

If you need a *little* extra money, you may trade character points for it – either at the time of creation or in play. Each point yields 10% of the campaign's average starting wealth. Money obtained this way can be saved, invested, gambled, spent on equipment, etc. You are free to spend as many points as you wish, but if you plan to spend more than 10 points, you would be better off just buying Wealth!

Unlike Wealth, points traded for money do not appear on your character sheet – they are *gone*. If you exercise this option during character creation, you are worth fewer points than your associates (but you are better equipped!).

You can also spend points on specific *equipment,* if it's key to your character concept. See *Signature Gear,* p. 85.

Later Earnings

You can depend on your adventures to bring in money . . . or you can get a job (see p. 516). Remember that in many worlds, unemployment is cause for grave suspicion and bad reaction rolls.

If a poor PC becomes wealthy, the GM should require the player to "buy off" the disadvantage with character points – see p. 121.

CREATING A CHARACTER

snakes, or whatever you want. However, you *must* give specifics. Reputation is, by definition, something noteworthy; there is no such thing as a "generic" reputation.

Reaction Modifier

Specify the reaction-roll modifier that you get from people who recognize you. This determines the base cost of your reputation. For every +1 bonus to reaction rolls (up to +4), the cost is 5 points. For every -1 penalty (up to -4), the cost is -5 points.

People Affected

The size of the group of people who might have heard of you modifies the base cost:

Almost everyone in your game world (but *not* those from other universes – at least, not until they have met you!): ×1.

Almost everyone in your game world *except* one large class (everyone but the French, everyone but Elves, everyone but offworld visitors): ×2/3.

Large class of people (all people of a particular faith, all mercenaries, all tradesmen, etc.): ×1/2.

Small class of people (all priests of Wazoo, all literate people in 12th-century England, all mages in modern Alabama): ×1/3.

If the class of people affected is so small that, in the GM's opinion, you would not meet even one in the average adventure, your reputation isn't worth points. This depends on the setting; for instance, mercenary soldiers are rare in some game worlds, common in others.

Frequency of Recognition

Either your name or your face is enough to trigger a "reputation roll" to see if the people you meet have heard of you. Roll once for each person or small group you meet. For a large group, the GM may roll more than once if he likes. The frequency with which you are recognized modifies the cost of your reputation:

Tech Level and Starting Wealth

Tech level (p. 22) determines starting wealth, as technologically advanced societies tend to be richer. Below is a comparison of TLs and suggested starting wealth.

TL0	Stone Age (Prehistory and later). $250.
TL1	Bronze Age (3500 B.C.+). $500.
TL2	Iron Age (1200 B.C.+). $750.
TL3	Medieval (600 A.D.+). $1,000.
TL4	Age of Sail (1450+). $2,000.
TL5	Industrial Revolution (1730+). $5,000.
TL6	Mechanized Age (1880+). $10,000.
TL7	Nuclear Age (1940+). $15,000.
TL8	Digital Age (1980+). $20,000.
TL9	Microtech Age (2025+?). $30,000.
TL10	Robotic Age (2070+?). $50,000.
TL11	Age of Exotic Matter. $75,000.
TL12+	Whatever the GM likes! $100,000.

GURPS gives wealth and prices in "$" for convenience. The $ can stand for "dollars," "credits," "pennies," or even units of barter. In a contemporary setting, $1 is a modern U.S. dollar. In other periods, $1 equates roughly with the amount of local currency needed to buy a loaf of bread or equivalent staple – *not* with historical U.S. dollars.

For example, in a high medieval society, each $ might be a copper farthing. In WWII-era America, each $ would convert to $0.10 in deflated 1940s-era dollars. And in a cyberpunk world with hyperinflation, each $ might equal $1,000 in grossly devalued 2030-era dollars! The *GURPS* $ is a constant, however. Variations in starting wealth by TL reflect increased prosperity due to civilization's progress – not inflation.

Worldbooks might give starting wealth, wages, and prices in local currency – historical U.S. dollars, British pounds, pieces of eight, etc. In such cases, they will always give a conversion factor to constant $.

Tech Level and Equipment

You enter play with "starting wealth" appropriate to the *campaign* TL. If you are from a higher TL, you may start with access to the equipment of your *personal* TL. However, *the price of an item of equipment is doubled for every TL by which its TL exceeds that of the campaign!*

For instance, a TL8 character in a TL3 game world starts with the same $1,000 as everyone else at TL3. If he wants a TL8 assault rifle that normally costs $1,500, it costs him 32 times as much (five TLs of difference results in five doublings, or a factor of 32) – or $48,000 – since the rifle is *far* more valuable in a low-tech setting. He'd need to start with some Wealth!

There is no guarantee that high-TL adventurers will *continue* to have access to high-tech gear in play. If you want a piece of gear, then you should buy it when you start out. If your TL8 adventurer is dropped into a TL3 world with 100 rounds of ammunition for his assault rifle, then he had better use it wisely. Once it's gone, it's gone . . .

Classless Meritocracies

In many societies, especially feudal ones, Status is the primary form of social rank. However, some societies, notably modern and futuristic ones, claim to be "classless." This does not mean that social rank doesn't exist! It just means that merit – most often in the form of wealth, education, or public service – replaces entitlement or birthright as the determiner of relative social position.

In a classless society, the GM may wish to limit the amount of Status that PCs can buy *directly* to only two levels. This represents some combination of higher education, professional license (such as in law or medicine), respected family name, and cultural achievements (anything from "rock star" to "poet laureate"). The only way to obtain higher Status is to get it for "free" from high Wealth (p. 25) or Rank (p. 29).

In a society where some form of Rank – not Status – is the official yardstick of power, it takes finesse to turn high Status to your advantage. For instance, you might come from a "good" family and have a decent education, allowing you to buy Status 2 outright. You might also be rich (Multimillionaire 1) for +2 Status and hold local office (Administrative Rank 3) for +1 Status. This would give you Status 5 in total. To overrule a senior bureaucrat with Administrative Rank 6 and Status 2, though, you'll have to use your social connections. You might have more clout in high society (Status 5 vs. Status 2), but he outranks you in the eyes of the law (Rank 6 vs. Rank 3)!

All the time: ×1.

Sometimes (roll of 10 or less): ×1/2.

Occasionally (roll of 7 or less): ×1/3.

Of course, your reputation extends only within a certain area. If you travel far enough away, the GM may require you to "buy off" the disadvantage points you received for a bad reputation. (There is no corresponding bonus for losing a good reputation.) Apply multipliers for people affected and frequency of recognition, and then drop all fractions at the end.

Multiple Reputations

You may have more than one reputation, and your reputations can overlap. The GM should check each one before determining how an NPC reacts to you. Your total reaction modifier from reputations cannot be better than +4 or worse than -4 in a given situation.

Multifaceted Reputations

A single reputation can give different reaction modifiers with different groups, provided the groups do not overlap. Set the reaction modifier for each group, modify the cost for the size of the group, and then add up the resulting costs. Modify this total for frequency of recognition. The reputation is an advantage if the net point cost is positive, a disadvantage if negative. The final point cost may be 0, but you should still record it on your character sheet!

Example 1: Sir Anacreon has a reputation for fearless monster-slaying. This earns him a +2 reaction from those who recognize him. Everyone has heard of him (no modifier), and he is recognized on a roll of 10 or less (×1/2). He has a 5-point advantage.

Example 2: The Green Dragon has a reputation as a crimefighter. He gets +3 reactions from honest citizens – which is almost everyone except the large class of *dishonest* citizens (×2/3) – for 10 points. He receives a -4 reaction from the underworld – a large group (×1/2) – for -10 points. The net point cost for his reputation is 0 points. If his player wished, he could specify a frequency of recognition, but the final cost would still be 0 points.

IMPORTANCE

Your formally recognized *place* in society is distinct from your personal fame and fortune. To influence others through established channels (as opposed to relying on popularity or bribery), you must purchase one or more types of social rank, each of which has unique benefits and drawbacks.

Status

5 points/level

Status is a measure of social standing. In most game worlds, Status levels range from -2 (serf or street person) to 8 (powerful emperor or god-king), with the average man being Status 0 (freeman or ordinary citizen). If you do not specifically buy Status, you have Status 0. Status costs 5 points per level. For instance, Status 5 costs 25 points, while Status -2 is -10 points. Status also costs money to maintain (see p. 516).

Status is not the same as personal popularity (see *Reputation,* p. 26) or the popularity of your racial or ethnic group (see *Social Regard,* p. 86, and *Social Stigma,* p. 155). Status can sometimes influence others' reactions, but its main effect is to spell out where you stand in the social pecking order. In short, Status represents *power.*

High Status

Status greater than 0 means you are a member of the ruling class in your culture. Your family may be hereditary nobles (e.g., Plantagenet, Windsor), successful businessmen or politicians (Rockefeller, Kennedy), or some other type of big shots. You may even have achieved Status by your own efforts. As a result, others *in your culture only* defer to you, giving you a bonus on all reaction rolls.

High Status carries various privileges, different in every game world; your GM will give you this information. Note that any high-Status person is a likely target for kidnappers and social climbers, and that some criminal types *hate* "the ruling class."

Low Status

Status less than 0 means you are a serf or a slave, or simply very poor. This is not the same thing as Social Stigma (p. 155). In medieval Japan, for instance, a woman could have high Status, but still get a -1 on reactions due to the Social Stigma of being female. A modern-day criminal could theoretically have *any* level of Status in conjunction with the Social Stigma of a criminal record.

The interaction of Status, Social Stigma, and Reputation can give interesting results. For instance, a person who is obviously from a lower social class, or even a disdained minority group, might earn such a reputation as a hero that others react well to him.

Status as a Reaction Modifier

When the GM makes a reaction roll (see p. 494), the relative Status of the characters involved can affect the reaction. The GM can roleplay NPCs as he likes, of course, but here are some general guidelines:

Higher Status usually gives a reaction bonus. When dealing with a social inferior, apply the difference between your Status levels as a reaction bonus – except, of course, when dealing with someone who resents Status. For instance, if you have Status 3, those of Status 1 react to you at +2, and those of Status 0 react at +3.

Lower Status may give a penalty. If you are dealing with a higher-Status NPC who is basically friendly, your Status doesn't matter (as long as it's positive). After all, the king has a far higher Status than his knights, but he reacts well to them . . . most of the time. But if the NPC is neutral or already angry, lower Status makes it worse ("How dare you, a mere knight, tell me my battle plan is foolish?"). Again, apply the difference in Status levels as a reaction modifier, but in this case it gives a penalty.

Negative Status usually gives a penalty. If your Status is so low as to be negative, those of higher Status *always* react badly to you. Apply the difference between your Status and the NPC's as a reaction penalty, but no worse than -4.

Recognizing Status

Status only affects reaction rolls if it is obvious to those around you. In some settings, your bearing, dress, and speech communicate your Status. Indeed, if you have very high Status, your *face* may be easily recognized – or perhaps the gaggle of servants that surrounds you gets the message across.

In other societies, you will have to produce physical proof (ID cards, signet rings, etc.), pass a test, or submit to ultra-tech or magical scans

before you will be recognized. Status costs no fewer points in such societies; you may get fewer reaction bonuses, but you can also live a normal life, and it is far more difficult for someone to impersonate you.

Rank

5 or 10 points/level

Specific sectors of society – e.g., the civil service, the military, and certain powerful religions – often have internal ranking systems, distinct from Status. If an organization like this has significant social influence, or access to useful resources, then its members must pay points for their rank within the organization.

Rank comes in levels. Each Rank has authority over those of lower Rank – regardless of personal ability. In most cases, there are six to eight levels of Rank. The GM should determine the highest Rank available to starting characters, usually Rank 3-5.

Unlike Status, Rank costs no money to maintain. On the other hand, almost all forms of Rank come with a Duty (see p. 133). Rank often has stringent prerequisites, too –

typically one of the traits given under *Privilege* (p. 30) or a minimum skill level. These things have their own point costs, not included in the cost of the Rank.

In a given society, there are usually *several* systems of Rank; the precise varieties depend on the game world. In most cases, you may hold more than one kind of Rank, although the GM is free to rule that holding one sort of Rank precludes holding another.

Rank may coexist with Status. If so, then high Rank grants additional Status at no extra cost: +1 to Status at Rank 2-4, +2 to Status at Rank 5-7, and +3 to Status at Rank 8 or higher. This represents society's respect for senior members of important social institutions. If you hold multiple types of Rank, then you may claim a Status bonus for each of them.

Alternatively, one form of Rank might replace Status; for instance, Religious Rank in a theocracy. In societies like this, Status *does not exist.* Each level of Rank gives all its usual benefits *plus* the effect of an equivalent level of Status.

Special Rules for Rank

A number of special situations might arise in play for those with Rank.

Temporary Rank

Those of higher Rank may *temporarily* increase your Rank for a predetermined amount of time – until the end of a project, battle, etc. This process is called *brevetting* in the case of Military Rank. To keep temporary Rank, you must meet all the usual requirements and pay the appropriate point cost.

Courtesy Rank

Those who have formerly held Rank may retain that Rank as "Courtesy Rank" for only 1 point per level. Those who *currently* hold a title that carries little real authority may also take Courtesy Rank. Courtesy Rank is for social situations only; it gives you a fancier title.

Rank for Spies

Officers of national intelligence services often possess a special category of Military Rank, distinct from that of line soldiers. Employees of civilian intelligence agencies usually possess some variety of Administrative Rank instead. Finally, some counterintelligence officers are actually police, and hold Police Rank. Those playing spies should consult with the GM before purchasing Rank of any kind!

Rank is worth 5 points per level if it coexists with Status, or 10 points per level if it replaces Status. Common varieties of Rank include:

Administrative Rank: Position within a governmental bureaucracy. When dealing with other administrators, differences in Rank work just like differences in Status (see p. 28). At TL5 and higher, a large bureaucracy might have *several* varieties of Rank: one per government department, and possibly extra categories for the senate, judiciary, etc. (Defense or law-enforcement officials use Military or Police Rank instead.) Note this on your character sheet; e.g., Administrative Rank (Judiciary).

Merchant Rank: Position within a national or transnational organization of merchants. This could be anything from the mercantile culture of the Aztecs (where Merchant Rank verged on being Status) to the "merchant marine" of a modern or futuristic society (where Merchant Rank often parallels Military Rank during wartime).

Military Rank: Position within a military organization. Each organization is structured differently. In general, personnel that are not specifically leaders will be Rank 0-2, while low-level officers and senior enlisted men will be Rank 3-4. Rank 5 and higher is normally limited to major commands and duties where the officer is responsible for extremely valuable or rare resources. Limited-duty officers, specialists, and personnel with little *actual* responsibility or command authority have a lower Rank in *GURPS* terms, despite possibly possessing titles identical to those of a higher Rank; represent this with one or more levels of Courtesy Rank (see *Courtesy Rank*, p. 29)

Police Rank: Position in a police force. Each agency has its own variety of Rank. You must buy Legal Enforcement Powers (p. 65) before you can buy Police Rank; this is the difference between a patrol officer (Police Rank 0, for 0 points) and an ordinary citizen (*no* Police Rank, also 0 points). Note that in a police state, there is no difference between Police Rank and Military Rank.

Religious Rank: Position in a religious hierarchy. Each religion has its own variety of Rank. You must buy Clerical Investment (p. 43) before you can buy Religious Rank; this is the difference between a novice (Religious Rank 0, for 0 points) and a layperson (*no* Religious Rank, also 0 points). Other common requirements include a minimum level of Theology skill and being of a particular sex or race. Differences in Rank work just like differences in Status (see p. 28) when dealing with co-religionists and those who respect your faith.

Example of Character Creation (cont'd)

ISWAT feeds and clothes Dai, and issues him the equipment he needs on a mission, but does *not* let him fetch his loot from Yrth. Thus, he does not *personally* own much. We give him Wealth (Poor), for -15 points. This gives 1/5 starting wealth for TL8, or $4,000. Still, by Yrth standards (starting wealth at TL3 is only $1,000), he lives in more luxury than he knew as a master thief!

Looking at the traits listed under *Privilege* and *Social Restraints*, we choose two to reflect Dai's job. ISWAT is *powerful*, and its agents' Legal Enforcement Powers (p. 65) reach across time and space, for 15 points. But these powers come with a Duty (p. 133), which occurs on 15 or less and is extremely hazardous, for -20 points.

Dai's wealth and influence are worth a net -20 points. This lowers his running point total to 143 points.

PRIVILEGE

You may buy special privileges within your society – e.g., a hard-to-obtain license, an "in" with an influential social group, or an exemption from certain laws – that allow you more latitude in your actions. Such advantages are not directly linked to Rank or Status. For instance, a spy with low Rank might have a "license to kill," while his commander, a bureaucrat with much higher Rank, is bound by all the rules of polite society.

Privileges include the advantages of Claim to Hospitality (p. 41), Clerical Investment (p. 43), Legal Enforcement Powers (p. 65), Legal Immunity (p. 65), Security Clearance (p. 82), Social Regard (p. 86), and Tenure (p. 93).

SOCIAL RESTRAINTS

Your social situation can instead *deprive* you of freedom. This can take many forms: an onerous obligation; the need to hide your deeds or lifestyle in order to avoid persecution; or widespread disdain for your cultural group, occupation, or social class. Such traits are considered disadvantages – see Duty (p. 133), Secret (p. 152), and Social Stigma (p. 155). All of these traits are externally imposed. If you are limited by your *values*, see *Self-Imposed Mental Disadvantages* (p. 121) instead.

FRIENDS AND FOES

You can *claim* to know just about anyone – and maybe you really do! Your life history should include at least some details about your relationships – good, neutral, or bad – with other people in the game world.

It costs points to have associates you can rely on for assistance during an adventure. Likewise, individuals who complicate your life or *actively* seek to thwart you, personally, are worth points as disadvantages. Note that these NPCs need not be *people* – they might be spirits, animal sidekicks, or robots.

ASSOCIATED NPCs

Some friends and foes physically enter play when they appear. These "Associated NPCs" have personalities, life histories, and character sheets, just like PCs. In each case, the GM will interview you regarding the attitude, character story, and general abilities of the NPC, and then use this information to create a character sheet.

Character sheets for Associated NPCs – like those of all NPCs – are for the GM's eyes only. You will *not* have access to them! When these NPCs become involved in the game, the GM plays their roles and control their actions. Thus, even your closest associates are never 100% predictable.

Buy advantageous Associated NPCs as Allies (p. 36) or Patrons (p. 72). Disadvantageous ones include Dependents (p. 131) and Enemies (p. 135). The GM's word is final in all cases. The GM is free to forbid an Associated NPC that he feels would be disruptive, unbalanced, or inappropriate. He might even choose to forbid entire classes of NPCs – Dependents, Enemies, Patrons, etc. – if he feels they would unduly disrupt the flow of the game.

CONTACTS

You may also have associates who provide useful information or very minor favors, but who do not become physically involved in dangerous adventures. They appear only for long enough to help out, and then quickly depart. The GM will roleplay them and give them personalities, but since they are no more likely than any other friendly NPC to get involved in the action, they do not require full character sheets. Purchase such NPCs as Contacts (p. 44) or Contact Groups (p. 44).

IDENTITIES

By now, you should have a good idea of what you look like and who you are . . . but this might be only one of several faces that you show the world. Most people have just one identity – but a criminal, spy, super, or vigilante might have multiple identities.

A *functional* alternate identity costs points; see *Alternate Identity* (p. 39). On the other hand, keeping your identity a secret can be troublesome and expensive enough to qualify as a Secret Identity disadvantage (p. 153). And if you have *no* legal identity, you are Zeroed (p. 100).

Pseudonyms

In many countries – including the present-day United States – it is legal to use a false name for privacy as long as you do not attempt to defraud or interfere with public records. You can rent an apartment as "Mr. Smith," paying cash, without problems. But you can't get a driver's license, etc., legally. This sort of "weak identity" costs no points, and is popular with rock stars and actors (who often use a "stage name"), writers (in the form of a *nom de plume*), and traveling royalty.

Temporary Identities

Anyone can have a hasty or low-quality Alternate Identity (p. 39).

While useful, such a false identity will eventually be noticed and eliminated (and the user sought after!). This kind of identity is not considered an advantage, and costs no points; buy it with cash.

A standard Temporary Identity is guaranteed to be good for one week. At the end of that week, the GM rolls 3d. On a roll of 8 or less, the authorities have discovered the false records. Otherwise, the identity holds up for another week and the process repeats itself, but the "discovery roll" is at a cumulative +1 for every week past the first (9 or less at the end of the second week, 10 or less at the end of the third week, and so on).

The price of a Temporary Identity is negotiable, and depends on your contacts, skills, and the setting. The cheaper the identity, the more frequently the GM will roll – a really cheap one might only be good for a *day*, with rolls every day! More expensive identities, lasting longer or starting at a lower number, might also be available.

Someone who is Zeroed (p. 100) *can* use a Temporary Identity.

Alternate Identity vs. Secret Identity

A Secret Identity (p. 153) isn't the same as an Alternate Identity (p. 39). If there are no false records to back up a Secret Identity, it doesn't count as an Alternate Identity. And if you use an Alternate Identity only to hold a secret bank account (for instance), and never try to "live" that persona, it isn't a Secret Identity.

CHAPTER TWO
ADVANTAGES

An "advantage" is a useful trait that gives you a mental, physical, or social "edge" over someone else who otherwise has the same abilities as you. Each advantage has a cost in character points. This is fixed for some advantages; others can be bought in "levels," at a cost per level (e.g., Acute Vision costs 2 points/level, so if you want Acute Vision 6, you must pay 12 points). Advantages with "Variable" cost are more complicated; read the advantage description for details.

You can start out with as many advantages as you can afford – although some advantages are forbidden to certain kinds of characters. You can also add advantages in play, if the GM permits. For instance, all the beneficial social traits in Chapter 1 (Status, Wealth, etc.) are advantages, and you could realistically acquire any of these in the course of the game. Magic and high technology can often grant advantages as well. For information on adding advantages in play, see Chapter 9.

TYPES OF ADVANTAGES

Advantages fall into several broad categories, each of which affects who can possess those advantages and how they work in play.

Mental 🧠, Physical 💪, and Social 🤝

Mental advantages originate from your mind, or perhaps even your *soul*. They stay with you even if your mind ends up in a new body due to possession, a brain transplant, etc. Magical, psionic, and spiritual traits usually fall into this category. Most mental advantages work automatically, but a few require a roll against IQ, Perception, or Will to use. Mental advantages are marked 🧠.

Physical advantages are part of your body. You lose these traits if your mind moves to a new body – and if another mind takes over *your* body, the body's new owner gains your physical advantages. Advantages provided by bionics and similar implants usually fall into this category. Make a HT roll to activate any physical advantage that does not work automatically. Physical advantages are marked 💪.

Social advantages are associated with your identity. Whether identity is a facet of mind or of body depends on the game world. In a fantasy setting, a demon might possess a duke and "become" a respected noble instead of a feared demon, while in a far-future society, people might routinely "upload" into new bodies with no effect on social standing. As with all things, the GM's word is final. Note that this category includes Rank, Status, Wealth, and related traits from Chapter 1. Social advantages are marked 🤝.

Many exotic and supernatural advantages (see below) could belong to more than one of these categories. This is noted (e.g., as 🧠/💪) where especially appropriate. The GM has the final say. The 🧠, 💪, and 🤝 markers are meant to assist GM judgment, not replace it.

Exotic 👁, Supernatural ☄, and Mundane

Exotic advantages are traits that ordinary humans cannot have without ultra-tech body modification or similar tampering; for instance, extra arms or death-ray vision. Nonhumans will often have exotic advantages on a racial basis, but this does *not* entitle them to add such traits freely. You need the GM's permission to add exotic traits that do not appear on your racial template (see Chapter 7). Exotic advantages are marked 👁.

Supernatural advantages are impossible in nature and cannot be justified by science – or even "super-science." They rely on divine intervention, magic, psionics, etc. The classic example is magical talent (see *Magery*, p. 66). Supernatural traits differ from exotic ones in that *anyone* might be supernaturally gifted – even a "normal" human, if the GM permits. Having a trait like this does not automatically mark you as an alien or a mutant. Supernatural advantages are marked ✦.

Mundane advantages are inborn or learned edges and knacks that anyone might have. There are normally no restrictions on who may possess a mundane advantage. Mundane advantages are not specially marked – if you don't see ♥ or ✦, the advantage is mundane and available to anyone *with the GM's permission.* This last point is important! Some mundane traits are intended for cinematic campaigns (see *The Cinematic Campaign,* p. 488); the GM may forbid them in realistic games. Cinematic traits are always clearly indicated in the text.

ADVANTAGE ORIGINS

When you select exotic or supernatural advantages, you must also choose an in-game justification for those abilities: biology, high technology, a divine gift, etc. Explaining your capabilities in terms that have meaning in the game world will give you a better "feel" for your character and give the GM some additional "adventure hooks."

Origins are usually just special effects. For instance, if you can sprout claws, they use the rules under Claws (p. 42) whether they are natural, cybernetic, or a gift from the Tiger God. Sometimes, though, you will encounter things that can only affect or be affected by a specific class of abilities. Furthermore, the GM may rule that talents with certain origins are more or less effective in a particular situation. In those cases, it is important to know *how your advantage works.*

Most characters have only one origin for all of their abilities, but you may choose a separate origin for each

of your advantages if you wish, subject to GM approval. The GM sets the origins available in his campaign. Examples include:

Biological: Inborn features (unique to you or part of your racial makeup) and mutations. Medical science can detect and analyze these traits, and – at higher tech levels – add or remove them through genetic engineering, implants, or surgery.

Chi: Powers that originate from the "inner strength" of martial artists and yoga masters (also known as *ki* and *prana*). Disease and similar afflictions can sometimes weaken such abilities –

for instance, by throwing your *yin* and *yang* out of balance.

Cosmic: Abilities that emanate from the universe itself or otherwise defy explanation. This is reserved for gods, powerful spirits, supers, etc. If your ability produces effects that *only* other cosmic powers can counteract, this is an enhancement; see *Cosmic* (p. 103).

Divine: Gifts from the gods (if *you* are a god, use Cosmic). In areas of low "sanctity" for your god – e.g., the temple of a rival god, or a foreign land where your god is unknown – you might find your abilities reduced or unavailable.

Potential Advantages

You will sometimes see an advantage you would like to have but that would not make sense at the start of your career – or that you cannot afford on your starting points! Or you might just want to start your adventuring career with unrealized potential, like countless fictional heroes. In either situation, the GM may choose to let you set aside 50% of the cost of an advantage as a "down payment" against acquiring the advantage later on.

When you take a *potential advantage* like this, sit down with the GM and work out the in-game conditions under which you will acquire the desired trait. When these conditions are met, you must use bonus character points to pay the other half of the price as soon as possible; see *Improvement Through Adventure* (p. 290). The GM is free to assess partial or uncontrollable benefits befitting the trait until you finish paying for the full, controllable advantage.

Examples of potential advantages include:

Heir: You stand to inherit wealth or a title. The GM decides when you will come into your inheritance. At that time, you acquire Status, Wealth, or other social privileges worth twice the points set aside for this trait. Until then, you enjoy extra money, reaction modifiers, etc. equal to *half* what you stand to gain. For instance, if you stood to inherit +2 to Status [10] and Comfortable wealth [10], Heir would cost 10 points, and give +1 to Status and a 50% bonus to starting wealth.

Schrödinger's Advantage: You can specify that at some critical juncture in an adventure, just when all seems lost, you will suddenly discover a new ability – worth twice the points you have set aside – that will help you out of trouble. You must immediately pay the remaining points to use your new ability. This is a *powerful* option. To keep things fair, points set aside this way provide no benefit until you discover your hidden talent.

Secret Advantage: You have an advantage *you don't know about!* The GM picks an advantage or set of advantages worth twice the points you have set aside . . . but he will not tell you what it is, or even give you a clue! The GM will reveal the truth at a suitably dramatic moment. Until then, the advantage provides the usual benefits – but it isn't under your control, so you won't be able to rely on it. The advantage functions normally once revealed and paid for.

High-Tech: Nonbiological implants in biological characters, as well as *all* abilities of cyborgs, robots, and vehicles. Sensors can detect and analyze such traits, and certain high-tech countermeasures might be able to neutralize them.

Magic: Talents that draw upon magical energy, or *mana*. You need not be a wizard yourself; this category includes such lasting sorcerous effects as personal enchantments. If your gifts do not function at all in areas without mana, and function at -5 to die rolls in low mana (like spells; see p. 235), then this is a limitation (see p. 110): Mana Sensitive, -10%.

Psionic: Advantages that originate from the power of the mind. In most settings where psi powers exist, there are drugs, gadgets, and specialized anti-psi powers that can detect and defeat them. As a result, they are bought with a special limitation; see Chapter 6.

Spirit: Abilities enabled by invoking spirits. You only *seem* to be the focus of the effects; in reality, invisible supernatural beings are doing your bidding. Obviously, if the spirits cannot reach you, your abilities do not work.

TURNING ADVANTAGES OFF AND ON

An advantage that never inconveniences you (e.g., Intuition), that has to be on at all times to be of benefit (e.g., Resistant), or that reflects a permanent trait of your species (e.g., Extra Arms) is *always on*. You cannot turn it off.

Most other advantages are *switchable:* you can turn them off and on at will. To do so requires a one-second Ready maneuver, with activation or deactivation occurring as soon as you execute the maneuver. Unlike certain skills and magic spells, this does not require concentration; switching an advantage is second nature, and cannot be "interrupted." The default condition (while sleeping, unconscious, etc.) is "on."

Attacks – notably Affliction (p. 35), Binding (p. 40), and Innate Attack (p. 61) – are only "on" while you are attacking. An advantage like this requires a one-second Attack maneuver to use; you *cannot* switch it on continuously without a special enhancement.

Exceptions to these guidelines are noted explicitly.

ADVANTAGE LIST

360° Vision 👹 👽
25 points

You have a 360° field of vision. You have *no* penalty to defend against attacks from the sides or rear. You can attack foes to your sides or rear without making a Wild Swing, but you are at -2 to hit due to the clumsy angle of attack (note that some Karate techniques do not suffer this penalty). Finally, you are at +5 to detect Shadowing attempts, and are never surprised by a danger that comes from behind, unless it also is concealed from sight.

Extra eyes are merely a special effect of this trait – you can have any number of eyes, but the point cost remains the same.

Special Limitations

Easy to Hit: Your eyes are on stalks, unusually large, or otherwise more vulnerable to attack. Others can target your eyes from within their arc of vision at only -6 to hit. -20%.

3D Spatial Sense
see *Absolute Direction,* below

Absolute Direction 👹/👹
5 or 10 points

You have an excellent sense of direction. This ability comes in two levels:

Absolute Direction: You always know which way is north, and you can always retrace a path you have followed within the past month, no matter how faint or confusing. This ability does not work in environments such as interstellar space or the limbo of the astral plane, but it *does* work underground, underwater, and on other planets. This gives +3 to Body Sense and Navigation (Air, Land, or Sea). (*Note:* The navigational sense that guides migratory creatures to their destination is too crude to qualify; treat it as a 0-point feature.) *5 points.*

3D Spatial Sense: As above, but works in three dimensions. This ability *is* useful in deep space – although it does not help you if you travel across dimensions. You get the skill bonuses given for Absolute Direction, plus +1 to Piloting and +2 to Aerobatics, Free Fall, and Navigation (Hyperspace or Space). *10 points.*

Special Limitations

Requires Signal: You rely on signals from a navigational satellite network (like Earth's GPS) or similar system. Your ability does not function in the absence of such a system, and it can be jammed. -20%.

Absolute Timing 🖤
2 or 5 points

You have an accurate mental clock. This ability comes in two levels, both of which are somewhat cinematic:

Absolute Timing: You always know what time it is, with a precision equal to the best personal timepieces widely available in your culture (but never better than a few seconds). You can measure elapsed time with equal accuracy. Neither changes of time zone nor sleep interferes with this ability, and you can wake up at a predetermined time if you choose. Being knocked unconscious, hypnotized, etc. *may* prevent this advantage from working, and time travel *will* confuse you until you find out what the "new" time is. *2 points.*

Chronolocation: As above, but time travel does not interfere – you always know what time it is in an absolute sense. Note that things like Daylight Savings Time and calendar reform can still confuse you! When you travel in time, the GM may tell you, "You have gone back exactly 92,876.3 days," and let you – or your character – deal with questions like, "What about leap year?" *5 points.*

Acute Senses 🖤
2 points/level

You have superior senses. Each Acute Sense is a separate advantage that gives +1 per level to all Sense rolls (p. 358) you make – or the GM makes for you – using that one sense.

Acute Hearing gives you a bonus to hear something, or to notice a sound (for instance, someone taking the safety off a gun in the dark). *2 points/level.*

Acute Taste and Smell gives you a bonus to notice a taste or smell (for instance, poison in your drink). *2 points/level.*

Acute Touch gives you a bonus to detect something by touch (for instance, a concealed weapon when patting down a suspect). *2 points/level.*

Acute Vision gives you a bonus to spot things visually, and whenever you do a visual search (for instance, looking for traps or footprints). *2 points/level.*

With the GM's permission, you may also buy Acute Sense advantages for specialized senses such as Scanning Sense and Vibration Sense.

You cannot usually buy Acute Senses in play – raise your Perception instead. However, if you lose a sense, the GM may allow you to spend earned points on other Acute Senses to compensate. For instance, if you are blinded, you might acquire Acute Hearing.

The GM determines which exotic and supernatural traits are allowed – and to whom – in his campaign.

Administrative Rank
see *Rank*, p. 29

Affliction 🖤🖤
10 points/level

You have an attack that causes a baneful, *nondamaging* effect: blindness, paralysis, weakness, etc. This might be an ultra-tech beam weapon, a chemical spray, a supernatural gaze attack, or almost anything else. Specify the details when you buy the advantage.

By default, Affliction is a ranged attack with 1/2D 10, Max 100, Acc 3, RoF 1, Shots N/A, and Recoil 1, although you can apply modifiers to change these statistics (see pp. 101-116).

If you hit, your victim gets a HT+1 roll to resist. Apply a penalty equal to the level of the Affliction (so Affliction 1 gives an unmodified HT roll). The victim gets a bonus equal to his DR *unless* the Affliction has one of the following modifiers: Blood Agent, Contact Agent, Cosmic, Follow-Up, Malediction, Respiratory Agent or Sense-Based. To reduce the effects of DR, add the Armor Divisor enhancement. The victim gets a further +3 if he is beyond 1/2D range.

If the victim makes his HT roll, he is unaffected. If he fails, he suffers the effects of the Affliction. By default, he is stunned (see p. 420). He may roll vs. HT+1 once per second to recover, but once again at a penalty equal to the level of the Affliction (DR has no effect on this roll).

If your Affliction causes an effect other than stunning, this is a special enhancement (see below). You can inflict more than one effect by giving your Affliction multiple special enhancements. These effects occur simultaneously, except where noted.

Successive Afflictions that produce the same effects are not normally cumulative. Use the single *worst* effect.

Use the special enhancements below to create specific Afflictions. Many *Attack Enhancements and Limitations* (p. 102) are also logical. For instance, a blinding flash is Sense-Based (p. 109); most drugs have Follow-Up (p. 105), Blood Agent (p. 102), or Contact Agent (p. 103); supernatural attacks like the "evil eye" use Malediction (p. 106); and touch attacks call for Melee Attack (p. 112).

If an Affliction produces two or more effects due to the special enhancements below, some of these effects may be *secondary*. Secondary effects occur only if the victim fails his HT roll by 5 or more or rolls a critical failure. A secondary effect is worth 1/5 as much; e.g., Secondary Heart Attack is +60% rather than +300%.

Once you have chosen all the modifiers on your Affliction, describe the nature of the attack as detailed for *Innate Attack* (p. 61).

Special Enhancements

Advantage: The victim immediately experiences the effects of a specific physical or mental advantage. Advantages with instantaneous effects affect the target *once*, as soon as he is hit, if he fails his HT roll; e.g., Warp immediately teleports the subject. Advantages that can be switched on and off (such as Insubstantiality) are automatically "on" for one minute per point by which the victim fails his HT roll, and are *not* under the subject's control. This is worth +10% per point by which the advantage is worth; e.g., Insubstantiality would be +800%! If the advantage comes in levels, specify the level.

Attribute Penalty: The victim suffers *temporary* attribute loss. This is +5% per -1 to ST or HT, or +10% per -1 to DX or IQ. For instance, an attack that caused DX-3 and IQ-2 would be +50%. Lower all skills based on reduced attributes by a like amount. ST penalties also reduce BL and damage, while IQ reductions also apply to Will and Perception. Secondary characteristics are not otherwise affected; for instance, HT reduction does not affect Basic Speed or FP. Penalties last for one minute per point by which the victim fails his HT roll.

Coma: The victim collapses, profoundly unconscious, and will likely die in days unless treated; see *Mortal Conditions* (p. 429). +250%.

Cumulative: Repeated attacks *are* cumulative! You must take this in conjunction with Attribute Penalty, or with an Advantage, Disadvantage, or Negated Advantage Enhancement that inflicts a "leveled" trait. +400%.

Disadvantage: The victim temporarily gains one or more specific physical or mental disadvantages (but *not* self-imposed mental disadvantages – see p. 121). This is worth +1% per point the temporary disadvantages are worth; e.g., Paranoia [-10] is worth +10%. If a disadvantage comes in levels, specify the level. The disadvantages last for one minute per point by which the victim fails his HT roll.

Heart Attack: The victim suffers an incapacitating heart attack, and will die in minutes unless treated; see *Mortal Conditions* (p. 429). +300%.

Incapacitation: The victim is incapacitated for a number of minutes equal to the margin of failure on his HT roll. After that, he is stunned until he can make a HT roll (roll once per second). If you combine Incapacitation with other effects (such as Irritant), those effects occur after the Incapacitation wears off; they replace the stunning and last for the same length of time the Incapacitation did. Incapacitation can take the form of any of the following: Daze, +50%; Hallucinating, +50%; Retching, +50%; Agony, +100%; Choking, +100%; Ecstasy, +100%; Seizure, +100%; Paralysis, +150%; Sleep, +150%; or Unconsciousness, +200%. See *Incapacitating Conditions* (p. 428) for the game effects.

Irritant: The victim suffers an impairing but non-incapacitating condition *instead of* being stunned. It lasts for a number of minutes equal to the margin of failure on his HT roll. The possibilities are Tipsy +10%; Coughing, +20%; Drunk, +20%; Moderate Pain, +20%; Euphoria, +30%; Nauseated, +30%; Severe Pain, +40%; or Terrible Pain, +60%. For definitions, see *Irritating Conditions* (p. 428).

Negated Advantage: The victim *loses* a specific advantage for one minute per point by which he failed his HT roll. There is no effect if the victim lacks that advantage! This enhancement is worth +1% per point the advantage is worth. If the advantage comes in levels, you must specify the level negated.

Stunning: May only accompany Advantage, Attribute Penalty, Disadvantage, or Negated Advantage. If the victim fails to resist, he is stunned (per an unmodified Affliction) *in addition to* the effects of the other enhancement(s). +10%.

Allies 🤝

Variable

Many fictional heroes have partners – loyal comrades, faithful sidekicks, trusted retainers, or lifelong friends – who accompany them on adventures. These partners are "Allies."

The other PCs in your adventuring party are, in a sense, "allies." But they can be unreliable allies indeed. Often they are chance acquaintances, first encountered at a roadside tavern only hours ago. They have their own hidden goals, ethics, and motives, which might not coincide with your own.

An NPC Ally, on the other hand, is wholly reliable. Perhaps you fought side by side in a long war, trained under the same master, or grew up in the same village. The two of you trust each other implicitly. You travel

---

Frequency of Appearance

Whether you pay points for a useful relationship with an NPC or collect points for a troublesome one, it is unlikely that the NPC will be a constant presence. Each friend or foe has a *frequency of appearance*, and will figure into a given adventure only if the GM rolls less than or equal to that number on 3d at the start of the adventure. How the NPC interacts with you if the roll succeeds depends on the nature of the relationship.

Frequency of appearance multiplies the point cost for an Associated NPC (see p. 31) *after* determining power level and group size (as applicable), but *before* you apply any special modifiers:

Constantly (no roll required): *×4*. The NPC is always present. This level is reserved for NPCs – usually Allies – that are implanted, worn like clothing, or supernaturally attached.

Almost all the time (roll of 15 or less): *×3*.

Quite often (roll of 12 or less): *×2*.

Fairly often (roll of 9 or less): *×1*.

Quite rarely (roll of 6 or less): *×1/2 (round up)*.

together, fight back-to-back, share rations in hard times, and trade watches through the night.

Your Ally is usually agreeable to your suggestions, but he is not your puppet. He *will* disagree with you from time to time. An Ally may try to dissuade you from a plan that seems foolish to him – and if he can't talk you out of the plan, he may refuse to cooperate. An Ally may even cause problems for you: picking fights, landing in jail, insulting a high noble . . . Of course, the Ally will also try to bail you out when *you* make mistakes.

The GM will not award you bonus character points for any play session in which you betray, attack, or unnecessarily endanger your Ally. Blatant, prolonged, or severe betrayal will break the trust between you and your Ally, and he will leave you permanently. If you drive your Ally off in this way, the points you spent on him are *gone*, reducing your point value. Leading your Ally into danger is all right, as long as *you* face the same danger and are a responsible leader.

The point cost for an Ally depends on his power and frequency of appearance. Only PCs who take NPCs as Allies pay points for the privilege. Two PCs can be mutual "allies" for free, as can two NPCs – and NPCs *never* pay points for PCs as Allies. An Ally is specifically a skilled NPC associate for one PC.

Ally's Power

Consult the following table to determine how many points you must spend on your Ally. "Point Total" is the Ally's point total expressed as a percentage of the PC's starting points; "Cost" is the cost of the Ally. If the Ally's point total falls between two percentages, use the *higher*.

Point Total	Cost
25%	1 point
50%	2 points
75%	3 points
100%	5 points
150%	10 points

Allies built on more than 150% of the PC's starting points are not allowed; treat such NPCs as Patrons (see p. 72). *Exception:* The progression above extends indefinitely for *nonsentient* (IQ 0) Allies; each +50% of the PC's starting points costs a further +5 points.

Allies built on no more than 100% of the PC's starting points may *also* be Dependents (see p. 131). Add the cost of Ally and Dependent together, and treat the combination as a single trait: an advantage if the total point cost is positive, a disadvantage if it is negative.

Ally Groups

You may purchase as many Allies as you can afford. Each Ally is normally a separate advantage, but you can treat a group of related Allies as a single trait to save space on your character sheet. For a group of *individuals* – with their own unique abilities and character sheets – add the costs of the individual Allies to find the cost of the group, adjust the total cost for frequency of appearance, and then apply any special modifiers.

For a group of more than five *identical* and *interchangeable* allies that share a single character sheet – for instance, an army of low-grade thugs or a swarm of robot drones – find the point cost to have one member of the group as an Ally, and then multiply that cost as follows to find the cost of the group:

Size of Group	Multiplier
6-10	×6
11-20	×8
21-50	×10
51-100	×12

Add ×6 to the multiplier per tenfold increase in number (e.g., 100,000 Allies would be ×30). The GM may require an Unusual Background (p. 96) if you wish to have hordes of

Allies, or even prohibit groups larger than a certain size – although he might permit an army or other large group as a *Patron*. Frequency of appearance multipliers and special modifiers (if any) apply to the final cost of the entire group.

Frequency of Appearance

Choose a frequency of appearance (see p. 36). If your Ally appears at the start of an adventure, he accompanies you for the duration of that adventure.

Allies in Play

As with Dependents (p. 131), the GM will adjust your Ally's abilities in order to keep his point total a fixed percentage of your own as you earn points. This will keep his value as an advantage constant. The *GM* decides how the Ally evolves, although he might ask you for your input.

If your Ally dies through no fault of yours, the GM will not penalize you. You may put the points spent on the deceased Ally toward a new Ally. The new relationship should normally develop gradually, but the GM might allow an NPC to become an Ally on the spot if you have done something that would win him over (e.g., saving his life). This is especially appropriate in cultures where debts of honor are taken seriously!

There is no penalty for amicably parting ways with your Ally. You may use the points spent on him to buy a new Ally met during play. At the GM's discretion, you may trade in any remaining points for money (see p. 26), reflecting parting gifts.

Familiars

Wizards, telepaths, and so on are often supernaturally linked to special Allies known as *familiars*. These are usually animals or spirits.

Your Ally is usually agreeable to your suggestions, but he is not your puppet. He will disagree with you from time to time.

Work out a familiar's basic abilities with the GM, starting with the racial template of an ordinary creature of its kind. If its racial IQ is 5 or less, raise it to at least 6. Consider buying off Cannot Speak, if applicable. Most familiars have supernatural advantages: Extra Lives for a cat (it has nine lives, after all!), Mindlink and Telesend for a familiar that can transmit its thoughts, etc.

Once you have determined the familiar's abilities, work out its point total and its base value as an Ally. Select frequency of appearance as usual. This may be *how often your familiar is available* (on a failed appearance roll, it is sleeping, reporting to a demon lord, etc.) or *how often its powers work* (on a failure, it is no more capable than an ordinary member of its species, and cannot use or grant special powers) – your choice.

This kind of Ally usually has one or more special modifiers. Minion, Summonable, and Sympathy are common. Unwilling is typical of demonic or otherwise evil familiars. Take Special Abilities only if your familiar grants *you* powers; e.g., extra Fatigue Points with which to fuel spells or exotic or supernatural advantages that emulate the familiar's own abilities (such as Flight, for a bird). You have no access to these abilities on a failed appearance roll; if your familiar is stunned, unconscious, or dead; or in areas where your special link does not function (GM's decision). Buy these abilities with a -40% Accessibility limitation: "Granted by familiar."

You can apply the following enhancements and limitations *after* calculating group cost (if applicable) and multiplying for frequency of appearance:

Special Enhancements

Minion: Your Ally continues to serve you regardless of how well you treat him. This might be due to programming, fear, awe, or lack of self-awareness. Examples include robots, zombies, and magical slaves. You are free of the usual obligation to treat your Ally well. Mistreatment might result in an inconvenient breakdown (mental or physical), but the Ally will not leave. See *Puppet* (p. 78) for additional options. +0% if the Minion has IQ 0 or Slave Mentality (p. 154), as the benefits of total loyalty are offset by the need for close supervision; +50% otherwise.

Special Abilities: Your Ally wields power out of proportion to his point value. Perhaps he has extensive political clout or access to equipment from a TL higher than your own; perhaps he grants *you* exotic powers. Don't apply this enhancement simply because your Ally has exotic abilities. If his powers are very uncommon, you will *already* be paying extra: your Ally requires an Unusual Background, which raises his point total and his value as an Ally. +50%.

Summonable: You conjure your Ally instead of rolling to see whether he appears at the start of an adventure. To do so, take a Concentrate maneuver and roll against frequency of appearance. On a success, your Ally appears nearby. On a failure, you cannot attempt to summon him again for one full day. Dismissing your Ally is a free action, but you may only dismiss him if he is physically present. +100%.

Special Limitations

Sympathy: If you are stunned, knocked out, mind-controlled, etc., your Ally is similarly affected. The reverse is also true, so you should take special care of your Ally! -25% if the death of one party reduces the other to 0 HP; -50% if the death of one party automatically *kills* the other. If your wounds affect your Ally, but your Ally's wounds don't affect you, reduce these values to -5% and -10%.

Unwilling: You have obtained your Ally through coercion (e.g., blackmail or magical binding). You do not have to treat him as well as you would a normal Ally. However, he *hates* you and is likely to act accordingly, reducing his overall reliability level. If you endanger such an Ally or order him to do something unpleasant, he may rebel (GM's option) if the consequences of doing so would be less severe than those of doing your bidding. An Ally who rebels is *gone*, along with the points you spent on him. -50%.

Altered Time Rate 🌑 🌑
100 points/level

Your rate of time perception is faster than that of a normal human. The first level of this advantage lets you experience time *twice* as fast as a normal – that is, you experience two subjective seconds for each real second that passes. Each level past the first increases this ratio by one: three times as fast at level 2, four times as fast at level 3, and so on.

Each level of Altered Time Rate lets you take one additional maneuver on your turn in combat, allowing you to cast spells quickly by taking multiple Concentrate maneuvers, run very fast by taking multiple Move maneuvers, etc. Your turn doesn't come any sooner, however! This advantage affects how fast you move *when you react*, but not how quickly you react in the first place.

Out of combat, Altered Time Rate allows you the luxury of extensive planning, even in crisis situations, as everything seems to happen in slow motion. You may always attempt a Sense roll, or an IQ-based skill roll to make plans or recall information (GM's decision), at no penalty to additional actions.

In order to do anything that depends on someone else's reactions, you must deliberately "slow down" and function at his speed. This applies both when making a Feint in combat and when making an Influence roll (see p. 359) out of combat. For instance, if you choose to Feint, that is all you can do on your turn – you cannot take extra actions. (On the other hand, you could make an All-Out Attack followed by an Attack in order to beat down his defenses through sheer blinding speed!)

Alternate Identity
5 or 15 points per identity

You have multiple, seemingly legal identities. Each time you purchase this trait, your fingerprints (or other biometrics used to verify identity in your world) are registered under another name, and you have an extra set of identity documents (birth certificate, licenses, passport, etc.) good enough to pass close inspection. These identities may also have valid credit cards and bank accounts, but *you* must supply the money – additional wealth is not included in the package!

If an intelligence or law-enforcement agency attempts to identify you with no clue as to your name – for instance, using biometrics or photoanalysis – there is an equal chance for each of your identities to come up. The search will stop . . . unless they have reason to believe you are a ringer. If the search continues, your other identities will eventually surface, and you will be unmasked. Once a government agency determines who you really are, your Alternate Identities are lost for good.

There are two types of Alternate Identity:

Legal: Some spies and undercover policemen – and even supers, in settings where they are backed by the government – may have a legal Alternate Identity. This requires at least 10 points in Legal Enforcement Powers, Legal Immunity, Police Rank, Security Clearance, etc.; the GM sets the precise prerequisites. If a super has official permission to conceal his original name (e.g., to protect his family) and to hold property in his "super" name, then that is a legal Alternate Identity combined with a Secret Identity (see p. 153). *5 points.*

Illegal: A criminal or foreign agent may have an illegal Alternate Identity. This has the advantage of being *completely* unknown when you first start out, and of course it cannot be revoked by the government. On the other hand, should it ever be discovered, you will face a stiff fine, a jail sentence, or execution, depending on the time and place. *15 points.*

Ambidexterity
5 points

You can fight or otherwise act equally well with either hand, and never suffer the -4 DX penalty for using the "off" hand (see p. 14). Note that this does *not* allow you to take extra actions in combat – that's Extra Attack (p. 53). Should some accident befall one of your arms or hands, assume it is the left one.

Amphibious ♔ ☻

10 points

You are well-adapted to movement in the water. You do not suffer skill penalties for working underwater, and you can swim at your full Basic Move. You still require air (but see *Doesn't Breathe*, p. 49). Typical features include smooth, seal-like skin and webbed fingers and toes.

If you can move *only* in the water, take the Aquatic disadvantage (p. 145) instead.

Animal Empathy ☻

5 points

You are unusually talented at reading the motivations of animals. When you meet an animal, the GM rolls against your IQ and tells you what you "feel." This reveals the beast's emotional state – friendly, frightened, hostile, hungry, etc. – and whether it is under supernatural control. You may also use your Influence skills (see p. 359) on animals just as you would on sapient beings, which usually ensures a positive reaction.

This ability frequently accompanies some level of Animal Friend (see *Talent*, p. 89), and often Sense of Duty (Animals) or Vow (Vegetarianism).

Animal Friend

see Talent, p. 89

Appearance

see *Appearance Levels*, p. 21

Above-average appearance is treated as an advantage.

Arm DX ♔ ☻

12 or 16 points per +1 DX

Some of your arms have extra DX relative to the DX of your body. This DX applies only to things done with those arms or hands. It does *not* affect Basic Speed! If a task requires two or more hands, and they don't have the same DX, use the *lowest* DX. Combat skills rely on bodily DX, and do not benefit from this DX at all.

Arm DX costs 12 points per +1 DX for one arm and 16 points per +1 DX for two arms. To raise the DX of three or more arms, buy up overall DX. If you bought your DX with the No Fine Manipulators limitation, apply this limitation to Arm DX as well.

Arm ST ♔ ☻

3, 5, or 8 points per +1 ST

Some of your arms have extra ST relative to the ST of your body. This ST applies only to efforts to lift, throw, or attack with those arms or hands. It does *not* affect HP or overall Basic Lift! If a task requires multiple hands, and they don't have the same ST, use the *average* ST.

Arm ST costs 3 points per +1 ST for one arm, 5 points per +1 ST for two arms, and 8 points per +1 ST for three arms. To raise the ST of four or more arms, buy up overall ST. If you bought your ST with the No Fine Manipulators or Size limitations, apply the same limitation(s) to Arm ST.

Artificer

see *Talent*, p. 89

Binding ♔ ☻

2 points/level

You have an attack that can hold your target in place. Specify how this works when you buy the advantage: entangling your victim in vines, tying him up with webs, freezing him inside a block of ice, turning the ground to quicksand beneath his feet, etc.

Binding is a ranged attack with 1/2D –, Max 100, Acc 3, RoF 1, Shots N/A, and Recoil 1. You can add modifiers to change these statistics (see pp. 101-116).

On a hit, your victim is grappled (see p. 370) and rooted in place. He cannot select the Move or Change Posture maneuvers or change facing, and is at -4 to DX. The ST of this effect is equal to your Binding level, but you can *layer* additional attacks on a successfully bound victim. Each extra layer gives +1 to ST.

To break free, the victim must win a Quick Contest of ST or Escape skill against the ST of your Binding. Each attempt takes one second. If the victim fails to break free, he loses 1 FP but may try again. Alternatively, he may try to destroy the Binding. Innate Attacks hit automatically; other attacks are at -4. External attacks on the Binding take no penalty, but risk hitting the victim on a miss (see *Striking Into a Close Combat*, p. 392). The Binding has DR equal to 1/3 your level (rounded down). Each point of damage reduces ST by one. At ST 0, the Binding is destroyed and the victim is freed.

To simulate vines, webs, and so forth, add one or more of Area Effect (p. 102), Persistent (p. 107), and Wall (p. 109) – and possibly some of the special modifiers below.

Special Enhancements

Engulfing: Your attack *pins* the target. He cannot move his limbs or speak; his only options are to use purely mental abilities, to attack the Binding with an Innate Attack, or to try to break free using ST (*not* Escape skill). If he tries to break free and fails, he is only allowed a repeated attempt every 10 seconds – and on a 17 or 18, he becomes so entangled that he cannot escape on his own! +60%.

Only Damaged By X: Only specific damage types can damage your Binding. +30% for one of burning, corrosion, crushing, or cutting; +20% for any two; +10% for any three.

Sticky: Your Binding is treated as Persistent (p. 107), but only affects those who actually touch the original target of your attack. +20%.

Unbreakable: Your Binding cannot be destroyed. The only way to escape is to break free. +40%.

Special Limitations

Environmental: Your Binding manipulates an existing condition or object in the environment, and won't work in its absence. This is worth from -20% (victim must be touching the ground) to -40% (victim must be standing in dense vegetation), at the GM's option.

One-Shot: You cannot layer your Binding to increase its ST. -10%.

Blessed ☻ ↗

10 or more points

You are attuned to a god, demon lord, great spirit, cosmic power, etc. This can take various forms, but in all cases, you will lose this advantage if you fail to act in accordance with your deity's rules and values.

Blessed: You sometimes receive wisdom from your deity. After communing with your god (meditating, praying, etc.) for at least one hour, you see visions or witness omens that have some bearing on future events. Work out the details with your GM; for instance, the God of Fire might require you to stare into flames for an hour, after which you hear a voice in the flames. The GM rolls secretly against your IQ to determine whether you gain any useful insight from this experience. The ritual is fatiguing, however; at the end of the hour, you lose 10 FP. As a side benefit, followers of your deity sense your special status and react to you at +1. *10 points.*

Very Blessed: As above, but your IQ roll to interpret visions is at +5 and the reaction bonus from your god's followers is +2. *20 points.*

Heroic Feats: Your blessing gives you the ability to perform a particular heroic feat. Once per game session, you may add 1d to *one* of ST, DX, or HT (other traits, such as Basic Move, are at the GM's discretion). You must specify which trait is boosted when you buy the advantage. This bonus lasts 3d seconds, after which your abilities revert to normal and you suffer any penalties amassed during the "heroic" period. (For instance, if your blessing boosts HP and you are reduced to -5 × your normal HP but not -5 × your "blessed" HP, you will die when the bonus HP wear off unless you receive some sort of healing.) *10 points.*

The GM may choose to allow other blessings as well.

Brachiator 🤸 🌑

5 points

You can travel by swinging on vines, tree branches, ropes, chandeliers, etc. You get +2 to Climbing skill, and can move at half your Basic Move while brachiating.

Breath-Holding 🤸 🌑

2 points/level

You are adept at holding your breath. Each level doubles the length of time you can do so (see *Holding Your Breath*, p. 351). Normal humans may not take this advantage – to be a world-record diver, learn Breath Control (p. 182). Nonhumans and supers *can* combine this advantage with Breath Control!

Business Acumen
see *Talent*, p. 89

Catfall 🤸 🌑

10 points

You subtract five yards from a fall automatically (treat this as an automatic Acrobatics success – don't check again for it). In addition, a successful DX roll *halves* damage from any fall. To enjoy these benefits, your limbs must be unbound and your body free to twist as you fall.

Chameleon 🤸 🌑

5 points/level

You can change your surface pattern to blend into your surroundings. In any situation where being seen is a factor, you get +2 per level to Stealth skill when perfectly still, or +1 per level if moving. Clothing reduces this bonus to +1 per level when you are motionless, with no bonus if you are moving (unless the clothing is, in the GM's opinion, camouflaged relative to your current environment).

Chameleon does not normally help in the dark or against someone relying upon senses other than sight. However, you can specify that your ability is effective against a particular visual or scanning sense (e.g., Infravision or Radar) *instead* of normal vision.

Special Enhancements

Extended: Your ability affects more than one visual or scanning sense. Each sense beyond the first is +20%.

Special Limitations

Always On: You cannot turn this ability off. Strangers react at -1; the flickering effect is irritating. -10%.

Channeling 🌑 ⚡

10 points

You can become a conduit for the spirit world, allowing spirits to speak through you. To do so, you must enter a trance, achieved through one minute of concentration and a Will roll (at +2 if you have Autotrance, p. 101). You are unaware of the world around you while you are in this state.

Once you have entered your trance, any spirit in the immediate vicinity can enter your body and use it to speak or write messages. The GM controls what the spirit does or says. The spirit answers questions put to it by others, but it is not bound to tell the truth.

This is a minor form of possession: the spirit can use your body only to communicate. However, if it has the Possession ability (p. 75), it is considered to be touching you, and can attempt *full* possession while you are in a trance. You are considered "wary," and thus get +5 to resist.

Charisma 🌑

5 points/level

You have a natural ability to impress and lead others. Anyone can acquire a semblance of charisma through looks, manners, and intelligence – but *real* charisma is independent of these things. Each level gives +1 on all reaction rolls made by sapient beings with whom you actively interact (converse, lecture, etc.); +1 to Influence rolls (see *Influence Rolls*, p. 359); and +1 to Fortune-Telling, Leadership, Panhandling, and Public Speaking skills. The GM may rule that your Charisma does not affect members of extremely alien races.

Chronolocation
see *Absolute Timing*, p. 35

Claim to Hospitality 🤝

1 to 10 points

You belong to a social group that encourages its members to assist one another. When you are away from home, you may call on other members of this group for food, shelter, and basic aid.

The point cost depends on the extent and wealth of the group. A single friend with a house in another city is worth 1 point; a small family, 2 points; a society of merchants along an important trade route, 5 points; and a vast alliance of wealthy figures, such as "every merchant in the world," 10 points. In the appropriate situation, members of the group should be easy to find (14 or less after 1d-1 hours of searching), but the chance of meeting one at random is small (6 or less to meet one in a small crowd in an appropriate place).

Claim to Hospitality mainly saves the cost and trouble of finding lodging while "on the road" (although if you are wealthy, you might be expected to give gifts to your hosts), but there are side benefits. Members of the group are friendly to each other

(+3 reactions), and may provide advice, introductions, and *small* loans, if asked. The level of assistance might occasionally approach that of Contacts (p. 44). If you expect anything more, though, buy Allies (p. 36) or Patrons (p. 72).

This advantage cuts both ways. If you take it, you can be asked, when at home (at the GM's whim), to provide NPCs with exactly the same sort of hospitality you claim while away. This may become an adventure hook! If you refuse such aid, you will eventually get a bad name and lose this advantage.

Clairsentience 🧠 ⚡

50 points

You can displace all of your *ranged* senses (for humans: sight, hearing, and smell) to a point outside your body. This "viewpoint" must be a specific location within 10 yards. You can modify this range with Increased Range (p. 106) or Reduced Range (p. 115). You can double your range temporarily by spending 2 FP per minute.

To initiate Clairsentience, pick the desired viewpoint (which *can* be inside something) and its facing, concentrate for one minute, and then make an IQ roll. If the viewpoint is out of sight, you must specify distance and direction, and the roll is at -5.

On a success, you can use your ranged senses as if you were physically present at the viewpoint (this means you cannot sense the environment around your body!). Your vision ignores darkness penalties completely. You cannot see *through* solid objects, but if your viewpoint were inside (for example) a closed chest, you would see what was inside despite the lack of light. If you are using or subjected to range-dependent abilities (e.g., spells), calculate all ranges from your *body*, not your *viewpoint*. You can maintain Clairsentience for as long as you like.

On failure by 1, your senses go to some other viewpoint of the GM's choosing. On any greater failure, nothing happens at all. *Critical* failure cripples your ability for 1d hours.

To return your displaced senses, move them elsewhere, or change their facing (usually only important for vision), you must concentrate for one second and make another IQ roll.

However, a viewpoint inside a moving object (e.g., a car) will move with that object with no special concentration on your part. You can only have one viewpoint at a time – you cannot put hearing in one location, vision in another, etc.

Special Limitations

Clairaudience: Only your sense of hearing is displaced. -30%.

Clairosmia: Only your sense of smell is displaced. -60%.

Clairvoyance: Only your sense of sight is displaced. -10%.

ESP: Your ability is part of the ESP psi power (see p. 255). -10%.

Visible: Your senses have a visible manifestation – for instance, a floating face. -10%.

Claws 💪 👽

Variable

You have claws. This advantage modifies all your hands and feet; there is no discount for claws on only some of your limbs. There are several variations:

Blunt Claws: Very short claws, like those of a dog. Add +1 per die to the damage you inflict with a punch or kick; e.g., 2d-3 becomes 2d-1. *3 points.*

Hooves: Hard hooves, like those of a horse. Add +1 per die to the damage you inflict with a kick, and give your feet (only) +1 DR. *3 points.*

Sharp Claws: Short claws, like those of a cat. Change the damage you inflict with a punch or kick from crushing to cutting. *5 points.*

Talons: Longer claws – up to 12" long. Change the damage you inflict with a punch or kick from crushing to your choice of cutting or impaling (choose before you roll to hit). *8 points.*

Long Talons: Huge claws, like sword blades extending from your body! Treat these as Talons, but damage is +1 per die. *11 points.*

Clerical Investment 🤝
5 points

You are an ordained priest of a recognized religion. You enjoy a number of privileges that a layman lacks, notably the authority to preside over weddings, funerals, and similar ceremonies. This gives you a +1 reaction bonus from co-religionists and those who respect your faith, and entitles you to use a title – Father, Sister, Rabbi, etc.

Remember that not all clerics are "good"! Aka'Ar, high priest of the unholy Cult of Set, is also a vested priest. The blessings and marriages he performs are as meaningful to his followers as those of a vicar are to his parish. And – if Set so wills – Aka'Ar can perform exorcisms as potent as those of a Christian priest, if not more so. After all, Aka'Ar has a better working knowledge of demons . . .

Clerical Investment is purely social in nature. It does *not* confer miraculous powers. If you wish to wield divine power by proxy, take Blessed (p. 40), Power Investiture (p. 77), or True Faith (p. 94).

Clerical Investment *includes* Religious Rank 0 (see p. 30). If you want more influence within your church, buy up your Rank.

Clinging 👕 👽
20 points

You can walk or crawl on walls and ceilings. You can stop at any point and stick to the surface without fear of falling. Neither feat requires a roll against Climbing skill, provided the surface is one you can cling to. Move while clinging is half your Basic Move.

If you are falling and try to grab a vertical surface to break your fall, the GM must first decide whether there is anything in reach. If there is, make a DX roll to touch the surface, and then make a ST roll at -1 per 5 yards already fallen. If you succeed, you stop your fall. Otherwise, you continue to fall – but you may subtract 5 yards from the height of the fall thanks to the slowing effect of the failed Clinging attempt. Variations in gravity affect these distances; e.g., in 0.5G, the ST roll would be at -1 per *10* yards.

Special Limitations

Specific: You can only cling to a particular substance. Common materials, such as brick, metal, rock, or wood, are -40%; uncommon materials, such as adobe, ice, or rubber, are -60%; absurd materials, such as chocolate, are -80%.

Combat Reflexes 👤
15 points

You have extraordinary reactions, and are rarely surprised for more than a moment. You get +1 to all active defense rolls (see *Defending*, p. 374), +1 to Fast-Draw skill, and +2 to Fright Checks (see *Fright Checks*, p. 360). You never "freeze" in a surprise situation, and get +6 on all IQ rolls to wake up, or to recover from surprise or mental "stun." Your *side* gets +1 on initiative rolls to avoid a surprise attack – +2 if you are the leader. For details, see *Surprise Attacks and Initiative* (p. 393).

Combat Reflexes is included in Enhanced Time Sense (p. 52). If you have ETS, you cannot also take Combat Reflexes.

Common Sense 👤
10 points

Any time you start to do something the GM feels is *STUPID*, he will roll against your IQ. A successful roll means he must warn you: "Hadn't you better think about that?" This advantage lets an impulsive *player* take the part of a thoughtful character.

Compartmentalized Mind 👤 👽
50 points/level

Your mental coordination gives you, in effect, more than one mind. Each mind – or "compartment" – functions independently and at full capability. Your compartments are identical, but hypnotism, magic, psionics, and the like affect them *separately* (e.g., one compartment could be hypnotized without affecting any of the others).

This advantage does not allow your *body* to perform more than one task. A normal character may select one maneuver on his turn in combat. This may be physical or mental. Each level of Compartmentalized Mind adds one extra *mental* maneuver to this allotment. For instance, Compartmentalized Mind 1 would let you perform one mental maneuver and one physical maneuver (e.g., Concentrate on a spell *and* Attack) or two mental maneuvers (e.g., Concentrate on *two* spells), but never more than one physical maneuver – for that, see *Extra Attack* (p. 53).

If one compartment is under external influence, roll a Quick Contest of Will to see whether it gains control of the body. The compartment currently in control of the body rolls at +1. Battling compartments may attempt to use mental powers on each other. Treat them as *completely separate minds* for this purpose, each with your IQ, Will, and mental abilities (such as Mind Shield).

Two variations on this advantage are available for vehicles built as characters:

Controls: Each level buys one set of controls. Controls let an operator perform his *own* physical or mental maneuvers using *your* abilities (e.g., Innate Attack or Radar), as per the rules for vehicular combat (see p. 467). The operator directs *all* actions of an IQ 0 vehicle with this advantage. Physical limits still apply; for instance, a vehicle can make no more attacks than it has ready weapons. Resolve conflicts between operators by rolling a Quick Contest of vehicle operation skill. *25 points/level.*

Dedicated Controls: As Controls, but each set of controls handles a specific task; e.g., "tail gunner." The person manning them can't operate anything else. *10 points/level.*

Constriction Attack 👕 👽
15 points

Your musculature is optimized for crushing your opponents – whether by "hugging" like a bear or constricting like a python. To use this ability, you must first successfully grapple your intended victim, whose Size Modifier (p. 19) cannot exceed your own. On your next turn, and each successive turn, roll a Quick Contest: your ST vs. your victim's ST or HT, whichever is *higher.* If you win, your victim takes damage equal to your margin of victory; otherwise, he takes no damage.

Contact Group 🤝

Variable

You have a network of Contacts (see *Contacts*, below) placed throughout a particular organization or social stratum. You must specify a corporation, criminal syndicate, military unit, police department, or similar organization, *or* the underworld, merchants, upper class, etc. of *one particular town*. Broader Contact Groups are not allowed.

You may request information from a Contact Group exactly as you would an individual Contact, using the same rules for frequency of appearance, effective skill, and reliability. The difference is that a Contact Group's effective skill reflects ability at an entire *category* of skills – e.g., "business skills" if your Contact Group is a corporation, or "military skills" if your Contact Group is a military unit – as opposed to one specific skill. You must define this area of knowledge when you purchase the Contact Group, and it must be appropriate to the organization.

The GM rolls against the group's effective skill when you request any information that it could reasonably provide. However, this is an abstract success roll, not a roll against a specific skill. For instance, a police Contact Group could provide ballistics comparisons, criminal profiles, legal advice, police records, and introductions to criminals. It would not specifically use Forensics, Criminology, Law, Administration, or Streetwise skills for this, but the information provided might be appropriate to *any* of these "police skills."

To determine the point cost of a Contact Group, select its effective skill, frequency of appearance, and reliability level just as you would for a simple Contact, then multiply the resulting cost by 5.

Contacts 🤝

Variable

You have an associate who provides you with useful information, or who does *small* (pick any two of "quick," "nonhazardous," and "inexpensive") favors for you. The point value of a Contact is based on the skill he uses to assist you, the frequency with which he provides information or favors, and his reliability as a person.

Effective Skill of Contact

First, decide on the type of Contact you have. He might be anything from a wino in the right gutter to a head of state, depending on your background. What is important is that he has access to information, knows you, and is likely to react favorably. (Of course, offering cash or favors is never a bad idea; the GM will set the Contact's "price.")

Next, choose the useful skill your Contact provides. This skill *must* match the Contact's background; e.g., Finance for a banker or Forensics for a lab technician. Since the GM rolls against this skill when you request aid from your Contact, you should select a skill that can provide the results you expect. If you want ballistics comparisons, take a Contact with Forensics, not Finance!

After that, select an *effective* skill level. This reflects the Contact's connections, other skills, Status, etc. It need not be his *actual* skill level (the GM will set this, if it matters). For instance, the president of a local steel mill might have business-related skills of 12-14, but his effective skill might be 18 because of his position in the company. This skill level determines the Contact's base cost:

Effective Skill	Base Cost
12	1 point
15	2 points
18	3 points
21	4 points

Add 1 point to these costs for Contacts who can obtain information using supernatural talents (ESP, magical divination, etc.). This is common for spirits, wizards, etc.

Frequency of Appearance

Select a frequency of appearance, as explained under *Frequency of Appearance* (p. 36), and apply its multiplier to the base cost of the Contact. When you wish to reach your Contact, the GM rolls against his frequency of appearance. On a failure, the Contact is busy or cannot be located that day. On a 17 or 18, the Contact cannot be reached for the entire *adventure!* On a success, the GM will roll against the Contact's effective skill once per piece of information or minor favor you request.

No Contact may be reached more than once per day, even if several PCs share the same Contact. If you have several questions to ask, you should have them all in mind when you first reach your Contact. The Contact answers the first question at his full effective skill. Each subsequent question is at a cumulative -2. Don't overuse your Contacts!

A Contact can never supply information outside his area of knowledge. Use common sense. Likewise, the GM must not allow a Contact to give information that short-circuits an important part of the adventure.

You must explain how you normally get in touch with your Contact. Regardless of frequency of appearance, you cannot reach your Contact if those channels are closed.

Reliability

Contacts are not guaranteed to be truthful. Reliability multiplies the Contact's point cost as follows:

Completely Reliable: Even on a critical failure on his effective skill roll, the Contact's worst response will be "I don't know." On an ordinary failure, he can find information in 1d days. ×3.

Usually Reliable: On a critical failure, the Contact lies. On any other failure, he doesn't know now, ". . . but check back in (1d) days." Roll again at that time; a failure then means he can't find out at all. ×2.

Somewhat Reliable: On a failure, the Contact doesn't know and can't find out. On a critical failure, he lies – and on a natural 18, he lets the opposition or authorities (as appropriate) know who is asking questions. ×1.

Unreliable: Reduce effective skill by 2. On any failure, he lies; on a critical failure, he notifies the enemy. ×1/2 (round up; minimum final cost is 1 point).

Money Talks

Bribery, whether cash or favors, motivates a Contact and increases his reliability level. Once reliability reaches "usually reliable," further levels of increase go to effective skill; bribery cannot make anyone completely reliable!

A cash bribe should be about equivalent to one day's income for a +1 bonus, one week's income for +2, one month's for +3, and one year's for +4. Favors should be of equivalent worth, and should always be something that you actually play out in the game.

The bribe must also be appropriate to the Contact. A diplomat would be insulted by a cash bribe, but might welcome an introduction into the right social circle. A criminal might ask for cash but settle for favors that could get you in trouble. A police detective or wealthy executive might simply want you to "owe him one" for later . . . which could set off a whole new adventure, somewhere down the road.

Contacts in Play

You may add new Contacts in play, provided you can come up with a good in-game justification. The GM might even turn an existing NPC into a Contact for one or more PCs – possibly in lieu of character points for the adventure in which the PCs developed the NPC as a Contact. For instance, the reward for an adventure in which the party helped solve a bank robbery might be a knowledgeable, reliable police Contact.

Examples of Contacts

The list of all possible Contacts – and their skills – would fill an entire book.

Here are just a few examples:

Business. Business owners, executives, secretaries, and even the mailroom flunky can supply information on business dealings. They generally provide a business skill, such as Accounting, Administration, or Finance. A mail boy or typist might have effective skill 12; the president's secretary has skill 15; a senior executive or accountant has skill 18; and the CEO, president, or chairman of the board has skill 21.

Military. This could be anyone from an enlisted grunt to a general. Such Contacts might provide information on troop movements, details on secret weapons or tactics, or top-level strategy. This could take the form of Savoir-Faire (Military), Strategy, or Tactics skill – or perhaps a technical skill, such as Engineer. A Rank 0 soldier would have effective skill 12, a Rank 1-2 NCO would have skill 15, a Rank 3-5 officer would have skill 18, and a Rank 6 or higher officer would have skill 21.

Police. Anyone connected with law enforcement and criminal investigations: beat cops, corporate security, government agents, forensics specialists, coroners, etc. Typical skills are Criminology, Forensics, Intelligence Analysis, and Law. Beat cops and regular private security officers have effective skill 12; detectives, federal agents, and records clerks are skill 15; administrators (lieutenants, captains, Special Agents in Charge, etc.) are skill 18; and senior officers (sheriffs, chiefs of police, District Superintendents, Security Chiefs, etc.) are skill 21.

Street. Thugs, fences, gang members, mobsters, and the like can provide information on illicit activities, local criminal gossip, upcoming crimes, etc. Most provide Streetwise skill. "Unconnected" crooks (those who are not part of the local criminal organization) have effective skill 12; "connected" ones are skill 15; mob lieutenants and other powerful criminals are skill 18; and an actual crime lord (e.g., the Don, clan chief, or Master of the Thieves' Guild) has skill 21.

Courtesy Rank

see *Rank*, p. 29

Cultural Adaptability 👤

10 or 20 points

You are familiar with a broad spectrum of cultures. When dealing with those cultures, you never suffer the -3 "cultural unfamiliarity" penalty given under *Culture* (p. 23). This is definitely a cinematic ability! Point cost depends on the scope of your familiarity:

Cultural Adaptability: You are familiar with all cultures of your race. *10 points.*

Xeno-Adaptability: You are familiar with all cultures in your game world, regardless of race. *20 points.*

Cultural Familiarity

see p. 23

Cybernetics 💪

Variable

Treat most cybernetic implants as equivalent advantages: Infravision for a bionic eye, Damage Resistance for dermal armor, etc. Some implants may qualify for the Temporary Disadvantage limitation (p. 115); suitable temporary disadvantages include Electrical (p. 134) and Maintenance (p. 143). These apply *to the implant*, not to your overall capabilities.

Damage Resistance 💪👽

5 points/level

Your body itself has a Damage Resistance score. Subtract this from the damage done by any physical or energy attack *after* the DR of artificial armor (you can normally wear armor over natural DR) but *before* multiplying the injury for damage type. By default, natural DR *does not* protect your eyes (or windows, if you are a vehicle) or help against purely mental attacks, such as telepathy.

Normal humans cannot purchase DR at all. Creatures with natural armor can buy DR 1 to 5. Thick skin or a pelt would be DR 1; pig hide, armadillo shell, a *heavy* pelt, or scales like those of a lizard would be DR 2; rhinoceros hide or a pangolin's armor plates would be DR 3; alligator scales or elephant hide would be DR 4; and a giant tortoise would have DR 5. Robots, supers, supernatural entities, etc. can purchase *any* amount of DR, subject to GM approval.

Many special modifiers are available to change the basic assumptions of this advantage.

Special Enhancements

Absorption: You can absorb damage and use it to enhance your abilities. Each point of DR stops one point of damage and turns it into one character point that you can use to improve traits (anything but skills) temporarily. You store these points in a "battery" with capacity equal to DR (e.g., DR 10 gives a 10-point battery). Once this battery is full, each point of DR will still stop one point of damage, but will not convert it into a character point. You do not have to use stored points immediately, but you cannot reallocate points once used. You lose absorbed points – unused ones first – at the rate of one

---

Limited Defenses

When you buy Damage Resistance – or *any* advantage that protects against damage (as opposed to non-damaging effects) – you may specify that it is only effective against certain damage types. This is a limitation that reduces the cost of the advantage. Attacks fall into four rarity classes for this purpose:

Very Common: An extremely broad category of damage that you are likely to encounter in almost any setting. *Examples:* ranged attacks, melee attacks, physical attacks (from any material substance), energy attacks (e.g., beam weapons, electricity, fire, heat and cold, and sound), or all damage with a specified advantage origin (chi, magic, psionics, etc.). -20%.

Common: A broad category of damage. *Examples:* a standard damage type (one of burning, corrosion, crushing, cutting, impaling, piercing, or toxic), a commonly encountered *class* of substances (e.g., metal, stone, water, wood, or flesh), a threat encountered in nature *and* produced by exotic powers or technology (e.g., acid, cold, electricity, or heat/fire), or a refinement of a "Very Common" category (e.g., magical energy). -40%.

Occasional: A fairly specific category of damage. *Examples:* a common substance (e.g., steel or lead), any one specific class of damage that is usually produced *only* by exotic abilities or technology (e.g., particle beams, lasers, disintegrators, or shaped charges), or a refinement of a "Common" category (e.g., magical electricity, piercing metal). -60%.

Rare: An extremely narrow category of damage. *Examples:* charged particle beams, dragon's fire, piercing lead, ultraviolet lasers, or an uncommon substance (e.g., silver or blessed weapons). -80%.

Unless specified otherwise, limited DR works only against *direct* effects. If you are levitated using magic and then dropped, the damage is from the fall; "DR vs. magic" would not protect. If a magic sword struck you, "DR vs. magic" would only protect against the magical component of its damage. Similarly, "DR vs. trolls" would not help against a boulder hurled by a troll – the damage is from a boulder, not a troll. Be sure to work out such details with the GM before setting the value of the limitation. If the GM feels that a quality would *never* directly influence damage, he need not allow it as a limitation!

point per second. You lose enhanced abilities as the points drain away. (*Exception:* If you are missing HP or FP, you can heal yourself. Restoring one HP drains 2 stored points *immediately*; restoring one FP drains 3 points. Such healing is permanent. Only HP or FP in excess of your usual scores drain away.) You cannot absorb damage from your own ST or attack abilities. +80% if absorbed points can only enhance one trait (determined when you create your character) *or* can only heal; +100% if you can raise *any* trait.

Force Field: Your DR takes the form of a field projected a short distance from your body. This protects your entire body – including your eyes – as well as anything you are carrying, and reduces the damage from attacks *before* armor DR. Effects that rely on touch (such as many magic spells) only affect you if carried by an attack that does enough damage to pierce your DR. +20%.

Hardened: Each level of Hardened reduces the armor divisor of an attack by one step. These steps are, in order: "ignores DR," 100, 10, 5, 3, 2, and 1 (no divisor). +20% per level.

Reflection: Your DR "bounces back" any damage it *stops* at your attacker. The remaining damage affects you normally. The attacker doesn't get an active defense against the first attack you reflect back at him, but gets his usual defenses against subsequent reflected attacks. Reflection only works vs. direct hits! It cannot reflect damage from explosions, fragments, poison gas, or anything else that affects an entire area. This enhancement is mutually exclusive with Absorption. +100%.

Special Limitations

Ablative: Your DR stops damage *once*. Each point of DR stops one point of basic damage but is destroyed in the process. Lost DR "heals" at the same rate as lost HP (including the effects of Regeneration, p. 80). Use this to represent supers who can absorb massive punishment but who lack the mass to justify a large HP score. -80%.

Can't Wear Armor: Your body is designed in such a way that you cannot or will not wear body armor or clothing. -40%.

Directional: Your DR only protects against attacks from one direction. -20% for the front (F); -40% for the back (B), right (R), left (L), top (T), or underside (U). Humanoids may only take this limitation for front and back.

Flexible: Your DR is not rigid. This leaves you vulnerable to blunt trauma (see p. 379). -20%.

Limited: Your DR applies only to certain attack forms or damage types. See *Limited Defenses* (box) for details.

Partial: Your DR only protects a specific hit location. This is worth -10% per -1 penalty to hit that body part (see p. 398). For instance, an animal with butting horns and a thick skull might have "Skull only," for -70%. "Torso only" is -10%, and also protects the vital organs. When you take this limitation for arms, legs, hands, or feet, the DR protects *all* limbs of that type. If it only protects one limb, the limitation value doubles (e.g., arms are -2 to hit, so a single arm would be -40%). If you have arms, legs, etc. with different penalties, use the least severe penalty to calculate limitation value.

Semi-Ablative: When an attack strikes semi-ablative DR, every 10 points of basic damage rolled removes one point of DR, regardless of whether the attack penetrates DR. Lost DR "heals" as for Ablative (and you cannot combine the two). -20%.

Tough Skin: By default, Damage Resistance is "hard": armor plate, chitin, etc. With this limitation, your DR is merely tough skin. Any effect that requires a scratch (e.g., poison) or skin contact (e.g., electrical shock or Pressure Points skill) affects you if the attack carrying it penetrates the DR of any armor you are wearing – even if it does exactly 0 damage! Your *natural* DR, being living tissue, provides no protection at all against such attacks. This limitation includes all the effects of the Flexible limitation (see above); you cannot take both. It is mutually incompatible with Force Field. -40%.

"Layered" Defenses

You may have multiple "layers" of DR with different combinations of modifiers. You must specify the order of the layers – from outermost to innermost – when you create your character. You may not change this order once set.

Danger Sense 🗝

15 points

You can't depend on it, but sometimes you get this prickly feeling right at the back of your neck, and you know something's wrong . . . If you have Danger Sense, the GM rolls once against your Perception, secretly, in any situation involving an ambush, impending disaster, or similar hazard. On a success, you get enough of a warning that you can take action. A roll of 3 or 4 means you get a little detail as to the nature of the danger.

Danger Sense is included in Precognition (p. 77); if you have the latter trait, you cannot also have Danger Sense.

Special Limitations

ESP: Your ability is part of the ESP psi power (see p. 255). -10%.

Daredevil 🗝

15 points

Fortune seems to smile on you when you take risks! Any time you take an unnecessary risk (in the GM's opinion), you get a +1 to all skill rolls. Furthermore, you may reroll any critical failure that occurs during such high-risk behavior.

Example: A gang of thugs opens fire on you with automatic weapons. If you crouch down behind a wall and return fire from cover, Daredevil gives no bonuses. If you vault over the wall and charge the gunmen, screaming, it provides all of its benefits!

Dark Vision 🗝 👁

25 points

You can see in absolute darkness using some means other than light, radar, or sonar. You suffer no skill penalties for darkness, no matter what its origin. However, you cannot see colors in the dark.

Special Enhancements

Color Vision: You *can* see colors in the dark. +20%.

Destiny 👤 ⚡

Variable

Your fate is preordained. This is considered an advantage if you are destined for great things – although this might not always be clear, and might even be inconvenient at times. For a *disadvantageous* Destiny, see p. 131.

When you choose this advantage, you may only specify its point value. The GM will secretly determine the nature of your Destiny, according to its point value and the dictates of the campaign. You might discover some clues about your Destiny via magical divination or similar techniques, but you are highly unlikely to learn its full extent until it is fulfilled. Note also that a Destiny may *change* as the campaign develops.

Be aware that this advantage gives the GM absolute license to meddle with your life – the GM *must* make the Destiny work out! Working out a good Destiny and making sure it comes to pass require considerable ingenuity on the part of the GM. The GM may wish to forbid this advantage if he feels it would send the campaign off the rails.

The point value of the Destiny determines its impact:

Great Advantage: You are fated to achieve greatness within your lifetime. In the end, everyone will know and praise your name! Sooner or later, something will happen to bring this Destiny to fruition. Note that this does not guarantee "success." If you choose to jump in front of an assassin's knife during your first game session, the GM might just decide the Destiny is fulfilled . . . you died a hero! *15 points.*

Major Advantage: As above, but to a lesser extent. Alternatively, you might be doomed to die in a particular place or in a particular fashion: at sea, by the hand of an emperor, underground, or whatever. You can be grievously wounded – even maimed – under other circumstances, but you *will not die.* If you avoid the circumstances that would fulfill your Destiny, knowingly or otherwise, you might find that Fate has a few surprises. The sea might flood your home while you sleep, the general against whom you march might be the future emperor, or Mt. Vesuvius might bury you under tons of ash. *10 points.*

Minor Advantage: You are fated to play a small part in a larger story, but this part will reflect to your credit. In game terms, you are guaranteed one significant victory. *5 points.*

If you fulfill your Destiny and survive, it's over – but you might feel its repercussions for years to come. In general, the GM should let you put the character points spent on an advantageous Destiny toward a positive Reputation. A Destiny that goes unnoticed once fulfilled is not much of a Destiny!

Detect 👤/👹 👽

Variable

You can detect a specific substance or condition, even when it is shielded from the five human senses. This requires one second of concentration, after which the GM will secretly make a Sense roll for you (see *Sense Rolls*, p. 358). The range modifiers from the *Size and Speed/Range Table* (p. 550) apply. You may buy a special Acute Sense (p. 35) to improve the roll, thereby increasing your effective range.

On a success, the GM tells you the direction to the nearest significant source of the substance, and give you a clue as to the quantity present. On a failure, you sense nothing.

Detect also includes the ability to *analyze* what you detect. This requires an IQ roll; the better the roll, the more precise the details. For instance, if you had Detect (Metal), you could tell gold from iron on a successful IQ roll, and might learn details – such as whether the gold is in the form of ore or bars, and its precise purity – on a critical success.

The base cost of Detect is as follows:

Rare (sorceresses, fire magic, zombies, gold, radar, radio): *5 points.*

Occasional (spellcasters, magic, undead, precious metal, electric fields, magnetic fields, radar *and* radio): *10 points.*

Common (humans, supernatural phenomena, supernatural beings, metal, electric *and* magnetic fields): *20 points.*

Very Common (all life, all supernatural phenomena *and* beings, all minerals, all energy): *30 points.*

Note that the ability to detect certain phenomena can often justify other advantages. For instance, Detect (Magnetic Fields) could explain Absolute Direction.

Special Enhancements

Precise: On a successful Sense roll, you also learn the distance to whatever you detect. +100%.

Signal Detection: You can detect an active transmission of some sort, such as a radio, radar, or laser; see *Scanning Sense* (p. 81) and *Telecommunication* (p. 91). You suffer no range penalties, but must be within twice the signal's own range and (if the signal is directional) within in its path. +0%.

Special Limitations

Vague: You can only detect the presence or absence of the target substance. Direction and quantity are revealed only on a critical success, and you cannot analyze what you detect. This limitation is mutually exclusive with Precise. -50%.

Digital Mind 👹 👽

5 points

You are a sentient computer program – possibly an artificial intelligence or an "upload" of a living mind. By default, you inhabit a body that includes a computer with Complexity equal to at least half your IQ; see *Computers* (p. 472).

You are *completely immune* to any power defined as "Telepathic," and to magic spells that specifically affect living minds. However, computer viruses and abilities that affect Digital Minds can affect you; you can be taken offline (or even stored, unconscious, as data); and those with Computer Hacking or Computer Programming skill can gain access to your data . . . and possibly read or alter your consciousness!

You are likely to have the Machine meta-trait (p. 263), but this is not mandatory, as you could be a computer-like mind inside an organic body (e.g., a bio-computer or a brain implant). The Reprogrammable disadvantage (p. 150) is also common for Digital Minds, as is the Automaton meta-trait (p. 263), but you do not *have* to possess either trait. Many *advantages* are also possible but not automatic:

Computing Power: If you operate faster than a human mind, buy Enhanced Time Sense (p. 52). If you can add advantages or skills temporarily by running programs, buy Modular Abilities (p. 71).

Copies: If you can run multiple copies of your mind on a single computer system, buy Compartmentalized Mind (p. 43). If you can create loyal copies that run on *other* systems, buy Duplication (p. 50) with the Digital limitation. If you have copies backed up offline, buy Extra Life (p. 55).

Uploading: If you can actively "upload" yourself into other computers, buy Possession (p. 75) with the Digital limitation. If you can do this *easily*, buy extra bodies as Puppets (p. 78).

Discriminatory Hearing ♣ 👽

15 points

You have a superhuman ability to distinguish between sounds. You can *always* identify people by voice, and can recognize individual machines by their "sound signature." You may memorize a sound by listening to it for at least one minute and making a successful IQ roll. On a failure, you must wait at least one full day before making a repeated attempt.

You get +4 (in addition to any Acute Hearing bonuses) on any task that utilizes hearing, and receive +4 to Shadowing skill when following a noisy target.

To simulate the passive sonar used by submarines, add a -30% Accessibility limitation, "Only underwater."

Discriminatory Smell ♣ 👽

15 points

Your sense of smell is far beyond the human norm, and can register distinctive odors for practically everything you may encounter. This allows you to recognize people, places, and things by scent. You may memorize a scent by sniffing it for at least one minute and making a successful IQ roll. On a failure, you must wait at least one full day before making a repeated attempt.

You get +4 (in addition to any Acute Taste and Smell bonuses) on any task that utilizes the sense of smell, and receive +4 to Tracking skill.

If you actually become ill when exposed to the odor of a particular substance, take the Temporary Disadvantage limitation (p. 115). The most common effect is Revulsion (p. 151), but the GM may choose to allow other temporary disadvantages.

Special Enhancements

Emotion Sense: You can detect a person or animal's emotional state by odor. This functions as the Empathy advantage (p. 51), but you must be within 2 yards of the subject. +50%.

Discriminatory Taste ♣ 👽

10 points

This talent functions in most ways like Discriminatory Smell (above), but enhances the sense of taste instead, so tracking is not possible. You must ingest a small quantity of the material to be examined; for a living subject, this means bodily fluids. This gives you an IQ roll to recognize the taste, identify whether a substance is safe to eat, etc. You can perform a detailed "analysis" with a roll against a suitable skill (Chemistry, Cooking, Pharmacy, Poisons . . .). You get +4 (in addition to any Acute Taste and Smell bonuses) on any task that utilizes the sense of taste.

Doesn't Breathe ♣ 👽

20 points

You do not breathe or require oxygen. Choking and strangulation attempts cannot harm (or silence!) you, and you are immune to inhaled toxins. You are still affected by contact poisons, pressure, and vacuum; take Sealed (p. 82), Pressure Support (p. 77), and Vacuum Support (p. 96), respectively, to resist those threats.

Destiny is considered an advantage if you are destined for great things – although this might not always be clear, and might even be inconvenient at times.

Special Limitations

Gills: You can extract oxygen from water, allowing you to remain submerged indefinitely. You suffocate if the water contains no dissolved oxygen. You are immune to strangulation and "the bends." If you can *only* survive underwater, and suffocate in air as quickly as a normal human would drown underwater, Doesn't Breathe (Gills) is a 0-point feature; otherwise, -50%.

Oxygen Absorption: As Gills, but you can absorb oxygen through the surface of your body whether it is in the air, a liquid, or another medium. Your body does not absorb poisonous gases, but you will suffocate if there is *no* oxygen available. You can use breathing equipment in space (your lungs are capable of working normally). You may not have the Sealed advantage. -25%.

Oxygen Combustion: As Oxygen Absorption, but you *cannot* breathe underwater or anywhere else fire cannot burn. -50%.

Oxygen Storage: You need to breathe, but you can go for extended periods of time without doing so; perhaps you store oxygen (like a whale) or have superior blood oxygenation. This differs from Breath-Holding in that you are completely immune to "the bends" *while your oxygen supply holds out.* If you can effectively "hold your breath" for 25 times as long as usual, this is -50%; 50 times, -40%; 100 times, -30%; 200 times, -20%; 300 times, -10%.

Doesn't Eat or Drink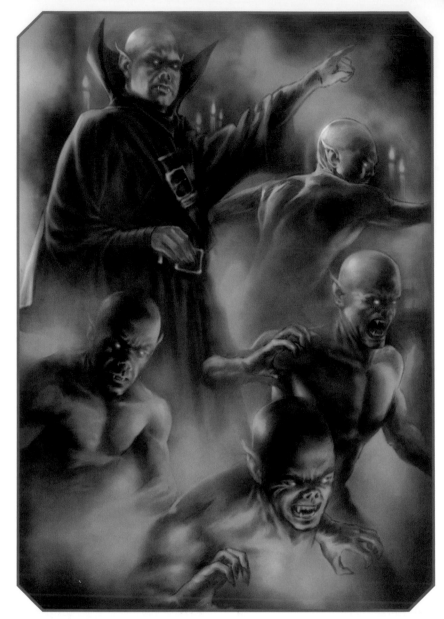

10 points

You do not require food, water, or fuel. Your body is powered in some other manner: solar power, ambient magical energy, etc. A sufficiently rare energy source might qualify you for Dependency (p. 130).

Doesn't Sleep

20 points

You do not have to sleep at all. You can ignore all ill effects from missed nights of rest.

Dominance

20 points

You can "infect" others with a supernatural condition – vampirism, lycanthropy, etc. – and exert absolute control over them. This trait is only appropriate for supernatural beings that spread their "curse" through infection, and only affects members of susceptible races (typically your original race and very similar races). The GM is the judge of which curses are spread this way and who is susceptible.

When you buy Dominance, you must specify *one* natural attack – Claws, Innate Attack, Vampiric Bite, etc. – that delivers the infection. Anyone you damage this way must roll 3d vs. the HP of injury he received (maximum one roll per day). If he rolls under the damage amount, he becomes infected, and will change into the same kind of creature as you in 2d days, or at the GM's discretion, without suitable supernatural intervention. The GM is free to impose additional conditions for infection; for instance, the victim might have to suffer three attacks, or share your blood, or even *die* before making the roll above.

Once the transition is complete, the victim acquires your supernatural racial template (Vampire, Werewolf, etc.) *plus* Slave Mentality (p. 154). He becomes your subordinate. If he goes on to infect others, *his* victims will acquire the same traits and serve you as well.

Dominance itself costs 20 points, but to control a new victim, you must have sufficient unspent points to buy

him as an Ally (p. 36) with the enhancements "Minion" (due to his Slave Mentality) and "Special Abilities" (because he can create new servitors for you). You can choose any frequency of appearance, and may improve this later on with earned points. If you lack the points to buy your victim as an Ally – even at a frequency of "6 or less" – he will still be infected but he will not become your slave.

Dominance persists until you die (*truly* die, for undead), *or* your slave grows in power and you cannot (or choose not to) spend the points to keep him as an Ally, *or* the GM rules the curse is broken via supernatural means. If any of these things occur, your victim will lose Slave Mentality

and become free-willed. You may use the points spent on your former Ally to dominate new victims.

See *Infectious Attack* (p. 140) for the disadvantageous form of Dominance.

Double-Jointed

see *Flexibility,* p. 56

Duplication

35 points/copy

You can split into two or more bodies ("Dupes"), each possessing your full knowledge and powers (but not copies of your equipment, unless you buy a special enhancement). It takes one second and a Concentrate maneuver to separate or merge. When your Dupes merge, your FP and HP are the *average* of all your copies' FP and HP at that time. Your combined self remembers everything experienced by any Dupe.

Dupes have no special ability to coordinate with one another. For that, buy Telesend (see *Telecommunication*, p. 91). If your Telesend works only with your Dupes, you may take the Racial limitation. You may combine Telesend with a Mindlink (p. 70) with your Dupes, in which case you are in constant telepathic contact – no die rolls required.

If one of your Dupes dies, all the others immediately take 2d damage and are stunned. This is mental stun if you define Duplication as a mental trait, physical stun if you define it as a physical trait. The IQ or HT roll to recover is at -6. You also lose the points you spent for that Dupe. The GM may allow you to buy back a dead Dupe with unspent points. Alternatively, an Extra Life (p. 55) will let you bring back *any one* dead Dupe. Your point value drops by the price of the Extra Life, but this is cheaper than buying back a Dupe.

Special Enhancements

Duplicated Gear: Your Dupes appear with copies of Signature Gear (p. 85) that you are *carrying* or *wearing*. Duplicated equipment vanishes when you merge, even if it becomes separated from you. Treat your equipment's HP, ammunition, energy supply, etc. just like your own HP and FP when you merge. +100%.

No Sympathetic Injury: If one of your Dupes is killed, the others are not stunned or hurt. +20%.

Special Limitations

Digital: Your Dupes are software copies of your *mind*, not physical copies of your body. They can possess other computers or occupy spare Puppets (p. 78). You may only take this limitation if you have both Digital Mind (p. 48) and Possession (Digital) (p. 75). -60%.

Shared Resources: Your Dupes do not share your full FP and HP; instead, you must distribute your FP and HP among them. For instance, if you had 15 HP and one Dupe, you could split your HP 7 and 8, 2 and 13, or in any other combination that totaled 15. You need not distribute FP and HP proportionally; with 15 HP

and 15 FP, you could give one copy 3 FP and 9 HP and the other 12 FP and 6 HP. When your bodies re-combine, *add* their FP and HP instead of averaging. -40%.

Eidetic Memory 👤
5 or 10 points

You have an exceptionally good memory. Anyone may attempt an IQ roll to recall the general sense of past events – the better the roll, the truer the memory, but the details are sketchy. With this talent, you automatically succeed at these "memory rolls," and you often recall *precise* details. This trait comes in two levels:

Eidetic Memory: You automatically remember the general sense of everything you concentrate on, and can recall specific details by making an IQ roll. It is possible to "learn" this advantage in play (bards and skalds often acquire it to recall poems and songs). *5 points.*

Photographic Memory: As above, but you automatically recall specific details, too. Any time you, the *player* forget a detail your *character* has seen or heard, the GM or other players must remind you – truthfully! *10 points.*

This trait affects recall, not comprehension, and so does not benefit skills. However, it gives a bonus whenever the GM requires an IQ roll for learning: +5 for Eidetic Memory, +10 for Photographic Memory.

Elastic Skin 👥👽
20 points

You can alter your skin and facial features (but *not* clothing or makeup) to duplicate those of another member of your race or a very similar race. This takes 10 seconds, and requires a Disguise roll if you try to duplicate a particular individual. It takes three seconds to return to your original form. This ability gives +4 to all Disguise rolls.

Empathy 👤
5 or 15 points

You have a "feeling" for people. When you first meet someone – or are reunited after an absence – you may ask the GM to roll against your IQ. He will tell you what you "feel" about that person. On a failed IQ roll, he will *lie!*

This talent is excellent for spotting impostors, possession, etc., and for determining the true loyalties of NPCs. You can also use it to determine whether someone is lying . . . not what the truth is, but just whether they are being truthful with you.

This advantage comes in two levels:

Sensitive: Your ability is not entirely reliable; the IQ roll is at -3. You get +1 to your Detect Lies and Fortune-Telling skills, and to Psychology rolls to analyze a subject you can converse with. *5 points.*

Empathy: Your ability works at full IQ, and the bonus to Detect Lies, Fortune-Telling, and Psychology is +3. *15 points.*

This advantage works only on sapient (IQ 6+), *natural* beings. The equivalent talents for animals, plants, and supernatural entities are Animal Empathy (p. 40), Plant Empathy (p. 75), and Spirit Empathy (p. 88), respectively.

Enhanced Defenses 👤
Variable

You are unusually adept at evading attacks! This may be due to careful observation of your foe, focusing *chi*, or anything else that fits your background. There are three versions:

Enhanced Block: You have +1 to your Block score with either Cloak or Shield skill. You must specialize in one particular Block defense. *5 points.*

Enhanced Dodge: You have +1 to your Dodge score. *15 points.*

Enhanced Parry: You have +1 to your Parry score. You may take this advantage for bare hands (5 points), for any one Melee Weapon skill (5 points), or for *all* parries (10 points). *5 or 10 points.*

This talent is definitely cinematic! The GM might require Trained By A Master (p. 93) or Weapon Master (p. 99) as a prerequisite. He may choose to allow warriors to buy this trait with earned points. He might even permit multiple levels of each Enhanced Defense, in which case the point cost is per +1 bonus. Note that bonuses larger than +3 are almost certainly unbalanced, even in "over-the-top" games!

Enhanced Move ♟ 👽
20 points/level

You can really move! Each level of Enhanced Move *doubles* your top speed in *one* environment: Air, Ground, Space, or Water. You may also take a half-level of Enhanced Move, either alone or with any whole number of levels; this costs 10 points and multiplies Move by 1.5.

Example 1: A super buys Enhanced Move 4 (Ground), for 80 points. He multiplies his Move by 2 × 2 × 2 × 2 = 16. If his Basic Move were 8, he could run at 128 yards/second (262 mph).

Example 2: An avian race has Enhanced Move 2.5 (Air), for 50 points. All members of the race multiply their top airspeed by 2 × 2 × 1.5 = 6.

(Air) requires Flight (p. 56). Enhanced Move (Space) requires Flight with the Space Flight or Newtonian Space Flight enhancement, and affects movement in space – not airspeed. To move faster in air *and* in space, buy both Enhanced Move (Air) and Enhanced Move (Space).

Special Enhancements

Handling Bonus: You get a bonus to DX or vehicle operation skill (e.g., Driving) for the sole purpose of maintaining control at speeds above your Basic Move. +5% per +1, to a maximum of +5.

Special Limitations

Handling Penalty: You have a penalty to DX or vehicle operation skill at high speeds. -5% per -1, to a maximum of -5.

Extra Attack: The "default" assumption in **GURPS** *is that you can make one attack per turn, no matter how many limbs you have.*

Your multiplied Move is your *top speed*. Record it in parentheses after your Enhanced Move trait; for instance, the super in the example above would write "Enhanced Move 4 (Ground Speed 128)." You can always choose to accept a slightly lower top speed if you want your speed to match that of a real-world or fictional creature or vehicle with a known top speed. This does not give you back any points.

Enhanced Move does *not* affect Basic Speed, Basic Move, or Dodge. Its benefits apply only when moving along a relatively straight, smooth course (see *Sprinting*, p. 354). It does have some defensive value, however: those who attack you with ranged attacks must take your speed into account when calculating speed/range modifiers (see p. 550).

Most forms of Enhanced Move have prerequisites. Enhanced Move (Water) requires Amphibious (p. 40) or Aquatic (p. 145). Enhanced Move

Newtonian: This is a limitation for Enhanced Move (Space). Your space "top speed" is actually your "delta-v": the *total* velocity change you can manage before running out of reaction mass. Once you have made velocity changes equal to your top speed, you must refuel before you can change velocity again. -50%.

Road-Bound: This is a limitation for Enhanced Move (Ground). Your Enhanced Move is effective only on a smooth, flat surface, such as a road or building floor. This is often taken in conjunction with the Wheeled disadvantage (p. 145). -50%.

Enhanced Time Sense 👤 👽
45 points

You can receive and process information dramatically faster than the human norm. This improves your *mental* speed – notably your reaction time – but not how fast you physically

move once you react. This has several game benefits.

First, Enhanced Time Sense (ETS) includes Combat Reflexes (p. 43), and provides all the benefits of that advantage. You cannot buy Combat Reflexes if you have ETS; the two advantages are not cumulative.

In combat, you automatically act before those without ETS, *regardless* of Basic Speed. If more than one combatant has ETS, they act in order of Basic Speed, and they *all* get to act before those who lack ETS.

You can perceive things that happen too fast for most people to discern. For example, you cannot be fooled by a projected image, because you can see the individual frames of the film. If secret information is being sent as a high-speed "burst," you can detect it if you're monitoring the transmission (you cannot necessarily *decipher* it, but you know it's there). At the GM's discretion, you get a Sense roll to spot objects moving so fast that they are effectively invisible; for instance, bullets in flight. ETS is extremely valuable if you possess magical or psionic defenses that work at the speed of thought.

If you have ETS, your rapid thought processes always allow you to ponder a problem thoroughly and respond in the manner you think best. You never suffer skill penalties for being mentally "rushed" – although you still need the usual amount of time to complete a physical task, and suffer the usual penalties for hasty work. The GM can almost *never* tell you to make up your mind *right now*. (But don't abuse this privilege by taking half an hour to decide what to do in each turn in combat!)

The exception is when something happens so fast that most people can't perceive it at all. In that case, the GM is justified in asking you for an immediate response, since those without ETS get *no* response.

ETS does not "slow down" the world from your viewpoint. You can still enjoy a movie by simply ignoring the frames, much as a literate person can choose whether or not to notice the individual letters in the words he's reading. ETS also does not let you violate the laws of physics. Some things (e.g., laser beams) simply travel too fast for you to react.

Enhanced Tracking ♈ ☻
5 points/level

You can "track" more than one target – whether with a built-in sensor array or eyes that can swivel independently, like those of a chameleon. An Aim (p. 364) or Evaluate (p. 364) maneuver normally applies to a single target. Each level of Enhanced Tracking allows your maneuver to apply to one additional target. You can only track targets that you can detect, and you cannot Aim at more targets than you have ready weapons to Aim with.

Extended Lifespan ♈ ☻
2 points/level

An average life cycle is defined as maturity at age 18, with aging effects (see p. 444) starting at age 50 and accelerating at ages 70 and 90. Each level of Extended Lifespan *doubles* all these values. Note that if you need to take more than seven levels of this trait (giving maturity at age 2,304 and the onset of aging at age 6,400), it is more efficient to take Unaging (p. 95).

Extra Arms ♈ ☻
Variable

In *GURPS*, a limb with which you can manipulate objects is an *arm*, regardless of where it grows or what it looks like. A normal arm can strike a blow that inflicts thrust-1 crushing damage based on ST. The human norm is two arms for 0 points. Extra arms have a base cost of 10 points apiece.

Coordination

You can use extra arms freely for multiple *noncombat* tasks. For instance, with three arms, you could perform a one-handed task (e.g., use a computer mouse) and a two-handed task (e.g., type) simultaneously. You need Enhanced Tracking (p. 53) to perform tasks that require attention to events in more than one place at a time, however.

You can also use all of your arms in concert for a *single* combat maneuver where extra arms would be helpful; e.g., grappling in close combat. And if you have at least three arms, you can use a shield normally with one arm and still wield a two-handed weapon, just as a normal human fighter can use a shield and one-handed weapon at the same time.

No matter how many arms you have, though, you do not get additional attacks (or other extra maneuvers) in combat unless you buy Extra Attacks (see below).

Close Combat With Extra Arms

Extra arms give a huge advantage in close combat. You cannot punch with more than one arm at a time unless you have Extra Attack, but you may *grapple* with all of your arms at once. Each extra arm of regular length or longer, over and above the generic set of two, gives +2 to any attempt to grapple or break free from a grapple. Having more arms than your opponent also gives +3 on any attempt to pin or resist a pin.

Special Enhancements

Extra-Flexible: Limbs with this enhancement are more flexible than human arms, like tentacles or an elephant's trunk. These limbs can always reach and work with other limbs, regardless of body positioning, general layout, or "right" and "left." +50%.

Long: Your arm is longer *in proportion to your body* than a human arm relative to the human body. This increases your effective SM for the purpose of calculating reach with that arm (see *Size Modifier and Reach*, p. 402). This *does* affect the reach of melee weapons wielded in that hand. Each +1 to SM also adds +1 per die to swinging damage. +100% per +1 to SM.

Special Limitations

Foot Manipulators: Your "arm" is really an unusually dextrous leg. You cannot walk while you are manipulating objects with it (although you can sit, float, or fly). This is a Temporary Disadvantage limitation, the disadvantage being Legless (p. 141). This kind of arm is usually – but not always – Short (see below). -30%.

No Physical Attack: The limb can manipulate but cannot punch or wield melee weapons, and gives no bonus in close combat. It can still wield a firearm or similar ranged weapon. -50%.

Short: The arm has reach "C" (close combat only), and lacks the leverage to use any weapon that must be swung. Subtract one yard from the reach of any melee weapon wielded by that limb. If *all* of your arms are short, you are at -2 on any attempt to grapple. -50%.

Weak: The arm has less than your full body ST for lifting, striking, and grappling. -25% if the arm has half your body ST, or -50% if it has 1/4 your body ST (round down in both cases).

Weapon Mount: Instead of an arm, you have a "hardpoint" where you can mount a weapon. This may be biological, mechanical, or a hybrid of the two, depending on whether you are a living being, a machine, or a cyborg. You cannot use this mount for any purpose other than bearing a weapon. This limitation is incompatible with Feet Manipulator, No Physical Attack, Short, and Weak. -80%.

Modifying Beings With One or Two Arms

Beings with one or two arms *can* use the special modifiers above. Point cost is equal to 1/10 the percentile modifier per affected arm. Thus, enhancements become advantages and limitations become disadvantages. For instance, Short is -50%, so it is worth -5 points per arm. Someone with two short arms would have a -10-point disadvantage.

Those with one arm can only apply these modifiers once, but also get the -20 points for One Arm (p. 147). For instance, an elephant's trunk would be Extra-Flexible (+50%), Long (+100%), and Weak (-50%). These modifiers total +100%, for a 10-point advantage. The -20 points for One Arm would make the net cost -10 points.

Extra Attack ♈
25 points/attack

You can attack more than once per turn. The "default" assumption in *GURPS* is that you can make *one* attack per turn, no matter how many limbs you have. Each Extra Attack allows one additional attack per turn. You may not have more attacks than you have limbs (arms, legs, etc.), natural weapons (Strikers, Teeth, etc.), and attack powers (Afflictions, Bindings, and Innate Attacks) with which to attack. The GM's word on what constitutes an "attack" is final.

A normal human can purchase *one* Extra Attack. This lets him attack with both hands at once, and represents unusually good coordination. Supers and nonhumans have no such limitation. A super-powered cop could buy two Extra Attacks, enabling him to shoot rays from his eyes, fire his pistol, and swing his nightstick all at once. A dragon might take four Extra Attacks and attack *five* times with any combination of his four clawed limbs, teeth, horns, tail, and fiery breath!

Extra Attack is exactly that: an extra Attack maneuver on your turn in combat. It does not eliminate the -4 penalty for an "off" hand (see *Ambidexterity*, p. 39) or let you take multiple Aim maneuvers (see *Enhanced Tracking*, p. 53). You may use some of your attacks for Feint maneuvers, but you many not take multiple actions of other kinds – that requires Altered Time Rate (p. 38).

Extra Attacks and All-Out Attack

When an individual with Extra Attacks makes an All-Out Attack, he must select *one* type of bonus for *all* his attacks that turn. He could not, for instance, take All-Out Attack (Determined) with one attack and All-Out Attack (Strong) with another. If he chooses All-Out Attack (Double) to increase his number of attacks, he gets *one* additional attack.

Extra Attacks and Rapid Strike

You may use *one* of your melee attacks to make a Rapid Strike (see p. 370) on your turn, at the usual penalty. Your remaining attacks are in addition to this Rapid Strike, and receive no penalty. You may not use Rapid Strike with two or more attacks in one turn.

Extra Head 💪 👽

15 points/head

You have more than one head, each with fully functional ears, eyes, mouth, etc. Each Extra Head gives you one Extra Mouth (p. 55) and one level of Enhanced Tracking (p. 53) at no extra charge. Each head also contains an extra brain with a complete copy of your memories, personality, and skills. These extra brains are "backups," however, and do *not* grant

additional mental actions – for that, take Compartmentalized Mind (p. 43).

You cannot suffer more than 2 × (your HP/number of heads) points of injury from any single attack to your head or neck. Any head blow that causes unconsciousness only knocks out that one head; the others continue to function! A critical head blow that would normally kill you simply destroys that head, inflicting the maximum injury noted above and crushing, severing, or exploding the head (GM's option).

Special Limitations

Extraneous: Your Extra Head grants Extra Mouth and Enhanced Tracking, but does not contain a backup brain. A single blow to an Extraneous head can do no more than HP/(1.5 × number of heads) points of injury, but blows to your *real* head can cause stun, knockout, or death even if your other heads are unharmed. -20%.

Extra Legs 💪 👽

Variable

If you can walk on a limb but cannot use it to manipulate objects, it is a leg in *GURPS* (for legs that double as arms, see *Extra Arms*, p. 53). A normal leg can kick for thrust/crushing damage at your usual reach (1 yard for a human). The human norm is two legs, which costs 0 points. It costs points to have more than two legs:

Three or four legs: If you lose a leg, you can continue to move at half Move (round down). Loss of a second leg causes you to fall. *5 points.*

Five or six legs: Each leg lost reduces Move by 20% until only three legs are left. At that point, your Move is 40% normal. Loss of another leg causes you to fall. *10 points.*

Seven or more legs: Each leg lost reduces Move by 10% until only three legs are left. At that point, your Move is 40% normal. Loss of another leg causes you to fall. *15 points.*

You can apply the following modifiers to *all* your legs:

Special Enhancements

Long: Your legs are longer *in proportion to your body* than human legs relative to the human body. This increases your effective SM for the purpose of calculating reach when kicking (see *Size Modifier and Reach,* p. 402) and when clambering over obstacles. +100% per +1 to SM.

Special Limitations

Cannot Kick: You cannot use your legs to kick for damage. -50%.

Modifying Beings With Two Legs

The modifiers above *can* be applied to creatures with only two legs. Point cost is equal to 1/10 the percentile modifier. For instance, a human with Cannot Kick (-50%) would have a -5-point disadvantage.

Extra Life 👤👽

25 points/life

You can come back from the dead! No matter how sure your foes were that they killed you, you didn't *really* die. Work out the details with the GM. Every time you come back from the dead, you use up one Extra Life – remove it from your character sheet and reduce your point total by 25 points. The GM may wish to let players spend earned points to buy Extra Lives in play.

Special Limitations

Copy: When you die, you revert to a "backup copy." To create this copy takes minutes or hours, possibly at a special facility. Details are up to the GM. Make a copy of your character sheet whenever you update your backup. If you die, you revert to those

statistics, losing any traits or character points acquired since then. Note that a copy exists *before* you die. You must tell the GM where you store it. You will return to life at that location . . . and if your enemies discover where you store your copy, they may tamper with it! -20%.

Requires Body: You come back in disembodied state – for instance, as a spirit or a digital copy on a computer. All your experiences and abilities are intact (unless you took Copy), but you cannot interact with the physical world *at all* until you acquire a new body. This might be a clone, an undead corpse, or even a robot "shell." -20%, or -40% if the required body is illegal, rare, or expensive (GM's decision).

Extra Mouth 👹👽

5 points/mouth

You have more than one functional mouth, which can be anywhere on your body. All of your mouths are capable of breathing, eating, and speaking. An Extra Mouth lets you bite more than once if you have Extra Attacks (p. 53). If you have Compartmentalized Mind (p. 43), you can carry on multiple conversations, or cast two spells that require spoken words. Other benefits include being hard to silence or suffocate, and being able to sing in harmony with yourself!

Fashion Sense

see p. 21

Favor 🤝

Variable

You saved someone's life, kept silent at the right time, or otherwise did someone a good turn. Now he owes you one.

A Favor is a one-shot Ally, Contact, Contact Group, or Patron. Work out the point cost of the parent advantage, and then divide it by 5 (round up) to get the cost of the Favor. The catch is that the NPC(s) in question will help you out once . . . and *only* once.

When you wish to "collect" on your Favor, the GM rolls against the frequency of appearance of the underlying advantage. On a failure, you couldn't reach your "friend" in time, or he couldn't comply, but you still

have your Favor coming. You may try again on a later adventure.

On a success, you get what you want (subject to the limits of the advantage). But this discharges the obligation: remove the Favor from your character sheet and reduce your point total appropriately. However, if the roll is a 3 or 4, your "friend" still feels indebted to you, and you retain the Favor . . . at least until next time.

You may buy a Favor in play, just like any trait of this kind. The GM may also wish to include a Favor as part of the reward for a successful adventure.

Fearlessness 👤

2 points/level

You are difficult to frighten or intimidate! Add your level of Fearlessness to your Will whenever you make a Fright Check or must resist the Intimidation skill (p. 202) or a supernatural power that induces fear. You also subtract your Fearlessness level from all Intimidation rolls made against you.

Filter Lungs 👹👽

5 points

Your respiratory system can filter out ordinary contaminants; e.g., dust, pollen, smoke, and even tear gas (but not nerve gas or other contact agents). You suffer no ill effects from such things. This is especially useful in polluted cities and on alien worlds. Note that if you have Doesn't Breathe (p. 49), you do not need this advantage!

Fit 👹

5 or 15 points

You have better cardiovascular health than your HT alone would indicate. This comes in two levels:

Fit: You get +1 to all HT rolls (to stay conscious, avoid death, resist disease or poison, etc.). This does *not* improve your HT attribute or HT-based skills! You also recover FP at twice the normal rate. *5 points.*

Very Fit: As above, but the bonus to HT rolls is +2. In addition, you *lose* FP at only half the normal rate. *15 points.*

In both cases, this advantage applies only to FP lost to exertion, heat, etc. It has no effect on FP spent to power psi or magic spells.

Flexibility ✊

5 or 15 points

Your body is unusually flexible. This advantage comes in two levels:

Flexibility: You get +3 on Climbing rolls; on Escape rolls to get free of ropes, handcuffs, and similar restraints; on Erotic Art skill; and on all attempts to break free in close combat (see p. 391). You may ignore up to -3 in penalties for working in close quarters (including many Explosives and Mechanic rolls). *5 points.*

Double-Jointed: As above, but more so. You cannot stretch or squeeze yourself abnormally, but any part of your body may bend any way. You get +5 on Climbing, Erotic Art, and Escape rolls, and on attempts to break free. You may ignore up to -5 in penalties for close quarters. *15 points.*

Flight ✊ 👽

40 points

You can fly. The "default" is full-fledged, self-powered flight without wings or gliding surfaces. This works at any altitude where there is still significant atmosphere – but in the upper atmosphere, you'll need a way to survive in very thin, cold air (e.g., Doesn't Breathe and Temperature Tolerance). You *cannot* fly in a trace atmosphere or vacuum.

Your flight Move is Basic Speed × 2 (drop all fractions). As explained in *Move in Other Environments* (p. 18), you can adjust this for ±2 points per ±1 yard/second. For very high speeds, take Enhanced Move (Air). If you do not have any of the Controlled Gliding, Gliding, Lighter Than Air, Small Wings, Space Flight Only, or Winged Flight limitations, you can also "fly" at half-speed underwater. Flight includes the ability to hover at Move 0 as well.

Flight does not confer the ability to do complex acrobatics and tight turns; for that, buy Aerobatics skill (p. 174). Flight skill (p. 195) improves endurance.

You can alter most of the above assumptions through special modifiers.

Special Enhancements

Newtonian Space Flight: As Space Flight (below), except that your space Move – or your space top speed, if you have Enhanced Move (Space) – is actually your "delta-v": the total velocity change you can manage in space before running out of reaction mass. For instance, you could accelerate up to your delta-v and stay there (like a missile), or to *half* your delta-v and then decelerate to a stop at the end of your trip (like a conventional spacecraft). Once you have made velocity changes equal to your delta-v, you must refuel before you can change your velocity in space again. +25%.

Space Flight: You can fly in space or a vacuum (such as on the moon). Your space Move is Basic Speed × 2. If you want to be able to accelerate constantly to reach a higher top speed, like a rocket, buy Enhanced Move (Space) (p. 52). This will let you accelerate or decelerate each turn by an amount equal to your space Move, up to your enhanced top speed. For a "realistic" space move that lets you accelerate *indefinitely* in a vacuum (up to the speed of light), you'll want Enhanced Move 25-27 (Space). This is incompatible with *all* other special modifiers except Space Flight Only. +50%.

Special Limitations

Cannot Hover: You must always move at least 1/4 your top airspeed (round up) when flying. This is incompatible with Controlled Gliding and Gliding. -15%.

Controlled Gliding: Like Gliding (below) in most respects, but you can gain altitude by riding updrafts or "thermals." A typical ascent rate is one yard per second. You can locate thermals, if any are present, on a successful IQ or Meteorology roll (one attempt per minute). -45%.

Gliding: You cannot gain altitude. With a running leap, you can launch yourself with an air Move equal to Basic Move. Each turn, you can change velocity by up to 10 yards/second × local gravity in Gs (Earth's gravity is 1G). To accelerate, you must descend by 1 yard for each 1 yard/second added to velocity; top speed is Basic Move × 4 (but you can go faster if towed). To decelerate, you must fly level. If you do not descend at least 1 yard, you *automatically* decelerate by 1 yard/second that turn. When working out turning radius, your basic air Move is 10 × local gravity in Gs. Each level of Enhanced Move (Air) *either* doubles top speed *or* halves deceleration in level flight (e.g., one level means you only lose 0.5 yard/second in level flight); specify which when you buy it. -50%.

Lighter Than Air: You fly by becoming lighter than air (or gaseous). A wind moves you 1 yard/second, in the direction it is blowing, per 5 mph of wind speed. If the wind happens to be blowing in the direction you wish to travel, this adds to your Move; otherwise, your Move goes down as you fight against the breeze. -10%.

Low Ceiling: You cannot fly very high. This does not limit speed in any way, but the GM may require Aerobatics rolls to dodge obstacles near the ground. A 30-foot ceiling is -10%; a 10-foot ceiling is -20%; and a 5-foot ceiling is -25%.

Small Wings: As Winged (below), except that your wingspan is no more than half your height. You use your wings to steer and to stabilize your flight – not to lift. If your wings are crippled in flight, roll against Aerobatics skill (or default) to land safely. -10%.

Space Flight Only: You can only take this in conjunction with Space Flight or Newtonian Space Flight. You can fly *only* in space; you have air Move 0 in atmosphere. You require a boost to reach space from any planet with an atmosphere, and are incapable of atmospheric reentry. -75%.

Winged: You use large wings or skin flaps to fly. Wingspan is at least twice your height. In order to take off, land, or maneuver, you must have an open area with a radius equal to your wingspan in all directions. If your wings are bound, or if a wing is crippled (more than 1/3 of your wings, if you have more than two), you cannot fly. Treat wings as arms for the purpose of targeting and crippling. If you wish to strike blows or manipulate objects with your wings, you must pay for them as Strikers or Extra Arms in addition to the cost of Flight. -25%.

Gadgeteer 👤

25 or 50 points

You are a natural inventor. You can modify existing equipment and – given sufficient time and money – invent entirely new gadgets as described under *Gadgeteering* (p. 475).

This lets you design gadgets *quickly*, and makes it easy to realize higher-TL innovations. This advantage comes in two levels:

Gadgeteer: You are a "cinematic" gadgeteer, but your work still takes days or months, and requires a good deal of money and expensive equipment. *25 points.*

Quick Gadgeteer: You can throw together wondrous gadgets in minutes or hours, and can get by with scrounged-together spare parts that cost a few percent of what a "realistic" inventor would have to spend. This level is definitely unsuitable for realistic campaigns! *50 points.*

G-Experience 💡

1 to 10 points

You have experience working in one or more gravitational fields other than your native one, and your reflexes adapt quickly to the way objects move and fall in those fields. You suffer only half the usual DX penalty for different gravity (see *Different Gravity,* p. 350). In situations where low gravity would make a task *easier,* you roll at full DX, plus the bonus for low gravity, plus an extra +1. For instance, if a normal person would get +2 to catch a ball in low gravity, you would get +3.

This trait costs 1 point per gravity field with which you have experience. For instance, an Earth native who works on the moon might have G-Experience (0.16G). To enjoy the benefits of G-Experience in *all* gravity fields, buy G-Experience (All) for 10 points.

Gifted Artist
see *Talent,* p. 89

Gizmos 💡

5 points/gizmo

You always seem to have just the piece of gear you need. Once per game session per level of this advantage, you may pull out one small item of equipment that you *could* have been carrying. This "Gizmo" remains undefined until you reveal it. It does not even "enter play" until you take it out; thus, it cannot be damaged, lost, stolen, or found in a search.

A Gizmo must be small enough to fit in an ordinary coat pocket, and must meet one of three criteria:

1. An item you own but did not specifically state you were carrying. For instance, if you own a handgun, and get ambushed while driving to church, you could pull out your pistol – even if the police searched your vehicle five minutes ago and found no weapons!

2. An item that you *probably* own, and that is in keeping with your character concept, but that is minor or ignorable enough to leave unspecified. For instance, a policeman might happen to be carrying a spare handcuff key, while a wizard might have some eye of newt. The GM has the final say, but should be lenient if the item you wish to have is consistent with your character story.

3. An inexpensive device widely available at your tech level. For instance, if you need to light the fuse on some dynamite, you could pull out a box of matches – and they would work, even if you just took an involuntary swim in the creek.

Each Gizmo you can use per game session (maximum of three) costs 5 points. Note that this ability is not realistic! The GM may wish to limit it further, or forbid it, in a realistic campaign.

Gadgeteers and Gizmos

Those with the Gadgeteer advantage (p. 56) have more latitude. In addition to the usual items available, a Gadgeteer may specify that his Gizmo is one of his inventions (which must still be small). Instead of pulling an existing gadget "out of his pocket," a Gadgeteer can use his Gizmo to let him *build* what he needs on the spot. He must still possess or find the appropriate materials, and know any required skills. The GM should roll secretly against the relevant skill, at -2 or worse. A failed roll means the device doesn't work (this still "uses up" the Gizmo). A critical failure means the device backfires spectacularly!

Green Thumb

see *Talent*, p. 89

Gizmos: You may pull out one small item of equipment that you could have been carrying. This "Gizmo" remains undefined until you reveal it. It cannot be lost, stolen, or found in a search.

Growth ♋ ♥

10 points/level

You can grow – *really* grow! As your size increases, so must your ST (or you would collapse under your own weight). Your equipment *doesn't* change size!

Each level of Growth lets you increase your Size Modifier by +1. Find your final height from the *Size Modifier Table* (p. 19). Increases in SM affect your arm and leg length when calculating reach and determining whether you can negotiate obstacles; see *Size Modifier and Reach* (p. 402). It takes one second to modify your SM

by +1 (or by -1 as you return to normal size).

If you attempt to grow in a room, vehicle, container, etc. that isn't large enough to hold you, your growth normally stops. However, if *maximum* thrust damage for your current ST is greater than the wall or ceiling's DR, you burst through it. This takes one second per point of DR.

You must buy the ST necessary to support your form separately. This is 5 × final height in *yards*. If your ST increases with height and is only available when you grow, you may buy it with the Size limitation (see *Strength*, p. 14). Use your *maximum* SM to determine the limitation value. At intermediate SMs, find your height as a fraction of your maximum height. This is the fraction of your extra ST available to you at that SM (round down).

Example: A 6'-tall character (SM 0) has Growth 4. He can grow to SM +4, giving him a maximum height of 10 yards. He must buy ST 50 to support himself. If he has ST 15 and gains +35 ST only at full height, he may buy his +35 ST with a -40% Size limitation. At SM +1, he will be 3 yards tall. This is 30% of his final height, so he will have 30% of +35 ST, or +10 ST, for ST 25. Similarly, he'll be 5 yards tall with ST 32 at SM +2, 7 yards tall with ST 39 at SM +3, and 10 yards tall with ST 50 at SM +4.

Special Modifiers

Maximum Size Only: You can only assume normal or maximum size.

Instead of growing at +1 SM per second, you grow to your maximum SM – or revert back to your usual SM – in *one* second. The limitation of no intermediate SMs (restricting your use of this ability in close quarters) cancels out the enhancement of rapid growth (a useful benefit in combat). +0%.

Gunslinger ♟

25 points

You can make uncannily precise shots without aiming. This ability works with any weapon that uses Beam Weapons, Gunner, Guns, or Liquid Projector skill. It gives no bonuses when using muscle-powered missile weapons (but the GM is free to introduce a low-tech version that works with Blowpipe, Bow, Crossbow, Sling, etc.).

When firing single shots (RoF 1-3) from a one-handed weapon, you get the Accuracy bonus of your weapon *without* the need for an Aim maneuver. When using a two-handed weapon or automatic fire, you get *half* the Accuracy bonus (round up) without the need to Aim. If you *do* Aim, you always get full Acc, and bracing, scopes, and additional seconds of Aim provide the usual benefits.

This ability is intended for cinematic games with an "action movie" ambience. The GM may wish to forbid it in a completely realistic campaign.

Hard to Kill ♋♥

2 points/level

You are incredibly difficult to kill. Each level of Hard to Kill gives +1 to HT rolls made for survival at -HP or below, and on any HT roll where failure means instant death (due to heart failure, poison, etc.). If this bonus makes the difference between success and failure, you collapse, apparently dead (or disabled), but come to in the usual amount of time – see *Recovering from Unconsciousness* (p. 423). A successful Diagnosis roll (or a Mechanic roll, for machines) reveals the truth.

Example: Bruno has HT 12, 15 HP, and Hard to Kill 4. He takes 45 points of damage, which reduces him to -30 HP. He must make two HT rolls to survive: one at -15 HP, one at -30 HP. He rolls an 11 for the first one, but on the second roll, he gets a 14. This is above his HT (12), but below his modified

HT (12 + 4 = 16). He passes out, and his foes leave him for dead. Roughly a day later, he'll regain consciousness – injured, but not dead!

In a realistic campaign, the GM may wish to limit characters to Hard to Kill 1 or 2.

Hard to Subdue ♟
2 points/level

You are hard to knock out. Each level of Hard to Subdue gives +1 to any HT roll to avoid unconsciousness – whether as a result of injury, drugs, or ultra-tech weapons – and to resist supernatural abilities that cause unconsciousness. In a realistic campaign, the GM may wish to limit characters to Hard to Subdue 1 or 2.

Healer
see *Talent*, p. 89

Healing ♟ 👽
30 points

You have the ability to heal others. You must be in physical contact with the subject. To activate your power, concentrate for one second and make an IQ roll. Roll at -2 if the subject is unconscious.

You can use Healing in two ways:

Heal Injuries: On a success, you can heal any number of HP. This costs you 1 FP per 2 HP healed (round up). Failure costs 1d FP, but you can try again; critical failure *also* causes the recipient 1d damage. Even 1 HP of healing will stop bleeding. By rolling at -6, you can repair a crippled but whole limb if you *completely* heal the HP lost to the crippling injury. For instance, to heal a hand crippled by 4 points of damage, make an IQ-6 roll and spend 2 FP. Each healer gets only one attempt per crippled limb. Healing cannot restore *lost* limbs or bring back the dead.

Cure Disease: This requires an IQ roll at a modifier determined by the GM – from +1 for the common cold to -15 for AIDS. The FP cost is equal to twice the penalty, minimum 1 FP. For instance, it would cost 6 FP to cure a disease that calls for an IQ-3 roll.

If used more than once per day on a given subject, apply a cumulative -3 per *successful* healing of the same type

(injury or disease) on that subject. This penalty accumulates until a *full* day has passed since the most recent healing.

Healing works on your own race and on all "similar" races. In a fantasy campaign, for instance, all warm-blooded humanoid races (elves, dwarves, orcs, halflings, etc.) would be "similar."

Special Enhancements

Faith Healing: Your power works by channeling spiritual energy. This lets you cure *anyone* the spirits or gods deem worthy of healing, regardless of race. However, you (and possibly your subject) must behave in a manner consistent with the interests and moral codes of your supernatural allies, or this ability will not work. You may not combine Faith Healing with Own Race Only or Xenohealing. +20%.

Xenohealing: You can heal beings quite dissimilar from yourself. Examples, assuming you are human: All Mammals, +20%; All Earthly Life, +40%; All Carbon-Based Life, +60%; Anything Alive, +80%; Anything Animate (including undead, golems, etc.), +100%.

Special Limitations

Disease Only: You can only cure disease. -40%.

Injuries Only: You can only heal injuries. -20%.

Own Race Only: This is only available in campaigns with multiple sapient races. -20%.

Psychic Healing: Your ability is part of the Psychic Healing psi power (see p. 256). -10%.

Hermaphromorph ♟ 👽
5 points

You can switch among fully functional neuter, male, and female forms. The process takes 10 seconds (Preparation Required, Takes Extra Time, and Takes Recharge are common limitations).

High Manual Dexterity ♟
5 points/level

You have remarkably fine motor skills. Each level (to a maximum of four) gives +1 to DX for tasks that

require a delicate touch. This includes all DX-based rolls against Artist, Jeweler, Knot-Tying, Leatherworking, Lockpicking, Pickpocket, Sewing, Sleight of Hand, and Surgery, as well as DX-based rolls to do *fine* work with Machinist or Mechanic (e.g., on clock-work). This bonus *doesn't* apply to IQ-based tasks or large-scale DX-based tasks, nor does it apply to combat-related die rolls of any kind.

High Pain Threshold ♟
10 points

You are as susceptible to injury as anyone else, but you don't *feel* it as much. You *never* suffer a shock penalty when you are injured. In addition, you get +3 on all HT rolls to avoid knockdown and stunning – and if you are tortured physically, you get +3 to resist. The GM may let you roll at Will+3 to ignore pain in other situations.

High Pain Threshold is *included* in Supernatural Durability (p. 89); if you have the latter advantage, you cannot take this one.

High TL
see p. 23

Higher Purpose ♟ 🏹
5 points

You are driven to exceed your normal limits in one specific pursuit. You must state this exactly as if it were a Code of Honor disadvantage (p. 127): "Defend all women," "Slay all demons," etc. If, in the GM's judgment, you are unfaltering in your pursuit of your Higher Purpose, you get +1 to all die rolls that pertain *directly* to the pursuit of your cause. If you deviate from your Higher Purpose, you lose this bonus . . . and the GM is free to penalize you for bad roleplaying just as if you had ignored a Code of Honor.

A Higher Purpose must be *specific*. Higher Purposes such as "Fight evil" or "Oppose authority figures" are too broad to be balanced. In addition, a Higher Purpose must entail genuine risk and inconvenience. The GM should not allow pragmatic Higher Purposes like "Faithfully serve my superiors." All Higher Purposes are subject to GM approval.

Hyperspectral Vision ♋ 👽

25 points

Your vision extends across the infrared, visible, and ultraviolet portions of the spectrum. This integrated picture often reveals details that are invisible to those who merely possess normal vision, Infravision (p. 60), or Ultravision (p. 94).

Hyperspectral Vision grants near-perfect night vision: you suffer no vision or combat penalties if there is *any light at all*. In total darkness, it functions exactly like Infravision. This trait also gives +3 on all Vision rolls; on all rolls to spot hidden clues or objects with Forensics, Observation, or Search skill; and on all Tracking rolls.

If you possess Hyperspectral Vision, you *cannot* also have Infravision or Ultravision. This trait is essentially a higher level of both those advantages. Its game effects *replace* the specific effects of those traits.

As described, this trait emulates realistic TL7+ sensors. The GM may permit supers to take the two special enhancements below. Neither is appropriate for real-world sensors!

Special Enhancements

Extended Low-Band: You perceive radiation below the infrared, allowing you to "see" microwave, radar, and radio sources. This gives no special ability to *understand* radio signals! +30%.

Extended High-Band: You sense radiation above the ultraviolet, allowing you to "see" X-ray and gamma ray sources. +30%.

Illuminated 👤 ↗

15 points

You are an "Illuminatus" in the original sense of the word – you are enlightened. You *know* what's going on, and you know it *intuitively*.

You can discern other Illuminati on sight, with no possibility of error. Furthermore, whenever the GM requires a roll against a skill such as Current Affairs, Hidden Lore, or Intelligence Analysis to tell whether a certain strange occurrence is truly a coincidence or the result of a conspiracy, you may roll against the *higher* of your IQ and the specific skill in

question. Finally, you can perceive and communicate with supernatural beings who are tied to Illuminated conspiracies in your game world (GM's decision). This gives you no special ability to control them, but they recognize you and treat you with a certain respect: +3 on reaction rolls.

The only drawback is that other Illuminati and spiritual beings are able to perceive *your* Illuminated nature, and there's nothing you can do about it except stay out of sight.

This advantage is best suited to mystical or fantastic campaigns. It is rarely appropriate in "mundane" conspiracy campaigns. The GM is the final judge of who may possess this trait.

Improved G-Tolerance ♋

5 to 25 points

You can function under a wide range of gravities. For a normal human, the penalties for non-native gravity accrue in increments of 0.2G; see *Different Gravity* (p. 350). A larger increment costs points: 5 points for 0.3G, 10 points for 0.5G, 15 points for 1G, 20 points for 5G, and 25 points for 10G. Normal humans are limited to 10 points in this trait.

Independent Income

see p. 26

Indomitable 👤

15 points

You are impossible to influence through ordinary words or actions. Those who wish to use Influence skills on you (see *Influence Rolls*, p. 359) must possess a suitable advantage: Empathy (p. 51) if you are a human or similar being, Animal Empathy (p. 40) if you're a beast, Plant Empathy (p. 75) if you're a plant, or Spirit Empathy (p. 88) if you're a demon, ghost, etc. Everyone else – however convincing – fails automatically. This trait often accompanies Unfazeable (p. 95).

Infravision ♋ 👽

0 or 10 points

You can see into the infrared portion of the spectrum, allowing you to detect varying degrees of heat. This lets you fight at no penalty even in absolute darkness, *if* your target emits

heat (this includes all living beings and most machines). It also gives you +2 on all Vision rolls to spot such targets, since their heat stands out from the background. You can follow a heat trail when tracking: add +3 to Tracking rolls if the trail is no more than an hour old.

Infravision does *not* let you distinguish colors, and only allows you to judge the general size and shape of heat-emitting objects, including living beings (for instance, you might have trouble telling two people of the same size apart). Roll at -4 to distinguish objects of similar size and shape. The GM may also require a Vision-4 roll to read by reflected heat. Sudden flashes of heat (e.g., a flare, fiery explosion, or infrared laser) can blind you, just as a flash of light can blind ordinary vision.

Cost depends on your capabilities:

You can only see using Infravision, and are subject to its limitations at all times: *0 points*.

You can switch freely between normal vision and Infravision: *10 points*.

Injury Tolerance ♋ 👽

Variable

You have fewer physiological weaknesses than ordinary living beings. The cost of this advantage depends on the precise frailties eliminated. Note that some forms of Injury Tolerance include others, and that Diffuse, Homogenous, and Unliving are mutually incompatible.

Diffuse: Your body is fluid or particulate, composed of a swarm of smaller entities, or perhaps made of pure energy. This makes you immune to crippling injuries and reduces the damage you suffer from most physical blows; see *Injury to Unliving, Homogenous, and Diffuse Targets* (p. 380). Most foes (GM's decision) cannot slam or grapple you! Diffuse includes all the benefits of No Blood, No Brain, and No Vitals. *100 points*.

Homogenous: Your body has no vulnerable internal organs, bones, muscles, or other mechanisms. As a result, you are less susceptible to piercing and impaling attacks; see *Injury to Unliving, Homogenous, and Diffuse Targets* (p. 380). Homogenous includes the benefits of No Brain and No Vitals. This trait is intended for entities such as iron golems, trees, and slimes. *40 points.*

No Blood: You do not rely upon a vital bodily fluid (like blood) for survival. You do not bleed (see *Bleeding,* p. 420), are unaffected by blood-borne toxins, and are immune to attacks that rely on cutting off blood to part of your body. *5 points.*

No Brain: Your brain – if you have one – is distributed throughout your body, or isn't your true seat of consciousness. Your opponents cannot target it for extra damage. You may have a head, but a blow to the skull or eye is treated no differently than a blow to the face (except that an eye injury can still cripple that eye). *5 points.*

No Eyes: You lack eyes or other vulnerable optics, but can somehow see despite this (unless of course you suffer from Blindness, p. 124). As you have no eyes, they cannot be attacked. You are also immune to blinding attacks. *5 points.*

No Head: You have no head at all. This *includes* the benefits of No Brain. As well, you lack "skull" and "face" hit locations, and have no need for head armor. You can still see, speak, hear, smell, taste, etc. unless you take the appropriate disadvantages. Specify how you do this (supernaturally, technologically, via organs on your torso, etc.). It is common – but not mandatory – for those with No Head to have No Neck, No Eyes, or both. *7 points.*

No Neck: You have no neck. As a result, you have no "neck" hit location, and cannot be decapitated, choked, or strangled. *5 points.*

No Vitals: You have no vital organs (such as a heart or engine) that attackers can target for extra damage. Treat hits to the "vitals" or "groin" as torso hits. *5 points.*

Unliving: Your body is not composed of living flesh. You take reduced damage from piercing and impaling attacks, but are not quite as resilient as if you were Homogenous; see *Injury to Unliving, Homogenous, and Diffuse Targets* (p. 380). This trait is intended mainly for machines and corporeal undead. *20 points.*

Innate Attack ♣ ♠

Variable

You have a natural or built-in attack with which you can inflict physical damage (for nondamaging attacks, see *Affliction,* p. 35, and *Binding,* p. 40). Examples include a dragon's fiery breath, a robot's built-in blaster, and a god's ability to hurl lightning bolts.

By default, this is a ranged attack with 1/2D 10, Max 100, Acc 3, RoF 1, Shots N/A, and Recoil 1, although you can apply modifiers to change these statistics (see pp. 101-116).

An Innate Attack inflicts 1d damage per level. Its cost per level depends on the *type* of damage it inflicts:

Burning (burn)

Your attack inflicts damage using flame, an energy beam, or localized electrical burns. It may ignite fires! *5 points/level.*

Corrosion (cor)

Your attack involves acid, disintegration, or something similar. For every 5 points of basic damage you inflict, reduce the target's DR by 1, in addition to regular damage. (Living beings heal natural DR at the same rate as HP.) *10 points/level.*

Crushing (cr)

Your attack inflicts damage through blunt impact, like a bludgeoning weapon or an explosive blast. It is likely to cause knockback (p. 378), and is more effective at inflicting blunt trauma (p. 379) than other types of damage. *5 points/level.*

Cutting (cut)

Your attack inflicts lacerations, like those caused by an axe or broken glass. Multiply penetrating damage by 1.5. Cutting attacks can inflict blunt trauma and cause knockback. *7 points/level.*

Fatigue (fat)

Your attack is nonlethal. It might involve a low-amperage electric shock or a "mind blast," or even inflict a weakening effect such as hypothermia or starvation. It reduces FP, not HP, and cannot affect machines. *10 points/level.*

Alternative Attacks

If you have multiple Innate Attacks, you may define them as being the *same* basic attack, but with different settings, ammo types, etc. Determine the cost of these "alternative attacks" as usual, but only pay full price for the *most expensive* attack. Buy additional attacks at 1/5 cost (round up).

This can save a lot of points, but there are drawbacks. First, since the attacks represent a single ability, you cannot use them simultaneously, even if you are capable of multiple attacks. This also prevents you from combining them with the Link enhancement (p. 106). As well, any critical failure or malfunction that disables one of your attacks disables *all* of them. Finally, if your most expensive attack is somehow drained or neutralized, none of the cheaper attacks will work.

You may also apply this rule to multiple Afflictions (p. 35) or Bindings (p. 40), or any combination of these with Innate Attacks that you cannot use simultaneously. With the GM's permission, you can apply this rule to multipurpose Strikers (p. 88) as well.

Impaling (imp)

Your attack inflicts stab wounds, like a spear or an arrow. *Double* penetrating damage in flesh! Impaling attacks can target the eyes and vital organs, can inflict blunt trauma, and may slip through high-tech flexible armor. *8 points/level.*

Piercing

Your attack involves a fast, blunt projectile, such as a bullet, or is sharp but too small to qualify as impaling, like a dart or a stinger. It may inflict blunt trauma, and can target the eyes and vital organs. There are four subclasses of piercing attack:

Small Piercing (pi-): Use this for very low-energy projectiles (e.g., blowgun darts), or for attacks that tend to punch through the target and leave a small wound channel (e.g., armor-piercing bullets). Against flesh, *halve* damage that penetrates DR. *3 points/level.*

Piercing (pi): Use this for most rifle and pistol bullets. *5 points/level.*

Large Piercing (pi+): Use this for attacks similar to large-caliber solid bullets, or for smaller projectiles that create large wound channels (e.g., hollow-point bullets). Multiply penetrating damage in flesh by 1.5. *6 points/level.*

Huge Piercing (pi++): Use this for attacks that leave an even larger wound channel than large piercing. *Double* penetrating damage in flesh! *8 points/level.*

Toxic (tox)

Your attack inflicts cellular damage, in the manner of disease, poison, or radiation. It cannot normally affect machines. The modifiers Cyclic (p. 103), Onset (p. 113), and Resistible (p. 115) are usual, but not required. *4 points/level.*

Partial Dice

You do not have to buy whole-numbered dice of damage. Each ±1 to damage counts as ±0.3 dice. Round the final cost *up.* For instance, an Innate Attack that does 1d+2 damage counts as 1.6 dice. If it were crushing (5 points/die), it would cost 1.6 × 5 = 8 points.

Some attacks do only *1 point* of damage. This counts as 0.25 dice. Once again, round cost *up.* Such attacks can still be deadly – especially if they involve the Follow-Up (p. 105) or Cyclic (p. 103) enhancement!

Special Modifiers

Many special modifiers for Innate Attack appear under *Attack Enhancements and Limitations* (p. 102). You can use these to create almost *any* attack – built-in guns, lasers, jets of liquid fire, gale-force winds, etc. – and to duplicate the capabilities of weapons listed in *GURPS* books.

Fatigue and toxic attacks intended to simulate poison or disease *require* modifiers. Noxious agents on Claws (p. 42), Teeth (p. 91), darts, etc. use Follow-Up (p. 105). Gases and sprays use Respiratory Agent (p. 108) or Contact Agent (p. 103), often with Area Effect (p. 102), Cone (p. 103), or Jet (p. 106). Attacks that depend on touch or on skin contact use Blood Agent (p. 102) or Contact Agent, plus one of Aura (p. 102) or Melee Attack (p. 112).

Regardless of other modifiers, Innate Attacks are treated as ranged attacks unless given the Melee Attack limitation; then they're considered melee weapons.

Description

After applying all relevant modifiers, name and describe the attack. You can be as general as "dragon fire" or as specific as "9mm machine pistol cybernetically implanted in right arm." At the GM's discretion, the description can imply additional noncombat abilities; for instance, a jet of high-pressure water could put out fires. The GM has the final say as to whether your description fits the campaign setting, and may modify the attack if necessary.

Insubstantiality 🧠/💪 👽

80 points

You can become intangible, passing through solid objects as though they weren't there. In this state, gravity does not affect you – you can move in *any* direction at full Move (and make no noise when you move). You can perceive the tangible world, and speak normally to those within it, but you *cannot* pick up normal objects or affect them in any way.

Physical and energy attacks cannot harm you, but you're still vulnerable

ADVANTAGES

to psionic and (nonmaterial) magical attacks. Likewise, your physical and energy attacks cannot affect physical opponents. Your psi abilities and magic spells *can* affect the physical world, but at -3 to all skill rolls.

Although you can pass through solids, you must still breathe. When moving through a solid object, treat this as if you were swimming underwater for purposes of suffocation. You cannot materialize inside a solid object.

Your "natural" form (physical or insubstantial) is considered a special effect. You must take this advantage if you can change between a physical and an insubstantial form.

This trait can represent any number of abilities from folklore and fiction. You should work out its origins (see p. 33) and special effects with the GM – perhaps you "vibrate" out of synch with reality, phase into a different dimension, or become a spirit. This determines your appearance, which may be transparent, misty . . . or completely normal (but you can't be *invisible* without the Invisibility advantage). Your physical and energy attacks affect other beings using the same form of Insubstantiality, and their attacks affect you. The GM may rule that certain materials, energy barriers, magic spells, etc. are impenetrable to your particular form of Insubstantiality.

Special Enhancements

Affect Substantial: If you have *any* abilities that can affect the substantial world when you are insubstantial – including magic, psionics, or powers with the Affects Substantial enhancement (p. 102) – this advantage costs more. +100%.

Can Carry Objects: Normally, you cannot carry *anything* while insubstantial. This enhancement lets you carry objects, including clothing and armor. They become physical if dropped. You cannot materialize these objects inside other objects or characters. No encumbrance is +10%; Light, +20%; Medium, +50%; Heavy, +100%.

Partial Change: You can turn part of your body substantial while other parts remain insubstantial, or vice versa. Thus, you could reach through a wall and tap someone on the shoulder. If you also have Can Carry Objects, you can materialize your

hand, pick up material objects, and carry them while insubstantial. +20%, or +100% if you can turn an item you are carrying substantial without dropping it (this requires turning your hand substantial, too).

Special Limitations

Always On: You are always insubstantial and cannot materialize. If you have this limitation, there is no -3 to use magic or psionics. -50%.

Usually On: Similar to Always On, but you can materialize for short periods with great effort. Materialization costs 1 FP per *second*. -40%.

Intuition 👤

15 points

You usually guess right. When faced with a number of alternatives, and no logical way to choose among them, you can ask the GM to let you use your Intuition. The GM makes a secret IQ roll, with a bonus equal to the number of "good" choices and a penalty equal to the number of "bad" choices. On a success, he steers you to a good choice; on a critical success, he tells you the *best* choice. On a failure, he gives you no information; on a critical failure, he steers you toward a *bad* choice. The GM can modify this as he sees fit for other situations where Intuition might logically help. Only one roll per question is allowed.

The GM should never allow Intuition to short-circuit an adventure – for instance, by letting the intuitive detective walk into a room, slap the cuffs on the guilty party, and close the case. At the most, Intuition would point the detective in the direction of a good clue. GMs who don't think they can control Intuition should not allow it in their games.

Intuitive Mathematician
see *Lightning Calculator*, p. 66

Invisibility 👤/💪 👽

40 points

You are invisible. Unlike most advantages, this one is "always on" unless you take a special enhancement. You still make noise, leave footprints, and have a scent – and by default, anything you *carry* remains visible. If you are carrying nothing, you get a +9 to Stealth in any situation where being seen would matter.

Individuals using paranormal remote viewing (crystal balls, Clairvoyance, etc.) cannot see you if you would be invisible to their normal vision. *Devices* with these powers can still sense you, as can paranormal abilities that detect enemies, life, and so on nonvisually.

Invisibility only works against *one* sort of vision. Types include electromagnetic vision (which encompasses ordinary vision, Infravision, Ultravision, and radar), sonar, magnetic fields, and anything else the GM comes up with. If you are invisible to electromagnetic vision, you do not cast a shadow and don't show up in mirrors.

Special Enhancements

Affects Machines: You are invisible even to machines. You cannot be photographed, and you don't show up on cameras or other detectors. Devices such as pressure plates still notice you, but you could walk past a robot sentry undetected. Electronically targeted weapons get no bonuses to hit you. +50%.

Can Carry Objects: The objects you carry, including clothing and armor, become invisible. They regain visibility when put down. No encumbrance is +10%; Light, +20%; Medium, +50%; Heavy, +100%.

Extended: You are invisible to more than one type of vision (for instance, electromagnetic vision *and* magnetic fields). +20% per additional type of vision.

Switchable: You are normally visible, but can become invisible at will. +10%.

Usually On: You are normally invisible, but can become visible for short periods with great effort. Turning visible costs 1 FP per *second*. +5%.

Special Limitations

Machines Only: Similar to Affects Machines, but you are *only* invisible to machines. Living beings can see you normally. -50%.

Substantial Only: Your invisibility only hides you in the material world. Insubstantial beings (ghosts, etc.) can see you normally. -10%.

Visible Reflection: You can be seen in mirrors! -10%.

Visible Shadow: You cast a shadow! -10%.

Jumper 👤 🏃

100 points

You can travel through time *or* to parallel worlds (sometimes known as "timelines") merely by willing the "jump." Decide whether you are a *time-jumper* or a *world-jumper*. To do both, you must buy Jumper (Time) and Jumper (World) separately, at full cost.

To initiate a jump, you must visualize your destination, concentrate for 10 seconds, and make an IQ roll. You may hurry the jump, but your roll will be at -1 per second of concentration omitted (-10 to jump with no preparation at all). Regardless of IQ, a roll of 14 or more always fails. On a success, you appear at your target destination. On a failure, you go nowhere. On a critical failure, you arrive at the *wrong* destination, which can be any time or world the GM wishes!

You appear at your destination at exactly the same place you left your previous time or world – or as close as possible. When jumping through time, this means the same place at a different time. When jumping between worlds, this means the same place at the same time, but on a parallel world.

If there is no corresponding "safe" location within 100 yards of your destination – for instance, if you jump while on an airplane to a destination with no plane at your location, or from a half-mile deep mine to a destination with no corresponding mine – the jump will *fail* and you will know why it failed. This does not prevent you from jumping into other types of danger, such as radiation, gunfire, or wild animals. If you have Danger Sense, the GM should roll before you make a hazardous jump; on a success, you get a warning.

This ability always costs at least 1 FP to use, whether it succeeds or fails. Particularly "distant" times or worlds might cost more, perhaps up to 10 FP, at the GM's discretion. If you are a machine, this ability does not cost *you* FP – but if you have passengers, *each* of them must pay the FP cost.

For an example of how Jumper might work in a particular game world, see *World-Jumpers* (p. 544).

Carrying Things

You can carry up to Basic Lift when you travel, plus any Payload (see p. 74). Take the Extra Carrying Capacity enhancement (below) if you wish to carry more weight, or bring along other people.

However, if multiple Jumpers *of the same kind* are in physical contact, when one jumps, the others can "hitch a ride" if they wish – even if the Jumper who initiates the jump does *not* want company. Only the person initiating the jump makes a die roll; wherever he ends up, the others do, too.

If you are a world-jumper, "hitching a ride" is the only way to visit a *new* parallel world (save for a critical failure!). However, once you reach a world, you can memorize its "feel" by concentrating and spending character points to "learn" that world as an IQ/Easy skill. This takes one hour per point you wish to spend. Use this skill in place of IQ when you travel to that world in the future. You never *have* to memorize a world, but if you do not, you roll at IQ-3 to attempt to return.

Time-jumpers have no similar restriction.

You can improve this ability with practice, spending points to add enhancements or remove limitations. GMs who do not want the PCs jumping multiple times per adventure are free to impose *mandatory* limitations (e.g., Limited Use) that cannot be bought off.

Special Enhancements

Extra Carrying Capacity: You can carry more than your Basic Lift. If your carrying capacity is high enough, you may transport *one* person with you. Light encumbrance is +10%; Medium, +20%; Heavy, +30%; Extra-Heavy, +50%.

New Worlds: This is only available for world-jumpers. You can deliberately aim for worlds you haven't visited. The IQ roll is always at -3 or worse (GM's decision). Of course, it is always possible that the desired destination *does not exist*, in which case the attempt automatically fails – although the GM will not tell you why. All FP costs are doubled when using this enhancement. +50%.

Omni-Jump: This is only available if you are both a world-jumper and a time-jumper! You must apply it to *both* Jumper advantages. This lets you move between times *and* timelines on

a single IQ roll – for instance, from the present day in our timeline to 1066 A.D. in a parallel timeline where the Norman invasion of England failed. +10%.

Tracking: You can travel to the "home" time or world of any man-made artifact you can hold or touch. Time-jumpers will arrive shortly after the item was created; world-jumpers will arrive at the current date on the item's home timeline. Any such attempt is at IQ-2, and each Jumper only gets one try per artifact. +20%.

Tunnel: You always create a portal (of about your size) when you jump. Others may pass through it, even if they can't jump. The portal lingers for 3d seconds, which can be good or bad – it means enemies can follow you! +40%.

Warp Jump: This enhancement is only available if you have the Warp advantage (p. 97). You must apply it to both Jumper and Warp. When you jump, you can simultaneously use Warp to appear *anywhere* at your destination. Two die rolls are necessary – one per ability – and it is possible for one to succeed while the other fails, or for both to fail. +10%.

Special Limitations

Cannot Escort: This is only available for world-jumpers. Other Jumpers cannot "hitch a ride," even if you want to bring them along. -10%.

Cannot Follow: This is only available for world-jumpers. You cannot "hitch a ride" with another Jumper. -20%.

Drift: You do not arrive in exactly the location you left from. You won't arrive in thin air or underground, but you may show up anywhere within 10 miles of your planned destination. The better your IQ roll when you jump, the closer you will be to where you wanted to arrive, but it's the GM's call as to exactly where you appear. -15%.

Limited Jump: You can only travel a certain distance through time, or a certain number of "removes" between parallel worlds, per jump. To go further, you must make multiple hops. The GM must set the value of this limitation for his campaign; it will be more of a handicap in some settings than in others. A suggested value is -10%.

Maximum Range: You can only jump a certain *total* distance through time, or a certain number of "removes" between parallel worlds, no matter how many hops you make. Like Limited Jump, the GM must set the value of this limitation.

Naked: You can carry nothing when you jump! You always arrive naked. -30%.

Stunning: You are always mentally stunned after a jump. -10%.

Language Talent 👤

10 points

You have a knack for languages. When you learn a language at a comprehension level above None, you automatically function at the next-highest level; thus, you can purchase a language at Accented level for 2 points or at Native level for 4 points. For full language rules, see *Language* (p. 23).

Legal Enforcement Powers 🤝

5, 10, or 15 points

You are a law enforcer, with the accompanying powers and restrictions. In some times and places, this amounts to a license to kill. In others, it's little more than the right to carry a badge and write parking tickets.

The point cost depends on the kinds of laws you enforce, the size of your jurisdiction, how answerable you are for your actions, and the degree of respect you must show for the civil rights of others:

● You have local jurisdiction, the ability to arrest suspected criminals, the power to perform searches with an appropriate warrant, and *possibly* the right to carry a concealed weapon. *Examples:* a Victorian bobby or a modern policeman. *5 points.*

● As above, but you also have national or international jurisdiction, *or* are not obligated to respect the civil rights of others, *or* are free to engage in covert investigations, *or* may kill with relative impunity. *Examples:* an FBI agent or a medieval Royal Guardsman. *10 points.*

● You have three or more of the above abilities. *Examples:* a *Gestapo*, KGB, or *Stasi* agent. *15 points.*

Legal Enforcement Powers almost always require an appropriate Duty (p. 133). In some cases, a Reputation (positive, negative, or mixed) is also appropriate. All levels of Legal Enforcement Powers *include* Police Rank 0 (see p. 30). To become a senior law enforcer, buy more Rank.

Legal Immunity 🤝

5 to 20 points

You are exempt from some or all of the laws of your society. Should you break the law, ordinary law enforcers do not have the power to charge you. Only one particular authority – your own church or social class, a special court, perhaps even your ruler – can judge or punish you.

The point cost depends on how sweeping the immunity is (GM's judgment):

● You are not subject to ordinary laws, but the rules that govern your behavior are just as strict. *Examples:* a medieval abbot or a modern UN observer. *5 points.*

● As above, but the laws that apply to you are *less* strict than those that apply to most people. *Example:* a medieval bard (see below). *10 points.*

● You can do nearly anything you please provided you don't injure the nation, church, or other power that granted you Legal Immunity in the first place. *Examples:* a medieval duke or an international diplomat (see below). *15 points.*

For an extra 5 points, you may add "diplomatic pouch" privileges: you can send and receive mail or objects that the ordinary authorities cannot legally stop or examine.

Two classes of Legal Immunity are of special interest to adventurers:

Bardic Immunity: You have the right to sing what you please without fear of serious consequences. You may even sing a grossly insulting song to the king – you might get banished for it, but you can't be whipped, imprisoned, or killed. Anyone who violates your immunity risks damage to his name and reputation. Other bards will compose and distribute vicious satires about him, giving him a bad Reputation. They might even expose a Secret, if he has one! This advantage applies to the content of your performances and *nothing* else. It is only available to true bards, in fantasy/medieval settings. To qualify for this advantage, you must spend at least 1 point apiece on the Performance, Poetry, and Singing skills. *10 points.*

Diplomatic Immunity: You are an international diplomat. You may ignore the laws of all countries except your own. While abroad, you cannot be prosecuted for *any* crime, no matter how grave; the local police may arrest you, but they cannot press charges. The only recourse for a foreign government is to declare you *persona non grata.* This means you must leave the country at once, ending your current assignment – and possibly your career. Foreign powers may request your extradition for normal prosecution, but your government is unlikely to comply. This trait always comes with a Duty (p. 133) to a government agency, and often has some level of Administrative Rank (p. 30) as a prerequisite. *20 points.*

Less Sleep 🔱

2 points/level

You need less sleep than most people. A normal human requires 8 hours of sleep per night. Each level of this advantage – to a maximum of four levels – lets you get by with one hour less than this, giving you a few extra hours each day in which to study or work on other projects.

Lifting ST 🔱 👤

3 points per +1 ST

You have lifting capacity out of proportion to your mass. This is common for vehicles and supers. Add your Lifting ST to your ordinary ST when you determine Basic Lift (p. 15) for the purposes of carrying, lifting, pushing, and pulling. Lifting ST also adds to ST in situations where you can apply slow, steady pressure (grappling, choking, etc.). Lifting ST *does not* boost ST (or Basic Lift) for the purpose of determining HP, throwing distance, or damage inflicted by melee attacks or thrown weapons.

If you bought your ST with the Size limitation, apply the same limitation to Lifting ST. The No Fine Manipulators limitation does *not* give a discount, however.

Lightning Calculator 👤

2 or 5 points

You have the ability to do math in your head, instantly. This talent comes in two levels:

Lightning Calculator: You, the *player,* may use a calculator at any time, to figure anything you want – even if your *character* is fleeing for his life! For simple math problems, the GM may just say that your character knows the answer. *2 points.*

Intuitive Mathematician: As above, but your ability is not limited to arithmetic. You can perform astrogation without a computer, do any level of engineering design in your head, and solve differential equations almost instantaneously. You never need a calculator; you yourself are far faster than that, and even faster than many computers. *5 points.*

True mathematical geniuses will have one of the above traits and one or more levels of Mathematical Ability (see *Talent,* p. 89).

Longevity 💪

2 points

Your lifespan is naturally very long. You fail aging rolls (see p. 444) only on a 17 or 18 – or only on an 18, if your modified HT is 17 or better!

Luck 👤

Variable

You were born lucky! There are three progressively more "cinematic" levels of Luck:

Luck: Once per hour of *play,* you may reroll a single bad die roll twice and take the best of the three rolls! You must declare that you are using your Luck immediately after you roll the dice. Once you or anyone else has made another die roll, it is too late to use Luck. If the GM is rolling in secret

(e.g., to see if you notice something), you may tell him you are using your Luck ahead of time, and he must roll three times and give you the best result. *15 points.*

Extraordinary Luck: As above, but usable every 30 minutes. *30 points.*

Ridiculous Luck: As above, but usable every *10 minutes! 60 points.*

Your Luck only applies to your own success, damage, or reaction rolls, *or* on outside events that affect you or your whole party, *or* when you are being attacked (in which case you may make the attacker roll three times and take the *worst* roll!).

You cannot share Luck. If Strong Sam is trying to kick open a door, Lucky Lou can't stand behind him and transfer his Luck. He'll have to kick that door himself.

Once you use Luck, you must wait an hour of real time (30 minutes for Extraordinary Luck, 10 minutes for Ridiculous Luck) before using it again. You cannot use Luck at 11:58 and then again at 12:01. And you cannot save up Luck. You cannot play for hours without using Luck and then use it several times in a row!

Special Limitations

Active: Your Luck is a conscious supernatural power. You must declare that you are using it *before* you roll the dice. It cannot be used "after the fact" to reroll a bad result. -40%.

Aspected: Your Luck applies only to one specific class of *related* tasks, such as athletics, social interactions, or skills you use at your job. "Combat" is a valid choice, but it only affects weapon skill rolls, active defenses, and ST or DX rolls for close combat – not DX rolls to avoid tripping, HT rolls to survive, etc. -20%.

Defensive: You can only use your Luck to reroll failed active defense rolls, resistance rolls, or HT rolls to resist the effects of injury, or to make an opponent reroll a *critical* hit against you. -20%.

Magery 👤 ⚡

5 points for Magery 0, +10 points/level

You are magically adept. This advantage comes in levels. You must purchase Magery 0 before buying higher levels of Magery.

Magery 0: This is basic "magical awareness," a prerequisite for learning magic in most worlds. The GM makes a Sense roll (p. 358) when you first *see* a magic item, and again when you first *touch* it. On a success, you intuitively know that the item is magical. A roll of 3 or 4 also tells you whether the magic is helpful or dangerous, and about how strong it is. Those without Magery do *not* get this roll! *5 points.*

Magery 1+: Higher levels of Magery make it *much* easier to learn and use magic. Add your Magery to IQ when you learn spells. For instance, if you have IQ 14, Magery 3 lets you learn spells as if you had IQ 17. Add your Magery level to Perception when you roll to sense magic items, and to IQ when you learn Thaumatology skill (p. 225).

Reduce the time required to learn new spells in play (but *not* the point cost) by 10% per Magery level, to a minimum of 60% of the usual time at Magery 4. For instance, with Magery 3, you would learn spells in 70% the usual time.

Powerful spells require a minimum level of Magery as a prerequisite, so be sure to skim the *Spell List* (pp. 242-253) when deciding how much Magery you need. Note that high Magery lets you produce powerful results with even the most basic spells; see *Magery and Effect* (p. 237). The GM sets the maximum Magery allowed to PCs. Magery 3 is about right for "classic fantasy." *10 points/level (on top of the 5 points for Magery 0).*

Mages in Nonmagical Settings

The use of Magery becomes tricky in nonmagical backgrounds. You still have the ability to sense magic, but until you gain experience with magic, the GM should not say, "That idol is magical," but, "That idol looks very strange to you, very sinister. You sense there is something special about it."

If you are from a nonmagical culture, you do not start with any spells, but you can still learn magic if you find an opportunity. When you enter a magical world, those who can detect your aura recognize you as a potential magic-user. How they react depends on the setting.

Magery 0 costs 5 points for *all* mages, but you may apply *one* of the limitations below to the 10 points/level for Magery 1+. Limited Magery is sometimes known as "aspected Magery."

Special Limitations

Dance: You must be free to use bodily motions in order to cast spells. You are not freed from rituals requiring movement as your spell level increases (see *Magic Rituals*, p. 237). However, you need not speak *at all* to cast your spells. -40%.

Dark-Aspected: You can only use your powers in darkness. Regardless of the time of day or night, any light greater than candlelight or starlight deprives you of your abilities, though your aura reveals that you are a mage. -50%.

Day-Aspected: You can use your powers only when the sun is in the sky – on average, from 6 a.m. to 6 p.m. During solar eclipses, you have no powers! The effects of other astronomical events are up to the GM. When the sun is down, you have *none* of your magical abilities, although a look at your aura reveals that you are a mage. You are not affected by being in buildings, underground, and so on; only the sun's position matters. You know automatically (if you are awake) when it is one minute to sunrise and one minute to sunset. -40%.

Musical: You must use a musical instrument in order to cast spells. You can never cast spells silently. -50%.

Night-Aspected: You can only use your powers when the sun is not in the sky – on average, from 6 p.m. to 6 a.m. When the sun is up, you have *none* of your magical abilities, although a look at your aura reveals that you are a mage. You are not affected by being in buildings, underground, and so on; only the sun's position matters. You know automatically (if you are awake)

when it is one minute to sunrise and one minute to sunset. -40%.

One College Only: Your Magery only benefits the spells of a single college and the Recover Energy spell (p. 248). You learn other spells as though you were a nonmage, and can only cast them in high-mana areas. You may still count such spells as prerequisites for spells in your own college. You cannot detect magic items unless they contain at least one spell of your college, in which case you roll normally for detection on first sight and first touch. -40%.

Solitary: Your magical abilities are at -3 for every sapient being within five yards of you, and -6 for anyone touching you. As partial compensation, you get a roll vs. IQ to notice any time a sapient creature enters or leaves the five-yard area around you – but this only works on a single person. If there is already someone standing next to you, you won't notice if someone else approaches. -40%.

Song: You must be able to sing in order to cast your spells. You are *not* freed from the ritual of speaking to cast spells as your spell level increases (see *Magic Rituals*, p. 237). -40%.

Magic Resistance, and its precise level, can be recognized by any mage who looks at your aura, or by anyone who casts a spell on you. If you have even one level of Magic Resistance, you can't cast spells at all.

Magic Resistance 🧠 ➹
2 points/level

You are less likely to be affected by magic. Subtract your Magic Resistance from the skill of anyone casting a spell on you, and add it to your roll to resist any spell that offers a resistance roll. For instance, if you have Magic Resistance 3, wizards have -3 to cast spells on you and you get +3 to resist. In addition, you may roll against HT + Magic Resistance to resist the effects of magical elixirs. You *cannot* "turn off" this advantage

to let friendly wizards cast spells on you (e.g., to heal you) or to benefit from helpful elixirs!

Magic Resistance only interferes with spells *cast directly on you.* It provides no benefit against Missile spells (which are cast on the wizard's hand and *hurled* at you), attacks by magic weapons, or information-gathering spells that aren't cast directly on *you.* It also has no effect on supernatural powers other than magic; e.g., divine miracles, psionics, or the innate powers of spirits.

Magic Resistance, and its precise level, can be recognized by any mage who looks at your aura, or by anyone who casts a spell on you.

You *cannot* combine Magic Resistance with Magery. If you have even one level of Magic Resistance, you can't cast spells at all (although you can still use magic weapons).

Special Enhancements

Improved: You Magic Resistance does not interfere with your *own* ability to cast spells. This allows you to possess both Magery and Magic Resistance. +150%.

Mana Damper 🧠 ➹
10 points/level

You negate magical energy ("mana") in your vicinity, making it difficult or impossible for others to cast spells. You can *never* cast spells yourself, nor can you have any level of Magery.

Each level of Mana Damper (to a maximum of three) reduces the local mana level by one step, but only for you and people or things that you're carrying. For instance, a wizard could throw a fireball at you unhindered, but he would find it difficult to use magic to turn you to stone or read your mind. For details, see *Mana* (p. 235).

Special Enhancements

Area Effect: Your ability affects everything in an area centered on you. The first level of Area Effect gives you a radius of one yard. Each level after the first doubles this radius as usual; see *Area Effect* (p. 102). +50%/level.

Switchable: You can switch this power off – for instance, to let a friendly wizard affect you or operate within your area of effect. +100%.

Mana Enhancer 👤 ⚡

50 points/level

You radiate magical energy, or "mana." Each level of Mana Enhancer (to a maximum of two) increases the local mana level by one step, but only for you and people or things that you're carrying. If more than one character with Mana Enhancer could increase the mana level, apply only the *highest* increase; do not add the effects together.

This ability does not directly confer the ability to cast spells; for that, take Magery (p. 66). However, if you can raise the mana level to "high" or better, you can cast many spells *without* Magery! For details, see *Mana* (p. 235).

This ability has its drawbacks: you cannot have Magic Resistance, and mages get an IQ + Magery roll to sense that you possess this trait. In some game worlds, this combination may force you to hide from unethical wizards!

The GM should keep this trait under strict control, as it is powerful and easily abused in fantasy settings.

Special Enhancements

Area Effect: Your ability affects everything in an area centered on you. The first level of Area Effect gives you a radius of one yard. Each level after the first doubles this radius as usual; see *Area Effect* (p. 102). +50%/level.

Switchable: You can switch this power off in order to deprive enemy wizards of its benefits (or simply to hide from them!). +100%.

Mathematical Ability
see *Talent*, p. 89

Medium 👤 ⚡
10 points

You can perceive and communicate with spirits – particularly spirits of the dead. You don't see them visually, but you know when they're nearby. You can speak with any spirit in your presence, provided you share a language. You can also call spirits to you; there is no guarantee that they will answer your summons, but they will hear it. Note that this trait does *not* give you a reaction bonus with spirits, or any power to control their behavior.

Merchant Rank
see *Rank*, p. 29

Metabolism Control 💪 👽
5 points/level

You can control normally involuntary biological functions such as pulse, blood flow, digestion, and respiration. Each level of Metabolism Control gives +1 on any HT roll that would benefit from such control (GM's decision), including bleeding rolls (see *Bleeding*, p. 420) and rolls to recover from (not *resist*) disease and poison.

You can also enter a deathlike trance. Anyone unfamiliar with your metabolism must win a Quick Contest of Diagnosis vs. your HT + Metabolism Control to discover that you aren't dead. In this state, each level of Metabolism Control reduces by 10% the amount of oxygen you need to stay alive (at level 10 or higher, you *don't breathe at all*), and *doubles* the amount of time you can safely go without food or water. You are unaware of your surroundings while in your trance, but awaken automatically if injured. You may also set a mental "alarm clock" to awaken you after a certain amount of time has passed.

This ability is incompatible with the Machine meta-trait (see p. 263).

Special Limitations

Hibernation: You can only use the trance ability, and get no bonus to HT rolls. Furthermore, you *automatically* enter a trance when exposed to certain environmental conditions – great cold, drought, etc. Work this out with the GM. In such conditions, you must make a Will roll to *avoid* hibernation. You can induce hibernation voluntarily. To do so, roll vs. Will-4 hourly until you succeed. You cannot set a precise "wake up" time. Set a duration, then multiply by (2d+3)/10. -60%.

Microscopic Vision 💪 👽
5 points/level

You can see details that would normally be invisible without a magnifying glass or a microscope. Each level increases magnification by a factor of 10: 5 points gives 10×, 10 points gives 100×, and so on. This magnification only applies to objects within 1 foot.

Level 1 suffices for ordinary forensic investigation. Level 3 (1,000×) is equivalent to the best optical microscopes. Level 5 (100,000×) is comparable to an electron microscope, capable of imaging viruses. Level 6 (1,000,000×) is on par with a scanning-tunneling or atomic force microscope, and can study an object's atomic structure.

Military Rank
see *Rank*, p. 29

Mimicry 👤 👽
10 points

You can duplicate any *simple* sound (alarm, gunshot, etc.) by listening to it for one second and making a successful IQ roll. You can also imitate voices by spending at least 10 seconds listening to them – live, recorded, or remotely – and making an IQ roll.

This trait gives you no special ability to stun or deafen others with loud sounds, or to speak unpronounceable magic words. Buy any such capabilities separately.

Mind Control 👤 👽
50 points

You can mentally dominate those you can *see* or *touch*. To use this ability, concentrate for one second and then roll a Quick Contest: your IQ vs. your subject's Will.

Modifiers: Range penalties to the subject (see p. 550); -1 per slave *already* under your control; +2 if you concentrate for a full minute, or +4 if you concentrate for a full hour.

If you win, your victim will obey your every command until you free him. In effect, he temporarily gains the Reprogrammable disadvantage (p. 150), with you as his master. Your control persists for as long as you take uninterrupted Concentrate maneuvers. Once you stop, your control lingers for one minute per point by which you won the Quick Contest. (To increase this, add Extended Duration, p. 105.) If you are incapacitated (stunned, knocked out, etc.), or attempt to force the subject to act against his principles (e.g., commit suicide or harm a loved one), roll another Quick Contest. If your victim wins, he breaks free. Roll at the moment of truth – you can march him to the edge of a cliff, but he doesn't roll until he's about to leap.

If you lose, you cannot attempt to control that subject again for 24 hours, and he feels a sense of mental coercion emanating from you. On a critical failure, you also lose control of *anyone else* under the influence of this ability!

Mind Control often has limitations: Accessibility (Only on opposite sex), Sense-Based (for hypnotic voices, eyes, scents, etc.), and so on. It may also have attack modifiers, subject to the restrictions that apply to attacks with Malediction (p. 106). Finally, you may apply the Cybernetic and Cybernetic Only modifiers from Mind Reading (see below).

Special Enhancements

Conditioning: You can reconstruct the subject's psyche and implant suggestions. In effect, you can add or remove *any* mundane mental disadvantage. Add Delusions for false memories, or Amnesia to wipe memories. Your victim must be under your control, cooperative, and conscious. Roll a second Quick Contest. You are at -1 per full -5 points of disadvantages changed, but you may substitute Brainwashing skill (p. 182) for IQ. Duration in *days* is equal to your margin of victory. If you win *and* roll a critical success, the conditioning is permanent! A conditioned subject who is no longer under your direct control imposes no penalty on the use of Mind Control on others. Note that another person with this ability can use it to undo your work. +50%.

No Memory: Your victims have no memory of anything that occurred while under your control. +10%.

Special Limitations

Conditioning Only: You cannot use regular Mind Control – only Conditioning (above). Uncooperative victims must be restrained before you can use your ability. -50%.

Puppet: Your victims have no initiative while under your control, and temporarily acquire Slave Mentality (p. 154). -40%.

Telepathic: Your ability is part of the Telepathy psi power (see p. 257). -10%.

Mind Probe 👤👽

20 points

You can perform a deep "mind probe." In effect, you can force the subject to answer any *one* specific question that he can answer with a brief sentence. To attempt a probe, you must first either touch your subject or successfully read his mind with Mind Reading (below). You must also share a language with him.

To use Mind Probe, you must concentrate for one second and roll a Quick Contest of your IQ (or Interrogation skill, if higher) vs. your subject's Will. If you win, you rip the answer from his mind. The answer is what the subject *believes* to be true – if he doesn't know, he'll tell you. If you lose, you may try again, at a cumulative -2 per repeated attempt to ask the *same* (or very similar) question in the past hour. Should you critically fail, you cannot probe that person again for 24 hours.

You may use Mind Probe to ask as many questions as you wish, but each question is a new use of your ability, and requires a second of concentration and its own Quick Contest.

Special Modifiers

The special enhancements and limitations given for Mind Reading (below) are also available for Mind Probe.

Mind Reading 👤👽

30 points

You can eavesdrop on others' surface thoughts. You must be able to see or touch the subject to affect him. Concentrate for one second and roll a Quick Contest of IQ vs. the subject's Will. Modify the roll for range penalties to the subject (see p. 550).

If you win, you can "hear" everything the subject says, subvocalizes, or *actively* thinks about as a voice in your head. Received thought comes at the speed of speech. If you do not understand the language, or if your subject isn't sapient, you only pick up feelings, images, and general intent. You can maintain Mind Reading for as long as you wish without further concentration. If you switch to another person, you must stop reading your current subject and roll a Quick Contest with the new subject. To read multiple subjects at once, take Compartmentalized Mind (p. 43).

If you lose, you may try again, at a cumulative -2 per repeated attempt on that subject in the past hour. Should you critically fail, you cannot read that person again for 24 hours.

Mind Reading is often psionic in origin, but it is just as likely to be a magical, divine, or even technological ability.

The Sense-Based *limitation* (p. 115) – especially Touch-Based – is common. If you take Hearing-Based, you can only read the thoughts of someone whose words you can hear, but can function as a "truthreader" or (with Universal) a "universal translator."

You can "hear" everything the subject says, subvocalizes, or actively thinks about.

Special Enhancements

Cybernetic: You can affect entities with the Digital Mind trait (p. 48), including all ordinary computers. Your IQ roll has a penalty equal to the system's Complexity. A nonsentient system does not resist; just roll vs. IQ - Complexity to succeed. +50%.

Sensory: You can also tap into your subject's senses. This lets you experience everything he experiences. If he is tortured, knocked out, or killed, the GM may require a Will roll to avoid stunning – or perhaps even a Fright Check! +20%.

Universal: You automatically understand thoughts, even those of nonsapient subjects and those with whom you do not share a language. +50%.

Special Limitations

Cybernetic Only: As for Cybernetic, but you can *only* read Digital Minds. -50%.

Racial: Your ability only works on those of your own race or a *very* similar race (for instance, humans are similar to elves, but not to dogs or trolls). Combine this with the Sense-Based limitation (Touch or Scent) to represent a race that can share thoughts through biochemical means. -20%.

Sensory Only: As for Sensory, but you can't read thoughts at all. -20%.

Telecommunication: Your ability only works on those with whom you are presently in contact via Telecommunication (p. 91). -20%.

Telepathic: Your ability is part of the Telepathy psi power (see p. 257). -10%.

Mind Shield 🧠 👽

4 points/level

You have a "shield" that warns you of and defends against mental attacks. Add your Mind Shield level to IQ or Will whenever you resist an advantage with the Telepathic limitation (see Chapter 6) and whenever you resist a spell listed under *Communication and Empathy Spells* (p. 245) or *Mind Control Spells* (p. 250).

Your shield also resists attempts to locate your mind using magic or psionics. Such abilities must win a Quick Contest against your Will + Mind Shield level to find you.

You may voluntarily lower your Mind Shield if you wish – for instance, to let a friend read your mind. Lowering or raising your shield is a free action, but it must take place at the start of your turn. Mind Shield *does* protect you while you are asleep or unconscious, unless you fell asleep or were knocked out while your shield was voluntarily lowered.

Special Limitations

Cybernetic: Your shield protects against computer-related attacks – e.g., the "Digital" form of Possession and the "Cybernetic" form of Mind Probe or Mind Reading – *instead* of magic and psi. This limitation is only available to those with Digital Mind (p. 48). -50%.

Telepathic: Your ability is part of the Telepathy psi power (see p. 257). -10%.

Mindlink 🧠 ⚡

Variable

You have a permanent telepathic rapport with someone – often a twin, loved one, hive member, etc. You automatically succeed at all attempts to contact him with Telesend (see *Telecommunication*, p. 91) and Mind Reading (p. 69), provided he chooses not to resist or has Slave Mentality. Mindlink does *not* allow automatic contact across interstellar distances (more than 0.1 light-year), nor can it reach other dimensions, parallel worlds, etc.

Mindlink costs 5 points for a single person, 10 points for 2-9 people, 20 points for 10-99 people, 30 points for 100-999 people, and so on – add 10 points per tenfold increase in the number of people.

As a rule, the GM should only permit PCs to buy Mindlinks with Allies, Contacts, and Dependents; duplicates (see *Duplication*, p. 50); and other PCs (if their players permit).

Special Modifiers

You may give Mindlink the same modifiers as your Mind Reading or Telesend advantage. In most cases, the GM should *require* this.

Modular Abilities ♟/♟ ☻
Variable

You have a pool of character points that you can reallocate under certain conditions. You may rearrange these points to add a skill (spell, technique, etc.) or mental advantage temporarily – or to improve such a trait, if you already have it. When you do, you lose any abilities to which those points were *previously* assigned.

This advantage comes in "slots." A slot can hold *one* skill or mental advantage at a time. Each slot has a fixed base cost, plus a cost per point in the pool for that slot. Both costs depend on the type of Modular Abilities you have.

Computer Brain: Your abilities are actually computer programs. The GM decides whether a program exists for a given ability. If you have Telecommunication (p. 91), you may *download* programs, usually from a network. How long this takes depends on the speed of data transfer in the setting – a second per character point works well. In some worlds, you must pay for such programs; $100 per character point is typical. *Cost per slot: 6 points base + 4 points per point of abilities.*

Chip Slots: As above, but the programs come on physical chips that you must plug into a socket – usually in your skull. It takes three seconds to insert or remove a chip. Chips typically have negligible weight, but cost $100 to $1,000 per point of abilities. *Cost per slot: 5 points base + 3 points per point of abilities.*

Super-Memorization: You gain new abilities through rapid study. This takes a second per character point. You can "forget" a memorized ability instantly. You can only memorize abilities if you have a suitable reference work (book, film, tape, etc.). The GM

determines the cash cost of such works. *Cost per slot: 5 points base + 3 points per point of abilities.*

Cosmic Power: You simply wish new abilities into being. This takes one second *per ability.* Unlike other Modular Abilities, you only ever have one "slot," and can rearrange your points into as many or as few abilities as you wish, to the limit of your advantage. *10 points per point of abilities.*

Example: Alex buys two Chip Slots at a base cost of 5 points/slot. This costs 10 points. One slot can hold a chip with a single ability worth up to 2 points, and costs 6 points. The other can hold up to 5 points, and costs 15 points. Total cost is 31 points. This appears on Alex's character sheet as "Chip Slots 2 (2, 5)." Alex will have to buy, borrow, or steal the chips he uses – but he need not pay character points for them.

Use Preparation Required (p. 114) to increase the time needed to rearrange your points, and Limited Use (p. 112) to represent an ability that you forget immediately after using it.

Special Enhancements

Physical: Your ability is not limited to skills and mental advantages. +50% for physical advantages only, or +100% for any mental or physical ability.

Special Limitations

Spells Only: Your ability only works with magic spells, which must usually be "memorized" from a grimoire. This is mutually exclusive with Physical. -20%.

Virtual: The abilities gained only apply in virtual reality, astral space, or another limited realm. -50%.

Musical Ability
see *Talent*, p. 89

Neutralize ♟ ☻
50 points

You can neutralize the psi powers of a single psionic individual. This is an active ability with an ongoing effect on the subject. It does not *have* to be psionic – it might represent a magical or high-tech way to drain psi abilities.

To use Neutralize, you must touch the subject (requires an Attack maneuver) and win a Quick Contest of Will. If you succeed, you successfully neutralize all your victim's psionic powers (see Chapter 6) for a number of minutes equal to your margin of victory. This has no effect on the subject's psionic *Talents.* Once you have neutralized someone, you cannot affect him again until his power recovers. A critical failure with this ability cripples it for 1d hours.

Special Enhancements

Power Theft: When you successfully neutralize a psi, you acquire his powers! You gain all the psionic abilities you neutralized – including their enhancements and limitations – for the duration. You can't use Neutralize again until these powers wear off. +200%.

Special Limitations

One Power: You can only neutralize a specific psionic power; e.g., ESP or Telepathy. See Chapter 6 for a list of standard psi powers. -50%.

Nictitating Membrane ♟ ☻
1 point/level

You have a transparent lens over your eyes that you can open and close like an eyelid. This lets you see normally underwater, and protects your eyes from sand, irritants, etc. Each level of Nictitating Membrane provides your eyes (only) with DR 1 and adds +1 to all HT rolls concerned with eye damage.

Night Vision ♟
1 point/level

Your eyes adapt rapidly to darkness. Each level of this ability (maximum nine levels) allows you to ignore -1 in combat or vision penalties due to darkness, provided there is at least some light.

Example: Night Vision 4 would completely eliminate darkness penalties up to -4, and would reduce a penalty of -7 to only -3.

Regardless of level, Night Vision only works in partial darkness. It has no effect on the -10 for *total* darkness (for that, get *Dark Vision*, p. 47).

Obscure ✊ 👁

2 points/level

You produce an effect that actively "jams" one particular sense, making it difficult to detect you and everything in your vicinity. You must specify the affected sense. This can be one of the five human senses or a sensory advantage such as Infravision, Radar, or one particular Detect. Examples include Obscure (Vision) for fog, Obscure (Hearing) for white noise, and Obscure (Radar) for electronic jamming.

Obscure affects a two-yard radius centered on you. Add the Area Effect enhancement (p. 102) to increase this radius. The affected sense is at -1 per level of Obscure to detect anything within your radius. Ten levels will block the sense completely. The *boundaries* of the zone are easily detected by the affected sense, however; roll at +1 per level.

Special Enhancements

Defensive: You are unaffected by your own Obscure ability. +50%.

Extended: Each *related* sense (Infravision as well as normal vision, Sonar as well as normal hearing, etc.) blocked beyond the first is +20%.

Ranged: You produce your obscuring effect at a distant point rather than around your body. This is a ranged attack with 1/2D –, Max 100, Acc 3, RoF 1, Shots N/A, and Recoil 1. Duration is 10 seconds. You can apply other modifiers to change these statistics. Unlike the usual Ranged enhancement (p. 107), this modifier lets you use your ability again before its duration has expired (e.g., to simulate multiple smoke grenades); thus, it is more expensive. +50%.

Stealthy: Your ability works invisibly, like a magical zone of silence. There is no bonus to detect the boundaries of your area of effect. +100%.

Special Limitations

Always On: You cannot turn this ability off. -50%.

Oracle 👤 ⚡

15 points

You are sensitive to omens, and see hidden significance in such things as the way plants grow, the behavior of animals, and even changes in the weather and the sky. Once per day, you may check the omens. This normally requires at least an hour, but if the GM has something in particular he wants to communicate, he may arbitrarily put it in your path. The GM rolls twice, in secret, when you use this ability: once to determine whether you discover the omen, once to see if you interpret it correctly.

Discovery: To detect an omen requires a Sense roll. On a success, you discover the omen; on a critical success, you get +5 on the subsequent interpretation roll. On a failure, you find nothing of oracular significance. On a critical failure, the GM *lies* – he tells you that you have found an omen, but this is, in reality, a product of your own fears or wishes.

Interpretation: To interpret an omen requires an IQ roll. On a success, the omen is very general; e.g., "an enemy approaches" or "a great power, long dormant, is stirring." On a critical success, the information is more specific: "you risk the wrath of the king," "seek out the mage in the tower," etc. On a failure, the omen is simply too vague to be useful. On a critical failure, you blatantly misinterpret the omen – possibly in a dangerous manner.

This ability differs from Precognition (p. 77), which requires no interpretation.

Outdoorsman

see *Talent,* p. 89

Parabolic Hearing ✊ 👁

4 points/level

You can "zoom in" on a particular sound or area, and can filter out background noise from sounds of interest to you. Each level of Parabolic Hearing *doubles* the distance at which you can clearly hear any given sound (see *Hearing,* p. 358).

Patrons 🤝

Variable

A "Patron" is an NPC – or even an entire *organization* – that serves as your advisor, employer, mentor, or protector. An employer must be exceptional to qualify as a Patron, though; a Patron is much more than an ordinary boss!

Power

The base point cost of a Patron depends on its power. Use the categories below as a guide, but note that some Patrons won't fit neatly into any of them. The GM's word is final.

You can move your consciousness from body to body. In theory, you could live forever this way . . . however, you cannot survive outside a living host.

A powerful individual (usually built on at least 150% of the PC's starting points) or a fairly powerful organization (assets of at least 1,000 times starting wealth for the world). *10 points.*

An extremely powerful individual (built on at least twice the PC's starting points) or a powerful organization (assets of at least 10,000 times starting wealth). *Examples:* a limited manifestation of a minor god, a billionaire, or a big-city police department. *15 points.*

An ultra-powerful individual (built on as many points as the GM wants!) or a very powerful organization (assets of at least 100,000 times starting wealth). *Examples:* a super, a limited manifestation of a major god, or a big city. *20 points.*

An extremely powerful organization (assets of at least 1 million times starting wealth). *Examples:* a large corporation or a very small nation. *25 points.*

A national government or giant multinational organization (net worth basically incalculable), or a true god who appears personally to intervene on your behalf. *30 points.*

Note that the *base* cost to have a deity as a Patron is comparable to that for a powerful mundane Patron, but divine power requires the Special Abilities enhancement (see below), which will greatly increase the *final* cost of a divine Patron!

Frequency of Appearance

Choose a frequency of appearance, as explained under *Frequency of Appearance* (p. 36). If the GM determines that your Patron appears at the start of an adventure, he *may* design the adventure to include an assignment or aid from the Patron. He may also choose to leave out your Patron, if its appearance would make no sense or disrupt the adventure.

However, if the GM determined that your Patron *could* have appeared, and you try to contact your Patron during the adventure (for help, advice, etc.), then the contact is likely to be successful and you may receive aid. (Within reason – if you're locked in a dungeon without any means of communication, you won't be contacting *anybody*.) You will not know whether your Patron is "available" on a given adventure until you attempt to request aid. As a rule, you should only be able to reach your Patron for help once per adventure.

Remember that a powerful Patron could be helpful without actually intervening! A Chicago hood who can say, "I'm from Big Eddie," or a crimefighter who can flash a Q-clearance card, may carry some extra weight in a tough spot.

Party Patrons

Often, several PCs – perhaps the entire party – share a Patron (they are all agents of the same government, servants of the same cult, etc.). No matter how many characters share a Patron, the cost is *not* shared; each character must pay full price for the Patron. On the other hand, the GM will make an appearance roll for each character at the start of each adventure – and if the Patron appears for *any* of them, then it is usually available for *all* of them. The GM should scale the quality and quantity of the aid provided in proportion to the number of successful appearance rolls.

Drawbacks of Patrons

If your Patron is an army, corporation, feudal lord, etc., you may owe it a Duty (p. 133). A god or similar Patron may require a stringent code of behavior in return for its aid; see *Self-Imposed Mental Disadvantages* (p. 121). A Patron might also have powerful foes that are now *your* foes; this can give you an Enemy (p. 135). Such factors can cut the effective cost of a Patron significantly, and turn it from a benefit to a considerable liability!

Employers and Patrons

Not every employer is a Patron. If you can depend on your employer to get you out of trouble (at least sometimes), it might really be a Patron. Otherwise, it's just a job. For example, a small police department is a 10-point Patron if, as most do, it takes care of its own. But the U.S. Army, though powerful, is not a likely Patron – at least for an ordinary trooper. You *could* say, "The Colonel takes care of his men." But you could just as easily say, "I'm on my own if I get in trouble," and play a soldier who does not have a Patron.

Examples of Patrons

• A powerful wizard as Patron to warriors (or young wizards) whom he sends to find magical items or slay foes.

• A crime lord as Patron to freelance thieves or assassins.

• A minor deity as Patron to a traveling Righter of Wrongs.

• A local police department as Patron to a private detective. (They might find him annoying at times, but he helps them out, and vice versa.)

• A local ruler (in any world) as Patron to an adventurer.

• A large company as Patron to a troubleshooter or spy.

• A super-crimefighter or politician as Patron to a news reporter.

• Any intelligence organization as occasional Patron to a freelance operative, or full-time Patron to its own agents. (The difference between this and ordinary jobs is that you can't quit . . .)

You can apply the following modifiers *after* multiplying for frequency of appearance.

Special Enhancements

Equipment: Your Patron supplies useful equipment that you can use for your own purposes, and that you would otherwise have to buy. This enhancement only applies if the equipment is *yours* once given. A soldier with a military Patron would not pay extra for his weapons, since when he goes off duty, he can't take them along. An adventurer in the employ of a generous noble who hands out useful "gifts" *would* pay extra. +50% if the equipment is worth no more than the average starting wealth in the campaign, or +100% if it is worth more than that.

Highly Accessible: You can attempt to contact your Patron at any time – even when you are locked in a dungeon, lost in the desert, etc. This is most appropriate if your Patron is a spirit, a god you can petition via prayer, etc. +50%.

Special Abilities: Your Patron wields power out of proportion to its wealth or point value. +50% if your Patron has extensive social or political power (e.g., the Governor of New York or the Pope), or +100% if your Patron has magical powers in a nonmagical world, possesses equipment from a TL greater than yours, grants you special powers, or has unusual reach in time or space (e.g., a super, spirit, or god).

Special Limitations

Minimal Intervention: Your Patron is less useful than its power level would suggest. On a successful appearance roll, the GM makes a reaction roll for your Patron to determine whether it actually provides aid; see *Requests for Aid* (p. 562). On a Neutral or better reaction, you receive the aid your Patron thinks you *need* – which may or may not be what you *want*. This is the classic modifier for gods who have many other minions to aid, and frequently accompanies the Pact limitation (see p. 113). -50%.

Secret: Your Patron works behind the scenes. You do not know who it is and you cannot request aid directly. You might be able to call for help in such a way that the Patron gets the message (GM's decision), but there is no guarantee that the Patron will take action. The only evidence of this kind of Patron is minor incidents and "lucky breaks." This may take the form of information, equipment, or even direct aid . . . but only when it suits the Patron, and always in an untraceable way. A Patron like this often regards its aid as an investment on which it expects some return; therefore, it might not have your best interests at heart! Only the GM knows any of these details. *You* know nothing other than the fact that you have a Patron. -50%.

Unwilling: You obtained your Patron through coercion (e.g., blackmail). It provides aid only because there is no other choice, and it *definitely* does not have your best interests at heart! You will eventually make one request too many (GM's judgment – perhaps if the appearance roll comes up 18) and lose the Patron: remove the Patron from your character sheet and lower your point value accordingly. Since a Patron is by definition more powerful than you are, taking an Unwilling Patron is risky. If the Patron can find a way to break your "hold," it will, and may well become an Enemy! -50%.

Payload ♟ ☻

1 point/level

You can carry cargo or occupants inside your body! This might be a superficial feature (e.g., a surgically implanted "flesh pocket" or a natural pouch like that of a kangaroo) or an actual internal compartment. The latter is not just for machines – a zombie might have a colony of spiders or snakes living in its body, for example.

Each level of Payload lets you carry up to Basic Lift/10 lbs. inside you. Those without Injury Tolerance (Homogenous) (p. 60) or the Machine meta-trait (p. 263) should ask the GM's permission before taking more than five levels of Payload. You must allocate your Payload between cargo and occupants when you buy the advantage:

Cargo: 20 lbs. of cargo space is roughly equal to one cubic foot of capacity. A typical car has about 10-20 cubic feet of storage space; a semi-trailer has about 2,400 cf.

Occupants: A human-sized being requires about 200 lbs. of capacity. For others, take average racial weight and increase it by 1/3. An actual *cabin* requires 10 times that weight. Your defensive advantages (DR, Sealed, etc.) also protect your occupants. If your occupants can control you, buy Controls separately – see *Compartmentalized Mind* (p. 43).

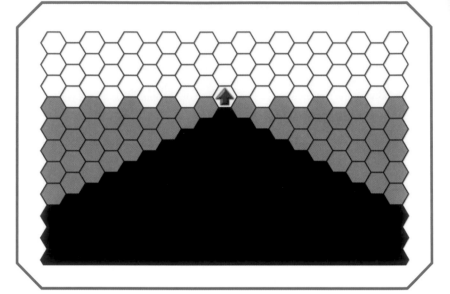

Treat your Payload as part of your body, *not* as encumbrance or carried weight, when calculating Move and using advantages with limited carrying capacity, such as Invisibility, Jumper, and Warp.

Machines that can push or pull large *external* loads – or pick them up and carry them with arms, cranes, etc. – have Lifting ST (p. 65), not Payload. Ordinary cars and trucks have Payload, but forklifts, tugboats, and the like should buy Lifting ST to represent their abilities.

Special Limitations

Exposed: Your Payload cannot be concealed and is not protected by your defensive advantages. You can apply this to any portion of your Payload. The main use of this limitation is to create motorcycles and similar unenclosed vehicles. -50%.

Penetrating Vision ♟ ☻

10 points/level

Penetrating Vision (sometimes called "X-ray vision") lets you see through solid objects. Each level of this advantage allows you to see through up to six inches of normal matter. You can just barely see the outline of the substance you are looking through – not enough to impair vision in any way. Penetrating Vision automatically works in conjunction with all your other vision advantages (Infravision, Ultravision, etc.).

Special Limitations

Blockable: Some substance completely blocks your vision. Common substances, such as plastic, stone, or wood, are -30%; less common materials, such as brick or asphalt, are -20%; one specific material, such as lead, is -10%.

Specific: Your ability only works through one particular substance. Common materials, such as brick, metal, or wood, are -40%; uncommon materials, such as ice or adobe, are -60%; absurd materials, such as chocolate or silk, are -80%.

Perfect Balance ♟

15 points

You can always keep your footing, no matter how narrow the walking surface, under normal conditions. This lets you walk along a tightrope, ledge, tree limb, or other anchored surface without having to make a die roll. If the surface is wet, slippery, or unstable, you get +6 on all rolls to keep your feet. In combat, you get +4 to DX and DX-based skill rolls to keep your feet or avoid being knocked down. Finally, you get +1 to Acrobatics, Climbing, and Piloting skills.

Peripheral Vision ♟

15 points

You have an unusually wide field of vision. You can see a 180° arc in front of you without turning your head, and have 30° of peripheral vision to either side of *that*. This gives you a 240° "arc of vision" for observation and ranged attacks. The figure above shows the arc of vision for a normal character (white) and for someone with Peripheral Vision (gray plus white).

If you are playing with a battle map, you can make melee attacks into "side" ("right" and "left") hexes as well as "front" hexes – although a one-handed attack to the opposite side (e.g., attacking your left hex with your right hand) is clumsy and considered a Wild Swing (see p. 388). You still cannot attack a foe directly behind you except with a Wild Swing.

This also helps on defense! If you are attacked from a "side" hex, you defend at no penalty. Even against attacks from the rear, your active defense is only at -2.

Out of combat, you get +3 to all rolls to detect Shadowing attempts or ambushes from behind, and the GM will *always* make a Vision roll for you to spot dangers "behind your back."

Special Limitations

Easy to Hit: Your eyes are on stalks, unusually large, or otherwise more vulnerable to attack. Others can target your eyes from within their arc of vision at only -6 to hit. -20%.

Permeation ♣ ◆

Variable

You can move through a particular solid material as if it didn't exist. You do not open a passage behind you; observers just see you "melt" into the surface and disappear. You need Penetrating Vision (p. 74) to see where you're going. You must still breathe (unless you have Doesn't Breathe), which limits trips to the length of time you can hold your breath (see *Holding Your Breath*, p. 351).

Permeation differs from Insubstantiality. You are affected by gravity, and you are limited to normal movement; if you lack Flight or another movement advantage, you must walk at your Basic Move. Furthermore, you can be affected by any attack that can reach you within a solid object. You also remain vulnerable to attacks *with* the material you can pass through, unless you purchase Damage Resistance to such attacks.

Cost depends on how often you are likely to encounter the material you can permeate *in the form of a barrier*. For instance, paper might be a "Common" substance, but since walls of paper are uncommon, it is treated as "Rare" for the purpose of Permeation.

Very Common: Earth (including clay, mud, and sand), metal, stone (including brick, concrete, and plaster), wood, and other ubiquitous structural materials. *40 points.*

Common: Concrete, plastic, steel, and other specific, common structural materials. *20 points.*

Occasional: Glass, ice (including snow), sand, and anything else that a normal person could eventually break or tunnel through using muscle power, as well as somewhat unusual structural materials, such as aluminum and copper. *10 points.*

Rare: Bone, flesh, paper, and other materials rarely encountered in large quantities or as barriers. *5 points.*

Special Enhancements

Can Carry Objects: Normally, you cannot carry *anything* while moving through matter. This enhancement lets you carry objects, including clothing and armor. If dropped, they "pop" into open space at the point where you entered the material. You cannot leave things *inside* solid matter! No encumbrance is +10%; Light, +20%; Medium, +50%; Heavy, +100%.

Tunnel: You can leave a tunnel (of about your size) behind you, if you choose. This rearranges the object you are moving though without inflicting damage, and does not work at all on living targets. For an ability that *can* rip holes in objects and people, see *Innate Attack* (p. 61). +40%.

Photographic Memory

see *Eidetic Memory,* p. 51

Pitiable

see p. 22

Plant Empathy ♀

5 points

You have an unusual rapport with growing things. On encountering a plant, the GM will roll against your IQ. On a success, he will give you a general sense of its health and whether it is natural or supernatural in origin. Furthermore, this advantage functions as Empathy (p. 51) with respect to *sentient* plants, and allows you to use your Influence skills (see p. 359) on such entities, which will usually ensure a positive reaction.

This ability frequently accompanies some level of Green Thumb (see *Talent,* p. 89) and often Sense of Duty (Plants) or Vow (Use plant material only if gathered without severe injury to the plant).

Police Rank

see *Rank,* p. 29

Possession ♀ ◆

100 points

You can move your consciousness from body to body. In theory, you could live forever this way, moving from dying bodies to healthy ones. However, *you cannot survive outside a living host.* Should your current body die, *you* will die! Thus, you must keep your current host alive . . . at least until you can find a replacement.

To possess a new host, you must concentrate for one second and physically touch him. Attempts to possess your own Puppet (p. 78) succeed automatically. In all other cases, roll a Quick Contest: your IQ vs. the subject's Will. Your victim resists at +5 if he is in combat with you or otherwise wary of you, so it is best to be subtle.

If you lose or tie, you are mentally stunned for 1d seconds. In addition, you may *never* attempt to possess that subject again – he is "immune" to you.

If you win, you take over your victim's body, completely suppressing his personality. Your *previous* host regains control of his body (if sentient) after 1d seconds of mental stun, and "comes to" with no memory of the possession.

You gain your new host's ST, DX, and HT (and secondary characteristics calculated from these scores), as well as his physical advantages and disadvantages. You keep your own IQ, Perception, and Will, and all of your mental traits. Your social traits *may* apply, depending on the laws and values of your society.

Skills are a special case. Your IQ-, Perception-, and Will-based skills are unchanged. Other skills remain at the same *relative* skill level. For instance, if you have Acrobatics at DX+3, then you would have Acrobatics-12 in a DX 9 body and Acrobatics-14 in a DX 11 body.

If you occupy a sentient host, you have sufficient access to his memories for the first few hours of the takeover to learn his name and daily routine, but not enough to learn IQ-based skills. To recall a specific fact from the host's memories, you must roll vs. IQ, at -1 per *hour* since the takeover. Only one attempt is allowed for any given memory!

Telecontrol: You remotely control your new host as if he were a puppet, leaving your original body in a trance. You may choose to return to your body at any time, and *must* do so if your host falls unconscious or dies (but not if he sleeps). As a result, you do not die if your host dies. +50%.

implant, telepresence, or similar technology. -40%.

No Memory Access: You have no access to your host's memories. -10%.

Parasitic: You enter your host's body *physically*. You must have Permeation (Flesh) (p. 75) to do this, unless your host has sufficient Payload (p. 74) to contain you – and your victim must have a higher Size Modifier than you. After entering your victim's body, you may attempt to possess him. He resists with the *higher* of HT or Will. You aren't forced out if you lose, but he is "immune" to you, so you need to find another host soon. While you are in someone else's body, he (if he is still uncontrolled) or his friends might be able to use technological means to detect you – and possibly remove you. Attacks that penetrate or ignore your host's DR can injure you, but his HP act as extra DR for this purpose. If you are microbial, you should purchase Injury Tolerance (Diffuse) (p. 60), which will protect you. The host nourishes you, and may have to eat extra food as a result. You can choose to leave at any time, the same way you entered. You may also temporarily release your host while continuing occupation. If you do, you will have to win a new Quick Contest to regain control. -60%.

Puppet Only: You may possess your own Puppets automatically, but you cannot possess anyone else. -30%.

Spiritual: You must have the Spirit meta-trait (p. 263) to take this limitation. Your spirit body merges with and occupies the body of your host. It remains insubstantial during the possession, traveling inside the host but otherwise inaccessible to you and effectively mindless. It can be injured as detailed under Parasitic, but only by attacks that affect insubstantial things. A genuine exorcist can cast you out by winning a Quick Contest of his exorcism ability vs. your Will. You cannot return to a body you have been cast out of for at least 24 hours. You may choose to release your host at any time. If you are exorcised or leave voluntarily, the host recovers after 1d seconds of mental stun. -20%.

Telepathic: Your ability is part of the Telepathy psi power (see p. 257). -10%.

> *Precognition: You cannot control the content of these flashes – you just know that something interesting or important might happen, at some unspecified future date.*

If you occupy a host for a long time, or hop between multiple bodies, the GM is free to adjust your point value to reflect the most expensive body you regularly occupy. For more on this subject, see Chapter 9.

With suitable modifiers, Possession can represent diverse abilities seen in speculative fiction. Note that the Digital, Magical, Parasitic, Spiritual, and Telepathic limitations are mutually exclusive.

Special Enhancements

Assimilation: When you enter a new body, you may choose to "forget" any of your current skills and use the points this frees up – and any unspent points – to learn ST-, DX-, or HT-based skills known by the host, at up to (host's level)-1. For instance, if you do not know Acrobatics, but your host knows it at DX+3, you can pick it up at DX+2 . . . if you have enough points. Skills forgotten in order to learn new skills are gone. Skills learned from your host will move from body to body with you. +10%.

Chronic: When you exit a host, you can leave a "back door" that lets you possess him again *without* a Quick Contest. This lets you buy your former host as a Puppet. You can only use this enhancement if you have enough unspent points to buy a Puppet at the time you leave your host. +20%.

Mind Swap: Your host's mind moves into your previous body instead of being suppressed – in effect, you "trade places." +10%.

Special Limitations

Digital: This limitation is only available to Digital Minds (p. 48). You take over computers, not living bodies. The target system must be connected to your current host computer via a network, and you must have *complete* access to it – voluntary or otherwise (see *Computer Hacking,* p. 184). The target computer's hardware must be complex enough to run your computer program; in general, its Complexity must be at least half your IQ (round up). You can also take over a computer using a *copy* of yourself while leaving the original intact! However, unless you have the Digital version of Duplication (p. 50), any system you take over this way becomes an independent NPC that thinks it is *you.* This can be good or bad – the duplicate could become any type of Associated NPC (see p. 31). -40%.

Magical: Your advantage is an innate magic talent. If the subject is protected by a spell that repels hostile magic, you must *win* a Quick Contest of your IQ vs. that spell before you can make a possession attempt. If your victim has Magic Resistance, it subtracts from your IQ *and* adds to his Will during the actual possession attempt. -10%.

Mindlink Required: You can only possess someone with whom you have a Mindlink. If the link is ever jammed, out of range, etc., the possession ends. If the Mindlink has the Telecommunication limitation, Mindlink Required can represent control via an

Power Investiture 👤 ⚡
10 points/level

A deity – god, demon lord, great spirit, cosmic power, etc. – has empowered you to cast "clerical" spells. Add your Power Investiture to your IQ when you learn spells granted by the deity who bestowed this advantage. For instance, IQ 12 and Power Investiture 2 (Thor) would let you learn spells granted by the god Thor (and *only* Thor) as if you had IQ 14.

You may only learn clerical spells from a fixed list set by your deity, who may even dictate which specific spells you learn. The GM determines this list and takes on the role of your deity when you wish to learn new spells. However, because you are channeling divine will as opposed to studying magic, *clerical spells do not have prerequisites.*

In general, the more Power Investiture you have, the "holier" you are. The maximum level of Power Investiture depends on your deity, as determined by the GM. Minor deities who have a limited ability to transfer power to their chosen, or a small range of possible spell effects, might grant only one level, while major deities might be more generous.

Note that Power Investiture is a measure of your bond with your deity, while Clerical Investment (p. 43) and Religious Rank (p. 30) measure social power. These need not be related. Power Investiture *might* be restricted to high-ranking clerics . . . but a deity can grant power to anyone it wants (possibly to the chagrin of the church!).

In some cases, you can add or increase Power Investiture in play. What this entails depends on the deity. To gain, keep, or improve Power Investiture, you nearly always have to take *and adhere to* one or more of the traits listed under *Self-Imposed Mental Disadvantages* (p. 121). If you break these vows, you will lose some or all of your powers – perhaps until you have made proper penance, perhaps permanently. In effect, Power Investiture comes with a built-in Pact limitation (see p. 113); do not apply this modifier again.

You may also need to meet certain *physical* requirements. Some deities only empower men, women, eunuchs, virgins . . . the GM should be creative. Should you lose a special requirement

(such as virginity), your Power Investiture may be diminished or lost, reducing your point value accordingly.

You can have both Magery and Power Investiture (unless your deity forbids this), but Magery does not improve clerical spells and Power Investiture does not aid magical spells. The clerical and magical versions of a given spell are *entirely different spells*, and clerical spells never count as prerequisites for magical spells. If you know both versions of a spell, they do not affect one another.

Power Investiture is one possible way to handle "holy powers." It is most appropriate in settings where priests are divinely inspired wizards. For other views of divine gifts, see *Blessed* (p. 40) and *True Faith* (p. 94).

Precognition 👤 ⚡
25 points

You receive glimpses of future events. You *cannot* control the content of these flashes – you just know that something interesting or important might happen, at some unspecified future date. You might learn this through visions, voices, or "sudden knowledge." A vivid premonition of a terrible event might even require a Fright Check (p. 360)!

Precognition only gives information that your "future self" could learn and that would matter to you. For instance, if you're in New York, you are unlikely to have a premonition about a random murder in Los Angeles. But if the victim was a friend, or if the killing was important enough to make national news, you might "flash" on it.

Nothing about the future is *certain*, though. Even if the GM has made up his mind, he could reconsider . . . although something *related* to the premonition should still happen. In most settings, predicted events *will* occur unless you take specific action to prevent them. (But the GM is free to rule that the future is immutable in his setting!)

Whenever the GM feels a premonition would be appropriate, he will secretly make an IQ roll for you – usually during an encounter with a person or object. For instance, meeting someone with an important event in his future might set off a premonition related to that event, especially if it would

affect *you* in some way. Similarly, seeing a picture of a place could set off a vision involving that location.

A *deliberate* attempt to use Precognition requires 10 minutes of concentration, 2 FP, and an IQ roll at *-8*. You can attempt to read your own future, or that of another person. To deliberately read the future of someone else, you must be able to touch him.

Precognition is normally limited to "seeing" into the near future – perhaps a week or so. At the GM's option, however, a critical success or a *very* important event might result in visions from much further in the future.

Note that Precognition *includes* Danger Sense (p. 47) – do not take both.

Special Limitations

Can't See Own Death: Your Precognition cannot detect people or events that the GM believes have a high probability of causing your death. Your ability does *not* include Danger Sense. -60%.

ESP: Your ability is part of the ESP psi power (see p. 255). -10%.

One Event: Your ability works only for a particular type of event: events involving you personally (if you scanned another, you would only see a significant event if you were involved); disasters; events related to death; events related to love, etc. This limitation is mutually exclusive with Can't See Own Death. -40%.

Pressure Support 🦀 👽
5 to 15 points

Every character has a "native pressure." For ordinary humans, this is the pressure of Earth's atmosphere ("1 atmosphere"). A native pressure other than 1 atmosphere is a 0-point feature, but if you can survive for a prolonged period of time at a *wide range* of pressures, you have an advantage. This trait comes in three levels:

Pressure Support 1: You can survive at pressures between your native pressure and 10 times that. (This would enable a human to survive on most of Earth's continental shelves.) *5 points.*

Pressure Support 2: You can withstand pressures between your native pressure and 100 times that. (This would enable a human to survive anywhere in Earth's oceans, save the deepest trenches.) *10 points.*

Pressure Support 3: You are *immune* to the effects of high pressure. *15 points.*

Pressure Support lets your body stay at a constant internal pressure with respect to a constant and uniform external pressure. This protects against attacks that manipulate ambient pressure or crush the entire body, but provides no defense against *localized* or *transient* pressure changes. In particular, Pressure Support does not reduce or prevent damage from crushing attacks or explosions of any kind.

Those with Pressure Support often have the Sealed advantage (p. 82), but this is not required.

Protected Sense 🖐️👽

5 points/sense

One of your ranged senses is protected against overload. It rapidly adapts to the most intense of stimuli, allowing you to function normally after a maximum of two seconds of impairment. You will never suffer permanent damage to that sense as a result of excessive sensory input, and you get +5 to rolls to resist temporary damage and Sense-Based attacks targeting that sense.

Protected Senses cost 5 points apiece. Protected Vision resists glare and eye damage from lasers, and lets Dark Vision, Infravision, and Night Vision adjust instantly from bright light to darkness. Protected Hearing protects against loud noises. Protected Taste/Smell filters out strong odors and tastes (but not toxins). The GM may permit other Protected Senses (Detect, Scanning Sense, etc.), with suitable justification.

Psi Static 👤⚡

30 points

You are a psionic "null." Psionic abilities cannot directly affect you or anything you are carrying or wearing. For instance, a telekinetic could throw a rock at you, but he could not levitate you or grab a sword from your hand.

Special Enhancements

Area Effect: You emit static in an area centered on you. The first level of Area Effect extends your static to everything within one yard. Each level after the first doubles this radius as

usual; see *Area Effect* (p. 102). +50%/level.

Switchable: You can switch this advantage off in order to allow friendly psis to affect you or operate within your area of effect. +100%.

Special Limitations

Resistible: Your ability is not absolute. A psi can "burn" through your static and affect those protected by it by winning a Quick Contest of Will with you. If the attacking psi ability *already* requires a Quick Contest, the attacker rolls only once but the target gets +5 to resist. -50%.

Psychometry 👤⚡

20 points

You can sense the history of a place or inanimate object – its use, its user's personality, etc. This is usually a supernatural gift of some sort (such as psi), but it could also represent a technological "time-scanning" power that can see the past.

To use Psychometry, you must touch the subject item or location, concentrate for one second, and make an IQ roll. This roll is at no penalty for an event that occurred the same day, -1 for one that occurred up to 10 days ago, -2 if up to 100 days ago, -3 if up to 3 years ago, -4 if up to 30 years ago, -5 if up to 300 years ago, and so on. At the GM's option, you might notice very strong "vibes" on an IQ-4 roll, even if you *aren't* concentrating.

On a success, you receive the general sense of emotions and events tied to the object or place . . . *if* it is linked to emotionally charged events (an uneventful history might leave no impressions at all). This is not always a good thing – a terrifying impression might require a Fright Check (p. 360)! On a critical success, you experience an actual vision. No matter how well you roll, you *cannot* detect magic, spirits, etc. Still, a magic item, ghostly haunt, or ritual site is likely to have an emotionally charged history, giving strong impressions.

On a failure, you receive no impressions at all, and cannot attempt to read that object or place again for 24 hours.

Special Limitations

ESP: Your ability is part of the ESP psi power (see p. 255). -10%.

Puppet 👤👽

5 or 10 points

Prerequisites: Possession and either Ally or Dependent.

A Puppet is an Ally (p. 36) or Dependent (p. 131) who cannot resist your Possession advantage (p. 75). When you use Possession on him, you succeed automatically! This may be due to his nature or some special knowledge you have: a curse, his true name, the key to his mind, etc.

A Puppet will always have IQ 0, *or* owe you a Duty (p. 133), *or* be Reprogrammable (p. 150). If he has a Duty, it must be Involuntary, and its frequency must be identical to the Puppet's own frequency of appearance as an Ally or Dependent.

Each Puppet costs 5 points. You can buy an *entire group* of related Allies as Puppets for 10 points. These costs are for the Puppet advantage only; you must pay for your Ally or Dependent separately. It is common but not mandatory for such Allies to have the Minion enhancement or the Unwilling limitation.

Racial Memory 👤👽

15 or 40 points

You have access to the memories of your direct ancestors (or earlier software generations, for Digital Minds). This ability comes in two forms:

Racial Memory (Passive): Your talent is vague and totally passive. The GM secretly makes an IQ roll for you in any situation that your ancestors might have encountered. On a success, you get a feeling of *déjà vu* about the situation. It is up to you to interpret this. A critical success gives a vivid replay of ancient ancestral memories. On a failure, nothing happens. A critical failure results in a wrong impression. *15 points.*

Racial Memory (Active): You may use this advantage *actively.* If you want to know something, the GM first determines whether or not your ancestors knew the answer. Then he rolls against your IQ to see if you can gain access to the information. If your ancestors didn't have the answer and the roll succeeds, you will know that. On a critical failure, you will believe your ancestors didn't know, even if they really did. This requires one turn of absolute concentration (the GM may require more elaborate preparations to recall very ancient memories). *40 points.*

Radiation Tolerance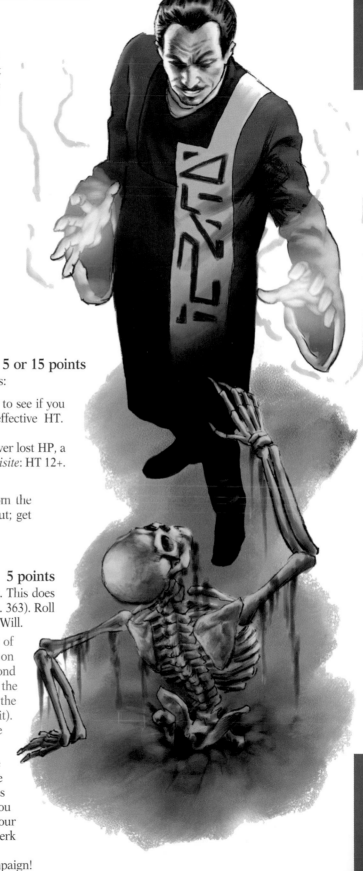

Variable

Your cells or circuits are resistant to radiation. The cost of this advantage depends on the divisor of the effective dose of radiation you receive – *after* dividing by the Protection Factor (PF) of artificial protection such as armor.

Divisor	*Cost*
2	5 points
5	10 points
10	15 points
20	20 points
50	25 points
100	30 points
200	35 points
500	40 points
1,000	45 points

Rank

see p. 29

Rapid Healing

5 or 15 points

Your wounds heal quickly. This trait comes in two levels:

Rapid Healing: Whenever you roll to recover lost HP *or* to see if you can get over a crippling injury, you get +5 to your effective HT. *Prerequisite:* HT 10+. *5 points.*

Very Rapid Healing: As above, but when you roll to recover lost HP, a successful HT roll means you heal *two* HP, not one. *Prerequisite*: HT 12+. *15 points.*

Note that this advantage does not hasten recovery from the *short-term* effects of injury, such as stunning and knockout; get Recovery (p. 80) for that.

Rapier Wit

5 points

You can use witty repartee to stun your foes in combat. This does not require a combat maneuver – talking is a free action (p. 363). Roll a Quick Contest of Public Speaking skill vs. your opponent's Will.

Modifiers: -2 if your target has the Clueless or No Sense of Humor disadvantage; any modifier the GM assigns based on your description of the verbal attack; -1 per opponent beyond the first to affect a group (and you must know something the *entire group* has in common; e.g., they're all flunkies of the same household or members of the same military unit). Opponents with the Unfazeable advantage (p. 95) are *immune* to Rapier Wit.

If you win, your opponent is mentally stunned (see p. 420). A critical success causes one HP of physical damage as well – your victim injures himself accidentally (drops something on his foot, chokes on his own tongue, etc.). If you lose, there is no effect. On a critical failure, you enrage your opponent, possibly triggering such disadvantages as Berserk and Bloodlust!

This advantage is usually only appropriate in a *silly* campaign!

Reawakened 🧠 ✦

10 points

You can "remember" skills (spells, techniques, etc.) learned during previous lives. You must purchase these abilities normally; Reawakened is just a special Unusual Background (p. 96) that explains how you learned them without a teacher. This trait is only available if reincarnation is a fact in the setting (GM's decision).

Recovery 💪 👽

10 points

You recover from unconsciousness very quickly. When determining the length of time you remain unconscious for *any* reason, divide by all times by 60: hours become minutes, minutes become seconds . . . even a month-long coma becomes a mere 12-hour sleep.

Reduced Consumption 💪

2 points/level

You can go for a long time without food and water, or fuel – although you still require these things. (For indefinite endurance, see *Doesn't Eat or Drink*, p. 50.) This advantage comes in four levels:

Reduced Consumption 1: You require 2/3 as much food and water, or fuel, as usual ("two meals a day"). *2 points.*

Reduced Consumption 2: You require 1/3 as much food and water, or fuel, as usual ("one meal a day"). *4 points.*

Reduced Consumption 3: You require food and water only once per week ("one meal a week," or about 5% as much). *6 points.*

Reduced Consumption 4: You require food and water only once per month ("one meal a month," or about 1% as much). *8 points.*

Note that one or even two levels of this advantage might be appropriate for ascetics in cinematic games!

Special Limitations

Cast-Iron Stomach: You require the standard *amount* of food and water, but the *quality* is irrelevant. You can eat rotten vegetables and fuzzy blue-green meat, and drink dishwater and sour milk. Instead of reducing how often you must eat, reduce your demands on life support (and your food costs) by a like amount: to 2/3 normal at level 1, 1/3 normal at level 2, 5% normal at level 3, and 1% normal at level 4. You get a bonus equal to your level (+1 to +4) to resist the effects of food-borne poisons or diseases not tailored expressly for you, but -3 on reactions from anyone watching you eat! -50%.

Food Only: You require less food, but the usual amount of water. -50%.

Water Only: You require less water, but the usual amount of food. -50%.

Regeneration 💪 👽

Variable

Your wounds heal in mere hours, minutes, or seconds! To regenerate lost *limbs*, you will also need Regrowth (below) – but Regeneration will greatly accelerate that ability. Regeneration includes Rapid Healing (p. 79) at no extra cost.

You cannot have Regeneration if you have Slow Healing (p. 155) or Unhealing (p. 160). Regeneration *is* compatible with Draining (p. 132), but it does *not* restore the daily HP loss due to that disadvantage.

The cost of this trait depends on your regeneration speed:

Regeneration (Slow): You recover 1 HP every 12 hours, in addition to normal healing. *10 points.*

Regeneration (Regular): You recover 1 HP per hour. *25 points.*

Regeneration (Fast): You recover 1 HP per minute. *50 points.*

Regeneration (Very Fast): You recover 1 HP per second. *100 points.*

Regeneration (Extreme): You recover 10 HP per second. *150 points.*

Special Enhancements

Heals Radiation: You shed accumulated rads at *10 times* the rate at which you heal missing HP. For instance, Regeneration (Regular) removes 10 rads per hour. This *will* heal "permanent" radiation damage. +40%.

Special Limitations

Radiation Only: As Heals Radiation, but you *only* shed rads – you do not heal HP. -60%.

Regrowth 💪 👽

40 points

You can regrow lost limbs and organs! A lost ear, finger, toe, claw, tentacle tip, etc. regrows in 1d weeks; a lost hand or foot in 1d+1 months; and a lost eye, arm, or leg in 2d+2 months. If you also have Regeneration (above), Regrowth works *much* faster: all lost body parts regrow in the time it takes you to heal to full HP.

Special Limitations

Minor: You can only regrow ears, fingers, toes, and other small bits – not hands, feet, eyes, etc. -50%.

Religious Rank

see *Rank*, p. 29

Reputation

see p. 26

A positive Reputation is an advantage and should be noted as such on your character sheet.

Resistant 💪

Variable

You are naturally resistant (or even immune) to noxious items or substances that are not direct, physical attacks. This gives you a bonus on all HT rolls to resist incapacitation or injury from such things.

The bonus from Resistant applies to all rolls to resist noxious effects within a particular category – usually some combination of disease, poison, and environmental syndromes (altitude sickness, the bends, space sickness, etc.). It also applies to rolls to resist *attacks* that use these effects. This includes Afflictions with one of Blood Agent, Contact Agent, Follow-Up, or Respiratory Agent, and Innate Attacks that have such modifiers *and* inflict toxic or fatigue damage.

Resistant does *not* protect against effects that Damage Resistance or Protected Sense either stop or provide a HT bonus to resist. This includes Afflictions and Innate Attacks that do not have any of the modifiers given above.

The base cost for Resistant depends on the rarity of the effects it counteracts:

Very Common: A broad category within the noxious items described above. *Example:* Metabolic Hazards (all threats that only affect the living, including all disease and poison, plus such syndromes as altitude sickness, bends, seasickness, and jet lag). *30 points.*

Common: A group of related items encountered as often in nature as in an attack, *or* some other suitably broad subset of "Very Common." *Example:* Poison (all toxins, but not asphyxiants or corrosives) or Sickness (all diseases and environmental syndromes). *15 points.*

Occasional: A group of closely related items more often encountered in nature than as a deliberate attack, *or* a subset of a "Common" group. *Examples:* Disease (all bacteria, viruses, fungus infections, etc.) or Ingested Poison. *10 points.*

Rare: A specific item or environmental syndrome, *or* a subset of an "Occasional" group. *Examples:* Acceleration (blackouts due to extreme G-forces), Altitude Sickness, Bends (decompression sickness), Seasickness, or Space Sickness; Nanomachines. *5 points.*

(+3) [5]. Anything more would be superhuman. Golems, robots, undead, and other beings that are not truly "alive" *must* take Immunity to Metabolic Hazards [30]; this is already included in the Machine meta-trait (p. 263). When in doubt, the GM's word is final.

Mental Resistance: It is possible to be Resistant to a purely mental threat. This works as described above, except that the bonus applies to resistance rolls against IQ and Will instead of HT. "Psionics" is an allowed category, and is considered Very Common.

Scanning Sense ✷ ✦
Variable

You can emit energy, bounce it off objects, and analyze the returned signal to build up a "picture" of your surroundings. This lets you discern size and shape, but not color or fine detail (such as writing). It has *nothing* to do with the normal human sense of sight, and requires no light. As a result, you may ignore darkness penalties in combat. Perception is limited to a 120° arc in front of you.

Resistant does not protect against effects that Damage Resistance or Protected Sense either stop or provide a bonus to resist.

Multiply base cost to reflect your degree of resistance:

You are *totally* immune to all noxious effects, and never have to make resistance rolls (write this as "Immunity" on your character sheet): ×1.

You have +8 to all HT rolls to resist: ×1/2.

You have +3 to all HT rolls to resist: ×1/3.

Drop all fractions from the final cost.

An ordinary human could believably have any level of resistance to a *mundane* "Rare" item, such as Seasickness. He might also have Resistant to Disease (+3) [3], Resistant to Disease (+8) [5], or Resistant to Poison

Your sense is "active." Anyone who can sense the signal you emit can detect you, out to *twice* your own range. Unlike other sensory advantages, however, you can turn this ability off; see *Turning Advantages Off and On* (p. 34).

Below are several varieties of Scanning Sense. Each is a *separate* advantage, with its own special rules. Where these rules contradict the general ones given above, follow the special rules. Each sense also has a base range. To adjust this, take Increased Range (p. 106) or Reduced Range (p. 115).

Radar: Your Scanning Sense uses radio waves. Base range is 2,000 yards. You can only detect large (human-sized or larger), dense objects. On a

Sense roll, you get a general idea of the relative size of the object, and whether it is moving, but nothing more precise. You cannot get an actual "image" with Radar, or use it to aim attacks. Radar works best on flying targets; roll at -4 to spot anyone who is not silhouetted against the sky. Radar does not work at all underwater. *20 points.*

Imaging Radar: Your Scanning Sense uses millimeter-wave radar. Base range is 200 yards. You can spot small objects and determine their shape, but you must make a Sense roll to distinguish fine relief (e.g., to identify a face). Imaging Radar can see through thin fabric or vegetation. You get +3 to locate objects like concealed weapons, and may ignore penalties for spotting objects hidden behind light brush. Ordinary radar detectors detect Imaging Radar at -4. Imaging Radar does not work underwater. *20 points.*

Ladar: Your Scanning Sense uses a laser beam. Base range is 200 yards. Ladar is very similar to Imaging Radar, but the beam is narrower and offers better resolution. This gives -4 on rolls to *locate* objects of interest, but +4 on rolls to *identify* them. Only specialized ladar detectors can detect Ladar, and at -4 even then. Ladar cannot penetrate dense smoke or solid objects. It has 10-50% range in falling rain or snow, and 1% range underwater. *20 points.*

Para-Radar: Your Scanning Sense uses energy unknown to 21st-century science. Treat Para-Radar as Imaging Radar, except that it functions in *any* environment! Ordinary radar detectors cannot detect Para-Radar, although some ultra-tech sensors might be able to do so. *40 points.*

Sonar: Your Scanning Sense uses ultrasonic sound waves. Base range is 2,000 yards underwater. You can spot small objects and determine their shape, but you must make a Sense roll to distinguish fine relief (e.g., to identify a face). Sonar does not function if you are deafened, and can be "jammed" or fooled by a very loud noise (e.g., an explosion). Individuals with Ultrahearing can detect Sonar. Sonar is much less effective in air: range is only 20 yards multiplied by air pressure in atmospheres (one atmosphere on Earth). Sonar is completely ineffective in vacuum. *20 points.*

Special Enhancements

Extended Arc: You can scan an arc greater than 120°. A 240° arc (as described for Peripheral Vision, p. 74) is +75%; a 360° arc (as described for 360° Vision, p. 34) is +125%.

Low-Probability Intercept (LPI): This is only available for Radar and Sonar. You can switch this enhancement on and off. Turning it on makes your signal difficult to detect. This halves range, but your Scanning Sense can only be detected at 1.5 times the *halved* range. +10%.

Multi-Mode: This is only available for Radar. You can switch between Radar and Imaging Radar. (This is much cheaper than buying the two advantages separately, because they overlap to some extent.) +50%.

Penetrating: This is only available for Para-Radar. You can "see" *inside* any object within range. This functions exactly as Penetrating Vision 2 (p. 74). +50%.

Targeting: By taking an Aim maneuver, you can "lock onto" any object within range and determine its precise range and speed – just as if you had a high-tech rangefinder. This gives you +3 to hit that target with an *aimed* ranged attack. +20%.

Special Limitations

Targeting Only: As Targeting, but you can *only* use your sense to "lock onto" targets already spotted with another sense; you cannot use it to spot things. -40%.

Sealed

15 points

You are encased in a gas- and liquid-impermeable layer. This makes you waterproof, and grants complete immunity to corrosive or toxic agents that must touch skin or exposed machinery to work. You must still breathe, unless you also have Doesn't Breathe (p. 49); however, your exterior breathing apparatus (nose, snorkel, etc.) is protected by this trait. Likewise, you are *not* automatically pressurized; for that, take Pressure Support (p. 77) or Vacuum Support (p. 96).

Security Clearance

Variable

A government agency or corporation trusts you with access to sensitive

information that would otherwise be "off limits" to someone of your Rank or Status. For instance, a general "cleared" for military secrets commensurate with his Military Rank would not have to buy Security Clearance separately, but a civilian with exactly the same level of access would have to pay points for the privilege.

Point cost depends on your degree of access:

• You have access to a relatively narrow range of secrets on a "need to know" basis. *Example:* a strategic bomber pilot, who might know secrets about aircraft, weapons, and targets. *5 points.*

• You have *either* free access to a narrow range of secrets *or* "need to know" access to a broad range of secrets. *Example:* a counterintelligence officer, who would have limited access to *many* secrets, as part of his job is to protect them. *10 points.*

• You have free access to a broad range of secrets. *Example:* a cinematic secret agent, who will know almost any secret the plot requires him to know. *15 points.*

Halve these values (round up) if the organization that grants the Security Clearance is of relatively minor importance (e.g., a small corporation or municipal government).

You cannot receive a security clearance without a thorough background check. The GM is free to forbid this advantage to any PC who has a suspicious past (including such traits as Debt or Secret) or an unstable personality (for instance, Paranoia or Sadism).

See Invisible ♟ ☻
15 points

You can see objects or individuals that are normally invisible. Buy this advantage separately for each kind of invisibility.

Sensitive

see *Empathy*, p. 51

Sensitive Touch ♟ ☻
10 points

Your fingertips or equivalent organs are extremely sensitive, allowing you to sense residual heat in a chair, faint vibrations in the floor as someone approaches, etc. You get +4 (in addition to any Acute Touch bonuses) on any task that utilizes the sense of touch; e.g., a Forensics roll to note the similarities or differences between two pieces of fabric, or a Search roll to feel out tiny concealed objects.

Serendipity ♟
15 points/level

You have the knack of being in the right place at the right time. Each level of this trait entitles you to one fortuitous but plausible coincidence per game session. The details are up to the GM. For instance, the GM might declare that one of the guards you need to talk your way past just happens to be your cousin, or that there is a sports car idling in front of the bank just as you run outside in pursuit of the fleeing bank robbers.

From time to time, the GM may rule that a single *implausible* coincidence counts as some or all of your lucky breaks for a given session (e.g.,

the mechanic at the local garage has all the parts you need to complete your ultra-tech contragrav belt).

You are free to *suggest* serendipitous occurrences to the GM, but he gets the final say. Should he reject all your suggestions but fail to work Serendipity into the game session, you will get your lucky breaks next game session.

Shadow Form ♟ ☻
50 points

You can become a two-dimensional shadow. This lets you slip along walls and floors – and through the thinnest cracks (anything wide enough to fit your shoulders through) – at your usual ground Move. You can also defy gravity, creeping up walls and across ceilings at half Move.

Physical attacks do half damage to you in this form. Energy attacks do normal damage, except for light-based attacks, which do 50% extra damage. Magic, psi, and other purely mental abilities affect you normally.

You are subject to a few major restrictions while in this form. You cannot walk through three-dimensional space; you *must* slide along an object. Furthermore, you cannot perform any purely physical attacks or actions, and you cannot carry ordinary items or affect them in any way. You *can* use magic, psi, and similar abilities, however.

If you cannot switch out of Shadow Form, Shadow Form is a *disadvantage* worth -20 points. This will make it difficult to interact with others! You may still add enhancements, but they will work like limitations, reducing the value of the disadvantage. For instance, a +50% enhancement would reduce the value of the disadvantage by 50%, to -10 points.

Special Enhancements

Can Carry Objects: You may carry objects. They take Shadow Form when picked up and return to normal when put down. You still may not affect non-shadow objects. No encumbrance is +10%; Light, +20%; Medium, +50%; Heavy, +100%.

Shapeshifting ♟ ☻
Variable

You can physically change into one or more forms different from your

native form. To shift between forms, you must concentrate for 10 seconds. To speed this up, add Reduced Time (p. 108).

Fatigue, injury, crippling, and afflictions carry over between forms – although HP and FP losses scale in proportion to the HP and FP of the form. For instance, if you suffer 10 HP of damage and a broken leg in a form that has 20 HP, you will have 5 HP of damage and a broken leg when you switch to a form that has only 10 HP.

If you are knocked out or killed, you *immediately* revert to your native form (which will also be unconscious or dead). In addition, you must specify a single, reasonably common external influence that can force you to return to your native form against your will. This should suit the advantage's origin: a Dispel Magic spell if your ability is magical, exorcism if a spirit power, strong magnetic fields if technological, etc.

Shapeshifting comprises two different traits: Alternate Form and Morph.

Alternate Form
Variable

Like the werewolf of folklore, you can assume a specific form other than your own. This can be *anything* built with points: humanoid, animal, robot, etc. Create your alternate form as a racial template (p. 260); however, you can switch it "on" and "off." This template need not be a "stock" template. For instance, if you wish to retain human intelligence in beast form, you could shift into a template that lacks the beast's low IQ (although this increases the template cost and hence the cost of Alternate Form). The GM is the final judge of what templates are allowed as Alternate Forms.

While it is turned on, your Alternate Form's racial template *replaces* your native racial template. Apply its racial traits – attribute modifiers, racial advantages and disadvantages, etc. – *instead* of those of your native race. Personal traits (including all attribute levels, advantages, disadvantages, and skills bought over and above racial norms) remain intact, although your skill levels are affected by changes to the controlling attribute scores.

If the Alternate Form's racial template has traits that conflict with your personal traits, the traits of your Alternate Form take precedence. For instance, if you become a dolphin with No Manipulators, you will temporarily lose personal advantages that affect your hands, such as High Manual Dexterity, while you are in dolphin form – and some skills (for instance, Lockpicking) will be relatively useless, although you do remember them.

If you have a single Alternate Form, it costs 15 points for a racial template worth no more than your native racial template. A more powerful form costs 15 points *plus* 90% of the difference in cost between your native template and that of your Alternate Form.

If you have multiple forms, pay full cost for the *most expensive* form. The less powerful Alternate Forms cost a flat 15 points apiece. Minimum cost per form is still 15 points.

Example: Consider four racial templates: a -100-point "cuddly critter," a 0-point human, an 80-point "ravenous beast," and a 100-point troll. A human who can turn into a cuddly critter pays 15 points, as the cuddly critter template is worth less than his native template. A cuddly critter who can turn into a human pays 15 + (0.9 × 100) = 105 points, since the human racial template is worth 100 points *more* than his own. A human who can become a troll also pays 15 + (0.9 × 100) = 105 points. A human who can assume any of the other three templates would pay full cost for his most expensive form, the troll: 105 points. The ravenous beast and cuddly critter forms would cost the minimum 15 points apiece. Total cost would be 135 points.

Were-Creatures: To create the classic "were-creature," start by purchasing any trait that applies in *both* forms – Infectious Attack, Vulnerability (Silver), etc. – as a personal trait. Next, buy an animal template as an Alternate Form. Since most beast templates are worth 0 or fewer points, this will usually cost 15 points, but powerful creatures (e.g., bears and tigers) may cost more. If the beast form is savage, the template should include such traits as Berserk, Bestial, and Bloodlust. Finally, apply limitations

such as Emergencies Only (p. 112), Unconscious Only (p. 115), and Uncontrollable (p. 116) to Alternate Form, as applicable. If you can only change during the full moon, add a -40% Trigger limitation (p. 115) as well.

Shapeshifting Races: When creating an entire race that has Alternate Form, work out the details of Alternate Form *last*. Total the cost of all the race's traits *other than* Alternate Form, subtract this total from the cost of the template the race transforms into, and use the difference to calculate the cost of Alternate Form for the race. Add the cost of Alternate Form to that of the race's other abilities to determine final racial cost.

Example: Forest Dwarves can turn into sapient bears. Excluding Alternate Form, the racial traits of Forest Dwarves total 25 points. The bear template is worth 125 points. The difference is 125 - 25 = 100 points. Thus, the cost of Alternate Form is 15 + (0.9 × 100) = 105 points. This makes the Forest Dwarf template worth 25 + 105 = 130 points.

Special Limitations

Cosmetic: You can assume a second, distinct appearance with *no* change in abilities or racial template. -50%.

Morph

Variable

This ability is similar to Alternate Form, but not limited to specific racial templates. You can assume *any* racial template, within certain limits.

First, the racial template must already exist in your game world. The *GM* might design the template himself or take one from a **GURPS** worldbook, but *you* cannot design totally new templates for the purpose of Morph (you can adjust existing ones, though; see below).

Second, you can only turn into a living being, or a formerly living being such as a vampire. To change into a machine requires a special enhancement.

Finally, the template's point value must be within a limit determined by the number of points you have in Morph.

If you can assume any racial template worth no more than your native one, Morph costs 100 points. This

makes *many* forms available – anything no more powerful than your native form. For a human, this includes cats, insects, owls, and wolves. If you can assume more powerful forms, add the difference between the maximum racial template cost and the cost of your native template to the base 100 points. For instance, a human who can take on any racial template worth up to 75 points would pay 175 points for Morph. You may improve this limit with earned character points.

You can always take on the form of a being you can *see* or *touch*, provided its racial template cost does not exceed your maximum. Once you have assumed a form, you can opt to memorize it by concentrating for one minute. This allows you to shapeshift into that form at any time. You can memorize a number of forms equal to your IQ. If all your "slots" are full, you must overwrite a previously memorized form (your choice) to add the new form.

As with Alternate Form, the racial template of whatever you turn into *replaces* your native racial template. You may not add traits to templates, but you may freely *omit* racial mental disadvantages (e.g., Bestial), and you may always choose to drop the racial IQ modifier from a template and use your own IQ. Such changes raise the cost of animal templates, which are cheap due to limited mental capabilities. If you intend to do this, you should spend more than the minimum 100 points on Morph.

Morph includes the ability to make cosmetic changes. This lets you impersonate a specific member of any race you can turn into. You can *always* impersonate someone who is present – but to assume his form later on, you must commit a memory "slot" to that form. With enough points in Morph, you can use this function to improve appearance. For instance, 115 points in Morph would let you give yourself any appearance from Horrific to Handsome. Cosmetic changes still take the usual 10 seconds.

Shapeshifting Races: Members of a race with the Morph ability must subtract the point cost of Morph from racial cost when determining what forms they can assume.

Example: Blue Blobs have a racial Morph ability worth 125 points – the basic ability, plus 25 points of extra capacity. This lets them assume forms worth 25 points more than their native one. With their other traits, their total racial cost is 175 points. However, for the purpose of Morph, they are considered to have a racial cost of 175 - 125 = 50 points. With their 25 points of additional capacity, Blue Blobs can turn into creatures worth up to 75 points.

Special Enhancements

Unlimited: You can become *anything* the GM has defined with a racial template. This lets you turn into robots, vehicles, etc. as well as living beings. Most ordinary inanimate objects – such as bricks and toasters – are worth 0 points or less. With the GM's permission, you can become a typical example of an object like this without the need for a specific racial template. +50%.

Special Limitations

Cosmetic: You can only change your outward appearance. Your abilities and racial template are unaffected. -50%. This limitation includes Mass Conservation, but not Retains Shape.

Mass Conservation: All your forms have the same weight. If the weight of your native form falls outside the *normal* racial weight range for a race, you simply cannot become a member of that race. The GM should be merciless when enforcing this limitation – no 150-lb. mice or elephants! -20%.

Retains Shape: You can only assume forms with the same number of limbs, body layout, posture, etc. as your native form. This would limit a human Morph to humanoids (e.g., elves and giants), a wolf Morph to horizontal quadrupeds, and a bird Morph to other birds. -20%.

Shrinking ♟ ☻
5 points/level

You can shrink at will. Each level of Shrinking lets you change your Size Modifier by -1, at the rate of -1 SM per second. You return to normal size at the same rate. By default, you cannot carry *any* equipment, not even clothing, when you shrink. The ability to carry objects while shrunk is an enhancement.

When you shrink, find your new height from the *Size Modifier Table* (p. 19). Every -6 to SM reduces height by a factor of 10. Reduce Move, reach, damage (with unarmed attacks, Innate Attacks, or shrunken weapons), HP, and DR in proportion to height. Every full -2 to SM also reduces weight by a factor of 10; for odd-numbered levels, treat the extra -1 as an additional factor of 3 (e.g., -3 to SM reduces weight by a factor of 30).

Example: A 5'10"-tall character (SM 0) has Shrinking 12. This lets him shrink until he has SM -12, reducing his height by a factor of 100 (to about 0.7"). However, at that size he has only 1% his usual Move, reach, HP, and DR, and must divide any damage he inflicts by 100. His weight goes down by a factor of 1,000,000!

Special Enhancements

Affects Others: You can bring your friends with you when you shrink! +50% per person you can affect at the same time.

Can Carry Objects: You may carry objects. This is limited to equipment you are actually carrying or wearing when you shrink. Such items regain normal size when put down; at the GM's option, they might sweep you aside as they grow, or even return to normal size beneath you, stranding you high above the ground! No encumbrance is +10%; Light, +20%; Medium, +50%; Heavy, +100%.

Full Damage: You inflict full damage when shrunk. (GMs be warned: this makes for an almost perfect assassin.) +100%.

Full DR: You retain full DR when shrunk. +30%.

Full HP: You retain full HP when shrunk. +30%.

Full Move: You retain full Move when shrunk. +30%.

Signature Gear 🤝
Variable

You have distinctive, valuable possessions unrelated to your wealth level. This gear is as much a part of your personal legend as are your reputation and skills. You *must* explain where it came from: you won your starship in a card game, inherited your magic sword from your mentor, etc.

For equipment normally bought with money, such as weapons and armor, each point in Signature Gear gives goods worth up to 50% of the average campaign starting wealth (but never cash). For anything built as a character, use the rules under *Allies* (p. 36) instead. It is up to the GM whether to treat android companions, faithful steeds, custom vehicles, etc. as equipment (with a cash cost) or characters (with a point cost).

If you misplace Signature Gear or sell it unwillingly, or an NPC steals or confiscates it, the GM must give you an opportunity to recover it in the course of the adventure. If it is truly lost forever through no fault of your own, the GM will give you back your points (or replace the item with another of equal value). However, should you sell or give away your Signature Gear of your own free will, it is *gone*, along with the points spent on it!

Silence ♟ ☻
5 points/level

You can move and breathe noiselessly. You get +2 per level to Stealth skill when you are perfectly motionless, or +1 if moving (even in armor, etc.). These bonuses help only in the dark, or against listening devices, blind creatures, and others who must rely on hearing to find you.

Single-Minded ☻
5 points

You can really concentrate! You get +3 to success rolls for any lengthy mental task you concentrate on to the exclusion of other activities, if the GM feels such focus would be beneficial. You tend to ignore everything else while obsessed (roll vs. Will to avoid this), and have -5 to all rolls to notice interruptions.

The GM may rule that certain complex tasks (e.g., inventing, magic, and social activities) *require* you to divide your attention. This trait has no effect in such situations.

Slippery ♟ ☻
2 points/level

You are hard to hold! You might be slimy, molecularly smooth, or surrounded by a force field that negates friction. Each level of this trait (maximum five levels) gives +1 on all ST, DX, and Escape rolls to slip restraints, break free in close combat, or squeeze through narrow openings.

Smooth Operator
see *Talent*, p. 89.

Snatcher 👤 ⭡

80 points

You have the power to find almost any small item you desire in an alternate world and "snatch" it across the dimensions to you. The items you snatch do not come from your own world, but from some nameless parallel; therefore, you can never intentionally take something away from a specific other person. Note that this talent does not allow you to *visit* alternate worlds in person – only to steal from them.

To make a snatch, you must first concentrate for 10 seconds and clearly visualize the item you want. The item must be able to fit in one hand, and cannot weigh more than 5 lbs. You should have a hand free (if your hands are tied, you roll at -3), and others can see you making "reaching" motions with that hand.

Next, make an IQ roll for the snatch attempt. If you are trying for *information* in any form, the GM makes this roll for you (see below). Regardless of IQ, a roll of 14 or more always fails.

On a success, the desired item appears in your hand – or sitting within arm's reach, if you prefer. On a failure, you obtain nothing. On a critical failure, you snatched the wrong item! This item is not immediately dangerous unless you were *trying* for something dangerous.

Regardless of success or failure, each snatch attempt costs 2 FP.

Items Available

In theory, you can get *anything*. In practice, some things are so hard to find that it is little use trying for them. You have a good chance of getting any item that exists, or that *ever* existed, in your own world – or any reasonably similar item. If the desired item is unusual, the GM may apply a penalty to the IQ roll:

Item is significantly different from anything that ever appeared in your own world: -1 or more (GM's option). You could visualize "a perfect diamond, bright green, the size of a hen's egg, carved into the shape of a typewriter," but you might be rolling at -20!

Item is unique or almost unique in any one world (e.g., the Hope Diamond): -3 or worse (GM's option).

You cannot clearly visualize what you want: -4 or worse (GM's option). Even on a "success," you might not get what you were really hoping for.

You *cannot* get an item that works by natural laws wholly different from those in your world. For instance, if your world is nonmagical (or has no magic *that you know of*), you cannot snatch a magic item, because you are unable to visualize it properly; you would get a pretty but powerless mundane item. Similarly, if you are from a low-TL world, you could not get a laser pistol; you wouldn't be able to visualize it well, and your best effort would be a broken or toy gun. (A generous GM might bend this rule on a critical success . . . and then let the poor Snatcher try to figure out how to use his amulet or laser pistol without killing himself.)

Information is not available except in the form of "ordinary" textbooks, reports, etc. You can grab a history book, but you can't ask for "The Book of What Happens Next in My Adventure." Note that the GM makes the roll if information is requested. If the roll fails by 5 or more, the information comes from an alternate world with different history, physics, etc., and *is* wrong – maybe subtly, maybe not subtly at all!

Repeated Attempts

If your snatch attempt is unsuccessful, you can immediately try to snatch the same or a similar object again. These "repeated attempts" are made at a cumulative -1 to the IQ roll. Each repeated attempt costs 4 FP instead of the usual 2 FP. To eliminate these penalties, wait one hour between attempts.

The GM should be strict about attempts to circumvent this. For instance, a ".45 pistol" is not very different from a ".357 pistol" for the purpose of this advantage. Furthermore, *ignore* critical successes on repeated attempts made in quick succession. If the snatch being attempted is very difficult, there is little choice but to wait an hour between attempts.

Duration

The objects you snatch remain until you voluntarily return them or use your Snatcher ability again. To keep objects indefinitely, take the Permanent enhancement (below).

Special Enhancements

Permanent: Objects you snatch *don't* vanish when you use your ability again. The GM is free to forbid this enhancement, as it allows a single Snatcher to amass boundless wealth by snatching small, valuable objects. +300%.

Special Limitations

Less Weight: Your weight limit is lower than 5 lbs.

Limit	Cost Modifier
3 lbs.	-5%
2 lbs.	-10%
1 lb.	-15%
4 oz.	-25%
1 oz.	-30%

Specialized: You can only grab a certain type of object, or cannot touch a certain class of thing. *Examples:* Only metal, -5%; Only money, -10%; Only weapons, -10%; Only information, -20%; No metal, -20%; Only blue things, -25%. The GM sets the limitation value using the guidelines under *Accessibility* (p. 110).

Stunning: You are mentally stunned after a successful snatch. -10%.

Unpredictable: On a failed IQ roll, you get *something*, but it isn't what you wanted. The worse the failure, the more different the item is. If you wanted a loaded pistol, failure by 1 might bring an unloaded pistol. Failure by 2 could mean a water pistol, failure by 3 a book on "How to Shoot," and so on . . . with a critical failure bringing a live hand grenade. *Any* critical failure is dangerous, regardless of what you were looking for! -25%.

Social Chameleon 👤

5 points

You have the knack of knowing exactly what to say – and when to say it – around your social "betters." You are exempt from reaction penalties due to differences in Rank or Status. In situations where there would be no such penalty, you get +1 on reactions from those who demand respect (priests, kings, etc.). This is a cinematic advantage!

Social Regard 🤝

5 points per +1 reaction

You are a member of a class, race, sex, or other group that your society holds in high regard. To be an advantage, this must be obvious to anyone who meets you. This is the opposite of Social Stigma (p. 155); membership in a given social group cannot result in both Social Regard and Social Stigma.

Social Regard costs 5 points per +1 to reaction rolls, to a maximum of +4. This is not a Reputation, despite the similarities in cost and effect. You are treated well because of *what* you are, not because of *who* you are. Think of it as "privilege by association."

The way you are treated on a good reaction roll will depend on the type of Regard:

Feared: Others will react to you much as if you had successfully used Intimidation skill (p. 202). Those who like you stand aside, while those who dislike you flee rather than risk a confrontation. You are met with silent deference, and perhaps even respect, but *never* friendly familiarity. *Examples:* a god among men or an Amazon warrior.

Respected: You receive polite and obsequious deference, much as if you had high Status (p. 28), regardless of your *actual* Status. Social interactions other than combat usually go smoothly for you – but there will be times when the kowtowing gets in the way. *Examples:* a member of a priest caste or a ruling race.

Venerated: Total strangers react to you in a caring way. They give up seats, let you ahead of them in lines, and receive your every word as pearls of wisdom. They also take great pains to prevent you from putting yourself in danger or even discomfort – even when you *need* to do so! *Example:* an elderly person in many societies.

Speak Underwater
5 points

You can talk normally while submerged, and you can understand what others say while underwater.

Special Enhancements

Interface Crossing: You can talk to those outside of the water while submerged, and can understand people on the surface talking to you. +50%.

Speak With Animals
25 points

You can converse with animals. The quality of information you receive depends on the beast's IQ and the GM's decision on what the animal has to say. Insects and other tiny creatures might only be able to convey emotions such as hunger and fear, while a chimp or a cat might be able to engage in a reasonably intelligent discussion. It takes one minute to ask one question and get the answer – *if* the animal decides to

speak at all. The GM may require a reaction roll (+2 to reactions if you offer food).

The GM is free to rule that alien, unnatural, or mythical beasts don't count as "animals" for the purpose of this advantage.

Special Limitations

Specialized: You can only communicate with *certain* animals. "All land animals" (including birds, insects, and land-dwelling mammals and reptiles) or "All aquatic animals" (including amphibians, fish, mollusks, crustaceans, and cetaceans) is -40%; one class (e.g., "Mammals" or "Birds"), -50%; one family (e.g., "Felines" or "Parrots"), -60%; one species (e.g., "House Cats" or "Macaws"), -80%.

Speak With Plants
15 points

You can communicate empathically with plants. All earthly plants are IQ 0, but a large tree might be "wiser" than the average ivy, at the GM's whim. A plant might know how recently it was watered or walked on, or something else that directly bears on its well-being, but would be unable to relate an overheard phone conversation. Any normal plant will always cooperate, within the limits of its ability. A mutant cabbage from Mars might require a reaction roll!

Special Rapport 👤🗡

5 points

You have a unique bond with another person. This acts as a potent version of Empathy (p. 51) that works only with one person, without regard to distance. You *always* know when your partner is in trouble, in pain, lying, or in need of help, no matter where he is. This requires no IQ roll. Your partner receives the same benefits with respect to you.

Both partners in a Special Rapport must buy this advantage. Your partner need not be a lover, or even a close friend, but the GM has the final say. In particular, the GM may wish to forbid PCs from buying Special Rapports with powerful NPCs who would otherwise qualify as Patrons (or allow it, but require an Unusual Background).

can get a feeling for the general intentions of any spirit you encounter by making a successful IQ roll. As well, your Influence skills (Diplomacy, Sex Appeal, etc.) work normally on spirits, which sets you aside from most mortals. Spirit Empathy does *not* prevent evil or mischievous spirits from seeking to harm you, but at the GM's option, it might make it easier to detect and counter their plots.

Special Limitations

Specialized: You are naturally in tune with the customs and moods of one specific class of spirits. Possibilities include angels, demons, elementals, faerie, ghosts, and anything else the GM wishes to allow. -50%.

Stretching is ideal for machines with telescoping mechanisms. A super with a "rubber body" should add some combination of Elastic Skin, Double-Jointed, Morph, and Super Jump.

Spines 🛡👽

1 or 3 points

You have sharp spines, like those of a porcupine or an echidna, located on strategic parts of your body. This is defensive weaponry, intended to discourage attackers; you cannot use your Spines actively. However, you get a DX-4 roll to hit *each* foe in close combat with you once per turn, as a free action. Roll at +2 against foes who attacked you from behind. Those who grapple or slam you are hit immediately and automatically – and those who slam you take *maximum damage!*

Short Spines: One or two inches long. Do 1d-2 impaling damage. Reach C. *1 point.*

Long Spines: One or two *feet* long. Do 1d impaling damage. Reach C. *3 points.*

Spirit Empathy 👤🗡

10 points

You are in tune with spirits, and receive the benefits of Empathy (p. 51) when dealing with them. You

Status

see p. 28

High Status is an advantage, and should be noted on your character sheet.

Stretching 🛡👽

6 points/level

You can stretch your body in any direction. Each level of Stretching lets you increase your effective SM by +1 with any body part *without* increasing your overall SM. You can elongate your arms to increase reach (but *not* swinging damage, as Stretching gives no extra mass or muscle), your legs to negotiate obstacles, your neck to see over barriers, etc. For more information, see *Size Modifier and Reach* (p. 402). Your body parts grow or shrink at the rate of ±1 SM per second.

By itself, Stretching is ideal for machines with telescoping manipulators. A super with a "rubber body" should add some combination of Elastic Skin (p. 51), Double-Jointed (p. 56), Morph (p. 84), and Super Jump (p. 89).

Striker 🛡👽

5, 6, 7, or 8 points

You have a body part that you can use to strike an aimed blow, but *not* to manipulate objects (see *Extra Arms*, p. 53) or walk on (see *Extra Legs*, p. 54). This might be a set of horns or protruding tusks, a heavy tail, a stinger, or any number of other natural weapons.

Your Striker can attack at reach C ("close combat only"), inflicting thrust damage at +1 per die; e.g., 2d-1 becomes 2d+1. Damage is *crushing* or *piercing* for 5 points, *large piercing* for 6 points, *cutting* for 7 points, or *impaling* for 8 points. See *Innate Attack* (p. 61) for details.

Roll against DX or Brawling to hit with your Striker. You can also use it to parry as if you had a weapon. Use the *higher* of (DX/2) + 3 or your Brawling parry.

Special Enhancements

Long: Your Striker is long relative to your body. This increases your effective SM for the purpose of calculating reach (see *Size Modifier and Reach*, p. 402). +100% per +1 to SM if you can attack at any reach from C to maximum, or +75% per +1 to SM if you can only attack at maximum reach (and *never* in close combat).

Special Limitations

Cannot Parry: You cannot parry with your Striker. -40%.

Clumsy: Your Striker is unusually inaccurate. This is common for tails and similar Strikers aimed from outside your usual arc of vision. -20% per -1 to hit.

Limited Arc: Your Striker can only attack straight ahead, straight behind, etc. Specify a direction when you buy the Striker. If your target isn't in the right place, and you cannot maneuver to put him there, *you cannot attack him at all.* -40%.

Weak: Your Striker is unusually blunt or light, or simply incapable of using your full ST. It inflicts only basic thrust damage, without the +1 per die. -50%.

Striking ST 🛡👽

5 points per +1 ST

You can strike more powerful blows than your ST score would indicate. Add Striking ST to base ST solely for the purpose of calculating thrust and swing damage (see *Damage Table*, p. 16). Striking ST has no effect on HP or Basic Lift. If you bought your ST with the No Fine Manipulators or Size limitation, apply the same limitation(s) to Striking ST.

Subsonic Hearing ✇ 👽 ●
0 or 5 points

You can hear very low-frequency sounds (under 40 Hz), such as the rumble of distant storms, the vibrations from incipient earthquakes, and the approach of stampeding herd beasts, armored vehicles, or dragons. This gives +1 to Tracking skill if your quarry is moving on the ground. Cost depends on your capabilities:

You can hear very low-frequency sounds only: *0 points*.

You can hear very low-frequency sounds *and* other sounds: *5 points*.

Note that Subsonic Hearing is included in the cost of Subsonic Speech (below); you cannot take both traits.

Subsonic Speech ✇ 👽 ●
0 or 10 points

You can converse using extremely low-frequency sounds. This trait *includes* Subsonic Hearing, above. Subsonic speech is slow (half-speed), and even if the frequency is shifted into the normal range, subsonic speakers are at -2 to Fast-Talk and any other skill where versatile speaking is important. However, subsonic speech carries twice as far as normal speech. Cost depends on your capabilities:

You can only communicate via Subsonic Speech: *0 points*.

You can switch between regular speech and Subsonic Speech at will: *10 points*.

Super Climbing ✇ 👽 ●
3 points/level

You can climb very quickly. Each level of Super Climbing gives you +1 Move when climbing or using the Clinging advantage (p. 43).

Super Jump ✇ 👽 ●
10 points/level

You can make superhuman leaps! Each level of Super Jump *doubles* the distance and height you can achieve when jumping (see *Jumping*, p. 352). Your Move while jumping is the *greater* of your normal ground Move and 1/5 your maximum long jump distance (thus, your maximum jump never takes more than five seconds). For instance, if your long jump were 100 yards, your jumping Move would be the greater of 20 and your normal ground Move.

You can jump at a foe in order to slam him. Figure the slam at your maximum jumping Move! You don't need to make a separate roll to jump accurately.

Finally, if you fall a distance less than or equal to your maximum high jump, you take *no* damage. You can increase this distance by five yards with a successful Acrobatics roll.

Super Luck 👤 ➹
100 points

You are not just lucky – you have limited control over probability. Once per hour of play, you may *dictate* the result of any one die roll you make (or the GM makes for you) instead of rolling the dice. Wholly impossible attempts cannot succeed (your effective skill level must be at least 3), but you can choose any result that would be possible – however improbable – on a single normal die roll.

You can have Super Luck and any degree of "normal" Luck, but no one can take Super Luck more than once!

Supernatural Durability ✇ ➹
150 points

Like a vampire or psycho killer from a horror movie, you can "shake off" most wounds. Injury comes off HP as usual, and you suffer knockback, but you are *completely immune* to shock, physical stun, and knockout. You don't need High Pain Threshold – this ability includes that one, and is far more potent!

As long as you have 0 or more HP, you are also immune to crippling injuries, and have your full Move. Below 0 HP, you are at half Move and Dodge, and can be crippled, but you won't *die* unless you are wounded by an attack to which you are specifically vulnerable (see below). The sole exception to this is a *single attack* that inflicts an injury of 10×HP or more. That much damage at once will blow you apart, killing you.

To die, you must first be wounded to -HP or worse. After that, one specific item can kill you. You must specify this when you buy Supernatural Durability. Valid categories appear under *Limited Defenses* (p. 46); the item that can kill you must be of "Occasional" rarity or higher. If wounds from this item ever reduce your HP to the point where a normal human would have to make HT rolls to survive, *you* must make those HT rolls or die. If this item wounds you to -5×HP, you die automatically. If you are already below -5×HP from other damage, *any* wound from this item will kill you. Any item to which you have a Vulnerability (p. 161) can also kill you in this way.

Talent 👤
Variable

You have a natural aptitude for a set of closely related skills. "Talents" come in levels, and give the following benefits:

● A bonus of +1 per level with all affected skills, even for default use. This effectively raises your relative skill level with *those skills only;* thus, this is an inexpensive way to be adept at small class of skills. (Generalists will find it more cost-effective to raise attributes.)

● A bonus of +1 per level on all reaction rolls made by anyone in a position to notice your Talent, if he would be impressed by your aptitude (GM's judgment). To receive this bonus, you must demonstrate your Talent – most often by using the affected skills.

● A reduction in the time required to learn the affected skills in play, regardless of *how* you learn them. Reduce the time required by 10% per level of Talent; e.g., Animal Friend 2 would let you learn animal-related skills in 80% the usual time. This has no effect on the *point cost* of your skills.

You may never have more than four levels of a particular Talent. However, overlapping Talents *can* give skill bonuses (only) in excess of +4.

Cost of Talents

The cost of a Talent depends on the size of the group of skills affected:

Small (6 or fewer related skills): 5 *points/level.*

Medium (7 to 12 related skills): 10 *points/level.*

Large (13 or more related skills): 15 *points/level.*

Skills with multiple specialties are considered to be *one* skill for this purpose. Once you buy a Talent, the list of affected skills is fixed. (*Exception:* The GM may rule that a Talent affects new skills appearing in later **GURPS** supplements, or skills he invents in the course of the campaign, if the Talent would logically be of value to those skills.)

Examples of Talents

The following Talents are considered standard, and exist in most campaigns:

Animal Friend: Animal Handling, Falconry, Packing, Riding, Teamster, and Veterinary. *Reaction bonus:* all animals. *5 points/level.*

Artificer: Armoury, Carpentry, Electrician, Electronics Repair, Engineer, Machinist, Masonry, Mechanic, and Smith. *Reaction bonus:* anyone you do work for. *10 points/level.*

Business Acumen: Accounting, Administration, Economics, Finance, Gambling, Market Analysis, Merchant, and Propaganda. *Reaction bonus:* anyone you do business with. *10 points/level.*

Gifted Artist: Artist, Jeweler, Leatherworking, Photography, and Sewing. *Reaction bonus:* anyone buying or critiquing your work. *5 points/level.*

Green Thumb: Biology, Farming, Gardening, Herb Lore, and Naturalist. *Reaction bonus:* gardeners and sentient plants. *5 points/level.*

Healer: Diagnosis, Esoteric Medicine, First Aid, Pharmacy, Physician, Physiology, Psychology, Surgery, and Veterinary. *Reaction bonus:* patients, both past and present. *10 points/level.*

Mathematical Ability: Accounting, Astronomy, Cryptography, Engineer, Finance, Market Analysis, Mathematics, and Physics. *Reaction bonus:* engineers and scientists. *10 points/level.*

Musical Ability: Group Performance (Conducting), Musical Composition, Musical Influence, Musical Instrument, and Singing. *Reaction bonus:* anyone listening to or critiquing your work. *5 points/level.*

Outdoorsman: Camouflage, Fishing, Mimicry, Naturalist, Navigation, Survival, and Tracking. *Reaction bonus:* explorers, nature lovers, and the like. *10 points/level.*

Smooth Operator: Acting, Carousing, Detect Lies, Diplomacy, Fast-Talk, Intimidation, Leadership, Panhandling, Politics, Public Speaking, Savoir-Faire, Sex Appeal, and Streetwise. *Reaction bonus:* con artists, politicians, salesmen, etc. – but only if you are not trying to manipulate *them. 15 points/level.*

Custom Talents

At the GM's option, you may create your own Talent with a custom skill list. However, the GM's word is law when determining which skills are "related" and how may points the Talent is worth. Talents should always be believable inborn aptitudes. For instance, Sports Talent might make sense – some athletes really do seem to have a gift – but the GM ought to forbid Ninja Talent or Weapon Talent (but see *Weapon Master*, p. 99).

Teeth ❦ ☻

0, 1, or 2 points

Anyone with a mouth has *blunt* teeth that can bite for thrust-1 crushing damage. This costs 0 points, and is typical of most herbivores. You have a more damaging bite:

Sharp Teeth: Like those of most carnivores. Inflict thrust-1 *cutting* damage. *1 point.*

Sharp Beak: Like that of a bird of prey. Inflicts thrust-1 *large piercing* damage. *1 point.*

Fangs: Like those of a *Smilodon.* Inflict thrust-1 *impaling* damage. *2 points.*

Telecommunication 🗣/❦ ☻

Variable

You can communicate over long distances without speaking aloud. You can send words at the speed of ordinary speech or pictures at the speed at which you could draw them. To establish contact requires one second of concentration and an IQ roll. After that, no concentration is required. You can maintain multiple contacts, but the IQ roll is at a cumulative -1 per contact after the first.

Telecommunication works amid even the loudest noises, although interference and jamming can disrupt your signal. Those with suitable equipment may attempt to locate, intercept, or jam your transmission. This requires an Electronics Operation (Communications) roll for an electromagnetic signal, an Electronics Operation (Psychotronics) roll for a psionic signal, and so forth.

Each variety of Telecommunication is a *separate advantage* with its own benefits and drawbacks. Some forms have limited range, which you can adjust using Increased Range (p. 106) or Reduced Range (p. 115).

Infrared Communication: You communicate using a modulated infrared beam. Base range is 500 yards in a direct line of sight. The short range and line-of-sight requirement make jamming and eavesdropping almost impossible under normal circumstances. You can only communicate with those who have this advantage or an infrared communicator. *10 points.*

Laser Communication: You communicate using a modulated laser beam. Base range is 50 miles in a direct line of sight. The narrow beam and line-of-sight requirement make it extremely hard to eavesdrop on you. You can only communicate with people who have this advantage or a laser communicator. *15 points.*

Radio: You communicate using radio waves. Base range is 10 miles. Your signal is omnidirectional, but because you can shift frequencies, eavesdroppers must still roll vs. Electronics Operation (Communications) to listen in. A side benefit of this ability is that you can receive AM, FM, CB, and other ordinary radio signals on an IQ roll (takes one second). Note that radio-frequency "noise" from lightning and unshielded electronics can interfere with Radio. Radio does not work *at all* underwater. *10 points.*

Telesend: You can transmit thoughts directly to others via magic, psi, or other exotic means (be specific!). Your subject receives your thoughts even if he lacks this ability. Range is theoretically unlimited, but the IQ roll to use this ability takes the range penalties given under *Long-Distance Modifiers* (p. 241). If you cannot see or otherwise sense your subject, you have an additional penalty: -1 for family, lovers, or close friends; -3 for casual friends and acquaintances; or -5 for someone met only briefly. *30 points.*

Special Enhancements

Broadcast: This enhancement is only available for Telesend. It lets you send your thoughts to everyone in a radius around you. This requires an IQ roll at the long-distance modifier for the desired radius, plus an additional -4. +50%.

Short Wave: This is only available for Radio. You can bounce your signal off a planet's ionosphere (if the planet has one). This lets you transmit to (or receive from) any point on the planet. Note that solar flares, weather, etc. can disrupt short-wave communications. +50%.

Universal: Your messages are automatically translated into your subject's language. The GM may limit this enhancement to individuals from advanced tech levels, or restrict it to Telesend. +50%.

Video: You are not limited to simple pictures! You can transmit real-time video of anything you can see. +40%.

Special Limitations

Racial: Your ability only works on those of your own race or a *very* similar race, per *Mind Reading* (p. 69). -20%.

Receive Only: You can receive but not send. This limitation is not available for Telesend. -50%.

Send Only: You can send but not receive. This limitation is not available for Telesend. -50%.

Telepathic: Your ability is part of the Telepathy psi power (see p. 257). -10%.

Vague: You cannot send speech or pictures. You can only send a simple code (e.g., Morse code) – or general concepts and emotions, in the case of Telesend. -50%.

Telekinesis 🧠/💪 👽
5 points/level

You can move objects without touching them. In effect, you manifest an invisible force that acts under your conscious direction at a distant point. Specify how you do this; possibilities include magnetism, psionic psychokinesis, an ultra-tech "tractor beam," or a supernatural "poltergeist effect."

You can manipulate distant objects just as if you were grasping them in a pair of hands with ST equal to your Telekinesis (TK) level. You can move any object you have strength enough to lift, at a Move equal to your TK level, modified as usual for encumbrance level (see *Encumbrance and Move*, p. 17). Regardless of level, maximum range is 10 yards. To modify range, take Increased Range (p. 106) or Reduced Range (p. 115).

Telekinesis requires constant concentration to use. In combat, this means you must take a Concentrate maneuver on your turn. Your TK may then perform *one* standard maneuver as if were a disembodied pair of hands at some point within your range: a Ready maneuver to pick up an object; a Move maneuver to lift and carry it; an Attack maneuver to throw it, or to grab or strike directly; and so on.

Example: On your turn in combat, you take a Concentrate maneuver and state that your TK is taking an Attack maneuver to grab a gun from a foe. The following turn, you can Concentrate again and specify that your TK is taking an Aim or Wait maneuver to cover your enemy with the gun, an Attack maneuver to shoot him, or a Move maneuver to bring the gun to your hand.

No rolls are necessary for ordinary lifting and movement. For more complex actions, the GM might require you to make a DX or skill roll. In situations where you would roll against ST, roll against your TK level instead.

All of the above assumes that you are using TK to perform a task at a distance. TK can also discreetly assist you with such skills as Gambling (especially to cheat!), Lockpicking, and Surgery. In general, anything that would benefit from High Manual Dexterity (p. 59) gets a +4 bonus if you can successfully make an IQ roll to use your TK properly. On a failure, the GM may assess any penalty he feels is appropriate.

Grappling and Striking: You can use TK to attack a foe directly. Roll against DX or an unarmed combat skill to hit. Your foe defends as if attacked by an invisible opponent (see *Visibility*, p. 394). If you grapple, your foe cannot grab hold of the TK force, but he *can* try to break free as usual – and if he also has TK, he can take a Concentrate maneuver and use his TK level instead of his ST. The turn after you grapple a foe using TK, your TK can use a Move maneuver to pick him up off the ground, provided you have enough TK to lift his weight. Someone in this position can't do anything that relies on ground contact (run, retreat, etc.), but can perform any other action that is possible while grappled.

Telekinesis: Possibilities include magnetism, psionic psychokinesis, an ultra-tech "tractor beam," or a supernatural "poltergeist effect."

Levitation: If you have enough TK to lift your own body weight, you can levitate. Take the Concentrate maneuver and have your TK take Move maneuvers to propel your body. For true psychokinetic flight, take Flight (p. 56) with the Psychokinetic limitation (below).

Throwing: By applying a TK impulse for a fraction of a second, you can *throw* objects faster (and farther) than you can move them. Take a Concentrate maneuver and have your TK take an Attack maneuver. This works just as if you were throwing the object with ST equal to your TK level. Roll against Throwing or Thrown Weapon skill to hit, depending on the object being hurled. For 1/2D and Max purposes, measure range from the *object* (not yourself!) to the target; for the purpose of *range penalties*, use the *sum* of the distance from you to the object and from the object to the target. Once you throw something, you have "released" your telekinetic grip – your TK must take a Ready maneuver to pick it up again.

Special Limitations

Magnetic: Your TK is "super magnetism," and only affects ferrous metals: iron (including steel), nickel, and cobalt. -50%.

Psychokinetic: Your ability is part of the Psychokinesis psi power (see p. 256). This makes it mental (🧠) rather than physical (💪). -10%.

Visible: Your TK is not an invisible force, but a disembodied hand, glowing "tractor beam," or similar. This makes it much easier for others to defend against your TK attacks (do not use the *Visibility* rules). -20%.

Telescopic Vision 💪 👽
5 points/level

You can "zoom in" with your eyes as if using binoculars. Each level lets you ignore -1 in range penalties to Vision rolls at all times, or -2 in range penalties if you take an Aim maneuver to zoom in on a particular target. This ability can also function as a telescopic sight, giving up to +1 Accuracy per level with ranged attacks provided you take an Aim maneuver for seconds equal to the bonus (see *Scopes* under *Firearm Accessories*, p. 411).

The benefits of this trait are not cumulative with those of technological aids such as binoculars or scopes. If you have both, you must opt to use one or the other.

Special Limitations

No Targeting: Your field of vision is broad and not "zeroed" to your ranged attacks. You get no Accuracy bonus in combat. -60%.

Temperature Control 🧠/💪 👽
5 points/level

You can alter the ambient temperature. Heating or cooling is limited to 20° per level, and occurs at a rate of 2° per level per second of concentration. You can affect a two-yard radius at a distance of up to 10 yards. Use Increased Range (p. 106) or Reduced Range (p. 115) to modify range; add levels of Area Effect (p. 102) to increase radius.

This ability never does damage directly. For that, buy Innate Attack – usually either burning (for flame) or fatigue (for attacks that damage by altering body temperature).

Special Limitations

Cold: You can only decrease the temperature. -50%.

Heat: You can only increase the temperature. -50%.

Psychokinetic: Your ability is part of the Psychokinesis psi power (see p. 256), often called "cryokinesis" (for cold) or "pyrokinesis" (for heat). -10%.

Temperature Tolerance ♋

1 point/level

Every character has a temperature "comfort zone" within which he suffers no ill effects (such as FP or HP loss) due to heat or cold. For ordinary humans, this zone is 55° wide and falls between 35° and 90°. For nonhumans, the zone can be centered *anywhere*, but this is a 0-point feature for a zone no larger than 55°. A larger zone is an advantage. Each level of Temperature Tolerance adds HT degrees to your comfort zone, distributed in any way you wish between the "cold" and "hot" ends of the zone.

Temperature Tolerance confers no special resistance to attacks by fire or ice unless the only *damage* is a result of a rise or fall in the ambient temperature. In particular, it cannot help you if your *body temperature* is being manipulated.

In a realistic campaign, the GM should limit normal humans to Temperature Tolerance 1 or 2. However, high levels of this trait are likely for nonhumans with fur or a heavy layer of fat.

Temporal Inertia ♟ ⚡

15 points

You are strongly rooted in probability. If history changes, you can remember both versions. If you are involved in a genuine time paradox, you are not erased, even if the rest of your world is! You have a place in the new timeline, whatever it is, and remember all your experiences – even the ones that never happened. (In an extreme case, you have two complete sets of memories, and must make an

IQ roll any time you have to distinguish between them under stress . . . you might need Acting skill to stay out of the lunatic asylum.)

There is a drawback: there is a "you" in any parallel or split timeline you encounter, and he is as similar to you as the timeline allows.

This trait is only worthwhile in a campaign in which paradoxes or changes in history – erasing past events or whole timelines – are possible. See *Unique* (p. 160) for the opposite of this advantage.

Temporary Rank

see *Rank*, p. 29

Tenure 🤝

5 points

You have a job from which you cannot normally be fired. You can only lose your job (and this trait) as the result of extraordinary misbehavior: assault, gross immorality, etc. Otherwise, your employment and salary are guaranteed for life. This is most common among modern-day university professors, but also applies to judges, priests, senators, etc. in many societies.

Terrain Adaptation ♋ 👽

0 or 5 points

You do not suffer DX or Move penalties for one specific type of unstable terrain: ice, sand, snow, etc. Cost depends on your capabilities:

You can function normally on one specific type of unstable terrain, but suffer the DX and Move penalties that most characters experience on that terrain type when you traverse solid ground: *0 points.*

You can function at full DX and Move both on solid ground *and* on one particular type of unstable terrain: *5 points.*

You must buy this ability separately for each terrain type.

Terror 👤 ⚡

30 points + 10 points per -1 to Fright Check

You can unhinge the minds of others. There are many way this effect can manifest: a chilling howl,

mind-warping body geometry, or even divine awe or unbearable beauty. When you activate this ability, anyone who sees you or hears you (choose *one* when you buy this trait) must roll an immediate Fright Check (see *Fright Checks*, p. 360).

Modifiers: All applicable modifiers under *Fright Check Modifiers* (p. 360). You can buy extra penalties to this Fright Check for 10 points per -1 to the roll. Your victims get +1 per Fright Check after the first within 24 hours.

If a victim succeeds at his Fright Check, he will be unaffected by your Terror for one hour.

Add the Melee Attack limitation (p. 112) if your Terror affects only those you touch.

Special Limitations

Always On: You cannot turn off your Terror to engage in normal social activities. This limitation often accompanies the extreme levels of Appearance – usually Hideous or worse, but possibly also Transcendent! -20%.

Trained By A Master 👤

30 points

You have been trained by – or are – a true master of the martial arts. Your exceptional talent means you have *half* the usual penalty to make a Rapid Strike (see *Melee Attack Options*, p. 370), or to parry more than once per turn (see *Parrying*, p. 376). These benefits apply to *all* your unarmed combat skills (Judo, Karate, etc.) and Melee Weapon skills.

Furthermore, you can focus your inner strength (often called "chi") to perform amazing feats! This permits you to learn Flying Leap, Invisibility Art, Power Blow, and many other skills – anything that requires this advantage as a prerequisite (see Chapter 4).

The GM is free to set prerequisites for this advantage if he wishes. Common examples from fiction include Judo, Karate, Melee Weapon skills, Philosophy, and Theology.

This ability is definitely "larger than life." The GM may wish to forbid it in a realistic campaign.

True Faith 👤 ⚡

15 points

You have a profound religious faith that protects you from "evil" supernatural beings such as demons and vampires. To enjoy this protection, you must actively assert your faith by wielding a physical symbol revered by *your* religion (e.g., crucifix, Torah, or Koran), chanting, dancing, or whatever else is appropriate to your beliefs. If you wish to use this ability in combat – to repel zombies, for instance – then you must choose the Concentrate maneuver each turn, and can do nothing else.

For as long as you assert your faith, no malign supernatural entity (GM's judgment as to what this covers) may approach within one yard of you. If one is forced into this radius, it must leave by the most direct route possible, as if it suffered from Dread (p. 132). If it cannot leave without coming closer, it must make a Will roll. On a success, it may run past you to escape, pushing you aside if necessary (but using only the minimum force required to escape). On a failure, the monster is cowed. It must cower, helplessly, and cannot move, defend itself, or take any other action.

To keep True Faith, you must behave in a manner consistent with your religion. You will nearly always have to take *and adhere to* one or more of the traits listed under *Self-Imposed Mental Disadvantages* (p. 121). In effect, True Faith comes with a built-in Pact limitation (p. 113); do not apply this modifier again. You do *not* have to be kind, loving, or law-abiding, however. A violent bigot or religious terrorist can be just as sincere in his religious devotion as a saintly ascetic.

Tunneling 👹 👽

30 points + 5 points per point of Tunneling Move

You can bore through earth and stone, spewing rubble behind you. The passage you dig is wide enough for you to walk through. You move through stone at half normal Tunneling Move. The GM may wish to assess a chance that your tunnel collapses behind you. Roll each minute vs. the *highest* of Engineer (Mining), Prospecting-3, and IQ-4 to dig a stable tunnel. This can be modified upward for hard rock and

downward for soft rock or loose earth. Each halving of your Tunneling Move gives +1 on this roll.

Ultrahearing 👹 👽

0 or 5 points

You can hear sounds in the frequencies above the normal range of human hearing (20 kHz). This allows you to hear dog whistles, sonar, motion detectors, etc. You can detect active sonar at *twice* its effective range. Cost depends on your capabilities:

You can hear only high-frequency sounds: *0 points.*
You can hear high-frequency sounds *and* other sounds: *5 points.*

This advantage is included in Ultrasonic Speech, below; if you have Ultrasonic Speech, you cannot take this as well (but don't need to).

Ultrasonic Speech 👹 👽

0 or 10 points

You can converse in the ultrasonic range. This advantage *includes* Ultrahearing, above. Note that many creatures find it intensely annoying or even painful to be within earshot of sustained ultrasonic pitches! Cost depends on your capabilities:

You can only communicate via Ultrasonic Speech: *0 points.*
You can switch between regular speech and Ultrasonic Speech at will: *10 points.*

Ultravision 👹 👽

0 or 10 points

You can see ultraviolet light (UV). Solar UV is present outdoors during the day, even under cloud cover, but is stopped by window glass or any solid barrier (earth, stone, etc.). Fluorescent lamps also emit UV. Provided UV is present, you can make out more colors than those with normal vision. This helps you discern outlines; spot trace quantities of dust, dyes, etc.; and identify minerals and plants. You get +2 to all Vision rolls made in the presence of UV, as well as to all Forensics, Observation, and Search rolls to spot clues or hidden objects.

At night, a small amount of UV reaches the ground from the stars. This doesn't let you see in the dark, but it does let you ignore -2 in darkness penalties (cumulative with Night Vision). UV penetrates farther underwater than visible light. This lets you halve all vision penalties underwater (but in *total* darkness, you are as blind as anyone else).

Cost depends on your capabilities:

You can only see UV, and are *blind* indoors, underground, or anywhere else there is no UV, even when there are normal light sources present: *0 points*.

You can see both visible light and UV: *10 points*.

Unaging ♟ ♦

15 points

You never grow old naturally and cannot be aged unnaturally. Your age is fixed at any point you choose and will never change. You never have to make aging rolls.

Special Enhancements

Age Control: You can "age" in either direction at will, at up to 10 times the normal rate. +20%.

Unfazeable ♟

15 points

Nothing surprises you – at least, nothing that's not obviously a threat. The world is full of strange things, and as long as they don't bother you, you don't bother them.

You are exempt from Fright Checks, and reaction modifiers rarely affect you either way. You treat strangers with distant courtesy, no matter how *strange* they are, as long as they're well-behaved. You have the normal reaction penalty toward anyone who does something rude or rowdy, but you remain civil even if forced to violence. Intimidation (p. 202) just does not work on you.

You are not emotionless – you just never display strong feelings. The stereotypical aged kung fu master or English butler has this trait.

You must roleplay this advantage fully, or the GM can declare that it has been lost. In a campaign where Fright Checks are an hourly occurrence, the GM can charge 20 points – or more! – or disallow Unfazeable altogether. This advantage is incompatible with all Phobias.

Universal Digestion ♟ ♦

5 points

You have remarkably adaptable digestive processes that let you derive nutrition from any nontoxic animal or plant protein, no matter how alien or fantastic. This enables you to subsist on things that would normally be harmless but non-nutritious. You have no special resistance to poison, though; for that, buy Resistant (p. 80). One side benefit of this trait is that you can quickly and safely dispose of any nontoxic, organic evidence by *eating* it!

Unkillable ♟ ♦

50 to 150 points

You cannot be killed! You are subject to *all* the other effects of injury. You feel pain, your wounds slow you, and you can be stunned or knocked out. You lose the use of any limb that receives a crippling wound, and you might even lose the limb itself. You can even lose attribute levels, advantages, etc. to disease, injury, or poison. However, you will only *die* if your body is physically destroyed – and sometimes not even then.

This advantage comes in three levels:

Unkillable 1: Injury affects you normally, but you need never make a HT roll to stay alive. You can survive (and even function, if you remain conscious) down to -10×HP, at which point your body is physically destroyed and you die. As long as you are alive, you heal at your usual rate – typically 1 HP/day, modified for any Regeneration (p. 80) you may have. Crippled limbs do heal, but *severed* limbs are gone for good unless you have Regrowth (p. 80). *50 points.*

Unkillable 2: As Unkillable 1, but you do not die at -10×HP. Once you reach -10×HP, you are reduced to an indestructible skeleton and automatically fall unconscious. You sustain no further damage from *any* attack. Once the damage stops, you heal normally – even if you've been hacked to pieces – and any severed body parts will grow back. You regain consciousness once you have *positive* HP. Note that your enemies can imprison your remains while you are unconscious, or even expose them to a source of continuous damage (fire is a common choice) to prevent you from healing. *100 points.*

Unkillable 3: As Unkillable 2, except that at -10×HP, you become a ghost, an energy pattern, or some other incorporeal form that cannot be contained or damaged through normal means. At this stage, you fall unconscious and heal normally. Once you are at *full* HP, your fully intact body will coalesce in a location of the GM's choosing. *150 points.*

With the GM's permission, if you have Unkillable 2 or 3 and are taken to -10×HP, you can trade in Unkillable and use the points to buy a spirit or undead racial template (if such things exist in the setting), becoming a ghost, revenant, etc. once you heal all your HP.

By default, you age normally, and will eventually die of old age. To be truly *immortal*, combine Unkillable with Unaging (above) – and possibly one or more of Doesn't Breathe (p.49), Injury Tolerance (p. 60), Regeneration (p. 80), and Resistant (p. 80).

Special Limitations

Achilles' Heel: Damage from one particular source (possibly one to which you have a Vulnerability, p. 161) can kill you normally. You must make normal HT rolls to survive at -HP and below, and die automatically if this damage takes you below -5×HP. The limitation value depends on the rarity of the attack, as defined under *Limited Defenses* (p. 46): -10% if "Rare," -30% if "Occasional," or -50% if "Common" or "Very Common."

Hindrance: A specific substance (e.g., silver or wood) prevents healing – whether by natural means or Regeneration – for as long as it remains in your body. Once you pass out from your injuries, you stay dormant until this substance is removed. The limitation value depends on the rarity of the substance: -5% if "Rare," -15% if "Occasional," or -25% if "Common."

Reincarnation: This is only available for Unkillable 2 or 3. When reduced to -10×HP, you recover at your usual rate, but you wake up in an entirely new body with new abilities. The GM creates the new form (or may allow you to do so), but you always retain the Unkillable advantage. -20%.

Trigger: This is only available for Unkillable 2 or 3. Once reduced to -10×HP, you require some substance (such as human blood) or condition (such as a ritual) before you will start to heal. Until then, you will remain dormant. The limitation value depends on the rarity of the trigger: -25% if "Rare," -15% if "Occasional," or -5% if "Common" or "Very Common."

Unusual Background 🧠
Variable

This is a "catch-all" trait that the GM can use to adjust the point total of any character with special abilities that are not widely available in the game world. "Special abilities" might mean cinematic traits, magic spells, exotic advantages (for a human), supernatural advantages (for *anyone*), or almost anything else – it depends on the setting. Players are free to suggest Unusual Backgrounds to the GM, but the GM decides whether a proposed Unusual Background is acceptable, and if so, what its cost and benefits are.

Example 1: "Raised by wizards" to justify access to magic spells might be a 0-point special effect in a fantasy world where magic is common, a 10-point Unusual Background in a conspiracy campaign where magic is known but kept secret, and a 50-point Unusual Background – or simply forbidden – in a horror game where a PC who wields supernatural power would reduce the suspense.

Example 2: "Daughter of the God of Magic" to justify the Unkillable advantage would be an Unusual Background in *any* setting, and would be worth as much as the advantage itself – 50 points or more – if the GM allowed it at all.

Not every unusual character concept merits an Unusual Background. The GM should only charge points when the character enjoys a tangible benefit. For instance, it would be unusual for a human to be raised by wolves, but unless this gave him special capabilities (such as Speak with Animals), it would be background color, worth 0 points.

Vacuum Support 🦀 👽
5 points

You are immune to deleterious effects associated with vacuum and decompression (see *Vacuum*, p. 437). This advantage does not give you an air supply; buy Doesn't Breathe (p. 49) for that.

Those with Vacuum Support usually have the Sealed advantage (p. 82), and often have Radiation Tolerance (p. 79) and Temperature Tolerance

(p. 93), but none of these traits are *required*.

Vampiric Bite 🦀 👽
30 points + 5 points per extra HP drained

You can bite people and drain their life force, healing your own wounds in the process. You can only feed if your victim is helpless (pinned, stunned, unconscious, etc.), grappled, or willing. If he is wearing armor, your biting damage must penetrate its DR. Once you've bitten through your victim's DR, you can drain 1 HP *per second* from him. For every 3 HP stolen, you heal 1 HP or 1 FP (your choice). You cannot raise your HP or FP above normal this way.

The basic Vampiric Bite described above costs 30 points. You may buy increased HP drain for 5 points per additional HP drained per second; for instance, to drain 10 HP per second, pay 75 points.

Vampiric Bite also lets you bite in combat *without* feeding. Treat this as Teeth (Sharp Teeth) or Teeth (Sharp Beak) (p. 91) – your choice. You do not need to purchase that advantage separately.

Versatile 🧠
5 points

You are extremely imaginative. You get a +1 bonus on any task that requires creativity or invention, including most rolls against Artist skill, all Engineer rolls for new inventions, and all skill rolls made to use the Gadgeteer advantage.

Very Fit
see *Fit*, p. 55

Very Rapid Healing
see *Rapid Healing*, p. 79

Vibration Sense 🦀 👽
10 points

You can detect the location and size of objects by sensing vibrations with your skin, whiskers, or antennae. You must specify whether this ability works in the air or in the water.

Vibration Sense is *not* a substitute for vision. You can locate an opponent in the dark, but you cannot detect details (e.g., whether he is armed). In

a perfectly still, dark chamber, you would have only a vague notion of the size of the area, but you would be able to sense a barrier before you ran into it, and could find openings by sensing the flow of air or water.

To use Vibration Sense, make a Sense roll. Consult the *Size and Speed/Range Table* (p. 550) and apply *separate* bonuses for the target's size and speed, and a penalty for the range to the target. Wind (in air) or swift currents (in water) will generate "noise" that interferes with your sense. Find the speed of the wind or current on the table and assess the relevant speed *penalty*.

A successful roll reveals the rough size, location, speed, and direction of movement of the target. It does not provide any information about the object's shape, color, etc. Once you have detected something, you may target it with an attack. The modifiers that applied to your Sense roll also apply to your attack roll, but can never give you a bonus to hit.

Note that if you are outside the element (air or water) where your ability functions, or if you are wearing a sealed suit, this ability does not work at all!

Special Enhancements

Universal: Your Vibration Sense works both in the air and in the water. +50%.

Visualization 🧠 ⚡
10 points

You can improve your chances at a task by visualizing yourself successfully performing it. The closer your mental picture is to the actual circumstances, the greater the bonus. The visualization must be detailed and must involve a clear and specific action. This makes it useless in combat, where the situation changes faster than you can visualize it.

To use this talent, you must concentrate for one minute. You, the *player,* must describe the scene you visualize (which can include senses other than sight) and the results you hope to achieve. Then make an IQ roll.

You get a +1 bonus to the action you visualized for every point by which you succeed – *if* the circumstances correspond almost exactly to the visualization. If they are not quite the same, which will almost always be true, halve the bonus (minimum +1). And if something is clearly *different*, divide the bonus by 3 (no minimum). The GM can assess a further bonus of up to +2, or a penalty of any size, for a good or bad description!

Voice

10 points

You have a naturally clear, resonant, and attractive voice. This gives you +2 with the following skills: Diplomacy, Fast-Talk, Mimicry, Performance, Politics, Public Speaking, Sex Appeal, and Singing. You also get +2 on any reaction roll made by someone who can hear your voice.

Walk on Air

20 points

Air, smoke, and other gases are like solid ground beneath your feet, allowing you to walk up and down "invisible stairs" at your ground Move. This won't work in a vacuum – there has to be *some* kind of air present. If you get knocked down or slip, you fall! You may attempt one DX roll per second of falling. If you succeed, you stop in thin air, unharmed. Otherwise, you hit the ground for normal falling damage (see *Falling*, p. 431).

Walk on Liquid

15 points

You can walk on the surface of any liquid as if it were solid ground. You move at your usual ground Move. This doesn't protect you from any damage that you would take from coming into contact with the liquid, however. You can't traverse volcanic lava or boiling acid without taking damage!

Warp

100 points

You have the ability to teleport, traveling from point to point without moving through the intervening space. To do so, you must be able to see your destination with your own eyes, *or* view it remotely (via closed-circuit TV, someone else's eyes using Mind Reading with the Sensory enhancement, etc.), *or* visualize it clearly (which is only possible if you have visited it previously in person).

You can carry up to Basic Lift when you travel, plus any Payload (p. 74). To carry more, or to bring along other people, take the Extra Carrying Capacity enhancement (below).

Make an IQ roll to activate your ability, modified as follows:

Distance: Distance penalties appear on the table below. If actual distance falls between two values, use the *higher.*

Distance	Penalty
10 yards	0
20 yards	-1
100 yards	-2
500 yards	-3
2 miles	-4
10 miles	-5
100 miles	-6
1,000 miles	-7

Add an additional -1 for each 10× increase in distance.

Preparation Time: The amount of time taken to prepare for the teleport affects the IQ roll, as follows:

Preparation Time	IQ Modifier
None	-10
1 second	-5
2 seconds	-4
4 seconds	-3
8 seconds	-2
15 seconds	-1
30 seconds	0
1 minute	+1
2 minutes	+2
4 minutes	+3
8 minutes	+4
15 minutes	+5
30 minutes	+6
1 hour	+7
2 hours	+8
4 hours	+9
8 hours	+10

This table is *not* open-ended; +10 is the maximum possible bonus.

Removal: If you have a "second-hand" view of the destination, you are at -2 per level of removal. For instance, seeing it on TV or through someone else's eyes would give -2, while seeing it on a television set that you are viewing through someone else's eyes would give -4. There is an additional -2 to teleport to a place you have visited but cannot see.

Fatigue Points: Apply a bonus of +1 per FP spent. You must declare this before you roll, and you lose the FP whether you succeed or fail. You never *have* to spend FP, but it is usually a good idea if you must travel far or without much preparation.

On a success, you appear at your target destination. On a failure, you go nowhere and strain your power: you are at -5 to use it again in the next 10 minutes. On a critical failure, you arrive at the *wrong* destination. This can be anywhere the GM wishes! It need not be dangerous, but it should seriously inconvenience you. In addition, your power temporarily "burns out" and will not function again for 1d hours.

You *can* use Warp to evade attacks in combat. Once per turn, you may teleport to any location you can see within 10 yards, instantly. This is considered a dodge. Of course, the IQ roll will be at -10 for instant use, so you might want to spend FP to improve your odds!

You can improve this ability with practice, spending points to add enhancements or remove limitations. You *cannot* take Reduced Fatigue Cost or Reduced Time (p. 108); instead, take Reliable (below) so that you will need less time or fewer FP to teleport reliably.

Special Enhancements

Blind: You can teleport to a specific set of coordinates (distance and direction) without seeing or having visited the destination. This gives you an extra -5 to your IQ roll! You must pay *two* FP per +1 bonus when using this enhancement. +50%.

Extra Carrying Capacity: You can carry more than your Basic Lift. If your carrying capacity is high enough, you may transport *one* person with you. Light encumbrance is +10%; Medium, +20%; Heavy, +30%; Extra-Heavy, +50%.

Wild Talent: You can simply do things without knowing how. It does apply to skills that normally have no default, provided you meet any advantage requirements. It has no effect on skills you already know.

Reliable: Your power is stable and predictable. Each level of this enhancement gives +1 to the IQ roll to use this ability, allowing you to teleport with little preparation (e.g., in combat) or over long distances without spending as many FP to improve your odds. +5% per +1, to a maximum of +10.

Warp Jump: This enhancement is only available if you have the Jumper advantage (p. 64). You must apply it to both Jumper and Warp. If you are both a time- and world-jumper, and wish to use Warp with both abilities, buy this enhancement twice. When you jump, you can simultaneously use Warp to appear *anywhere* at your destination. Two die rolls are necessary – one per ability – and it is possible for one to succeed while the other fails, or for both to fail. +10% per linked Jumper advantage.

Special Limitations

Hyperjump: You physically move through "hyperspace" or "jump space" to journey between destinations. This is not true, instantaneous teleportation; you have an effective speed, which means the trip takes time. On long trips, you will need to address life-support needs! In addition, you cannot activate Hyperjump in atmosphere and you cannot travel distances shorter than one light-second (186,000 miles, -10 to IQ). This effectively limits you to space travel. There is one benefit to Hyperjump: if you possess

Navigation (Hyperspace) skill, you may substitute it for IQ. -50% if your effective speed is the speed of light (every 186,000 miles traveled takes one second); -25% if you can travel one light-year (-17 to IQ) per day.

Naked: You can carry nothing when you teleport! You always arrive naked. -30%.

Psionic Teleportation: Your ability is part of the Teleportation psi power (see p. 257). -10%.

Range Limit: You cannot teleport more than a certain distance per hop. Choose a range and find its distance penalty above. The limitation is worth -5% × (10 + penalty); e.g., 10 yards (-0) would be -50%, while 100 miles (-6) would be -20%. A range limit of more than 100,000 miles is not a meaningful limitation.

Wealth

see p. 25

Above-average Wealth is an advantage, and should be noted on your character sheet.

Weapon Master 👤

Variable

You have a high degree of training or unnerving talent with a particular class of muscle-powered weapons (swords, bows, etc. – *not* guns). Available classes are:

All muscle-powered weapons. *45 points.*

A large class of weapons. *Examples:* all bladed weapons, all one-handed weapons. *40 points.*

A medium class of weapons. *Examples:* all swords, all ninja weapons. *35 points.*

A small class of weapons. *Examples:* fencing weapons (main-gauche, rapier, saber, and smallsword), knightly weapons (broadsword, mace, shield, and lance). *30 points.*

Two weapons normally used together. *Examples:* broadsword and shield, rapier and main-gauche. *25 points.*

One specific weapon. *20 points.*

In all cases, if a weapon can be thrown, the benefits of this advantage also apply when throwing that weapon.

When using a suitable weapon, add +1 *per die* to basic thrust or swing damage if you know the relevant

weapon skill at DX+1. Add +2 per die if you know that skill at DX+2 or better. You also have *half* the usual penalty to make a Rapid Strike (see *Melee Attack Options*, p. 369), or to parry more than once per turn (see *Parrying*, p. 376). None of these benefits apply to default use.

You are familiar with – if not proficient in – every weapon within your class. This gives you an improved default: DX/Easy weapon skills default to DX-1, DX/Average ones to DX-2, and DX/Hard ones to DX-3. Note that these skills are no easier to *learn*, and may not be "bought up" from the improved defaults in order to save points.

Finally, you may learn any cinematic skill that names this advantage as a prerequisite (see Chapter 4) – e.g., Blind Fighting and Power Blow – *if* you could reasonably use that skill with your weapons of choice. The GM is the final arbiter in all cases.

This trait is best suited to a "cinematic" swashbuckling game. The GM may wish to forbid it in a realistic campaign.

Wild Talent 👤 🏹

20 points/level

You can simply *do* things without knowing how. Once per game session per level of this advantage, you may attempt a roll against *any* skill, using your score in the appropriate attribute: IQ for IQ-based skills, DX for DX-based skills, etc. You do not

incur any default penalties, but situational and equipment modifiers apply normally, as do any modifiers for advantages or disadvantages. Tech level is irrelevant: a TL3 monk could make an IQ roll to use Computer Programming/TL12!

Wild Talent *does* apply to skills that normally have no default, provided you meet any advantage requirements. For instance, you could cast unknown magic spells provided you had Magery, or use unknown cinematic martial-arts skills provided you have Trained By A Master.

Wild Talent has *no effect* on skills you already know.

Special Enhancements

Retention: You can learn the skills you use! To do so, you must have one unspent character point available when you attempt the skill roll. On a success, you may buy the skill at the one-point level. You cannot improve a skill learned this way for one month, during which time you use it at -2. On a critical success, you can start improving the skill *immediately,* and there is no -2. On a failure, you cannot learn the skill; on a critical failure, you also lose your unspent character point! Regardless of success, if you lack any of the skill's prerequisites, your skill is at -4 until you acquire them, and you *cannot* improve the skill in the interim. This enhancement does not let you learn skills from a TL higher than your own. +25%.

Special Limitations

Emergencies Only: Your Wild Talent only works in life-threatening situations, such as mortal combat. To use it, you must ask for a particular *result* related to your predicament. Your request must be specific (e.g., "Get him away from me."), but you cannot specify a skill (e.g., "Use Judo" or "Cast the Command spell"). The GM will then choose a skill that could bring about the desired result. He is not limited to mundane skills; he may choose a spell if you have Magery, a cinematic martial-arts skill if you have Trained By A Master, and so forth. Once the GM has chosen, roll against the governing attribute, as usual. If the GM feels you *already* have skills equal to the task, he will advise you on which skill to use. This still counts as one of your uses of Wild Talent! -30%.

Focused: You can only use (and if you have Retention, learn) one specific class of skills. Options include Mental (mundane skills based on IQ, Perception, or Will), Physical (mundane skills based on ST, DX, or HT), Magical (spells), and Chi (cinematic martial-arts skill). -20%.

Xeno-Adaptability
see *Cultural Adaptability*, p. 46

Zeroed 🤝

10 points

You do not officially exist. Even the highest authorities in the land know nothing about you. In a fantasy setting, you are a "mysterious wanderer"; magical divination cannot discover conclusive details about your past or true identity. In a high-tech world, you don't appear in the public records – and if computer databases exist, they contain no evidence of your existence. You must provide a reason for this; e.g., your parents hid you away at birth, you are legally dead, or you somehow managed to destroy all the records (explain how!).

To maintain this status, you must deal strictly in cash or commodities. Credit and bank accounts must be blind (keyed to pass-code, not a person – the "Swiss bank account") or set up through a Temporary Identity (see p. 31).

If the authorities investigate you, they will initially assume that there has been an error. They will become increasingly concerned as no information can be found about your life. Eventually, they will attempt to apprehend you. If they can't find you, then they're likely to give up. But if they catch you, you are in for a thorough interrogation, possibly involving torture, mind probes, or worse. After all, a nonperson has no rights . . . and it will be very difficult for your allies to prove that you are being held, as you don't officially exist!

PERKS

A "perk" is a very minor advantage, worth only 1 point. Perks cannot be modified with enhancements or limitations, and they can be added in play without upsetting game balance. Otherwise, perks use the same rules as other advantages.

The GM is encouraged to create new perks. No perk should provide wealth, social standing, or combat bonuses. A perk can provide a modest bonus (up to +2) to an attribute, skill, or reaction roll in relatively rare circumstances. The GM may allow more generous bonuses, if they apply only in *extremely* rare situations.

Accessory 🔧 👽

Your body incorporates a tool or other useful gadget (e.g., a siren or a vacuum cleaner) that provides minor, noncombat benefits not otherwise covered by a specific advantage.

Alcohol Tolerance 🔧

Your body metabolizes alcohol with remarkable efficiency. You can drink steadily for an indefinite period with no major detrimental effects. *Binging* affects you as it would anyone else. You get +2 on all HT rolls related to drinking.

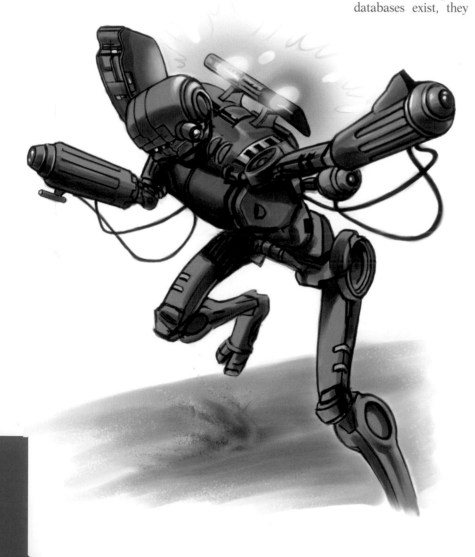

Autotrance ♟

You can enter a trance at will. This requires one minute of complete concentration and a successful Will roll, at -1 per additional attempt per hour. This trance gives +2 on rolls to contact spirits, etc. You must make a Will roll to break your trance. If you fail, you can try again every five minutes.

Deep Sleeper ♛

You can fall asleep in all but the worst conditions, and can sleep through most disturbances. You never suffer any ill effects due to the quality of your sleep. You get an IQ roll to notice disturbances and awaken, just like anyone else; success is automatic if you have Combat Reflexes.

Fur ♛ ☻

You have fur. This prevents sunburn. Thicker fur might justify 1-3 levels each of Damage Resistance (p. 46) and Temperature Tolerance (p. 93), while spiky "fur" might grant Spines (p. 88). You must buy these other traits separately.

Honest Face ♛

You simply look honest, reliable, or generally harmless. This has nothing to do with your reputation among those who know you, or how virtuous you *really* are! People who don't know you will tend to pick you as the one to confide in, or *not* to pick you if they are looking for a potential criminal or troublemaker. You won't be spot-checked by customs agents and the like unless they have another reason to suspect you, or unless they are truly choosing at random. You have a +1 to trained Acting skill for the sole purpose of "acting innocent."

No Hangover ♛

No matter how much you drink, you will never get a hangover. This does not mitigate the effects of intoxication – it just eliminates the unpleasant aftereffects.

Penetrating Voice ♛

You can really make yourself heard! In situations where you want to be heard over noise, others get +3 to

their Hearing roll. At the GM's option, you get +1 to Intimidation rolls if you surprise someone by yelling or roaring.

Sanitized Metabolism ♛ ☻

You are totally *clean*. Your body produces minimal, sanitized waste products, and you never suffer from bad breath, excessive perspiration, or unsightly skin problems. This gives -1 to attempts to track you by scent and +1 to reaction rolls in close confines (cramped spaceships, submarines, elevators, etc.).

Shtick ♟/♛

You have a cool move or slick feature that sets you apart from the masses. This provides no combat or reaction bonuses, and you can't use it to earn money, but it might occasionally give you some minor benefit in play (GM's discretion). *Example:* your clothing is always spotless, even after combat or swimming the Nile; you can run, climb, fight, etc. while wearing high heels without suffering any special penalty for bad footing.

MODIFIERS

A *modifier* is a feature that you can add to a trait – usually an advantage – to change the way it works. There are two basic types of modifiers: *enhancements* and *limitations*. Adding an enhancement makes the underlying trait more useful, while applying a limitation attaches additional restrictions to your ability.

Modifiers adjust the base cost of a trait in proportion to their effects. Enhancements *increase* the cost, while limitations *reduce* the cost. This is expressed as a percentage. For instance, a +20% enhancement would increase the point cost of an advantage by 1/5 its base cost, while a -50% limitation would reduce it by half its base cost.

You can apply any number of modifiers to a trait. Total them to find the net modifier, and then apply this modifier to the base cost of the trait. Round the resulting cost *up* to the next-highest whole number. For example, a +10% enhancement, a +40% enhancement, a -30% limitation, and a -45% limitation would give a net modifier of -25%. This would reduce the cost of a 10-point advantage to 7.5 points, which would round up to 8 points.

Modifiers can *never* reduce cost by more than 80%. Treat a net modifier of -80% or worse as -80%. Thus, no matter how many limitations you take, you cannot lower the cost of a trait to less than 1/5 its base cost.

The GM has the final say as to which traits you can modify, and in what ways. Some combinations make no sense (imagine Unaging with the Limited Use limitation!), others have potential for abuse, and still others might not suit the campaign. Percentile modifiers can also result in a lot of extra math. GMs who prefer to keep things simple may wish to prohibit modifiers altogether.

Special Modifiers

Many advantages, and some disadvantages, offer "special enhancements" and "special limitations." These modifiers are generally applicable only to the specific trait(s) with which they are described. However, the GM may choose to extend the special modifiers of one particular trait to other, very similar traits.

Range, Area, and Duration for Advantages

When applying modifiers, you occasionally need to know the range, area of effect, or duration of an advantage for which one or more of these quantities is not specified - for instance, when applying an enhancement that gives a range to an ability that normally has none. Assume that *range* is 100 yards, *area* is a circle 2 yards in radius (and 12' high, should volume matter), and *duration* is 10 seconds, unless the advantage specifies otherwise. Exceptions will be noted.

ENHANCEMENTS

You can apply enhancements to advantages, and more rarely to basic attributes and secondary characteristics. The GM might even permit specific enhancements on certain *skills*, but this is difficult to justify unless the skill functions much as an advantage (which is sometimes true of racially innate skills possessed by non-humans).

Accurate 🔫

+5%/level

Your attack is unusually accurate. Each +1 to Accuracy is a +5% enhancement.

Affects Insubstantial 🔫

+20%

Your ability affects insubstantial targets *in addition to* normal, substantial things.

Note to GMs: This enhancement is *very* powerful. It lets insubstantial characters affect the material world with little fear of retribution. Feel free to disallow it, restrict it to NPCs, or to make sure that *lots* of foes have the Affects Insubstantial enhancement!

Area Effect 🔫

+50%/level

Your ability works as an area power instead of affecting a single target. Everything in the area suffers the attack's damage or other effects. On a miss, use the scatter rules (p. 414) to see where the area is centered. Active defenses don't protect against an area attack, but victims may attempt to dive for cover or dodge and retreat to leave the area. For more information, see *Area and Spreading Attacks* (p. 413).

Radius	Modifier
2 yards	+50%
4 yards	+100%
8 yards	+150%
16 yards	+200%

Attack Enhancements and Limitations

Some enhancements and limitations are intended only for Affliction, Binding, and Innate Attack, and for advantages modified with the Ranged enhancement (p. 107). They are called "attack" modifiers. Certain of these have additional restrictions; e.g., Armor Divisor applies only to Affliction and Innate Attack. Attack enhancements and limitations are marked 🔫.

Turning Enhancements Off and On

When you use an enhanced trait, you must use *all* of its enhancements unless a particular enhancement – or the underlying ability itself – explicitly allows you to turn an enhancement "off." (The extended capabilities that many enhancements provide might have no effect in certain situations, but they are still *on.*) To be able to pick which enhancements are "on" at any given moment, take the Selectivity enhancement (p. 108).

Affects Substantial

+40%

Your ability affects substantial targets even when *you* are insubstantial. It also affects insubstantial creatures normally. (Do not add this enhancement to magical or psi abilities; these can already affect the substantial world at -3.)

Further levels continue to double the radius. If applied to an advantage that *already* covers an area, each level doubles the base radius.

Area Effect is a prerequisite for Mobile (p. 107), Persistent (p. 107), Selective Area (p. 108), Bombardment (p. 111), and Emanation (p. 112).

Armor Divisor 🔫

Variable

Your attack can pierce more armor than its base damage would indicate.

Armor Divisor	Modifier
(2)	+50%
(3)	+100%
(5)	+150%
(10)	+200%

Only Innate Attacks and Afflictions can have this enhancement. Armor Divisor is a "penetration modifier"; you cannot combine it with other penetration modifiers, such as Contact Agent (p. 103) and Follow-Up (p. 105).

Aura 🔫

+80%

Your attack takes the form of a malefic aura that affects anyone you touch (reach C) or who touches you. If a weapon strikes you, your aura affects the weapon. You can switch the aura on or off at the start of your turn (if not, take Always On, p. 110). You *must* take Aura in conjunction with Melee Attack (p. 112) at the -30% level (reach C), and you cannot claim the extra -5% for "cannot parry" – an aura cannot parry in the first place.

The classic example of an Aura is the sheath of flame surrounding a fire elemental. See *Body of Fire* (p. 262) for how to write this up.

Based on (Different Attribute) 🔫

+20%

This enhancement is only available for abilities that allow a resistance roll against ST, DX, IQ, HT, Perception, or Will. It moves the resistance roll from the usual attribute or characteristic to a different one, specified when you buy the ability. This is considered an enhancement because it lets you fine-tune your ability to be more effective against targets with known weaknesses.

Blood Agent 🔫

+100%

On an attack with Area Effect or Cone, this is an *enhancement*. See the Blood Agent limitation (p. 110) for details.

Cone

Variable

Your attack spreads to affect everyone in a cone-shaped area. Cones use special rules; see *Area and Spreading Attacks* (p. 413). Decide on the maximum width of the cone, in yards, at the attack's maximum range. Cone costs +50% *plus* +10% per yard of maximum width.

You cannot combine Cone with Area Effect, Aura, Jet, Melee Attack, Rapid Fire, or Emanation.

Contact Agent

+150%

On an attack with Area Effect or Cone, this is an *enhancement*. See the Contact Agent limitation (p. 111) for more information.

Cosmic

Variable

Your ability operates on a "higher level" than is usual in your game world. This allows it to work under all circumstances, and possibly even ignore opposing powers! The value of the enhancement depends on the underlying trait:

Ability other than an attack or a defense. Your ability is not subject to the usual built-in restrictions. For instance, your Healing might cure otherwise "incurable" diseases, your Insubstantiality might allow you to penetrate barriers that would block other insubstantial beings, or your Shapeshifting might be immune to negation by external forces. +50%.

Defense or countermeasure. Your defensive trait provides its usual benefits against offensive abilities modified with the Cosmic enhancement. +50%.

Attack with a lingering special effect. Your attack has an enduring effect that only another Cosmic power can counteract; e.g., a burning Innate Attack that sets fires that water cannot extinguish, or a toxic Innate Attack that inflicts Cyclic (below) damage that medical technology cannot halt. This does *not* negate the target's protection! DR still affects Innate Attack, a HT roll is still allowed for a Resistible (p. 115) attack, etc. +100%.

Irresistible attack. Your attack *does* negate the target's protection; e.g., an Innate Attack that ignores DR, or Mind Control that ignores Mind Shield. The target may still attempt an active defense against the attack, if applicable. You cannot combine this enhancement with other "penetration modifiers," such as Follow-Up (p. 105). +300%.

Cyclic

Variable

This enhancement is only available for Innate Attacks that inflict burning, corrosion, fatigue, or toxic damage. It represents an attack that persists *on the victim*: acid, disease, liquid fire, poison, etc. (For attacks that linger in the environment, see *Persistent*, p. 107.)

A Cyclic attack damages its target normally – but once the target has been exposed, the attack damages him *again* each time a set interval passes! All penetration modifiers (e.g., Contact or Follow-Up) continue to apply; for instance, a Cyclic attack with Follow-Up continues to ignore DR. Worst of all, the victim cannot recover HP or FP lost to a Cyclic attack until the attack stops damaging him!

Guided: You steer your attack to the target using your own skill. This lets you ignore all *range* penalties to hit! If the target is so distant that your attack needs multiple turns to reach it (see below), you must take a Concentrate maneuver each turn. If you lose sight of the target while the attack is en route, your attack automatically misses. +50%.

Homing: Your attack steers itself. Decide how it seeks its target: with ordinary vision or a sensory advantage such as Detect (p. 48), Infravision (p. 60), Night Vision (p. 71), Scanning Sense (p. 81), or Vibration Sense (p. 96). The attack uses this sense for the purpose of combat modifiers; e.g., radar ignores darkness but can be jammed. To "lock on," you must Aim at the target and make an unmodified skill roll. Do not roll against your skill to hit. Instead, use the attack's skill of 10 – plus Accuracy, if you made your skill roll – and ignore all range penalties. Homing costs a base +50%, *plus* 1% per point the chosen homing mechanism would cost if bought as an advantage (without any modifiers); e.g., Infravision costs 10 points, making Homing (Infravision) +60%. Ordinary vision uses the base +50%.

If a Guided or Homing attack has a 1/2D statistic, read this as the attack's *speed* in yards/second. The attack can hit a target at up to its 1/2D range on the turn you launch it. It requires multiple turns to reach more distant targets. Do *not* halve damage, but defer the attack roll until the attack reaches its target.

For more information, see *Guided and Homing Weapons* (p. 412).

Increased Range

+10%/level

You may add this enhancement to any advantage that has a range; e.g., Innate Attack or Scanning Sense. Each level increases range as follows:

Range Multiple	Modifier
2×	+10%
5×	+20%
10×	+30%
20×	+40%
50×	+50%
100×	+60%

Further levels follow the same "2-5-10" progression.

If applied to a ranged attack, each level increases 1/2D *and* Max. You may increase 1/2D or Max individually at half cost (that is, "Increased 1/2D" and "Increased Max" are +5%/level). However, you cannot increase 1/2D past Max. At most, you can make 1/2D *equal* to Max – this means the attack has *no* 1/2D range. For attacks that already have no 1/2D range, you can increase Max for +5%/level.

Jet 🔫

+0%

Your attack is a continuous stream, like a flamethrower. Treat it as a melee weapon with a very long reach rather than as a ranged weapon. Do not apply penalties for target range and speed.

An attack with Jet has no Acc, and has 1/2D 5 and Max 10 instead of its usual range. Increased Range increases range by 100% per level instead of its usual effects.

Jet is incompatible with Area Effect, Aura, Cone, Follow-Up, Melee Attack, and Rapid Fire.

Link

+10% or +20%

You can use two or more advantages simultaneously, as if they were a single ability. For +10%, your abilities are permanently linked into a single power, and must be used together – you *cannot* use them separately. For +20%, you can also use them separately. You must add this enhancement to *all* the abilities you wish to link.

If you link two attacks into one and give them identical Malf., 1/2D, Max, Acc, RoF, Shots, and Recoil, you can treat them as a *single* attack with one attack roll but separate rolls for damage. This is not the same as the Follow-Up enhancement (p. 105)!

Low or No Signature 🔫

+10% or +20%

An attack normally has a "signature": a flash of light, a sound, etc. If left unspecified, this is assumed to be similar to a gunshot or a stroke of lightning – that is, a brilliant flash and a loud report. This enhancement makes your attack less obvious.

Low Signature: The attack is no more easily identifiable as an attack than the loud pop of a champagne cork; e.g., a suppressed pistol shot. +10%.

No Signature: The attack is almost completely unnoticeable; e.g., a blowgun's dart. Alternatively, it is utterly undetectable by normal means, but leaves a magical or psionic trace. +20%.

Malediction 🔫

Variable

Your attack is not a conventional ranged attack; it works more like a Regular spell (p. 239). It lacks Malf., 1/2D, Max, Acc, RoF, Shots, and Recoil statistics, and cannot have any enhancement or limitation that modifies those statistics. Most important, the target's DR has *no effect* on the attack's damage, resistance roll, or other effects!

Malediction requires a Concentrate maneuver rather than an Attack maneuver to use. It can target any victim you can see or otherwise clearly perceive. To determine if the attack succeeds, roll against your Will, applying the range penalties detailed below. Your foe may choose to resist; if so, resolve the attack as a Quick Contest of Will. You must *win* to affect the victim.

When enhancing an Affliction, the Quick Contest above *replaces* the usual resistance roll. You roll against Will, but your target rolls against HT – or other attribute, if the attack has Based on (Different Attribute) – modified as usual for the Affliction. For instance, an Affliction that allows a HT-1 roll to resist would result in a Quick Contest of your Will vs. the target's HT-1.

The value of Malediction depends on the range modifiers it uses. If it takes -1 per yard of range, like a Regular spell, it costs +100%. If it uses the range penalties on the *Size and Speed/Range Table* (p. 550), it costs +150%. And if it uses the penalties given under *Long-Distance Modifiers* (p. 241), it costs +200%.

Malediction is a "penetration modifier"; you cannot combine it with other penetration modifiers, nor with modifiers that apply only to conventional ranged attacks.

Mobile

+40%/level

You may only add this enhancement to an attack that has both Area Effect (p. 102) *and* Persistent (below). The area of effect moves under your control. Move equals thc level of the enhancement (Move 1 at +40%, Move 2 at +80%, and so on), and cannot exceed the attack's Max range.

To move the area of effect, you must take a Concentrate maneuver. To make the mobile area autonomous, add Homing (which causes it to attack the nearest valid target) and possibly Selective Area (so it only seeks out enemies). Buy these enhancements *twice* if they're intended to apply to both the initial attack roll and the autonomous area.

Mobile is mutually exclusive with Drifting (p. 105).

Overhead

+30%

Your attack can alter its angle to strike from a different side of the target – usually the top. This bypasses any cover that does not provide overhead protection, and negates attack penalties to hit crouching, kneeling, sitting, or prone targets. (If you are already above or below your target, adjust this appropriately.) Use this to represent a rain of fire, a missile that swoops up and then dives down at the last moment, an airburst grenade, etc.

Persistent

+40%

You may only add this enhancement to an Area Effect (p. 102) attack. This causes the area of effect to remain in place for 10 seconds, continuing to damage (or attack and *possibly* damage, if taken with Bombardment, p. 111) anyone entering or passing through it. Use Extended Duration to increase the duration.

Ranged

+40%

This enhancement gives range to an advantage that normally affects your immediate area, or that requires a touch to affect others. By default, it has 1/2D 10, Max 100, Acc 3, RoF 1, Shots N/A, and Recoil 1. Duration is 10 seconds, unless the ability lists another duration (like Neutralize or Possession) or is instantaneous (like Healing), and you cannot use the ability again until all existing effects have worn off. You can apply other modifiers to change the ranged combat statistics and duration.

This enhancement is normally restricted to Healing, Mana Damper, Mana Enhancer, Neutralize, Possession, and Psi Static. The GM is free to allow it on other traits, but it should *never* modify body weaponry (such as Strikers or Vampiric Bite) or abilities that already have a range.

Rapid Fire

Variable

An Innate Attack's base Rate of Fire (RoF) is 1. Consult the table below to find the cost for a higher RoF:

RoF	Cost
2	+40%
3	+50%
4-7	+70%
8-15	+100%
16-30	+150%
31-70	+200%
71-150	+250%
151-300	+300%

Two special options are available for attacks with this enhancement:

Multiple Projectile: Each shot splits into multiple projectiles after you attack, like a shotgun blast or forked lightning. Express this as a multiplier following RoF; for instance, RoF 3×4 means each of three shots fired divides into four individual projectiles. Modifier cost is based on the RoF times the multiplier; e.g., RoF 3×4 costs the same as RoF 12.

Selective Fire: You may designate a RoF 5+ attack as Selective Fire, allowing it to fire as if it had RoF 1-3. This costs an extra +10%.

Reduced Fatigue Cost

+20%/level

You may only take this enhancement for abilities that cost FP, and never in conjunction with the special modifier "Usually On." You can take it any number of times. Each level cuts the cost to use the ability by 1 FP. If you must "maintain" the ability by spending FP on a regular basis, reduce this maintenance cost by a like amount.

Reduced Time

+20%/level

You may only add this enhancement to abilities that require time to activate. You can take it any number of times. Each level halves the time required to use the ability (round up). Once time is reduced to one second, a further level of Reduced Time makes the ability *instantaneous* – using it is a free action.

Note that you *cannot* add Reduced Time to attack powers, to traits that list any kind of special modifier that affects activation time, or to Magery (to reduce casting times).

Respiratory Agent

+50%

Your attack must be inhaled to have any effect, but it ignores *all* DR. Only Doesn't Breathe and Filter Lungs protect completely – although a victim who makes a Sense roll to notice the attack in time may hold his breath (see *Holding Your Breath*, p. 351). To make your attack less noticeable, take Low Signature (p. 106).

You may only add this enhancement to an Affliction or to an Innate Attack that inflicts toxic or fatigue damage, and you *must* combine it with one of Area Effect (p. 102), Cone (p. 103), or Jet (p. 106). Persistent (p. 107) is common but not required.

Respiratory Agent is a "penetration modifier"; you cannot combine it with other penetration modifiers, such as Follow-Up (p. 105).

Selective Area

+20%

You may add this enhancement to any Area Effect (p. 102) or Cone (p. 103) attack. It lets you choose which targets within your area are actually affected.

Selectivity

+10%

This enhancement lets you turn a trait's *other* enhancements off and on at will. For instance, if you had an attack with Area Effect, you could turn this enhancement off to affect only one other person. You must specify which enhancements you wish to ignore *before* you activate the ability. The default assumption is that you are always using all of your enhancements.

By allowing you to select which enhancements you use, Selectivity permits you to have multiple versions of the same ability without having to buy the ability multiple times. This can be extremely useful when creating comic-book supers!

Sense-Based ✈

Variable

Your attack is channeled through your victim's senses, allowing it to ignore DR! You must specify the sense(s) affected. Examples include vision, hearing, smell, and exotic senses such as Detect. This is worth +150%, plus an extra +50% per sense after the first; e.g., Vision and Hearing-Based would be +200%.

Your attack only affects someone who is using the targeted sense. For instance, a Vision-Based attack cannot affect a blind subject or someone with his eyes closed, while a Smell-Based attack doesn't work underwater or on a target with a gas mask. Advantages (such as Protected Sense, p. 78) and equipment that protect the sense in question either negate the attack completely or, in the case of attacks that allow a roll to resist (such as Afflictions, Maledictions, and Resistible attacks), give a bonus to the resistance roll.

The most common Sense-Based attack is an Affliction that knocks out the sense it is based on; for instance, Affliction (Blindness; Vision-Based) for a blinding flash. However, Sense-Based attacks can also be deadly, like a banshee's wail or basilisk's gaze.

Sense-Based is a "penetration modifier"; you cannot combine it with other penetration modifiers, such as Follow-Up (p. 105).

Exception: You *can* combine Sense-Based with Malediction (p. 106). In conjunction with Malediction, or when added to an ability that already ignores DR (e.g., Mind Control or Mind Reading), Sense-Based becomes a *limitation*. It is worth -20% if it works through one sense, -15% if two senses, or -10% if three senses. If it works through more than three senses, it is not a significant limitation.

Side Effect ✈

Variable

You may only add this enhancement to an Innate Attack, and you cannot combine it with penetration modifiers other than Armor Divisor. If *any* damage penetrates the target's DR, he must make a HT roll, at -1 per 2 points of penetrating damage, or suffer a "side effect."

Choose the side effects from the effects described for Affliction (p. 35). Valid choices are stunning, Attribute Penalty, Disadvantage, and Incapacitation. The cost of Side Effect is a base +50%, *plus* the cost of the Affliction enhancements. For instance, stunning would be +50%, while Disadvantage (Blindness) would be +100%.

You may specify more than one side effect. If the victim gets a single resistance roll against all of them, treat them as a single Side Effect enhancement, totaling their cost. If the victim must resist each effect individually, take a separate Side Effect enhancement for each effect.

Stunning wears off normally, while other effects last (20 - HT) minutes, minimum 1 minute. If Incapacitation is combined with other effects, the other effects last for *another* (20 - HT) minutes after the Incapacitation wears off.

Symptoms ✈

Variable

Symptoms are effects that occur if the cumulative damage (HP or FP loss) inflicted by the enhanced Innate Attack exceeds a fraction of the victim's basic HP or FP. The victim does *not* get a HT roll to resist Symptoms! The GM should consider limiting Symptoms to attacks that inflict 1d damage or less.

Choose Symptoms from the following effects described as enhancements for Affliction (p. 35): Advantage, Attribute Penalty, Disadvantage, Irritant, and Negated Advantage. If the threshold for the Symptom is 2/3 the victim's basic HP, use the cost under Affliction. If the threshold is 1/2 basic HP, *double* this cost. If it's 1/3 basic HP, *triple* this cost.

Example: Blindness is worth +50% as an Affliction, but as a Symptom that occurs when the victim has lost half his HP to an Innate Attack, it is a +100% enhancement.

Unlike Afflictions, Symptoms abate only when the damage that caused them is healed. In the example above, the Blindness would only end when the victim's HP healed past the halfway point.

An Innate Attack can have multiple Symptoms, representing different effects that that occur at different damage thresholds.

Underwater ✈

+20%

Attacks are assumed to be usable in air or in vacuum, but ineffective in liquid. This enhancement lets an attack work underwater at 1/10 range.

Variable ✈

+5%

You can reduce the level of your attack. For example, if you have an Innate Attack that normally does 3d damage, you could reduce it to 1d or 2d damage. You must indicate this before you make your attack roll.

Wall ✈

+30% or +60%

You may only add this enhancement to an attack that has both Area Effect (p. 102) and Persistent (p. 107).

For +30%, you can set up your Area Effect as a wall filled with the substance or effect of your ability. This affects anyone or anything passing through it. You get a three-yard-long by one-yard-wide wall per yard of radius in your area.

For +60%, your wall works as above, but you can form it into any shape you choose.

You must define your wall as either *permeable* or *rigid*:

Permeable: The wall is composed of liquid, gas, energy, or an amorphous solid (e.g., thorn bushes). It impedes vision, and inflicts damage on anyone who attempts to cross it, but an intruder can traverse it provided he is not stunned, knocked out, killed, etc. by its effects. Anything effective against the substance of the wall will disperse it; e.g., water or a fire extinguisher could extinguish a wall of fire.

Rigid: The wall is a material barrier. This is only possible for Innate Attacks that deal crushing, cutting, impaling, or piercing damage. Each yard of wall has DR 3 and 1/2 HP per die of damage (round up); e.g., a 6d attack produces a wall with DR 18 and 3 HP. The wall does no damage itself, but the damage type applies to the injury inflicted on anyone crashing into it.

LIMITATIONS

You can apply limitations to almost *any* trait (although as with enhancements, skills are normally off-limits). When you apply a limitation to a disadvantage, you reduce its value *as a disadvantage;* e.g., a -10% limitation on a -25-point disadvantage would make it a -22.5-point trait, which rounds to -22 points. Limited disadvantages are worth fewer points because they affect you under more restricted circumstances.

Remember that no matter how many limitations you take, you cannot reduce the cost of a trait by more than 80%. That is, when totaling modifiers, treat net modifiers below -80% as -80%.

> *You can apply limitations to almost any trait. When you apply a limitation to a disadvantage, you reduce its value as a disadvantage. Limited disadvantages are worth fewer points because they affect you under more restricted circumstances.*

Accessibility

Variable

Accessibility is a catchall limitation you can use to cover any restriction not specifically defined elsewhere. Accessibility limitations fall into two broad categories: those that limit the *targets* your ability can affect and those that limit the *situations* in which it works.

If your ability can only affect certain targets, the limitation depends on how common the target group is. "Only on women," "Only on men," or anything else that covers about half of the population is worth -20%. "Only on Electrical" or "Only on machines" is worth -20% in a technological setting. "Only on sea creatures" is worth -30% – unless the campaign is set on a world mostly covered with water, in which case it isn't worth more than -10%. "Only on aliens" is worth -30% or -40%, depending on the world. "Only on psis" is worth -50% in

most settings. "Not on redheads" is identical to "On everyone but redheads," and is worth -10%.

The same yardstick applies to limitations based on the situation. "Only at day" or "Only at night" is worth -20%. "Only in direct sunlight" is worth -30%. "Only in water" is worth -30% on Earth – but more on a desert planet and less on an ocean world. "Only during full moon" or "Only during new moon" is worth -40%. And "Useless under stress" is a whopping -60%, since it makes the ability worthless in most adventuring situations!

You can also link situational Accessibility to your actions. The more unusual, difficult, or obnoxious the required action is, the greater the limitation value. Some examples:

Only in altered body form (Invisible, Insubstantial, etc.): *-10%.*
Only while playing trumpet: *-20%.*
Only while flying, Only while swimming, Only in hypnotic trance: *-30%.*
Only by one side of split personality: *-40%.*

In all cases, if the ability is only weakened (half power) instead of becoming useless, *halve* the value of the limitation.

The GM shouldn't allow meaningless Accessibility limitations. For instance, buying a helpful ability with the limitation "Only on friends" gives no cost break. Buying it with "Only on enemies" would be interesting, though! Likewise, the GM should reject any proposed limitation that is already implicit in the ability. For instance, "Only while flying" is not an acceptable limitation for Enhanced Move (Air).

Always On

Variable

You cannot switch your advantage off. You may only add this to an ability that can normally be switched off *and* that is inconvenient if you can't turn it off. It is worth -10% if the effects are social or cosmetic, -20% if they are physically inconvenient, and -40% if they are dangerous (to you!). Always On appears as a "special limitation" for most of the traits to which it would apply. The GM can add new costs as appropriate for other abilities.

Armor Divisor

Variable

Your attack can pierce less armor than its base damage would indicate. "Divisor" is the factor by which you divide. "DR Multiplier" is an equivalent calculation – multiply your opponent's DR by this number.

Divisor	DR Multiplier	Modifier
(0.5)	2	-30%
(0.2)	5	-50%
(0.1)	10	-70%

In addition, if you have *any* level of this limitation, targets that have DR 0 (e.g., bare flesh) get DR 1 against your attack.

Only Innate Attacks and Afflictions can have this limitation. Armor Divisor is a "penetration modifier"; you cannot combine it with other penetration modifiers, such as Contact Agent (p. 103) and Follow-Up (p. 105).

Blood Agent

-40%

Your attack must reach a mucous membrane (eyes, open mouth, nose, etc.) or an open wound to have any effect *at all*. DR *always* stops it.

This limitation is intended for Afflictions, and for Innate Attacks that inflict fatigue or toxic damage. It is especially appropriate for poisonous spit or spray. In conjunction with Aura (p. 102), it can also represent an attack that is delivered via intimate physical contact.

Exception: If the attack also has Area Effect (p. 102) or Cone (p. 103), Blood Agent works as described above and also when inhaled (like Respiratory Agent, p. 108). This lets it ignore *all* DR. Only targets with the

Sealed advantage (p. 82) – or with one of Doesn't Breathe (p. 49) or Filter Lungs (p. 55) *and* one of Nictitating Membrane (p. 71) or Protected Vision (p. 78) – are immune. This powerful ability converts Blood Agent into a +100% *enhancement* when combined with Area Effect or Cone!

This is a "penetration modifier"; you cannot combine it with other penetration modifiers, such as Follow-Up (p. 105).

Bombardment 🔫

Variable

You may only take this limitation in conjunction with Area Effect (p. 102) or Cone (p. 103). The attack does not automatically hit everyone in the area. Instead, it attacks each potential target in the area at an effective skill, which sets the value of the limitation.

Effective Skill	Modifier
14	-5%
12	-10%
10	-15%
8	-20%

Modify effective skill for target size only – not for range or for any other factor. Determine hit location randomly. If the target is under cover, the cover protects normally against the damage.

This limitation is intended for attacks like electrical or ice storms, which could affect some but not all individuals within a given area.

Contact Agent 🔫

-30%

Your attack must touch bare skin or porous clothing to have any effect *at all*. DR *always* stops it.

This enhancement is intended for Afflictions, and for Innate Attacks that inflict fatigue or toxic damage. Taken with Aura (p. 102), it can represent a "contagious" attack that spreads via skin contact.

Exception: If the attack also has Area Effect (p. 102) or Cone (p. 103), Contact Agent lets it ignore *all* DR. Only targets with the Sealed advantage (p. 82) are immune. This powerful ability converts Contact Agent into a +150% *enhancement* when combined with Area Effect or Cone!

This is a "penetration modifier"; you cannot combine it with other penetration modifiers, such as Follow-Up (p. 105).

Costs Fatigue

Variable

Your ability costs FP to use. This is worth -5% per FP per use. What constitutes a "use" depends on the underlying trait.

For abilities that produce instantaneous effects (e.g., Innate Attack), you must pay this FP cost every time you trigger the ability.

For advantages that produce continuing effects (e.g., Flight), you must pay this FP cost to activate the ability for one minute. However, once you have paid this initial cost, you need only pay *half* as many FP (round up) per minute to keep the ability active. If an advantage that produces continuing effects only lasts one *second*, and you must pay the cost to maintain it every second, this doubles the value of the limitation to -10% per FP.

Damage Limitations 🔫

Variable

You may add the following limitations to an Innate Attack:

No Blunt Trauma (nbt)

-20%

An attack that inflicts crushing, cutting, impaling, or piercing damage normally inflicts blunt trauma (see p. 379). Add this limitation if it does not.

No Knockback (nkb)

-10%

An attack that inflicts crushing or cutting damage normally inflicts knockback (see p. 378). Add this limitation if it does not.

No Wounding (nw)

-50%

The attack inflicts basic damage, and may cause knockback and blunt trauma, but its penetrating damage has no wounding effect (HP or FP loss). Apply this limitation to a crushing attack to represent effects such as a mighty gust of wind or jet of water. Use it with impaling, piercing, or cutting attacks that are carriers for Afflictions or Innate Attacks (usually those that inflict fatigue or toxic damage) with the Follow-Up modifier (p. 105); this represents small poison darts, stings, etc. that can slip through armor without inflicting grievous wounds.

Dissipation ⌐

-50%

You may only take this limitation in conjunction with Area Effect (p. 102) or Cone (p. 103). The further the victim is from the center of the area or the apex of the cone, the less effective your attack is. See *Area and Spreading Attacks* (p. 413) for details.

Emanation ⌐

-20%

You may only take this limitation in conjunction with Area Effect (p. 102). It means the effect has no range or Accuracy, but radiates from your body (without affecting *you*, if the effect is a bad one). This is incompatible with Melee Attack and ranged attack modifiers.

Emergencies Only

-30%

Your ability is triggered by your fear or excitement; you cannot use it under "routine" conditions. The GM is the final arbiter. He may rule that multiple successive failures of your power make you angry enough that it begins to work, but this is entirely up to him.

Full Power in Emergencies Only: If your ability works at half power under normal conditions, but at full power under stress, this limitation is not worth as much. For traits that come in levels, "half power" means half as many levels. The GM must decide what this means for other traits (half range, duration, bonuses, etc.). -20%.

Extra Recoil ⌐

-10% per +1 Recoil

By default, a ranged attack has Recoil 1, making it virtually recoilless (see p. 271). You may give an attack with Rapid Fire (p. 108) a higher Recoil (Rcl) as a limitation.

Recoil (Rcl)	Modifier
2	-10%
3	-20%
4	-30%
5+	-40%

Inaccurate ⌐

-5%/level

Your attack benefits little from careful aiming. Most attacks start with Accuracy (Acc) 3. Each -1 to Acc is

a -5% limitation. You may not reduce Acc below 0.

Limited Use

Variable

You can use your ability only a limited number of times in a 24-hour period. For most advantages, each "use" is 1 minute of activation. For an attack, each "use" gives shots equal to your RoF, with a minimum one shot per use; for instance, three uses of an attack with RoF 2 would give six shots. The value depends on the number of uses you get.

Uses Per Day	Modifier
1	-40%
2	-30%
3-4	-20%
5-10	-10%

More than 10 uses per day is not a significant limitation.

Two special options are available for attacks (and optionally, other abilities) that have this enhancement:

Fast Reload: You can replace all your uses in 3 to 5 seconds simply by replenishing ammunition. The GM determines the weight and cost of the ammunition. This halves the value of the limitation; e.g., three or four uses would be worth only -10%.

Slow Reload: As above, except if you have two or more shots (not uses!) you must reload each shot individually (taking 3 or more seconds *per shot*). If you have only one shot, it must take at least 6 seconds to reload – possibly longer, if using this limitation to represent a very slow-firing weapon such as a flintlock. This makes the limitation worth 5% less than usual; e.g., three or four uses would be worth only -15%.

Melee Attack ⌐

Variable

Your attack functions as a melee weapon. It has no range, but allows you to parry, use Rapid Strike, Feint, etc. It lacks Malf., 1/2D, Max, Acc, RoF, Shots, and Recoil statistics, and may not have any enhancement or limitation that modifies these statistics. Instead, it has a Reach statistic.

Reach	Modifier
C	-30%
1 *or* 2	-25%
C, 1, *or* 1, 2, *or* 2, 3	-20%
1-4 (like a whip)	-15%

If your attack cannot parry, it is worth an extra -5%.

Mitigator

Variable

You may only apply this limitation to a disadvantage. A particular item or substance – the *mitigator* – temporarily negates your disadvantage. The more effective the mitigator, the fewer points you get for the disadvantage. Use the following guidelines:

Mitigator is *vulnerable,* and easily stolen, broken, or misplaced (e.g., a pair of glasses). -60%.

Mitigator is a drug or other treatment that you must take *daily.* -60%.

Mitigator is a *weekly* treatment. -65%.

Mitigator is a *monthly* treatment. -70%.

This assumes your treatments are available at pharmacies. If you require a special (and possibly expensive) prescription, add +5% to the values above; e.g., -70% becomes -65%. If you can only get your treatments from one specific source, such as an experimental drug program, add +10%; e.g., -70% becomes -60%.

Example 1: Bad Sight is worth -25 points. Glasses cure Bad Sight while worn, but are breakable, for a -60% Mitigator limitation. This reduces Bad Sight to -10 points.

Example 2: Jan has AIDS, and would die in a month without treatment. This level of Terminally Ill is normally worth -100 points. Fortunately, Jan is on an experimental drug plan that is holding him in remission. The treatments are weekly (-65%) but impossible to find outside his program (+10%), for a -55% Mitigator limitation. This reduces Terminally Ill to -45 points. As long as Jan stays with the program, his countdown to death is halted.

Nuisance Effect

Variable

Your ability has a "side effect" that causes you *serious* inconvenience. The GM must approve this limitation and determine its value in each case, and should ruthlessly forbid effects that are abusive or that do not genuinely limit the ability's value. A few guidelines (a given trait can have more than one of these drawbacks):

• Your ability earns a reaction penalty from those around you. Perhaps it makes you look disgusting, or requires you to perform some sort of distressing ritual. *-5% per -1 to reactions (maximum -4)*.

• Your ability makes you *obvious*, limiting stealth and attracting enemies. *-5%*.

• Your ability physically inconveniences you – it attracts stinging insects, causes your armor to rust, makes you ravenously hungry, etc. *-5%*.

You cannot take a valuable power as a Nuisance Effect. For instance, "Kills everyone within a mile" is not an acceptable Nuisance Effect! Neither can you claim a limitation for a *harmless* nuisance. If your Terror advantage attracts gerbils instead of frightening them, this is amusing but not a limitation.

Onset

Variable

You must "stack" this limitation with one of Blood Agent, Contact Agent, Follow-Up, Malediction, or Respiratory Agent. It delays the damage or affliction caused by the attack until some time after exposure. The delay determines the value of the limitation.

Delay	Modifier
1 minute	-10%
1 hour	-20%
1 day	-30%
1 week (or more)	-40%

Delays that fall between two values use the smaller limitation; e.g., 30 minutes is -10%. If you can *control* the onset time, take Delay (p. 105) instead.

A variant limitation is *Exposure Time*, which is only available for attacks with Aura or Persistent. Use it to represent radioactivity, mildly toxic gases, etc. It works just like Onset, except that the victim must be exposed for the *entire period* to suffer the effect (or repeat it, if you continue exposure). This is worth an extra -20%; e.g., 1 minute is -30%.

Pact

Variable

A Higher Power – god, spirit, etc. – grants your ability under the condition that you follow a *strict* moral code. This code must take the form of one or more of the traits listed under *Self-Imposed Mental Disadvantages*

(p. 121). These disadvantages give you the usual number of points. Should you ever stray from the path, your ability immediately ceases to function until you repent. The limitation value is numerically equivalent to the point cost of the required disadvantages; e.g., a -10-point Vow gives a -10% Pact limitation.

Preparation Required

Variable

Your ability requires special preparation before you can use it. Perhaps you have to meditate first, or perform some ritual to focus concentration. This limitation is particularly appropriate for supernatural traits such as Channeling (p. 41) and Medium (p. 68).

You cannot use an unprepared ability. To prepare, take the Concentrate maneuver for the required amount of time. You need not specify how you plan to use your ability while you are preparing it, but you must specify which ability you are preparing if you have more than one trait with this limitation.

You can use a prepared ability normally – either immediately or at a later time. However, you can only have *one* advantage with this limitation prepared at a time, and it becomes unprepared immediately after use, regardless of success or failure (but if your ability has continuing effects, you can maintain them once activated).

The value of this limitation depends on the time required to prepare the ability.

Preparation Time	Modifier
1 minute	-20%
10 minutes	-30%
1 hour	-50%
8 hours	-60%

Weakened Without Preparation: Your ability works if you do not prepare it beforehand, but at half duration, range, effect, etc. This does not make sense for all advantages (GM's decision as to when it does). Weakened Without Preparation is worth exactly half as much as listed above.

Examples of Modified Attacks

Banshee's Wail: Affliction 3 (HT-2; Area Effect, 64 yards, +300%; Emanation, -20%; Hearing-Based, +150%; Heart Attack, +300%; Limited Use, 1/day, -40%; Selective Area, +20%) [243].

Dragon's Breath: Burning Attack 4d (Cone, 5 yards, +100%; Limited Use, 3/day, -20%; Reduced Range, ×1/5, -20%) [32].

Hand of Death: Toxic Attack 6d (Contact Agent, -30%; Costs Fatigue, 2 FP, -10%; Delay, Variable, +20%; Low Signature, +10%; Melee Attack, Reach C, -30%; Resistible, HT-4, -10%) [12].

Implanted 9mm SMG: Piercing Attack 3d-1 (Accurate +2, +10%; Extra Recoil +1, -10%; Increased Range, ×20, +40%; Limited Use, 3 uses/30 shots, Fast Reload, -10%; Rapid Fire, RoF 10, +100%) [33].

Lightning Bolt: Burning Attack 6d (Side Effect, Stunning, +50%; Surge, +20%) [51].

Mind Blast: Affliction 1 (Will; Based on Will, +20%; Malediction 2, +150%; Secondary Unconsciousness, +40%; Telepathic, -10%) [30].

Poison Bite: Sharp Teeth [1], plus Toxic Attack 2d (Cyclic, 1 hour, 5 cycles, resistible, +40%; Follow-Up, Sharp Teeth, +0%; Resistible, HT-3, -15%) [10].

Reduced Range

-10%/level

You may add this limitation to any advantage that has a range; e.g., Innate Attack or Scanning Sense. It comes in three levels, depending on the range divisor.

Range Divisor	Modifier
2	-10%
5	-20%
10	-30%

If applied to a ranged attack that has a 1/2D range, each level reduces both 1/2D *and* Max. You may reduce 1/2D only at half value (that is, "Reduced 1/2D" is -5%/level). You may not reduce Max independently.

Resistible

Variable

This limitation is only available for Innate Attacks that inflict fatigue or toxic damage. You must combine it with one of Blood Agent, Contact Agent, Follow-Up, Respiratory Agent, or Sense-Based. It represents poison, disease, or a similar effect that a sufficiently healthy victim can resist or "shrug off."

The victim gets a HT roll to avoid the effect. A resistance roll against HT-5 is worth -5%. Each +1 to the roll is a worth another -5% (e.g., HT-4 is -10%, and HT+4 is -50%).

If the attack is also Cyclic (p. 103), the victim rolls before each cycle (including the first). Success means the attack ends without further injury; failure means the target takes damage normally and the attack continues.

Sense-Based

Variable

On an attack with Malediction or an ability that *normally* ignores DR (e.g., Mind Control), this is a *limitation*. See the Sense-Based enhancement (p. 109) for details.

Takes Extra Time

-10%/level

You can only apply this limitation to abilities that require time to activate *and* that work fast enough to be useful in an emergency (e.g., combat). This is up to the GM, who is free to restrict this limitation to advantages that take only 1 or 2 seconds to activate.

For abilities that require a Ready or Concentrate maneuver, each level of Takes Extra Time *doubles* the time required. Activation occurs at the end of this time. For instance, Takes Extra Time 1 on an advantage that usually requires a one-second Ready maneuver would increase the Ready time to 2 seconds.

For attacks, the first level of Takes Extra Time results in a one-second Ready maneuver *before* you can make your Attack maneuver. Successive levels double the Ready time.

Takes Recharge

Variable

Your ability requires "recharging" after each use. It is unavailable during the recharge period. Value depends on the time between uses: five seconds (or twice the time required to use the ability, if longer) is -10%, 15 seconds (or 5 times the time required to use the ability, if longer) is -20%, and one hour (or 10 times the time required to use the ability, if longer) is -30%. Longer recharge times are not valid as limitations (but see *Limited Use*, p. 112).

Temporary Disadvantage

Variable

You may add this limitation to any advantage that can be switched off and on at will, *and* that takes at least one second to switch. When you switch on the advantage, you suffer one or more disadvantages until you switch it off again. This limitation is worth -1% per point the temporary disadvantages are worth, to a maximum of -80%.

Example: You can use your feet as hands, but can't walk while doing so. This is Extra Arms 2 (20 points) with Temporary Disadvantage: Legless (-30%), for 14 points.

The *point break* due to Temporary Disadvantage cannot exceed 80% of the value of the original disadvantage.

Example: You have Altered Time Rate 1 (100 points) with Temporary Disadvantage: Hemophilia (-30%) – you *bleed* faster, too! Since Hemophilia is worth -30 points normally, the most it can be worth as a Temporary Disadvantage is -24 points;

therefore, it reduces the cost of Altered Time Rate by 24 points (to 76 points) and not by 30 points (to 70 points).

You may only take Temporary Disadvantages that could logically inconvenience you for the period of time the advantage is normally on. In the case of mental disadvantages (Berserk, Lecherousness, etc.), if a failed self-control roll indicates that you give in to the disadvantage, you will suffer the disadvantage's effects until the GM rules you have regained your composure – which might be long after you deactivate the advantage with this limitation!

You can also use this limitation to remove an advantage temporarily. This is worth -1% per point the negated advantage is worth, and the point break cannot exceed 80% of the deactivated advantage's cost. Only one of the involved advantages can take this limitation – you *cannot* take two advantages, both with this limitation, each of which negates the other when used.

Trigger

Variable

Your advantage requires exposure to a specific substance or condition (e.g., a dose of a drug) to function. One dose or exposure is required per one-minute "use." Cost depends on the rarity of the Trigger:

Very Common (available almost anywhere): -10%.
Common (expensive, somewhat hard to find): -20%.
Occasional (very expensive and hard to find): -30%.
Rare (cannot be bought; must be found or made): -40%.

Multiply the limitation value by 1.5 if the Trigger is illegal, addictive, or otherwise dangerous.

Unconscious Only

-20%

You may only take this limitation in conjunction with Uncontrollable (below). You cannot consciously activate your ability *at all*; it can only come into play under GM control, as a result of stress. Like Uncontrollable, you may buy this off later on, as you gain control over your ability.

Uncontrollable

-10% or -30%

Your ability tends to manifest itself at undesirable or inappropriate times. Whenever the GM rules that you are in a stressful situation – including any situation that requires a Fright Check or a self-control roll for a mental disadvantage – you must make a Will roll to keep your ability under control, even if you did not intend to use it! You need only roll once per stressful situation, but a roll of 14+ always fails, regardless of Will.

On a failure, the GM takes over your ability, playing it as though it were an entity of a prankish or hostile nature. The actions of your ability will often reflect your "suppressed desires," as reflected in your quirks and mental disadvantages.

An ability that cannot inflict damage – for instance, Flight or Jumper – will activate unexpectedly. This is inconvenient and embarrassing, but not overly dangerous. After each uncontrolled act, you get another Will roll to control your power. This goes on until you make a Will roll. In this case, Uncontrollable is worth -10%.

A harmful ability goes after obvious foes first, and will never turn on *you* . . . but nobody else is safe! After each uncontrolled act (or *before* an attack on a Dependent or other loved one), you get another Will roll to control your power. This continues until you make a Will roll or destroy everything around you! For destructive powers, Uncontrollable is worth -30%.

You may buy this limitation off later on, as you gain control over your ability.

Unreliable

Variable

Sometimes your ability works and sometimes it doesn't! It just comes and goes, and you've never identified why. This is completely separate from any roll *normally* needed to activate the ability. You can have skill 20 and still have problems making it work!

Every time you want to use the power, you must roll the activation number (see below) or less on 3d. Once you succeed, the ability will work for that particular use. When you cease to use it, you must make another activation roll to start it again.

If you cannot activate your ability on your first attempt, you may try again once per second after that, at no penalty. Each successive attempt costs one FP. If you are reduced to three or fewer FP, you must rest until *all* FP are regained before you can attempt to use your ability again.

Example of Character Creation (cont'd)

Dai's main advantage is that he can teleport. This is Warp (p. 97), which costs 100 points! But Dai has two special limitations to lower the cost. First, his Warp is *psionic*, so "anti-psi" can keep it from working. This gives the Psionic Teleportation limitation, worth -10%. Second, his ability has a very short range: 10 yards. That's a Range Limit limitation worth -50%. These limitations mean that Dai gets Warp at 60% off, for 40 points.

We decide to give Dai another psi ability useful to a thief: a "sixth sense" that warns him of traps and similar dangers. This is Danger Sense (p. 47), with the ESP special limitation. Danger Sense costs a basic 15 points, but the -10% limitation reduces this to 13.5 points, which rounds up to 14 points.

Even without his psi abilities, Dai is a gifted thief. His specialty is second-story work, so we add Flexibility (p. 56), for 5 points, because it gives a big bonus when climbing; Perfect Balance (p. 74), for 15 points, so he won't lose his balance and fall off; and Absolute Direction (p. 34), for 5 points, to help him negotiate back alleys and rooftops.

Since we want Dai to be able to disappear into a crowd, we throw in the 1-point Honest Face perk (p. 101) – he doesn't "look like a thief."

Dai's advantages total 80 points, raising his current point total to 223 points.

Activation Number	Modifier
5	-80%
8	-40%
11	-20%
14	-10%

Unreliable works differently when applied to attacks which are *also* gadgets or built-in firearms. Instead of requiring an activation roll, it gives a Malfunction number worse than 17.

Malf.	Modifier
12	-25%
13	-20%
14	-15%
15	-10%
16	-5%

Untrainable

-40%

You may only apply this limitation to abilities that normally require a skill to use. You can't learn to control your power well. You learn all skills associated with it as though the relevant attribute were only 8 (or at one less than its usual value, if already at 8 or worse), and your maximum skill level is 10.

GADGET LIMITATIONS

The GM may require you to pay points for any "gadget" that grants traits that usually cost points (attribute levels, advantages, etc.). However, he should charge points *only* for items that even the most advanced technology could not produce (e.g., a ring that bestows Luck) – and even then, only if those items are not for sale at *any* price in the game world.

In particular, the GM should never charge points for ordinary, manufactured equipment – or even for special equipment, if it is for sale – unless it happens to be Signature Gear (p. 85). Body armor, a rifle, and night-vision goggles effectively bestow Damage Resistance, Innate Attack, and Infravision, respectively . . . but since *anyone* could buy these items, they have a cash cost, not a point cost.

Traits bestowed by items have their usual point cost. You can give them any logical combination of modifiers, plus one or more of the special limitations below.

Breakable

Variable

Your foes can destroy the item. Once destroyed, it will cease to grant you its benefits until repaired. Add the following elements together to find the final limitation value.

Durability: The easier the object is to break, the greater the limitation. Decide on the gadget's weight and DR.

DR	Modifier
2 or less	-20%
3-5	-15%
6-15	-10%
16-25	-5%
26 or higher	0%

If the object is a machine that can break down (as opposed to a simple artifact, like a ring or a hat), add another -5%. See *Damage to Objects* (p. 483) to determine HP and the effects of damage.

Reparability: You can normally repair your gadget if it breaks; the GM chooses the skill(s) needed to make repairs. If you *cannot* repair it, and it requires inconvenient time, effort, or expense to replace (GM's decision), it is worth an additional -15%.

Size: The item's Size Modifier affects Vision rolls to identify it out of combat and rolls to hit it in combat.

SM	Modifier
-9 or less	0%
-7 or -8	-5%
-5 or -6	-10%
-3 or -4	-15%
-1 or -2	-20%
0 or more	-25%

Can Be Stolen

Variable

Your foes can take this item from you, depriving you of its benefits. This is only a limitation if the item is *obviously* powerful and likely to be the target of theft! The value of the limitation depends on how hard it is to steal:

Easily snatched with an unopposed DX roll (e.g., a hat): -40%.

Thief must win a Quick Contest of DX (e.g., a bracelet) or ST (e.g., a wand) with you: -30%.

Can only by taken by stealth or trickery (e.g., a coin in a pocket): 20%.

Must be forcefully removed (e.g., a suit of armor): -10%.

Halve the value of the limitation if the gadget will not immediately work for the thief.

Unique

-25%

You may only take this limitation in conjunction with Breakable or Can Be Stolen. Normally, you can replace a broken or stolen gadget – although this might require significant time and effort (GM's decision). If the item is Unique, *you cannot replace it!* Character points spent for the item are lost for good if it is broken or stolen.

The GM is free to add as many new advantages as he can think of. Players take note: You may invent new advantages only with the GM's permission.

NEW ADVANTAGES

The GM (no doubt with the enthusiastic advice of the players!) is free to add as many new advantages as he can think of. What follows are some guidelines on how to balance the costs of such advantages in light of the traits in this chapter.

Players take note: *these rules are for GMs. You may invent new advantages only with the GM's permission.*

MODIFYING EXISTING ADVANTAGES

GURPS has a *lot* of advantages. Often, one of these is similar to what you had in mind, in which case you can "tweak" an existing ability instead of inventing a new one.

Rename

The advantage you're looking for might already exist, but under a moniker you dislike or find unintuitive. In this case, creating a "new" advantage is just a matter of changing the name! For instance, if you want a Light Intensification advantage that lets those who have it see in the dark, just rename "Night Vision" to "Light Intensification."

Redefine

Many "new" advantages amount to existing advantages with revised special effects. If an existing advantage provides the right ability with the wrong justification, use the game mechanics and point cost of the existing trait but come up with a new explanation for how it works. For instance, Night Vision assumes natural, dark-adapted eyes, but you are free to explain it as ultra-tech implants, if that suits your campaign better.

Combine

Still other "new" advantages are *combinations* of existing traits. If a mix of advantages (possibly with a few disadvantages, to bring the cost down) collectively provide the effects you want, just group them together, add their costs, and rename the whole thing.

For instance, you might lump together Acute Vision 5 [10], Night Vision 5 [5], and Colorblindness [-10] as the "Cat's Eye Mk. V" implant. Players would just list "Cat's Eye Mk. V [5]" on their character sheet.

Note that this is identical to the way meta-traits work in Chapter 7.

Modify

The game mechanics for an existing advantage will sometimes be almost, but not quite, what you want. In that case, start with the nearest existing advantage, apply enhancements and limitations that add the desired effects, and present the final product as an entirely new advantage.

For instance, suppose undead beings in your campaign can see the Spectral Plane. This gives them Night Vision with the side effects that they see ghosts and have glowing red eyes. You *could* write this as "Night Vision 5 (Affects Insubstantial, +20%; Temporary Disadvantage: Unnatural Feature, -5%) [6]," but it would be simpler to write "Spectral Vision [6]" on character sheets and leave the design details in your notes.

Fine-Tune

After applying the above processes to achieve the effects you seek, you might wish to add some "color" or adjust the cost – perhaps by adding minor side effects, such as small modifiers to certain success rolls. The guidelines and examples under *Perks* (p. 100) and *Quirks* (p. 162) can be useful here.

For instance, you might want "Spectral Vision" to cost a nice, round

5 points, but you don't want to make the ability to see ghosts a freebie. To justify shaving the cost down to 5 points, you toss in a -1 to Vision rolls made in bright daylight. After all, everyone knows the undead don't like sunlight!

DESIGNING ENTIRELY NEW ADVANTAGES

There are times when nothing less than a totally new advantage will do. Advantages in **GURPS** usually grant one of four basic types of abilities (although a single advantage often qualifies in more than one category).

1. Situational bonuses to attributes. Handle attribute bonuses by assuming that each +1 is worth 10 points for ST or HT, or 20 points for DX or IQ, and then modifying the cost downward to reflect how often the bonus applies. See *Accessibility* (p. 110) for inspiration. For instance, Rapid Healing is basically +5 HT (base cost 50 points) that only applies to rolls to recover from damage. Since most people go to great pains to avoid damage, and since rolls for natural recovery rarely matter in settings with magical, psionic, or

ultra-tech healing, the point value of the bonus is reduced to 1/10 of normal, for a net cost of 5 points.

2. Bonuses to skill rolls. In general, simply work out the equivalent Talent (p. 89) and add its cost to the advantage. If the advantage modifies *one* skill, then assume it is worth 2 points per +1 to skill, to a maximum of +3 to skill for 6 points.

3. Bonuses to reaction rolls. Work out reaction bonuses as described for *Reputation* (p. 26). You may include a bonus that applies to a very small class of people (e.g., "anyone with a Ph.D. in Comparative Anatomy from Harvard," unless the campaign happens to be set at Harvard Medical School) for free as a "special effect." Note that these bonuses need not be *actual* Reputations – they could as easily be due to looks, a psionic aura, or mind-control lasers.

4. Unique abilities that those without the advantage do not have in any measure. You should price these abilities by comparison. Examine other traits in the rules and assign a similar cost for an advantage that is about equal in power. Reduce or increase the cost if the ability is slightly more or less powerful than the one to which you are comparing it. For instance, "automatically makes all normal Vision rolls" is about as useful as "automatically makes all Fright Checks," so you might price that ability along the lines of Unfazeable, for 15 points.

Finalizing the Cost

To determine the final cost of a new advantage, add up the costs of all the abilities it grants. If the advantage is extremely rare, and those who have it could reliably use it as a surprise tactic or as a means of making money, increase its final cost by up to 100%. Conversely, if the GM wants it to be extremely common, he may reduce its final cost by as much as 50%. Use fine-tuning (above) to further adjust the cost.

The GM is the final arbiter when it comes to the cost of new advantages. He is free to charge an Unusual Background – over and above the cost of the advantage – for any new advantage he wishes to restrict to a certain class of characters. This is *in addition to* any "built-in" rarity modifier.

CHAPTER THREE

DISADVANTAGES

A "disadvantage" is a problem or imperfection that renders you less capable than your attributes, advantages, and skills would indicate. In addition to the traits in this chapter, this includes anything with a negative point cost in Chapter 1: low Status, below-average Wealth, etc.

You are probably wondering, "Why would I want to give my character disadvantages?" There are two good reasons:

1. Each disadvantage has a *negative* cost in character points. Thus, disadvantages *give you extra character points*, which let you improve your character in other ways. But note that disadvantages limit you in proportion to their cost. Be sure to read the disadvantage description in full to know what you are getting into!

2. An imperfection or two makes your character more interesting and realistic, and adds to the fun of roleplaying!

Disadvantages for Heroes

Two kinds of disadvantages are particularly suitable for heroic PCs. Roleplayed well, they might limit the *character's* choices, but they should make the *player's* experience more fun.

"Good" Disadvantages

It might seem strange that virtues such as Truthfulness and Sense of Duty are listed as "disadvantages." In the real world, we regard such traits as advantages! Their disadvantage value in **GURPS** comes from the fact that these virtues limit your freedom of action. For instance, someone with Truthfulness will have trouble lying, even for a good cause; therefore, within the framework of the game, he has a disadvantage. This has one very worthwhile benefit: if you want to create a wholly heroic character, you don't have to take any "character flaws" at all. You can get points by choosing only those disadvantages that are actually virtuous!

Tragic Flaws

Many of the greatest heroes of history and literature had a "tragic flaw." Alcoholism, great ugliness, bad temper, compulsive behavior, and even drug addiction – all are found in the *heroes* of fact and fiction. So don't assume that your heroes have to be perfect . . . try giving them significant problems to overcome.

RESTRICTIONS ON DISADVANTAGES

Your GM might wish to "cap" the extra points you can gain from disadvantages; see *Disadvantage Limit* (p. 11). This limit applies to the total points you can get from *all* traits with negative point costs, from Chapter 1 (reduced attributes, low Status, etc.) or the list below. Mandatory disadvantages assigned by the GM *don't* count against this limit.

Most GMs will want to enforce two additional restrictions:

Negated Disadvantages

You cannot take a disadvantage that one of your advantages would mitigate or negate! For instance, if you have Acute Hearing, you cannot take Hard of Hearing. Contradictory disadvantages, such as Curious and Incurious, are also mutually exclusive. The GM has the final say as to which traits are compatible.

TYPES OF DISADVANTAGES

Like advantages, disadvantages are classified according to how they work in play and who can have them.

Mental 🧠, Physical 💪, and Social 🤝

Mental disadvantages originate from your mind or soul. They stay with you if your mind ends up in a new body. This category includes the vast majority of "magical," "psionic," and "spiritual" traits. Mental disadvantages are marked 🧠.

Physical disadvantages are associated with your body. You can escape them by moving to a new body! If another mind occupies your body, the new owner gains your physical disadvantages.

adventure fiction, so they are included in the interest of good NPC creation.

Secret Disadvantages

You may give your character a disadvantage unknown both to him and to *you*. Choose a point value and tell the GM. The GM will select a disadvantage and give you its value plus an additional -5 points (e.g., Unluckiness, normally worth -10 points, gives -15 points as a secret disadvantage) . . . but he will not give you any hints as to what it is! When your disadvantage finally becomes obvious in the course of play (GM's decision), you must buy off the extra -5 points as soon as possible.

The GM must pick a secret disadvantage carefully. It should be something that you could believably not know about. If it is a mental disadvantage, the conditions that trigger it should never have arisen (Berserk, Bloodlust, Combat Paralysis, the less-common Phobias, and Split Personality all work well here). Most physical disadvantages are too obvious – although something like Hemophilia *might* go unnoticed.

You can only list one secret disadvantage on your character sheet, but this might represent more than one trait. The GM is free to select multiple, related disadvantages worth the appropriate number of points.

Villain Disadvantages

Some disadvantages – Sadism, for instance – are not at all suitable for a "hero," and the GM is free to forbid them to PCs. But they are often found in the more fiendish villains of

You can acquire a physical disadvantage during play, most likely due to accident or combat. In this case, you immediately suffer the bad effects of the disadvantage. Unlike starting disadvantages, however, physical handicaps acquired in play do *not* "give

back" points with which to buy abilities – they just lower your point value!

Example: If you start out blind, you start with an extra 50 points . . . but if an explosion blinds you during the game, you're just blind and that's that. Reduce your point total by 50 points to reflect your new disadvantage. You *should not* keep the same point total and take 50 points of compensating advantages!

Physical disadvantages are marked 💪.

Social disadvantages are associated with your identity. Should it become important to know whether they go with mind or body, the GM's word is final. Note that this category includes below-average Status, Wealth, and so forth from Chapter 1. Social disadvantages are marked 🤝.

The GM is the final judge of which category a disadvantage belongs in. It is possible to interpret certain disadvantages in more than one way!

Exotic ☠, Supernatural ⚡, and Mundane

Exotic disadvantages are forbidden to normal humans. Nonhumans may acquire such traits from their racial template (see Chapter 7), but they still need the GM's permission to take additional exotic disadvantages. Exotic disadvantages are marked ☠.

Supernatural disadvantages are the result of divine intervention, magic, psionics, etc. With the GM's permission, *anyone* might be cursed in this way – but only if supernatural powers exist in the game world. Supernatural disadvantages are marked ⚡.

Mundane disadvantages are everything else. They are inborn, acquired, or self-imposed handicaps that anyone might have. Mundane disadvantages are not marked in any special way. Assume that a disadvantage with neither ☠ nor ⚡ is available to anyone.

SELF-CONTROL FOR MENTAL DISADVANTAGES

Many mental disadvantages do not affect you constantly – you may attempt to control your urges. An asterisk (*) appears next to the point cost of any disadvantage that offers a chance to resist. For each disadvantage like this, you must choose a *self-control number:* the number you must roll on 3d to avoid giving in. This modifies point value as follows:

You resist quite rarely (roll of 6 or less): *2 × listed cost.*
You resist fairly often (roll of 9 or less): *1.5 × listed cost.*
You resist quite often (roll of 12 or less): *listed cost.*
You resist almost all the time (roll of 15 or less): *0.5 × listed cost.*

Drop all fractions (e.g., -22.5 points becomes -22 points).

The "default" self-control number is 12: you must roll 12 or less on 3d to avoid giving in to your problem. This lets you use disadvantage costs as written. Choose a self-control number of 15 if you wish to have a tendency toward a disadvantage instead of a full-blown case. A self-control number of 9 will regularly limit your options. A self-control number of 6 can be *crippling* (especially with genuine psychiatric problems).

Note your self-control number in parentheses after the name of the disadvantage on your character sheet. For instance, if you can resist Berserk on a roll of 9 or less, write this as "Berserk (9)."

> *Many mental disadvantages do not affect you constantly – you may attempt to control your urges.*

Self-Control Rolls

In circumstances that are likely to trigger your problem, you may opt to roll 3d against your self-control number to see whether your disadvantage actually affects you. If you roll less than or equal to this number, you resist your disadvantage – this time. Otherwise, you suffer the listed effects. This is called a *self-control roll.*

Like all success rolls, self-control rolls are subject to modifiers. Exceptionally mild or severe stimuli can give bonuses or penalties. Drugs and afflictions can make you more or less likely to give in. Other disadvantages can make you irritable, reducing your odds of resisting. See the disadvantage descriptions for details.

Example: Your self-control number is 15, but you are in a highly stressful situation that gives -5 to your self-control roll. You must roll 10 or less to resist your disadvantage.

You never *have* to try a self-control roll – you can always give in willingly, and it is good roleplaying to do so. However, there will be times when you really need to resist your urges, and that is what the roll is for. Be aware that if you attempt self-control rolls too often, the GM may penalize you for bad roleplaying by awarding you fewer earned points.

Optionally, the GM may permit you to use one unspent character point to "buy" an automatic success on a self-control roll. Points spent this way are gone for good, but there will be times when staying on the straight and narrow is worth the sacrifice. In this case, the GM should *not* penalize you for bad roleplaying, because you are penalizing yourself!

Note that high Will helps you make Fright Checks and resist supernatural emotion control, but it does *not* improve self-control rolls – not even for disadvantages with effects identical to these things. Mental disadvantages represent an aspect of your personality that you cannot simply will (or reason) away. This is part of what makes them disadvantages!

"Buying Off" Disadvantages

You may use bonus points to "buy off" many disadvantages – whether you started with them or acquired them in play. This costs as many points as the disadvantage originally gave you. If the GM permits, you may buy off leveled disadvantages one level at a time. Likewise, you can buy off those with self-control numbers gradually, by raising the self-control number. In both cases, the point cost is the difference between your former level and your current one. For more on buying off disadvantages, see Chapter 9.

Self-Imposed Mental Disadvantages

Certain mental disadvantages – Code of Honor (p. 127), Disciplines of Faith (p. 132), Fanaticism (p. 136), Honesty (p. 138), Intolerance (p. 140), Sense of Duty (p. 153), Trademark (p. 159), and Vow (p. 160) – are not psychiatric problems, but beliefs or codes of conduct. Such "self-imposed mental disadvantages" share three features that distinguish them from other mental disadvantages:

● They can be "bought off" with earned points at *any* time. People really do wake up in the morning and resolve to live their lives differently for no apparent reason!
● They cannot be caused by Afflictions (p. 35), drugs, brain surgery, and similar "quick and dirty" behavior alteration. Such techniques can create a pacifist or a maniac, but you need magic, Mind Control (p. 68), or prolonged Brainwashing (p. 182) to impose anything as complex as a code of conduct.
● They can be used with the Pact limitation (p. 113) as conditions to which you *must* adhere to retain certain supernatural powers.

DISADVANTAGE LIST

Absent-Mindedness 🧠
-15 points

You have trouble focusing on anything not of immediate interest. You have -5 on all IQ and IQ-based skill rolls, save those for the task you are currently concentrating on. If no engaging task or topic presents itself, your attention will drift to more interesting matters in five minutes, and you will ignore your immediate surroundings until something catches your attention and brings you back. Once adrift in your own thoughts, you must roll against Perception-5 in order to *notice* any event short of personal physical injury.

You may attempt to rivet your attention on a boring topic through sheer strength of will. To do so, make a Will-5 roll once every five minutes. "Boring topics" include small talk, repetitive manual tasks, guard duty, driving on an empty highway . . .

Absent-minded individuals also tend to forget trivial tasks (like paying the bills) and items (like car keys and checkbooks). Whenever it becomes important that you have performed such a task or brought such an item, the GM should call for a roll against IQ-2. On a failure, this detail slipped your attention.

Example: An absent-minded detective is in a shootout. He was involved in gunplay earlier in the day, in which he fired four rounds, so the GM calls for an IQ-2 roll. The detective fails the roll, and discovers too late that he forgot to reload his weapon, so his revolver has only two bullets left!

This is the classic disadvantage for eccentric geniuses.

Addiction 🧠/💪
Variable

You are addicted to a drug, which you must use daily or suffer withdrawal. The value of this disadvantage depends on the cost, effects, and legality of the drug:

Cost (per day)

Cheap (up to 0.1% of average starting wealth): *-5 points.*

Expensive (up to 0.5% of average starting wealth): *-10 points.*

Very expensive (more than 0.5% of average starting wealth): *-20 points.*

Effects

Incapacitating or hallucinogenic: *-10 points.*

Highly addictive (-5 on withdrawal roll): *-5 points.*

Totally addictive (-10 on withdrawal roll): *-10 points.*

Legality

Illegal: *+0 points.*

Legal: *+5 points.*

Examples: Tobacco is cheap, highly addictive, and legal; a chain-smoker has a -5-point Addiction. Heroin is very expensive, incapacitating, totally addictive, and illegal; a heroin addict has a -40-point Addiction.

Non-Chemical Addictions: You can take Addiction to an activity instead of a drug – for instance, telepathic contact or spending time in virtual reality. If this costs money, price the Addiction based on its daily cost. If it is free (e.g., telepathic contact), treat it as "Cheap" if it you can do it almost anywhere (telepathic contact with *anyone*) or as "Expensive" if restrictive conditions apply (telepathic contact with one specific person). Such Addictions almost always cause psychological dependency (see *Withdrawal*, below).

Effects of Drugs

A *stimulating* drug leaves you feeling energized . . . until it wears off. Then you are depressed and irritable. An *incapacitating* drug renders you unconscious (or just blissfully, uselessly drowsy) for about two hours. A *hallucinogenic* drug renders you useless for work or combat, though you might be active and talkative. Some drugs (e.g., tobacco) have none of these effects, while others have unique effects. Side effects are also possible. For detailed rules, see *Addictive Drugs* (p. 440).

Withdrawal

Sometimes, voluntarily or otherwise, you must try to give up your Addiction. Addiction to a drug that causes *psychological dependency* is a mental disadvantage; withdrawal from such a drug requires a series of Will rolls, and may result in mental problems. Addiction to a drug that induces *physiological dependency* is a physical disadvantage; withdrawal is a function of your HT, and may cause physical injury. For details, see *Drug Withdrawal* (p. 440). Should you successfully withdraw from an Addiction, you must immediately buy off this disadvantage.

Minor Addictions

For an Addiction worth only -5 points, the GM may rule that the expense, stigma, and detrimental long-term effects of use are the whole of the disadvantage, and waive the usual withdrawal rules. This is appropriate for such drugs as tobacco and caffeine. If forced to go without, you must make a Will or HT roll as usual, but the only effects on a failure are general anxiety, irritability, or restlessness. This manifests as a temporary -1 to DX, IQ, self-control rolls, or reaction rolls (GM's choice) – not as insanity or injury. Successive failures prolong the duration of the effects; they do not increase the size of the penalty. If you can make 14 successful rolls in succession, you must buy off your Addiction.

It is also possible to create a 0-point Addiction using these rules. Such Addictions are *always* Minor Addictions, and you may take them as -1-point quirks (see *Quirks*, p. 162).

Alcoholism 💪
-15 or -20 points

You are an alcohol addict. Alcoholism uses the Addiction rules (above). It is cheap, incapacitating, and usually legal, so it would normally be a -10-point Addiction. But it is also *insidious;* therefore, it is worth -15 points – or -20 points if it is illegal.

Most of the time, you may confine your drinking to the evenings, and therefore function normally (for game purposes). However, *any time* you are in the presence of alcohol, you must roll vs. Will to avoid partaking. A failed roll means you go on a "binge" lasting

2d hours, followed by a hangover; see *Drinking and Intoxication* (p. 439). Alcoholics on a binge are characterized by sudden mood swings – from extreme friendliness to extreme hostility – and may attack friends, talk too freely, or make other mistakes.

The other drawback of Alcoholism is that it is hard to get rid of. Should you manage to "withdraw," you no longer need to drink daily . . . but you must still make a Will+4 roll whenever you are in the presence of alcohol. A failed roll does not reinstate the addiction, but does set off a binge. (Three binges in a week *will* reinstate the addiction.) Thus, there is no normal way to "buy off" this disadvantage.

Continued Alcoholism will steal your abilities. You must roll yearly against HT+2 until you withdraw. Failure means you lose a level from one of your four basic attributes – roll randomly to determine which.

Amnesia ♀

-10 or -25 points

You've lost your memory. You can't remember any of your past life, including your name. This disadvantage comes in two levels:

Partial Amnesia: You, the *player,* can see your character sheet, but the GM may reserve up to -30 points of your disadvantage allotment for "secret" disadvantages of his choosing. You know that you can use certain skills, but have no idea where you learned them. You are likely to have enemies – and possibly friends – that you can't remember. If you turn yourself in to the police, they can perform their standard ID checks . . . but you might turn out to be a wanted criminal. Even if you aren't, finding out your name won't restore your memory! *-10 points.*

Total Amnesia: The only traits you can specify during character creation are those you could see in a mirror. The GM assigns everything else – and holds onto your full character sheet until your memory returns! You have *no* idea of your full abilities. Since the GM knows your quirks and mental traits, and you *don't,* he will sometimes overrule your statements about what you're doing. He will also make all skill rolls for you, because you have no idea what you can do until you try

it! Your IQ-based skill rolls are at -2 unless the GM feels that memory would have no effect at all on the task at hand. *-25 points.*

You can only buy off Amnesia if there is some reason why you might recover your memory; e.g., meeting an old friend, reliving some fateful event, or the ever-popular blow to the head. In most cases, the cure will be related to the cause of the memory loss. Particularly twisted GMs might enjoy making the cause in question some form of brainwashing. In this case, one of the hidden disadvantages will probably be an Enemy with sufficient resources to have arranged the brainwashing in the first place.

Appearance

see p. 21

Below-average appearance is a disadvantage, and should be noted as such on your character sheet.

Bad Back ♥

-15 or -25 points

For whatever reason, your spinal column is in bad shape. During strenuous physical activity, you may "throw your back" and suffer crippling pain or further injury. Whenever you make a ST roll, and whenever you roll 17 or 18 on an attack or defense roll in melee combat, or on a roll for an "athletic" skill such as Acrobatics, make a HT roll as well.

Modifiers: Any modifiers to the success roll for the activity that triggered the HT roll. For a long task that allows the luxury of planning, you can try to minimize the strain on your back; a successful IQ-2 or Physiology+4 roll gives +2 on the HT roll.

On a failure, you throw your back. Consequences depend on the severity of your case:

Mild: You are at -3 DX until you rest or someone helps you; a First Aid-2 roll will reset your back. You are also at -3 IQ, but during the next second only (for your next turn, in combat). On a critical failure, you are at -5 DX and must make a Will roll to perform *any* physical action. *-15 points.*

Severe: The HT roll is at -2. On a failure, DX and IQ are both at -4 until you receive rest or help; you are in

constant agony. On a critical failure, you take 1d-3 damage and are at -6 DX and -4 IQ. *-25 points.*

High Pain Threshold (p. 59) halves all DX and IQ penalties (drop fractions), but does not eliminate them completely.

Bad Grip ♥

-5 points/level

You have a penalty on tasks that require a firm grip. Each level (maximum three levels) gives -2 with such tasks. This penalty is *overall* – not per hand. Affected tasks include melee weapon use, climbing, catching things, and anything else the GM deems requires a firm grip (e.g., an Acrobatics roll to catch a trapeze).

This disadvantage is mutually exclusive with No Fine Manipulators (p. 145).

Bad Sight ♥

-25 points

You have poor vision. This applies to *all* your visual senses: regular vision, Infravision, Ultravision, etc. You may be nearsighted or farsighted – your choice.

Nearsighted: You cannot read small print, computer displays, etc., more than a foot away, or road signs, etc., at more than about 10 yards. You are at -6 to Vision rolls to spot items more than one yard away. When making a melee attack, you are at -2 to skill. When making a ranged attack, *double* the actual distance to the target when calculating the range modifier. *-25 points.*

Farsighted: You cannot read text except with great difficulty (triple normal time). You are at -6 to Vision rolls to spot items within one yard, and you have -3 to DX on any close manual task, including close combat. *-25 points.*

Special Limitations

Mitigator: At TL5+, you can acquire glasses that compensate totally for Bad Sight *while they are worn.* At TL7+, contact lenses are available. In both cases, remember that accidents can happen . . . and that enemies can deprive you of these items. If you are starting at a tech level in which vision can be corrected, you *must* take this limitation. -60%.

Bad Smell ♟

-10 points

You exude an appalling odor that you cannot remove, such as the stench of death and decay. This causes a -2 reaction from most people and animals (although pests or carrion-eating scavengers might be unusually *attracted* to you!). You can mask the smell with perfumes, but the overpowering amount needed results in the same reaction penalty.

Bad Temper ☻

-10 points*

You are not in full control of your emotions. Make a self-control roll in any stressful situation. If you fail, you lose your temper and must insult, attack, or otherwise act against the cause of the stress.

Berserk ☻

-10 points*

You tend to rampage out of control when you or a loved one is harmed, making frenzied attacks against whoever or whatever you see as the cause of the trouble. If you also suffer from Bad Temper (above), *any* stress may trigger Berserk.

Make a self-control roll any time you suffer damage over 1/4 your HP in the space of one second, and whenever you witness equivalent harm to a loved one. If you fail, you go berserk. You go berserk automatically if you fail a self-control roll for Bad Temper! You may *deliberately* go berserk by taking the Concentrate maneuver and making a successful Will roll. Once you are berserk, the following rules apply:

● If armed with a hand weapon, you must make an All-Out Attack each turn a foe is in range. If no foe is in range, you must use a Move maneuver to get as close as possible to a foe – and if you can Move and Attack, or end your Move with a slam, you will.

● If the enemy is more than 20 yards away, you may attack with a ranged weapon if you have one, but you may not take the Aim maneuver. If using a gun, you blaze away at your maximum rate of fire until your gun is empty. You cannot reload unless your weapon – and your Fast-Draw skill – lets you reload "without thought" (can

take no more than one second). Once your gun is empty, you must either draw another gun or charge into melee combat.

● You are immune to stun and shock, and your injuries cause no penalty to your Move score. You make all rolls to remain conscious or alive at +4 to HT. If you don't fail any rolls, you remain alive and madly attacking until you reach -5×HP. Then you fall – dead!

● When you down a foe, you may (if you wish) attempt another self-control roll to see if you snap out of the berserk state. If you fail (or do not roll), you remain berserk and attack the next foe. Treat any friend who attempts to restrain you as a foe! You get to roll again each time you down a foe, and you get one extra roll when no more foes remain. If you are still berserk, you start to attack your friends . . .

Once you snap out of the berserk state, all your wounds immediately affect you. Roll at normal HT to see whether you remain conscious and alive.

Special Enhancements

Battle Rage. You go berserk in *any* combat situation, regardless of whether you have been injured. To avoid this, you must make a self-control roll when you first enter combat (even a barroom brawl or a boxing match). +50%.

Bestial ☻ 👽

-10 or -15 points

You think and react like a wild animal. You have no concept of "civilized" standards of morality or propriety, and no concept of property. You fight or flee from those who frighten or threaten you. You cannot learn skills that, in the GM's opinion, rely on "civilized" notions of art or social interaction, and you have no default with such skills.

You are not necessarily out of control; you simply react in an animalistic manner. You will usually ignore those who leave you alone (unless they're food!), and might even come to display affection for those who treat you with special kindness. You cannot understand property in the human sense, but (depending on your race) you might understand territory and

avoid doing damage to objects on another's territory. Whether you regard humans as individuals with territory rights is an open question! You might also understand dominance, and respect or even obey a human who has proved to be stronger than you.

You cannot take an Odious Personal Habit for your beast-like behavior; that's included in the cost of Bestial. But if your behavior is extremely repugnant to humans – equivalent in severity to a -15-point Odious Personal Habit – the GM might rule that Bestial is worth -15 points instead of the usual -10. You are free to take Odious Personal Habits *unrelated* to beast-like behavior (including "eats humans"), however.

Bestial is not necessarily tied to low IQ, but roleplaying a character who is both Bestial and remarkably intelligent would be a major challenge requiring a lot of thought and effort. The GM may therefore choose to restrict Bestial to characters with IQ scores under 10 (or even under 6!), or simply reserve it for NPCs.

Note that the Wild Animal meta-trait (p. 263) includes this disadvantage.

Blindness ♟

-50 points

You cannot see *at all*. In unfamiliar territory, you must travel slowly and carefully, or have a companion or guide animal lead you. Many actions are impossible for you; the GM should use common sense.

You are at -6 to all combat skills. You *can* use hand weapons, but you *cannot* target a particular hit location. If using a ranged weapon, you can only attack randomly, or engage targets so close that you can hear them. All this assumes you are accustomed to blindness. If you *suddenly* lose your eyesight, you fight at -10, just as if you were in total darkness. In either case, you suffer no *extra* penalties for operating in the dark.

If you have Blindness, you cannot purchase superhuman vision abilities. If you see in a spectrum other than the visible one, you have the 0-point version of Infravision (p. 60) or Ultravision (p. 94) – not Blindness and the 10-point version of one of those advantages. Note that Scanning Sense

(p. 81) and Vibration Sense (p. 96) are *not* vision; you may take either of these traits in conjunction with Blindness, at the usual point costs.

Bloodlust

-10 points*

You want to see your foes *dead*. In battle, you must go for killing blows, and put in an extra shot to make sure of a downed foe. You must make a self-control roll whenever you need to accept a surrender, evade a sentry, take a prisoner, etc. If you fail, you attempt to kill your foe instead – even if that means breaking the law, compromising stealth, wasting ammo, or violating orders. Out of combat, you never forget that a foe is a foe.

This may seem a truly evil trait, but many fictional heroes suffer from it. The hero is not a fiend or sadist; his animosity is limited to "legitimate" enemies, be they criminals, enemy soldiers, or feuding clansmen. He often has a good reason for feeling as he does. And, in an ordinary tavern brawl, he would use his fists like anyone else. On the other hand, a gladiator or duelist with Bloodlust would be very unpopular, a policeman would soon be up on charges, and a soldier would risk a court-martial.

Bully

-10 points*

You like to push people around whenever you can get away with it. Depending on your personality and position, this might take the form of physical attacks, intellectual harassment, or social "cutting." Make a self-control roll to avoid gross bullying when you know you shouldn't – but to roleplay your character properly, you should bully anybody you can. Since nobody likes a bully, others react to you at -2.

Callous

-5 points

You are merciless, if not cruel. You can decipher others' emotions, but you do so only to manipulate them – you don't *care* about their feelings or pain. This gives you -3 on all Teaching rolls, on Psychology rolls made to help others (as opposed to deduce weaknesses or conduct scientific research), and on any skill roll made to interact with those who have suffered the consequences of your callousness in the past (GM's decision). As well, past victims, and anyone with Empathy, will react to you at -1. But ruthlessness has its perks: you get an extra +1 to Interrogation and Intimidation rolls when you use threats or torture.

Cannot Learn

-30 points

You cannot spend earned character points to add or improve DX, IQ, skills, or mental advantages, nor can you acquire new techniques (see *Techniques*, p. 229) or familiarities (see *Familiarity*, p. 169) to accompany existing skills. You are stuck with your starting abilities!

You can still increase your ST and HT, and add physical advantages (with the GM's permission). As well, Cannot Learn doesn't prevent you from *temporarily* acquiring skills using the Modular Abilities advantage (p. 71). Those with computer brains often possess both traits.

This trait is most suitable for golems, mindless undead, robots, and other automata.

Cannot Speak

-15 or -25 points

You have a limited capacity for speech. This trait comes in two levels:

Cannot Speak: You can make vocal sounds (bark, growl, trill, etc., as appropriate), but your speech organs are incapable of the subtle modulations required for language. You may still have the Mimicry or Voice advantage, or the Disturbing Voice disadvantage (but *not* Stuttering). Most animals have this trait. *-15 points.*

Mute: You cannot vocalize *at all*. All communications with others must be nonverbal: writing, sign language, Morse code, telepathy, etc. Time spent communicating this way counts at *full* value for study of the related skills (see Chapter 9). No roll is required (or allowed!) when you try to communicate with PCs who don't know your sign language – roleplay this on your own! You cannot have any other voice-related traits. *-25 points.*

Charitable

-15 points*

You are acutely aware of others' emotions, and feel compelled to help those around you – even legitimate enemies. Make a self-control roll in any situation where you could render aid or are specifically asked for help, but should resist the urge. If you fail, you *must* offer assistance, even if that means violating orders or walking into a potential trap.

Chronic Depression 🧠
-15 points*

You've lost your will to live. You'd commit suicide, but it seems like so much trouble. Make a self-control roll to do *anything* but acquire and consume the minimum necessities for survival (for instance, to motivate yourself to go to a movie, attend a job interview, or keep a date), or whenever you must choose between two or more actions. If you fail, you take the path of least resistance. This usually means staying put and doing nothing.

If your self-control number is sufficiently low, you will find it almost impossible to do anything at all for yourself, unless someone physically drags you out of your lair. If somebody shows up and demands that you go out and do something with him, make a self-control roll. If you fail, you go along with his plan out of apathy.

You may eventually replace this disadvantage with another one of equivalent value that is more conducive to self-esteem. The GM need only allow this evolution if you roleplay it convincingly. The GM may also require you to roleplay *both* disadvantages (the new one constantly, the Chronic Depression whenever the GM decides to bring it into play) during the transition period.

You may also *acquire* this disadvantage in play. If you violate a self-imposed mental disadvantage (see p. 121), or lose a Dependent, the GM may replace that disadvantage with this one.

Chronic Pain ♥
Variable

You have an injury, disorder, or illness that leaves you in severe pain on a regular basis – perhaps even *constantly*. Examples include arthritis, bone cancer, migraines, and pieces of shrapnel embedded in the body (an "old war wound").

Roll against the frequency of appearance for your Chronic Pain once per day. If you roll below this number, you suffer a bout of pain. The timing of this attack is up to the GM, but it usually occurs during waking hours – you might wake up with it, or it might be set off by stress (fatigue, exertion, etc.) during the day.

While in pain, reduce your DX and IQ by the amount specified for the severity of your pain (see below). Reduce self-control rolls to resist disadvantages such as Bad Temper and Berserk by the same amount – someone in pain is more likely to lose his cool. If the GM rules that the attack occurs while you are trying to sleep, you suffer penalties for sleep deprivation instead of the usual effects of this disadvantage.

Chronic Pain attacks endure for a fixed "interval," after which you may attempt a HT roll to recover. If you succeed, you have dealt with your pain . . . today. If you fail, the attack continues for another interval, after which you may attempt another HT roll. And so on.

Find the point cost of Chronic Pain by choosing a severity and then multiplying the given cost to reflect the interval and frequency of attacks. Drop all fractions.

Severity

Mild: -2 to DX, IQ, and self-control rolls: *-5 points*.

Severe: -4 to DX, IQ, and self-control rolls: *-10 points*.

Agonizing: -6 to DX, IQ, and self-control rolls: *-15 points*.

Interval

1 hour: ×*0.5*.
2 hours: ×*1*.
4 hours: ×*1.5*.
8 hours: ×*2*.

Frequency of Appearance

Attack occurs on a roll of 6 or less: ×*0.5*.

Attack occurs on a roll of 9 or less: ×*1*.

Attack occurs on a roll of 12 or less: ×*2*.

Attack occurs on a roll of 15 or less: ×*3*.

Chummy 🧠
-5 or -10 points

You work well with others and seek out company. This trait comes in two levels:

Chummy: You react to others at +2 most of the time. When alone, you are unhappy and distracted, and suffer a -1 penalty to IQ-based skills. *-5 points*.

Gregarious: You usually react to others at +4. You are *miserable* when alone, and use IQ-based skills at -2 – or at -1 if in a group of four or less. *-10 points*.

If your self-control number is sufficiently low, you will find it almost impossible to do anything at all for yourself, unless someone physically drags you out of your lair.

Clueless 🧠
-10 points

You totally miss the point of any wit aimed at you, and are oblivious to attempts to seduce you (+4 to resist Sex Appeal). The meanings of colloquial expressions escape you. Sophisticated manners are also beyond you, giving -4 to Savoir-Faire skill. You have many minor habits that annoy others (e.g., leaving the turn signal on while driving from Chicago to Albuquerque), and may take one or two of these as quirks. Most people will react to you at -2.

Unlike No Sense of Humor (p. 146), you may make jokes – albeit lame ones – and you can appreciate slapstick and written humor. However, you rarely "get" verbal humor, *especially* if you are the target (roll vs. IQ-4 roll to realize you're the butt of the joke). And unlike Gullibility (p. 137), you normally realize when someone is trying to take advantage of you, except in social situations. You are no more susceptible to Fast-Talk than normal, save when someone is trying to convince you that an attractive member of the appropriate sex is interested in you . . .

This disadvantage is most appropriate for ivory-tower geniuses, aliens from Mars, etc.

Code of Honor 🗣

-5 to -15 points

You take pride in a set of principles that you follow at all times. The specifics can vary, but they always involve "honorable" behavior. You will do nearly anything – perhaps even risk death – to avoid the label "dishonorable" (whatever that means).

You must do more than pay lip service to a set of principles to get points for a Code of Honor. You must be a true follower of the Code! This is a disadvantage because it often requires dangerous – if not reckless – behavior. Furthermore, you can often be forced into unfair situations, because your foes know you are honorable.

Code of Honor is not the same as Duty (p. 133) or Sense of Duty (p. 153). A samurai or British grenadier marches into battle against fearful odds out of duty, not for his personal honor (though of course he would lose honor by fleeing). The risks you take for your honor are solely on your *own* account.

The point value of a particular Code of Honor depends on how much trouble it is liable to get you into and how arbitrary and irrational its requirements are. An informal Code that applies only among your peers is worth -5 points. A formal Code that applies only among peers, or an informal one that applies all the time, is worth -10 points. A formal Code that applies all the time, or that requires suicide if broken, is worth -15 points. The GM has the final say! Some examples:

Code of Honor (Pirate's): Always avenge an insult, regardless of the danger; your buddy's foe is your own; never attack a fellow crewman or buddy except in a fair, open duel.

Anything else goes. This is also suitable for brigands, bikers, etc. *-5 points.*

Code of Honor (Professional): Adhere to the ethics of your profession; always do your job to the best of your ability; support your guild, union, or professional association. This is most suitable for lawyers and physicians (Hippocratic Oath), but dedicated tradesmen, merchants, and so forth may have a similar Code. *-5 points.*

Code of Honor (Gentleman's): Never break your word. Never ignore an insult to yourself, a lady, or your flag; insults may only be wiped out by an apology or a duel (*not* necessarily to the death!). Never take advantage of an opponent in any way; weapons and circumstances must be equal (except in open war). This only applies between gentlemen. A discourtesy from anyone of Status 0 or less calls for a whipping, not a duel! *-10 points.*

Code of Honor (Soldier's): An officer should be tough but fair, lead from the front, and look out for his men; an enlisted man should look out for his buddies and take care of his kit. Every soldier should be willing to fight and die for the honor of his unit, service, and country; follow orders; obey the "rules of war"; treat an honorable enemy with respect (a dishonorable enemy deserves a bullet); and wear the uniform with pride. *-10 points.*

Code of Honor (Chivalry): As Code of Honor (Gentleman's), except that flags haven't been invented. Respond to any insult to your liege-lord or to your faith. Protect any lady, and anyone weaker than yourself. Accept any challenge to arms from anyone of greater or equal rank. Even in open war, sides and weapons must be equal *if* the foe is also noble and chivalrous. *-15 points.*

Cold-Blooded 🗣 👽

-5 or -10 points

Your body temperature fluctuates with the temperature of the environment. You are less susceptible to damage from high or low body temperature (+2 HT to resist the effects of temperature), and require only 1/3 the food needed by a warm-blooded being of equal mass, but you tend to "stiffen up" in cold weather.

After 30 minutes in cold conditions (or one hour if you have any level of

Temperature Tolerance), you get -1 to Basic Speed and DX per 10° below your "threshold temperature" (see below). At temperatures below 32°, you must roll vs. HT or take 1 HP of damage. Warm clothing gives +2 to this roll.

You regain lost Basic Speed and DX at the rate of one point of each per hour once you return to a warm climate. Double this rate in an exceptionally warm environment.

Point value depends on your "threshold temperature":

You "stiffen up" below 50°: *-5 points.*

You "stiffen up" below 65°: *-10 points.*

Colorblindness 🗣

-10 points

You cannot see any colors at all (this is *total* colorblindness). In any situation requiring color identification (e.g., gem buying, livery identification, or pushing the red button to start the motor), the GM should give you appropriate difficulties. Certain skills are always harder for you. In particular, you are at -1 on most Artist, Chemistry, Driving, Merchant, Piloting, and Tracking rolls.

Combat Paralysis 🗣

-15 points

You tend to "freeze up" in combat situations, and receive -2 to all Fright Checks. This has *nothing* to do with Cowardice (p. 129) – you may be brave, but your body betrays you.

In any situation in which personal harm seems imminent, make a HT roll. Do not roll until the instant you need to fight, run, pull the trigger, or whatever. Any roll over 13 is a failure, even if you have HT 14+. On a success, you can act normally. On a failure, you are mentally stunned (see *Effects of Stun*, p. 420). Make another HT roll every second, at a cumulative +1 per turn after the first, to break the freeze. A quick slap from a friend gives +1 to your cumulative roll.

Once you unfreeze, you will not freeze again until the immediate danger is over. Then, in the next dangerous situation, you may freeze once again.

This trait is the opposite of Combat Reflexes (p. 43). You cannot have both.

Compulsive Behavior
-5 to -15 points*

You have a habit – often a vice – that wastes a good deal of your time or money. You *must* indulge at least once per day, if at all possible, and do so *any* time you have the opportunity unless you can make a self-control roll. You seek to avoid any situation where you know you will be unable to indulge for more than a day. You must make a self-control roll to enter into such a situation; if you succeed (or are forced into the situation), you suffer from Bad Temper (p. 124) the whole time, with the same self-control roll as your Compulsive Behavior. It's bad roleplaying to try to avoid your compulsion regularly!

The point value of this disadvantage depends on how much your habit costs and how much trouble it is likely to get you into. The GM is the final judge. Examples include:

Compulsive Carousing: You cannot resist the urge to party! Once per day, you must seek out a social gathering and lounge around – feasting, drinking, singing, and joking – for at least an hour. If you are not invited, you crash the party; if there is no party, you attempt to liven things up. Money is no object! If you have it, you will spend it. You try almost any mind-altering substance without a second thought, never refuse a social drink, and aren't particularly picky about your romantic partners. You get +1 to reactions from like-minded extroverts, but -1 or worse from sober-minded citizens – and *-4* in puritanical settings. *-5 points* (-10 points* in puritanical settings).

Compulsive Gambling: You cannot pass up an opportunity to gamble. Bets, wagers, games of chance, and even lotteries hold an uncanny fascination for you. If there is no game of chance or bet going, you will start one. You try any gambling game proposed to you, whether you know it or not. You do not *have* to have the Gambling skill, but if you don't, you will need a steady source of wealth! If you are prevented from gambling – for instance, by traveling with nongamblers – you will quickly earn a reaction penalty (-1 per -5 points in this disadvantage, after the self-control multiplier) by constantly talking about gambling and attempting to draw others into games or wagers. *-5 points.*

Compulsive Generosity: You are too open-handed. If a beggar asks for cash, you give – and where others give copper, you give silver. You always listen to larger requests for financial aid, if they are even remotely plausible, and you must make a self-control roll whenever you hear a good hard-luck story (if you are broke when asked, you apologize profusely). You aren't a complete sucker – you just feel guilty about being better off than others. In a society with a lot of beggars around, increase your cost of living:

Self-Control Number	Cost of Living Increase
6	20%
9	15%
12	10%
15	5%

This may earn you a +1 reaction bonus from pious folk; if you are poor yourself, the reaction bonus may be even higher. This trait is incompatible with Miserliness. *-5 points.*

Compulsive Lying: You lie constantly, for no reason other than the joy of telling the tale. You delight in inventing stories about your deeds, lineage, wealth – whatever might impress your audience. Even when exposed as a liar, you cling to your stories tenaciously, calling your accuser a liar and a scoundrel. Make a self-control roll to tell the pure, unvarnished truth. If you fail, you *lie* – no matter how dire the consequences. When you roll to tell the truth to your fellow party members, roll out of sight of the other players. Thus, they can never be sure they are getting accurate information. *-15 points.**

Compulsive Spending: Cash just runs through your fingers! You enjoy being seen as a big spender, are too fond of luxury, or find the experience of buying to be fun – perhaps all three. Make a self-control roll whenever someone offers you a purchase that matches any of your quirks or interests, and the cash in your pocket is more than twice the asking price. If you fail, you buy. This raises your cost of living, and gives you a penalty to Merchant skill when you bargain or haggle:

Self-Control Number	Cost of Living Increase	Merchant Skill Penalty
6	80%	-4
9	40%	-3
12	20%	-2
15	10%	-1

Compulsive Spending is not limited to the wealthy! A poor farmer can be a spendthrift. This trait is incompatible with Miserliness (it's the opposite!), but you *can* combine it with Greed. *-5 points.**

Compulsive Vowing: You never simply *decide* to do something; you must make it an oath. Although these vows are often trivial in nature, you approach them all with the same solemnity and dedication. You may tack extraneous vows onto legitimate ones. *-5 points.**

Confused 🧠

-10 points*

To you, the world seems a strange and incomprehensible place most of the time. You are not necessarily stupid, but you are slow to pick up on new facts or situations.

In particular, you respond poorly to excessive stimulation. When alone in the peace and quiet of your own home, you function normally. But in a

strange place, or when there's a commotion going on, you must make a self-control roll. On a failure, you freeze up instead of taking decisive or appropriate action. This often prevents you from making Tactics rolls and engaging in other sorts of long-range planning. The GM should adjust the self-control roll in accordance with the stimuli in the area. To resist confusion from two friends chatting quietly in a familiar room would require an unmodified roll, but a nightclub with flashing lights and pounding music might give -5, and a full-scale riot or battle would give -10!

If this disadvantage strikes in combat, you must take the Do Nothing maneuver each turn. You are not stunned, and if you are *directly* and physically attacked, you can defend yourself normally. You can even launch a counterattack against *that one foe*. But you never act – only react.

Cowardice 🧠

-10 points*

You are extremely careful about your physical well-being. Make a self-control roll any time you are called on to risk physical danger. Roll at -5 if you must risk *death*. If you fail, you must refuse to endanger yourself unless threatened with *greater* danger!

Cowardice gives a penalty to Fright Checks whenever physical danger is involved:

Self-Control Number	Fright Check Penalty
6	-4
9	-3
12	-2
15	-1

In some times and places, soldiers, police, etc., react to you at a similar penalty if they know you are a coward.

Curious 🧠

-5 points*

You are naturally very inquisitive. This is not the curiosity that affects *all* PCs ("What's in that cave? Where did the flying saucer come from?"), but the *real* thing ("What happens if I push *this* button?").

Make a self-control roll when presented with an interesting item or situation. If you fail, you examine it –

push buttons, pull levers, open doors, unwrap presents, etc. – even if you *know* it could be dangerous. Good roleplayers won't try to make this roll very often . . .

In general, you do everything in your power to investigate *any* situation with which you aren't 100% familiar. When faced with a *real* mystery, you simply cannot turn your back on it. You try to rationalize your curiosity to others who try to talk you out of it. Common Sense doesn't help – you know you are taking a risk, but you're curious anyway!

Cursed 🧠 ☄

-75 points

Like Unluckiness (p. 160), but worse. When anything goes wrong for your party, it happens to you, first and worst. If something goes right, it misses you. Any time the GM feels like hosing you, he can, and you have no complaint coming, because you are Cursed. You can't buy this off just by spending points – you must determine what has cursed you and deal with it, and *then* spend the points.

Deafness 💪

-20 points

You cannot hear *anything*. You must receive information in writing (if you are literate) or sign language. However, time you spend communicating this way counts at *full* value for study of the skills used (Gesture, Lip-Reading, etc.); see Chapter 9.

Debt

see p. 26

Decreased Time Rate 🧠 👽

-100 points

This is the disadvantageous counterpart to Altered Time Rate (p. 38). You experience time half as fast as normal: one subjective second for every two real seconds that pass. You only get a turn every *two* seconds in combat! (Gaming groups that enjoy extra detail might wish to give characters with Decreased Time Rate "half-turns" instead: splitting a Move maneuver across two turns, *declaring* an Attack maneuver one turn and *rolling to hit* the next, etc.)

Delusions 👤

-5 to -15 points

You believe something that simply is not true. This may cause others to consider you insane. And they may be right! If you suffer from a Delusion, you *must* roleplay your belief at all times. The point value of the Delusion depends on its nature:

Minor: This Delusion affects your behavior, and anyone around you will soon notice it, but it does not keep you from functioning more-or-less normally. Those who notice your Delusion will react at -1. *Examples:* "Squirrels are messengers from God." "The Illuminati are watching me constantly – but only to *protect* me." "I am the rightful Duke of Fnordia, stolen at birth by Gypsies and doomed to live among commoners." *-5 points.*

Major: This Delusion *strongly* affects your behavior, but does not keep you from living a fairly normal life. Others will react at -2. *Examples:* "The government has *all* phones tapped." "I have Eidetic Memory and Absolute Direction." *-10 points.*

> *A GM who wants to shake up his players can have a Delusion turn out to be true. (And remember: the GM won't tell you that you are not really crazy. You can be right and still be crazy . . .)*

Severe: This Delusion affects your behavior so much that it may keep you from functioning in the everyday world. Others react to you at -3, but they are more likely to fear or pity you than to attack. A Delusion this severe can keep you from participating meaningfully in the campaign; therefore, you should always clear it with the GM first. *Examples:* "I am Napoleon." "I am immortal." "Ice cream makes machines work better, especially computers. Spoon it right in." *-15 points.*

Depending on your behavior, the same Delusion could be a quirk (-1 point) or worth -5, -10, or -15 points. Consider "Everything colored purple is alive." If you pat purple things and say hello, that's a quirk. If you won't discuss serious matters with purple things in the room, it's a Minor Delusion. If you picket the Capitol demanding Civil Rights For Purple Things, that's Major. If you attack purple things on sight, that's Severe!

Regardless of how insane you really are, you may not get more than -40 points, total, from Delusions.

A GM who wants to shake up his players can have a Delusion turn out to be *true.* This does not suit all Delusions. Of those listed above, for instance, the ones about squirrels, ice cream, and Napoleon seem unlikely. But the Illuminati might really exist, or Gypsies might really have stolen the heir to the throne of Fnordia . . . Have fun!

If your Delusion turns out to be true, you don't have to buy it off until the other players realize it's true. (And remember: the GM *won't* tell you that you are not really crazy. You can be right and *still* be crazy . . .)

Dependency 💪 👽

Variable

You must regularly ingest a substance (e.g., a drug or magic potion), touch or carry an object (e.g., a holy shrine or magical amulet), or spend time in an environment (e.g., your coffin or your home country, planet, or plane) in order to survive. If you fail to do so, you start to lose HP and will eventually die. Point value depends on the rarity of the item you depend on:

Rare (cannot be bought; must be found or made): *-30 points.*
Occasional (very expensive or hard to find): *-20 points.*
Common (expensive, somewhat hard to find): *-10 points.*
Very Common (available almost anywhere): *-5 points.*

Add -5 points to these values for items that are *illegal* in your game world.

Apply a multiplier based on the frequency with which you must receive the item:

Constantly: You must carry and use the substance at all times – for example, an exotic atmosphere. Lose 1 HP per minute without the substance. ×5.
Hourly: Lose 1 HP per 10 minutes after missing an hourly dose. ×4.
Daily: Lose 1 HP per hour after missing a daily dose. ×3.
Weekly: Lose 1 HP per six hours after missing a weekly dose. ×2.
Monthly: Lose 1 HP per day after missing a monthly dose. ×1.
Seasonally: Lose 1 HP per three days after missing a seasonal dose (a "season" is three months for this purpose). ×1/3 (drop all fractions).
Yearly: Lose 1 HP per two weeks after missing a yearly dose. ×1/10 (drop all fractions).

If you need to touch an object or spend time in an environment, you must do so for time equal to your damage interval in order to avoid damage. For instance, to avoid losing 1 HP per hour to a daily Dependency on rest in your coffin, you must spend at least one hour per day in your coffin. To avoid losing 1 HP every two weeks to a yearly Dependency on visiting your home planet, you must visit your home planet for at least two weeks per year.

With the GM's permission, normal humans may take this disadvantage to represent the special requirements of certain chronic illnesses.

Not every life-support requirement qualifies as Dependency. Use Maintenance (p. 143) if you require *skilled care* – not a substance, object, or environment – to avoid HT loss (not injury). Use Restricted Diet (p. 151) for special dietary requirements that result in slow starvation as opposed to rapid HP loss when you are forced to do without.

Special Enhancements

Aging: You age unnaturally without the item you depend on. For each HP lost, you also age two years (even if you are normally Unaging). +30%.

Dependents 🤝

Variable

A "Dependent" is an NPC for whom you are responsible; e.g., your child, kid brother, or spouse. You *must* take care of your Dependents. Furthermore, your foes can strike at *you* through them. (If you have both an Enemy and a Dependent, and the dice indicate that both appear, then the GM can build an entire adventure around this theme!)

If your Dependent ends up kidnapped or otherwise in danger during play, you *must* go to the rescue as soon as possible. If you don't go to his aid immediately, the GM can deny you bonus character points for "acting out of character." Furthermore, you never earn any character points for a game session in which your Dependent is killed or badly hurt.

Three factors determine the disadvantage value of a Dependent: his *competence*, his *importance* (to you!), and his *frequency of appearance*.

Competence

Specify the number of points your Dependent is built on. The more points you use to "build" your Dependent, the more competent he will be, and the *fewer* points he will be worth as a disadvantage. "Point Total" is the Dependent's point total as a fraction of the PC's, except for the last line, which is absolute; "Cost" is the number of character points the disadvantage is worth.

Point Total	Cost
No more than 100%	-1 point
No more than 75%	-2 points
No more than 50%	-5 points
No more than 25%	-10 points
0 or fewer points	-15 points

The *same person* can be both a Dependent and an Ally (p. 36)! Add the cost of Ally and Dependent together, and treat the combination as a single trait: an advantage if the total point cost is positive, a disadvantage if it is negative. You must use the same point total for him in both cases, but frequency of appearance can differ. Roll separately for his appearance as a Dependent and as an Ally. If he appears as a Dependent, he shows up in a way that causes you trouble (e.g., he's captured). If he appears as an Ally, he manages to be helpful and take care of himself. If he appears as both, he is helpful *and* troublesome at the same time; for instance, he uses his skills to assist you, but also wanders off, is singled out by the enemy, or otherwise causes problems equal to the assistance he offers.

Importance

The more important your Dependent is to you, the more you multiply his intrinsic "nuisance value" and worth in points.

Employer or acquaintance: You feel a responsibility toward this person, but you may weigh risks to him in a rational fashion. ×1/2.

Friend: You must always try to protect this person. You may only risk harm to him if something very important (such as the safety of many other people) is at stake. ×1.

Loved one: The Dependent is a relative or a lover. You may not put *anything* before his safety! ×2.

Frequency of Appearance

Choose a frequency of appearance, as explained under *Frequency of Appearance* (p. 36). This should fit the "story" behind the Dependent. If the Dependent were your infant child, for instance, it would be odd for him to appear "quite rarely"!

Multiple Dependents

You cannot earn points for more than two Dependents. However, if you have a *group* of Dependents, you may count the entire group as your two Dependents. Work out the value of an average member of the group as a Dependent, and then claim twice this point value.

Example: A vigilante who is a schoolteacher by day could have "generic dependents": all pupils. They are young (-10 points), around "quite often" (×2), and count as "friends" (×1), for -20 points each. However, the two-Dependent limit lets the hero claim -40 points' worth of Dependents. (And if one gets hurt, there are always others.)

Dependents in Play

As you earn points, the GM will scale your Dependent's abilities proportionally to keep his point total a fixed percentage of your own. Thus, his value as a disadvantage will not change. Children grow up, adults earn money, and everyone learns new skills. Dependents who spend a lot of time around you might become adventurers in their own right. You are free to suggest reasonable improvements for your Dependents, but the GM's word is final.

If your Dependent is killed, or so seriously injured that the GM decides he is effectively out of the campaign, you *must* make up the bonus points you got for him. You have three options: buy off the amount by spending earned character points, take a new disadvantage (e.g., Chronic Depression, p. 126), or get a new Dependent. New Dependents are usually inappropriate, but a mental disability brought on by the loss is a good solution. (Ever since the octopus got Amy, you've been afraid of the ocean . . .)

Examples of Dependents

- For anyone: elderly relatives, teachers, friends, children, younger brothers or sisters, lovers, husbands or wives.
- For crimefighters: young sidekicks, reporters, or wards.
- For wizards: apprentices.
- For ship captains (ocean- or space-going): ensigns or cabin boys.
- For soldiers: orphans or new recruits.
- For criminals or mad scientists: incompetent henchmen.

Destiny 💭 🏃

Variable

A disadvantageous Destiny functions identically to an advantageous one (see p. 48), save that it always leads to something *bad* – but perhaps not immediately, and not without a chance to gain honor by dealing with it well. A fated, tragic death can be an end worthy of a hero! This kind of Destiny comes in three levels:

Minor Disadvantage: You are fated to play a small part in a larger story, and you will not come off so well. You are guaranteed at least one tragic experience or embarrassing failure – although these things are unlikely to result in your death except under the most desperate and heroic of circumstances. *-5 points.*

Major Disadvantage: You are fated to play a key role in a sorry turn of events. For instance, you might be late with a message that could save the day . . . or execute the only competent general in a threatened province, causing its loss to barbarian invaders. Still, you will survive. *-10 points.*

Great Disadvantage: Death stalks you. Something out there has your name on it. It knows where you are and it's getting closer all the time. You will either die or be ruined, and your fall will have terrible repercussions for others. This kind of Destiny is not suitable for every campaign! The GM does not have to allow it – and if he does, he should plan on letting the campaign take a radical turn, or *end*, when the Destiny is fulfilled. *-15 points.*

You *must* buy off a disadvantageous Destiny as soon as it is fulfilled. This is automatic if the outcome strips you of Allies, Status, Wealth, etc. worth the same number of points. If you lack the points to buy off your Destiny, you gain Unluckiness (p. 160), regardless of the point value of the Destiny. It is up to the GM whether you can buy off the Unluckiness! Alternatively, the GM might assign you a new bad Destiny, Divine Curse (below), or other supernatural disadvantage.

Disciplines of Faith 🧠
-5 to -15 points

You live by a strict set of rules in order to achieve a greater understanding of your faith. This might be a personal decision or a requirement of your religion. Such rules are optional in many faiths, though – indeed, some religions might *forbid* them as excesses! Disciplines of Faith are often a prerequisite for abilities that channel divine power: Power Investiture, True Faith, etc.

Some examples of Disciplines of Faith:

Asceticism: You have renounced the comforts of society to lead a life of self-denial and self-discipline. This often involves some sort of isolation in bleak, austere settings. It might even involve sporadic bouts of severe self-punishment to excise the mortal taint of earthly desire. You must try to transcend *all* need for worldly possessions,

and in any event cannot have above-average Wealth, or Status beyond that granted by your Religious Rank (if any). *-15 points.*

Monasticism: You lead a life apart from worldly concerns. You are completely devoted to religious pursuits, which often involves the denial of ego and self. You must spend at least 75% of your time sequestered from the world, and cannot have above-average Wealth, or Status beyond that granted by your Religious Rank (if any). *-10 points.*

Mysticism: You engage in deep meditation and trance-like contemplation, with the aim of obtaining a closer union with the divine. You spend most of your time engaged in these rituals, complete with chanting and any other necessary trappings. Individuals other than devout co-religionists will consider you a bit mad, and will react at -2. *-10 points.*

Ritualism: You adhere strictly to elaborate rituals regarding every aspect of life – from waking to eating to bathing to sex. Each ritual has its proper place, time, words, trappings, and ceremony. Your fundamental belief is that, through the perfect performance of these rituals, you bring each aspect of your life closer to the divine. *-5 points.*

Disturbing Voice 💪
-10 points

Your voice is naturally unpleasant or obviously artificial. Details can vary. You might be a robot, or use a technological aid to mitigate the Mute disadvantage. Your voice might be raspy, hollow, or squeaky, or your speech might be monotonous and without inflection. The game effects in all cases are identical to those of Stuttering (p. 157), although you do not necessarily stutter.

This trait is the opposite of the Voice advantage (p. 97); you cannot have both.

Divine Curse 🧠 ⚡
Variable

You suffer from a curse placed by a god or similar supernatural force. The curse might be on just you, on your entire family, or even on your nation or race.

Divine Curse can take any form the GM desires. It can be a continuing commandment (e.g., "You may never sleep at night," -10 points), a misfortune (e.g., "Every child born to you will die young," -5 points), or even a particularly nasty disadvantage such as Berserk, Blindness, or Epilepsy (at the usual cost). What makes it distinct from other disadvantages is the potential for removal. The curse was given for a reason, and you can try to uncover this reason and atone in play, thereby lifting the curse.

The GM should judge the point value of Divine Curse on a case-by-case basis, using existing disadvantages as guidelines: the more encompassing or debilitating the curse, the higher its value. Curses that result in standard disadvantages should never be worth more points than those disadvantages. Price commandments as if they were Vows. The terms of atonement will often be nearly as bad as the curse itself, or require great effort to discover and satisfy. *Halve* the point value if this is not the case.

Draining 💪 ⚡
Variable

Once per day, at a specific time – sunrise, noon, sunset, midnight, etc. – you take 2 HP of damage. You can do nothing to prevent this, and cannot heal the damage naturally (even if you have Regeneration!), technologically, or supernaturally. The *only* way to regain your lost HP is to receive a daily dose of a particular substance. Point cost depends on the rarity of this substance:

Rare (e.g., a special potion): *-15 points.*

Occasional (e.g., virgin's blood): *-10 points.*

Common (e.g., human blood): *-5 points.*

Add -5 points to these values for items that are *illegal* in your game world.

This is not the same as Dependency (p. 130). You can have both!

Dread 🧠 ⚡
Variable

You suffer from a supernatural aversion that compels you to keep a certain, minimum distance from a particular item or substance. If outside forces bring you and the item you dread closer together than that, you must move away as fast as you can, by the most direct route possible. You may do *nothing* else until you are beyond the range of your Dread. If you cannot put at least that much distance between yourself and the object of your Dread, your Dread will render you helpless!

You can instantly sense the presence of the dreaded substance as soon as you enter the forbidden radius. You do not know exactly where it is, but you know what direction it lies in and are compelled to go exactly the other way.

Base value of Dread is -10 points, which prohibits you from coming within one yard of the dreaded substance. A larger radius gives an additional -1 point per yard, to a maximum of -20 points at 11 yards. Find the final disadvantage value by multiplying the point value for your range to reflect the rarity of the substance, as described for *Weakness* (p. 161).

Special Limitations

Cannot Be Trapped: You cannot enter the forbidden zone of your own volition, but if carried there by an outside force, you no longer feel your Dread. You can act normally in the forbidden zone until you leave the substance's presence, at which time the prohibition reactivates. -50%.

Duty

Variable

If your occupation and social situation saddle you with a significant personal obligation toward others, and occasionally require you to obey hazardous orders, you have a "Duty." Duty most often accompanies Rank (p. 29), a Patron (p. 72), or one of the traits discussed under *Privilege* (p. 30).

A particularly arduous job might qualify as a Duty, but most ordinary jobs would not. A wholly self-imposed feeling of duty is not a Duty, either (but it can still be a disadvantage; see *Sense of Duty,* p. 153). Finally, you cannot claim points for a Duty toward Dependents (p. 131); the points you get for Dependents *already* reflect your obligations in this regard.

The GM may restrict the Duties allowed in a campaign, or even forbid them entirely, if he feels they would unduly disrupt the flow of the adventure.

If you have a Duty, the GM rolls at the beginning of each adventure to see whether it comes into play. Being "called to duty" could delay your plans . . . or be the *reason* for the adventure! Alternatively, your master might give you a secret agenda to pursue, or his associates might harass you while you are officially "on leave." If you try to avoid your Duty, your GM is within his rights to penalize you for bad role-playing.

The basic point cost of a Duty depends on the frequency with which comes up in play:

Almost all the time (roll of 15 or less): *-15 points*. At this level, the GM may rule that you are *always* on duty.

Quite often (roll of 12 or less): *-10 points*.

Fairly often (roll of 9 or less): *-5 points*.

Quite rarely (roll of 6 or less): *-2 points*.

This cost is for an occasionally hazardous Duty imposed through normal social means. If this does not describe your Duty, you should modify the cost:

Extremely Hazardous: You are *always* at risk of death or serious injury when your Duty comes up. There are significant penalties if you refuse to take these risks: dismissal in disgrace, imprisonment, perhaps even death. The GM has the final say as to whether a given Duty is "extremely hazardous" in his campaign. *-5 points*.

Involuntary: Your Duty is enforced by threats to you or your loved ones, or is imposed by exotic mind control, a curse, etc. This is unrelated to how hazardous the Duty is when you carry it out – the danger here lies in what will happen if you *don't* carry it out! A Duty can be Involuntary *and* either Extremely Hazardous or Nonhazardous. *-5 points*.

Nonhazardous: Your Duty never *requires* you to risk your life. This option is mutually exclusive with Extremely Hazardous. *+5 points*. (If this raises the cost of your Duty to 0 points or more, the obligation is too trivial to qualify as a Duty.)

Examples

Example 1: A mayor is indebted to the crime lord who got him elected. His benefactor rarely calls on him for favors (-2 points), but since the mayor faces blackmail or violence if he refuses to comply, his Duty is Involuntary. Duty (Crime Lord, 6 or less; Involuntary) is worth -7 points.

Example 2: A commando is always on duty (-15 points). He might see only a handful of combat assignments in his whole career, but these will be *deadly*. And his daily routine calls for him to jump out of planes, hike through snake-infested jungles, and train with live ammo. A commando has Duty (Army, 15 or less; Extremely Hazardous), for -20 points.

Dwarfism

see p. 19

Dyslexia

-10 points

You have a *crippling* reading disability. Even simple maps and road signs are beyond you. You start with a written comprehension level of "None" in your native language. This is included in Dyslexia; you get no extra points for it. Furthermore, you may never improve your written comprehension level beyond "None" in *any* language. For more on language comprehension, see *Language* (p. 23).

You can learn "book-learned" skills at normal speed if you have a teacher to substitute for your inability to use texts. Attempts to learn such a skill without a teacher progress at 1/4 speed – *if* the skill is one you can teach yourself without books. The GM's word is final in all cases. In traditional fantasy settings, magic is a book-learned skill, and Dyslexia prevents you from ever becoming a wizard.

Note that this is a *severe* case. Mild dyslexia is not significant in game terms, except possibly as a quirk.

Easy to Kill

-2 points/level

You have a health problem or structural weakness that leaves you prone to catastrophic system failure if you suffer enough damage. Each level of Easy to Kill gives -1 to HT rolls made for survival at -HP or below, and on any HT roll where failure would mean instant death (e.g., heart failure). This does *not* affect most normal HT rolls – only those to avoid certain death. You may not reduce your HT roll below 3. For instance, if you have HT 10, you are limited to Easy to Kill 7.

Easy to Read

-10 points

Your body language betrays your true intentions. This is *not* the same as Truthfulness (p. 159). You have no moral problem with lying, and may even possess Fast-Talk at a high level, but your face or stance gives the game away.

Easy to Read gives *others* +4 on all Empathy, Body Language, and Psychology rolls to discern your intentions or the truth of your words. As well, they get +4 to their IQ, Detect Lies, and Gambling rolls in any Quick Contest with your Acting, Fast-Talk, or Gambling skill when you try to lie or bluff. (If you *also* have Truthfulness, your Fast-Talk skill is at -5 on top of this.) This is a crippling disadvantage for a would-be spy, con man, or gambler!

This *is* a mental disadvantage, despite its physical manifestations; with enough practice, you can "buy it off."

Electrical

-20 points

Your body contains unshielded electronics, or relies on electrical power for its vital energy. This makes you susceptible to attacks that only affect electrical systems, such as spells, advantages, and ultra-tech weapons that drain power or produce "surge" effects, and the electromagnetic pulse from a nuclear blast. A critical hit from an electrical attack causes you to "short-circuit," rendering you unconscious in addition to any other damage effects.

This disadvantage usually accompanies the Machine meta-trait (p. 263), but this is not required. Afflictions and Innate Attacks that *only* affect those with this trait are possible. Apply the -20% Accessibility limitation "Only on Electrical" to all such attacks.

Enemies

Variable

An "Enemy" is an NPC, group of NPCs, or organization that actively works against you, personally, on your adventures. Some Enemies want to kill you . . . others have more devious goals.

Determine the nature of your Enemy when you create your character, and explain to the GM why the Enemy is after you. The GM is free to fill in additional details as he sees fit.

Three factors determine the disadvantage value of an Enemy: its *power*, its *intent*, and its *frequency of appearance*.

Power

The more powerful the Enemy, the more points it is worth as a disadvantage. The GM sets this value. Note that when your Enemy is an organization, the point value is based on the number of individuals who are after *you* – not on the total size of the group!

One person, less powerful than the PC (built on about 50% of the PC's starting points). *-5 points.*

One person, equal in power to the PC (built on about 100% of the PC's starting points), or a small group of less-powerful people (3 to 5 people). *Examples:* A mad scientist, or the four brothers of the man you killed in a duel. *-10 points.*

One person, more powerful than the PC (built on at least 150% of the PC's starting points), or a medium-sized group of less-powerful people (6 to 20 people). *Examples:* a single superhuman or a city police department (which numbers in the hundreds, but they're not all after you at once). *-20 points.*

A large group of less-powerful people (21 to 1,000 people), or a medium-sized group that includes some formidable or superhuman individuals. *Examples:* the FBI or the Mafia. *-30 points.*

An entire government, a whole guild of powerful wizards, an organization of supers, or some other utterly formidable group. *-40 points.*

Special Cases

There are two special cases for which you should adjust the costs given above *before* multiplying for intent and frequency of appearance:

Evil Twin: Your Enemy looks and sounds like you, and perhaps even uses your name, but acts completely opposite. Often, others will think you suffer from Split Personality (p. 156), and react appropriately (-3 to reactions). You might never meet your Evil Twin, but you *will* hear about him – usually when you're taking the blame for something you didn't do. Normally, an Evil Twin has exactly the same skills and abilities as you, but his mental disadvantages are opposite or skewed. This makes him an even match: a -10-point Enemy. If he is more capable than you, he is worth extra points, because he is better equipped to make you look insane, and you are less able to predict and thwart his actions.

Evil Twin is more skilled than you *or* possesses abilities that you do not (GM decides): *-5 points.*

Evil Twin is more skilled than you *and* possesses abilities that you do not (GM decides): *-10 points.*

Unknown: You know you have an Enemy, but you have no idea who it is. Tell the GM the power level of your Enemy. He will create the Enemy in secret and give you *no details whatsoever!* The advantage of surprise increases your Enemy's effective power level, and hence its disadvantage value. *-5 points.*

Intent

The more unpleasant the Enemy's intentions, the more you multiply its worth in points.

Watcher: Your Enemy stalks you or spies on you. This is annoying, and makes it hard to keep secrets, but it is rarely more than a minor inconvenience. *Examples:* an aggressive journalist dogging a politician, detectives shadowing a suspected criminal. ×1/4.

Rival: Your Enemy wishes to upstage or inconvenience you, or plays cruel practical jokes on you (this is typical of most Evil Twins), but stops short of anything that would do lasting harm. *Examples:* a politician's bitter political rival, detectives harassing a suspected criminal. ×1/2.

Hunter: The Enemy intends to arrest, bankrupt, injure, or otherwise harm you in some lasting way – or simply wants to kill you. *Examples:* an assassin gunning for a politician, detectives out to arrest a suspected criminal. ×1.

Frequency of Appearance

Choose a frequency of appearance, as explained under *Frequency of Appearance* (p. 36). Roll at the beginning of each adventure, or at the start of each *session* of a continuing adventure.

Limits on Enemies

You may not take more than two Enemies, or claim more than -60 points in Enemies. (If the whole U.S. government is out to get you, the fact that your old college professor has lost his mind, and is *also* after you, pales to insignificance.)

Enemies in Play

If the dice indicate that an Enemy should show up, the GM must decide how and where the Enemy becomes involved. If an Enemy is very powerful, or if a number of *different* Enemies show up at the same time, this may influence the whole adventure.

If you take an extremely powerful Enemy, you are likely to be jailed or killed before long. So it goes. You can get a 60-point bonus by taking Enemy (FBI, 12 or less; Hunter), but your every adventure will be that of a hunted criminal. Even with an extra 60 points, your career may be short.

If you start with a *weak* Enemy, or play cleverly, you might manage to eliminate your foe or permanently change his attitude toward you. But as the saying goes, "There ain't no such thing as a free lunch." If you get rid of an Enemy, you have three choices:

1. Pay enough character points to buy off the original bonus you got for that Enemy.

2. Take a disadvantage to make up for the point bonus. For instance, you might have been kicked in the head during the final battle, leaving you partially deaf. Or a giant spider might have attacked you, leaving you with arachnophobia. The new disadvantage should have the same point cost as your former Enemy (or less, if you want to buy off *part* of the disadvantage). If you cannot think of a good substitute disadvantage, the GM will be more than happy to supply one!

3. Take a new Enemy of equal value. You might have destroyed the fiendish Dr. Scorpion – but his brother is continuing his evil work.

Epilepsy ⚜

-30 points

You suffer from *severe* epilepsy. You are subject to seizures during which your limbs tremble uncontrollably and you cannot speak or think clearly.

Make a HT roll whenever you are in a stressful situation (especially if your life or the life of a friend is threatened). If you have any sort of Phobia, exposure to the object of your fear counts as a stressful situation; roll vs. HT once every 10 minutes. On a failure, you suffer a seizure that lasts 1d minutes and costs you 1d FP. You can do *nothing* during that time.

You may attempt to induce a seizure through autohypnosis. This requires one minute of concentration and a successful Will or Autohypnosis roll. Seizures near areas charged with supernatural energies might produce visions. Whether these are *useful* is up to the GM.

Low-tech individuals who do not understand "fits" may be awed by them, and perhaps even believe your seizure represents a communication from the gods. Make a reaction roll at +1. A reaction of "Very Good" or better indicates religious awe! "Poor" or worse causes the observers to flee – not to attack (unless they had other provocation).

Extra Sleep ⚜

-2 points/level

You need more sleep than most people. A normal human requires 8 hours of sleep per night. Each level (maximum of four levels) means you need one additional hour of sleep. Thus, you must go to bed early or sleep in for a few hours each day. This gives you less time each day in which to study or work on other projects.

Fanaticism ⚜

-15 points

You believe so strongly in a country, organization, philosophy, or religion that you put it ahead of *everything* else. You might even be willing to die for it! If the object of your Fanaticism demands obedience to a code of behavior or loyalty to a leader, you oblige willingly and unquestioningly. You *must* roleplay your unwavering dedication.

Fanaticism does not make you mindless or evil. A glaring priest of Set, brandishing his bloody dagger, is a fanatic. But so is a kamikaze pilot, exchanging himself for an aircraft carrier. And so is a patriot who says, "Give me liberty or give me death!" Fanaticism is a state of mind; it is *what* you are fanatic about that makes the difference.

Extreme Fanaticism: This is an advanced case of Fanaticism. You get +3 on Will rolls to resist Brainwashing, Interrogation, and supernatural mind control in any situation where failure to resist would lead to betrayal of your cult or organization. On the other hand, you will not hesitate to die for your cause, and will undertake suicide missions "matter-of-factly." This is still worth -15 points. Your willingness to die is offset by the significant bonus to Will (which will apply a good deal of the time, if you are roleplaying properly).

Fat

see p. 19

Fearfulness ⚜

-2 points/level

You are nervous and timid. Subtract your Fearfulness from your Will whenever you make a Fright Check, and whenever you must resist the Intimidation skill (p. 202) or a supernatural power that causes fear. As well, add your Fearfulness level to all Intimidation rolls made against you.

You may not reduce your Will roll below 3. For instance, if you have Will 11, you are limited to Fearfulness 8.

This trait is the opposite of Fearlessness (p. 55); you cannot have both.

Flashbacks ⚜

Variable

You tend to experience "flashbacks" when under stress. These are vivid hallucinations, full-participation replays of memories, or similar phenomena. You should choose the *type* of flashback you experience when you take this disadvantage. The *content* of each episode is up to the GM.

In any situation that the GM feels is stressful, he will roll 3d. On a 6 or less, you have a flashback. The GM will roll whenever you miss a Fright Check or make the roll exactly, and whenever you fail a self-control roll for another stress-related disadvantage. The flashback occurs *in addition to* any other results!

Point value depends on the severity of the flashback:

Mild: Duration is 2d seconds. The attendant hallucinations give -2 on all skill rolls, but they are minor – you realize that you are experiencing a flashback. *-5 points.*

Severe: Duration is 1d minutes. The hallucinations give -5 on all skill rolls, and seem *real. -10 points.*

Crippling: Duration is 3d minutes. The hallucinations are so severe that they preclude all skill use. The flashback seems completely, 100% real, and can be potentially fatal, as you are receiving *no* input from the real world. *-20 points.*

Fragile ⚜ ♦

Variable

You are susceptible to wounding effects that do not apply to normal humans. Attacks do not injure you any more than usual (that's Vulnerability, p. 161), but enough penetrating damage can trigger results more catastrophic than stunning, unconsciousness, or bleeding. Possibilities include:

Brittle: You are brittle (like a creature of ice or crystal) or rotten (like a decaying undead monster). Whenever an injury cripples one of your limbs or extremities, it *breaks off.* If you can make a HT roll, it falls off in one piece; otherwise, it shatters or liquefies irrecoverably. Furthermore, should you fail any HT roll to avoid death, you are instantly destroyed – you shatter, melt, decay to goo, etc., and instantly go to -10×HP. *-15 points.*

Combustible: Your body burns more easily than flesh. Perhaps it is dry, resinous, or made of wood. Make a HT roll to avoid catching fire whenever you receive a major wound from a burning or explosive attack. You catch fire *automatically* if such an attack inflicts 10+ HP of injury. Once aflame, you suffer 1d-1 injury per second until you extinguish the fire by immersion in water, rolling on the ground (takes 3 seconds), etc. *-5 points.*

Explosive: Your body contains explosives, compressed gas, or something else unstable. On any critical failure on the HT roll for a major wound, you explode! You also explode if you fail any HT roll to avoid death by 3↓. Treat this as a 6d×(HP/10) crushing explosion. The blast instantly reduces you to -10×HP, regardless of the damage it *inflicts*. *-15 points.*

Flammable: Your body contains something highly flammable: gasoline, hydrogen gas, etc. Make a HT roll to avoid catching fire, with effects as per Combustible, after a major wound from *any* kind of attack. Roll at -3 for a burning or explosive attack, -3 if the attack struck the vitals, and -6 if both. Once you are burning, a critical failure on any HT roll to avoid death means you explode as described for Explosive. You may be Combustible as well. If so, any burning or explosive attack that inflicts either a major wound or 10+ HP of injury *automatically* sets you ablaze. *-10 points.*

Unnatural: You are summoned, conjured, or a magical or weird-science "construct" (e.g., demon, golem, or undead). You *automatically* fail the HT roll to stay alive if reduced to -HP or below, as that much damage severs your ties with the force that animates you. *-50 points.*

It sometimes makes sense to take more than one of the above (in particular, Explosive and Flammable often occur together). The GM must personally approve any combination of Fragile with Injury Tolerance (p. 60), as these traits are in many ways opposites.

Frightens Animals 🧠 ⚡
-10 points

Animals react to you with fear and aggression. Horses do not permit you to ride them, dogs shy away from you or attack savagely, and your mere scent is enough to panic most creatures. You get -4 on all reaction rolls made by animals. Anyone who sees how animals react to you – and those with Animal Empathy – reacts to you at -1. Note that guards or police with guard animals, "sniffer" dogs, etc. decide how to deal with you based on the *animal's* reaction roll, not their own!

If your disadvantage is due to lycanthropy, vampirism, or a similar trait, observers get +1 on all rolls to deduce your secret!

G-Intolerance 💪
-10 or -20 points

You function well under a narrow range of gravities. For a normal human, the penalties for non-native gravity accrue in increments of 0.2G; see *Different Gravity* (p. 350). An increment of 0.1G is worth -10 points. An increment of 0.05G is worth -20 points.

This disadvantage is only allowed in campaigns that feature regular space travel.

Gigantism
see p. 20

Gluttony 🧠
-5 points*

You are overly fond of good food and drink. Given the chance, you must always burden yourself with extra provisions. You should never willingly miss a meal. Make a self-control roll when presented with a tempting morsel or good wine that, for some reason, you should resist. If you fail, you partake – regardless of the consequences.

Greed 🧠
-15 points*

You lust for wealth. Make a self-control roll any time riches are offered – as payment for fair work, gains from adventure, spoils of crime, or just bait. If you fail, you do whatever it takes to get the payoff. The GM may modify this roll if the money involved is small relative to your own wealth. Small sums do not tempt you much if you are rich, but if you are *poor,* you get -5 or more on your self-control roll if a rich prize is in the offing. If you have Honesty (p. 138), your self-control roll is at +5 for a shady deal and +10 for outright crime. However, it is almost a foregone conclusion that you will eventually do something illegal.

Gregarious
see *Chummy*, p. 126

Guilt Complex 🧠
-5 points

You feel personally responsible for those who play a significant role in your life. This includes adventuring companions, employers, subordinates, Allies, Dependents, and those toward whom you have a Duty or a Sense of Duty. If *anything* bad happens to someone like this, you will be wracked by anxiety and guilt – even if there was nothing you could have done to avert the disaster.

If the mishap was not your fault, you will suffer the effects of Chronic Depression (p. 126) for (15 - Will) days, minimum one day. Use your Will as your effective self-control number. If the mishap *was* your fault, the effects of Chronic Depression will last (20 - Will) days, minimum two days, and your effective self-control number is Will-3.

Others may attempt to help you overcome your feelings of guilt by making Fast-Talk or Psychology rolls. The GM is free to modify their rolls, depending on how convincing they sounded. Roleplay it!

Gullibility 🧠
-10 points*

There's one born every minute, and you're it. You believe everything you hear. You'll swallow even the most ridiculous story, if it's told with conviction. Make a self-control roll, modified by the plausibility of the story, whenever you are confronted with a lie – or an improbable truth, for that matter. If you fail, you believe what you were told!

A lie well told, or involving something you have no familiarity with ("My father is the chief of police in this town, and he won't stand for this!") gives -6 to the self-control roll. A lie concerning a topic you are familiar with ("Didn't you know they bred ducks in your village, Torg?") gives -3. You believe even a totally outlandish tale ("Of course the Eskimos are descended from Spanish conquistadors; everyone knows that!"), if you fail an unmodified self-control roll.

You also suffer a -3 penalty on any Merchant skill roll, or in any situation in which your credulity might be exploited. You can *never* learn the Detect Lies skill.

Ham-Fisted

-5 or -10 points

You have unusually poor motor skills. You suffer a penalty to any DX-based roll to do fine work using the skills listed under *High Manual Dexterity* (p. 59), and to Fast-Draw skill. For -5 points, the penalty is -3; for -10 points, it is -6. This does *not* affect IQ-based tasks or large-scale DX-based tasks, nor does it modify combat-related die rolls other than Fast-Draw.

You are also a messy eater, can't tie a necktie properly, and so on. At the GM's option, you get -1 per level of this trait on any Influence or reaction roll where being tidy or well-groomed would matter.

This disadvantage is mutually exclusive with High Manual Dexterity.

Hard of Hearing

-10 points

You are not deaf, but you have some hearing loss. You are at -4 on any Hearing roll, and on any skill roll where it is important that you understand someone (if you are the one talking, this disadvantage doesn't affect you).

Hemophilia

-30 points

You are a "bleeder." Even a small wound *will not heal* unless well-bandaged – and you may bleed to death. Any untreated wound bleeds at a rate equal to its original damage every minute. For instance, an untreated 3 HP wound bleeds for 3 HP of damage per minute until stanched.

First Aid is enough to staunch most wounds, but an impaling wound to the torso causes slow internal bleeding. It does damage every minute, as above, until you receive First Aid. Furthermore, it *continues* to do damage equal to its original damage once per *day* until properly treated. Only a Surgery roll or supernatural healing can stop internal bleeding or restore HP lost to it. If proper treatment is not available, you will soon die.

If you suffer from this disadvantage, your HT score may not exceed 10.

Hidebound

-5 points

You find it difficult to come up with an original thought. You have a -2 penalty on any task that requires creativity or invention, including most rolls against Artist skill, all Engineer rolls for new inventions, and all skill rolls made to use the Gadgeteer advantage.

Honesty

-10 points*

You *must* obey the law, and do your best to get others to do so as well. In an area with little or no law, you do not "go wild" – you act as though the laws of your own home were in force. You also assume that others are honest unless you *know* otherwise (make an IQ roll to realize someone might be dishonest if you haven't seen proof).

This is a disadvantage, because it often limits your options! Make a self-control roll when faced with the "need" to break unreasonable laws; if you fail, you *must* obey the law, whatever the consequences. If you manage to resist your urges and break the law, make a second self-control roll afterward. If you fail, you must turn yourself in to the authorities!

You *may* fight (or even start a fight, if you do it in a legal way). You may even kill in a legal duel or in self-defense – but you may never *murder*. You may steal if there is great need, but only as a last resort, and you must attempt to pay your victims back later. If you are jailed for a crime you did not commit, but treated fairly and assured of a trial, you will not try to escape.

You always keep your word. (In a war, you may act "dishonestly" against the enemy, but you will not be happy about it!) However, you *are* allowed to lie if it does not involve breaking the law. Truthfulness (p. 159) is a separate disadvantage.

Honesty has its rewards, of course. If you stay alive and in one place long enough for your honesty to become known, the GM should give you +1 on any noncombat reaction roll – or +3 if a question of trust or honor is involved. This is essentially a free Reputation (see *Reputation*, p. 26).

Horizontal ♟♥

-10 points

You have a horizontal posture, like a cat. You can stand on your hind legs for short periods, but find this very uncomfortable. You can use one hand (if you *have* hands) while standing on your other limbs, or two hands while sitting on your haunches; in both cases, your ground Move is 0 while doing so. You can carry but not use an object in one hand if moving at half Move. If you are human-sized, you take up two hexes on a battle map.

A horizontal build does not let you put your full weight behind a kick. As a result, your thrusting damage is at -1 *per die* when you kick. Ignore this penalty if you have Claws (p. 42) – that trait includes the necessary adaptations to strike at full power. The penalty *does* apply if you have Hooves, however.

Do *not* take this disadvantage if you are Aerial or Aquatic (see *No Legs*, p. 145). If you are fully adapted to a three-dimensional environment, body posture is irrelevant.

Hunchback ♟

-10 points

You have a spinal deformity that forces you into a twisted or hunched position, usually resulting in a noticeable hump or lump on one or both shoulders. This reduces height by 6" without changing weight or build. Normal clothing and armor will fit badly, giving you -1 to DX; to avoid this, you must pay an extra 10% for specially made gear.

Most people find you disturbing to see and react at -1. This penalty is cumulative with regular appearance modifiers (see *Physical Appearance*, p. 21), and you may have no better than Average appearance. Your appearance is also *distinctive*, which gives you -3 to Disguise or Shadowing skill, and +3 to others' attempts to identify or follow you.

Realistic hunchbacks should have the Bad Back disadvantage (p. 123) as well, but this is not required.

Impulsiveness ♥

-10 points*

You hate talk and debate. You prefer action! When you are alone, you act first and think later. In a group, when your friends want to stop and discuss something, you should put in your two cents' worth quickly – if at all – and then do *something*. Roleplay it! Make a self-control roll whenever it would be wise to wait and ponder. If you fail, you *must* act.

Increased Consumption ♟

-10 points/level

One "meal" keeps you going for a much shorter period of time than it would a normal human. This is suitable for small creatures that must eat often, or for machines that rapidly exhaust their fuel or energy supply.

Increased Consumption 1: You must eat six meals a day. If you have the Machine meta-trait (p. 263), you have a 4-hour endurance.

Increased Consumption 2: You must eat 12 meals a day. If you have the Machine meta-trait, you have a 2-hour endurance.

Increased Consumption 3: You must eat 24 meals a day. If you have the Machine meta-trait, you have a 1-hour endurance.

. . . and so on, doubling consumption and halving endurance for each additional level. A single level of this

trait is appropriate for normal humans who have a build of Overweight or heavier (see *Build*, p. 19), or the Gluttony disadvantage (p. 137).

Increased Life Support ♟♥

Variable

Your environmental requirements in a life-support situation are greater than those of a normal human. Some examples:

Extreme Heat/Cold: You require a temperature above 200° or below 0°. *-10 points.*

Massive: You require more than a ton of additional weight in order to survive aboard a spacecraft or a submarine, or in any other setting where resources and space are limited. If you can wear an environment suit, this always weighs at least a ton. *-10 points.*

Pressurized: You require a separate pressurized compartment to survive. *-10 points.*

Radioactive: You are radioactive or require a radioactive environment. *-10 points.*

The GM may allow other kinds of Increased Life Support. These should worth no more than -10 points apiece unless they are *extremely* exotic. Add together the value of multiple special requirements, but note that the total disadvantage value cannot exceed -40 points.

Increased Life Support represents the *logistical* inconvenience of special life-support requirements, while Dependency (p. 130), Maintenance (p. 143), and Restricted Diet (p. 151) all reflect the *health* effects of doing without such requirements. The same requirement can qualify in both categories if it has consequences for both health and logistics. But note that a Dependency you can satisfy with a one-ounce inhaler of a drug does not let you claim Increased Life Support for a pressurized cabin full of the stuff! The GM's word is final.

With the GM's permission, normal humans may take this disadvantage to represent the special requirements of certain chronic illnesses.

Incurious 🗫

-5 points*

You hardly ever notice things unrelated to the business at hand. Make a self-control roll when confronted with something strange. If you fail, you *ignore* it! You react at -1 to new things.

Indecisive 🗫

-10 points*

You find it difficult to make up your mind. As long as there is a single path before you, you are fine, but as soon as there is a choice, you begin to dither. Make a self-control roll whenever a choice confronts you, modified downward by the number of alternatives you can see: -2 if there are two choices, -3 if there are three, etc. If you fail, you do *nothing*. Roll again every minute (or every *second* in combat or a similar high-stress situation) until you make up your mind, after which you may act normally until the next time you face a decision.

If you are Indecisive *and* Confused (p. 129), you must roll as described above to decide on a course of action. When you finally succeed, you must make *another* self-control roll – this one for Confused – to see whether you can act on your decision immediately.

Infectious Attack 🗫 ⚡

-5 points

You have an infectious supernatural condition. This works identically to the Dominance advantage (p. 50), except that you do not control those you infect and cannot add them as Allies. This is a disadvantage, because enemies who survive (or *don't* survive!) violent encounters with you become stronger through the "gift" of supernatural powers, and are completely free to use their new abilities to seek vengeance for what you have done to them.

To prevent PCs with this trait from turning their friends into powerful monsters for free, the GM should consider making infected PCs pay points for supernatural racial templates gained this way. If they cannot afford such a template, the GM is free to balance its point cost with supernatural drawbacks such as Cursed, Dread, Revulsion, and Weakness.

Innumerate 🗫

-5 points

You have little or no grasp of mathematics. You cannot learn – and get no default with – Computer Programming, Economics, or any of the skills that benefit from Mathematical Ability (see *Talent*, p. 89). You effectively have Incompetence (p. 164) in those areas. This has many frustrating side effects: you must use your fingers to count or perform arithmetic, you have no idea if the results computed by calculating machines are correct (making them basically useless), and you are easily cheated by dishonest merchants (-4 to rolls to notice you've been had).

In "innumerate" cultures, including many cultures at TL4 or below, this disadvantage is widespread, and the GM should not count it against the campaign disadvantage limit (if any). In societies that prize technological or mercantile ability, Innumerate individuals are liable to have a Social Stigma *as well*. This is worth an additional -5 points and gives -1 to reaction rolls.

Insomniac 🗫

-10 or -15 points

You go through periods where falling asleep is very difficult. During such an episode, you must make a HT-1 roll once per night. On a success, you fall asleep easily, ending that episode of insomnia. On a failure, you lose two hours of sleep that night (and suffer all the usual effects; see *Missed Sleep*, p. 426) and the episode continues for another night. On a critical failure, you get *no* sleep that night. Point value depends on severity:

Mild: The GM secretly rolls 3d for the number of days between episodes. *-10 points.*

Severe: The GM rolls 2d-1 for the number of days between episodes. *-15 points.*

Regardless of severity, whenever you suffer prolonged stress, the GM can require a HT roll. Failure means an episode starts immediately.

Intolerance 🗫

Variable

You dislike and distrust some (or all) people who are different from you.

You may be prejudiced on the basis of class, ethnicity, nationality, religion, sex, or species. Victims of your Intolerance will react to you at -1 to -5 (GM's decision). Point value depends on the *scope* of your Intolerance.

If you are thoroughly intolerant, you react at -3 toward *anyone* not of your own class, ethnicity, nationality, religion, or species (pick one). On a "Good" reaction, you tolerate the person and are as civil as possible (but are stiff and cold toward him). On a "Neutral" reaction, you still tolerate him, but make it plain in words and deeds that you don't care to be around him and consider him inferior or offensive. On any worse reaction, you attack or refuse to associate with the victim. Total Intolerance of this kind is worth -10 points.

Intolerance directed at only one *specific* class, ethnicity, nationality, religion, sex, or species is worth from -5 points for a commonly encountered victim to -1 point (a nasty quirk) for a rare victim.

Invertebrate 🗫 👽

-20 points

You have no spine, exoskeleton, or other natural body support. Use your full Basic Lift for the purpose of pushing, but only 1/4 your BL to calculate the weight you can lift, carry, or pull. This trait has a small side benefit, however: you can squeeze through much smaller openings than your size might suggest!

Note that this trait differs somewhat from the biological term "invertebrate."

Jealousy 🗫

-10 points

You react poorly toward those who seem smarter, more attractive, or better off than you! You resist any plan proposed by a "rival," and *hate* it if someone else is in the limelight. (Jealousy goes well with Megalomania.) If an NPC is jealous, the GM will apply a -2 to -4 reaction penalty toward the victim(s) of his jealousy.

Killjoy 🗫

-15 points

Your brain's pleasure center is burned out or absent. You cannot appreciate the taste of good food, the joy of sex, the savage beauty of combat, and so on. You might not even remember what these pleasures were like! You can "go through the motions," but you have -3 on all Carousing, Connoisseur, Erotic Art, and Gambling rolls. Others react to you at -1 to -3 in any situation where your lack of appreciation becomes obvious (GM's decision). A bad reaction indicates ridicule from cultured folk, rejection by a lover, etc. – not violence.

Some ultra-tech societies might use surgery to inflict this state as a form of punishment! If so, you *won't* plot your revenge . . . because there won't be any pleasure in it.

Kleptomania

-15 points*

You are compelled to steal – not necessarily things of value, but anything you can get away with. Make a self-control roll whenever you are presented with a chance to steal, at up to -3 if the item is especially interesting to you (not necessarily *valuable*, unless you are poor or have Greed). If you fail, you must try to steal it. You may keep or sell stolen items, but you may not return or discard them.

Klutz

-5 or -15 points

You have an uncanny affinity for gross physical blunders. You do not necessarily have a low DX (you may have up to DX 13 and still select this trait) but you are more awkward than your DX would suggest. This disadvantage comes in two levels:

Klutz: Make a DX roll to get through the day without doing a pratfall, dropping books, or knocking over shelves filled with fragile items. This is rarely life-threatening, but it is inconvenient and often expensive. The GM should be creative in inventing minor torments. You should especially avoid laboratories, explosives, china shops, etc. *-5 points.*

Total Klutz: As above, but in addition, *any* failure on a DX roll or DX-based skill roll is considered a *critical* failure for you! *-15 points.*

This trait might seem silly, but it need not be. Most realistic TL7-8 robots have this disadvantage!

Lame

-10 to -30 points

This disadvantage assumes that you are a member of a race with legs. If your *entire race* is legless, see *No Legs* (p. 145).

You have some degree of impaired mobility:

Crippled Legs: You have all of your legs, but some of them are damaged. For a human, this means one bad leg. You are at -3 to use any skill that requires the use of your legs, including all Melee Weapon and unarmed combat skills (but not *ranged* combat skills). You *must* reduce your Basic Move to half your Basic Speed (round down), but you get full points for this (see *Basic Move*, p. 17). *-10 points.*

Missing Legs: You have lost some, but not all, of your legs. For a human, this means you have one leg. You are at -6 to use any skill that requires the

use of your legs. Using crutches or a peg leg, you can stand up and walk slowly. You *must* reduce Basic Move to 2, but you get full points for this. You can still kick, but between the standard -2 for a kick and the -6 for this disadvantage, you do so at DX-8!

Without your crutches or peg leg, you cannot stand, walk, or kick. *-20 points.*

Legless: You are missing *all* of your legs, no matter how many you started out with. You are at -6 to use any skill that requires the use of your legs, and you cannot stand, kick, or walk at all. You *must* reduce Basic Move to 0, but you get full points for this. *-30 points.*

Paraplegic: You have all of your legs, but they are paralyzed. The effects and point value are identical to Legless. Unlike a Legless character, you can be struck in the legs for damage. This is balanced by the fact that it isn't inconceivable that you could regain the use of your legs (a Legless character is out of luck). *-30 points.*

Technological Assistance

A muscle-powered wheelchair or wheeled platform has ground Move equal to 1/4 your ST (round down), but cannot pass through narrow doorways, negotiate staircases or steep curbs, enter most vehicles, etc.

If you have advanced prosthetics that cancel this disadvantage while worn, apply a Mitigator limitation (p. 112) to Lame and any reduced Basic Move. If surgery or ultra-tech replacement parts eliminate this disadvantage completely, you must pay back the points you received for Lame and reduced Basic Move.

Laziness 👤

-10 points

You are violently averse to labor. Your chances of getting a raise or promotion in *any* job are halved. If you are self-employed, halve your monthly pay (see *Jobs,* p. 516). You must avoid work – especially hard work – at all costs. Roleplay it!

Lecherousness 👤

-15 points*

You have an unusually strong desire for romance. Make a self-control roll whenever you have more than the briefest contact with an appealing member of the sex you find attractive – at -5 if this person is Handsome/Beautiful, or at -10 if Very Handsome/Very Beautiful. If you fail, you must make a "pass," using whatever wiles and skills you can bring to bear. You must then suffer the consequences of your actions, successful or not: physical retribution, jail, communicable disease, or (possibly) an adoring new friend.

Unless the object of your affection is Very Handsome/Very Beautiful, you need not roll more than once a day to avoid making a pass. If someone turns you down very firmly (e.g., a black eye, or an arrest for sexual harassment) the GM may give you a bonus to future self-control rolls regarding that individual . . .

Note that you are likely to change your standards of attractiveness if no truly attractive members of the appropriate sex are available!

Lifebane 👤 ⚡

-10 points

You have a supernatural aura of death about you. Grass dies in your footprints and will never grow there again, larger plants wilt instantly in your presence, and insects and other tiny creatures die if they get within a yard of you. Your aura has *no effect* on animals that weigh more than a few ounces, on very large plants such as trees (but the leaves closest to you might die, and a tree you pass daily for years will eventually be affected), on ordinary life forms controlled by supernatural means (e.g., insect swarms conjured up using magic), or on supernatural entities of any kind.

Lifebane gives -2 on reaction rolls made by anyone in a position to notice it. If it stems from demonic powers, vampirism, etc., observers get +2 on all rolls to deduce your secret! This trait makes it difficult to use stealth- or invisibility-related abilities outdoors, too: +2 on rolls to locate you in most outdoor environments. It has its side benefits, however. For instance, you need never buy insect repellent!

Light Sleeper 🏋

-5 points

You do not sleep as soundly or as easily as most people. Whenever you must sleep in an uncomfortable place, or whenever there is more than the slightest noise, you must make a HT roll in order to fall asleep. On a failure, you can try again after one hour, but you will suffer all the usual effects of one hour of missed sleep (see *Missed Sleep,* p. 426).

You usually wake up if there is activity going on around you (but you are stunned unless you have Combat Reflexes). If you wish to continue sleeping, you must *fail* a Sense roll. If you wake up, you must make HT rolls to get back to asleep, as above. This can occasionally be to your advantage, but the most likely effect is that you miss sleep whenever inconsiderate companions trade watches or return from a night on the town.

Loner 👤

-5 points*

You require a great deal of "personal space." Make a self-control roll whenever anyone lingers nearby, watches over your shoulder, etc. If you fail, you lash out at that person just as if you had Bad Temper (p. 124). Loner NPCs always react to others at a penalty.

Self-Control Number	Reaction Penalty
6	-4
9	-3
12	-2
15	-1

Low Empathy 👤

-20 points

You cannot understand emotions *at all.* This doesn't prevent you from having and showing emotions of your own (unless you have something like No Sense of Humor) – your problem is that you don't really *understand* them. As a result, you have difficulty interacting socially.

You may not take the Empathy advantage, and suffer a -3 penalty on all skills that rely in whole or in part on understanding someone's emotional motivation, including Acting, Carousing, Criminology, Detect Lies, Diplomacy, Enthrallment, Fast-Talk, Interrogation, Leadership, Merchant, Politics, Psychology, Savoir-Faire, Sex Appeal, Sociology, and Streetwise. You can still have these skills – you just aren't as good at them as someone without this disadvantage.

Low Empathy is common in androids, demons, golems, the undead, and some aliens. It is also appropriate for certain humans! This trait is mutually exclusive with the somewhat similar disadvantages Callous (p. 125) and Oblivious (p. 146), both of which assume *some* understanding of emotions, however flawed.

Low Pain Threshold 🏋

-10 points

You are very sensitive to pain of all kinds. *Double* the shock from any injury; e.g., if you take 2 HP of damage, you are at -4 to DX on your next turn. You roll at -4 to resist knockdown, stunning, and physical torture. Whenever you take a wound that does more than 1 HP of damage, you must make a Will roll to avoid crying out. This can give away your presence, and may earn you a -1 reaction from "macho" individuals.

Low Self-Image 💀

-10 points

You lack self-confidence and underrate your abilities to such a degree that it interferes with your performance. You are at -3 to all skill rolls whenever you believe that the odds are against you or others expect you to fail (GM's judgment). For instance, if you're a mechanic, you have no penalty to repair an engine in your shop . . . but you are at -3 to make the same repairs on the road, in the rain, with only a portable tool kit, and an enemy hot on your trail – on top of the usual modifiers that would apply in that situation!

Low TL

see p. 22

Lunacy 💀

-10 points

The moon has a dramatic and inconvenient effect on your personality. During the full moon, you are extremely emotional and volatile (-2 to all Will and self-control rolls), while on nights of the new moon, you are very passive (you temporarily suffer from the Laziness disadvantage, p. 142). While the moon is waxing, you are focused and pleasant; while it is waning, you are apathetic and a little touchy. Roleplay it!

Magic Susceptibility 💀 🗡

-3 points/level

Magic is more likely to affect you. Add your Magic Susceptibility to the skill of anyone casting a spell on you, and subtract it from your roll to resist any spell that you can resist. For instance, if you have Magic Susceptibility 4, wizards have +4 to cast spells on you and you get -4 to resist.

Magic Susceptibility only makes you more vulnerable to spells *cast directly on you*. It does not affect Missile spells, attacks by magic weapons, or information-gathering spells that aren't cast directly on *you*. It also has no effect on supernatural powers other than magic; e.g., divine miracles, psionics, or the innate powers of spirits. Magic Susceptibility works normally against Area spells; do not double its effects as you would those of Magic Resistance (p. 67).

Magic Susceptibility, and its precise level, can be recognized by any mage who looks at your aura or by anyone who casts a spell on you. You may have no more than five levels of Magic Susceptibility.

You can combine Magic Susceptibility with Magery but *not* with Magic Resistance.

Maintenance 💪

Variable

You require skilled attention at regular intervals to avoid HT loss. Examples include a robot that needs a mechanic, a chronically ill person who needs a doctor's attention, or a god that requires devout prayer.

Decide on the care you require and the skill needed to provide it. Possibilities include electronic maintenance (use Electronics Repair), mechanical maintenance (use Mechanic), medical care (use Physician), and physical repairs (use Carpentry, Electrician, etc.). You may specify an advantage or disadvantage instead; e.g., a god might require worshippers with Disciplines of Faith. You can split Maintenance between multiple skills; for instance, a robot might require Electronics Repair *and* Mechanic.

Those who maintain you must have access to the appropriate facilities: a mechanic needs tools, worshippers must pray at a temple, etc. No resources are *consumed*, however; for that, take Dependency (p. 130).

Each installment of maintenance takes one hour. The base point value depends on the number of people needed to perform it:

Number of People	Point Value
1	-10
2	-20
3-5	-30
6-10	-40
11-20	-50
21-50	-60
51-100	-70

Add another -10 points per *full* doubling of the number of people required; e.g., a god that requires 10,000 worshippers would have a base -130-point disadvantage. Extra man-hours of maintenance may substitute for extra people, if the GM approves.

The frequency with which you require maintenance modifies this base cost.

Maintenance Interval	Multiplier
Monthly	1/5
Bi-weekly	1/3
Weekly	1/2
Every other day	3/4
Daily	1
Twice daily	2
Three to five times daily	3
Constant	5

If you miss a maintenance period, your HT attribute drops by 1 and you must make a HT roll. Failure results in some additional incapacity of the GM's choosing. Critical failure means a potentially fatal outcome; e.g., a human might suffer a heart attack, or a vehicle's brakes might fail while it is moving.

To restore lost HT and capabilities requires suitable intervention and skill rolls (repairs if you're a machine, surgery if you're a living being, etc.). If you require an unusual form of maintenance, this might call for exotic measures!

Manic-Depressive 💀

-20 points

Your moods are on a seesaw. You bounce back and forth between bubbling enthusiasm and morose withdrawal. At the beginning of each play session, roll 1d. On 1-3, you are in your manic phase; 4-6 indicates depression. Every five hours of game time thereafter, roll 3d. A 10 or less indicates that you begin a mood swing. Over the next hour, you shift from your current phase to the opposite one. You remain in the new phase for at least five hours, after which you must again roll 3d.

In the manic phase, you suffer the effects of Overconfidence (p. 148) and Workaholic (p. 162). You are friendly, outgoing, and excited about whatever it is you're doing. In the depressive phase, you suffer the effects of Chronic Depression (p. 126). You are not interested in doing anything but lying in bed, sitting in a dark room and moping, etc. Your effective self-control number for these effects is equal to your Will.

Emergencies can also cause mood swings; in that case, the switch is immediate. On a roll of 10 or less on 3d, you change phases. This can be good (an emergency jars you into action) or bad (a problem triggers depression and you become worthless).

Megalomania
-10 points

You believe you are a superman, that you have been chosen for some great task, or that you are destined to conquer. You must choose a grand goal – most often conquest or the completion of some fantastic task. You must let nothing stand between you and this goal.

You may attract followers with Fanaticism, but nobody else enjoys hearing you talk about your brilliance and great plans. Young or naive characters, and fanatics looking for a new cause, react to you at +2; others will react at -2.

This is a better disadvantage for NPCs than it is for PCs.

Miserliness
-10 points*

You are preoccupied with conserving your wealth. You must always hunt for the best deal possible. Make a self-control roll any time you are called on to spend money. If the expenditure is large, this roll may be at -5 or worse (GM's decision). If you fail, you refuse to spend the money. If you absolutely *must* spend the money, you should haggle and complain interminably. Note that you may have both Greed (p. 137) and Miserliness!

Missing Digit
-2 or -5 points

You are missing a finger or thumb.

Missing Finger: Gives -1 DX with that hand (only). *-2 points.*
Missing Thumb: Gives -5 DX with that hand (only). *-5 points.*

Mistaken Identity
see p. 21

Motion Sickness
-10 points

You are miserable whenever you are in a moving vehicle, be it an automobile, train, airplane, balloon, ship, or spacecraft. You may never learn any vehicle-operation skill. You must roll vs. HT as soon as you are aboard a moving vehicle. On a failure, you vomit and are at -5 on all DX, IQ, and skill rolls for the rest of the journey. On a success, you are merely miserably queasy and at -2 on DX, IQ, and skill rolls. Roll daily on long journeys.

Mundane Background
-10 points

You have a complete lack of experience with the supernatural and the weird. When you first enter play, you can only have mundane skills and equipment. Magic spells, cinematic skills, etc. are off-limits. So are Hidden Lore and Occultism! You *can* have supernatural advantages, but you can neither use them nor learn any skills that would allow you to use them. In fact, you have no idea that you possess such talents, save perhaps for the odd dream now and then. You must buy off this disadvantage if you wish to use supernatural advantages actively or learn *any* skill related to the supernatural or the weird.

Mundane Background is only available in settings with supernatural or weird elements! It is not a valid disadvantage in perfectly mundane game worlds.

Mute
see *Cannot Speak,* p. 125

Neurological Disorder
Variable

You suffer from one of several neurological disorders that cause tremors, involuntary movements, facial contortions, etc. Point value depends on severity:

Mild: Your condition is obvious to anyone who observes you for more than a few seconds. You are at -2 to tasks that involve fine manipulation (see *High Manual Dexterity,* p. 59), and such tasks take twice the normal time. You also have -2 to social skills such as Acting, Leadership, Performance, Public Speaking, and Sex Appeal in any situation where your condition would be apparent (GM's decision). *-15 points.*

Severe: You find it difficult to function in normal society. You are at -4 to tasks that involve fine manipulation, and such tasks take four times as long. Your DX and Basic Move cannot exceed your racial average (DX 10 and Move 5 for a human), and might be lower. You get -4 to social skills whenever your condition becomes apparent. *-35 points.*

Crippling: You find it almost impossible to function in normal society. You are at -6 to tasks that involve fine manipulation, and such tasks take six times as long. Your DX and Basic Move cannot exceed 80% of your racial average (DX 8 and Move 4 for a human), and might be *considerably* lower. You get -6 to social skills most of the time. *-55 points.*

Many other symptoms are possible, including *gross* motor impairment (buy down DX or Move), involuntary vocalizations (treat as Noisy, p. 146), and facial contortions (reduce appearance level; see *Physical Appearance,* p. 21). Violent tics and *profane* involuntary vocalizations might qualify as Odious Personal Habits (p. 22).

Night Blindness
-10 points

You have poor night vision. If the vision or combat penalty for poor lighting is between -1 and -4 for most people, your penalty is the *worse* of double the usual penalty or -3. If the usual penalty is -5 or worse, you function as though you were completely blind (see *Blindness,* p. 124). If you have Acute Vision (p. 35), it only applies in situations with no darkness penalty.

This trait is mutually exclusive with both Night Vision (p. 71) and Dark Vision (p. 47).

Nightmares
-5 points*

You are tormented each night by horrible nightmares. Sometimes they're so harrowing that they affect your efficiency during waking hours. Make a self-control roll each morning upon awakening. If you fail, you suffered nightmares; this costs you 1 FP that you can only recover through sleep. On a roll of 17 or 18, you are left shaking, and are at -1 to all skill and Perception rolls for the entire day.

These nightmares can be so vivid that they're indistinguishable from reality. The GM might choose to play them out in the game, starting out like a normal scenario and steadily becoming more horrible. The victim should only gradually come to suspect that he is dreaming. Such dreams can have a dramatic effect on the dreamer's waking life, such as temporary Obsessions or Phobias, or even a psychosomatic loss of HP or attribute levels.

If other PCs are involved in the nightmare, they're completely unaffected by anything that occurs there (but if the nightmare takes a long time to play out, the GM might wish to reward the players with a bonus character point as a token of appreciation for their time – maybe two points if they roleplayed the dream-situation particularly well). It's the GM's option whether to let the other players know in advance that the scenario is a dream. Either way can lead to unique and fascinating roleplaying.

No Depth Perception ♛
-15 points

You have two eyes, but you lack effective binocular vision and cannot visually judge distances. This might be due to a vision disorder or a quirk of your racial neurology. The game effects are identical to One Eye (p. 147); you may not take both disadvantages.

No Fine Manipulators ♛ ☻
-30 or -50 points

Your body lacks hands and possibly limbs. Point value depends on the extent of your limitation:

No Fine Manipulators: You have no body part more agile than paws or hooves. You cannot use your limbs to make repairs, pick locks, tie knots, wield weapons, etc., or even to grasp firmly. You may only select this trait if you have *nothing* approaching the human hand in terms of overall versatility. If you have a beak, tongue, prehensile tail, etc. that is as good as a hand, you do not have No Fine Manipulators! *-30 points.*

No Manipulators: You have *no* limbs. The only way for you to manipulate objects is to push them around with your body or head. You can still move, and are capable of rolling, wriggling, bouncing, etc. at your Basic Move unless you buy it down to 0. *-50 points.*

Note that this trait is limited to non-humans and supers. Either level qualifies you to buy ST and DX with the -40% No Fine Manipulators limitation.

No Legs ♛ ☻
Variable

This disadvantage assumes that your race lacks legs. If your race has legs, but you are missing yours, see *Lame* (p. 141).

You are a member of a legless race. There are several different forms of this trait, but in all cases, you cannot kick, cannot be struck in the legs in combat, and need not wear leg armor. The point costs below assume that the benefit of having no legs for foes to target in combat balances the drawback of being unable to kick.

Aerial: You cannot move on land, but you can hover, glide, or fly. You *must* purchase the Flight advantage (p. 56). Calculate Basic Speed as usual and use twice this value to determine your basic *air* Move, as described for Flight. Your *ground* Move is 0. *0 points.*

Aquatic: You cannot move on land, but you are adapted to movement on or in water, like a ship or a fish. Calculate Basic Move and use this as your basic *water* Move. Your *ground* Move is 0. You suffer no skill penalties for working in or under water. *0 points.* If your mobility depends on fins, masts, paddles, or sails that you can't armor, *or* you can't dive: -5 *points.* If both: *-10 points.*

Bounces, Rolls, or Slithers: You move on land without using legs, like a snake or a wheel-form robot. Work out Basic Move and use it as your ground Move, just as a legged character would. *0 points.*

> These nightmares can be so vivid that they're indistinguishable from reality. The GM might choose to play them out in the game, starting out like a normal scenario and steadily becoming more horrible.

Semi-Aquatic: You "walk" on flippers, like a seal. Use Basic Move as your basic *water* Move and 1/5 this as your *ground* Move – that is, reverse the normal relationship between ground and water Move. You suffer standard skill penalties in the water. *0 points.*

Sessile: Your base is anchored where you sit, like a tree or a building. You can't move under your own power in *any* environment, and lack the option of using a moving platform (although you can *be* moved, with considerable effort). Your Basic Move is automatically 0, and you get no extra points for this. You can still have manipulators. If so, you wield weapons at no DX penalty, because unlike those with the Lame disadvantage, you have a very stable base! *-50 points.*

Tracked or Wheeled: You have tracks or wheels *instead* of legs. Specify how many – one to four, or any higher *even* number. If using hit locations, treat each track or wheel as if it were a leg. You can neither jump nor negotiate obstacles that require arms and legs working together (e.g., a ladder or rope). You always leave a visible trail (giving others a Tracking bonus: +1 for Wheeled, +2 for Tracked). Tracks are also *noisy* (+2 to all Hearing rolls to detect you), but let you handle rough terrain more easily. Tracked and Wheeled do *not* reduce Move; in fact, you may buy up to three levels of Enhanced Move (Ground). This disadvantage usually accompanies the Machine meta-trait (p. 263). *-20 points.*

No Manipulators

see *No Fine Manipulators*, p. 145

No Sense of Humor 💭

-10 points

You never get any jokes; you think everyone is earnestly serious at all times. Likewise, you never joke, and you *are* earnestly serious at all times. Others react at -2 to you in any situation where this disadvantage becomes evident.

No Sense of Smell/Taste 💪

-5 points

This affliction – known as *anosmia* – prevents you from smelling or tasting *anything*. Thus, you are unable to detect certain hazards that ordinary people spot quickly. However, the disability has its advantages . . . you need never worry about skunks, and can always eat what is set before you.

Nocturnal 💪 👽 👁

-20 points

You can only be active when the sun is below the horizon. This represents more than a preference for night over day! As soon as dawn starts to break, you become lethargic – and when the sun clears the horizon, you fall paralyzed and comatose until the sun goes down again.

Note that this is *not* the same as the biological term "nocturnal."

Special Enhancements

Permanent Paralysis: You turn to stone or suffer some other permanent incapacitation if struck by the sun's rays. Only one specific power or item – most often a powerful magic spell – can reverse this effect. Details are up to the GM. +100%.

Noisy 💪

-2 points/level

You make a *lot* of noise! Perhaps you're a ghost with clanking chains, a cyborg with a rasping ventilator, or a machine with a loud engine . . . or perhaps you're absurdly inept at stealth.

You make noise constantly – even when standing still – unless you are comatose (for animate beings) or powered down (for machines). Each level gives +2 to Sense rolls to hear you or -2 to your Stealth rolls, as the situation warrants. In some circumstances (e.g., at the opera), each level might also give -1 to reactions! You may not take more than five levels of Noisy without the GM's permission.

Non-Iconographic 💭

-10 points

You are incapable of processing abstract images and symbols. Graphical computer interfaces, maps, heraldic devices, and magical runes are completely meaningless to you. Like Dyslexia (p. 134), this is a structural shortcoming of your *brain;* you cannot normally buy it off.

You cannot learn Cartography, Heraldry, Symbol Drawing, or any similar skill used mainly to design or arrange patterns and symbols. You also cannot use graphical computer interfaces; you are limited to text interfaces and immersive virtual realities. Finally, since you cannot grasp magical symbols, you cannot learn magic save through oral tradition.

Note that you can process *text* without difficulty, and may learn written languages normally (see *Language*, p. 23).

Numb 💪

-20 points

You have no sense of touch. You have a limited degree of pressure sense – enough to feel your weight and stand up and walk without falling over – but you cannot distinguish textures by touch at all. Feats that depend on touch alone (e.g., touch-typing, or untying your hands behind your back) are impossible for you.

When performing a task that requires hand-eye coordination, you suffer all the effects of one level of Ham-Fisted (p. 138) unless you take twice as long to perform the action *and* can clearly see what you're doing. If you also have Ham-Fisted, add its effects.

You experience pain, temperature, and shock as acutely as anyone else, unless you also have High Pain Threshold (p. 59), but you won't know *where* you were injured without looking. Instead, you feel pain as generalized shock throughout your entire body. As a result, you cannot perform First Aid on yourself if you can't see the injury.

Oblivious 💭

-5 points

You understand others' emotions but not their *motivations*. This makes you awkward in situations involving social manipulation. You are the classic "nerd"! You have -1 to use or *resist* Influence skills (see *Influence Rolls*, p. 359): Diplomacy, Fast-Talk, Intimidation, Savoir-Faire, Sex Appeal, and Streetwise.

Obsession 💭

-5 or -10 points*

Your entire life revolves around a single goal. Unlike Compulsive Behavior (p. 128), this is not a daily habit, but an overpowering fixation that motivates all of your actions. And unlike Fanaticism (p. 136), this does not necessarily imply a set of philosophical beliefs.

You must rationalize *all* of your actions as an attempt to reach your goal. Make a self-control roll whenever it would be wise to deviate from your goal. If you fail, you continue to pursue your Obsession, regardless of the consequences.

Point cost depends on the time needed to realize your goal. A short-term goal (e.g., assassinating someone) is worth -5 points, while a long-term goal (e.g., becoming President) is worth -10 points. In both cases, modify the base cost to reflect your self-control number. If your Obsession causes others to react badly, take Odious Personal Habit (p. 22) or Delusion (p. 130) as well.

Should you ever reach your goal, you must either substitute a new goal or buy off your Obsession.

Odious Personal Habits

see p. 22

On the Edge 💭

-15 points*

You take *grossly* unreasonable risks in the face of mortal danger. Make a self-control roll whenever you face a life-threatening situation: piloting a burning vehicle, staring down an entire street gang while armed only with a toothbrush, etc. If you fail, you may not back down from the challenge – but you may roll again after every success roll or reaction roll relating to the situation. This might be once per second in a potential combat situation but only once per day on a dangerous space mission.

In combat, make a self-control roll every time you take your turn. If you fail, you must make an All-Out attack or engage in some other kind of near-insane, suicidal behavior.

Most people think you're crazy if they witness this behavior, giving -2 on reaction rolls. Individuals who value bravery over self-preservation (GM's decision) will react at +2.

One Arm

-20 points

You have only one arm. You cannot use two-handed weapons, wield two weapons at once (or a weapon and a shield), or perform any task that *requires* two arms. You get -4 on tasks that are *possible* with one arm but that are usually executed with two (e.g., most Climbing and Wrestling rolls). You have no penalty on tasks that require only one arm. In all cases, the GM's ruling is final. When in doubt, try a quick reality check if possible!

If you originally had two arms, assume that you lost the left arm if you were right-handed, or vice versa.

If you are a nonhuman who only had one arm to begin with, your "arm" need not be an arm at all – it can be *any* appendage capable of fine manipulation. For instance, a parrot that used its beak and tongue would have One Arm (and *not* No Fine Manipulators).

If you have advanced prosthetics that cancel One Arm while worn, apply a Mitigator limitation (p. 112). Should you ever eliminate One Arm completely through surgery or an ultra-tech replacement limb, you must pay back the points you received for it.

One Eye

-15 points

You have only one eye. Either you are missing an eye (in which case you may wear a glass eye or cover the missing eye with a patch) or you have only a single, cyclopean eye. You suffer -1 to DX in combat and on any task involving hand-eye coordination, and -3 on ranged attacks (unless you Aim first) and on rolls to operate any vehicle faster than a horse and buggy.

Some cultures regard those who are missing an eye as unattractive. If this is generally true in your game world, losing an eye will *also* reduce your appearance by one level (see *Physical Appearance*, p. 21). If you start with this trait, assume that it is already factored into your appearance – do not apply an additional reaction modifier.

One Hand

-15 points

You have only one hand. For the most part, use the rules under *One Arm* (above). The difference is that you may make unarmed parries with a handless arm, and possibly strap something to it (e.g., a shield).

Good-quality prosthetic replacements use the rules under *One Arm*. Not all prosthetics are good enough to count as Mitigators, though. A low-tech mechanical replacement gives you -2 (for a grabber) or -4 (for a hook or claw) on tasks involving that hand. A hook or claw also counts as an undroppable large knife in combat (use Knife skill), and gives +1 to Intimidation skill if waved at your foes. In some societies, such crude replacements will reduce appearance as described under *One Eye* (above).

Overconfidence 👤

-5 points*

You believe that you are far more powerful, intelligent, or competent than you really are. You may be proud and boastful or just quietly determined, but you must roleplay this trait.

You must make a self-control roll any time the GM feels you show an unreasonable degree of caution. If you fail, you *must* go ahead as though you were able to handle the situation! Caution is not an option.

You receive +2 on all reaction rolls from young or naive individuals (who believe you are as good as you say you are), but -2 on reactions from experienced NPCs.

Overconfidence is like Megalomania (p. 144) on a smaller scale. Robin Hood was overconfident – he challenged strangers to quarterstaff duels. Hitler was a megalomaniac – he invaded Russia! Heroes are rarely megalomaniacal but often overconfident.

Overweight

see p. 19

Pacifism 👤

Variable

You are opposed to violence. This can take several forms. Choose *one* of the following:

Reluctant Killer: You are psychologically unprepared to kill *people*. Whenever you make a deadly attack (e.g., with a knife or a gun) against an obvious person whose face is visible to you, you are at -4 to hit and may not Aim. If you cannot see the foe's face (due to a mask, darkness, or distance, or because you attacked from behind), the penalty is only -2, save in close combat. You have no penalty to attack a vehicle (even an occupied one), an opponent you do not believe is a *person* (including things with Horrific or Monstrous appearance), or a target you can't actually see (e.g., a set of map coordinates or a blip on a radar screen). If you kill a recognizable person, the effect on you is the same as for Cannot Kill (see below). You have no problem with your *allies* killing; you may even supply ammo, loaded weapons, and encouragement! You

just can't do the killing yourself. -5 *points.*

Cannot Harm Innocents: You may fight – you may even *start* fights – but you may only use deadly force on a foe that is attempting to do you serious harm. Capture is not "serious harm" unless you are already under penalty of death or have a Code of Honor that would require suicide if captured. You never intentionally do anything that causes, or even threatens to cause, injury to the uninvolved – particularly if they are "ordinary folks." This trait is especially appropriate for crime-fighters, supers, etc. -10 *points.*

Cannot Kill: You may fight – you may even *start* fights – but you may never do anything that seems likely to kill another. This includes abandoning a wounded foe to die "on his own"! You must do your best to keep your companions from killing, too. If you *do* kill someone (or feel responsible for a death), you immediately suffer a nervous breakdown. Roll 3d and be totally morose and useless (roleplay it!) for that many days. During this time, you must make a Will roll to offer any sort of violence toward *anyone*, for *any* reason. -15 *points.*

Self-Defense Only: You only fight to defend yourself or those in your care, using only as much force as necessary (no pre-emptive strikes allowed!). You must do your best to discourage others from starting fights. -15 *points.*

Total Nonviolence: You will not lift a hand against another intelligent creature, for any reason. You must do your nonviolent best to discourage violent behavior in others, too. You are free to defend yourself against attacks by animals, mosquitoes, etc. -30 *points.*

In a high-realism campaign, the GM might require all PCs to start out with Reluctant Killer or even Cannot Kill, giving them extra points but putting them at a disadvantage when facing hardened foes.

Paranoia 👤

-10 points

You are out of touch with reality, and think that everyone is plotting against you. You never trust anyone except old friends . . . and you keep an eye on them, too, just in case. Most people, understandably, react to you

at -2. A paranoid NPC reacts at -4 toward *any* stranger, and any "legitimate" reaction penalty (e.g., for an unfriendly race or nationality) is *doubled*. Paranoia goes very well with Delusions (p. 130), which of course have their own disadvantage value!

Phantom Voices 👤

-5 to -15 points

You are plagued by whispered phrases that only you can hear. These voices might be unintelligible, or they might repeat the same words over and over. Eventually, your sanity (such as it is) will start to erode.

In any situation that the GM feels is stressful, he may roll 3d. On a 6 or less, you hear voices. The GM will always roll whenever you miss a Fright Check or make the roll exactly, and whenever you fail a self-control roll for another stress-related disadvantage. The voices occur *in addition to* any other results!

Point value depends on the nature of the voices:

Annoying: You hear voices, but you are reasonably sure that they are not real, and they do not harm you directly. Still, most people who see you responding to unheard noises will react at -2. -5 *points.*

Disturbing: As above, but in addition, the voices can drown out normal sounds, and may even startle and frighten you (possibly requiring a Fright Check). -10 *points.*

Diabolical: The voices tell you to kill – yourself or others – or perform other terrible deeds. If you are already under stress, or under the influence of drugs, you might need to make a Will roll to avoid carrying out the "orders" (GM's discretion). -15 *points.*

Phantom Voices are usually due to mental problems, but they may also be symptomatic of some form of supernatural possession. If so, psychotherapy cannot reveal the cause, much less cure the problem. If you manage to exorcise the evil spirits, you are cured and must buy off this disadvantage.

Phobias 👤

Variable*

You are afraid of a specific item, creature, or circumstance. Many fears are reasonable, but a Phobia is an unreasonable, unreasoning, morbid fear. The point value depends on how common the object of your fear is – fear of darkness is far more troublesome than fear of left-handed plumbers.

Make a self-control roll whenever you are exposed to the object of your Phobia. If you fail, roll 3d, add the amount by which you failed your self-control roll, and look up the result on the *Fright Check Table* (p. 360). For instance, if your self-control number is 9 but you rolled a 13, roll 3d+4 on the table. The result from the table affects you immediately!

If you succeed, you have successfully mastered your Phobia (for now), but you are still shaken, and have a penalty to all DX, IQ, and skill rolls while the cause of your fear persists. The penalty depends on your self-control number.

Self-Control Number	Penalty
6	-4
9	-3
12	-2
15	-1

You must roll again every 10 minutes to see if the fear overcomes you.

Even the mere *threat* of the feared object requires a self-control roll, although this is at +4. If your enemies actually inflict the feared object on you, you must make an unmodified self-control roll, as described above. If you fail, you might break down, depending on the Fright Check results, but you won't necessarily talk. Some people can panic and fall apart, but still refuse to talk – just as some people do not talk under torture.

A phobic situation is by definition stressful. If you have other mental disadvantages that are triggered by stress, you are likely to have these reactions if you fail to resist a Phobia.

Some common phobias:

Being Alone (Autophobia): You cannot stand to be alone, and do anything in your power to avoid it. *-15 points.**

Blood (Hemophobia): The sight of blood gives you the screaming willies! You need to make a self-control roll during most combats . . . *-10 points.**

Cats (Ailurophobia): *-5 points.**

Crowds (Demophobia): Any group of over a dozen people sets off this fear unless they are all well known to you. The self-control roll is at -1 for over 25 people, -2 for a crowd of 100 or more, -3 for 1,000, -4 for 10,000, and so on. *-15 points.**

Darkness (Scotophobia): A common fear, but crippling. You should avoid being underground if possible; if something happens to your flashlight or torch, you might well lose your mind before you can relight it. *-15 points.**

Death and the Dead (Necrophobia): You are terrified by the idea of death. Make a self-control roll in the presence of any dead body (animals don't count, but *portions* of human bodies do). Roll at -4 if the body is that of someone you know, or -6 if the body is unnaturally animated in some way. A ghost (or apparent ghost) also requires a roll at -6. *-10 points.**

Dirt (Mysophobia): You are deathly afraid of infection, or just of dirt and filth. Make a self-control roll when you must do something that might get you dirty. Roll at -5 to eat any unaccustomed food. You should act as "finicky" as possible. *-10 points.**

Dogs (Cynophobia): This includes *all* canines: foxes, wolves, coyotes, wild dogs, etc. *-5 points.**

Enclosed Spaces (Claustrophobia): A common, crippling fear. You are uncomfortable any time you can't see the sky – or at least a very high ceiling. In a small room or vehicle, you feel the walls closing in on you . . . You need *air!* This is a dangerous fear for someone who plans to go underground. *-15 points.**

Fire (Pyrophobia): Even a burning cigarette bothers you if it comes within five yards. *-5 points.*

Heights (Acrophobia): You may not voluntarily go more than 15 feet above ground, unless you are inside a building and away from windows. If there is some chance of an actual fall, self-control rolls are at -5. *-10 points.*

Insects (Entomophobia): You are afraid of all "bugs." Large or poisonous ones give -3 to self-control rolls. Very large ones, or large numbers, give -6. Avoid hills of giant ants. *-10 points.*

Loud Noises (Brontophobia): You avoid any situation where loud noises are likely. A sudden loud noise requires an immediate self-control roll. A thunderstorm is a traumatic experience for you! *-10 points.*

Machinery (Technophobia): You can never learn to repair any sort of machine and refuse to learn to use anything more complicated than a crossbow or bicycle. Any highly technological environment calls for a self-control roll; dealings with robots or computers require a roll at -3, and hostility from intelligent machines requires a roll at -6. *-5 points at TL4 or below, -15 points at TL5 or above.*

Magic (Manaphobia): You can never learn to use magic, and you react badly to any user of magic. Make a self-control roll whenever you are in the presence of magic. This roll is at -3 if you are to be the target of friendly magic, and -6 if you are the target of hostile magic. (The magic does not have to be real, if *you* believe in it!) *-15 points in a setting where magic is common, -10 if it is known but uncommon, -5 if "real" magic is essentially unknown.*

Monsters (Teratophobia): Any "unnatural" creature sets off this fear. You have -1 to -4 on the self-control roll if the monster seems very large or dangerous, or if there are a lot of them. Note that the definition of "monster" depends on experience. An American Indian would consider an elephant monstrous, while an African pygmy would not! *-15 points.*

Number 13 (Triskaidekaphobia): You must make a self-control roll whenever you have to deal with the number 13 – visit the 13th floor, buy something for $13.00, etc. Roll at -5 if Friday the 13th is involved! *-5 points.*

Oceans (Thalassophobia): You are afraid of any large body of water. Ocean travel, or even air travel over the ocean, is basically impossible for you, and encounters with aquatic monsters are also upsetting. *-10 points.*

Open Spaces (Agoraphobia): You are uncomfortable whenever you are outside, and actually become frightened when there are no walls within 50 feet. *-10 points.*

Psionic Powers (Psionophobia): You are afraid of those with known psionic powers. An actual exhibition of power in your presence requires a self-control roll. You do not voluntarily allow anyone to use a psionic power on you. The power does not have to be real – all that matters is that *you* believe it is! *-15 points if psi powers are common, -10 if they are uncommon, -5 if they are essentially unknown.*

Reptiles (Herpetophobia): You come unglued at the thought of reptiles, amphibians, and similar scaly slimies. A very large reptile, or a poisonous one, gives -2 to self-control rolls; a horde of reptiles (such as a snake pit) gives -4. *-10 points.*

Sex (Coitophobia): You are terrified by the idea of sexual relations or the loss of your virginity. *-10 points*

Sharp Things (Aichmophobia): You are afraid of anything pointed. Swords, spears, knives, and hypodermic needles all give you fits. Trying to use a sharp weapon, or being threatened with one, requires a self-control roll at -2. *-15 points at TL5 or below, -10 at TL6 or above.*

Spiders (Arachnophobia): *-5 points.*

Strange and Unknown Things (Xenophobia): You are upset by any sort of strange circumstances, and in particular by strange *people*. Make a self-control roll when surrounded by people of another race or nationality; roll at -3 if the people are not human. If you lose control, you might well attack strangers out of fear. *-15 points.*

Sun (Heliophobia): *-15 points.*

Weapons (Hoplophobia): The presence of any sort of weaponry is stressful. Trying to use a weapon, or being threatened with one, requires a self-control roll at -2. *-20 points.*

Post-Combat Shakes 🗣
-5 points*

You are shaken and sickened by combat, but only *after* it's over. Make a self-control roll at the end of any battle. It is up to the GM to determine when a battle has truly ended, and he may apply a penalty if the combat was particularly dangerous or gruesome. If you fail, roll 3d, add the amount by which you failed your self-control roll, and look up the result on the *Fright Check Table* (p. 360). For instance, if your self-control number is 12 but you rolled a 14, roll 3d+2 on the table. The result from the table affects you immediately!

Pyromania 🗣
-5 points*

You like fires! You like to set fires, too. For good roleplaying, you must never miss a chance to set a fire, or to appreciate one you encounter. Make a self-control roll whenever you have an opportunity to set a fire.

Quadriplegic 🖐
-80 points

You are paralyzed in all your arms and legs, or lack limbs entirely. You can neither manipulate objects nor move yourself without assistance. You suffer all the bad effects of Paraplegic (see *Lame*, p. 141) and No Manipulators (see *No Fine Manipulators*, p. 145). If the GM is enforcing a disadvantage limit, Quadriplegic counts against the limit – but you may reduce ST and DX by up to four levels each *without* the resulting disadvantage points counting against the limit (points gained from further reductions count normally).

For rules governing prosthetic limbs and surgical cures, see *Lame* (p. 141) and *One Arm* (p. 147) for legs and arms, respectively.

Reprogrammable 🗣 👽
-10 points

You can be programmed to obey a master. If you have Slave Mentality (p. 154), you must obey slavishly, and remain strictly within the letter of your master's commands. If you lack Slave Mentality, you may interpret his orders creatively, as long as you remain within either their letter or spirit (your choice). If you are nonsentient (IQ 0), you have no interest in doing anything *but* following your programming!

You may have both Duty and Reprogrammable. If so, you must do your best to fulfill both obligations. Should the two come into conflict, your programming always comes first.

This trait is most appropriate for golems, mindless undead, robots, and similar automata. It is rarely suitable for PCs, and the GM may choose to forbid it entirely.

Reputation

see p. 26

A negative reputation counts as a disadvantage. Note it as such on your character sheet!

Restricted Diet ♥

-10 to -40 points

You require a specialized food or fuel that is hard to come by. Unlike Dependency (p. 130), you do not take damage if you go without . . . you just can't eat or refuel, which will eventually incapacitate you. Point value depends on the rarity of the item you consume:

Rare: Dragon's blood, exotic nutrient mixture, weapons-grade uranium. *-40 points.*

Occasional: Virgin's blood, rocket fuel, babies, radioactives. *-30 points.*

Common: Human flesh, gasoline, liquid hydrogen. *-20 points.*

Very Common: Fresh meat, *any* hydrocarbon fuel (gasoline, diesel, etc.), electric batteries, fresh blood. *-10 points.*

Restricted Diet *is* appropriate for normal humans with chronic gastrointestinal disorders.

Special Limitations

Substitution: You can try to consume a food or fuel similar to the one you require. For instance, a cyborg that requires exotic nutrients could try ordinary human food, or a machine that requires gasoline could try diesel. This sustains you, but you must make a HT roll after each meal or refueling. Failure means your HT attribute drops by one until you receive appropriate medical or mechanical

attention. Critical failure means an incapacitating reaction (GM's decision): severe immune response, engine failure, etc. Those who lack this limitation but for some reason attempt substitution derive no sustenance at all *and* must still make the HT roll above; treat success as failure and failure as critical failure. -50%.

Restricted Vision ♥

-15 or -30 points

You have an unusually narrow field of vision. A normal character can see a 120° arc in front of him without turning his head, and has 30° of peripheral vision to either side, giving him a 180° "arc of vision" for observation and ranged attacks. On a battle map, this means he has three "front" hexes, two "side" hexes ("left" and "right"), and a single "back" hex. Your vision is considerably more restricted. This comes in two levels:

No Peripheral Vision: Your arc of vision is a 120° wedge to the front. On a map, your "left" and "right" hexes become "back" hexes – that is, you have three "back" hexes, and get *no* defense against attacks originating from these hexes! *-15 points.*

Tunnel Vision: Your arc of vision is a *60°* wedge to the front. On a map,

your only "front" hex is the one directly ahead of you. The hexes to either side of this are "side" hexes: you are at -2 to defend against attacks from these hexes, and can only attack into those hexes with a Wild Swing. Everything else is a "back" hex, as above. *-30 points.*

Revulsion ♥ ⚡

-5 to -15 points

You have an incapacitating supernatural reaction to an ordinarily innocuous substance. If you touch or breathe the substance, you must immediately make a HT roll. On a failure, you are at -5 to all skills and attributes for the next 10 minutes. If you *ingest* the substance, you are at -5 to attributes and -10 to all skills and Sense rolls for 10 minutes. Point value depends on the rarity of the substance:

Occasional (leather, soap): *-5 points.*

Common (smoke, wood): *-10 points.*

Very Common (grass, metal): *-15 points.*

This reaction is physical in nature. For mental aversions, see *Dread* (p. 132).

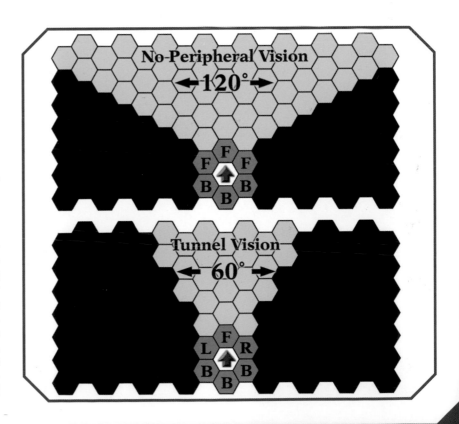

Sadism

-15 points*

You delight in cruelty . . . mental, physical, or both. Make a self-control roll whenever you have an opportunity to indulge your desires and know you shouldn't (e.g., because the prisoner is one who should be released unharmed). If you fail, you cannot restrain yourself. Those who become aware of your problem react at -3 unless they are from a culture that holds life in little esteem.

This is a particularly "evil" trait, more appropriate to villainous NPCs than to heroic PCs. The GM may completely prohibit Sadism if he does not want anyone roleplaying it in his campaign.

It is possible, though despicable, to possess both Bully (p. 125) *and* Sadism.

Secret

-5 to -30 points

A Secret is an aspect of your life or your past that you must keep hidden. Revelation would result in lasting negative consequences. The point value depends on the severity of those consequences:

Serious Embarrassment: If this information gets around, you can forget about ever getting a promotion, getting elected, or marrying well. Alternatively, revelation of your Secret might simply attract unwelcome public attention. *-5 points.*

Utter Rejection: If your Secret is revealed, it will change your whole life. Perhaps you will lose your job and be rejected by friends and loved ones. Perhaps admirers, cultists, long-lost relatives, or the press will harass you. *-10 points.*

Imprisonment or Exile: If the authorities uncover your Secret, you'll have to flee, or be imprisoned for a long time (GM's discretion). *-20 points.*

Possible Death: Your Secret is so terrible that you might be executed by the authorities, lynched by a mob, or assassinated (by the Mafia, CIA, etc.) were it revealed. You would be a hunted man. *-30 points.*

Frequency of Appearance

In general, a Secret appears in a particular game session if the GM rolls a 6 or less on 3d before the adventure begins. However, as for all other disadvantages of this type, the GM need not feel constrained by the appearance roll. If he thinks that the Secret should come into play, it does!

When a Secret appears in play, it is not automatically made public. The GM will give you a chance to prevent your Secret from being revealed. This might require you to cave in to blackmail or extortion, steal incriminating documents, or even silence the person who knows the Secret. Regardless of the solution, however, it's only temporary – the Secret will appear again and again until either you buy it off with earned character points or it is finally revealed.

Effects of Revelation

If a Secret is made public, there is an immediate negative effect ranging from serious embarrassment to possible death, depending on the severity of the Secret (see above). There is also a lasting effect: you suddenly acquire new, permanent disadvantages – or lose advantages – worth points equal to *twice* what the Secret was worth! These new disadvantages replace the Secret on your character sheet, and reduce your point value accordingly.

The GM chooses the new disadvantages and lost advantages, which should always be appropriate to the Secret. Most Secrets turn into Enemies (p. 135), negative Reputations (p. 26), and Social Stigmas (p. 155), or reduce or remove advantages described under *Wealth and Influence* (pp. 25-30). Some could even turn into mental or physical disadvantages.

DISADVANTAGES

Example: A city guardsman has a -20-point Secret: at night, he is a thief. When he is finally caught and brought to justice, his Secret is revealed and immediately replaced with *-40* points in disadvantages and lost advantages! The GM rules that he is stripped of his 5-point Legal Enforcement Powers (-5 points), gains Social Stigma (Criminal Record) (-5 points), and is punished by having his right hand chopped off (One Hand, -15 points) and being forced to pay reparations that reduce his Wealth from Average to Poor (-15 points).

Secret Identity 🤝
Variable

A Secret Identity is a special kind of Secret (above): it is another *persona* that you use for deeds that you don't want connected with your "public" self. Only your closest family and friends know, and you are willing to go to great lengths to keep your privacy. This is a disadvantage because it limits your behavior. It is difficult (and often illegal) to maintain a Secret Identity.

The GM will roll to see whether your Secret Identity factors into a game session, just as for any Secret. If it does, this usually takes the form of someone who threatens to expose your real identity. Anyone with Status 3 or higher gets an extra -10 points for a Secret Identity, because of the attention the media and public pay to his every move, but the GM will introduce a challenge to his identity on a roll of 7 or less instead of the usual 6 or less.

A Secret Identity otherwise works just like any other Secret, its point value depending on the severity of the consequences should it be exposed.

Self-Destruct 👽👤
-10 points

As soon as you reach your aging threshold (age 50 for a normal human), your organs and immune system begin to fail. You start to age rapidly, making aging rolls every *day* at -3 to HT.

You cannot get points for both this disadvantage and Terminally Ill (p. 158). If you are going to self-destruct *soon*, take Terminally Ill instead of Self-Destruct.

Selfish 👤
-5 points*

You are self-important and status-conscious, and spend much of your time striving for social dominance. Make a self-control roll whenever you experience a clear social slight or "snub." On a failure, you lash out at the offending party just as if you had Bad Temper (p. 124) – likely resulting in a bad reaction (-3 to the target's reactions toward you) and putting you in an awkward social situation.

Selfish NPCs react to perceived slights at a penalty:

Self-Control Number	Penalty
6	-5
9	-4
12	-3
15	-2

Selfless 👤
-5 points*

You are altruistic and self-sacrificing, and put little importance on personal fame and wealth. You must make a self-control roll to put your needs – even survival – before those of someone else. A Selfless *race* will have a "hive mentality."

Semi-Upright 👽👤
-5 points

You have a semi-upright posture, like a chimpanzee. You can stand up more-or-less comfortably, allowing you to use your forelimbs to bash enemies, hold babies, or even manipulate objects. You can manage a clumsy gait while upright (-40% to Move), but you must use all of your limbs to run at full Move. If you have DX 12 or more, you can carry a small object or two while walking.

Sense of Duty 👤
-2 to -20 points

You feel a strong sense of commitment toward a particular class of people. You will never betray them, abandon them when they're in trouble, or let them suffer or go hungry if you can help. This is different from a Duty (p. 133), which is imposed upon you. A Sense of Duty always comes from within.

If you are *known* to have a Sense of Duty, the GM will adjust the reactions of others by +2 when rolling to see whether they trust you in a dangerous situation. However, if you go against your Sense of Duty by acting against the interests of those you are supposed to be looking out for, the GM will penalize you for bad roleplaying.

The GM will assign a point value to your Sense of Duty based on the size of the group you feel compelled to aid:

Individual (the President, your wingman, etc.): *-2 points.*

Small Group (e.g., your close friends, adventuring companions, or squad): *-5 points.*

Large Group (e.g., a nation or religion, or everyone you know personally): *-10 points.*

Entire Race (all humanity, all elves, etc.): *-15 points.*

Every Living Being: *-20 points.*

You cannot claim points for a Sense of Duty toward Allies, Dependents, or Patrons. The point costs of these traits *already* take such a bond into account.

You *can* take a Sense of Duty toward adventuring companions. If you do, you must share equipment with and render aid to the other members of your adventuring party, and go along with majority decisions. The GM might make this mandatory in games where the party *needs* to get along. This gives everyone a "free" 5 points to spend . . . but if you start backstabbing, running off on your own, etc., the GM is free to overrule your actions and point to these bonus points as the reason why.

Shadow Form 👽👤
-20 points

See p. 83. If you cannot turn this ability off, it is a disadvantage.

Short Attention Span 👤
-10 points*

You find it difficult to concentrate on a single task for longer than a few minutes. Make a self-control roll whenever you must maintain interest in something for an extended period of time, or whenever a distraction is offered. If you fail, you *automatically* fail at the task at hand. The GM might give you a small bonus to the self-control roll in situations where concentration is crucial, such as when your survival is at stake.

Short Lifespan ♟♻

-10 points/level

Your lifespan is *much* shorter than the human norm. Each level of this disadvantage halves your lifespan (round down). This affects the age at which you reach maturity, the ages at which aging rolls begin and increase in frequency, and the interval between aging rolls; see the table (above right). No more than four levels are possible. Short Lifespan is often found in conjunction with Self-Destruct (p. 153).

Level	Maturity	Aging [Frequency of Aging Rolls]		
0 (Human)	18 years	50 years [1 year]	70 years [6 months]	90 years [3 months]
1	9 years	25 years [6 months]	35 years [3 months]	45 years [45 days]
2	4 years	12 years [3 months]	17 years [45 days]	22 years [22 days]
3	2 years	6 years [45 days]	8 years [22 days]	11 years [11 days]
4	1 year	3 years [22 days]	4 years [11 days]	5 years [5 days]

Shyness ♟

-5, -10, or -20 points

You are uncomfortable around strangers. Roleplay it! This disadvantage comes in three levels; you can buy it off one level at a time.

Mild: You are uneasy with strangers, especially assertive or attractive ones. You have -1 on skills that require you to deal with people, including Acting, Carousing, Diplomacy, Fast-Talk, Intimidation, Leadership, Merchant, Panhandling, Performance, Politics, Public Speaking, Savoir-Faire, Sex Appeal, Streetwise, and Teaching. *-5 points.*

Severe: You are very uncomfortable around strangers, and tend to be quiet even among friends. -2 the skills listed above. *-10 points.*

Crippling: You avoid strangers whenever possible. You may not learn the skills listed above *at all,* and are at -4 on default rolls on such skills. *-20 points.*

Skinny

see p. 18

Slave Mentality ♟

-40 points

You have no initiative, and become confused and ineffectual without a "master" to give you orders. You must make an IQ roll at -8 before you can take any action that isn't either obeying a direct order or part of an established routine. As well, you *automatically* fail any Will roll to assert yourself or resist social influence except in circumstances where the GM rules

that success might be possible, in which case you roll at -6.

This doesn't necessarily imply low IQ or Will. You might be intelligent enough to obey the command, "Program the computer to detect quarks," but if you were starving and found $10, you would have to roll vs. IQ-8 to decide to pick up the money and go buy food without being told to do so. Similarly, you might be strong-willed enough to make all your Fright Checks in the presence of terrifying monsters, yet roll at Will-6 to resist the unsubtle manipulations of an obvious con man.

This disadvantage is rarely appropriate for PCs, and the GM may choose to forbid it entirely.

Sleepwalker ♟

-5 points*

You walk in your sleep ("somnambulate"). This is merely annoying or embarrassing under most circumstances (unless you fall down the stairs), but it can be very dangerous to sleepwalk while encamped in hostile territory!

Sleepwalking is merely annoying or embarrassing under most circumstances, but it can be very dangerous to sleepwalk while encamped in hostile territory!

If sleepwalking would matter during an adventure, the GM will make a self-control roll for you whenever you go to sleep. If you fail, you sleepwalk sometime during the night. You wake up after walking for 1d minutes, or if someone awakens you. The GM will make DX rolls to see if you trip while going down stairs or walking over

rough ground – if this happens, you wake up suddenly and are mentally stunned.

You are considered to be in a hypnagogic state while sleepwalking, and thus are very susceptible to telepathic influences. If *you* possess supernatural abilities, you might use these while sleepwalking (e.g., if you have Warp, you might "sleepwarp" instead).

Sleepy ♟♻

Variable

This is a racial trait. Members of the race need to sleep more than the human norm of 1/3 of the time. Point value depends on the fraction of the time they must spend asleep:

Time Spent Asleep	Cost
1/2 of the time	-8 points
2/3 of the time	-16 points
3/4 of the time	-20 points
7/8 of the time	-26 points

The race's precise schedule is a "special effect." For instance, a race that sleeps 3/4 of the time might be awake and active for three days straight and then sleep for a full nine days.

This trait can also represent *hibernation.* For instance, if a race is awake and active on a human schedule for six months, and then hibernates for two months straight, then *on the average,* that's equivalent to sleeping 1/2 of the time.

Slow Eater ♥ ◉

-10 points

You spend a *lot* of your time eating. Each meal takes about two hours, as opposed to about 1/2 hour for most humans. This reduces the time available for study, long tasks, and travel on foot by 4 1/2 hours per day.

Slow Healing ♥

-5 points/level

Your body heals very slowly. Each level (maximum three levels) *doubles* the interval between HT rolls to regain lost HP: roll every two days for Slow Healing 1, every four days for Slow Healing 2, and every eight days for Slow Healing 3. Take Unhealing (p. 160) if you heal even more slowly. Each level also doubles the time allowed between Physician rolls when under the care of a competent physician (see *Medical Care*, p. 424).

Normal humans may take no more than one level of Slow Healing.

Slow Riser ♥

-5 points

You are not a "morning person." For one hour after you awaken from any sleep longer than a one-hour nap, you have -2 on all self-control rolls and -1 to IQ and IQ-based skills. Furthermore, whenever the GM assesses attribute penalties for missed sleep, you suffer an *extra* -1.

Social Disease ♥

-5 points

You have contracted a contagious, antibiotic-resistant bacteria, retrovirus, or similar disease. This is only transmitted by close, unprotected physical contact. Those who know about it react to you at -1 and automatically resist your seduction attempts. The disease isn't fatal – at least not immediately – but may produce physical symptoms (left to the imagination of the player or GM).

Social Stigma ✊

-5 to -20 points

You belong to a race, class, sex, or other group that your society deems inferior. To be worth points, this must be obvious from your physical appearance (a visible brand, tattoo, or magical mark counts), dress, manner, or speech; *or* easily learned by anyone who cares to check up on you (only valid in societies with free and easy access to information); *or* the result of public denouncement (e.g., by a powerful leader or media figure) that ensures that everyone you meet knows that you, personally, belong to the disdained group.

A Social Stigma gives you a reaction penalty (-1 per -5 points of Social Stigma), restricts your social mobility, or both. Examples include:

Criminal Record: You have been convicted of a crime that your society considers serious. You may be prohibited from legally acquiring certain items (e.g., weapons), taking certain kinds of employment, receiving security clearances, or even traveling outside your country. Many noncriminals who learn of your past react at -1; police, judges, vigilantes, and other law-and-order types usually react at -2. If you are also *wanted*, take an appropriate Enemy. *-5 points.*

Disowned: Your family has publicly snubbed you. This is only worth points in settings where family ties play a significant social role, and never applies to those who *voluntarily* part ways with their family. This Social Stigma comes in two levels:

● You would normally be an heir in your culture, but someone else has been named in your stead. This is embarrassing, but you may still count yourself as part of the family. This gives -1 on reaction rolls. *-5 points.*

● The head of your family – or your entire *clan* – has wholly and publicly disowned you. This gives -2 on reaction rolls. *-10 points.*

Excommunicated: Your church has cast you out. Followers of your faith react to you at -3. This is only a disadvantage if you are excommunicated by a powerful and widespread religion (most likely state-backed) that plays a significant role in day-to-day life. *-5 points.*

If your religion has true supernatural power, and you are surrounded by an aura that conveys your shame to co-religionists, angels, and anyone else who would care, no matter how well you disguise yourself, your Social Stigma is worth twice as much. *-10 points.*

Ignorant: You have not learned a skill required of all responsible adults in your society (that is, you have no points in the skill). Others look down upon you as a slacker or a fool. This gives -1 on reactions for each "expected" skill you lack, up to a maximum of four skills. This is only worth points in highly structured societies, or in primitive ones where individuals depend on one another for survival. *-5 points/skill.*

Minor: You are underage by your culture's standards. You suffer -2 on reaction rolls whenever you try to deal with others as an adult; they might like you, but they do not fully respect you. You might also be barred from nightclubs, vehicle operation, war parties, guild membership, etc., depending on the culture and setting. You must buy off this trait when you reach "legal age" (usually 18) for your time and place. *-5 points.*

Minority Group: You are a member of a minority that the dominant culture around you regards as "barbarians" or "inferior." You get -2 on all reaction rolls made by anyone except your own kind. In an area, profession, or situation where your minority is *especially* rare, you get +2 on reaction rolls made by your own kind. *-10 points.*

Monster: You are a large carnivore, magical abomination, or other being that is hated or feared regardless of *actual* appearance or disposition. This gives you -3 on all reaction rolls, and you are liable to be hunted on sight. However, you get +3 to Intimidation rolls in situations where you have the upper hand (GM's opinion). *Examples:* a bear or a vampire. *-15 points.*

Second-Class Citizen: You belong to a group that receives fewer rights and privileges than "full citizens." This gives -1 on all reaction rolls except from others of your own kind. *Examples:* a woman in 19th-century America, or members of some religions. *-5 points.*

Subjugated: You are a member of a slave nation or race. Within the overlords' culture, you have *no* rights, and suffer the negative effects of Second-Class Citizen *and* Valuable Property. If you manage to escape to freedom, you acquire the entire overlord nation or race as an Enemy. *-20 points.*

Uneducated: You are from a class, race, or subculture that lacks a cultural repository of wisdom, eschews formal schooling, and takes a dim view of activities that do not relate directly to survival or procreation. You receive -1 to reactions from more sophisticated folk in any situation where your lack of schooling would be apparent, and you may not start with any "book-learned" skills (GM's discretion; most IQ/Hard skills qualify). You may buy off this trait once you have lived in "civilized" parts for long enough (GM's decision). *-5 points.*

Valuable Property: Your society regards you as somebody's property rather than as a "legal person." This takes the form of limited freedom or lack of intellectual respect more than as a reaction modifier. *Examples:* a woman in 18th-century America or 16th-century Japan. *-10 points.*

Social Stigmas *must* bind those who take them. For example, a medieval Japanese lady must pay for her 10-point bonus by giving up her freedom of movement in many cases, and must defer to older male relatives when they are present. A black slave in 19th-century America is allowed to learn very little and own almost no property, and has little freedom of any kind unless he manages to escape. (If he does escape, he has traded his Social Stigma for a powerful Enemy!)

It is possible to have multiple Social Stigmas, provided they do not significantly overlap (GM's decision). For instance, a teenager who drops out of school and joins a street gang could believably end up with Minor, Uneducated, *and* Criminal Record.

Space Sickness 👽
-10 points

You are miserable in free fall. You can never learn Free Fall skill; you must always roll at default. In addition, you are at -4 on your HT roll to avoid "space adaptation syndrome" (see p. 434) – and if you fail the first HT roll, the only way for you to recover is to return to normal gravity.

This trait is only allowed in campaigns that feature regular space travel.

Split Personality 👤
-15 points*

You have two or more distinct personalities, each with its own set of behavior patterns. They may interpret their memories differently, and even use different names.

For each personality, select a "package" of mental disadvantages and up to five quirks. The GM may also permit variations in IQ, Perception, Will, and mental advantages, where these would make sense. Each package of mental traits must be worth the same number of points. When calculating the value of your character, count the "package price" *once* – not once for each personality. *All* your personalities have the same physical traits and skills (although some personalities might not use certain skills), and share any mental trait that is not part of one of these packages.

Example: Bob Smith has three personalities. "Col. Smith" is a stern disciplinarian with Delusion ("I am a military officer") [-10], Code of Honor (Soldier's) [-10], and the quirk "Stands on ceremony" [-1]. "Bobby" is a party animal with -2 to Will [-10], Compulsive Carousing (6) [-10], and the quirk "Sleeps all day and goes out at night" [-1]. "Smitty" is a trouble-maker with Overconfidence (12) [-5], Trickster [-15], and the quirk "Steals for fun" [-1]. All three personalities share all of Bob's other traits. Each package totals -21 points. Bob's player claims the -21 points *once*. With -15 points for Split Personality (12), the total point value is -36 points.

You must make a self-control roll in any stressful situation (but no more than once per hour of game time). On a failure, one of your other personalities emerges, and you behave according to its mental disadvantages and quirks. If there are several possibilities, the GM should either choose a personality appropriate to the situation or roll randomly.

All your personalities are somewhat shallow and affected, which gives -1 to reactions at all times. Those who witness a personality change will feel (possibly with justification) that you are a dangerous nutcase, and react at -3.

Squeamish 👤
-10 points*

You dislike "yucky stuff": little bugs and crawly things, blood and dead bodies, slime, etc. When exposed to such things, you react just as if you had a Phobia; see *Phobias*, p. 148. Note that you do *not* suffer from the standard fears of insects, reptiles, dirt, and the dead! What bothers you isn't huge bugs or reptiles, ordinary "clean" dirt, and ghosts; it's nasty creepy things, filth, and bits of grue.

Status
see p. 28

Status below 0 is a disadvantage. Almost everyone reacts negatively to you!

Stress Atavism 👤👽
Variable*

This disadvantage is normally available only to characters who are members of races "uplifted" from an animal state.

You temporarily "regress" when frightened, angered, fatigued, or injured. Make a self-control roll in those situations. On a failure, you behave like an animal, acting on impulse and instinct.

Once the stressful situation has passed, make a self-control roll every minute. If friends comfort you, roll at +2. If one of these people has Animal Empathy or Empathy, apply an additional +2. On a success, the attack ends and you return to normal. If you pass out from fatigue or injury before you succeed, you recover automatically when you wake up.

Point value depends on the severity of the attacks:

Mild: You have trouble speaking, and must roll vs. IQ to utter a sentence. You cannot operate complicated machinery, although you may attack wildly with weapons (-4 to hit). *-10 points.*

Moderate: You suffer from all of the above problems, and have trouble understanding commands from others as well: roll vs. IQ to *understand* a sentence spoken by someone else. If you are attacked or challenged, you must make a self-control roll to avoid acting "on instinct." *-15 points.*

Severe: You cannot speak or understand others, or use tools (except possibly as clubs), and automatically act on instinct at all times. You behave like your primitive ancestors! *-20 points.**

Stress Atavism may result in additional troublesome behavior. Pick a suitable mental disadvantage, halve its value (drop all fractions), and add this point cost to the above costs *before* applying the self-control multiplier.

Stubbornness

-5 points

You always want your own way. Make yourself generally hard to get along with – roleplay it! Your friends may have to make a lot of Fast-Talk rolls to get you to go along with perfectly reasonable plans. Others react to you at -1.

Stuttering

-10 points

You suffer from a stammer or other speech impediment. This gives -2 on any reaction roll where conversation is required, and -2 to Diplomacy, Fast-Talk, Performance, Public Speaking, Sex Appeal, and Singing. Certain occupations (interpreter, newsreader, etc.) are always closed to you.

Supernatural Features

Variable

You have disturbing features that mark you as a demon, vampire, or other supernatural being. You can pass for a normal mortal to casual observers, but closer inspection reveals that you are *not quite right.* This might give away your secret to the trained eye.

Supernatural Features differ from Unnatural Features (p. 22) in that they *aren't* usually obvious; they only become apparent under a specific set of circumstances. When they *are* noticed, though, they result in a reaction penalty. They also give those who know what to look for a bonus to any skill roll (against Hidden Lore, Occultism, etc.) made to identify your true nature.

Supernatural Features can accompany appearance levels Hideous through Transcendent (see *Physical*

Appearance, p. 21). You cannot get points for Supernatural Features if you are Monstrous or Horrific, however. If you look *that* scary, you're not hiding any secrets!

soul! -2 on reaction rolls made by those who notice; +2 on all rolls to deduce your secret. *-10 points.*

No Body Heat: You are cold to the touch. -1 on reaction rolls made by those who touch you, shake your hand, kiss you, etc.; +1 on all rolls to deduce your secret. *-5 points (-1 point if you can gain warmth temporarily; e.g., after feeding, for a vampire).*

No Reflection: You produce no reflection. You do not show up in mirrors, still water, and similar reflective surfaces, and technological devices such as cameras do not display your image. In some places and times, people will assume that you have no

No Shadow: You produce no shadow, regardless of the intensity or direction of the light source. -2 on reaction rolls made by those who notice; +2 on all rolls to deduce your secret. *-10 points.*

Pallor: You look like a corpse, with bloodless skin, sunken eyes, etc. -2 on reaction rolls made by anyone who can see you without makeup in good light; +2 on all rolls to deduce your secret. *-10 points (-5 points if you can gain the flush of life temporarily; e.g., after feeding, for a vampire).*

Supersensitive 🧠 ⚡

-15 points

You are telepathically sensitive to the presence of others *all the time*. You experience a constant, irritating buzz of low-level psychic noise. This does not imply any kind of useful telepathic ability – the thoughts and emotions you receive remain just below the threshold of conscious understanding.

If there are *any* sapient beings (IQ 6+) with 20 yards, you suffer -1 to DX and IQ. This becomes -2 for 10 or more people, -3 for 100 or more, -4 for 1,000 or more, and so on. If DX or IQ drops below half its original score because of this penalty, you collapse and can take no action until the "noise" goes away. Machine intelligences and individuals behind telepathic shielding (psionic, technological, or otherwise) do not bother you.

There is one beneficial side effect to Supersensitive: the psychic noise you receive warns you if there are people within 20 yards, and the noise level tells you roughly how many. The noise is too diffuse to let you determine their locations, however.

Susceptible ♥

Variable

You are extremely sensitive to a particular class of noxious items or substances; e.g., disease or poison. You have a penalty to all HT rolls to resist the negative effects of these things. You do not suffer extra damage, however; for that, see *Vulnerability* (p. 161).

If you are exposed to trace quantities of an item to which you are Susceptible – a dose so tiny that it would not affect most people – you must roll against HT+1, modified by your usual penalty for this disadvantage. If you fail, you suffer *half* the effects (fatigue, injury, attribute loss, period of incapacitation, etc.) you would suffer from a full dose. For instance, Susceptible to Poison would require a roll if you ingested highly diluted industrial waste in drinking water, while Susceptible to Disease would require a roll if you received a "live" vaccine (one that contains weakened microbes). Should there be any doubt as to exposure or effects, the GM's decision is final.

Point cost depends on the item's rarity *in the environment*:

Very Common (e.g., Disease, Poison): *-4 points/-1 to HT rolls.*

Common (e.g., Bacteria, Gases): *-2 points/-1 to HT rolls.*

Occasional (e.g., Intestinal Disease, Ingested Poison): *-1 point/-1 to HT rolls.*

You may not take more than five levels of Susceptible to a given item, or more than two separate Susceptible disadvantages, without the GM's permission. You cannot take more levels of Susceptible than would reduce your effective HT to 3. For instance, if your HT is 7, you are limited to four levels of Susceptible. If you have any form of Resistant (p. 80) that protects against a given item, you cannot also be Susceptible to that item.

This trait can simulate many common health problems. Use Susceptible to Disease for a weak immune system, Susceptible to Ingested Poison for a tendency not to vomit up noxious substances (a "weak vomit reflex"), etc.

Terminally Ill ♥

-50, -75, or -100 points

You are going to die . . . soon. This could be due to a nasty disease, a potent curse, an irremovable explosive device embedded in the base of your skull, or something else that will result in certain death. Point cost depends on how much time you have left:

Time Until Death	Cost
Up to one month	-100 points
Up to one year	-75 points
Up to two years	-50 points

More than two years is worth nothing. Anyone might be hit by a truck in that time!

If you acquire a "miracle cure," upload yourself into a new body, or otherwise extend your life past your termination date during the course of the campaign, you must buy off this disadvantage. If you cannot afford to do so, the GM is free to make up the difference with new disadvantages related to your illness or its cure (e.g., Chronic Pain, Dependency, Maintenance, or Susceptible).

If the GM is running a one-shot adventure or short campaign, he should disallow this disadvantage as meaningless.

> *A Trademark is an action separate from capturing the crooks, committing the crime, etc. Destroying files on a computer is not a Trademark; trashing them by substituting a "7" for each "5" is.*

Timesickness ♥

-10 points

Time travel, dimension travel, and teleportation make you ill. You cannot have psionic talents, magic spells, or technological skills that have to do with this kind of travel, nor can you learn the Body Sense skill. You must make a HT roll whenever you journey through time or across dimensions, and whenever you teleport. On a failure, you are effectively *stunned* for 1d hours (doubled on a critical failure!). On a success, you are only stunned for 1d×10 minutes.

Timesickness is only allowed if dimension travel, teleportation, or time travel occur regularly in the campaign. The GM may wish to permit a variation on this trait in settings with faster-than-light hyperdrives ("Hypersickness") or jump drives ("Jump Sickness").

Total Klutz

see *Klutz*, p. 141

Trademark 👤

-5 to -15 points

You have a special symbol – something that you leave at the scene of action, as a way of "signing your work." The classic fictional example is the carved initial "Z" of Zorro.

Simple: Your Trademark takes very little time to leave and cannot be used to trace your identity, but you absolutely *must* leave it. You cannot leave the scene until you do, even if your enemies are breaking down the door. A typical example is something left at the scene – a playing card, a small stuffed animal, etc. – as long as it can't be traced and takes little time. *-5 points.*

Complex: As above, but leaving your Trademark measurably increases your chances of being caught – initial carving, notes, traceable clues, etc. Leaving this sort of Trademark takes a minimum of 30 seconds. Anyone searching the scene receives +2 to Criminology and Forensics rolls to trace or identify you. *-10 points.*

Elaborate: Your trademark is so elaborate – dousing the captured thugs with a certain cologne, painting the entire crime scene pink, writing a long poem to the police – that it virtually ensures your eventual capture. The GM may give investigators clues *without* a successful Criminology or Forensics roll! *-15 points.*

You may have only one Trademark. Multiple actions (e.g., binding your victims with purple phone wire, painting a frog on the wall, *and* wrecking every computer in the building) simply give you a higher level of Trademark – they are *not* multiple Trademarks.

Note also that a Trademark is an action separate from capturing the crooks, committing the crime, etc. It's the particular *way* that it is done. Destroying files on a computer is not a Trademark; trashing them by substituting a "7" for each "5" is.

Trickster 👤

-15 points*

You crave the excitement of outwitting *dangerous* foes. This is not ordinary practical joking. Playing simple tricks on innocent or harmless folk is no fun at all – it has to be perilous! There may be no need for this at all (in fact, there probably isn't), but you need the thrill of a battle of wits and dexterity.

Make a self-control roll each day. If you fail, you must try to trick a dangerous subject: a skilled warrior, a dangerous monster, a whole *group* of reasonably competent opponents, etc. If you resist, you get a cumulative -1 per day to your self-control roll until you finally fail a roll!

Truthfulness 👤

-5 points*

You hate to tell a lie – or you are just very bad at it. Make a self-control roll whenever you must keep silent about an uncomfortable truth (lying by omission). Roll at -5 if you actually have to *tell* a falsehood! If you fail, you blurt out the truth, or stumble so much that your lie is obvious. You have a permanent -5 to Fast Talk skill, and your Acting skill is at -5 when your purpose is to deceive.

Uncontrollable Appetite 👤 ⚡

-15 points*

You consume something that you must obtain from other sapient beings through force or guile, and you have difficulty controlling your appetites. You must specify what it is you crave. This could be blood, "life force," sex, or anything else the GM permits.

Whenever you have an opportunity to indulge, you must make a self-control roll. Roll at -2 if someone deliberately tempts you, or if the item you feed on is available in large quantities within range of your senses. If feeding would restore lost HP, this roll is at -1 per missing HP. If you fail, you *must* feed. Make a second self-control roll to stop feeding once you have had your fill. If you fail, you go into frenzy and overindulge, which could kill your victim.

Unfit ⚕

-5 or -15 points

You have worse cardiovascular health than your HT alone would indicate. This comes in two levels:

Unfit: You get -1 to all HT rolls to remain conscious, avoid death, resist disease or poison, etc. This does *not* reduce your HT attribute or HT-based skills! As well, you lose FP at twice the normal rate. *-5 points.*

Very Unfit: As above, but the penalty to HT rolls is -2. In addition, you *recover* FP at only half the normal rate. You may not purchase any level of Resistant (p. 80). *-15 points.*

> *You have rotten luck. If the plot of the adventure calls for something bad to happen to someone, it's you. The GM may not kill you outright with "bad luck," but anything less than that is fine.*

In both cases, this disadvantage applies only to FP lost to exertion, heat, etc. It has no effect on FP "spent" to power psi or magic spells.

Unhealing ⚕ 👽

-20 or -30 points

You cannot heal *naturally*. You get no daily HT roll to recover lost HP, and you cannot recuperate from crippling injuries on your own. The First Aid skill can stop your bleeding, but neither it nor the Physician skill can restore missing HP. Technologies that accelerate natural healing (including herbs, drugs, etc.) are useless. This trait comes in two levels:

Partial: You can heal naturally if a rare condition is met (e.g., when you are immersed in blood or bathed in lava). You can also heal yourself by stealing HP from others using Vampiric Bite (p. 96), magic, or psionics. *-20 points.*

Total: You can *never* heal naturally, and you cannot steal HP from others. *-30 points.*

Depending on your nature, you might be able to regain lost HP and the use of crippled limbs *unnaturally* through surgery, repairs (if you're a machine), or exotic means (healing spells, alchemy, psionics, etc.).

Unique 👤 ✈

-5 points

You exist only in one timeline. If a time paradox occurs, you have no memory of it. If it is particularly severe, you are likely to vanish. In most settings, you would be unaware of this danger until it happened . . . and then nobody would even remember you! Thus, this disadvantage is usually inappropriate for PCs.

In an alternate-world campaign, being Unique means that you do not exist in any form in an alternate world, even one very much like your own. This deprives you of the chance to befriend "yourself" when you visit such a world. There is one benefit, though: you are effectively Zeroed (p. 100) at no point cost in any alternate world.

Unique is only a disadvantage in campaigns in which paradoxes or changes in history – erasing past events or whole timelines – are possible. See *Temporal Inertia* (p. 93) for the opposite of this trait.

Unluckiness 👤

-10 points

You have rotten luck. Things go wrong for you – and usually at the worst possible time. Once per play session, the GM will arbitrarily and maliciously make something go wrong for you. You miss a vital die roll, or the enemy (against all odds) shows up at the worst possible time. If the plot of the adventure calls for something bad to happen to someone, it's *you*. The GM may *not* kill you outright with "bad luck," but anything less than that

is fine. (For *lethally* bad luck, see *Cursed*, p. 129.)

If you wish, you may specify a recurring "theme" for your Unluckiness – for instance, your weapons tend to break, you're always 5 minutes late, or objects have a nasty habit of falling on your head. The GM should do his best to make your Unluckiness work this way. However, this is a characterization tool and not a hard-and-fast game mechanic. Bad luck can *always* manifest in other ways if the GM wants to keep you on your toes!

Unnatural Features

see p. 22

Unusual Biochemistry ⚕ 👽

-5 points

You can subsist on human food, but your biochemistry is sufficiently different from that of humans that drugs intended for humans don't work or have unpredictable effects. Drugs that are specific to your biochemistry work normally, but cost 10 times as much as usual.

When you receive a drug intended for humans, roll 1d:

1-3 – Normal effect.

4-5 – Normal effect, plus an additional harmful effect of the GM's choosing: lose 1d FP (sickness and nausea), suffer an amplified version of the drug's usual negative side effects, etc.

6 – No effect at all.

Very Fat

see p. 19

Very Unfit

see *Unfit*, above

Vow 👤

-5 to -15 points

You have sworn an oath to do (or not to do) something. Whatever the oath, you take it seriously; if you didn't, it would not be a disadvantage. This trait is especially appropriate for knights, holy men, and fanatics.

The point value of a Vow should be directly related to the inconvenience it causes you. The GM is the final judge. Some examples:

Minor Vow: Silence during daylight hours; vegetarianism; chastity (yes, for game purposes, this is *minor*). *-5 points.*

Major Vow: Use no edged weapons; keep silence at all times; never sleep indoors; own no more than your horse can carry. *-10 points.*

Great Vow: Never refuse any request for aid; always fight with the wrong hand; hunt a given foe until you destroy him; challenge every knight you meet to combat. *-15 points.*

Note that if you could represent your Vow using another disadvantage, you only get points for one of the two disadvantages (your choice). No one may get points for Vow (Poverty) *and* Wealth (Dead Broke), Vow (Never kill) *and* Pacifism (Cannot Kill), etc.

Many Vows end after a specified period of time. You must buy off such a Vow when it ends. Vows for a period of less than a year are frivolous! If you want to end a Vow before its stated time, the GM may exact a penalty; for instance, in a medieval world, you might have to undertake a quest by way of penance.

Vulnerability ♞ ☻
Variable

You take extra damage from a particular attack form. Whenever this type of attack hits you, the GM applies a special wounding multiplier to damage that penetrates your DR. Regular wounding multipliers (for cutting, impaling, etc.) *further* multiply the damage.

Example: A werewolf with Vulnerability (Silver ×4) is nicked with a silver knife for 1 point of cutting damage. The GM multiplies this by 4 for Vulnerability, giving 4 points of damage, and then multiplies by 1.5 for a cutting attack. The final injury is 6 HP.

Point value depends on the wounding multiplier and the rarity of the attack:

Vulnerability Table

Rarity of Attack	Wounding Multiplier		
	×2	×3	×4
Rare	-10 points	-15 points	-20 points
Occasional	-20 points	-30 points	-40 points
Common	-30 points	-45 points	-60 points
Very Common	-40 points	-60 points	-80 points

Use the categories under *Limited Defenses* (p. 46) to assess rarity. The GM has the final say on the rarity of a given attack form. You may not take more than two types of Vulnerability without GM permission.

You *cannot* have Vulnerability to anything against which you have a specific defense: Resistant, Damage Resistance limited to work only against that attack form, etc. You can have both Vulnerability and Supernatural Durability (p. 89), but this reduces the utility of Supernatural Durability.

Special Limitations

Fatigue Only: You are vulnerable to an attack that drains FP instead of HP, or to some form of mundane fatigue loss (e.g., ×2 FP from hot weather). -50%.

Weak Bite ♞ ☻
-2 points

Your jaw is not structured to make full use of your strength while biting. Calculate biting damage normally, then apply an extra -2 *per die.* This trait is common for large herbivores (e.g., horses), uncommon for small herbivores and omnivores, and very rare for carnivores.

Weakness ♞ ☻
Variable

You suffer injury merely by being in the presence of a particular substance or condition (which cannot be a food item or something equally easy to avoid). This injury comes off your HP *directly,* regardless of your DR or defensive advantages. The more quickly you take damage, the more points your Weakness is worth:

Frequency of Damage	Value
1d per minute	-20 points
1d per 5 minutes	-10 points
1d per 30 minutes	-5 points

Multiply the base value to reflect the rarity of the damaging substance or condition:

Rare (e.g., exotic radiation or minerals): ×1/2.

Occasional (e.g., microwave radiation, intense normal cold, airborne pollen): ×1.

Common (e.g., smoke, nearby magic, horses, loud noises): ×2.

Very Common (e.g., sunlight, living plants): ×3.

Example: An anaerobic organism takes 1d per minute from oxygen. The base value of a Weakness that inflicts 1d per minute is -20 points. Since oxygen is "Very Common," final cost is -60 points.

You may not take more than two types of Weakness without GM permission.

Special Limitations

Fatigue Only: Your Weakness drains FP instead of HP. -50%.

Variable: Your Weakness is sensitive to received intensity. You may specify one relatively common class of barriers that halves the rate at which you take damage (e.g., heavy clothing or sunscreen, for sunlight). On the other hand, intense sources (GM's decision) *double* the rate at which you suffer harm! -40%.

Wealth
see p. 25

Below-average levels of Wealth are a disadvantage; be sure to note them on your character sheet.

Weirdness Magnet ☻ ⚡
-15 points

Strange and bizarre things happen to you with alarming frequency. You are the one demons stop and chat with. Magic items with disturbing properties find their way to you. The only talking dog on 21st-century Earth comes to you with his problems. Dimensional gates sealed for centuries crack open just so that you can be bathed in the energies released . . . or perhaps the entities on the other side invite you to tea.

Nothing lethal happens to you, at least not immediately, and occasionally some weirdness is beneficial. But most of the time it is terribly, terribly inconvenient. People who understand what a Weirdness Magnet is (and that you are one) react to you at -2. The exceptions are parapsychologists, fringe cultists, unhinged conspiracy theorists, and thrill-seekers, who follow you around!

Workaholic ☻

-5 points

You tend to drive yourself past your limits, and find it hard to relax and turn away from your work. You always work at least half again as long as a normal working day. This often results in missed sleep (see *Missed Sleep*, p. 426). Most people regard you with respect at first (+1 to reaction rolls), but you eventually suffer -1 or -2 to reactions – especially from friends and loved ones who rarely get to spend time with you.

Wounded ☻

-5 points

You have an open wound that will not completely heal, for whatever reason (botched surgery, backfired healing spell, etc.). You are not missing any HP, but your wound serves as a path for infection and toxins, and may complicate new injuries.

A foe who knows about your wound may deliberately target it, at -7 to hit. Such attacks have a wounding multiplier of 1.5 (that is, you take 50% more damage). Blood agents that reach your wound affect you as if carried on a weapon that broke your skin. You must carefully dress your wound each day (requires a First Aid or Physician roll) or get -3 to all HT rolls to resist infection in a plague-ridden area.

At the GM's option, you may acquire a wound like this in play due to torture, scalping, etc. Certain wounds have other effects; for instance, scalping would cost you a level of appearance.

Example of Character Creation (cont'd)

Dai believes he can steal anything and escape any situation. He *definitely* suffers from Overconfidence (p. 148)! This trait is worth "-5 points*." The "*" indicates a trait that requires a self-control number. To avoid crippling Dai, we decide that he can set his attitude aside to weigh risks "quite often," or on a 12 or less. Overconfidence (12) is worth the listed cost: -5 points.

To play up Dai's twitchy, catlike side, we decide that because of his high Perception and Danger Sense, almost any little disturbance wakes him up. This gives him Light Sleeper (p. 142), for -5 points.

Finally, since an overconfident thief isn't a typical team player, Dai needs a reason to stay with ISWAT. We decide that he has come to see those in his squad as a replacement for the "family" slain by the Thieves' Guild. Although he'd never admit it, he would die rather than let anything bad happen to *this* family. We represent this with a Sense of Duty (p. 153) to his squad – a small group – for -5 points.

These disadvantages come to -15 points. This lowers Dai's running point total to 208 points.

Note that when we looked at Dai's wealth and influence, we chose Duty (ISWAT; 15 or less; Extremely Hazardous) and Wealth (Poor) – another -35 points of disadvantages. And Dai also got -20 points for ST 8 and -6 points for FP 10. In a campaign with a disadvantage limit, the entire -76 points from these traits would count against the limit.

Xenophilia ☻

-10 points*

You are instinctively fascinated and attracted by strangers and aliens, no matter how dangerous or frightening they appear to be. Make a self-control roll whenever you meet someone (or some*thing*) like this. If you fail, you assume that this person is interested in interacting with you socially. A xenophile finds himself offering drinks to glaring foreign soldiers, making passes at cute vampires, and shaking tentacles with Things Man Was Not Meant To Know while his companions are pointing weapons or running the other way . . .

As partial compensation, you get a bonus to Fright Checks when meeting strange creatures

Self-Control Number	Bonus
6	+4
9	+3
12	+2
15	+1

NPCs with this trait will react to exotic PCs at a similar bonus.

QUIRKS

A "quirk" is a minor feature that sets you aside from others. It has a negative point value, but it is not *necessarily* a disadvantage. For instance, a major trait like Greed is a disadvantage. But if you insist on being paid in gold, that's a quirk.

You may take up to five quirks at -1 point apiece . . . and if you do, you will have five more points to spend. You can also "buy off" a quirk later on by *paying* 1 point, but as a rule, you shouldn't do that. Quirks might have a small cost, but they are a big part of what makes a character seem "real"!

Quirks can be either mental or physical. This distinction implies for quirks exactly what it implies for advantages and disadvantages.

MENTAL QUIRKS

Mental quirks are minor personality traits. They are a contract between you and the GM: "I agree to roleplay these character foibles. In return, you agree to give me a few extra points to spend." However, you *must* roleplay them. If you take the quirk "Dislikes heights," but blithely climb trees and cliffs whenever you need to, the GM will penalize you for bad roleplaying. The points you lose this way will cost you much more than you earned for taking the quirk. So don't choose a quirk you aren't willing to roleplay!

This doesn't mean the GM should be inflexible about mental quirks. A player should be allowed to *change* a quirk if something happens during play to justify a noticeable change in his character's personality. The GM should also allow players to leave a few of their five "quirk slots" open during character creation and fill them in after the first couple of play sessions. The most interesting quirks often emerge as the *result* of roleplaying!

To qualify as a mental quirk, a personality trait must meet one of two criteria:

● It requires a specific action, behavior, or choice on your part from time to time. This need not take hours, or be especially inconvenient, but it must be something that you can act out in the course of the game; it *cannot* be totally passive.

● It gives you a *small* penalty very occasionally, or to a narrow set of actions. Negotiate the game effects with the GM. You may take almost any mundane mental disadvantage at quirk level, in which case the rules for that disadvantage are used as guidelines, although the effects will be much less severe.

Example: "Wears black" is not a valid quirk – it is completely passive, and there are no negative side effects. "Dresses like the stereotypical necromancer" *is* a permissible quirk if the player and GM agree that it gives -1 to reactions from unusually pious folk.

Attentive

You tend to stick to one task until it's done. You get a +1 bonus when working on lengthy tasks, but -3 to *notice* any important interruption!

Broad-Minded

A trivial form of Xenophilia (p. 162). You get along well with other races and species, and strange looks rarely bother you.

Careful

A quirk-level version of Cowardice (p. 129). You are naturally cautious, always on the lookout for danger. You dedicate extra time and money to preparations before venturing into a dangerous situation.

Chauvinistic

An extremely low level of Intolerance (p. 140). You are always aware of differences in sex, skin color, etc. even if you do not actually react poorly to others. Thin-skinned individuals might occasionally react to you at -1 as a result.

Code of Honor

You may take a minor Code of Honor (p. 127) as a quirk. For instance, you might insist on exhibiting "gentlemanly" behavior toward all females, or spurning "chauvinistic" behavior from all males.

Congenial

This is a milder version of Chummy (p. 126). You like company and you work well with others. You always choose group action over individual action.

Delusions

You may take a completely trivial Delusion (p. 130) as a quirk. This does not affect your everyday behavior, and is unlikely to be noticed by casual acquaintances, but you must *believe* it! *Examples:* "The Earth is flat." "The Pentagon controls the Boy Scouts and the health food stores." "Socks cause diseases of the feet."

Dislikes

You can have any of the Phobias on p. 148 at the level of a mere "dislike." If you dislike something, you must avoid it whenever possible, but it does not actually *harm* you as a Phobia would. Dislikes don't *have* to be watered-down Phobias. There is a whole world full of things to dislike: carrots, cats, neckties, violence, telephones, telephone *solicitors*, income tax . . .

Distractible

Quirk-level Short Attention Span (p. 153). You are easily distracted, and don't do well on long-term projects. You are at -1 when rolling to accomplish long tasks.

Dreamer

You have a -1 on any long task, because you tend to spend time thinking of better ways to do it, rather than working.

Dull

You are not quite Hidebound (p. 138), but you tend to stick with tried and true methods.

Habits or Expressions

Saying "Jehoshaphat!" or "Bless my collar-button" constantly. . . or carrying a silver piece that you flip into the air . . . or never sitting with your back to the door.

Humble

A weak form of Selfless (p. 153). You tend to put the concerns of others, or of the group, before your own.

Imaginative

You are a font of ideas, and are more than willing to share them with others! They may or may not be *good* ideas, of course . . .

Incompetence

You are *inept* at one specific skill. You cannot learn that skill, and your default is at an extra -4. You cannot be incompetent in a single specialty of a skill; if you are incompetent with Guns, for instance, you are incompetent with *all* guns. The GM may disallow Incompetence if the skill would be irrelevant to a given character, or is unlikely to play a role in the campaign.

Likes

If you like something, you will seek it out whenever possible. Gadgets, kittens, shiny knives, ceramic owls, fine art . . . whatever. This is not a compulsion – just a preference.

Minor Addiction

You may take Addiction (p. 122) as a quirk, if you are addicted to a drug that causes psychological dependency and works out to 0 points under the Addiction rules.

Nosy

A lesser version of Curious (p. 129). You are always poking your nose into corners and everyone else's business (which is likely to result in a small reaction penalty once in a while).

Obsessions

You may take an almost-rational and not especially unusual Obsession (p. 146) as a quirk, to reflect a minor goal. For instance, you hope to get just enough money to buy a farm (or boat, or spaceship, or castle) of your own.

Personality Change

This is quirk-level Split Personality (p. 156). You suffer from a full-blown mental disadvantage, but only in circumstances that are normally under *your* control; e.g., Bully when you drink too much, or Pyromania when you cast your Create Fire spell.

Proud

This is Selfish (p. 153) at quirk level. Individual success, wealth, or social standing concerns you greatly. NPCs with this quirk react at -1 to orders, insults, or social slights.

Responsive

A mild case of Charitable (p. 125). You are able to imagine the feelings and motivations of others – and all other things being equal, you are inclined to help them.

Staid

You may take this very low level of Incurious (p. 140) as a quirk. You are likely to ignore matters that don't immediately affect you.

Trademark

A quirk-level Trademark (p. 159) takes almost no time to leave, cannot be used to trace your identity, and can be overlooked when inconvenient.

Example of Character Creation (cont'd)

Now it's time to define Dai's quirks – five *minor* character traits that help to define his personality. We choose the following:

1. "Dislikes deep water." Thieves' Guild enforcers threw the young Dai off a pier, and he nearly drowned. To this day, he is leery of deep water.

2. "Loves high places." Given Dai's gifts, he can get to some very high places indeed. When he cases a joint, he *always* wants a view from the top.

3. "No drugs or alcohol." Dai is no Puritan, but growing up on the streets he saw too many people destroy themselves that way.

4. "Sensitive about his height." Dai is self-assured, but he cannot deny one *physical* shortcoming: he isn't very tall. This is a topic best avoided in conversation . . .

5. "Showoff." Dai isn't *quietly* overconfident. He has more than his fair share of natural talents, and is all too happy to demonstrate them.

Dai's quirks are worth -1 point apiece, or -5 points total. As a result, his point total becomes 203 points.

Uncongenial

A lesser version of Loner (p. 142). You prefer to be alone. You always choose individual action over group action.

Vow

A trivial Vow (p. 160) – e.g., never drink alcohol, treat all ladies with courtesy, or pay 10% of your income to your church – is a quirk.

PHYSICAL QUIRKS

Physical quirks are physical disadvantages that are only mildly or rarely limiting. They do not require roleplaying, but they give specific, *minor* penalties in play.

Unlike mental quirks, you cannot normally change physical quirks – that would make no more sense than exchanging One Eye for One Hand, under most circumstances. Also, you must define physical quirks when you create your character; you cannot use them to fill open "quirk slots" once the campaign begins.

Acceleration Weakness

You are susceptible to the bad effects of extreme acceleration, and get -3 to HT rolls to avoid them.

Alcohol Intolerance

Alcohol "goes right to your head." You become intoxicated much more quickly than normal. You get -2 on any HT roll related to drinking.

Bowlegged

You are bowlegged. This doesn't normally affect Move, but you have -1 to Jumping skill. This quirk may elicit a -1 reaction from those who think it looks funny.

Cannot Float

You always sink in water. This is most applicable to machines, but it might also afflict fantasy races or result from a curse.

Distinctive Features

You have a physical feature – e.g., "Brilliant blue hair" – that makes you stand out in a crowd. This gives -1 to your Disguise and Shadowing skills, and +1 to others' attempts to identify or follow you. Some Distinctive Features may stem from full-blown disadvantages. For instance, an albino (someone with no natural body pigment, resulting in pink eyes and pink-white hair and skin) would also have Weakness (Sunlight). Compare *Supernatural Features* (p. 157) and *Unnatural Features* (p. 22).

Horrible Hangovers

You suffer an additional -3 to any penalties the GM assesses for excessive drinking the previous evening, and add three hours to hangover duration.

Minor Addiction

You may take Addiction (p. 122) as a quirk, if you are addicted to a drug that causes physiological dependency and works out to 0 points under the Addiction rules.

Minor Handicaps

You may take most mundane physical disadvantages at quirk level; for instance, you could use a watered-down version of Lame for a "bum knee." Difficulties rarely crop up, but are genuinely inconvenient when they do. If you have this kind of handicap, the GM may give you -1 to attribute, skill, or reaction rolls, as appropriate, in situations where it would logically interfere.

Nervous Stomach

You have -3 to HT rolls to avoid illness (typically in the form of attribute penalties or vomiting) brought on by rich or spicy food, strong drink, etc.

Neutered or Sexless

You are missing sex organs that someone of your race, sex, and age would normally possess – or perhaps you are a genuinely sexless being that only *looks* like someone of a particular race and sex. This might qualify you for reduced appearance, Social Stigma, or Unnatural Features in some settings. However, there are minor benefits: you are immune to seduction and will never accidentally become a parent. This is more than simple sterility (which is a feature worth 0 points).

NEW DISADVANTAGES

The GM is welcome to develop new disadvantages. The guidelines given under *New Advantages* (p. 117) apply here as well – but note that it is easier to abuse disadvantages than advantages. A badly designed advantage might be too powerful, but it costs points, so it isn't a free lunch. On the other hand, a disadvantage that does not restrict the character *gives away points*. It *is* a free lunch! Remember the "golden rule" of disadvantage design:

A "disadvantage" that does not limit the character is not a disadvantage.

MODIFYING EXISTING DISADVANTAGES

You can turn existing disadvantages into new ones using the processes recommended for advantages: rename, redefine, combine, modify, and fine-tune. For instance, you could combine the modified disadvantage Weakness (Sunlight; 1d/30 minutes; Variable, -40%) [-9] with the quirk Distinctive Features [-1] and rename it "Albinism," giving you a new disadvantage worth -10 points. There are a few additional points to note when doing this kind of thing.

Some existing disadvantages are essentially "user-defined." This property makes them particularly useful for building "new" disadvantages. The most versatile traits of this kind are Addiction, Code of Honor, Compulsive Behavior, Delusions, Dependency, Destiny, Disciplines of Faith, Dread, Fanaticism, Increased Life Support, Intolerance, Maintenance, Obsession, Odious Personal Habits, Phobias, Restricted Diet, Revulsion, Sense of Duty, Susceptible, Unnatural Features, Vows, Vulnerability, and Weakness.

When combining multiple disadvantages to create new ones, remember that advantages can be added to the mix, reducing the value of the composite disadvantage. For instance, a positive Reputation can be associated with a "good" personality trait (such as Honesty or Sense of Duty) that is considered a disadvantage in **GURPS** because it restricts the hero's choice of actions. If the restrictions outweigh the reaction bonus, the overall trait is still a disadvantage.

Finally, when you apply limitations (pp. 110-116) to a disadvantage, remember that they *reduce* the points gained from the disadvantage. For instance, if you apply an Accessibility limitation worth -40% to a -15-point disadvantage, it becomes a -9-point disadvantage. See the "special limitations" throughout this chapter for examples of suitable limitations. (A few disadvantages have special enhancements that *increase* disadvantage value, but these are less common.)

BRAND-NEW PROBLEMS

The guidelines for creating totally new disadvantages are similar to those for designing entirely new advantages (p. 118):

1. Situational penalties to attributes. Assume that each -1 to an attribute is worth a basic -10 points for ST or HT, or -20 points for DX or IQ, and then reduce the final cost to reflect the limited circumstances under which the penalty applies. For instance, Susceptible to Poison (-2) is -2 to HT (base cost -20 points), reduced to 40% its normal value because it applies only to rolls to resist poison – which are common enough but still a specialized use of HT – for a net value of -8 points.

2. Penalties to skill rolls. Handle skill penalties using the Incompetence quirk (p. 164). This gives -1 point for each -4 to a specific skill. These skill penalties are *not* symmetrical with the skill bonuses given on p. 118. This is intentional! It reflects the reality that most players select skills for which their characters have an aptitude and ignore those at which their characters are inept. The Incompetence penalty can be changed to -3 or -5 without much effect on game balance, but it must apply to a reasonably common skill to be worth points at all.

Price a blanket penalty to an entire *group* of related skills exactly as if you were pricing a Talent (p. 89), but with minus sign in front of the cost. This makes a penalty to a group of skills a far more serious disadvantage than a penalty to one skill. This reflects the fact that it is difficult to work around ineptitude with *every* skill in a large, useful category.

3. Penalties to reaction rolls. Reaction penalties use the Reputation rules on p. 26. As explained for new advantages, these modifiers need not be *actual* Reputations – they could as easily be due to looks, a supernatural aura, etc.

4. Unique disabilities. You can only price unique disadvantages by comparison. Look at comparable disadvantages in the system and assign a similar point value, and then adjust it if the new disadvantage is more or less limiting than the existing one.

Finalizing the Cost

The final cost of a disadvantage equals the sum of the costs of its component parts, modified for rarity as the GM sees fit. A rare disadvantage is sometimes worth *more* points because it is less likely to be treatable, or because it is more likely to generate shock and disgust on a bad reaction roll. A common disadvantage may be worth fewer points by the same logic – that is, it is easy to circumvent using technology, or its social ramifications are mitigated by others' indifference.

In general, though, the point value of a disadvantage *won't* be that of the "opposite" advantage with a minus sign in front. This is mainly because most traits in **GURPS** are asymmetric, skewed toward the human norm and biased toward adventuring heroes. For instance, One Arm is a serious disadvantage worth -20 points because having only one arm severely limits skill use, while Extra Arms are a mere 10 points apiece because additional arms rarely benefit most skills. It is also important to realize that for adventurers, there are many qualities where *either* extreme is an effective disadvantage (for instance, Curious and Incurious) or advantage (consider Common Sense and Daredevil).

CHAPTER FOUR

SKILLS

A "skill" is a particular kind of knowledge; for instance, judo, physics, auto mechanics, or a death spell. Every skill is separate, though some skills help you to learn others. Just as in real life, you start your career with some skills and can learn more if you spend time training.

A number called "skill level" measures your ability with each of your skills: the higher the number, the greater your skill. For instance, "Shortsword-17" means a skill level of 17 with the shortsword. When you try to do something, you (or the GM) roll 3d against the appropriate skill, modified for that particular situation. If the number you roll is *less than or equal to* your modified score for that skill, you succeed! But a roll of 17 or 18 is an automatic failure. For more on skill rolls, modifiers, success, and failure, see Chapter 10.

Each skill is qualified in several ways to indicate what basic attribute represents talent with that skill, how easy the skill is to learn, any special restrictions on who can learn the skill, and whether the skill is broad or narrow in focus.

CONTROLLING ATTRIBUTE

Each skill is based on one of the four basic attributes or, more rarely, on Perception or Will. Your skill level is calculated directly from this "controlling attribute": the higher your attribute score, the more effective you are with *every* skill based on it! If your character concept calls for *many* skills based on a given attribute, you should consider starting with a high level in that attribute, as this will be most cost-effective in the long run.

Choosing Your Beginning Skills

Like attributes and advantages, skills cost points. You should spend at least a few of your starting character points on skills. It would be extraordinarily unusual for anyone – even a young child – to have *no* skills at all!

Your starting skills must suit your background. The greater your Wealth and Status, the more leeway the GM will allow you in skill choice – the rich and powerful can arrange to learn the most surprising things. You cannot start with *inappropriate* skills, however. The GM is free to forbid any skill that simply would not be available to someone of your background. For instance, a stone-age hunter could not be a jet pilot, a Victorian gentleman would need an excellent explanation (and an Unusual Background) to start out as a skilled sorcerer, and a futuristic adventurer would have difficulty finding training in "archaic" weapon skills . . . though a military background would help.

ST-based skills depend wholly on brawn, and are very rare. ST determines the power you can bring to bear with DX-based skills far more often than it affects skill levels directly.

DX-based skills rely on coordination, reflexes, and steady hands. This is representative of athletic and combat skills, and most vehicle-operation skills.

IQ-based skills require knowledge, creativity, and reasoning ability. This includes all artistic, scientific, and social skills, as well as magic spells.

HT-based skills are governed by physical fitness. This includes any activity influenced by hygiene, posture, or lung capacity.

Perception-based skills involve spotting subtle differences. This is typical of skills used to detect clues and hidden objects.

Will-based skills hinge on mental focus and clarity of thought. Most allow one to resist mental attacks, bring about an altered mental state, or focus "inner strength."

DIFFICULTY LEVEL

Some fields demand more study and practice than others. **GURPS** uses four "difficulty levels" to rate the effort required to learn and improve a skill. The more difficult the skill, the more points you must spend to buy it at a given skill level.

Easy skills are things that *anyone* could do reasonably well after a short learning period – whether because they are second nature to most people or because there isn't a whole lot to learn.

Average skills include most combat skills, mundane job skills, and the practical social and survival skills that ordinary people use daily. This is the most common difficulty level.

Hard skills require intensive formal study. This is typical of most "academic" skills, complex athletic and combat skills that require *years* of training, and all but the most powerful of magic spells.

Very Hard skills have prodigious scope, or are alien, counterintuitive, or *deliberately* shrouded in secrecy. The most fundamental of sciences, and many potent magic spells and secret martial-arts techniques, are Very Hard.

TECHNOLOGICAL SKILLS

Certain skills are different at each tech level (see *Technology Level*, p. 22). These "technological skills" are designated by "/TL." This means that when you learn the skill, you must learn it at a specific tech level (TL). Always note the TL when you write down such a skill; e.g., "Surgery/TL4" for the TL4 version of Surgery skill. Surgery/TL4 (cut his arm off with an axe) is nothing like Surgery/TL9 (graft on a replacement arm from his clone)!

You learn technological skills at your personal TL. You may also choose skills from a *lower* TL. You can only learn skills from a *higher* TL in play – and only if you have a teacher *and* the skill is not based on IQ. To learn IQ-based technological skills from a higher TL, you must first raise your personal TL.

Technological skills rely on language, tool use, or both. This means that only sapient characters – those with IQ 6 or higher – may learn them. *Exception:* Robots and the like can have IQ 5 or less and perform such skills by running programs . . . but of course *programming* isn't *learning*.

Tech-Level Modifiers

Technological skills work best with the specific artifacts and techniques of their own TL. When you work with equipment or concepts of a TL different from that of your skill, you suffer a penalty to your skill roll.

IQ-Based Technological Skills

IQ-based technological skills represent a studied technical understanding of the *specific* methods and tools common at a particular TL. There is a penalty to your skill roll when you use these skills with the equipment of a higher TL (which relies on scientific and engineering principles unknown to you) or a lower TL (which depends on principles that were, at best, a "historical footnote" during your training).

Equipment's TL	Skill Penalty
Skill's TL+4 or more	Impossible!
Skill's TL+3	-15
Skill's TL+2	-10
Skill's TL+1	-5
Skill's TL	0
Skill's TL-1	-1
Skill's TL-2	-3
Skill's TL-3	-5
Skill's TL-4	-7
Per extra -1 to TL	-2

Other Technological Skills

Technological skills based on attributes other than IQ let you *use* technology; they do not assume any real understanding of the science or engineering behind the tools. For instance, a TL5 gunslinger accustomed to firing a Colt Peacemaker might find a TL7 Colt Python a bit strange, but he would have little difficulty shooting it.

For skills like this, apply a flat penalty of -1 per TL of difference between the skill and the equipment. For instance, a TL5 gunman would be at -2 to shoot a TL7 revolver. It is irrelevant whether the equipment is more or less advanced – a TL7 policeman would be at -2 to fire a TL5 revolver, too.

Grouped Skills

A set of distantly related skills that use identical rules may appear under a single heading to avoid repetition. If a skill description does not say that you must specialize, and indicates that it represents a *collection* of skills, then the subentries represent stand-alone skills – not specialties. Use only the name of the relevant subentry when you refer to such skills.

Example: Hand-to-hand weapon skills are grouped under *Melee Weapon* (p. 208), but if you learn to use a shortsword, write "Shortsword," not "Melee Weapon (Shortsword)."

PREREQUISITES

Some skills have other skills as prerequisites. This is the case when an advanced skill is based on, and in some ways an outgrowth of, a basic one. To study the advanced skill, *you must have at least one point in the prerequisite skill.*

Certain skills also require that you know a prerequisite skill at a minimum skill level. Where this is the case, you must spend the points required to learn the prerequisite skill at the specified level before you can learn the advanced skill.

A few skills have advantages as prerequisites. In order to learn such a skill, you *must* possess the required advantage. If you do not have the advantage, and cannot acquire it in play, you can *never* learn that skill.

SPECIALTIES

An entry on the skill list may represent an entire category of closely related skills that share a single skill name. Examples include Armoury (p. 178) and Survival (p. 223). Skills like this are marked with a dagger (†) in the list on pp. 174-228. The skills within such a category are called "specialties." When you buy a general skill of this kind, you *must* specify which specialty you are learning. On your character sheet, note the name of the specialty in parentheses after the general skill name; e.g., "Armoury (Small Arms)" or "Survival (Arctic)."

You may learn skills like this any number of times, with a different specialty each time, because *each specialty is a different skill.* There is usually a favorable "default" between specialties

(see *Skill Defaults*, p. 173), which may let you purchase additional specialties more cheaply.

Optional Specialties

Many IQ-based skills – notably "academic" skills such as Literature and Physics – have countless subfields but do not *require* you to select a specialty. As written, if you learn a skill like this, you are a generalist, knowledgeable about every aspect of the skill. However, you may *opt* to specialize in a single, narrow area. You may only do this with an Average or harder IQ-based skill, and only if the GM agrees that the chosen subfield is logical given the skill and your TL.

Familiarity

Any skill used to operate equipment – e.g., Beam Weapons/TL11 (Pistol) or Driving/TL7 (Automobile) – takes a penalty when you are faced with an unfamiliar *type* of item. For instance, if you were trained on a laser pistol, a blaster pistol would be "unfamiliar." Assume that an unfamiliar piece of equipment gives -2 to skill except where an individual skill description specifies otherwise.

In general, if you have the skill to use a piece of equipment, you are considered *familiar* with a new make or model after you have had eight hours of practice with it. Some skills require more or less practice than this, so be sure to read the skill description.

There is no limit to the number of types of gun, car, plane, etc. you can become familiar with. Each of these items is called a "familiarity." If you have at least six familiarities for a given skill, the GM may roll against your skill when you pick up a new piece of equipment. On a success, you are already familiar with something similar and may use the new device at no penalty. The GM may also rule that a new item is so similar to a known one that it is familiar – for instance, two similar models of Colt revolver should be considered identical.

Equipment from another tech level will usually be unfamiliar. This gives both TL *and* familiarity modifiers. Practice can eliminate unfamiliarity penalties, but to shed TL penalties, you must relearn the operation skill at the equipment's TL. *Exception:* Improved or obsolete versions of items with which you are already familiar do *not* give unfamiliarity penalties.

Familiarity for Beginning Characters

Starting characters may specify two familiarities per point spent on a skill. For instance, if you have four points in Guns (Pistol), you can be familiar with up to eight handguns.

Both specialization and familiarity come into play with many skills, but they are not the same thing. Driving (Automobile) is a *specialty* of Driving: it is a separate skill from Driving (Locomotive), and to know both, you must pay points for both. "Volkswagen Bug" is a *familiarity* of Driving (Automobile): you can select it for free as one of your starting familiarities.

When you choose an optional specialty, write down the skill and its specialty just as if you were selecting a required specialty. You learn the specialized skill as if it were one level easier. Unless otherwise noted, prerequisites are unchanged. The general skill defaults to the specialized one at -2; roll against this whenever you must answer questions outside your field. Any skill that defaults to the general skill also defaults to all of its optional specialties, but at an additional -2.

Example: Chemistry is IQ/Hard and does not *require* a specialty. You could learn the *optional* specialty Chemistry (Analytical) as if it were one level easier, or IQ/Average. Your general Chemistry skill would default to Chemistry (Analytical)-2. Metallurgy, which normally defaults to Chemistry-5, would default to Chemistry (Analytical)-7.

BUYING SKILLS

In order to learn or improve a skill, you must spend character points. When you spend points on a skill, you are getting training to bring that skill up to a useful level. Skills are easy to learn at first – a little training goes a long way! But added improvement costs more.

The point cost of a skill depends on two things: its difficulty and the final skill level you wish to attain. Use the *Skill Cost Table* (below) to calculate a skill's point cost.

The first column shows the skill level you are trying to attain, *relative to the skill's controlling attribute* – DX for DX-based skills, IQ for IQ-based skills, and so forth. For instance, if your DX were 12, a level of "Attribute-1" would be DX-1, or 11; "Attribute+0" would be DX, or 12; and "Attribute+1" would be DX+1, or 13.

The next four columns show the character point costs to learn skills of different difficulties – *Easy, Average, Hard,* and *Very Hard* – at the desired skill level. Harder skills cost more points to learn!

Example: A warrior with DX 14 wishes to learn Shortsword (DX/Average) at level 17. Since skill 17 is equal to his DX+3, he goes to the "Attribute+3" row. Then he reads along the row to the "Average" column to find the point cost: 12 points.

> ## Skill Notation
>
> When you write down a skill with a single specialty, either required or optional, do so in the form "Skill Name (Specialty)"; e.g., Artist (Painting). If such a skill has multiple qualifiers, follow these guidelines:
>
> *Technological skills:* Place the tech level after the skill name and before the specialty; e.g., Engineer/TL8 (Civil).
> *Skills with both required and optional specialties:* If a skill that requires you to specialize also allows an optional specialty, write the required specialty before the optional specialty and separate the two with a comma; e.g., Artist (Painting, Oil).
> *Skills that require two specialties:* In the rare case where a skill requires you to select two specialties, separate them with a slash; e.g., Geography/TL7 (Physical/Earth-like).

There is no limit (except lifespan) to the amount of improvement possible with any skill. However, the useful maximum for most skills is between 20 and 30. Problems to challenge a greater skill are rare!

IMPROVING YOUR SKILLS

There are two direct ways to increase your skills in play: spend the bonus points you earn for successful adventuring on new or better skills, or dedicate game time to study, which gives you points you can use to add or improve the skills you studied. In either case, *the cost to improve a skill is the **difference** between the cost of the desired skill level and the cost of your current skill level.* For more information, see Chapter 9.

Free Increases in Skills

There is one way to increase many skills at once: pay the points to improve an attribute (see Chapter 9). If you do this, *all* your skills based on that attribute go up by the same amount, at no extra cost. For instance, if you raise DX by one level, all of your DX-based skills also go up by one level. Further improvements are based on the new DX value.

You can also base skills on "defaults" from other skills; see *Defaulting to Other Skills* (p. 173). Any skill bought up from such a default is likely to enjoy a free increase when you raise the skill to which it defaults.

Skill Cost Table

Your Final Skill Level	Difficulty of Skill			
	Easy	Average	Hard	Very Hard
Attribute-3	–	–	–	1
Attribute-2	–	–	1	2
Attribute-1	–	1	2	4
Attribute+0	1	2	4	8
Attribute+1	2	4	8	12
Attribute+2	4	8	12	16
Attribute+3	8	12	16	20
Attribute+4	12	16	20	24
Attribute+5	16	20	24	28
Extra +1	+4	+4	+4	+4

MEANING OF SKILL LEVELS

So you have Literature-9, Savoir-Faire-22, and Shortsword-13. What does that *mean*? What is good, bad, and average? That's very important when you create a character. It's also important if you're converting characters from another system into **GURPS,** or vice versa. There are two equally valid – but *different* – ways to make skill-level comparisons.

Base Skill vs. Effective Skill

Your unmodified skill level is called your *base skill*. It measures your odds of success at an "average" task *under adventuring conditions* – in other words, in a stressful situation where the consequences of failure are significant. Some examples:

> *Your base skill measures your odds of success at an "average" task in a stressful situation where the consequences of failure are significant.*

PROBABILITY OF SUCCESS

The easiest way to get a feel for your skill levels is to look at your odds of success. To use a skill, you must roll 3d against your skill level. This is called a "success roll" (see Chapter 10). For instance, if your skill is 13, you must roll 13 or less on 3d to succeed. The table below shows the *probability of success* at each skill level – that is, your chance of rolling less than or equal to a given number on 3d. Note that skill levels can be over 18, but a roll of 17 or 18 is automatically a failure. *Nobody* succeeds 100% of the time!

- Battles and chase scenes.
- Races against the clock.
- Situations where your health, freedom, finances, or equipment is at risk.

The GM may modify your skill level to reflect the difficulty of a task. Your final skill level, after applying all modifiers for the task at hand, is your *effective skill* for that task.

In nonadventuring situations when you have lots of time to prepare and face minimal risk, the GM may give you +4 or more to skill. (The GM might even declare such actions successful instead of wasting time on a skill roll; see *When to Roll,* p. 343). Ordinary people *almost always* receive this bonus at mundane tasks, even if they are working from default skill!

Example: An airline pilot has Piloting-12 – normally a 74% chance of success. For day-to-day flying, however, he rolls at +4. This makes his effective skill 16, for a 98% chance of success.

On the other hand, especially tough adventuring situations can result in penalties. See *Culture* (p. 23), *Language* (p. 23), *Tech-Level Modifiers* (p. 168), *Familiarity* (p. 169), *Equipment Modifiers* (p. 345), and *Task Difficulty* (p. 345) for some common modifiers. Be sure to take these factors into account when buying your skills.

RELATIVE SKILL LEVEL

Skill level reflects a combination of talent and training. For instance, a DX 17 warrior has a lot of raw talent. He could quickly learn Shortsword-17, as this is only DX level for him. A DX 10 fighter would need considerably more practice to become that skilled, as Shortsword-17 is DX+7 level for him.

Such details are often unimportant; two warriors with Shortsword-17 are equally good at smiting foes, regardless of whether their skill is due to talent or training. However, there are times when you need (or want) to know the difference.

It is easy to compare talent – just look at the controlling attribute for the skill. In the example above, the DX 17 swordsman is clearly more talented than the DX 10 fighter.

To compare training, you must look at *relative skill level*. You can calculate it quickly by subtracting controlling attribute from skill level. In our example, the DX 17 warrior has a relative skill level of 0, while the DX 10 fighter has a relative skill level of +7, and is better trained.

Relative skill level becomes important when using the next two rules; therefore, you might opt to note it in parentheses after your skill level; e.g., "Shortsword-17 (+7)."

Skill Level	Probability of Success	Skill Level	Probability of Success
3	0.5%	10	50.0%
4	1.9%	11	62.5%
5	4.6%	12	74.1%
6	9.3%	13	83.8%
7	16.2%	14	90.7%
8	25.9%	15	95.4%
9	37.5%	16+	98.1%

Choosing Your Skill Levels

Gauging what skill levels you need to survive is no easy task. Determining how much skill is *realistic* can be tricky as well. When creating a PC (or an NPC), bear the following guidelines in mind.

Ordinary Folks

For an "average" person, it is reasonable to assume attributes between 9 and 11, and from 20 to 40 points in "life skills" (varying with education and dedication). Most people spread these points fairly evenly over roughly a dozen skills. This will result in skill levels between 8 and 13. Skills used to earn a living tend toward the upper end of this range (12 or 13), while little-used skills and those originating from long-forgotten college courses are at the lower end (8 or 9).

Experts

Once your skill level reaches 14, additional levels of skill don't improve your odds of success much. Furthermore, it can cost a lot of points to acquire higher skill levels. If you are an adventurer, though, the investment is worthwhile, to help you overcome the penalties for difficult tasks. For instance, if you have Lockpicking-23, ordinary locks are no easier for you – you fail on a 17 or 18, no matter what. But when you run into a *hard* lock that gives -6 to skill, your effective skill is 17 and you *still* only fail on a 17 or 18!

Masters

If you are a "master" in your field, you might be tempted to increase your skill levels *ad infinitum*. However, a true master has a detailed understanding of every aspect of his calling, best represented by stopping at a masterful level (20 to 25) in the "main" skill and branching out into several "subsidiary" skills. An extreme level (anything over 25) in one skill tends to be excessive and unbelievable – and is frequently *less useful* than a lesser level combined with one or more subsidiary skills.

Example: Instead of improving Karate skill to 30, a kung fu master would be better off using those points to buy Karate at 25 and decent levels of Acrobatics, Judo, Meditation, etc.

Masters should also consider putting some points into advantages that negate skill penalties for adverse conditions. For instance, a kung fu master might buy Trained By A Master (reducing his penalties for multiple attacks and parries) and Combat Reflexes (improving his chances of defending himself), extending his capabilities in ways that high skill alone cannot.

To encourage players to develop their characters laterally instead of sinking all their points into just one or two skills, the GM might wish to consider limiting PCs to skill levels somewhere in the 20-25 range.

Using Skills With Other Attributes

The GM will sometimes find it useful to ask for a skill roll based on an attribute other than the controlling one for a skill. This is realistic; few skills really depend *just* on brains, *just* on agility, etc. To make a roll like this, simply add the *relative* skill level to the attribute you wish to use and make a success roll against the total.

Example: A warrior with DX 10, IQ 14, and Shortsword-17 has a relative skill level of +7 in Shortsword. If the GM asked for an IQ-based Shortsword roll, the swordsman would roll against 14 + 7 = 21 instead of his Shortsword skill of 17.

Some skill descriptions present situations where skill rolls using other attributes would be appropriate. The GM is encouraged to dream up more! A few examples:

● DX-based rolls against IQ-based repair skills to reach into tight corners; ST-based rolls against these skills to manhandle engine blocks and other heavy parts into place.

● IQ-based rolls against DX-based combat skills to feint an opponent, formulate tactics, or perform minor maintenance on weapons; ST-based rolls against these skills to disarm someone using brute strength rather than finesse.

● IQ-based rolls against DX-based vehicle-operation skills to recall traffic regulations, remember to change the oil, or identify the make and model of a vehicle; HT-based rolls against these skills to stay awake at the wheel.

Your relative skill level will sometimes modify ST for a specific task (e.g., kicking in doors). Only modify ST if your relative skill level is *positive* – you get a bonus for high skill, but you never get a penalty for low skill.

Using Skills Without Attributes

The GM might occasionally want two people with identical training to have similar odds of success *regardless* of their attributes, in a situation where training really does matter more than innate talent. In this case, just add relative skill level to a flat number – usually 10 – and roll against the result.

Example: Two accountants are vying for a promotion. One is talented, with IQ 14 and Accounting-18 (+4). The other is dull but experienced, with IQ 8 and Accounting-15 (+7). The GM decides to handle this as a Quick Contest: each accountant must attempt his Accounting roll, and the one who succeeds by the most will get the promotion. However, the boss cares about seniority above all, so the GM applies relative skill level – which reflects experience – to a flat base of 10. This leaves IQ out of the picture! The talented accountant rolls against 10 + 4 = 14, while his rival rolls against 10 + 7 = 17. Sometimes, life isn't fair . . .

SKILL DEFAULTS: USING SKILLS YOU DON'T KNOW

Most skills have a "default level": the level at which you use the skill if you have *no* training. A skill has a default level if it is something that everybody can do . . . a little bit. As a general rule, a skill defaults to its controlling attribute at -4 if Easy, -5 if Average, or -6 if Hard. There are exceptions to this, but not many.

Example: The "default" for Broadsword (DX/Average) is DX-5. If your DX is 11, and you have to swing a broadsword without training, then your "default" skill at Broadsword is 11 - 5 = 6. You need a roll of 6 or less to hit.

Some skills have *no* default level. For instance, Alchemy, Hypnotism, and Karate are complex enough that you cannot use them *at all* without training.

Regardless of your default skill level, you do not get the special benefits of a skill – especially combat bonuses such as improved damage, special defenses, and unpenalized off-hand use – when you use a skill at default. To enjoy these benefits, you must spend *at least one point* on the skill.

The Rule of 20

If a skill defaults to a basic attribute that is higher than 20, treat that attribute as 20 when figuring default skill. Superhuman characters get *good* defaults, but not *super* ones.

Who Gets a Default?

Only individuals from a society where a skill is known may attempt a default roll against that skill. For instance, the default for Scuba skill assumes you are from a world where scuba gear exists and where most people would have *some* idea – if only from TV – of how to use it. A medieval knight transported to the 21st century would not get a default roll to use scuba gear the first time he saw it!

Defaulting to Other Skills

Some skills default to *another skill* instead of or as well as an attribute.

Example: Broadsword defaults to Shortsword-2, because the two skills are very similar. A Shortsword skill of 13 gives you a "default" Broadsword skill of 11.

Double Defaults

A skill can't default to another skill known only by default. If Skill A defaults to Skill B-5, and Skill B defaults to IQ-5, does Skill A default to IQ-10? No.

Improving Skills from Default

If your default level in a skill is high enough that you would normally have to pay points for that level, you may improve the skill past its default level by paying only the *difference* in point costs between your new level and your default level.

Example: Suppose you have DX 12 and Shortsword at 13. Since Broadsword defaults to Shortsword-2, your default Broadsword skill is 11. Skill 11 is equal to DX-1 for you. This would have cost 1 point had you bought it directly. The next level (DX) costs 2 points. The difference is 1 point; to raise your Broadsword skill from its default level of 11 (DX-1) to 12 (DX), you need only pay 1 character point. You do not have to pay the full 2 points for DX level!

If you increase a skill, skills that default to it go up as well. However, if you have spent points to improve these defaults, you may not see an increase when you raise the skill to which they default. This is best illustrated with our running example:

Example: Suppose you spend the point to raise Broadsword to 12 (DX). Now you spend 4 more points on Shortsword, improving that skill

from 13 to 14 (from DX+1 to DX+2). Does your Broadsword skill also go up a level? No. Your new default from Shortsword is now 12 (Shortsword at 14, minus 2), but to go from level 12 to level 13 (from DX to DX+1) with Broadsword costs 2 points, and you've only spent 1 point on Broadsword. Keep track of that point, though. When you spend one more point on Broadsword, it goes up a level, too.

When two skills default to one another and you have improved both, you may switch the "direction" of your default if this would give you better skill levels. Redistribute the points spent on both skills as needed. You may *never* decrease either skill level this way, however; you must always spend enough points to keep each skill at its current level.

Example: Keeping Shortsword at 14, you spend a total of 22 points on Broadsword, improving your skill from its default of 12 (DX) to 18 (DX+6). You'd like to default Shortsword from Broadsword now, rather than vice versa. Taking the 8 points you spent on Shortsword and the 22 points you spent on Broadsword, you have 30 points to work with. First, buy Broadsword at 18 (DX+6) for 24 points. Then default Shortsword from Broadsword, getting 16 (that is, Broadsword-2). Finally, spend the remaining 6 points on Shortsword. This will be enough to raise Shortsword skill to 17 (and 2 more points will make that 18).

This feels like an abstract number shuffle, but it works. You're no better off than if you had started out with Broadsword skill, and you aren't penalized for learning Shortsword first.

SKILL LIST

The skill list is sorted alphabetically by skill name. Each entry gives the following information:

Name: The skill's name. Technological skills are noted as such; e.g., "Machinist/TL." Skills marked with a dagger (†) *require* you to choose a specialty (see *Specialties,* p. 169).

Type: The skill's controlling attribute and difficulty level; e.g., "IQ/Average."

Defaults: The attributes or other skills to which the skill defaults if you have not studied it. Where there is more than one possible default, use the most favorable. Some skills have *no* default – you *cannot* attempt to use these skills if you don't know them.

Prerequisites: Traits you must possess before you can spend points on the skill. If the prerequisite is another skill, you must have at least one point in that skill. Not all skills have prerequisites.

Description: An explanation of what the skill is for and how it works in play.

Modifiers: A list of common bonuses and penalties for use of the skill. The GM decides whether a particular modifier applies in a given situation. If an advantage or disadvantage *permanently* modifies base skill level rather than simply giving a bonus or a penalty for a specific task, add this permanent modifier to the skill level listed on your character sheet.

Accounting

IQ/Hard

Defaults: IQ-6, Finance-4, Mathematics (Statistics)-5, or Merchant-5.

This is the ability to keep books of account, to examine the condition of a business, etc. A successful Accounting roll (requires at least two hours of study, and possibly months to audit a large corporation) can tell you whether financial records are correct, and possibly reveal evidence of forgery, tampering, and similar criminal activity.

Modifiers: The time modifiers under *Time Spent* (p. 346) often apply; the Talents (p. 89) of Business Acumen and Mathematical Ability *both* provide a bonus.

Acrobatics

DX/Hard

Default: DX-6.

This is the ability to perform gymnastic stunts, roll, take falls, etc. This can be handy on an adventure, as tightrope walking, human pyramids, and trapeze swinging all have useful applications. Each trick requires a separate skill roll, at whatever penalties the GM sees fit. If you are performing stunts on a moving vehicle or mount, roll against the *lower* of Acrobatics and the appropriate Driving or Riding skill.

You may substitute an Acrobatics roll for a DX roll in any attempt to jump, roll, avoid falling down, etc. As well, you may attempt an Acrobatic Dodge in combat – a jump or roll that avoids an attack in a flashy way (see *Acrobatic Dodge,* p. 375). Finally, a successful Acrobatics roll will reduce the effective distance of any fall by five yards (see *Falling,* p. 431).

Two special versions of Acrobatics are also available:

Aerobatics: The ability to execute tight turns, loops, power dives, etc. in flight. You must be able to fly to learn this skill – although *how* you fly (magic, wings, jet pack, etc.) is irrelevant. Natural fliers might find flight to be as effortless as humans find walking, but they must still learn Aerobatics in order to engage in complex acrobatics. Add +2 to skill if you have 3D Spatial Sense (p. 34).

Aquabatics: The ability to engage in underwater acrobatics. *Prerequisites:* Swimming, *or* the Amphibious advantage (p. 40) or the Aquatic disadvantage (p. 145).

Acrobatics, Aerobatics, and Aquabatics default to one another at -4. Add +1 to these three skills if you have Perfect Balance (p. 74).

Acting

IQ/Average

Defaults: IQ-5, Performance-2, or Public Speaking-5.

This is the ability to counterfeit moods, emotions, and voices, and to lie convincingly over a period of time. A successful Acting roll lets you pretend to feel something that you do not. The GM may also require an Acting roll whenever you try to fool someone, play dead in combat, etc.

Impersonation is a special type of acting. To impersonate someone, you must first successfully disguise yourself (see *Disguise,* p. 187) – unless your victims cannot see you!

Note that Acting is *not* the same Fast-Talk (the art of the "quick con") or Performance (the skill of screen and stage acting).

Modifiers: +1 for every point of IQ you have over the person you are trying to fool (or the smartest one in the group), or -1 for every point of difference if your victim is smarter than you; -3 for Low Empathy (p. 142); -1 to -4 for Shyness (p. 154); -5 for Truthfulness (p. 159), but only if you are trying to deceive someone. *For impersonation only:* -5 if you are not well acquainted with your subject; -5 if those you wish to fool are acquaintances of the subject (-10 for *close* acquaintances).

Administration

IQ/Average

Defaults: IQ-5 or Merchant-3.

This is the skill of running a large organization. It is often a prerequisite for high Rank (p. 29). A successful Administration roll gives you a +2 reaction bonus when dealing with a bureaucrat, and allows you to predict the best way to go about dealing with a bureaucracy.

Aerobatics

see *Acrobatics,* above

Airshipman/TL

see *Crewman,* p. 185

Alchemy/TL

IQ/Very Hard

Defaults: None.

This is the study of magical transformations and transmutations. In a magical game world, an alchemist would be able to identify concoctions with magical effects ("elixirs"), such as love potions and healing unguents, and prepare them from suitable ingredients. This is a mechanical process, using the mana inherent in certain things; therefore, those without Magery can learn and use Alchemy, and Magery confers no benefit.

Animal Handling†
IQ/Average

Default: IQ-5.

This is the ability to train and work with animals. You *must* specialize in a category of animals – the more intelligent the animals, the narrower the category. Examples of interest to adventurers: Big Cats (jaguars, lions, tigers, etc.), Dogs, Equines (horses and donkeys), and Raptors (eagles, falcons, and hawks). The default between specialties is -2 within the same order (e.g., Dogs to Big Cats), -4 across orders (e.g., Dogs to Equines), and -6 for larger differences (e.g., Dogs to Raptors).

To train an animal, make an Animal Handling roll once per day of training. A failed roll means the animal learned nothing; a badly failed roll means you are *attacked*. The time it takes to train an animal depends on the beast's intelligence and tractability (see Chapter 16).

When working with a trained animal, roll against skill for each task you set the animal. This roll is at -5 if the animal is not familiar with you, -5 if the circumstances are stressful to the animal, and -3 or more if the task is a complex one. To put on an *entertaining* circus act, snake-charming show, etc., you must make a separate Performance roll!

This skill can also (sometimes) be used to quiet a wild, dangerous, or untrained animal. This roll is at -5 if the creature is wild or very frightened, or -10 if it is a man-eater or man-killer.

Finally, this skill gives an advantage in combat against animals within your specialty. If you have Animal Handling at level 15, an animal's attack and defense rolls are at -1 against you, because you can predict its behavior. At skill 20, the animal's rolls are at -2.

Anthropology†
IQ/Hard

Defaults: IQ-6, Paleontology (Paleo-anthropology)-2, or Sociology-3.

This is the science of evolution and culture. An anthropologist is knowledgeable in the ways of primitive (and not-so-primitive) societies. An Anthropology roll might explain, or even predict, unusual rituals and folk customs. This skill requires specialization by species (if left unspecified, assume the anthropologist's *own* species). Specialties usually default to one another at -2 to -5, although there may be no default for completely alien species.

Optional Rule: Wildcard Skills

The professor who has studied *every* science, the swordsman who can fight with *any* blade . . . cinematic fiction is full of heroes who know a little bit about everything in one broad area. The time required to list every last skill such a hero might need, and the difficulty of figuring out which skills to take (and which to *use*), might discourage many gamers from playing cinematic experts. Such broad expertise doesn't exist in real life, but it is all part of the fun in cinematic games!

A solution to this problem is "wildcard skills" or "bang skills": skills that cover extremely broad categories of ability. The names of these skills end in an exclamation point in order to distinguish them from normal skills; e.g., "Science!" is the skill of "all science." *Wildcard skills include and replace **all** specific skills within their area.* For instance, a hero could attempt a Science! roll whenever the adventure calls for a roll against Chemistry, Physics, or another science skill.

Wildcard skills that cover mainly intellectual pursuits are IQ-based, while those that pertain chiefly to physical actions are DX-based. Such skills have no default; to use them, you *must* spend points on them. Buy wildcard skills as Very Hard skills, but at *triple* the usual point cost. For instance, it would normally cost 8 points to buy an IQ/Very Hard skill at IQ level, so Science! skill at IQ level would cost 24 points.

The GM might choose to limit wildcard skills to those with a suitable Unusual Background – perhaps "Cinematic Hero." This Unusual Background should never be available to sidekicks and random thugs! To give each hero a well-defined dramatic niche, the GM might wish to limit PCs to one or two wildcard skills apiece (preferably those that emerge naturally from their character stories).

Some examples:

Detective! (IQ). Replaces Criminology, Detect Lies, Electronics Operation (Security and Surveillance), Forensics, Interrogation, Law, Observation, Research, Savoir-Faire (Police), Search, Shadowing, Streetwise, etc.

Gun! (DX). Replaces *all* specialties of Beam Weapons, Gunner, Guns, and Liquid Projector, as well as all related Fast-Draw skills. Make an IQ-based roll for Armoury pertaining to these weapons.

Science! (IQ). Replaces Astronomy, Bioengineering, Biology, Chemistry, Engineer, Geology, Mathematics, Metallurgy, Meteorology, Naturalist, Paleontology, Physics, Psychology, etc.

Sword! (DX). Replaces Broadsword, Force Sword, Jitte/Sai, Knife, Main-Gauche, Rapier, Saber, Shortsword, Smallsword, and Two-Handed Sword, as well as related Fast-Draw skills. Use in place of such skills as Acrobatics and Jumping for physical stunts while fighting.

Wildcard skills are useful for omniproficient characters. Someone who can pick up and play *any* instrument, or sight-read *any* choral work, would have the Music! skill. If he's gifted with several instruments and can pick up others easily (but does have to learn them first), that's the Musical Ability Talent.

Aquabatics

see *Acrobatics*, p. 174

Archaeology

IQ/Hard

Default: IQ-6.

This is the study of ancient civilizations. An archaeologist is at home with excavations, old potsherds, inscriptions, etc. An Archaeology roll lets you answer questions about ancient history, or identify artifacts and dead languages. It might even reveal information relating to the occult; e.g., Ancient Secrets and Things Man Was Not Meant To Know . . .

Architecture/TL

IQ/Average

Defaults: IQ-5 or Engineer (Civil)-4.

This is the ability to design buildings, and to deduce the design of buildings from their function (and vice versa). A successful Architecture roll lets you learn things about a strange building, find a secret room or door, etc.

Modifiers: -2 if the building is of a strange type; -5 if it is alien.

Area Knowledge†

IQ/Easy

Defaults: IQ-4 or Geography (Regional)-3*

* You have an IQ default only for Area Knowledge of a place where you live or once lived. Geography only gives a default for Area Knowledge of the specialty region.

This skill represents familiarity with the people, places, and politics of a given region. You usually have Area Knowledge only for the area you consider your "home base," whether that's a single farm or a solar system. If information about other areas is available, the GM may allow you to learn additional Area Knowledge skills.

The GM should not require Area Knowledge rolls for ordinary situations; e.g., to find the blacksmith, tavern, or your own home. But he could require a roll to locate a smith to shoe

Geographical and Temporal Scope

Skills such as Area Knowledge, Current Affairs (Regional) (p. 186), Geography (Regional) (p. 198), and History (p. 200) require specialization to specific places and times. In reality, this kind of knowledge is never "clear cut," and tends to spill over into related areas. The following penalties apply when you wish to use such a skill outside your specialty.

Distance

For an area far from your "stomping grounds," use the penalties under *Long-Distance Modifiers* (p. 241). However, the speed at which knowledge propagates increases as progressively more powerful tools for managing information appear: printing press, telephone, television, computers, faster-than-light radio, etc. To reflect this, at TL5 and above, the GM may choose to roll 3d against TL+1 (e.g., 9 or less at TL8) to determine whether you are familiar with the distant region from TV, the Internet, etc. On a success, you may *ignore* all distance penalties. (The GM might also wish to use this rule to determine whether a character's Reputation is known far from home in a high-tech setting.)

Time

Time is usually only a concern for History skill – but it could also apply to Area Knowledge skill in a time-travel game, or if someone has been away from home for a *long* time. Use the Long-Distance Modifiers once again, substituting *years* for *miles*. For each point of tech-level difference, *double* the time modifier (a two-TL difference would be ×4, etc.). This is because societies change drastically on all levels when technology increases.

Area Class

"Area classes" are defined under Area Knowledge skill: Neighborhood; Village or Town; City; Barony, County, Duchy, or Small Nation; Large Nation; Planet; Interplanetary State; and Galaxy. Area class becomes important in campaigns that involve a lot of travel. We assume here that the smaller areas are contained within the larger ones.

If you have specialized in a *larger* area and want information about a *smaller* area within it, the penalty is -2 for one class of difference, -4 for two, -8 for three, and so on, doubling each time.

If you have specialized in a *smaller* area and want information about a specific locale within the *larger* area containing it, the most appropriate solution is usually to use the distance penalties described above. However, questions having to do with the *entire* large area use a flat -2 per difference in levels.

Example: Someone with Area Knowledge (Earth) would be at -8 – due to three classes of difference – to know the mayor of Los Angeles. However, someone with Area Knowledge (Los Angeles) would be at -4 to know the location of Mount Rushmore. The same person would be at -10 to know the location of the Library of Congress in Washington, D.C.; the Library of Congress has more to do with Washington than with the United States as a whole, and it's more appropriate to resolve the question by considering distance.

Note that in a setting with multiple planes of existence, Area Knowledge skills for one reality can be dangerously unreliable in another. The GM decides the penalty that he will apply when you try to apply your knowledge of *your* San Francisco to *his* version.

your horse at 3 a.m., or to find the best ambush spot along a stretch of road. "Secret" or obscure information might give a penalty, require a Hidden Lore skill (p. 199), or simply be unavailable – GM's decision. For instance, Area Knowledge of Washington, D.C. gives you the location of the Russian Embassy, but not the KGB's current safe house.

The information covered by Area Knowledge often overlaps such skills as Current Affairs, Geography, Naturalist, and Streetwise. The difference is that Area Knowledge works for a single area: you know the habits of *this* tiger or gang boss, but have no special insight into tigers or gangs in general.

You can learn Area Knowledge for any sort of area. The larger the territory, the less "personal" and more general your knowledge becomes. Almost everyone will have Area Knowledge of *some* type. The "canonical" area classes are:

Neighborhood: For an urban area: the residents and buildings of a few city blocks. For a rural area: the inhabitants, trails, streams, hiding places, ambush sites, flora, and fauna of a few hundred acres.

Village or Town: All important citizens and businesses, and most unimportant ones; all public buildings and most houses.

City: All important businesses, streets, citizens, leaders, etc.

Barony, County, Duchy, or Small Nation: General nature of its settlements and towns, political allegiances, leaders, and most citizens of Status 5+.

Large Nation: Location of its major cities and important sites; awareness of its major customs, ethnic groups, and languages (but not necessarily expertise); names of folk of Status 6+; and a general understanding of the economic and political situation.

Planet: As for a large nation, but more general; knowledge of people of Status 7+ only.

Interplanetary State: Location of major planets; familiarity with all *known* races (but not necessarily expertise); knowledge of people of Status 7+; general understanding of the economic and political situation.

Galaxy: Location of the capitals of interplanetary states and the

homeworlds of major races; general awareness of all *major* races; knowledge of individuals of Status 8; general understanding of relations between interplanetary states.

Area Knowledge for anything larger than a galaxy would be meaninglessly vague.

Your IQ-4 default applies to *any* of these classes, as long as you have lived in the area. Defaults are limited by "common knowledge" at your tech level! A TL0 hunter would have a

default for every level up to "Village or Town," while a TL8 student would have defaults up to "Planet" level. You must live in an interplanetary or interstellar state to have defaults for levels above "Planet."

In some game worlds, Area Knowledge specialties may exist for parallel realities and other dimensions – Area Knowledge (Cyberspace), Area Knowledge (Dream Realms), etc. The knowledge such skills provide is left to the GM's judgment.

Armoury/TL†

IQ/Average

Defaults: IQ-5 or Engineer (same)-4.

This is the ability to build, modify, and repair a specific class of weapons or armor. (It does not include skill at design; for that, see *Engineer*, p. 190.) A successful roll lets you find a problem, if it isn't obvious; a second roll lets you repair it. Time required is up to the GM.

You *must* specialize in one of the following fields:

Battlesuits: All kinds of powered armor, along with any built-in weaponry.

Body Armor: Any kind of unpowered personal armor (but *not* shields). Also defaults to Smith (Bronze)-3 at TL1, to Smith (Iron)-3 at TL2-4, and to Machinist-3 at TL5+.

Force Shields: Any kind of force screen or deflector – be it personal or vehicular. This is the same skill as Electronics Repair (Force Shields).

Heavy Weapons: All weapons used with the Artillery and Gunner skills.

(Bronze)-3 at TL1, to Smith (Iron)-3 at TL2-4, and to Machinist-3 at TL5+.

Missile Weapons: Man-portable, pre-gunpowder projectile weapons of all kinds – bows, crossbows, slings, etc.

Small Arms: All weapons used with the Beam Weapons and Guns skills. Also defaults to Machinist-5 at TL5+.

Vehicular Armor: All kinds of armored vehicle hulls.

Most specialties default to one another at -4 – but above TL4, there is *no* default between Armoury specialties dealing with armor and Armoury specialties dealing with weapons. The technologies covered by each specialty vary with TL. For instance, Armoury (Small Arms) covers black-powder small arms at TL4, repeating small arms that fire cartridges at TL6, "smart" infantry weapons at TL8, and portable beam weapons at TL10.

The GM should strictly enforce penalties for unfamiliarity. Armoury/TL10 (Small Arms) might cover both beam weapons and portable railguns, but going from one to the other gives you -2 to skill until you familiarize yourself with all the differences.

Melee Weapons: Any weapon used with a Melee Weapon or Thrown Weapon skill, as well as all kinds of shields. Also defaults to Smith

Modifiers: -2 for an unfamiliar item within your specialty (e.g., plate armor when you're used to mail); equipment modifiers (p. 345).

Artillery/TL†

IQ/Average

Default: IQ-5.

This is the ability to use a heavy weapon, such as a trebuchet or a howitzer, for *indirect* fire – that is, to put fire onto a target area via a high ballistic arc or similar path. For *direct* fire, use Gunner skill (p. 198). Roll against Artillery skill to bombard the target.

Loaders can make ST-based Artillery rolls to improve the rate of fire of certain crew-served heavy weapons. See the appropriate weapon description for details.

You *must* specialize by weapon type. The available specialties vary by TL, but include one or more of:

Beams: Any kind of heavy energy weapon that is fired from orbit, bounced off a mirror, or otherwise used against targets you cannot see.

Bombs: All kinds of unpowered, free-falling munitions.

Cannon: Any kind of heavy projectile weapon – bombard, howitzer, naval gun, etc.

Catapult: Any kind of indirect-fire mechanical siege engine, such as a trebuchet.

Guided Missile: Any kind of seeking or remotely piloted missile.

Torpedoes: Any kind of powered underwater projectile.

There is *no* default between specialties, some of which (e.g., Torpedoes) cover weapons that bear little or no resemblance to true artillery. Artillery is a single skill only because all the weapons it covers use the same rules.

The weapons covered by each specialty will vary by TL. For instance, Artillery (Cannon) would cover primitive bombards at TL3, brass cannon at TL4, breech-loading howitzers at TL6, and orbital railguns at TL9+.

Familiarity is crucial here! Artillery (Cannon) covers both 81mm infantry mortars and 406mm naval guns, but going from one to the other will give -2 for weapon type (81mm vs. 406mm), -2 for fire-control (visual spotting vs. fire-direction center), and -2 for mount (bipod vs. naval turret), for a total of -6 to skill until you familiarize yourself with all the differences.

Note that Forward Observer skill (p. 196) is generally required to designate targets for Artillery skill.

Modifiers: All relevant combat modifiers; -2 for an unfamiliar fire-control system (e.g., map coordinates when you're used to satellite imagery) or mount (e.g., a naval turret when you're used to emplaced guns), or for an unfamiliar weapon of a known type (e.g., 155mm when you are used to 203mm); -4 or more for a weapon in bad repair.

Artist†

IQ/Hard

Default: IQ-6.

This skill represents talent at a visual art. A successful roll might let you create a recognizable likeness of a person or an object, or a work beautiful enough to sell (the GM should not allow a default roll for this use!). Time required is up to the GM.

Artist is based on IQ, but there are many situations in which the GM could logically ask for a DX-based roll, in which case modifiers for High Manual Dexterity (p. 59) or Ham-Fisted (p. 138) would apply. In rare cases, even a *ST*-based Artist roll might make sense – for instance, to work with a physically tough material.

You *must* specialize in an art form. Common specialties include:

Body Art: Tattooing, piercing, and scarification. Both this specialty and Painting suffice for henna or temporary tattoos, but cosmetic *surgery* requires Surgery skill (p. 223).
Calligraphy: Beautiful and decorative handwriting. You need not be literate!
Drawing: All forms of charcoal, ink, pastel, and pencil work.
Illumination: Decorating written text with miniature paintings and pictures.
Illusion: Creating believable or evocative illusions. *Prerequisite:* magical or psionic illusion ability of some kind.
Interior Decorating: Creating pleasing building interiors by selecting appropriate paints, fixtures, and furniture. *Default:* Architecture-3.
Painting: All forms of painting, whether on paper, canvas, or a wall, and whether with tempera, oil-based paint, or something more exotic (like blood).
Pottery: Working with various sorts of ceramics – especially clay.
Scene Design: Designing sets for the stage. *Default:* Architecture-3.
Sculpting: Creating three-dimensional art from ivory, stone, metal, etc.
Woodworking: All forms of fine woodwork, including cabinet-making and decorative carving. *Default:* Carpentry-3.

Calligraphy, Drawing, Illumination, and Painting default to one another at -2, and to or from Body Art at -4. Interior Decorating, Scene Design, and Woodworking default among themselves at -4. All other Artist specialties default to one another at -6.

An artist of any kind can take a further *optional* specialty (p. 169) in a particular medium or technique.

Many Artist specialties are used to earn a living rather than to create fine art, and some people regard them as "craft" skills, not "art" skills. It is up to *you* whether you focus on beauty, realism, or functionality.

Modifiers: Equipment modifiers (p. 345); -2 if the medium is unfamiliar (e.g., tempera when you are used to oils); -5 if the medium is difficult (e.g., marble, for a sculptor).

Astronomy/TL

IQ/Hard

Default: IQ-6.
Prerequisite: Mathematics (Applied).

This is the study of stars and other extraplanetary objects. An astronomer could answer questions about the Sun, the planets of the solar system, etc. An amateur who can locate stars and use a telescope, but not perform involved calculations, has an *optional* specialty (p. 169): Astronomy (Observational). This specialty does *not* require Mathematics as a prerequisite.

Autohypnosis

Will/Hard

Default: Meditation-4.

This skill allows you to tap reserves of inner strength by entering a trance-like state. It requires a concentration period of (20 - skill) seconds, minimum one second. You cannot talk or move during the initiation of the trance state. A successful skill roll allows you to do *one* of the following:

Improve Concentration. You get +2 to skill to perform a specific, lengthy mental task (e.g., break a code or write a computer program), but -2 to all unrelated IQ, Perception, and skill rolls. The task must be a relatively sedate one, done in a quiet place (library, lab, monastery, or placid wilderness).
Increase Will. You get +2 to Will (+5 on a critical success) for one hour. This applies to all attempts to resist interrogation, torture, or magical or psionic attack. This roll is at -2.
Negate Pain/Fatigue. Cancels the negative effects of being reduced to less than 1/3 of your FP or HP (but *not* the fatigue or injury itself). This roll is at -4, and you may only make one attempt per hour.

Axe/Mace
see *Melee Weapon,* p. 208

Battlesuit/TL
see *Environment Suit,* p. 192

Beam Weapons/TL†

DX/Easy

Default: DX-4.

This is the ability to use beam small arms. You *must* specialize by weapon type:

Pistol: Any handgun that fires an energy or particle beam.
Projector: Any energy weapon that emits an area-effect cone or field.
Rifle: Any long arm that fires an energy or particle beam.

These specialties default to one another at -4. Treat specific beam types (blaster, laser, stunner, etc.) as familiarities. Other modifiers are as per *Guns* (p. 198). In settings with both beam and projectile weapons, the Pistol and Rifle specialties of Beam Weapons default to the similarly named Guns specialties at -4, and vice versa.

See *Artillery* (p. 178) and *Gunner* (p. 198) for heavier beam weapons.

Bicycling

DX/Easy

Defaults: DX-4 or Driving (Motorcycle)-4.

This is the ability to ride a bicycle long distances, at high speeds, in rallies, etc. Roll at +4 if all you want to do is struggle along without falling off. An IQ-based Bicycling roll allows you to make simple repairs, assuming tools and parts are available.

Bioengineering/TL†

IQ/Hard

Default: Biology-5.

This is the ability to engineer living organisms with specific characteristics, or to create biotechnological products. You *must* specialize:

Cloning: The creation and growth of clones.
Genetic Engineering: The manipulation and modification of genes.
Tissue Engineering: The manufacture of organs and tissues.

These specialties default to each other at -4.

Biology/TL†

IQ/Very Hard

Defaults: IQ-6 or Naturalist-6.

This is the scientific study of the structure, behavior, and habitats of living organisms. You *must* specialize in the life of a particular planet type (see box). If you do not specify a planet type, your native planet type is assumed. The IQ default applies only to the planet type you grew up on. The default between different planet-type specialties is -4.

At TL6+, most biologists have an *optional* specialty (p. 169) as well. The most common options are biochemistry (the study of the chemical reactions that sustain life), botany (the study of plants), ecology (the study of environments), genetics (the study of heredity and genomes), marine biology (the study of ocean life), microbiology (the study of microscopic organisms), and zoology (the study of animals), but more obscure specialties are possible.

Planet Types

Biology, Geology (p. 198), and Meteorology (p. 209) *require* you to specialize by "planet type," as does the "Physical" specialty of Geography (p. 198). If you do not specify a planet type, your native planet type is assumed – so if the campaign will never leave your home world, save space and just write "Geology," "Biology," etc. *GURPS* sorts planets into six broad categories for these purposes.

Earthlike: Essentially, all habitable worlds.
Gas Giants: Jupiter/Uranus types.
Hostile Terrestrial: Venus types.
Ice Dwarfs: Comets and small moons composed almost entirely of snow or ice.
Ice Worlds: Rock worlds covered by a frozen "ocean."
Rock Worlds: Most moons, asteroids, etc.

Unless otherwise specified, all planet-type specialties for a given skill default to one another at -4.

Blind Fighting

Per/Very Hard

Defaults: None.
Prerequisites: Trained By A Master or Weapon Master.

You have learned to fight blindfolded or in absolute darkness. As a result, you can "sense" your targets without having to see them.

This skill enables you to use senses other than vision – mainly hearing, but also touch and even smell – to pinpoint exactly where your opponents are. A successful roll allows one melee attack or active defense without any penalties for lighting (even total darkness), blindness (temporary or permanent), or an invisible foe. However, attacks made in total darkness, while blind, or against invisible enemies have an extra -2 to target specific hit locations.

If you also know Zen Archery (p. 228), you can shoot targets without seeing them by making rolls on both skills at -6.

An opponent who knows you possess this ability can foil it by winning a Quick Contest of Stealth-4 vs. your Blind Fighting each turn. If he wins, you cannot detect him. However, Invisibility Art (p. 202) never works on you; it is completely useless against this skill.

Modifiers: Background noise gives a penalty: -1 for rain, -2 for heavy rain or a storm, -3 for a crowded, noisy area or heavy machinery, -4 for a full football stadium, or -5 in the middle of an artillery barrage. If you cannot hear *at all*, the roll is at -7, but you may still attempt a roll, as the skill is not completely based on hearing. Add your level of Acute Hearing to the roll. Add the *higher* of your ESP Talent (p. 256) or Telepathy Talent (p. 257).

Blowpipe

DX/Hard

Default: DX-6.

This is the ability to use a blowpipe. You can use this weapon to shoot small, usually poisoned, darts. You can also use it to blow powders at targets within one yard. Treat this as a melee attack, not as a ranged attack. Such attacks are always at +2 to hit.

Modifiers: -2 and up for wind, if outdoors.

Boating/TL†

DX/Average

Defaults: DX-5 or IQ-5.

This is the ability to handle a specific type of *small* watercraft. For large vessels that require multiple crewmen on a "bridge," use Seamanship (see *Crewman*, p. 185) and Shiphandling (p. 220).

Make a roll to get underway, to dock, and whenever you encounter a hazard. If using this skill at default, also roll when you first enter the boat – to avoid falling in the water!

You *must* specialize:

Large Powerboat: Any boat with an enclosed cabin and an inboard motor. Includes cabin cruisers, houseboats, and patrol boats. *Defaults:* Motorboat-2, Sailboat-4, or Unpowered-4. This specialty (only) also defaults to Seamanship-4.

Motorboat: Any open powerboat – notably speedboats and any of the boats used with the Sailboat or Unpowered specialty when outfitted with an outboard motor. *Defaults:* Large Powerboat-2, Sailboat-3, or Unpowered-3.

Sailboat: Any small watercraft moving under sail. *Defaults:* Large Powerboat-4, Motorboat-3, or Unpowered-3.

Unpowered: Any small watercraft that relies on muscle power, whether it is paddled, rowed, or poled. Includes canoes, rowboats, and rafts. *Defaults:* Large Powerboat-4, Motorboat-3, or Sailboat-3.

Modifiers: -2 for an unfamiliar boat within your specialty (e.g., a kayak when you're used to a rowboat); -3 or worse for foul weather, navigational hazards, etc.

Body Control

HT/Very Hard

Defaults: None.
Prerequisites: Trained By A Master, Breath Control, and Meditation.

This ability lets you affect involuntary bodily functions such as heart rate, blood flow, and digestion. One use of this skill is to enter a deathlike trance, during which only those who can win a Quick Contest of Diagnosis vs. your Body Control skill even realize that you are alive. This requires (30 - skill) seconds of concentration, minimum one second.

You can also use this skill to flush poisons from your body. To do so, you must first roll against Poisons (or Alchemy, Pharmacy, etc., as appropriate) to identify the poison. You cannot attempt this roll until you know you have been poisoned. In most cases, you only discover this when the first symptoms show! A successful Body Control roll – adjusted by any modifier to the HT roll to resist the poison –

flushes the poison in 1d hours, after which it has no further effect.

Finally, you may use the *higher* of this skill and basic HT to resist any Affliction, magic spell, or psionic attack that is normally resisted by HT.

Body Language

Per/Average

Defaults: Detect Lies-4 or Psychology-4.

This is the ability to interpret a person's facial expressions and body posture in order to gauge his feelings. You can use it like the Empathy advantage (p. 51) or Detect Lies skill (p. 187), but only on a subject you can *see*. You can also use it to get a rough idea of what a party member is doing or about to do in a situation where he cannot communicate with you directly (for instance, when using Stealth). You can only observe one subject at a time.

The ability to read body language in *combat* is a standard part of any Melee Weapon or unarmed combat skill; see *Feint* (p. 365).

Modifiers: All Vision modifiers; physiology modifiers (see box); +4 if your subject is Easy to Read (p. 134). Anything that makes the subject harder to "read" gives a penalty: baggy clothing gives -1, a shield or a voluminous cloak gives from -2 to -4,

and a mask gives -5 (and makes it *impossible* to use this skill if you cannot see the rest of the body!).

Body Sense

DX/Hard

Defaults: DX-6 or Acrobatics-3.

This is the ability to adjust quickly after teleportation or similar "instant movement." A successful roll lets you act normally on your next turn. A failed roll means disorientation: you may take no action other than defense for one turn. A critical failure means you *fall down,* physically stunned!

Modifiers: +3 for either level of Absolute Direction (p. 34). -2 if you changed facing, or -5 if you went from vertical to horizontal or vice versa (you cannot change *posture* during a teleport – only orientation).

Bolas

DX/Average

Defaults: None.

This is the ability to throw the *bolas:* a length of cord with two or more weights attached. Its primary uses are to stop herd animals and to hunt small game, but it can also entangle opponents in combat. See *Special Ranged Weapons* (p. 410) for bolas rules.

Physiology Modifiers

The following skills deal with the health, function, or vital points of living beings: Body Language, Diagnosis (p. 187), First Aid (p. 195), Physician (p. 213), Pressure Points (p. 215), Pressure Secrets (p. 215), and Surgery (p. 223). These skills work as written when working with members of *your* species. When dealing with a member of *another* species, apply the following modifiers:

Species with similar physiology: -2 (human vs. Elf) to -4 (human vs. troll).
Species with very different physiology, but still from your world: -5. This includes all normal animals.
Utterly alien species: -6 or worse (GM's option).
Machine: No roll possible! These skills do not work at all on creatures with the Machine meta-trait (p. 263).

A successful roll against a suitable skill lets you avoid these penalties. This roll is usually against the relevant racial specialty of Physiology, although Biology-4 suffices for common animals.

Bow

DX/Average

Default: DX-5.

This is the ability to use the longbow, short bow, and all similar bows. It also covers the compound bow, although a person who had never seen a compound bow would suffer a -2 unfamiliarity penalty.

Boxing

DX/Average

Defaults: None.

This is the skill of trained punching. Roll against Boxing to hit with a punch. Boxing does *not* improve kicking ability – use Brawling (p. 182) or Karate (p. 203) for that.

Boxing improves damage: if you know Boxing at DX+1 level, add +1 *per die* to basic thrust damage when you calculate punching damage. Add +2 per die if you know Boxing at DX+2 or better! Work out damage ahead of time and record it on your character sheet.

When you defend with bare hands, Boxing allows you to parry two *different* attacks per turn, one with each hand. Your Parry score is (skill/2) + 3, rounded down. Boxing parries are at -2 vs. kicks and -3 vs. weapons other than thrusting attacks. Boxing also gives an improved retreating bonus when you parry; see *Retreat* (p. 377). For more on barehanded parries, see *Parrying Unarmed* (p. 376).

Brain Hacking

see *Brainwashing,* below

Brainwashing/TL

IQ/Hard

Defaults: Special.
Prerequisite: Psychology.

This is the "black art" of technological personality alteration and mind control. Only intelligence, military, and security services teach it – and only to individuals with suitable Rank or Security Clearance. Even then, it is rare outside police states (except perhaps during wartime).

Brainwashing encompasses many techniques – some proven, others little better than witchcraft. Depending on the setting, these might include drugs, electroshock, hypnotism, sensory deprivation, sleep deprivation, social pressure, subliminal messages, or surgery . . . and most likely a combination of several of these.

Regardless of the techniques employed, brainwashing is handled as a Regular Contest (*not* a Quick Contest) between Brainwashing skill and the victim's Will. Roll once per day. Obviously, the brainwasher has a tremendous advantage: even if the victim wins *this* time, it is only a matter of time before he slips.

Results depend on how effective the GM deems brainwashing to be, but might include insanity, personality alteration, or suggestions that can be triggered by future events. In game terms, the victim can acquire almost any *mental* quirk or disadvantage.

In settings where neural interfaces exist, it might be possible to "hack" the victim's brain using a computer. This takes only a *fraction of a second* per attempt! Brain Hacking should be treated as its own skill, with Computer Hacking instead of Psychology as a prerequisite.

This skill normally has no default. However, GMs who wish to explore the gory details can specify the techniques used in their campaign and have Brainwashing default to one or more of Electronics Operation (Medical)-6, Hypnotism-6, Interrogation-6, Pharmacy-6, Psychology-6, or Surgery-6, as appropriate.

Brawling

DX/Easy

Defaults: None.

This is the skill of "unscientific" unarmed combat. Roll against Brawling to hit with a punch, or Brawling-2 to hit with a kick. Brawling can also replace DX when you attack with teeth, claws, horns, or other "natural weapons."

Brawling improves damage: if you know Brawling at DX+2 level or better, add +1 *per die* to basic thrust damage when you calculate damage with Brawling attacks – punches, kicks, claws, bites, etc. Work out damage ahead of time and record it on your character sheet.

Brawling includes the ability to use the blackjack or sap. An attack with such a fist load is considered a punch at +1 to damage.

When you defend with bare hands, Brawling allows you to parry two *different* attacks per turn, one with each hand. Your Parry score is (skill/2) + 3, rounded down. Brawling parries are at -3 vs. weapons other than thrusting attacks. For more on barehanded parries, see *Parrying Unarmed* (p. 376).

Breaking Blow

IQ/Hard

Defaults: None.
Prerequisite: Trained By A Master.

This skill allows you to find the weakest spot in any object when making a barehanded attack. Each attack requires a separate Breaking Blow roll. Roll against skill *after* you hit. Breaking Blow costs 1 FP per attempt, whether or not you hit.

On a success, your attack gains an armor divisor of (5) against any braced, inanimate, homogenous target (see *Injury to Unliving, Homogenous, and Diffuse Targets,* p. 380), and you may treat the target as if it were Fragile (Brittle) (p. 136) for this one attack.

In a cinematic game, you are not limited to inanimate targets. Your armor divisor affects any *artificial* armor or force field (*not* natural DR), and you may treat homogenous *opponents* as if they were Fragile (Brittle)!

On a failure, your attack gains no special benefits. On a critical failure, you do the damage to your own hand or foot.

Modifiers: -10 if used *instantly,* dropping to -5 after 1 turn of concentration, -4 after 2 turns, -3 after 4 turns, -2 after 8 turns, -1 after 16 turns, and no penalty after 32 turns. -1 if your target is wood or plastic, -3 if brick or stone, or -5 if metal or high-tech composites.

Breath Control

HT/Hard

Defaults: None.

This is the ability to breathe at maximum efficiency. On a successful skill roll, you can increase the time you can hold your breath for any reason (e.g., underwater) by 50%, or regain one FP in only two minutes (you cannot combine this with magic spells that restore FP).

Broadsword

see *Melee Weapon*, p. 208

Camouflage

IQ/Easy

Defaults: IQ-4 or Survival-2.

This is the ability to use natural materials, special fabrics and paints, etc. to hide yourself, your position, or your equipment. To see through your camouflage, an observer must win a Quick Contest of Vision or Observation skill (p. 211) vs. your Camouflage skill.

Depending on the circumstances, successful camouflage might hide its subject entirely or merely blur its outlines to make it harder to hit (-1 to attacker's skill). Camouflage will not improve your Stealth roll, but if you fail a Stealth roll while camouflaged, those who *heard* you must still see through your camouflage to *see* you.

Modifiers: Equipment modifiers (p. 345). Apply a *penalty* equal to the Size Modifier of a large object (e.g., -5 for a tank with **SM** +5). This makes it difficult to camouflage large objects, but remember that distant observers suffer large Vision penalties for range – see *Vision* (p. 358).

Captivate

see *Enthrallment*, p. 191

Carousing

HT/Easy

Default: HT-4.

This is the skill of socializing, partying, etc. A successful Carousing roll, under the right circumstances, gives you a +2 bonus on a request for aid or information, or just on a general reaction. A failed roll means you made a fool of yourself in some way; you get a -2 penalty on any reaction roll made by those you caroused with. If you do your carousing in the wrong places, a failed roll can have other dangers!

Modifiers: Up to +3 for buying drinks or other entertainment for your fellow carousers; -3 for Killjoy (p. 140); -3 for Low Empathy (p. 142); -1 to -4 for Shyness (p. 154).

Carpentry

IQ/Easy

Default: IQ-4.

This is the ability to build things out of wood. A successful roll lets you do one hour's worth of competent carpentry. A failed roll means the work was bad. The GM may require DX-based Carpentry rolls for certain kinds of fine work.

Modifiers: Equipment modifiers (p. 345); +5 if you are being supervised or assisted by someone with skill 15 or better.

Cartography/TL

IQ/Average

Defaults: IQ-5, Geography (any) -2, Mathematics (Surveying)-2, or Navigation (any)-4.

This is the ability to create and interpret maps and charts. Roll against this skill to map any location as you move through it. At TL7+, this skill includes knowledge of computer mapping techniques and generating maps from sensor information.

Chemistry/TL

IQ/Hard

Default: IQ-6 or Alchemy-3.

This is the study of matter. A chemist can identify elements and simple compounds (but not necessarily drugs, magical substances, etc.). Given proper equipment, he could conduct complex analyses and syntheses.

Climbing

DX/Average

Default: DX-5.

This is the ability to climb mountains, rock walls, trees, the sides of buildings, etc. See *Climbing* (p. 349) for details.

Modifiers: +2 for Brachiator (p. 41); +3 for Flexibility *or* +5 for Double-Jointed (p. 56); +1 for Perfect Balance (p. 74); a penalty equal to encumbrance level (e.g., -1 for Light encumbrance).

Cloak
DX/Average

Defaults: DX-5, Net-4, or Shield (any)-4.

This is the skill of using a cloak or a cape as a weapon. It covers the use of two types of cloak: the waist-length "light cloak" (any cloak, cape, or coat weighing less than 5 lbs.) and the full-length "heavy cloak" (any cloak weighing 5 lbs. or more).

Offensively, you can use a cloak to entangle an opponent – see *Special Melee Weapon Rules* (p. 404) for details. You can also snap a cloak in your opponent's face or simply use it to block his vision, either of which counts as a Feint maneuver.

Defensively, a cloak works much like a shield. It provides a Defense Bonus (+1 if light, +2 if heavy) and gives a Block defense equal to (skill/2) + 3, rounded down. A cloak is not as robust as a shield, though! A light cloak has only DR 1 and 3 HP, while a heavy cloak has DR 1 and 5 HP.

Combat Art or Sport
DX/Varies

Defaults: Special.

You can opt to learn most combat skills in nonlethal forms aimed at either exhibition (Combat Art skill) or competition (Combat Sport skill).

Combat Art skills emphasize graceful movements and perfect stances. Since these skills still give a default to full-fledged, lethal combat skills (see below), they are a logical choice for Pacifists who want *some* combat ability.

Combat Sport skills concentrate on speed of movement and nondamaging attacks. A failed skill roll means a foul that might disqualify you from a tournament! You can make an IQ-based roll against Combat Sport to recall *basic* tournament rules, but to become a qualified judge or referee, learn the relevant Games skill (p. 197).

Combat Art and Sport skills are DX-based, with the same difficulty level and defaults as the corresponding combat skill. A combat skill, its Art form, and its Sport form default among themselves at -3. For instance, Staff Art and Staff Sport are DX/Average skills that default to DX-5, just like Staff skill (p. 208). A fighter with Staff at 15 would have default Staff Art and Staff Sport skills of 12, while an athlete with Staff Sport at 15 would have Staff and Staff Art skills at 12 by default.

Computer Hacking/TL
IQ/Very Hard

Defaults: None.
Prerequisite: Computer Programming.

This is the skill of gaining illegal access to a computer system – usually using another computer over a communications network. A successful Computer Hacking roll allows you to gain surreptitious access to a system, or to find (or change) information on a system you have already broken into. On a critical failure, you fail to gain access *and* leave some sort of incriminating evidence of your attempt.

This skill is cinematic, and simulates the way computer intrusion works in many movies and novels. It does not exist in realistic settings! Realistic "hackers" should learn a combination of Computer Operation (to exploit OS loopholes and run intrusion software), Computer Programming (to *write* intrusion software), Cryptography, Electronics Operation (Communications or Surveillance), Electronics Repair (Computers), Fast-Talk (to convince legitimate users to reveal passwords), Research (to find documented security holes), and Scrounging (to "Dumpster dive" for manuals, passwords on discarded sticky notes, etc.).

Modifiers: Equipment modifiers (p. 345). -1 to -10 if you have been away from the field for a long time and have not had a chance to become familiar with the changes. Security measures give a penalty, from -1 for the cheapest commercial security software to -15 for the latest technology. Some measures *resist* your intrusion attempt; treat this as a Quick Contest of Hacking vs. the effective skill of the defenses.

Computer Operation/TL
IQ/Easy

Default: IQ-4.

This is the ability to use a computer: call up data, run programs, play games, etc. It is the only computer skill needed by most end users. Learn Computer Programming (below) to write software and Electronics Repair (Computers) (p. 190) to troubleshoot hardware.

This skill only exists in game worlds with computers. Individuals from settings without computers cannot even use it by default until they have had time to gain familiarity with computers! In settings where it is possible to "jack" your brain into a computer, Computer Operation includes the ability to use a neural interface, but new users initially suffer a -4 penalty for unfamiliarity (see *Familiarity,* p. 169).

Modifiers: -2 or more for an unfamiliar computer, operating system, or program.

Computer Programming/TL
IQ/Hard

Defaults: None.

This is the ability to write and debug computer software. A successful roll lets you find a bug in a program, determine a program's purpose by examining the code, answer a question about computer programming, or write a new program (time required is up to the GM).

In settings where artificial intelligence (AI) exists, those who wish to work with AI must learn Computer Programming (AI). There is no default between this skill and regular Computer Programming. When using Detect Lies, Fast-Talk, Psychology, Teaching, and similar "social" skills on an AI, roll against the *lower* of Computer Programming (AI) and the relevant skill.

Modifiers: -2 or more for an unfamiliar programming language (see *Familiarity,* p. 169). The time modifiers under *Time Spent* (p. 346) will often apply. When writing a program that deals with a specialized field of knowledge, the GM may require a roll against the *lower* of Computer Programming and your skill in that field (e.g., a Mathematics specialty for a complex mathematical program, or the lower of Teaching skill and a "subject" skill for an expert system that will assist users with a particular subject).

Connoisseur†

IQ/Average

Defaults: IQ-5 and others.

This skill represents an *educated* understanding of art and luxury items. It is vital to art dealers, critics, master thieves, and anyone who wishes to appear cultured. A successful roll lets you predict what critics will think of a piece of art, assess how much it will fetch on the market (+1 to Merchant skill when trading it), or impress the culturally literate (may give +1 to Savoir-Faire or reaction rolls, at the GM's option).

You *must* specialize. Specialties include Dance, Literature, Music, Visual Arts, and Wine. Each specialty defaults to skills used to *study* or *create* the art at -3: Connoisseur (Literature) defaults to Literature, Poetry, or Writing at -3; Connoisseur (Music) defaults to Group Performance (Conducting), Musical Composition, or Musical Instrument at -3; and so on.

Modifiers: Cultural Familiarity modifiers (p. 23); -3 for Killjoy (p. 140).

Cooking

IQ/Average

Defaults: IQ-5 or Housekeeping-5.

This is the skill of being a chef – you do not need it to heat water and open boxes, or to cook rat-on-a-stick over your campfire. A successful skill roll allows you to prepare a pleasing meal. Many chefs have an *optional* specialty (p. 169), such as baking, beverage making, or a particular variety of ethnic cuisine (e.g., Chinese or Martian).

Counterfeiting/TL

IQ/Hard

Defaults: IQ-6 or Forgery-2.

This is the art of duplicating banknotes and coins. It is only taught by the underworld and government agencies (although this is rare outside of rogue states, except in wartime). Time required varies from days to weeks (GM's option). The GM secretly rolls against your Counterfeiting skill for each "batch" of money.

A critical success means that the fakes *in that batch* are as good as the real thing.

An ordinary success means that your work is good but not perfect. Whenever you try to pass the counterfeit money, the GM makes a *second* skill roll for you, with all the same modifiers. If this roll fails, the recipient spots your handiwork. To successfully pass bogus currency to someone who has reason to be suspicious, you must win a Quick Contest of Counterfeiting vs. the *highest* of his Perception, Forensics, and Merchant.

Any failure on the initial Counterfeiting roll means that the first person to receive the money immediately realizes that it is bogus. Critical failure – on the initial roll or any subsequent roll – has other ramifications: the recipient is an undercover cop, an armed and angry citizen, etc.

Modifiers: Equipment modifiers (p. 345). Materials – ink, paper, presses, etc. – stolen from the legitimate mint can give from +1 (a few rolls of paper) to +10 (actual plates or molds). You *must* have a sample of the real thing or you cannot make the attempt at all!

Crewman/TL

IQ/Easy

Default: IQ-4.

This is the ability to serve as *crew* aboard a specific type of large vehicle. It includes familiarity with "shipboard life," knowledge of safety measures, and training in damage control (the use of emergency equipment to control flooding, fight fires, patch the hull, and so forth). Make a skill roll for basic map or chart reading, practical meteorology, or to recall laws and regulations that pertain to your vehicle.

This skill also lets you steer the vessel. It is easier than Piloting, Submarine, and similar skills because it *only* includes knowledge of how to steer. Specialists handle such activities as plotting courses and operating sensors. These experts report to the captain, who in turn tells you how to maneuver. Make a DX-based skill roll whenever you take the helm – but note that your effective skill cannot exceed your captain's Shiphandling skill (p. 220).

The *average* Crewman skill of an entire crew can be used as a measure of overall crew quality. The GM rolls against average skill whenever the vehicle arrives or departs, in unfavorable conditions, or in battle. Failure and critical failure results depend on the circumstances.

> *Connoisseur represents an educated understanding of art and luxury items. It is vital to art dealers, critics, master thieves, and anyone who wishes to appear cultured.*

There is a separate skill for each class of vessel:

Airshipman/TL: The skill of handling ballast, gas valves, mooring lines, etc. on a blimp, zeppelin, or other large airship.

Seamanship/TL: The skill of operating anchors, hatches, mooring lines, pumps, sails, windlasses, etc. aboard a large surface ship (but *not* a submarine).

Spacer/TL: The skill of working with airlocks, docking clamps, hull patches, pressure doors, etc. on a large spacecraft or space base.

Submariner/TL: The skill of handling pressure doors, pumps, valves, etc. aboard a submarine or in an undersea base.

Criminology/TL

IQ/Average

Defaults: IQ-5 or Psychology-4.

This is the study of crime and the criminal mind. A successful skill roll allows you to find and interpret clues, guess how criminals might behave, etc. Though this skill does not actually default to Streetwise, the GM might allow a Streetwise roll *instead* in certain situations – especially to predict or outguess a criminal.

Modifiers: -3 for Low Empathy (p. 142).

Crossbow

DX/Easy

Default: DX-4.

This is the ability to use all types of crossbows, including the pistol crossbow, prodd (which fires pellets or stones), repeating crossbow, and high-tech compound crossbow.

Cryptography/TL

IQ/Hard

Default: Mathematics (Cryptology)-5.

This is the ability to create and defeat encryption systems, codes, and ciphers. It is of use in wartime, espionage, and even business dealings. It covers all the techniques of your TL, which can range from unsophisticated substitution ciphers to state-of-the-art tactical encryption schemes.

Knowledge of a *specific* system, code, or cipher depends on your Security Clearance (p. 82) and allegiances (national, administrative, or both). In many settings, some level of Security Clearance is a prerequisite to learning this skill *at all*.

Treat an attempt to break an unknown code as a Quick Contest of Cryptography skill between the code-breaker and code-maker. The code-breaker must *win* to break the code. Repeated attempts are possible, but each attempt takes a day. The code-maker rolls only once, when he first creates the code.

Those with Cryptography skill may take an *optional* specialty (p. 169) in making or breaking codes. (The code-breaking specialty is often called "cryptanalysis.")

Cryptography normally has *no* IQ default, with two exceptions. Anyone can devise a trivial code or cipher by making an IQ-5 roll. This won't stall a professional for long, of course. Likewise, anyone can make an IQ-5 roll to attempt to break such a trivial code (but *not* a code devised by someone with Cryptography skill), using the Quick Contest system described above.

Modifiers: Mathematical Ability (p. 90). A computer with appropriate software gives a bonus (provided you know Computer Operation skill): +1 for a home computer, +2 for a minicomputer, +3 or +4 for a mainframe, and +5 or more for a supercomputer.

The *code-breaker* is at +5 if he has a sample of the code with translation, and -5 if the message to be decoded is shorter than 25 words. The *code-maker* receives a bonus for the time taken to create the code: consult the *Size and Speed/Range Table* (p. 550), look up the time in days in the Range/Speed column (substituting "days" for "yards"), and use the corresponding bonus.

Current Affairs/TL†

IQ/Easy

Defaults: IQ-4 or Research-4.

This is the ability to assimilate *quickly* whatever qualifies as "news" in your world, and to recall it as needed.

You *must* specialize in one of the following areas:

Business: Exchange rates, investment performance, etc.

Headline News: Usually *bad* news, such as assassinations, plagues, and wars.

High Culture: Information on galleries, operas, symphonies, and so forth.

People: The names of and gossip on celebrities, heads of state, and the like.

Politics: Election results, international treaties, etc.

Popular Culture: Hit songs, cool fashions, and hot products, among other things.

Regional: News of all kinds for a specific region (pick one). This is the definitive "town crier" skill at low TLs.

Science & Technology: New discoveries and inventions.

Sports: Scores for recent matches, names of star athletes, etc.

Travel: Where the "beautiful people" are going this year, and how much it all costs.

These specialties default to one another at -4. It is hard to bone up on one kind of news without learning about all the others!

On a successful Current Affairs roll, the GM will inform you of any news within your specialty that pertains to the current adventure (possibly including clues, on a good roll) or give you a small skill bonus (e.g., a success on Current Affairs (Sports) might give +1 to Gambling skill when betting on a boxing match).

Modifiers: -1 per *day* that you have been unable to access news media; -3 if you only have one source; +1 or more for "inside" access to the news (a subscription to an ordinary wire service is worth +1, while a job at an intelligence agency might give +3 or more).

Dancing
DX/Average
Default: DX-5.

This is the ability to perform dances appropriate to your own culture, and to learn new dances quickly. Note that certain physical handicaps make this skill effectively impossible!

Exotic dances abound in fiction and history: blade dancing, bull dancing, fire dancing, snake dancing, etc. The GM may decide that each is a separate DX/Average skill that defaults to Dancing-5.

Modifiers: Cultural Familiarity modifiers (p. 23); -5 if the dance is unfamiliar (a dance is familiar once you have successfully performed it three times).

Detect Lies
Per/Hard
Defaults: Perception-6, Body Language-4, or Psychology-4.

This is the ability to tell when someone is lying to you. It is not the same as Interrogation (p. 202); Detect Lies works in a casual or social situation. When you ask to use this skill, the GM rolls a Quick Contest of your Detect Lies skill vs. your subject's IQ (or Fast-Talk or Acting skill). If you win, the GM tells you whether the subject is lying. If you lose, the GM may lie to you about whether you were lied to . . . or just say, "You can't tell."

Modifiers: +1 for Sensitive *or* +3 for Empathy (p. 51), or -3 for Low Empathy (p. 142); +4 if your subject is Easy to Read (p. 134). If the subject is of a different species, the GM may assess a penalty – see *Physiology Modifiers* (p. 181).

Diagnosis/TL
IQ/Hard
Defaults: IQ-6, First Aid-8, Physician-4, or Veterinary-5.

This is the ability to tell what is wrong with a sick or injured person, or what killed a dead person. A successful roll gives some information about the patient's problem – *limited to realistic knowledge for your tech level*. It might not determine the exact problem (if the GM feels the cause is totally beyond your experience, for instance), but it always gives hints, rule out impossibilities, etc. No Diagnosis roll is required for *obvious* things, like open wounds and missing limbs!

Modifiers: Equipment modifiers (p. 345); physiology modifiers (p. 181); -5 for internal injuries; -5 or more for a rare disease.

Diplomacy
IQ/Hard
Defaults: IQ-6 or Politics-6.

This is the skill of negotiating, compromising, and getting along with others. You may substitute a Diplomacy roll for any reaction roll in a noncombat situation, as described under *Influence Rolls* (p. 359).

Unlike other Influence skills, Diplomacy never gives a worse result than if you had tried an ordinary reaction roll. Failure with Fast-Talk or Sex Appeal alienates the subject, but Diplomacy is usually safe.

A successful roll also allows you to predict the possible outcome of a course of action when you are negotiating, or to choose the best approach to take.

If you know Diplomacy at level 20 or better, you get a +2 bonus on all reaction rolls!

Modifiers: +2 for Voice (p. 97); -3 for Low Empathy (p. 142); -1 for Oblivious (p. 146); -1 to -4 for Shyness (p. 154); -2 for Stuttering (p. 157).

Disguise/TL†
IQ/Average
Defaults: IQ-5 or Makeup-3.

This is the art of altering your appearance using clothing, makeup, and prosthetics. You do not need this skill to don a quick disguise – e.g., to put on a lab coat when you enter a laboratory – but such disguises only fool the inattentive! A *good* disguise requires a Disguise roll and 30 minutes to an hour of preparation.

Roll a Quick Contest of Disguise skill vs. the Perception of *each person* your disguise must fool. Individuals with Criminology or Observation skill may substitute those skills for Perception when rolling to penetrate a disguise. The GM may allow other skills to be of use – for instance, Physician skill might help spot a rubber nose.

When combining Acting (p. 174) with Disguise (that is, when you must change your face *and* your personality), you need only make one roll for each person or group – but it must be the *harder* of the two rolls.

If there is more than one sapient species in your world, you *must* specialize by race – Disguise (Human) is nothing like Disguise (Bug-Eyed Monster). Disguise specialized in your own species is the most common form; just list this as "Disguise" on your character sheet. Disguise skills for physically similar species default to one another at -2 to -4.

Modifiers: Equipment modifiers (p. 345). +4 for Elastic Skin (p. 51). You are at -1 to -5 to disguise yourself as someone very different from you (GM's discretion). Distinctive appearance also gives a penalty – see *Build* (p. 18), *Unnatural Features* (p. 22), and specific disadvantages (e.g., Hunchback, p. 139) for details. Differences in Size Modifier usually make Disguise *impossible*.

You can also learn Disguise (Animals) to deceive nonsapient creatures. This involves wearing animal skins, smearing your body with musk or dung, etc. There is no default between this and other Disguise specialties. Use the following modifiers *instead* of those given above.

Modifiers: +2 if approaching from downwind; -1 for each animal over one of the same type being approached (-1 for every *10* in the case of herd animals); -1 to -3 if the skins are old or in poor condition. Make a Naturalist roll to recall the habits of the animal being imitated; success gives +1 to +3, while failure gives -1 to -3.

Diving Suit/TL
see *Environment Suit,* p. 192

Dreaming

Will/Hard

Default: Will-6.

This is the skill of controlling and remembering your dreams. A successful skill roll lets you experience vivid dreams about a subject of your choosing. Use the Fortune-Telling (Dream Interpretation) skill to *interpret* your dreams. In some game worlds, this might be a useful divinatory technique (GM's decision).

A Dreaming roll can also help you recall a previously forgotten piece of information, or something you witnessed but did not consciously note. This technique is much less reliable than Eidetic Memory (p. 51), though. The GM will describe your dreams to you, working clues into the narrative. It is up to you, the *player*, to spot these hints!

Finally, you can use this skill to combat malign supernatural influences on your dreams. Resolve this as a Quick Contest between your Dreaming skill and your harasser's skill at dream control. If you win, you shut out the external influence.

Driving/TL†

DX/Average

Defaults: DX-5 or IQ-5.

This is the ability to drive a specific type of ground vehicle.

Make an IQ-based Driving roll for basic map reading, to diagnose simple malfunctions, or to recall rules of the road.

You *must* specialize:

Automobile: Any vehicle with three or more wheels that weighs less than 5 tons and does not move on rails. *Defaults:* Heavy Wheeled-2 or other Driving at -4.

Construction Equipment: Any kind of bulldozer, crane, plow, etc. *Default:* other Driving at -5.

Halftrack: Any vehicle that moves on tracks *and* either wheels or skids. *Defaults:* Tracked-2 or other Driving at -4.

Heavy Wheeled: Any vehicle with three or more wheels that weighs 5 tons or more and does not move on rails. *Defaults:* Automobile-2 or other Driving at -4.

Hovercraft: Any kind of air-cushion vehicle. *Default:* other Driving at -5.

Locomotive: Any vehicle that moves on conventional or maglev rails. *Default:* other Driving at -5.

Mecha: Any kind of legged, bouncing, rolling, or slithering vehicle. *Defaults:* Battlesuit-3 or other Driving at -5.

Motorcycle: Any powered one- or two-wheeled vehicle, including those with sidecars. Large motorcycles often have a Minimum ST, just like a weapon (see p. 270). *Default:* Bicycling-4.

Tracked: Any vehicle that moves on tracks. *Defaults:* Halftrack-2 or other Driving at -4.

Note that the ability to "drive" a team of animals is not Driving, but Teamster (p. 225).

Modifiers: -2 or more for bad driving conditions; -2 or more for a vehicle in bad repair; -2 for an unfamiliar control system (e.g., an automatic when you are used to a manual); -4 or more for a vehicle of an unfamiliar type within your specialty (e.g., a race car when you are used to stock cars).

SKILLS

Dropping

DX/Average

Defaults: DX-3 or Throwing-4.

This is the skill of dropping heavy objects on your foes while flying. Treat this as a ranged attack made from above. Learn Dropping if you wish to drop boulders and similar projectiles on individual opponents while on the wing. Use Artillery (Bombs) to attack areas with explosive ordnance, etc.

Economics

IQ/Hard

Defaults: IQ-6, Finance-3, Market Analysis-5, or Merchant-6.

This is the study of the *theory* of money, markets, and financial systems. It is mainly an academic skill, but a successful skill roll allows you to predict the economic impact of events in the game world: the assassination of a political figure, the demolition of a power plant, the introduction of a new invention, etc. Adventurers with intelligence and military backgrounds frequently have some training in this skill.

Electrician/TL

IQ/Average

Defaults: IQ-5 or Engineer (Electrical)-3.

This is the skill of building, maintaining, and repairing electrical systems. Make a skill roll to diagnose an electrical fault, wire a building or vehicle, etc. Adventuring uses include damage control in combat (e.g., to restore power to a damaged vehicle system) and cutting the power to a building prior to clandestine activities.

Note that *electrical* and *electronic* systems are not the same thing. The equivalent skill for electronics is Electronics Repair (p. 190).

Modifiers: Equipment modifiers (p. 345).

Electronics Operation/TL†

IQ/Average

Defaults: IQ-5, Electronics Repair (same)-5, or Engineer (Electronics)-5.

This skill lets you use all electronic equipment *within a known specialty.*

Make a skill roll in an emergency situation or for "abnormal" use of equipment – not for ordinary, everyday use. (*Exception:* Unskilled users must always attempt their default roll!)

You *must* specialize. Available specialties vary by game world, but might include:

Communications (Comm): All forms of electronic communications technology: radios, satellite uplinks, laser communicators, etc. Includes knowledge of any standard, current communications codes appropriate to your background. These do not require a skill roll – although attempts to understand or use an unfamiliar code *do* require a roll. At TL5-7, this includes telegraphy: you can send or receive 2 words per minute (wpm) per point of skill at TL5, 3 wpm per point of skill at TL6-7.

Electronic Warfare (EW): All signals-intelligence and jamming equipment, including electronic countermeasures (ECM) and electronic counter-countermeasures (ECCM). In most game worlds, only intelligence agencies and the military teach this specialty – and only to individuals with suitable Military Rank (p. 30) or Security Clearance (p. 82).

Force Shields: Portable, vehicular, base, and starship force shields and deflectors.

Matter Transmitters (MT): All matter transmitters and teleporters. Critical failures can be disastrous, especially when transmitting living beings!

Media: All forms of audio, film, and video editing equipment. If three-dimensional video ("holographics") or sensory recordings ("sensies") exist in the setting, this specialty includes the ability to operate the relevant equipment. Treat different media as mutually unfamiliar technologies.

Medical: All manner of electronic diagnostic and life-support equipment.

Parachronic: Technological means of travel between dimensions or timelines.

Psychotronics: Psionic technology, such as telepathic shields and amplifiers.

Scientific: Laboratory electronics and survey gear. You are automatically familiar with the equipment used with any scientific skill on which you have spent at least one point.

Security: Both operating and circumventing all forms of alarms, security sensors, and area-surveillance technology.

Sensors: Most forms of long-range detection gear, from air-defense radar to starship sensor suites. Certain highly specialized sensors (such as sonar, below) have their own specialties.

Sonar: All types of acoustic detection and ranging gear (normally used underwater).

Surveillance: All forms of concealable or remote surveillance gear: "bugs," hidden cameras, long-range microphones, wiretaps, etc.

Temporal: All manner of time machines. Critical failures can be disastrous for the time travelers! Make separate rolls to "lock onto" and transfer the travelers.

These specialties default to one another at -4; however, the GM is free to rule that in *his* campaign, there is no default between exotic specialties (Parachronic, Psychotronics, etc.) and mundane ones (Media, Security, etc.). The technologies covered by a particular specialty vary with TL. For instance, Electronics Operation (Comm) covers telegraphs at TL5, telephones and radios at TL6, and digital communications systems at TL8 . . . and might cover faster-than-light or telepathic communicators at higher TLs.

Familiarity (p. 169) is crucial here! Electronics Operation/TL8 (Sensors) covers both thermographs on fighter jets and ground-penetrating radars on satellites, but going from one to the other gives you -2 for type (thermograph to radar) and -2 for implementation (jet to satellite), for a net -4 to skill until you familiarize yourself with all the differences.

Modifiers: Equipment modifiers (p. 345); -2 for an unfamiliar technology of a known type (e.g., radar when you are used to thermograph) or an unfamiliar implementation of a familiar technology (e.g., air-defense radar when you are used to weather radar); -1 to -10 if you have been away from the field for a long time (this varies by field) and have not had a chance to become familiar with the changes.

When choosing technological skills for your character, it can be helpful to bear in mind that such skills govern three distinct classes of activity:

Design. An inventor, gadgeteer, or mad scientist requires skills that let him design and build new inventions, redesign existing ones, and deduce the function of (and reverse-engineer!) unknown technologies. The key skill here is Engineer – specialized in the inventor's fields of interest – but Bioengineering (for biotechnology) and Computer Programming (for software) are equally appropriate.

Repair. A craftsman or technician needs skills that enable him to troubleshoot and repair known devices, perform major overhauls and upgrades, install new equipment, and customize existing gear. The most important skills of this type are Armoury, Electrician, Electronics Repair, Machinist, and Mechanic.

Use. A detective, soldier, spy, or similar professional needs skills that let him operate specialized equipment, conduct routine maintenance on his gear, and identify common makes and models (and their strengths and weaknesses). Such skills include Computer Operation, Electronics Operation, Environment Suit, Explosives, vehicle skills (Crewman, Driving, Shiphandling, etc.), and weapon skills (Artillery, Guns, etc.).

These skills form "design-repair-use triads"; e.g., Engineer (Electronics)-Electronics Repair-Electronics Operation for electronic devices, Engineer (Vehicle)-Mechanic-Driving for vehicles, and Engineer (Small Arms)-Armoury-Guns for firearms. Cinematic adventurers with great depth of knowledge often have *all three* skills in a triad!

Electronics Repair/TL†

IQ/Average

Defaults: IQ-5, Electronics Operation (same)-3, or Engineer (Electronics)-3.

This is the ability to diagnose and repair known types of electronic equipment. Time required for each attempt is up to the GM. You *must* specialize in one of the areas listed under Electronics Operation (above), or in Computers (Electronics Repair (Computers) defaults to Computer Operation-5). These specialties default to one another at -4.

Modifiers: Equipment modifiers (p. 345); -2 without plans or schematics; -2 for an unfamiliar technology or implementation (just as for Electronics Operation); -4 to *modify* a device away from its intended purpose.

Engineer/TL†

IQ/Hard

Defaults: Special.

Prerequisites: Mathematics (Applied) at TL5+, plus others as noted.

This is the ability to design and build technological devices and systems. A successful roll lets you design a new system, diagnose a glitch, identify the purpose of a strange device, or improvise a gadget to solve a problem. Time required for each attempt is up to the GM.

Note that engineers are *designers* and *inventors;* they are not necessarily skilled at the routine operation or maintenance of the things they design! For instance, Engineer (Small Arms) lets you design a new assault rifle, but you need Armoury skill to maintain it and Guns skill to shoot it.

You *must* specialize. Possible fields include:

Artillery: Designing whatever passes for artillery at your TL, from trebuchets to smart missiles. *Default:* Armoury (Heavy Weapons)-6.

Civil: Planning highways, aqueducts, buildings, etc. *Default:* Architecture-6.

Clockwork: Designing wind-up gadgetry – watches, mechanical men, and the like. *Default:* Mechanic (Clockwork)-6.

Combat: Building or removing fortifications, trenches, etc. *Default:* Explosives (Demolition)-6.

Electrical: Designing electrical systems, such as power cells and transmission lines. *Default:* Electrician-6.

Electronics: Designing and building electronic apparatus, from computers to starship sensor arrays. (The specific technologies involved – vacuum tubes, transistors, photonics, etc. – will depend on the tech level.) *Default:* Electronics Repair (any)-6.

Materials: Concocting new structural materials. *Prerequisites:* Chemistry or Metallurgy. *Defaults:* Chemistry-6 or Metallurgy-6.

Microtechnology: Designing micromachines. *Default:* Mechanic (Micromachines)-6.

Mining: Designing underground structures. *Defaults:* Explosives (Demolition)-6 or Geology (any)-6.

Nanotechnology: Designing nanomachines. *Default:* Mechanic (Nanomachines)-6.

Parachronic: Designing apparatus for crossing dimensions or timelines. *Prerequisite:* Physics. *Default:* Electronics Operation (Parachronic)-6, but there is *no* default if your society has not discovered dimensional travel.

Psychotronics: Designing psionic technology, such as telepathic shields and amplifiers. *Default:* Electronics Operation (Psychotronics)-6, but there is *no* default for individuals from backgrounds where psionics do not exist.

Robotics: Designing robotics and cybernetics. *Default:* Mechanic (Robotics)-6.

Small Arms: Designing personal firearms, such as guns and portable rocket launchers. *Default:* Armoury (Small Arms)-6.

Temporal: Designing time machines. *Prerequisite:* Physics. *Default:* Electronics Operation

(Temporal)-6, but there is *no* default for individuals from backgrounds without time travel!

Vehicle Type: Designing a single, broad class of vehicle. Examples include Engineer (Automobiles), Engineer (Ships), and Engineer (Starships). *Default:* Mechanic (same vehicle type)-6.

Engineer specialties normally default to one another at -4; however, the GM is free to rule that in *his* campaign, there is no default between exotic specialties (Nanotechnology, Parachronic, Psychotronics, etc.) and more mundane ones (Civil, Combat, Mining, etc.).

Modifiers: Equipment modifiers (p. 345). Up to +5 to build a gadget if you can give the GM a good description of what you want it to do.

"Kill the king!" is acceptable; "Kill the king if he doesn't accede to our demands!" is not.

Enthrallment
Will/Hard

Defaults: None.
Prerequisites: Charisma 1 and Public Speaking at 12+.

Bards in fantasy can often influence others through storytelling. The GM may choose to represent this ability using the four Enthrallment skills described below. Depending on the setting, these skills might be magical, psionic, or a cinematic form of hypnotism. Each has a time requirement, FP cost, and duration, and requires *two* skill rolls to use.

At the outset of the tale, roll vs. Public Speaking skill; if you can't grab your audience's attention early on, you won't have much of a chance of controlling them by the end. On a success, proceed to the Enthrallment skill roll; critical success gives +1 on that roll. On a failure, you may still attempt the Enthrallment roll, but at a penalty equal to your margin of failure. Critical failure means your Enthrallment attempt fails automatically.

After the time required to enthrall has passed, roll a Quick Contest of your Enthrallment skill vs. the Will of each audience member. If you win, you affect your audience – see the individual skill description for effects. If you lose or tie, there is no effect. However, if you *critically* fail, your audience instantly turns hostile!

You may never learn these skills at a skill level higher than your Public Speaking skill.

Audience Size: An "audience" can be one listener or a hundred – as many as can hear the tale. However, the number of audience members that you can enthrall at one sitting is limited to your Charisma level *squared*, to a maximum of 25 people at Charisma 5.

Modifiers: All four Enthrallment skills are at -3 for Low Empathy (p. 142). If the *player* actually tells a good tale, the GM should reward him with +1 to +3 to the Public Speaking and Enthrallment rolls!

Captivate
Will/Hard

Defaults: None.
Prerequisite: Suggest at 12+.

This skill allows you to tell a story so skillfully that those listening lose their will and do whatever you want them to do. In effect, they believe themselves to be *in* the tale, and are vulnerable to being manipulated by you, the teller of the tale.

If you win the Quick Contest, the audience becomes intensely loyal to you. They follow *any* direct order you give. In the absence of a direct order, they act in your best interest, *as they understand it.* If you tell someone to do something very hazardous, or that goes against his usual code of behavior (GM's decision), he gets a Will-5 roll to break the captivation. Otherwise, he is your loyal supporter for all intents and purposes.

Time: 30 minutes of uninterrupted storytelling.
Fatigue Cost: 8 FP, whether successful or not.
Duration: Captivation lasts until the subject becomes unconscious or falls asleep, *you* become unconscious or fall asleep, you attack the subject, or the subject loses half his HP to injury.

Persuade
Will/Hard

Defaults: None.

This ability allows you to bring an audience over to your point of view, granting you a bonus to your reaction rolls with them. You may use this skill whenever a reaction roll is called for.

If you win the Quick Contest, add your margin of victory to any reaction roll those in the audience make regarding you – for any reason – to a maximum of +3 (+4 on a critical success). If you critically fail, the best possible reaction is Poor (see p. 560).

Time: 1 minute.
Fatigue Cost: 2 FP, whether successful or not.
Duration: Until you do something to change the audience's opinion!

Suggest
Will/Hard

Defaults: None.
Prerequisite: Persuade at 12+.

This ability lets you give your audience a single, simple suggestion. A suggestion should have no complex grammatical clauses – just a subject, verb, object, and at most two modifiers. "Kill the king!" is acceptable; "Kill the king if he doesn't accede to our demands!" is not. A given subject gets +5 to resist if your suggestion goes against his personal safety, and +3 if it goes against his beliefs, convictions, or knowledge.

If you win the Quick Contest, the audience members try to act on the suggestion to the best of their abilities – each assuming that the idea was his own.

Time: 20 minutes of uninterrupted storytelling.
Fatigue Cost: 6 FP, whether successful or not.
Duration: 10 minutes – or longer, if you continue to talk to the audience and can make a successful Suggest roll every 10 minutes! Once the suggestion lapses, audience members only wonder why they acted the way they did if the suggestion was something they would never have done normally.

Sway Emotions
Will/Hard

Defaults: None.
Prerequisite: Persuade at 12+.

This ability allows you to instill the audience with any one emotion. Allowed emotions include anger, boredom, depression, disgust, fear, greed, hate, jealousy, joy, love, lust, patriotism, peace, sadness, and unrest.

If you win the Quick Contest, your audience experiences the emotion you select. How they act as a result is up to the GM.

Time: 10 minutes of uninterrupted storytelling.
Fatigue Cost: 4 FP, whether successful or not.
Duration: One hour.

Environment Suit/TL
DX/Average

Defaults: DX-5 and others.

This is training in the use of a specific class of protective suit. Suits designed to shield the wearer from environmental or battlefield hazards frequently incorporate gadgets (such as autoinjectors and sensors) and life-support equipment. Some suits even contain motors to enhance ST or Move. As a result, you do not merely wear such gear – you *operate* it.

Roll against Environment Suit skill to get into or out of your suit *quickly*. A successful roll halves the time required. To activate a specific subsystem of a suit, or to gauge whether a suit is in good repair, make an IQ-based skill roll instead.

When rolling against DX or any DX-based skill while suited up, use the *lower* of your Environment Suit skill and your actual skill level. For instance, if you have DX 14, Stealth-15, and Vacc Suit-13, you will function at DX 13 and Stealth-13 while wearing a spacesuit. Particularly ungainly suits might give -1 or more to DX on top of this, regardless of skill level. On the other hand, some sleek, ultra-tech suits might not limit skills *at all!*

However, Environment Suit is *strictly* the skill of donning and operating the suit. Familiarity with and knowledge of dangerous environments is covered by other skills: Free Fall, Hazardous Materials, Survival, etc.

Each suit type requires its own skill. Examples include:

Battlesuit/TL: All kinds of powered battle armor and exoskeletons. Battle armor and exoskeletons are similar but not identical. If you only have experience with one, you are at -2 to operate the other until you gain familiarity (see *Familiarity*, p. 169).

Diving Suit/TL: All types of *hard* diving suits (as opposed to the wetsuits and drysuits used with Scuba skill). This includes "open dress" gear at TL5 and "hard hat" gear at TL6, both of which use a sealed helmet and supplied air, but not always a full, sealed suit. At TL7+, this skill covers true underwater "hardsuits." The GM may require Swimming rolls to *maneuver* while wearing such a suit. *Default:* Scuba-2.

NBC Suit/TL: All forms of hazardous materials ("HazMat") gear – including sealed, unpowered body armor that can be buttoned down against nuclear-biological-chemical (NBC) threats. Without this skill, you run the risk of misusing the equipment and being exposed to contamination. To *improvise* NBC gear, make an IQ-based skill roll at -5 to -15 to skill.

Vacc Suit/TL: Any kind of spacesuit. In addition to true vacuum suits, this includes suits intended for use in high-pressure, corrosive, and poisonous atmospheres.

Battlesuit, NBC Suit, and Vacc Suit default among themselves at -2. Diving Suit defaults to or from any other Environment Suit skill at -4.

Note that unpowered, unsealed body armor *never* requires an Environment Suit skill.

Erotic Art
DX/Average

Defaults: DX-5 or Acrobatics-5.

This represents general knowledge of advanced sexual technique. IQ-, HT-, and even ST-based rolls are common. Precise game effects are left to the GM's discretion.

Modifiers: +3 for Flexibility *or* +5 for Double-Jointed (p. 56); -3 for Killjoy (p. 140).

Escape
DX/Hard

Default: DX-6.

This is the ability to slip out of ropes, handcuffs, and similar restraints. The first attempt to escape takes one minute; each subsequent attempt takes 10 minutes.

The GM may apply a penalty for particularly secure bonds. For instance, modern police handcuffs would give -5 to Escape. You suffer only *half* these penalties if you dislocate the restrained limb (usually an arm). This requires (20 - skill) minutes of concentration, minimum one minute and a Will roll. However, if you fail your Escape roll by 3 or more when dislocating a limb, the limb suffers 1d damage. On a critical failure, you automatically take enough damage to cripple the limb!

Modifiers: +3 for Flexibility *or* +5 for Double-Jointed (p. 56); any bonus for Slippery (p. 85).

Esoteric Medicine
Per/Hard

Default: Perception-6.

This is the skill of treating illness and injury with techniques grounded in esoteric theory rather than analytical science. It is usually associated with a magical or spiritual tradition. The particulars vary by tradition, but might include acupuncture, massage, alchemical or herbal preparations, or such exercises as breath control and meditation.

The effectiveness of Esoteric Medicine relative to Physician (p. 213) is up to the GM. It might be more effective (especially if it can channel real supernatural power), equivalent but different, or less effective. It should always be at least as good as First Aid (p. 195) – the attentions of a trained healer of *any* kind are preferable to bleeding to death! In TL5+ settings, Esoteric Medicine is often *perceived* as "quack" medicine, regardless of actual effectiveness.

This skill might represent Ayurvedic medicine, *chi* treatment, Hermetic medicine, yin/yang healing, or any other historical or fictional healing discipline. In settings where multiple forms of treatment exist, healers must specialize in one specific tradition.

Exorcism

Will/Hard

Defaults: Will-6, Religious Ritual (any)-3, Ritual Magic (any)-3, or Theology (any)-3.

This is the ability to drive a spirit from a possessed person or haunted location. It is not a magical skill, but a religious ritual. Exorcism is not specific to any one religion. A Malay witch doctor and a Catholic priest can both perform exorcisms; their relative effectiveness depends on the originating culture of the *spirit*.

The length of the ritual is 15 minutes × the spirit's HT. Some spirits wait patiently through the ritual, anticipating the combat to come; others try to distract or even attack you before you can complete the ritual. Once the ritual is complete, roll against Exorcism skill.

On a failure, the spirit remains and you must wait at least a week before you can repeat the ritual. On a critical failure, immediately roll 3d+10 on the *Fright Check Table* (p. 360). Even if you keep your sanity, you may *never* attempt to exorcise this particular spirit again.

On a critical success, you immediately banish the spirit. On a regular success, you meet your opponent in a Quick Contest: your Exorcism skill vs. the *higher* of the spirit's ST or Will.

When fighting a spirit in a living host, add higher of the ST or Will of the possession victim to your Exorcism skill as he tries to "push the spirit out."

If the spirit wins or ties, it retains its current status and you must wait at least a week before you can repeat the ritual. If you win, you drive the spirit from its haunt or victim. The spirit of a deceased mortal is laid to rest. For demons and similar entities, make a reaction roll. On a "Poor" or better reaction, the spirit flees in humiliation. On a "Bad" or worse reaction, the spirit immediately uses whatever resources it has to take vengeance on you and those nearby.

If the exorcism fails at any stage, make an IQ roll afterward. A success means that you learned something about the spirit that will help you in your *next* attempt to banish that foe, giving you +2 on later skill rolls. You may only claim this bonus once for a particular spirit.

Modifiers: -4 if you do *not* have one or more of Blessed (p. 40), Power Investiture (p. 77), or True Faith (p. 94); you might understand the ritual, but you lack holy support.

Expert Skill†

IQ/Hard

Defaults: None.

An Expert Skill represents cross-disciplinary knowledge of a single, narrow theme. When answering factual questions *on that theme*, you may substitute a roll against your Expert Skill for any IQ-based roll against any skill that has a default. Expert Skills do not exempt you from Cultural Familiarity (p. 23) or Language (p. 23) requirements, and never provide the ability to do practical tasks. Experts sometimes complement Expert Skills with related Area Knowledge skills (p. 176), but you must learn these separately.

You *must* specialize by theme, and the GM is free to forbid any theme he feels is too broad. Some examples:

Computer Security: Expertise at combating computer intrusion ("hacking"). Can stand in for Computer Operation, Cryptography, or Electronics Operation to spot "holes" in the security of a computer system. Use Computer Programming to patch or exploit such holes.

Conspiracy Theory: The study of interlocking networks of conspiracies. Can substitute for Anthropology, Geography, History, Literature, or Occultism to answer questions about conspiracies, and can also work as Intelligence Analysis for this purpose (only). This does *not* include hidden inner secrets, which are the province of Hidden Lore (p. 199).

Egyptology: The study of ancient Egypt. Can function as Anthropology, Archaeology, History, Linguistics, or Occultism for that purpose.

Epidemiology: The study of the spread of disease. Can serve as Biology, Diagnosis, Forensics, Geography, or Mathematics when deducing how a disease was spread.

Hydrology: The study of a planet's water. Can be used in place of Biology, Chemistry, Geography, Geology, or Meteorology to answer questions about precipitation, flooding, irrigation, etc.

Military Science: General expertise on military capabilities. Can substitute for Artillery, Armoury, Strategy, or Tactics to answer questions about – but not *use* – weapons or strategies.

Natural Philosophy: A general skill that usually replaces specific science skills (which might not even exist yet!) for scholars at TL1-4. Can be used in place of any science skill (e.g., Biology or Physics) to answer questions about how the universe is *believed* to work.

Political Science: The academic study of politics. Can substitute for Geography, History, Law, Politics, or Sociology when performing political analysis.

Psionics: The study of the psionic mind and brain. Can function as Biology, Diagnosis, Physician, Physiology, or Psychology when dealing with psi phenomena in living beings. *Cannot* substitute for Electronics Operation, Electronics Repair, and Engineer specialties that deal with psychotronics.

Thanatology: The esoteric study of death. Can stand in for Anthropology, Archaeology, Occultism, or Theology when dealing with death and the dead.

Xenology: General knowledge of the *known* races in your setting. Can substitute for Anthropology, History, Physiology, or Psychology to identify a member of a race different from your own, or to answer general questions about the race and its culture.

Explosives/TL†

IQ/Average

Defaults: IQ-5 and others.

This is the skill of working with explosives and incendiaries.

You *must* specialize:

Demolition: The ability to prepare and set explosives in order to blow things up. Make a roll whenever you use explosives in this way. A failure indicates an error. The gravity of the error depends on the amount by which you failed; a badly failed roll in close quarters can *blow you up!* Time required varies – it takes only a couple of seconds to set a prepared charge, but it might take *hours* to demolish a large bridge or a skyscraper. When setting an explosive trap, use this skill rather than Traps. Rolls to set a "trap" fuse (e.g., a land mine) instead of a timed fuse are at -2. *Defaults:* Engineer (Combat) or (Mining) at -3.

Explosive Ordnance Disposal (EOD): The ability to disarm and dispose of bombs and other explosives. When disarming a trap, roll a Quick Contest of your Explosives (EOD) skill vs. the Explosives (Demolition) skill of the person who created the device. A failure (or even a critical failure) does not necessarily mean an explosion – the GM can be much more creative than that! Sudden hissing noises, mysterious parts falling off, cramps, itches, and alarm bells are all possible in the right circumstances. It is best if the GM rolls the dice and describes the physical circumstances to the victim. Fright Checks are appropriate for the survivors of a failed EOD attempt! *Prerequisite:* DX 12+.

Fireworks: The skill of *making* pyrotechnic devices – fireworks, flares, smoke bombs, flash grenades, etc. Most of these things can be *used* by anyone. *Default:* Chemistry-3.

Nuclear Ordnance Disposal (NOD): The equivalent of Explosives (EOD) for nuclear devices. Disarming a military nuclear weapon is straightforward; disarming a homemade terrorist bomb might be more difficult. Only a critical failure *verified by a second critical failure* will result in a nuclear detonation. Any lesser failure will – at worst – detonate the high-explosive trigger and contaminate the immediate area with radioactive material . . . not that this is a great deal of consolation to those nearby.

Underwater Demolition (UD): The ability to prepare and set explosives underwater. This is otherwise identical to Explosives (Demolition).

You usually need Scuba skill – or at least Swimming skill – to get into a position where you can use this skill.

These specialties default to one another at -4 *except* for Demolition and UD, which default to one another at -2, and EOD and NOD, which also default to one another at -2.

Modifiers: Equipment modifiers (p. 345); -1 to -5 for distractions (e.g., enemy fire or swarms of biting ants) or physical motion (e.g., a rocking boat or speeding bus). The time modifiers under *Time Spent* (p. 346) will often apply.

Falconry

IQ/Average

Defaults: IQ-5 or Animal Handling (Raptors)-3.

This is the skill of "hawking": hunting small game with a trained hawk. It includes knowledge of hunting and training techniques, as well as how to care for a falcon. Finding a wild falcon's nest in spring requires a week's search and a successful Falconry roll; a nest has 1d-3 chicks.

Farming/TL

IQ/Average

Defaults: IQ-5, Biology-5, or Gardening-3.

This is the skill of growing things. It is usually used to earn a living, but you can also use it to answer theoretical questions about or solve problems related to agriculture.

Fast-Draw†

DX/Easy

Defaults: None.

This skill lets you *quickly* draw a weapon from its holster, sheath, or hiding place. A successful roll means you ready the weapon instantly. This does not count as a combat maneuver; you can use the weapon to attack on the same turn. On a failure, you ready your weapon normally but may do nothing else on your turn. A critical failure means you *drop* the weapon!

You *must* specialize in one of these weapon types: Force Sword, Knife, Long Arm (rifle, shotgun, submachine gun, etc.), Pistol, Sword (any one-handed blade larger than a knife), or

Two-Handed Sword. The GM may add Fast-Draw skills for other weapons (or even tools) that one could reasonably draw quickly.

In addition to the above specialties, there are two Fast-Draw skills that allow you to reload missile weapons quickly:

Fast-Draw (Arrow): Lets you ready a single arrow, bolt, or dart instantly. This reduces the time required to reload a bow, crossbow, or blowgun by one second.

Fast-Draw/TL (Ammo): Reduces the time required to reload any kind of gun or beam weapon. The exact benefits depend on your weapon, but a successful roll always shaves at least one second off the reload time. This skill varies greatly with TL! At TL4, it covers powder-and-shot drills; at TL6+, it includes speed-loading techniques for detachable magazines; and at higher tech levels, it involves quickly replacing energy cells and attaching power cables.

For the Arrow and Ammo specialties, failure means you drop the arrow or bolt, or accidentally discard one round of ammunition. On a critical failure, you drop the entire quiver, powder horn, ammo box, magazine, etc., scattering loose ammunition everywhere!

Modifiers: Combat Reflexes (p. 43) gives +1 to all Fast-Draw specialties; Ham-Fisted (p. 138) gives -3 per level.

Fast-Talk

IQ/Average
Defaults: IQ-5 or Acting-5.

This is the skill of talking others into doing things against their better judgment. It is not taught (intentionally, that is) in school; you study it by working as a salesman, confidence man, lawyer, etc. In any situation that calls for a reaction roll, you may make an Influence roll against Fast-Talk instead; see *Influence Rolls* (p. 359).

If you have Fast-Talk at level 20 or better, you get +2 on all reaction rolls where you're allowed to talk!

Note that Fast-Talk differs from Acting (p. 174). In general, Fast-Talk is used to get someone to make a snap decision in your favor, while Acting is used for long-term dissimulation.

However, there are situations in which the GM could allow a roll on either skill.

Modifiers: +2 for Voice (p. 97); -3 for Low Empathy (p. 142); -1 for Oblivious (p. 146); -1 to -4 for Shyness (p. 154); -2 for Stuttering (p. 157); -5 for Truthfulness (p. 159). The GM may ask you for details of the story you are using, rather than just let you say, "I'm using Fast-Talk." Your approach and the plausibility of the story may further modify the roll, at the GM's discretion.

Filch

DX/Average
Defaults: DX-5, Pickpocket-4, or Sleight of Hand-4.

This skill lets you steal objects that are sitting in plain sight . . . without being spotted. Roll against skill to shoplift, snatch documents off a desk, etc. If someone is *actively* watching the item you wish to snatch, you must win a Quick Contest of Filch vs. his Vision roll (or Observation skill, p. 211) to perform the theft unnoticed.

Filch only covers the theft itself. The GM might require rolls against Stealth to get close enough to make the attempt and Holdout to conceal stolen objects afterward.

Modifiers: +3 if the light is dim; +3 if you have a confederate to distract attention.

Finance

IQ/Hard
Defaults: Accounting-4, Economics-3, or Merchant-6.

This is the skill of managing money. It is a *practical* application of Economics (p. 189), much as Engineer skill is a practical application of Physics. A successful skill roll lets you broker a financial deal, raise capital for a new corporation, balance a budget, etc.

Modifiers: Business Acumen and Mathematical Ability *both* provide a bonus.

Fire Eating

DX/Average
Defaults: None.

This is the performance skill of extinguishing flames in your mouth without burning yourself. Make a skill roll for each item you wish to extinguish. On a success, you put out the flames. On a failure, you take 1d-3 damage (minimum 1) to your mouth.

This skill also includes fire *breathing:* igniting a stream of fuel blown from the mouth. At the GM's option, you may use this as an attack (1d-3 damage).

First Aid/TL

IQ/Easy
Defaults: IQ-4, Esoteric Medicine, Physician, or Veterinary-4.

This is the ability to patch up an injury in the field (see *Recovery*, p. 423). Make a skill roll to halt bleeding, suck out poison, give artificial respiration to a drowning victim, etc. Unusual problems must be identified using Diagnosis skill first.

Modifiers: Equipment modifiers (p. 345); physiology modifiers (p. 181).

Fishing

Per/Easy
Default: Perception-4.

This is the ability to catch fish – with a net, hook and line, or whatever method is used in your culture. If you have proper equipment and there are fish to be caught, a successful roll catches them. If you lack equipment, you can improvise.

Modifiers: Equipment modifiers (p. 345).

Flail

see *Melee Weapon,* p. 208

Flight

HT/Average
Default: HT-5.
Prerequisite: Flight advantage (p. 56).

This skill represents training for endurance flying. Use the *better* of Flight or HT when rolling to avoid fatigue due to flying. When traveling long distances, a successful Flight roll increases the distance traveled by 20%. If a group of fliers is traveling together, all must make the Flight roll in order to get the increased distance.

Flying Leap
IQ/Hard

Defaults: None.
Prerequisites: Trained By A Master or Weapon Master, and both Jumping and Power Blow.

This skill allows you to make incredible leaps. It costs 1 FP per attempt, successful or not.

On a success, you may immediately attempt a jump. Use the standard jumping rules (see *Jumping*, p. 352), but *triple* your jumping distance. On a failure, you may still attempt the jump, but you receive no bonus and make all jumping-related rolls at -5. On a critical failure, you fall down!

You may use Flying Leap to jump *into* someone as part of an attack. Such attacks are at an extra -2 to hit, but if you *do* hit, triple your ST for damage and knockback purposes. In a slam or collision, calculate Move from jumping distance as described for Super Jump (p. 89), and use this velocity to calculate damage.

Modifiers: -10 if used *instantly,* dropping to -5 after 1 turn of concentration, -4 after 2 turns, -3 after 4 turns, -2 after 8 turns, -1 after 16 turns, and no penalty after 32 turns.

Force Sword
see *Melee Weapon*, p. 208

Force Whip
see *Melee Weapon*, p. 208

Forced Entry
DX/Easy

Defaults: None.

This is the ability to kick in doors and windows, or demolish them with a crowbar, ram, or sledgehammer, without necessarily being adept at melee combat. Make a skill roll to hit an inanimate object with your foot or an impact weapon. Add +1 *per die* to basic thrust or swing damage if you have this skill at DX+1, +2 per die if you know it at DX+2 or better. Add a similar bonus (+1 or +2) to ST rolls made for forced entry. The damage bonus also applies when you use Melee Weapon skills to wreck inanimate objects *out of combat.*

For *subtle* break-ins, use Lockpicking skill (p. 206).

Forensics/TL
IQ/Hard

Defaults: IQ-6 or Criminology-4.

This is the ability to apply the principles of forensic science and criminalistics, such as the computation of bullet paths and the microscopic or chemical analysis of clues. Some disciplines require other skills. For instance, a forensic pathologist performing an autopsy would roll against Surgery skill.

Forgery/TL
IQ/Hard

Defaults: IQ-6 or Counterfeiting-2.

This is the ability to create falsified documents (identity cards, passports, etc.). It is not taught except by intelligence agencies and the underworld – although you can always study it on your own.

The time required to create a forgery ranges from days to weeks (GM decides). When you use a forged document, make your Forgery roll *each time* it is inspected – unless you roll a critical success on your first attempt. Failure means someone spots the forgery.

Some tasks require DX-based skill rolls, in which case modifiers for High Manual Dexterity (p. 59) or Ham-Fisted (p. 138) apply. The GM may allow Forgery to default to a suitable Artist specialty at -5 if you are doing the work entirely by hand.

Modifiers: Equipment modifiers (p. 345); +3 if you merely *altered* a genuine document; -5 if you did not have a sample to copy. The GM may also assign modifiers based on the severity of the inspection; a routine border check, for instance, would give a +5 bonus.

Fortune-Telling†
IQ/Average

Defaults: IQ-5, Fast-Talk-3, or Occultism-3.

This is the art of interviewing someone in order to learn more about his lifestyle and personality, and then using this information to make an "educated guess" about his future that you can pass off as supernatural divination. Suitable props – star charts, tea leaves, etc. – can enhance the illusion. Knowledge of traditional occult or religious beliefs (especially those of your subject) can also lend an air of legitimacy.

With the GM's permission, you can sometimes use Fortune-Telling in place of Fast-Talk (by making predictions that guide the subject toward a particular course of action), or Interrogation or Psychology (by asking the subject leading questions under the pretense of telling his fortune). This is only possible if the subject believes you are a genuine fortune-teller *and* you take the time to do a full "reading" for him.

You *must* specialize in a particular mantic art. Available specialties include Astrology, Augury (interpretation of natural omens, such as flocks of birds), Crystal Gazing, Dream Interpretation, Feng Shui, Palmistry, and Tarot.

This skill is *not* a paranormal talent, and the GM is under *no* obligation to supply you with hints of future events. You might wish to learn this skill if you have actual divinatory abilities, though, as it enables you to present your predictions in a culturally acceptable way. "I saw it in the stars" may be less likely to get you burned as a witch than "I cast a spell"!

Modifiers: +1 for Sensitive *or* +3 for Empathy (p. 51); any Charisma bonus; -3 if using Fortune-Telling in place of Fast-Talk, Interrogation, or Psychology.

Forward Observer/TL
IQ/Average

Defaults: IQ-5, Artillery (any)-5, and others.

This is the skill of being a "spotter" for artillery. It includes locating targets (with map and compass at TL6, global positioning systems and satellite imagery at TL7+), marking targets (using smoke, a laser designator, etc.), matching ordnance to target for best effect, and calling in corrections to any fire you personally observe.

Failure means the ordnance misses the target; critical failures result in severe "collateral damage" or "friendly fire" incidents. The very worst critical failures (GM's decision) drop the ordnance on *your* position!

At higher tech levels, Forward Observer is less about observing targets and more about operating specialized technology such as drones, GPS, and laser designators. To remotely pilot a drone or use a laser designator to direct "smart" munitions onto a target, make a DX-based skill roll. At TL7+, Forward Observer defaults to Electronics Operation (any)-5.

Modifiers: Equipment modifiers (p. 345); -2 if you are unfamiliar with the artillery (e.g., aircraft bombs when you are used to naval guns); -3 per 500 yards between you and the target – but divide the actual range by the magnification of any vision aid first.

People often stake vast sums on games, and it might be possible to earn a living as a professional gamer.

Free Fall
DX/Average
Defaults: DX-5 or HT-5.

This is the ability to operate in a free-fall (zero-gravity) environment. Roll against the *higher* of HT or Free Fall when you first enter free fall; see *Space Adaptation Syndrome* (p. 434) for the effects of failure. In addition, whenever you make a DX or DX-based skill roll in free fall, use the *lower* of Free Fall and your DX or skill. For instance, if you had Free Fall-14 and Karate-16, you would roll at 14 or less to land a punch.

Modifiers: +2 for 3D Spatial Sense (p. 34).

Freight Handling/TL
IQ/Average
Default: IQ-5.

This is the skill of supervising the loading and unloading of vehicles (*laborers* do not require this skill – just their foreman). A successful skill roll cuts the time required by 20%. Also roll against Freight Handling skill any time there is doubt as to whether an item of cargo was lost or damaged; on a success, it made the journey intact.

Gambling
IQ/Average
Defaults: IQ-5 or Mathematics (Statistics)-5.

This is skill at playing games of chance. A successful Gambling roll can (among other things) tell you if a game is rigged, identify a fellow gambler in a group of strangers, or "estimate the odds" in *any* tricky situation. When you gamble against the house, make a skill roll (the GM will secretly modify this roll if the odds are poor!). When you gamble against someone else, roll a Regular Contest (p. 349) of Gambling until one of you wins.

Sleight of Hand skill (p. 221) is helpful if you want to cheat! To *spot* a cheater, roll a Quick Contest of your Gambling or Vision roll, whichever is *higher*, vs. your opponent's Sleight of Hand skill (for card or dice tricks) or IQ (for other kinds of cheating).

Modifiers: +1 to +5 for familiarity with the game being played; -1 to -5 if the game is rigged against you; -3 for Killjoy (p. 140), since you don't care if you win or lose.

Games†
IQ/Easy
Default: IQ-4.

This is the ability to play a game *well.* It includes knowledge of rules, etiquette, and tournament regulations. You *must* specialize in a particular game; possibilities include traditional board games (such as chess, *Go, hnefatafl,* and *mankala*), card games, war games, and computer games.

Many cultures regard the ability to play one or more games skillfully as a worthwhile social accomplishment. People often stake vast sums on games, and it might be possible to earn a living as a professional gamer. Games may also be played to settle disputes. In a fantasy world, a powerful monster or wizard might even challenge a hero to a game – with his life or the lives of his companions at stake!

Knowledge of the rules of a given sport is also a Games skill, but unlike other Games skills, sports specialties only allow you to *judge* an event. To *play,* learn the associated Sports (p. 222) or Combat Sport (p. 184) skill. As a referee, roll against skill to adjudicate a match, spot a subtle foul, determine the winner in a "photo finish" situation, etc. As an athlete, you can use Games to make an Influence roll (see *Influence Rolls,* p. 359) when dealing with a referee or judge, but this use is always at -3 or worse.

When you take a sports specialty, specify both the sport and the league or tournament type; e.g., Games (NFL Football) or Games (Olympic Judo). The rules of different leagues within the same sport default to one another at -2.

Modifiers: Cultural Familiarity modifiers (p. 23). Long-lived games have a body of knowledge that grows through time; therefore, when gamers from different times compete, the player from later in the timeline gets +1 to effective skill.

Gardening
IQ/Easy
Defaults: IQ-4 or Farming-3.

This is the ability to care for plants on a small scale. (For large-scale crops, use Farming skill, p. 194.) A skill roll lets you grow food, medicinal herbs, attractive flowers and trees, etc.

Modifiers: -2 to -4 for an unfamiliar method (e.g., hydroponics or bonsai when you're used to your back yard), crop (herbs, trees, and vegetables all differ), or geographical region. These three penalties are cumulative!

Garrote
DX/Easy
Default: DX-4.

This is the ability to strangle a victim with a rope or a wire. See *Special Melee Weapon Rules* (p. 404) for details. Note that you cannot use a garrote to parry.

Geography/TL†

IQ/Hard

Defaults: IQ-6 and others.

This is the study of the physical, political, and economic divisions of a planet, and how they interact. It is part physical science, part social science. You *must* specialize:

Physical: The study of the physical properties of a planetary surface. A physical geographer could answer questions about climate, terrain, and so forth. You must further specialize by planet type; see *Planet Types* (p. 180). *Defaults:* Geology (same planet type)-4 or Meteorology (same planet type)-4.

Political: The study of political regions – their borders, natural resources, industries, etc. A political geographer could answer questions about land claims, overpopulation, regional economic disparities, transportation networks, etc. *Default:* Economics-4.

Regional: The study of *all* of the above, but specific to a single region: New York, the United States, planet Earth, etc. The depth of knowledge decreases with the size of the region (see *Area Knowledge*, p. 176). *Default:* the relevant Area Knowledge skill at -6.

These specialties default among themselves at -5.

Geology/TL†

IQ/Hard

Defaults: IQ-6, Geography (Physical)-4, or Prospecting-5.

This is the science dealing with the structure of planets – their crust, mantle, and core. A geologist knows about minerals, oil, ores, etc.; about earthquakes and volcanoes; and about fossils. In the field, he can attempt to find water by using an "eye for country" (see *Survival*, p. 223).

You *must* specialize by planet type. See *Planet Types* (p. 180) for details.

Gesture

IQ/Easy

Default: IQ-4.

This is the ability to communicate through improvised hand signals. A successful skill roll will let you convey one *simple* idea to another person, or understand one simple idea he is attempting to get across to you. Gesture is not suited to complex communication, however.

Modifiers: Cultural Familiarity modifiers (p. 23) definitely apply! Different cultures develop distinct gesture vocabularies.

Group Performance†

IQ/Average

Defaults: IQ-5 and others.

This is the ability to arrange a performance and direct a group of performers in its execution – in rehearsal, in a studio, or before a live audience. A successful roll means the performance is pleasing. You *must* specialize in a particular performing art. All specialties have prerequisites: the specific skills listed below, plus any *one* of Diplomacy, Intimidation, or Leadership.

Choreography: The ability to instruct and lead a group of dancers. *Prerequisite:* Dancing. *Default:* Dancing-2.

Conducting: The ability to coordinate a group of musicians. Choirs, swing bands, symphony orchestras, etc. are different familiarities; see *Familiarity* (p. 169). *Prerequisites:* Any two Musical Instrument skills, *or* one Musical Instrument and Singing. *Defaults:* Musical Instrument-2 or Singing-2.

Directing: The ability to direct a group of actors. Film, opera, television, and theater are different familiarities. *Prerequisite:* Performance. *Default:* Performance-5.

Fight Choreography: Similar to Choreography, but for Stage Combat (p. 222) instead of Dancing. *Prerequisite:* Stage Combat. *Default:* Stage Combat-2.

Gunner/TL†

DX/Easy

Default: DX-4.

This is the ability to use a heavy weapon, usually one mounted on a tripod or a vehicle, to make a *direct-fire* attack – that is, to aim and fire at a target to which you have a line of sight. For *indirect* fire, use Artillery skill (p. 178). Roll against Gunner skill to hit the target.

Make an IQ-based skill roll to take immediate action (e.g., clear a stoppage or restart a crashed targeting computer), should your weapon fail. Loaders can make ST-based skill rolls to improve the rate of fire of certain crew-served weapons; see individual weapon descriptions for details.

You *must* specialize by weapon type. The available specialties vary by TL, but include one or more of:

Beams: Any kind of heavy directed-energy weapon: laser, particle beam, etc.

Cannon: Any kind of heavy projectile weapon – e.g., the main gun of a tank or an ultra-tech railgun on a starship – that fires single shots.

Catapult: Any kind of large, direct-fire mechanical bolt-thrower, such as a ballista.

Machine Gun: Any kind of heavy projectile weapon capable of firing bursts.

Rockets: Any kind of free-flight rocket fired from a mount.

These specialties default to one another at -4. The weapons covered by each specialty vary by TL. For instance, Gunner (Machine Gun) covers hand-cranked Gatling guns at TL5, automatic machine guns at TL6, autocannon at TL7, and electromagnetic machine guns at TL9+.

Familiarity is crucial here! Gunner/TL7 (Machine Gun) covers both tripod-mounted machine guns and aircraft autocannon, but going from one to the other gives you -2 for weapon type (machine gun to autocannon), -2 for aiming system (open sights to HUD), and -2 for mount (tripod to hull mount), for a net -6 to skill until you familiarize yourself with all the differences.

Modifiers: All applicable ranged combat modifiers; -2 for an unfamiliar aiming system (e.g., a camera when you're used to open sights) or mount (e.g., a tripod when you're used to a turret), or for an unfamiliar weapon of a known type (e.g., .30-cal when you are used to .50s); -4 or more for a weapon in bad repair.

Guns/TL†

DX/Easy

Default: DX-4.

This is the ability to use a hand-held chemical-propellant or mass-driver projectile weapon. Roll against Guns skill to hit your target.

Make an IQ-based skill roll to take immediate action (e.g., eject a dud round), should your weapon fail.

You *must* specialize by weapon type. The available specialties vary by TL, but include one or more of:

Grenade Launcher (GL): Any large-bore, low-powered small arm that fires a bursting projectile. Includes under-barrel grenade launchers, flare pistols, and ultra-tech "tanglers."

Gyroc: Any kind of small arm that fires miniature rockets.

Light Anti-Armor Weapon (LAW): All forms of rocket launchers and recoilless rifles.

Light Machine Gun (LMG): Any machine gun fired from the hip or a bipod.

Musket: Any kind of *smoothbore* long arm (usually, but not always, a black powder weapon) that fires a solid projectile.

Pistol: All kinds of handguns, including derringers, pepperboxes, revolvers, and automatics, but *not* machine pistols.

Rifle: Any kind of *rifled* long arm – assault rifle, hunting rifle, sniper rifle, etc. – that fires a solid projectile.

Shotgun: Any kind of *smoothbore* long arm that fires multiple projectiles (flechettes, shot, etc.).

Submachine Gun (SMG): All short, fully automatic weapons that fire pistol-caliber ammunition, including machine pistols.

Most of these specialties default to one another at -2, but defaults involving GL, Gyroc, or LAW are at -4 in either direction. The weapons covered by each specialty vary by TL. For example, Guns (Rifle) covers muzzle-loaders at TL4, lever actions at TL5, and self-loaders at TL6+. In particular, *ammunition* varies with TL, from black powder and loose shot at TL4, to smokeless powder cartridges at TL6, to power cells and metallic slivers for TL9+ electromagnetic guns.

Familiarity is crucial here! Guns (Rifle) covers both bolt-action 12.7mm sniper rifles and 5.56mm assault rifles, but going from one to the other gives you -2 for weapon type (12.7mm to 5.56mm), -2 for action

(bolt-action to self-loader), and -2 for grip (bipod to hand-held), for a total of -6 to skill until you familiarize yourself with all the differences.

Modifiers: All applicable ranged combat modifiers; -2 for an unfamiliar action (e.g., an automatic when you're used to a revolver) or grip (e.g., a shoulder-fired antitank weapon when you're used to a bipod), or for an unfamiliar weapon of a known type (e.g., a 5.56mm rifle when you are used to a 7.62mm rifle); -4 or more for a weapon in bad repair.

Hazardous Materials/TL†

IQ/Average

Default: IQ-5.

This is the skill of transporting, storing, and disposing of hazardous materials ("HazMat"). It includes preparing the records that accompany HazMat shipments; applying and identifying warning labels and markings; and knowledge of countermeasures, antidotes, and containment and decontamination procedures. (To operate *personal* protective gear, use the NBC Suit skill, p. 192.)

You *must* specialize by type of HazMat. Common specialties are Biological, Chemical, and Radioactive, but more exotic options (e.g., Magical or Nanotech) may exist in some settings. Mundane specialties default to one another at -5; exotic specialties often have no default at all.

Whenever you deal with HazMat in any capacity, roll against the *lower* of the skill used for the task (Driving, Freight Handling, etc.) and the applicable Hazardous Materials specialty or default. Note that the IQ-5 default represents any layman's knowledge of household hazards. HazMat professionals *deliberately* keep certain aspects of this skill (notably HazMat markings) obscure to avoid alarming the general public. The default does not apply when dealing with such things.

Heraldry

IQ/Average

Defaults: IQ-5 or Savoir-Faire (High Society)-3.

This is the skill of recognizing and designing coats of arms, crests, flags,

tartans, and other emblems. A successful roll lets you recognize a knight or a noble from his banner or shield, create attractive and proper arms (without conflicting with existing designs), etc.

In some settings, you might have to specialize in a particular *type* of Heraldry: Coats of Arms (the usual specialty, described above), Corporate Logos (defaults to Current Affairs (Business)-3), or even Graffiti Tags (defaults to Streetwise-3).

Modifiers: Cultural Familiarity modifiers (p. 23). Up to +5 to recognize a well-known design, and down to -5 for an obscure design or one that was retired long ago.

Herb Lore/TL

IQ/Very Hard

Defaults: None.
Prerequisite: Naturalist.

This is the ability to manufacture herbal concoctions that have magical effects – healing balms, love potions, etc. It only exists in magical game worlds, where it functions much as Alchemy skill (p. 174). Unlike Alchemy, Herb Lore does *not* include the ability to analyze "elixirs." On the other hand, an expert at this skill can locate magical ingredients for free in the wild by making a few Naturalist rolls, while an alchemist requires rare and expensive materials (such as alkahest, dragon's blood, gemstones, and gold) to do his work.

Hidden Lore†

IQ/Average

Defaults: None.

This skill represents knowledge that is lost, deliberately hidden, or simply neglected. Whatever the reason, the general public is unaware of it. It is only available to those who study it specifically.

You *must* specialize in a particular body of secret knowledge. If you wish to enter play with Hidden Lore skills, you must account for this specific knowledge in your character story. The GM might even require you to purchase an Unusual Background before you can learn Hidden Lore skills. Of course, the GM is also free to *forbid* Hidden Lore skills to starting characters . . . or to PCs in general!

To acquire Hidden Lore in play, you must find a reliable source of relevant information. The GM may choose to tie skill increases in Hidden Lore to specific acts – such as reading moldy tomes – instead of allowing you to spend points freely. For instance, an ancient manuscript might let you spend up to eight points (and no more) on a specific Hidden Lore skill.

Remember that most Hidden Lore is secret because somebody powerful wants it kept that way. Thus, discussing or revealing your knowledge can be extremely hazardous.

Possible Hidden Lore specialties include:

Conspiracies: You know details about the conspiracies that underlie every aspect of society. This is factual knowledge (e.g., truths about the Illuminati), not the ability to *analyze* conspiracies. Only available in settings where vast conspiracies really do exist.

Demon Lore: You know the secrets of Hell, the goals of demons in the mortal world, and possibly even the names of specific demons.

Faerie Lore: You have detailed knowledge of the faeries and their secret kingdom(s).

Spirit Lore: You know about ghosts and other spirit entities – names, motivations, etc.

Hiking

HT/Average

Default: HT-5.

This skill represents training for endurance walking, hiking, and marching. It includes knowledge of how to pace yourself in different conditions, and how best to carry a pack. Make a Hiking roll before each day's march; on a success, increase the distance traveled by 20%. The GM may allow bonuses for good maps and good walking shoes, but not for terrain. If a party is traveling together, *all* must make the Hiking roll in order to get the increased distance. See *Hiking* (p. 351).

History†

IQ/Hard

Default: IQ-6.

This is the study of the recorded past (compare Archaeology skill,

p. 176). A successful skill roll lets you answer questions about history, and might (at the GM's option) allow you to remember a useful parallel: "Ah, yes. Hannibal faced a situation like this once, and here's what he did . . ."

You *must* specialize. There are two general classes of specialty:

● A limited geographical region – no larger than a small nation – over multiple eras. *Examples:* History (Bavarian), History (Irish), or History (New York State).

● A single *era* (e.g., Victorian period, 20th century) and *one* of a broad geographical region (e.g., Europe), a culture (e.g., Muslim), or an idea (e.g., economic, esoteric, or military). *Examples:* History (20th-Century American), History (Ottoman Muslim), or History (Napoleonic Military).

The sheer variety of possible specialties makes it impossible to list all possible defaults. In general, if two specialties overlap *at all*, then GM should permit a default at -2 to -4.

Hobby Skill

DX or IQ/Easy

Default: DX-4 or IQ-4, depending on the controlling attribute.

Many fields of study have little to do with adventuring or making a living – but people study them nonetheless. Each of these is a separate Hobby Skill. Those that require agility or a delicate touch (e.g., juggling, kite flying, needlepoint, and origami) are DX/Easy skills that default to DX-4, while those that focus on knowledge and trivia (e.g., comic books, rock music, science fiction, and tropical fish) are IQ/Easy skills that default to IQ-4.

A few points in a Hobby Skill can make roleplaying more fun – and possibly come in handy once in a while. You do not need a teacher to learn or improve a Hobby Skill. However, you *cannot* learn skills defined elsewhere in this chapter as Hobby Skills.

Holdout

IQ/Average

Defaults: IQ-5 or Sleight of Hand-3.

This is the skill of concealing items on your person or on other people

(usually with their cooperation). An item's size and shape govern its concealability. Some examples:

+4: A BB-sized jewel, a postage stamp.

+3: A pea-sized jewel.

+2: One lockpick, a huge jewel, a dime, a TL9+ computer disk, a letter.

+1: A set of lockpicks, a silver dollar.

0: A TL8 floppy disk or CD, without case.

-1: A dagger, a slingshot, the tiniest handgun or grenade.

-2: An average handgun (e.g., a Luger), a grenade, a large knife.

-3: A submachine gun, a shortsword, a short carbine.

-4: A broadsword, an assault rifle.

-5: A bastard sword, a battle rifle.

-6: A crossbow, a heavy sniper rifle.

Things that move or make noise give an additional -1 or more to skill.

Clothing also modifies effective skill. A Carmelite nun in full habit (+5 to skill) could conceal a bazooka or a battle-axe from an eyeball search. A Las Vegas showgirl in costume (-5 to skill) would have trouble hiding even a dagger. Of course, the showgirl might escape search entirely (unless the guards were bored) because "She obviously couldn't hide anything in *that* outfit!" Full nudity is -7 to skill.

A proper concealment holster helps conceal a weapon; use the equipment modifiers on p. 345. Clothing designed specifically to hide things gives a bonus of up to +4.

To spot a concealed item, roll a Quick Contest of Search skill vs. Holdout. Search defaults to Perception-5 if you haven't studied it. See *Search* (p. 219) for additional rules.

Housekeeping

IQ/Easy

Default: IQ-4.

This is the ability to manage a household. It covers both home economics and domestic chores: cleaning, cooking (but not *haute cuisine*, which requires the Cooking skill), minor repairs (any routine maintenance task that calls for a roll against Carpentry, Sewing, or a similar skill at +4 or better), etc. The main use of Housekeeping is to qualify for the job of "homemaker," but it can come in handy on adventures – for instance, to clean up evidence!

Hypnotism
IQ/Hard

Defaults: None.

This is the skill of inducing a suggestible state in another person through verbal or mechanical means. It requires five seconds and a successful skill roll to use. If you fail on a *cooperative* subject, you may try again. The second attempt takes five *minutes*, and the roll is at -5. If this attempt fails, you may not try to hypnotize the subject again that day.

A successful Hypnotism attempt puts the subject to sleep. This counts as an anesthetic for the purpose of Surgery. At the GM's option, further Hypnotism rolls might help the subject remember something he had forgotten, while Psychology rolls might help him get over mental problems.

A hypnotized individual is extremely suggestible. Roll a Quick Contest of Hypnotism vs. the victim's Will for each suggestion. The subject resists suggestions that threaten his life or his loved ones, or that go strongly against his character, at +5. You may also give "posthypnotic suggestions," instructing the subject to do something in response to a trigger after the hypnosis ends. The subject's resistance roll for such suggestions takes place when he encounters the trigger. He resists at +1 to Will per week since he was hypnotized.

You *cannot* use Hypnotism as an attack, except in highly cinematic games. You *can* use it on an unaware or unwilling subject out of combat, but he resists at Will+5. If he resists the initial attempt, he is considered uncooperative, and you may not make a second attempt that day. A subject who is unfamiliar with Hypnotism might not know what you attempted, but he suspects *something* – possibly witchcraft!

In all cases, a hypnotic trance lasts 1d hours unless you end it sooner.

Modifiers: +2 if you send hypnotic suggestions via Telesend (see *Telecommunication,* p. 91), since voices in the head are harder to ignore.

Immovable Stance
DX/Hard

Defaults: None.
Prerequisite: Trained By A Master.

This skill allows you to anchor yourself to the ground by properly channeling your *chi,* using secret balancing techniques, etc. Make a skill roll whenever an attack (e.g., a shove or the Push skill, p. 216) would result in knockback or a fall.

On a success, you neither experience knockback nor fall down. On a failure, you are knocked back but still get the usual DX roll to avoid falling down. On a critical failure, you automatically suffer full knockback *and* you fall down.

This skill also helps against attacks with the Judo skill (p. 203). If you fail your active defense (or choose not to defend) against a Judo throw, your attacker must *win* a Quick Contest of Judo vs. your Immovable Stance skill, or his throw fails.

Modifiers: -1 per yard of potential knockback; +4 for Perfect Balance (p. 74).

Innate Attack†
DX/Easy

Default: DX-4.

This skill represents trained ability with a "built-in" *ranged* attack: fiery breath, super-powered energy bolts, etc. Learn it to improve your odds of hitting with Afflictions (p. 35), Bindings (p. 40), Innate Attacks (p. 61), magical jets and missiles, and similar attacks that originate from *you* as opposed to a weapon in your hand. Roll against skill to hit.

You *must* specialize:

Beam: Any energy blast, magical jet, etc. emitted from the hands. To use this skill, you must have at least one unrestrained hand (although it need not be *empty*).
Breath: Any attack emitted from the mouth, such as dragon's fire or acidic sputum. To use this skill, you cannot be gagged and you *must* be facing your target.
Gaze: Any attack emitted from the eyes – heat vision, a petrifying stare, etc. To use this skill, you cannot be blindfolded and you *must* be facing your target.

Projectile: Any solid projectile or pseudo-solid energy bolt (e.g., Fireball spell) emitted from the hands. To use this skill, you must have at least one unrestrained hand (although it need not be *empty*).

These specialties default to one another at -2.

You use this skill to *direct* your attack, not to *activate* it; therefore, restrictions such as "you cannot be gagged" apply strictly to your ability to make ranged attacks. If you can trigger your attack while restrained, no skill roll is needed to attack your restraints!

You can only learn this skill for ranged attacks. Use Brawling (p. 182) to improve your odds with abilities that require a touch.

Intelligence Analysis/TL
IQ/Hard

Defaults: IQ-6 or Strategy (any)-6.

This is the ability to *analyze* and *interpret* intelligence data. It allows you to deduce enemy plans and capabilities, evaluate the accuracy of information, rate the reliability of sources, etc. In most game worlds, only intelligence, military, and security services teach this skill – often only to those with a minimum level of Rank or Security Clearance.

The GM makes *all* Intelligence Analysis rolls in secret. On a success, he provides details about the significance and accuracy of your data, or insights into what it means in terms of enemy planning. When you encounter deliberately falsified data, the GM rolls a secret Quick Contest: your Intelligence Analysis vs. the enemy's skill at disinformation (Forgery, Propaganda, etc.). If you win, the GM provides details on precisely what is wrong with the information. It is up to you to deduce what this means, however!

This skill has nothing to do with *gathering* intelligence. Use Current Affairs (p.186) and Research (p. 217) to sift through public sources; Forensics (p. 196) and Search (p. 219) to find physical clues; Observation (p. 211) for human surveillance; and Electronics Operation (p. 189) to work with the satellite imagery, communications intercepts, and related "technical means" common at TL7+.

You may take an *optional* specialty (p. 169) in one particular type of intelligence. A useful specialty at TL6+ is Intelligence Analysis (Traffic Analysis): identifying the purpose and organization of targets by examining intercepted communications traffic.

Modifiers: -1 to -5 for incomplete information; -3 if all your information comes from a single source; -3 for intelligence concerning an arcane scientific or bureaucratic principle, *unless* you have skill in that area (e.g., Engineer (Electronics) for intelligence regarding a radar installation).

Interrogation

IQ/Average

Defaults: IQ-5, Intimidation-3, or Psychology-4.

This is the ability to question a prisoner. Only intelligence agencies, police and prison services, the military, and the underworld teach this skill.

Roll a Quick Contest of Interrogation vs. the prisoner's Will for each question. This requires 5 minutes per question. If you win, you get a truthful answer. If you tie or lose, the victim remains silent or lies. If you lose by more than five points, he tells you a *good, believable* lie! The GM roleplays the prisoner (or, if *you* are the prisoner, the GM will roleplay the interrogator) and makes all die rolls in secret.

Modifiers: -5 if the prisoner's loyalty to his leader or cause is "Very Good" or "Excellent"; -3 for Low Empathy (p. 142); +2 for a lengthy interrogation (over two hours); +3 if you use severe threats; +6 if you use torture*. Increase these last two bonuses by +1 if you have the Callous disadvantage (p. 125)!

* "Torture" does not necessarily mean thumbscrews and the rack. Exposing a prisoner to the object of his phobia (see *Phobias*, p. 148) is an effective torture, as is a believable threat against a loved one. Note that torturing a prisoner is usually considered *vile* behavior, likely bringing retribution.

Intimidation

Will/Average

Defaults: Will-5 or Acting-3.

This is the skill of hostile persuasion. The essence of Intimidation is to convince the subject that you are able and willing, perhaps even eager, to do something awful to him.

You can substitute an Intimidation attempt for any reaction roll; see *Influence Rolls* (p. 359). *Exception:* You cannot intimidate someone who has the Unfazeable advantage!

The results of a successful Intimidation attempt depend on the target. An honest citizen probably cooperates, sullenly or with false cheer. A low-life might lick your boots (even becoming genuinely loyal). A really tough sort might react well without being frightened: "You're my kind of scum!" The GM decides, and roleplays it. If you rolled a critical success – or if the subject critically failed his Will roll – your victim must make a Fright Check in addition to the other results of the Influence roll!

Group Intimidation: You may attempt to intimidate up to 25 people at once, at -1 to skill per five people (or fraction thereof) in the group. Multiple intimidators can attempt to intimidate proportionally larger groups; for instance, three thugs could try to intimidate up to 75 people! Base the skill penalty on the size of the target group divided by the number of intimidators (round up). Resolve the outcome with a single Quick Contest: the *highest* effective Intimidation skill from among the intimidators vs. the *highest* modified Will in the target group.

Specious Intimidation: You can attempt a Quick Contest of Fast-Talk vs. the subject's IQ *before* your Intimidation attempt in order to appear to be intimidating when you can't back it up. If you win, you are at +3 on the subsequent Intimidation attempt, which can go a long way toward offsetting the high Will and Fearlessness of martial arts masters, world leaders, etc. If you tie or lose, however, your Intimidation attempt fails *automatically*, and you suffer a "Very Bad" reaction instead of just a "Bad" one!

Modifiers: +1 to +4 for displays of strength, bloodthirstiness, or supernatural powers (GM's judgment); increase this bonus by +1 if you are Callous (p. 125). Appearance (p. 21) matters: +2 if you are Hideous, +3 if Monstrous, or +4 if Horrific. Size also matters: add your Size Modifier and subtract the subject's. Appropriate Reputation modifiers (positive or negative) certainly count! You get -1 for Oblivious (p. 146) and -1 to -4 for Shyness (p. 154). Subtract the *subject's* Fearlessness (p. 55) from your roll. The GM may assign a +1 or -1 for especially appropriate or clumsy dialog. Requests for aid are always at -3 or worse.

Invisibility Art

IQ/Very Hard

Defaults: None.
Prerequisites: Trained By A Master, and both Hypnotism and Stealth at 14+.

This is the fabled skill, often attributed to ninja and other martial-arts masters, of being able to stand in plain sight without being noticed. It requires one second of concentration to activate. After that time, roll a Quick Contest once per *second:* your Invisibility Art vs. the Vision roll of each person who can see you.

Viewers must apply the current darkness penalty to their Vision roll. A viewer who is concentrating on something else or otherwise distracted is at -3; one who is specifically looking for intruders gets +3. If someone sees you and raises the alarm, by pointing and crying out, those who believe the warning get +3 on their *next* roll.

If you win, that person is unable to see you for one second. Otherwise, he can see you normally. Once someone notices you, he is unaffected by this skill until you can get out of sight somehow (which might be as easy as stepping into a shadow), whereupon you may try again.

Note that this skill does not work at all in combat. In particular, if you attack *anyone*, you will immediately become visible to *everyone!*

Modifiers: +3 if you use a smoke bomb or flash grenade before you attempt your roll (you appear to vanish in a cloud of smoke). Your movement modifies your skill roll rather than viewers' Vision rolls: no modifier if you stand still (Move 0), -1 if you move at a slow walk (Move 1), -2 at a fast walk (Move 2), or -5 at a run (Move 3+). If you stand *perfectly* still (requires a successful Breath Control or Meditation roll), you get +1.

Jeweler/TL

IQ/Hard

Defaults: IQ-6, Smith (Copper)-4, or Smith (Lead and Tin)-4.

This is the ability to work with precious metals, make jewelry, decorate weapons, etc. A successful skill roll allows you to identify a precious metal or gem, or determine the value of a precious bauble.

Jitte/Sai

see *Melee Weapon,* p. 208

Judo

DX/Hard

Defaults: None.

This skill represents *any* advanced training at unarmed throws and grapples – not just the eponymous Japanese martial art.

Judo allows you to parry two *different* attacks per turn, one with each hand. Your Parry score is (skill/2) + 3, rounded down. This parry is *not* at the usual -3 for parrying a weapon barehanded, greatly reducing the likelihood of injury when you defend against an armed foe. In addition, Judo gives an improved retreating bonus when you parry; see *Retreat* (p. 377). For complete rules for parrying barehanded, see *Parrying Unarmed* (p. 376).

On the turn immediately after a successful Judo parry, you may attempt to throw your attacker if he is within one yard. This counts as an attack; roll vs. Judo skill to hit. (Note that in an All-Out Attack, you cannot attempt two throws, but you can make one attempt at +4.) Your foe may use any active defense – he *can* parry your hand with a weapon! If his defense fails, you throw him.

When you throw a foe, he falls where you please. On a battle map, he lands in any two hexes near you. One of these hexes must be *his* starting hex, *your* hex, or any hex adjacent to one of those hexes. Your victim must roll against HT; a failed roll means he is stunned! If you throw him into someone else, that person must roll against the higher of ST+3 or DX+3 to avoid being knocked down.

Finally, you may use your Judo skill instead of your DX for any DX roll made in close combat except to draw a weapon or drop a shield. If you grapple a foe using Judo, and he fails to break free, you may make a Judo attack to throw him on your next turn, exactly as if you had parried his attack.

To use Judo, any hand with which you wish to parry or grapple must be empty. Because Judo relies heavily on footwork, all Judo rolls and Judo parries take a penalty equal to your encumbrance level. For instance, Heavy encumbrance would give you -3 to hit or to parry an enemy attack.

Jumping

DX/Easy

Defaults: None.

This skill represents trained jumping ability. When you attempt a difficult jump, roll against the *higher* of Jumping or DX. In addition, you may use half your Jumping skill (round down) instead of Basic Move when calculating jumping distance. For instance, Jumping-14 would let you jump if you had Basic Move 7. See *Jumping* (p. 352).

Karate

DX/Hard

Defaults: None.

This skill represents *any* advanced training at unarmed striking, not just the Okinawan martial art of *karate.* Roll against Karate to hit with a punch (at no -4 for the "off" hand), or Karate-2 to hit with a kick. You cannot use Karate to attack with claws, teeth, etc., or with a blackjack – use Brawling (p. 182) for that. Karate skill does let you make several special attacks, however; see *Special Unarmed Combat Techniques* (p. 403).

Karate improves damage: if you know Karate at DX level, add +1 *per die* to basic thrust damage when you calculate damage with Karate attacks: punches, kicks, elbow strikes, etc. Add +2 per die if you know Karate at DX+1 or better! Work out damage ahead of time and record it on your character sheet.

Karate allows you to parry two *different* attacks per turn, one with each hand. Your Parry score is (skill/2) + 3, rounded down. This parry is *not* at the usual -3 for parrying a weapon barehanded, greatly reducing the likelihood of injury when you defend against an armed foe. In addition, Karate gives an improved retreating bonus when you parry; see *Retreat* (p. 377). For more on parrying barehanded, see *Parrying Unarmed* (p. 376).

To use Karate, any hand with which you wish to strike or parry must be empty (but you are free to wear heavy gauntlets, brass knuckles, etc. to increase damage). Because Karate relies heavily on footwork, all Karate attacks and parries take a penalty equal to your encumbrance level. For instance, Heavy encumbrance would give you -3 to hit or to parry an enemy attack.

Kiai

HT/Hard

Defaults: None.
Prerequisites: Trained By A Master or Weapon Master.

You can channel your *chi* outward in a mighty shout (*kiai*) that freezes lesser foes. This counts as an attack, and costs 1 FP per attempt, successful or not.

Roll a Quick Contest: your Kiai skill vs. your target's Will. You are at -1 for every full two yards of distance. Your victim resists at +1 if he is Hard of Hearing, at +2 if Deaf! If you win, your target is mentally stunned (see *Effects of Stun,* p. 420).

This skill only works against a single victim; everyone can hear the shout, but your *chi* is focused on that one foe. However, a successful Kiai roll gives you +2 to Intimidation rolls vs. *everyone* within earshot.

Knife

see *Melee Weapon,* p. 208

Knot-Tying

DX/Easy

Defaults: DX-4, Climbing-4, or Seamanship-4.

This is the ability to tie a wide variety of knots quickly and efficiently. A successful skill roll lets you make a noose, tie someone up, etc. If you bind someone using this skill, he must win a Quick Contest of Escape vs. your Knot-Tying skill to free himself.

Modifiers: +1 per level of High Manual Dexterity (p. 59), or -3 per level of Ham-Fisted (p. 138).

Kusari

see *Melee Weapon,* p. 208

Lance

DX/Average

Defaults: DX-5 or Spear-3.
Prerequisite: Riding.

The ability to use the lance: a long, spear-like weapon wielded from horseback. This is *not* a Melee Weapon skill (see p. 208). You may not use a lance to parry – you must block or dodge enemy attacks.

Lasso

DX/Average

Defaults: None.

This is the skill of throwing the *lariat:* a long rope or thong with a sliding noose at one end. Its intended purpose is to snare animals, but it can also entangle opponents in combat – see *Special Ranged Weapons* (p. 410).

Law†

IQ/Hard

Default: IQ-6.

This skill represents knowledge of law codes and jurisprudence. A successful roll lets you remember, deduce, or figure out the answer to a question about the law. Few legal questions have clear-cut answers, however – even an expert will hedge his advice!

You *must* specialize. There are two general classes of specialty:

● The laws of a particular political region (e.g., Canada or France) *within a specific field* (constitutional, contract, criminal, police, etc.). *Examples:* Law (British Criminal), Law (Canadian Constitutional), and Law (U.S. Contract).

● A specialized body of law not associated with a political region. *Examples:* Law (Catholic Canon), Law (International), and Law (Space).

Specialties within the same *region,* such as Law (British Criminal) and Law (British Police), or *field,* such as Law (British Criminal) and Law (French Criminal), default to one another at -4. If both region and field differ, the default is -6 or worse.

In some times and places, a Quick Contest of Law (Criminal) between the defense and prosecution will determine the outcome of a trial. In others, Law functions as an Influence skill (see *Influence Rolls,* p. 359) used to sway the rulings of the judge.

Law enforcers nearly always have a point or two in Law (Police) for their region. This represents knowledge of "proper procedure" when it comes to arrests, evidence handling, interrogation, etc.

Leadership

IQ/Average

Default: IQ-5.

This is the ability to coordinate a group. Make a Leadership roll to lead NPCs into a dangerous or stressful situation. (PCs can decide for themselves if they want to follow you!)

You may attempt a Leadership roll in combat if you spend your turn doing *nothing* but giving orders and encouragement. On a success, everyone on your side who can hear you (*including* PCs) has +1 on all combat-related Fright Checks and loyalty checks, and on self-control rolls for disadvantages that would reduce combat efficiency (such as Berserk and Cowardice – or Bloodlust, if you wish to take prisoners). A critical success gives +2. The bonus lasts until your next turn, at which time you may roll again. A group can have only one leader, however! If multiple people attempt Leadership rolls, *no one* gets a bonus.

Note that a minimum level of Leadership is often a prerequisite for high Rank (p. 29).

Modifiers: Any bonus for Charisma (p. 41); -3 for Low Empathy (p. 142); -1 to -4 for Shyness (p. 154). -5 if the NPCs have never been in action with you; -5 if you are sending them into danger but not going yourself; +5 if their loyalty to you is "Good"; +10 if their loyalty is "Very Good." If their loyalty is "Excellent," you do not have to roll!

Leatherworking

DX/Easy

Default: DX-4.

This is the ability to work with leather to make belts, saddles, armor, etc. A successful skill roll lets you repair or create leather goods. Make an IQ-based roll to design items that are more artistic than functional.

Modifiers: Equipment modifiers (p. 345); +1 per level of High Manual Dexterity (p. 59), or -3 per level of Ham-Fisted (p. 138).

Lifting

HT/Average

Defaults: None.

This is the trained ability to use your strength to its best advantage when you lift. Roll once per lift. On a success, increase your Basic Lift by 5% per point by which you made your roll. This has no effect on encumbrance, or on how much you can carry. See *Lifting and Moving Things* (p. 353).

Light Walk

DX/Hard

Defaults: None.
Prerequisites: Trained By A Master, and both Acrobatics and Stealth at 14+.

This skill allows you to exert very little pressure when you walk. On a successful Light Walk roll, you leave no visible tracks. Tracking rolls to follow you *automatically* fail unless they rely on something more than sight; thus, a human tracker would be baffled, but bloodhounds would suffer no penalty at all.

You can also attempt to walk over fragile surfaces without falling through. Maximum Move under such circumstances is 1/3 normal (GM's decision). Thin ice would require an unmodified Light Walk roll, while rice paper would require a roll at -8!

Finally, a successful Light Walk roll can give a bonus to Stealth when your intention is to move quietly. This bonus equals half your margin of success, rounded down. Minimum bonus is +1.

Linguistics

IQ/Hard

Defaults: None.

This is the study of the principles upon which languages are based. A successful skill roll lets you identify a language from a snatch of speech or writing. As well, make a skill roll once per month when learning a language without a teacher. On a success, you learn at full speed rather than at 1/4 speed (see *Learning Languages*, p. 25).

Literature can be useful for finding clues to hidden treasure, sunken lands, Ancient Secrets, and the like.

Lip Reading

Per/Average

Default: Perception-10.

This is the ability to *see* what others are saying. You must be within seven yards, or have some means of bringing your point of view this close. A successful skill roll lets you make out one sentence of a discussion – assuming, of course, that you know the language. If your subjects suspect that you can read lips, they can hide their mouths or subvocalize to thwart you. A critical failure on a Lip Reading roll – if you are where your victims could see you – means that you stared so much you were noticed!

Modifiers: All Vision modifiers (see *Vision*, p. 358).

Liquid Projector/TL†

DX/Easy

Default: DX-4.

This is the ability to use a weapon that projects a stream of liquid or gas. Roll against Liquid Projector skill to hit your target.

Make an IQ-based Liquid Projector roll to take immediate action (e.g., patch a leak), should your weapon fail.

You *must* specialize by weapon type:

Flamethrower: Any weapon that projects *burning* liquid or gas. (This does *not* include plasma weapons, which are often called "flamers"; use Beam Weapons skill for those.)

Sprayer: Any weapon that emits a gas or atomized liquid (nerve gas, sleeping gas, etc.), including an ordinary spray can used as an improvised weapon.

Squirt Gun: Any weapon that fires a low-pressure stream of liquid at the rate of one squirt per pull of the trigger.

Water Cannon: Any weapon that fires a continuous jet of high-pressure liquid, usually but not always water, with the intent of causing knockback.

These specialties default to one another at -4. The weapons covered by each specialty vary by TL; e.g., Liquid Projector (Flamethrower) covers fire-siphons loaded with Greek fire at TL4, while at TL6, it covers backpack tanks that project thickened fuel.

Modifiers: All applicable ranged combat modifiers; -2 for heavy weapons when you are used to portable weapons (e.g., a flamethrower mounted on a tank when you are used to a backpack model), or for an unfamiliar weapon of a known type; -4 or more for a weapon in bad repair.

Literature

IQ/Hard

Default: IQ-6.

This is the study of the great writings. A student of literature would be knowledgeable in the realms of old poetry, dusty tomes, criticism, etc. This can be useful for finding clues to hidden treasure, sunken lands, Ancient Secrets, and the like. The work in question must be available in a language you read.

Modifiers: -5 if you're illiterate (see *Literacy*, p. 24) and relying on oral tradition, save in pre-literate cultures, where this is the norm.

Lockpicking/TL

IQ/Average

Default: IQ-5.

This is the ability to open locks without the key or combination. Each attempt requires one minute.

If you make the roll and open the lock, each point by which you succeeded shaves five seconds off the required time. (Safecracking and similar challenges can take more time, at the GM's discretion.)

Note that if the lock has a trap or alarm attached, you must make a separate Traps roll to circumvent it.

Modifiers: Equipment modifiers (p. 345); -5 if working by touch (e.g., in total darkness). Inside information gives a bonus at GM's discretion. If the GM requires a *DX*-based roll (for instance, to work with a particularly delicate mechanism), modifiers for High Manual Dexterity (p. 59) or Ham-Fisted (p. 138) will apply.

Machinist/TL

IQ/Average

Defaults: IQ-5 or Mechanic (any)-5.

This is the skill of making and modifying mechanical parts and tools. A successful skill roll lets you build parts from raw materials, manufacture tools for use with another skill (such as Armoury or Lockpicking), or modify any simple mechanical device not explicitly covered by another skill. The GM may require an inventor to make one or more Machinist rolls before attempting an Engineer roll to assemble a gadget.

Materials and component size vary significantly with tech level. A TL5 machinist works mainly with brass and steel components that can be seen with the naked eye; a TL10 machinist might work with carbon nanotubes.

Modifiers: Equipment modifiers (p. 345).

Main-Gauche

see *Melee Weapon*, p. 208

Makeup/TL

IQ/Easy

Defaults: IQ-4 or Disguise-2.

This is the skill of using theatrical makeup to enhance a performer's appearance. It is not just the ability to make someone look "pretty" – you can make yourself or others look older, younger, or of a different race or nationality. At TL6+, you can use prosthetics to further enhance the effect. However, you cannot make someone look taller or shorter than he actually is.

Market Analysis

IQ/Hard

Defaults: IQ-6, Economics-5, or Merchant-4.

This is the skill of predicting the short-term behavior of bond, stock, and currency markets – usually in order to make money! It is the main job skill of professional traders and speculators. Make a skill roll to determine current market trends. On a critical success, you also learn whether a trend will continue or reverse in the future. On a failure, you get no clear answer. On a critical failure, you guess *wrong*.

Modifiers: The Talents (p. 89) of Business Acumen and Mathematical Ability *both* provide a bonus.

Masonry

IQ/Easy

Default: IQ-4.

This is the ability to build things out of brick or stone.

Modifiers: Equipment modifiers (p. 345); -3 for simple engineering (erecting scaffolding, moving large blocks of stone, etc.) rather than masonry per se.

Mathematics/TL†

IQ/Hard

Defaults: IQ-6 and others.

This is the scientific study of quantities and magnitudes, and their relationships and attributes, through the use of numbers and symbols. You *must* specialize:

Applied: The branch of mathematics that interacts directly with the physical sciences and engineering, dealing with mathematical models of the behavior of physical systems. *Defaults:* Engineer (any)-5 or Physics-5.

Computer Science: The theoretical study of data structures and computation. Roll vs. skill to answer questions about what is *possible* with computers! This gives you no special ability to *use* computers! *Default:* Computer Programming-5.

Cryptology: The mathematical study of codes and ciphers. This gives you a *theoretical* understanding of encryption schemes, including how they change with TL and why some schemes are more effective than others. To create or break codes, use Cryptography skill (p. 186). *Default:* Cryptography-5.

Pure: Generic "academic" mathematics. Make a skill roll to answer any math-related question not covered by another specialty. Pure mathematics encompasses dozens of obscure subfields that will never affect the game. If you *must* be an expert in something like "non-selfadjoint operator algebras," you may further note an *optional* specialty (p. 169).

Statistics: The science of assembling and analyzing data for the purpose of calculating probabilities, constructing models, and making forecasts. Roll vs. skill to determine the odds of a particular outcome, given sufficient data about similar situations in the past.

Surveying: The science of determining the area of a portion of the Earth's surface, the lengths and directions of the bounding lines, and the contour of the surface. Make a skill roll to determine the dimensions of any area you can see. More complex determinations require specialized equipment. *Defaults:* Cartography-3 or Navigation (any)-4.

These specialties default to one another at -5.

Mechanic/TL†

IQ/Average

Defaults: IQ-5, Engineer (same)-4, or Machinist-5.

This is the ability to diagnose and fix ordinary mechanical problems. A successful skill roll will let you find or repair one problem.

You must pick a specialty from within *one* of these four categories:

Machine Type: Any one class of nonvehicular machine. Types include Micromachines (miniature machinery, invisible to the naked eye; TL9+), Nanomachines (*molecular*-scale machinery; TL10+), and Robotics (robots and automated factories; TL7+).

Motive System Type: Any one type of propulsion system, regardless of vehicle type. Types include Legged, Tracked, Wheeled, Rockets, and Reactionless Thrusters.

Power Plant Type: Any one type of power plant, no matter what it powers. Types include Clockwork, Steam Engine, Gasoline Engine, Diesel Engine, Gas Turbine, Fuel Cell, Fission Reactor, Fusion Reactor, and Antimatter Reactor.

Vehicle Type: The controls, hull, motive system, power plant, transmission, and even the paint job of *one specific type of vehicle* listed under a vehicle-operation skill such as Driving (p. 188), Piloting (p. 214), or Submarine (p. 223).

Mechanic specialties default to one another at -4, although the GM may modify this for particularly close or distant specialties. The systems covered by each specialty vary by TL. For instance, Mechanic (Light Airplane) covers single-engine biplanes at early TL6, small private jets at TL7, and so forth.

Familiarity is very important here. For instance, Mechanic/TL7 (Light Airplane) covers both propeller-powered seaplanes and small private jets, but going from one to the other gives you -2 for an unfamiliar item (prop-powered plane to jet) and -2 for an unfamiliar implementation (seaplane to regular plane), for a net -4 to skill until you familiarize yourself with all the differences.

Modifiers: -2 for an unfamiliar item within your specialty (e.g., a barge when you're used to battleships), or for an unfamiliar implementation (e.g., a powerboat engine when you're used to automobile engines); equipment modifiers (p. 345).

Meditation

Will/Hard

Defaults: Will-6 or Autohypnosis-4.

This is the ability to calm the emotions, control the mind, and relax the body. To use this skill, you must concentrate for (20 - skill) seconds, minimum one second, and then roll vs. skill. On a success, you enter a trance-like state, which you can maintain for hours.

A meditative trance is required for certain rituals and is a common preparation for prayer. In addition, the GM may permit you to meditate on a particular moral dilemma. On a successful Meditation roll, the GM will "enlighten" you, providing a hint as to which course of action "feels" right.

Melee Weapon

DX/Varies

Defaults: Special.

This is not one skill, but an entire *collection* of skills – one per class of closely related melee weapons. Melee Weapon skills are based on DX, and default to DX-4 if Easy, DX-5 if Average, or DX-6 if Hard. See specific skill descriptions for other defaults.

Make a Melee Weapon roll to hit an opponent in combat. You may also use these skills to parry. Your Parry defense is (skill/2) + 3, rounded down.

Melee weapons fall into broad categories on the basis of overall balance and function. When a rule refers to one of these categories, it applies to *all* weapons in that category and *all* Melee Weapon skills used to wield them. For instance, "fencing weapons" means "all weapons used with any of Main-Gauche, Rapier, Saber, or Smallsword skill."

Fencing Weapons

Fencing weapons are light, one-handed weapons, usually hilted blades, optimized for parrying. If you have a fencing weapon, you get an improved retreating bonus when you parry – see *Retreat* (p. 377). Furthermore, you have *half* the usual penalty for parrying more than once with the same hand (see *Parrying*, p. 376).

Note that fencing weapons are *light* and likely to break when used to parry a heavier weapon. They cannot parry flail weapons at all! You must be relatively mobile to capitalize on their speed and maneuverability: all attacks and parries take a penalty equal to your encumbrance level (e.g., Heavy encumbrance gives -3 to hit or to parry).

The skills in this category default to one another at -3. They also default to sword skills, as noted below.

Main-Gauche (DX/Average): Any weapon normally wielded with Knife or Jitte/Sai skill (see below), used in the "off" hand. With this skill, you may ignore the penalty for using the "off" hand on defense (*attacks* are still at -4) and the -1 for parrying with a knife. To wield a knife as a primary weapon, use Knife skill. *Defaults:* Jitte/Sai-4 or Knife-4.

Rapier (DX/Average): Any long (over 1 yard), light thrusting sword. *Default:* Broadsword-4.

Saber (DX/Average): Any light cut-and-thrust sword. Note that *cavalry* sabers are quite heavy, and use Broadsword instead. *Defaults:* Broadsword-4 or Shortsword-4.

Smallsword (DX/Average): Any short (up to 1 yard), light thrusting sword or one-handed short staff (such as the sticks used in the martial arts *arnis*, *escrima*, and *kali*). *Default:* Shortsword-4.

Flails

A *flail* is any flexible, unbalanced weapon with its mass concentrated in the head. Such a weapon cannot parry if you have already attacked with it on your turn. Because flails tend to wrap around the target's shield or weapon, attempts to *block* them are at -2 and attempts to *parry* them are at -4. Fencing weapons and knives cannot parry them at all! An unarmed fighter *can* parry a flail, but at -4 in addition to any penalty for parrying unarmed.

The skills in this category default to one another at -3.

Flail (DX/Hard): Any one-handed flail, such as a morningstar or nunchaku. *Default:* Axe/Mace-4.

Two-Handed Flail (DX/Hard): Any two-handed flail. *Defaults:* Kusari-4 or Two-Handed Axe/Mace-4.

Impact Weapons

An *impact* weapon is any rigid, unbalanced weapon with most of its mass concentrated in the head. Such a weapon cannot parry if you have already attacked with it on your turn.

The skills in this category default to one another at -3.

Axe/Mace (DX/Average): Any short- or medium-length, one-handed impact weapon, such as an axe, hatchet, knobbed club, or pick. *Default:* Flail-4.

Two-Handed Axe/Mace (DX/Average): Any long, two-handed impact weapon, such as a baseball bat, battleaxe, maul, or warhammer. *Defaults:* Polearm-4 or Two-Handed Flail-4.

Pole Weapons

Pole weapons are long (usually wooden) shafts, often adorned with striking heads. All require two hands.

Polearm (DX/Average): Any *very* long (at least 2 yards), unbalanced pole weapon with a heavy striking head, including the glaive, halberd, poleaxe, and countless others. Polearms become *unready* after an attack, but not after a parry. *Defaults:* Spear-4, Staff-4, or Two-Handed Axe/Mace-4.

Spear (DX/Average): Any long, balanced pole weapon with a thrusting point, including spears, javelins, tridents, and fixed bayonets. *Defaults:* Polearm-4 or Staff-2.

Staff (DX/Average): Any long, balanced pole *without* a striking head. This skill makes good use of the staff's extensive parrying surface when defending, giving +2 to your Parry score. *Defaults:* Polearm-4 or Spear-2.

Swords

A *sword* is a rigid, hilted blade with a thrusting point, cutting edge, or both. All swords are balanced, and can attack and parry without becoming unready.

Broadsword (DX/Average): Any *balanced*, 2- to 4-foot blade wielded in one hand – broadsword, cavalry saber, scimitar, etc. This skill also covers any stick or club of similar size and balance to these blades, as well as bastard swords, katanas, and longswords used one-handed. *Defaults:* Force Sword-4, Rapier-4, Saber-4, Shortsword-2, or Two-Handed Sword-4.

Force Sword (DX/Average): Any sword with a "blade" made of energy instead of matter. This generally refers to an ultra-tech weapon that projects energy from a powered hilt, but extends to similar effects produced using magic or psionics. *Default:* any sword skill at -3.

Jitte/Sai (DX/Average): Any tined, one-handed sword designed to catch *rigid* weapons. Jitte/Sai weapons are built for disarming, and give +2 in the Quick Contest to disarm an opponent (see *Knocking a Weapon Away*, p. 401). Furthermore, if you attempt to disarm on the turn *immediately* after you parry your opponent's weapon, you need not roll to hit his weapon first. Just state that you are attempting to disarm and move directly to the Quick Contest! This still counts as an attack. *Defaults:* Force Sword-4, Main-Gauche-4, or Shortsword-3.

Knife (DX/Easy): Any rigid, hilted blade less than one foot long, from a pocketknife to a bowie knife. A knife has a very small parrying surface, which gives you -1 to your Parry score. *Defaults:* Force Sword-3, Main-Gauche-3, or Shortsword-3.

Shortsword (DX/Average): Any *balanced,* one-handed weapon 1-2 feet in length – including the shortsword and any club of comparable size and balance (e.g., a police baton). *Defaults:* Broadsword-2, Force Sword-4, Jitte/Sai-3, Knife-4, Saber-4, Smallsword-4, or Tonfa-3.

Two-Handed Sword (DX/Average): Any *balanced,* two-handed blade over 4 feet in length: greatswords, zweihanders, etc. This skill also covers quarterstaffs wielded like swords, as well as bastard swords, katanas, and longswords used two-handed. *Defaults:* Broadsword-4 or Force Sword-4.

Whips

A *whip* is a flexible weapon made from a length of chain, leather, wire, etc. A whip can be up to seven yards long – but note that a whip two yards or more in length cannot strike at one yard or closer, and is slow to ready after an attack. A whip tends to wind around its target, making it an excellent disarming and entangling weapon. However, a whip's lack of rigidity makes it a poor parrying weapon. For details, see *Special Melee Weapon Rules* (p. 404).

The skills in this category default to one another at -3.

Force Whip (DX/Average): Any whip made of pure energy instead of matter. These are usually ultra-tech devices that project energy from a powered hilt, but magical or psi-tech versions are possible. Most force whips can lash the target but not ensnare him.

Kusari (DX/Hard): A weighted chain wielded in two hands. *Default:* Two-Handed Flail-4.

Monowire Whip (DX/Hard): A whip made of a weighted length of monomolecular wire attached to a handle.

Whip (DX/Average): Any ordinary whip.

Other Weapons

Some hand weapons defy easy classification. For instance:

Tonfa (DX/Average): A tonfa is a baton with a protruding handle on one side. It can function as a baton, but you can also grasp it by the handle and hold it against the forearm in close combat. This grip lets you jab for thrust+1 crushing damage and parry close-combat attacks at (skill/2) + 3, rounded down. Roll vs. skill to change grips. On a success, the grip change is a free action. On a failure, you must spend the entire turn changing grips. A critical failure means you throw your weapon away! *Default:* Shortsword-3.

Mental Strength
Will/Easy

Defaults: None.
Prerequisites: Trained By A Master or Weapon Master*.
* At the GM's option, a mage or psi may also learn this skill.

You can actively focus your mind to resist mental attacks. This skill replaces Will when you resist magic spells, psi powers, Hypnotism, Invisibility Art, Kiai, and similar abilities. Mental Strength does *not* replace most normal Will rolls. Furthermore, it does not work if you are stunned, asleep, or unconscious – for that, buy the Mind Shield advantage (p. 70).

Merchant
IQ/Average

Defaults: IQ-5, Finance-6, or Market Analysis-4.

This is the skill of buying, selling, and trading retail and wholesale goods. It involves bargaining, salesmanship, and an understanding of trade practices. It covers all types of merchandise, but many merchants have an *optional* specialty (p. 169) in a single class of goods.

Make a skill roll to judge the value of any piece of common goods, find out where any commodity is bought and sold, find the local fair market value of any commodity, etc.

When two merchants haggle, the GM may settle it with a Quick Contest. The winner adds or subtracts 10% of fair value, depending on whether he was trying to sell or buy.

If you have this skill at *any* level, you get +1 on reaction rolls when buying or selling. If you have this skill at level 20 or better, you get +2.

Modifiers: -3 for Gullibility (p. 137); -3 for Low Empathy (p. 142); -1 to -4 for Shyness (p. 154). -3 for illegal goods, unless you have Streetwise at 12+ or specialize in such goods; -2 in an unfamiliar area, until you have had time to familiarize yourself with local market conditions; Cultural Familiarity modifiers (p. 23). These last two modifiers "stack," and frequently occur together.

Metallurgy/TL
IQ/Hard

Defaults: Chemistry-5, Jeweler-8, or Smith (any)-8.

This is the study of metals and their properties. A successful roll lets you identify metals or alloys, or solve a problem concerning metals, their use, mining, or refining.

Meteorology/TL†
IQ/Average

Default: IQ-5.

This is the study of the weather, and the ability to predict it. It includes familiarity with technological aids such as barometers and satellite maps, but you can still function without your instruments. (If you can't, you're a meter-reader, not a meteorologist!)

When you wish to predict the weather, the GM rolls against your skill in secret. On a success, he tells the truth; on a failure, he answers randomly, or *lies.* Each skill roll predicts the weather for one day. If one day's roll fails, subsequent ones can't succeed. For instance, a three-day forecast would require three skill rolls: the first for tomorrow, the second for the next day, and the third for the day after that.

A successful roll also allows you to deduce what sort of *general* climate to expect when you visit a new area.

At TL4 or less, this skill is called Weather Sense, and you get +2 to skill in your home area. At TL5 and up, Meteorology is a scientific skill, and you *must* specialize by planet type; see *Planet Types* (p. 180) for details.

Modifiers: Time is a major factor! There is no penalty to predict tomorrow's weather, but you have -1 for 2 days, -2 for 3 days, -4 for 4 days, -6 for 5 days, and an additional -2 per day for each further day. Instrumentation becomes useful with the development of the barometer at TL4, after which equipment modifiers (p. 345) apply. You must know this skill at better than default to claim bonuses for good equipment.

Mimicry†

IQ/Hard

Defaults: IQ-6 and others.

This is the ability to imitate voices. The Voice advantage (p. 97) gives +2 to skill. You *must* specialize:

Animal Sounds: Lets you emulate a lion's roar, a wolf's howl, a frog's croak, etc. You can only imitate animals that have distinctive sounds. Make a skill roll to attract animals of the type mimicked – or predators that normally hunt those animals – if any are nearby. To fool *people*, you must win a Quick Contest of Mimicry vs. the listeners' Naturalist-3 or Perception-6. *Default:* Naturalist-6.

Bird Calls: Allows you to reproduce the whistles, chirps, and other sounds made by birds. Otherwise, this works as Animal Sounds. *Default:* Naturalist-6.

Speech: Enables you to imitate vocal sounds. This does not allow you to converse in a foreign language, but if you have heard it, you can reproduce the *sound* of it. If you are trying to mimic a specific person, roll at -3. Treat this roll as a Quick Contest vs. the IQ of anyone who knows the person mimicked well. *Defaults:* Acting-6 or Linguistics-4.

Animal Sounds and Bird Calls default to one another at -6. There is no default between these specialties and Speech.

Note that if you have the Mimicry *advantage* (p. 68), there is no need to learn this skill!

Mind Block

Will/Average

Defaults: Will-5 or Meditation-5.

This ability allows you to establish a mental block against psionic or magical attempts to eavesdrop on your thoughts and emotions. The techniques involved are wholly mundane – for instance, doing complicated mathematical calculations, or repeating poetry over and over again. With sufficient training, *anyone* can learn this skill.

To maintain a block, you must make a Mind Block roll once per minute. You must roll every *second* in combat or other stressful situations.

If you succeed, anyone who reads your mind must *win* a Quick Contest of his mind-reading ability vs. your Mind Block skill in order to get useful information. Otherwise, he gets nothing but poetry, multiplication tables, etc. However, if you ever critically fail a Mind Block roll, you thought about precisely what the mind reader wanted to know – in detail – right there in the forefront of your mind!

This skill only works against mind *reading*, not mind control or other mental attacks. If you have a supernatural mind shield, Mind Block acts as a last-ditch defense: only mental probes that pierce your magical or psionic defenses and contact your mind will encounter the block.

Modifiers: +2 if you do nothing but concentrate on blocking; -3 if you are mentally or physically stunned; -2 or more to hide *emotions* rather than thoughts, depending on how strong the GM rules your emotions are – it's hard to block your emotions while sneaking up on your most hated enemy!

Monowire Whip

see *Melee Weapon*, p. 208

Mount

DX/Average

Default: DX-5.

This is the trained ability to serve as a mount for a rider. If your Mount skill exceeds your rider's Riding level, he may use the average of the two skills (round *up*) whenever he must make a Riding roll. If you have *any* points in this skill, your rider gets a minimum +1 to skill. To throw an unwelcome rider, win Quick Contest of Mount vs. his Riding skill.

Musical Composition

IQ/Hard

Defaults: Musical Instrument-2, or to Poetry-2 for song.

This is the ability to compose a piece of music. A successful skill roll means the piece is a pleasant listening experience.

To compose for an ensemble or band *without* a conductor, you must have a skill level of IQ with at least one instrument in the composition and a skill level of IQ-2 with the rest. Roll at -1 per "instrument group" after the first used in the piece; e.g., a jazz composition for a saxophone section, drums, and bass would require a roll at -2.

To compose for an orchestra or band *with* a conductor requires Group Performance (Conducting) skill (p. 198) at IQ level. Roll at -1 per general *class* of instruments after the first used in the piece. Classes include brass, percussion, strings, and woodwinds. Treat choir, harp, organ, or piano as its own class.

This skill includes the ability to read, write, and transcribe music in your culture's notation system (if any). Treat different systems – and different musical traditions – as familiarities (see *Familiarity*, p. 169).

Musical Influence

IQ/Very Hard

Defaults: None.
Prerequisites: Musical Ability 1 and either Musical Instrument or Singing at 12+.

This cinematic skill allows you to influence the emotions of others by playing a musical instrument or singing. In some settings, this is a magical or psionic talent, or a special form of hypnotism, and works with *any* instrument, as well as with voice. In other settings, this skill is associated with a specific type of magical or ultra-tech instrument.

To attempt Musical Influence, you must first get your audience to sit and listen to your performance. You must also make a successful Musical Instrument or Singing roll. You may then roll against your Musical Influence skill. On a success, you can adjust the reaction roll of your audience – to you or to anyone present – up *or* down by an amount equal to your margin of success, to a maximum of +3 (+4 for critical success).

If you have only a few seconds, or if the audience is not paying full attention to your performance, you may adjust reaction rolls by ±1 at most, regardless of your margin of success.

Listeners who do not wish to be influenced may resist with Will. Hard of Hearing (p. 138) gives +4 to resist, and those with Deafness (p. 129) are completely immune. However, some science-fiction devices generate vibrations that affect the *body*, in which case a listener's sense of hearing is irrelevant.

It is up to the GM to determine whether this skill works on animals as well as sapient beings. In classic fantasy, it just might!

Musical Instrument†
IQ/Hard

Defaults: Special.

This is the ability to play a musical instrument. With a successful skill roll, you give a competent performance. You *must* specialize in a particular instrument. Defaults between specialties range from -3 for similar instruments to "no default" for utterly unrelated ones, such as Musical Instrument (Drums) and Musical Instrument (Harp).

This skill includes the ability to read music in your culture's notation system (if any). Treat different systems as familiarities (see *Familiarity*, p. 169).

Naturalist†
IQ/Hard

Defaults: IQ-6 or Biology-3.

This skill – crucial for fantasy druids and rangers – represents *practical* (as opposed to scientific) knowledge of nature in its many forms. It includes just enough Biology to tell dangerous plants and animals from benign ones; just enough Geology to locate a cave to shelter in; and just enough Meteorology to know when to take shelter. Roll vs. skill to do any of these things.

In settings where it is possible to visit other worlds, you must specialize by *planet*. The specialties for planets of the same type (see *Planet Types*, p. 180) default to one another at -4. Any larger difference results in no default.

Navigation/TL†
IQ/Average

Defaults: Special.

This is the ability to find your position through careful observation of your surroundings and the use of instrumentation. A successful roll tells you where you are or lets you plot a course.

You *must* specialize:

Sea: Navigation by the stars and ocean currents. *Modifiers:* +3 if you have Absolute Direction (p. 34), or a high-tech global positioning system or inertial compass; -5 (and no use of Astronomy default) if you lack high-tech aids, the weather is bad, and the stars are hidden. *Defaults:* Astronomy-5 or Seamanship-5.

Air: Navigation by the stars and by the terrain below. Modifiers are as for Navigation (Sea). *Default:* Astronomy-5.

Land: Navigation using landmarks and the stars; also called "orienteering." *Modifiers:* +3 if you have Absolute Direction or a high-tech substitute. *Defaults:* IQ-5, Cartography-4, or Mathematics (Surveying)-4.

Space: Navigating through ordinary interplanetary and interstellar space, usually at less than the speed of light (but some science-fiction "warp drives" let you travel at faster-than-light speeds in normal space). *Modifiers:* +2 for 3D Spatial Sense (p. 34). *Defaults:* Astronomy-4 or Mathematics (Applied)-4.

Hyperspace: Also called "astrogation." Similar to Navigation (Space), but used when traveling through "jump space" or "hyperspace." In settings with multiple faster-than-light drive technologies, there may be one Navigation specialty per drive type. Modifiers are as for Navigation (Space). *Defaults:* Astronomy-4 or Mathematics (Applied)-4.

Air, Land, and Sea default to one another at -2. Space and Hyperspace default to one another at -5. There are *no* defaults between these two groups.

Modifiers: -1 to -10 for being in an unfamiliar area (GM's discretion, but an unfamiliar world, star system, etc. should give at least -5); equipment modifiers (p. 345).

NBC Suit/TL
see *Environment Suit*, p. 192

Net
DX/Hard

Default: Cloak-5.

This is the ability to use a net as a thrown or melee weapon. For detailed net rules, see *Special Ranged Weapons* (p. 410).

Observation
Per/Average

Defaults: Perception-5 or Shadowing-5.

This is the talent of observing dangerous or "interesting" situations without letting others know that you are watching. Use this skill to monitor a location, a group of people, or your immediate surroundings for concealed or tactically significant details. This is not the same as gathering clues or making a hands-on search (use Forensics and Search, respectively) – you always use Observation from a distance.

A successful skill roll lets you gather information that is not specifically hidden. For instance, you could case a bank for obvious cameras before a robbery, learn the schedule of sentries, estimate the size of a crowd, or gauge the strength of troops moving in the open. The GM may require an Intelligence Analysis roll to *interpret* what you observe.

To spot deliberately hidden details – e.g., someone trying to sneak up on you, an armed man hiding in the crowd, or a concealed machine-gun nest – you must win a Quick Contest of Observation skill vs. the Stealth, Shadowing, or Camouflage skill (as appropriate) of the other party. The GM should roll the Contest in secret, and should *not* say, "You don't see the machine gun nest concealed in the bushes."

If your attempt fails, you get no details on an obvious item, or fail to spot a hidden one. On a critical failure, someone spots *you* and reacts poorly to the attention . . .

Modifiers: Acute Senses (p. 35), as appropriate; modifiers for cover, darkness, or size; -1 to -10 if the target is concealed by high-tech camouflage or "stealth" technology; +1 to +10 if you possess suitable surveillance devices (a thermograph to spot a concealed sniper, binoculars to observe troop movements, etc.) and succeed at the skill roll to operate them.

Occultism

IQ/Average

Default: IQ-5.

This is the study of the mysterious and the supernatural. An occultist is an expert on ancient rituals, hauntings, mysticism, primitive magical beliefs, psychic phenomena, etc. Note that an occultist does not have to *believe* in the material he studies!

In worlds where everyone knows that paranormal powers exist, Occultism covers lore about these powers and their users. A good roll might provide insights into phenomena that *aren't* related to known powers. However, Occultism provides no details on how talented individuals invoke their powers. For instance, a fantasy occultist would know what magic can accomplish, and could provide advice on slaying demons, but without Thaumatology skill (p. 225), he could not explain the gestures, words, and symbols used by wizards.

In campaigns where many supernatural forces coexist, the GM may *require* occultists to specialize in such fields as Demonology (the study of demons, possession, and pacts), Pneumatology (the study of spirits), and Vampirology (the study of vampires).

Packing

IQ/Average

Defaults: IQ-5 or Animal Handling (Equines)-5.

This is the ability to get loads on and off of pack animals quickly and efficiently. It also lets you get the best performance from pack animals on the road, judge such beasts before purchase, and select the best route for a pack train. If the beasts are ornery or badly trained (GM's judgment), you must make a successful Animal Handling roll before you can attempt a Packing roll. A caravan without at least one master packer (Packing at 15+) moves at 80% its normal speed.

Paleontology/TL†

IQ/Hard

Defaults: Biology-4 and others.

This is the science of fossil study. Make a skill roll to recognize fossils or to deduce an organism's habitat,

structure, etc. from fossil evidence. A successful roll – with equipment modifiers (p. 345) for lab facilities – identifies the approximate age of a fossil.

You *must* specialize:

Micropaleontology: The study of fossils too small to be seen with the naked eye. This skill *requires* a lab.

Paleoanthropology: The study of human fossils and tools, and the relation of primitive tribes to their habitats. Also defaults to Anthropology-2.

Paleobotany: The study of vegetable fossils.

Paleozoology: The study of prehistoric animals from fossilized bones, food, feces, footprints, etc.

These specialties default to one another at -2.

Note that an occultist does not have to believe in the material he studies!

Panhandling

IQ/Easy

Defaults: IQ-4, Fast Talk-2, or Public Speaking-3.

This is the art of effective begging: who to approach, how to approach them, and how to avoid legal entanglements. Roll once per hour of begging.

On a success, you net $2.00 times your margin of success. On a critical success, you get some sort of unexpected bonus – perhaps someone buys you dinner or gives you a useful or saleable item (e.g., a raincoat or a new pair of shoes). On a failure, you receive nothing. On a critical failure, you are assaulted or have a run-in with the law.

Modifiers: Any bonus for Charisma (p. 41); +3 for Pitiable (p. 22); -1 to -4 for Shyness (p. 154). You may, if you wish, apply the *opposite* of your usual appearance modifier – that is, a penalty for being attractive or a bonus for being unattractive – unless you are Horrific or Monstrous (p. 21). The GM may assign a bonus if there is a lot of foot traffic in the area, or a penalty if there is no one around.

Parachuting/TL

DX/Easy

Default: DX-4.

This is the ability to survive a parachute jump. Roll once per jump. Failure could mean anything from drifting off course to panic that makes you drop your gear (GM's option). A critical failure means the chute did not open or was fatally fouled (see *Falling*, p. 431). For a jump under bad conditions, make a second roll on landing – for instance, to survive an "ankle-breaker" landing without injury, or to dodge trees on the way down. Make an IQ-based roll to *pack* a parachute.

Modifiers: -2 if your body weight plus encumbrance exceeds your Basic Lift×10.

Parry Missile Weapons

DX/Hard

Defaults: None.

This skill lets you parry thrown or missile weapons with a ready melee weapon. If you are wearing wristbands or gloves with DR 2+, or have at least this much natural DR, you can also parry with your hands. Your Parry score is (skill/2) + 3, rounded down – but based on Parry Missile Weapons skill, *not* your Melee Weapon or unarmed combat skill.

Modifiers (to Parry): +4 to parry large thrown weapons (e.g., axes and spears); +2 to parry small thrown weapons (e.g., knives and shuriken); no modifier to parry arrows; -2 to parry smaller low-tech missiles (e.g., crossbow bolts and blowpipe darts). You cannot parry bullets or similar high-tech projectiles! (*Exception:* Enhanced Time Sense allows you to parry bullets at -5.)

Performance

IQ/Average

Defaults: IQ-5, Acting-2, or Public Speaking-2.

This is the ability to act on the stage or screen. It is different from Acting in that you are trying to impress and entertain people – not *deceive* them. If you studied this skill formally, it includes the knowledge expected of a professional actor from your culture and tech level (stage directions, actor-agent-producer relations, etc.).

Modifiers: +2 for Voice (p. 97); -1 to -4 for Shyness (p. 154); -2 for Stuttering (p. 157).

Persuade
see *Enthrallment*, p. 191

Pharmacy/TL†
IQ/Hard
Defaults: IQ-6 and others.

This is the skill of preparing medicines to treat illness. (To work with *noxious* drugs, use Poisons skill, p. 214.) You *must* specialize:

Herbal: The ability to make and administer remedies prepared from plants. Make a Naturalist roll to *locate* herbs. Before TL5, this is the only specialty available. It replaces Physician (below) and is frequently used in conjunction with Esoteric Medicine (p. 192). At TL5+, this specialty remains available, but Pharmacy (Synthetic) is much more common. *Prerequisite:* Naturalist. *Defaults:* Biology-5, Herb Lore-5, or Naturalist-5.

Synthetic: The skill of preparing drugs under "laboratory" conditions. To *prescribe* drugs, use Physician skill. This specialty is only available at TL5+. *Defaults:* Chemistry-5 or Physician-5.

Philosophy†
IQ/Hard
Default: IQ-6.

This is the study of a system of principles to live by. You *must* specialize in a particular school of philosophy; e.g., Confucianism, Marxism, or Stoicism. (If you study a *religious* philosophy, buy Theology skill, p. 226.) When confronted with someone who subscribes to this philosophy, a successful Philosophy roll might provide insights into his behavior.

You do not necessarily believe in the ideals of the philosophy you study. If you do, you may ask the GM to make a secret roll against your Philosophy skill when you are faced with a moral dilemma. On a success, the GM will "enlighten" you and provide a hint as to which course of action "feels" right given your beliefs.

Photography/TL
IQ/Average
Defaults: IQ-5 or Electronics Operation (Media)-5.

This is the ability to use a camera competently, use a darkroom (TL5+) or digital imaging software (TL8+), etc., and to produce recognizable and attractive photos. You may roll at default to use a camera, but not to develop film or prints in a darkroom.

Modifiers: -3 for an unfamiliar camera; -3 for a motion-picture camera.

Physician/TL
IQ/Hard
Defaults: IQ-7, First Aid-11, or Veterinary-5.

This is the ability to aid the sick and the injured, prescribe drugs and care, etc. Make a skill roll to hasten natural recovery from injury (see *Recovery*, p. 423), and whenever the GM requires a roll to test general medical competence or knowledge. Apply physiology modifiers (p. 181) if your patient is of a different species from you.

At TL4 and below, *this skill does not exist* in most game worlds. Instead, use Esoteric Medicine (p. 192), Pharmacy (Herbal) (above), or both.

At TL5+, medical knowledge is divided between Pharmacy (Synthetic) and Physician. A physician knows a great deal about drugs. He can identify most drugs fairly easily (at -5 without laboratory facilities but +3 if he takes the risk of smelling/tasting the substance), but he cannot *formulate* them unless he also learns Pharmacy.

Physics/TL
IQ/Very Hard
Default: IQ-6.
Prerequisite: Mathematics (Applied) at TL5+.

This is the science dealing with the properties and interactions of matter and energy. Beyond the basics (such as the behavior of moving bodies), a physicist's knowledge includes whatever is understood about electricity, gravity, heat, light, magnetism, radiation, and sound at his tech level.

At TL6+, most physicists have an *optional* specialty (p. 169): acoustics, astrophysics, geophysics, nuclear physics, optics, particle physics, quantum physics, relativity, solid-state physics, etc. Some settings offer exotic options, such as hyperspace physics (the science of hyperspace and jump points), parachronic physics (the study of other realities and timelines), paraphysics (the physics of psi phenomena), probability physics (the study of probability manipulation), and temporal physics (the science of time travel).

Physiology/TL†
IQ/Hard
Defaults: IQ-6, Diagnosis-5, Physician-5, or Surgery-5.

This is the study of the human body and its function. A physiologist knows how bones, muscles, and organs work, and where they are located. In settings with multiple sapient species, you *must* specialize by race. Defaults between species (if any) are up to the GM.

Pickpocket
DX/Hard
Defaults: DX-6, Filch-5, or Sleight of Hand-4.

This is the ability to steal a purse, knife, etc., from someone's person – or to "plant" something on him.

If your victim is aware someone may try to pick his pocket, or if he is generally wary, you must win a Quick Contest of Pickpocket vs. the *higher* of his Perception or Streetwise skill. To outwit a third party who is watching you and the victim, you must win a Quick Contest of Pickpocket vs. the watcher's Observation skill.

Modifiers: +5 if the victim is distracted; +10 if he is asleep or drunk; up to -5 for goods in an inner pocket; and up to -10 for a ring or similar jewelry.

Piloting/TL†

DX/Average

Default: IQ-6.

This is the ability to operate a specific type of aircraft or spacecraft. The default is to IQ, because it takes intelligence to figure out the controls in an emergency, but when you *learn* this skill, always base it on DX.

Roll against Piloting for takeoffs and landings, and in any hazardous situation. Failure by 1 indicates a rough job; failure by more indicates damage to the vehicle. A critical failure is a crash! If you have skill 15+, a critical failure requires an immediate second roll. Only if the second roll is a failure does a mishap occur. Otherwise, it was a "near thing," averted by experience. Air combat requires frequent Piloting rolls as well.

Make an IQ-based Piloting roll for basic map reading or practical meteorology, or to recall aviation laws and regulations.

Remotely piloted vehicles (RPVs) use this skill if the pilot uses some form of telepresence to mimic actually being in the cockpit. Otherwise, make a DX-based roll against the appropriate skill for the task the RPV is performing (e.g., Forward Observer for a surveillance drone).

You *must* specialize:

Aerospace: Any vehicle capable of atmospheric flight to and from orbit. *Defaults:* High-Performance Airplane-2 or other Piloting at -4.

Autogyro: Any rotor-equipped aircraft that uses its rotors for lift but not thrust. *Defaults:* Helicopter-3, any Airplane specialty at -4, or other Piloting at -5.

Contragravity: Any aircraft that relies on ultra-tech or magical levitation. *Defaults:* Vertol-3 or other Piloting at -5.

Flight Pack: Any "strap-on" aircraft. *Defaults:* Vertol-4 or other Piloting at -5.

Glider: Any kind of unpowered, winged aircraft. *Defaults:* Light Airplane or Ultralight at -2, or other Piloting at -4.

Heavy Airplane: Any winged aircraft weighing over 10 tons and flying at 600 mph or slower. *Defaults:* High-Performance Airplane or Light Airplane at -2, or other Piloting at -4.

Helicopter: Any aircraft that uses rotors for both lift and thrust. *Defaults:* Autogyro-2, Vertol-4, or other Piloting at -5.

High-Performance Airplane: Any winged aircraft capable of flying faster than 600 mph. *Defaults:* Aerospace, Heavy Airplane, or Light Airplane at -2, or other Piloting at -4.

High-Performance Spacecraft: Any space vehicle capable of accelerations of 0.1G or more. *Defaults:* Aerospace-4 or Low-Performance Spacecraft-2.

Light Airplane: Any winged aircraft weighing 10 tons or less and flying at 600 mph or slower. *Defaults:* Glider, Heavy Airplane, High-Performance Airplane, or Ultralight at -2, or other Piloting at -4.

Lighter-Than-Air: Any kind of airship or balloon. *Default:* other Piloting at -5.

Lightsail: Any spacecraft that uses a lightsail, regardless of thrust. *Default:* Low-Performance Spacecraft-4.

Low-G Wings: Muscle-powered strap-on wings used in a low-gravity environment with an atmosphere. Learn Flight (p. 195) for endurance flying. *Default:* Glider-4.

Low-Performance Spacecraft: Any space vehicle that accelerates at less than 0.1G. *Defaults:* Aerospace-4 or High-Performance Spacecraft-2.

Ultralight: Any winged aircraft weighing 0.5 tons or less and flying at 200 mph or slower. *Defaults:* Glider or Light Airplane at -2, other Airplane specialties at -4, or other Piloting at -5.

Vertol: Any aircraft that flies by brute-force application of thrust rather than by using rotors or wings. *Defaults:* Contragravity-3, Helicopter-4, or other Piloting at -5.

Modifiers: +1 for 3D Spatial Sense (p. 34); +1 for Perfect Balance (p. 74). -2 for an unfamiliar vehicle within your specialty (e.g., a twin-engine plane when you are used to single-engine craft); -2 or more for unusually primitive *or* extremely complex controls; -4 or more for a plane in bad repair; -2 or more for bad flying conditions.

Poetry

IQ/Average

Defaults: IQ-5 or Writing-5.

This is the ability to compose "good" poetry of any type native to your culture, in any language you know. A successful roll lets you write one good poem in an appropriate amount of time (GM's decision). A failed roll might mean that you couldn't get inspired – or that your audience just didn't care for your work (for whatever reason).

Modifiers: The time modifiers under *Time Spent* (p. 346) will often apply; Cultural Familiarity modifiers (p. 23); Language modifiers (p. 23).

Poisons/TL

IQ/Hard

Defaults: IQ-6, Chemistry-5, Pharmacy (any)-3, or Physician-3.

This skill represents practical knowledge of poisons. A successful skill roll lets you (among other things) recognize a poison-bearing plant in the wild; extract the poison in a useful form; recognize a poison by its taste in food or drink; identify a poison by observing its effects (+3 if *you* are poisoned); know a proper antidote; or recognize or prepare the antidote from its sources. Each of these feats requires a separate roll.

Modifiers: Acute Taste and Smell (p. 35) gives a bonus to notice or recognize a poison by taste or by scent. Likewise, Discriminatory Smell and Discriminatory Taste (p. 49) give +4 to these tasks when working by smell or by taste, respectively.

Polearm

see *Melee Weapon,* p. 208

Politics

IQ/Average

Defaults: IQ-5 or Diplomacy-5.

This is the ability to get into office and get along with other politicians. It has nothing to do with administration! You can only learn Politics in office or by working for someone in office. A successful skill roll will give you +2 on reactions from fellow politicians. The GM may opt to handle an election as a Quick Contest of Politics.

Modifiers: +2 for Voice (p. 97); -3 for Low Empathy (p. 142); -1 to -4 for Shyness (p. 154). In some jurisdictions, money is another important modifier . . .

Power Blow

Will/Hard

Defaults: None.
Prerequisites: Trained By A Master or Weapon Master.

This is the ability to draw on your inner strength to deliver a devastating blow in melee combat. Roll once per attack. Power Blow costs 1 FP per attempt, successful or not.

If successful, double your ST for damage purposes for the *next attack only.* This attack takes all normal modifiers, and must occur immediately after the Power Blow roll. If you know Power Blow at better than skill 20, you

can *triple* your ST by accepting an extra -10 to the skill roll.

You can also use this skill in noncombat situations. For instance, you could use Power Blow to double or triple your ST momentarily in order to move a heavy object. Such feats cost 1 FP and require a skill roll, as described above.

Modifiers: -10 if used *instantly,* dropping to -5 after 1 turn of concentration, -4 after 2 turns, -3 after 4 turns, -2 after 8 turns, -1 after 16 turns, and no penalty after 32 turns.

Pressure Points

IQ/Hard

Defaults: None*.
Prerequisites: Trained By A Master or Weapon Master.
* May default to Esoteric Medicine-4 in a cinematic campaign.

This is the art of striking pressure points in order to disable an opponent. To use this ability, you must make a successful attack with Karate (or other appropriate combat skill; see below). This attack is at -2 in addition to any hit location modifier (see *Hit Location,* p. 398). If at least one point of damage penetrates the target's DR, roll a Quick Contest of Pressure Points vs. the victim's HT.

If you win, you temporarily disable your target. A limb is paralyzed and effectively crippled for 5d seconds. A hit to a torso pressure point interferes with the victim's breathing, resulting in suffocation (see *Suffocation,* p. 436); he may roll against HT every second to recover. A hit to the face stuns the victim; he gets an IQ roll every second to recover. A blow to the skull blinds the victim for 2d seconds; see *Blindness* (p. 124).

You can also use Pressure Points with Judo. Roll the Quick Contest described above after successfully applying a lock. This is *in addition to* any other effects of the lock.

The GM may permit warriors to learn specialties of this skill for use with crushing weapons. Examples include Pressure Points (Bow) for use with blunt arrows, Pressure Points (Shortsword) for use with a baton, and Pressure Points (Staff) for use with a staff.

Modifiers: Physiology modifiers (p. 181).

Pressure Secrets

IQ/Very Hard

Defaults: None.
Prerequisites: Trained By A Master and Pressure Points at 16+.

This skill represents knowledge of the most vulnerable vital points of the human body. It allows you to maim and kill by crushing and tearing vital organs and nerve clusters with deadly precision.

To use this ability, you must make a successful unarmed attack. This attack is at -2 in addition to any hit location modifier (see *Hit Location,* p. 398). If you hit, make a Pressure Secrets roll.

On a success, any damage that penetrates DR is *doubled* – or *tripled* if you targeted the vital organs. In effect, your hands and feet have become impaling weapons!

You can also use this ability with locks and similar grappling attacks. This represents knowledge of exactly where to apply pressure to tear or sprain joints and ligaments. After applying the lock, make a Pressure Secrets roll. On a success, double the damage, shock, or harmful effects of the lock *for that turn.*

This skill is unrealistic and potentially unbalancing. The GM should carefully weigh its impact before allowing it, and may wish to make it very difficult for PCs to learn – or even restrict it to deadly NPC opponents.

Modifiers: Physiology modifiers (p. 181).

Professional Skill

DX or IQ/Average

Defaults: Special.

Many realistic job skills are more useful for making a living than for adventuring. Most such skills do not appear in this skill list – but you can still learn them if you want! Each is a separate Professional Skill. If your "adventuring" skills aren't useful for earning money, a Professional Skill can help you earn a steady income. To qualify for most jobs, you will need the relevant Professional Skill at 12+ (unless you are *supposed* to be incompetent!).

Most professions encompass a body of knowledge. The associated Professional Skills are IQ/Average and default to IQ-5, because the smarter you are, the better you can recall and employ the techniques used at your job. Examples include air traffic controller, barber, brewer, cooper, distiller, dyer, florist, game designer, journalist, prostitute, tanner, vintner, and zookeeper.

A few professions – glassblower, tailor, weaver, etc. – focus more on precision than on recall. These Professional Skills are DX/Average and default to DX-5.

At the GM's option, a given Professional Skill might also default to other skills. For instance, "Journalist" would logically default to Writing-3.

The skills associated with highly paid or respected professions often have prerequisites. For instance, "Air Traffic Controller" might require Electronics Operation (Sensors) skill. Like defaults, prerequisites are up to the GM.

You are free to create your own Professional Skills, subject to GM approval. They should be unique and well defined, *not* just a compilation of existing skills. For example:

Bartender

IQ/Average

Defaults: IQ-5 or Carousing-3.

This is the skill of maintaining a professional-quality bar and interacting with customers in a professional yet friendly way. A successful skill roll lets you mix drinks, recall local laws regarding alcohol, gauge the intoxication level of a customer, or calm an unruly drunk before the bouncer needs to get involved. At higher levels, this skill takes on an element of showmanship, allowing you to present drinks in unique and attractive ways, and to mix them with showy tricks and flourishes.

Propaganda/TL

IQ/Average

Defaults: IQ-5, Merchant-5, or Psychology-4.

This is the skill of indirect persuasion through the media. It is used for psychological warfare by intelligence and military organizations, and for advertising and marketing in the civilian world. Use familiarity (p. 169) to reflect the differences between these areas.

Propaganda works on groups, not individuals. The GM should set the effective Will of the target group based on its size, composition, and resistance to the desired outcome, and then use the *Influence Rolls* (p. 359) rules to determine the results. Success might inform the target audience or even alter its perceptions. Propaganda attempts nearly always take more time and exposure than ordinary Influence rolls, however; how much time is up to the GM.

Prospecting/TL

IQ/Average

Defaults: IQ-5 or Geology (any)-4.

This is the skill of finding valuable minerals. A successful Prospecting roll lets you locate minerals, judge good ore from a small sample (and gauge its commercial value), and find water by using an "eye for country," as described for Survival skill (p. 223).

This skill is "applied geology," and *requires* on-site examination. Prospecting from a distance – using maps, instrument readings, and extrapolation – uses Geology skill instead.

Modifiers: Equipment modifiers (p. 345); -1 in a new area of a familiar type, or -2 or more in an unfamiliar type of area, until you have been there for at least a month.

Psychology

IQ/Hard

Defaults: IQ-6 or Sociology-4.

This is the skill of *applied* psychology, which may be learned by academic study or lengthy observation of human nature. Roll against skill to predict the *general* behavior of an individual or small group in a particular situation – especially a stressful situation.

In settings with multiple sapient species, you *must* specialize by race. Defaults between specialties are up to the GM.

If the GM desires extra detail, he may rule that Psychology is split into two specialties: Applied (described above) and Experimental (for scientists who run rats in mazes and so forth). Applied defaults to Experimental-5; Experimental does not default to Applied, as a shrewd observer of people may lack training in scientific procedures.

Modifiers: +3 if you know the subject well; +3 if the subject is of a known deviant personality type; +1 for Sensitive *or* +3 for Empathy (p. 51), or -3 for Low Empathy (p. 142), if diagnosing a subject in your presence; -3 for Callous (p. 125), unless specifically rolling to deduce someone's weaknesses so you can exploit them.

Public Speaking

IQ/Average

Defaults: IQ-5, Acting-5, Performance-2, or Politics-5.

This is general talent with the spoken word. A successful skill roll lets you (for instance) give a good political speech, entertain a group around a campfire, incite or calm a riot, or put on a successful "court jester" act.

Public Speaking includes skill with debate, oratory, and rhetoric, as well as ability with less formal activities such as "punning" and storytelling. Not all speakers possess talent in all of these areas. You may take an *optional* specialty (p. 169) to represent this.

Modifiers: Any bonus for Charisma (p. 41); +2 for Voice (p. 97); -1 to -4 for Shyness (p. 154); -2 for Stuttering (p. 157); Cultural Familiarity modifiers (p. 23); Language modifiers (p. 24).

Push

DX/Hard

Defaults: None.
Prerequisite: Trained By A Master.

This skill allows you to channel your *chi* in order to "gently" push away an adversary or cause him to lose his balance. Roll against Push skill to hit. This counts as a barehanded attack (see *Shove*, p. 372), and your target may attempt any legal active defense.

If you hit, use the *higher* of your ST or your Push skill as your effective ST. Roll *swing* damage for that ST, and double the result. For instance, if you had ST 10 and Push-15, you would roll swing damage for ST 15 (2d+1), and double it. This damage inflicts knockback (see *Knockback*, p. 378) but *never* actual physical injury.

Rapier

see *Melee Weapon,* p. 208

Religious Ritual†

IQ/Hard

Defaults: Ritual Magic (same)-6 or Theology (same)-4.

This is the ability to perform religious rites – masses, funerals, weddings, etc. – before a congregation. You *must* specialize by religion. This skill includes detailed knowledge of the ritual motions, prayers, and trappings of the faith, as well as the ability to capture and hold the attention of worshipers. For religions that practice sacrifice, Religious Ritual also covers familiarity with sacrificial tools and methods.

To be a priest or holy man at TL1+, you must have both Religious Ritual *and* Theology skill (p. 226) for your religion. TL0 shamans need only learn Religious Ritual.

In worlds where priests can perform miracles, each *magical* ritual or spell is a separate skill, but certain "mundane" religious rituals – such as sacrifice – can give bonuses to spell rolls. You must always make a successful Religious Ritual roll to claim such a bonus. In other settings, a priest's magic is only as good as his ritual. If this is the case, your roll to work magic is against the *lower* of Religious Ritual and your actual spell skill.

Research/TL

IQ/Average

Defaults: IQ-5 or Writing-3.

Prerequisite: literacy in at least one language (see p. 24)*.

* At TL8+, Computer Operation is also a prerequisite.

This is the ability to do library and file research. Roll against skill to find a useful piece of data in an appropriate place of research . . . *if* the information is there to be found.

At the GM's option, when researching material connected with a "book-learned" skill such as Forensics, Literature, or Physics, you may roll against that skill at -2 instead, if that would be better than your Research skill or default (but this is *not* a general default level).

Modifiers: Language modifiers (p. 24), for research materials in a foreign tongue.

Riding†

DX/Average

Defaults: DX-5 or Animal Handling (same)-3.

This is the ability to ride a particular kind of mount. Make a skill roll when you first try to mount a riding animal, and again each time something happens to frighten or challenge the creature (e.g., a jump).

You *must* specialize by riding beast. Defaults between specialties vary from 0 to -10. For instance, if you have Riding (Horse), Riding (Mule) is essentially the same skill (no default penalty), Riding (Camel) would default at -3, Riding (Dolphin) at -6, and Riding (Dragon) at a whopping -10!

Modifiers: +5 if the animal knows and likes you; +1 or more for a mount with the Mount skill (p. 210); -10 if the animal has not been trained for riding.

Ritual Magic†

IQ/Very Hard

Default: Religious Ritual (same)-6.

This skill gives an understanding of the intellectual and mystical processes involved in the rituals of a particular tradition of spirit invocation. Make a skill roll to determine the purpose of a ritual conducted in your presence, the type of entity being summoned, etc.

You *must* specialize by tradition; e.g., Voodoo or Witchcraft. Specialties default to one another at -5. The processes involved are comparable, but the specific rituals and spirits differ significantly.

In worlds with working ritual magic, Ritual Magic skill is the primary skill of sorcerers. All rituals of power default to it! See the appropriate worldbook for details.

This is the skill of invoking spirits to produce magical effects for nonreligious reasons. The equivalent skill for the more direct, flashy magic of fantasy is Thaumatology (p. 225); knowledge of *religious* rites associated with a tradition is Religious Ritual (p. 217).

Running

HT/Average

Default: HT-5.

This skill represents training in both sprints and long-distance running. Roll against the *higher* of Running or HT to avoid fatigue or injury due to running. When racing someone of equal Move on foot, roll a Quick Contest of Running skill to determine the winner.

Note that you must have legs and be capable of land movement to learn this skill.

Saber

see *Melee Weapon*, p. 208

Savoir-Faire†

IQ/Easy

Defaults: IQ-4 and others.

This is the skill of appropriate behavior in a subculture that has an established code of conduct – for instance, high society or the military. When dealing with that social group, a successful skill roll lets you interact without embarrassing yourself, detect pretenders to high standing, and so

on. You may also substitute an Influence roll against Savoir-Faire for any reaction roll required in a social situation involving that subculture; see *Influence Rolls* (p. 359). Roll once per encounter.

You *must* specialize. Common specialties include:

Dojo: How to greet masters, wear weapons, and issue challenges at a karate *dojo*, kung fu *kwoon*, fencing *salle*, or similar academy of the martial arts. *Recognized* skill determines relative standing. In certain places and times, to flout tradition is to risk violent retribution! For competitive martial arts (only), this skill defaults to any relevant Games skill at -3.

High Society: The manners of those of "good" birth and breeding. Status determines relative standing. Roll against skill whenever you must impersonate someone more than three Status levels away from your own. If your Status is negative and you are trying to pass yourself off as someone of Status 1+, or vice versa, this roll is at -2.

Mafia: Proper conduct within a formal criminal organization. This includes such things as codes of silence and showing proper deference to "made men." These protocols often ape those of high society . . . but the penalties for misconduct are far more severe. *Default:* Streetwise-3.

Military: The customs, traditions, and regulations of military service. This also includes knowledge of the *unwritten* rules: what is acceptable even if not regulation, and what is forbidden although there is nothing in writing against it. Military Rank determines relative standing.

Police: As Savoir-Faire (Military), but for civilian police service. This gives knowledge of the *social* protocols for police officers; use Law (Police) for the *legal* protocols. Police Rank determines relative standing.

Servant: Knowledge of how to serve the upper class. Certain procedures are always done *just so* (the salad fork goes outside the dinner fork, the Duke is announced before the Earl, etc.), and certain attitudes in a servant are unacceptable.

Savoir-Faire (High Society) is the most common specialty, and you may list this as simply "Savoir-Faire" on your character sheet. Savoir Faire (High Society) and (Servant) default to one another at -2. There are no defaults between other types of Savoir-Faire.

Modifiers: Cultural Familiarity modifiers (p. 23). +2 if you are of higher standing than those you are trying to impress, or -2 if you are of lower standing ("standing" might mean Rank, Status, skill level, or something else). +2 if you seem to have important friends. -4 for Clueless (p. 126); -3 for Low Empathy (p. 142); -1 for Oblivious (p. 146); -1 to -4 for Shyness (p. 154).

Scrounging

Per/Easy

Default: Perception-4.

This is the ability to find, salvage, or improvise useful items that others can't locate. Each attempt takes an hour. You do not necessarily steal your booty; you just locate it – somehow – and then acquire it by any means necessary. Note that if you find something that is "nailed down," you must decide how to try to get it (which might require a roll on another skill).

Modifiers: As the GM sees fit, for the rarity of the item sought.

Scuba/TL

IQ/Average

Defaults: IQ-5 or Diving Suit-2.
Prerequisite: Swimming.

This is the ability to use self-contained underwater breathing apparatus (scuba). Roll when you first enter the water, and again every 30 minutes thereafter, to avoid inhaling water (treat as drowning; see *Suffocation*, p. 436). If you know this skill above default level, a successful roll also lets you spot problems with the equipment before you put it on.

Modifiers: -2 to -4 for unfamiliar scuba rigs; e.g., closed-circuit gear when you're used to open-circuit.

Seamanship/TL

see *Crewman*, p. 185

Search

Per/Average

Defaults: Perception-5 or Criminology-5.

This is the ability to search people, baggage, and vehicles for items that aren't in plain sight. The GM rolls once – *in secret* – per item of interest. For *deliberately* concealed items, this is a Quick Contest of your Search skill vs. the Holdout or Smuggling skill used to hide the item. If you fail, the GM simply says, "You found nothing." (It defeats the purpose to say, "You don't find the gun under his jacket.")

If more than one person is searching, roll separately for each searcher.

The GM should avoid unnecessary rolls. For instance, no human can get a sawed-off shotgun through a body search. Likewise, a knife or jewel simply cannot be found on a normally dressed person without an X-ray or skin search. In general, if the net bonus to the concealer's Holdout roll is +3 or more, a skin search is *required*. If his Holdout is at -2 or worse for size, a skin search will automatically find the hidden item.

Modifiers: +1 for a "pat-down" of an unresisting person (takes one minute), +3 for a thorough "skin search" of a person's hair and clothing (takes three minutes), or +5 for a complete search, including body cavities (takes five minutes). Bonuses for Acute Touch (p. 35) and Sensitive Touch (p. 83) apply to *all* hands-on searches. On a successful Electronics Operation (Security) roll, specialized sensors – metal detectors, X-ray machines, etc. – give from +1 to +5 to find items they can detect (a metal detector won't help you find plastic explosives!).

Sewing/TL

DX/Easy

Default: DX-4.

This is the ability to work with fabric using the tools of your tech level. A successful skill roll lets you repair damaged clothing (or any other item made of cloth), modify garments (useful when you must wear another person's clothing, perhaps to impersonate him), or create new clothing or costumes from suitable materials.

Make an IQ-based roll to *design* clothing, at +1 if you have Fashion Sense (p. 21).

Before TL7, someone knows this skill in almost every household. At TL7+, it is rare for anyone but a professional seamstress or tailor to know Sewing – most people work at default (at +4 for a simple task like reattaching a button) and discard items that they cannot mend.

Modifiers: Equipment modifiers (p. 345); modifiers for High Manual Dexterity (p. 59) or Ham-Fisted (p. 138).

Sex Appeal

HT/Average

Default: HT-3.

This is the ability to impress those who are attracted to members of your sex. It has as much to do with attitude as it does with looks. If you are not willing to "vamp" someone to get what you want, you won't have this skill – or *want* it.

You may substitute an Influence roll against Sex Appeal for any reaction roll made by someone who is attracted to members of your sex; see *Influence Rolls* (p. 359).

Usually, you may make only one attempt per "target," although the GM might allow another attempt after a few weeks.

Modifiers: +2 for Voice (p. 97); -3 for Low Empathy (p. 142); -1 for Oblivious (p. 146); -1 to -4 for Shyness (p. 154); -2 for Stuttering (p. 157). Apply any bonus for above-average appearance (p. 21) – or *double* the penalty for below-average appearance!

Shadowing

IQ/Average

Defaults: IQ-5, Observation-5, or Stealth-4 (on foot only).

This is the ability to follow another person through a crowd without being noticed. (In the wilderness, use Tracking and Stealth.) Roll a Quick Contest every 10 minutes: your Shadowing vs. the subject's Vision roll. If you lose, you lost the subject; if you lose by more than 5, you were seen.

Once the subject is aware you are shadowing him, roll a Quick Contest every five minutes: your Shadowing skill vs. his Shadowing or Stealth skill. If he wins, he eludes you. If he loses by more than 5, he *thinks* he eluded you. If you critically fail, you lose him *and* follow the wrong person.

Following someone in a vehicle is harder than shadowing on foot. Use the same rules, but you roll at -2 (and may not use your Stealth default).

Modifiers: -3 if the subject knows you. Distinctive appearance gives a penalty – see *Build* (p. 18), *Unnatural Features* (p. 22), and specific disadvantages (e.g., Hunchback, p. 139) for details. If you belong to a visibly different race than most of the people around you, the penalty is up to the GM; it is never smaller in magnitude than the *difference* between your Size Modifier and that of those around you.

Shield†

DX/Easy

Default: DX-4.

This is the ability to use a shield, both to block and to attack. Your active defense with any kind of shield – your Block score – is (skill/2) + 3, rounded down. You *must* specialize:

Shield: Any shield held in place with straps. Such shields have the advantage that you can hold (but not *wield*) something in your shield hand, but the disadvantage of being slow to put on or take off. This is the most common specialty – list it as "Shield" on character sheets.

Buckler: Any kind of shield, usually a small one, held in the hand. A buckler occupies one hand completely, but you can ready it in only one turn and drop it as a free action.

Force: Any shield with a blocking "surface" formed from energy rather than matter.

Shield, Shield (Buckler), and Shield (Force) default to one another at -2.

Shiphandling/TL†

IQ/Hard

Defaults: IQ-6 and others.
Prerequisites: see below.

This is the ability to act as the *master* of a large vessel. It involves directing the crew in the tasks necessary to control the vehicle's speed and direction. It also covers such duties as keeping the captain's log and inspecting the crew. Someone with Shiphandling skill (at better than default!) should stand watch at all times when the vessel is underway. Roll vs. skill when encountering hazards or maneuvering for battle.

A failed roll when encountering hazards means the vessel is damaged. This might mean anything from scratched paint to crippling damage that requires extensive repairs.

A failed roll in battle means the vessel did not go exactly where intended. The details depend on the vessel, the tech level, and the GM's judgment, but might include weapons being "masked" (unable to engage the enemy), a failed boarding attempt, or drifting out of formation with your fleet (which might deny you the benefits of area defenses, fire support, or tactical communications).

A critical failure under any circumstances means an appropriate disaster. Depending on the TL and situation, this could mean running aground, colliding with another vessel, being dismasted, losing your screws or rudder, or simply giving an order that your crew disregards. Whether they then save your ship for you, or mutiny and flee, is up to the GM.

You *must* specialize:

Airship: Blimps, zeppelins, and similar large airships. *Prerequisites:* Airshipman, Leadership, and Navigation (Air). *Defaults:* Airshipman-5 or Piloting (Lighter-Than-Air)-5.

Ship: Surface vessels, from tugboats to carriers. *Prerequisites:* Leadership, Navigation (Sea), and Seamanship. *Defaults:* Seamanship-5, or to Boating (Large Powerboat)-5 for ships with engines or Boating (Sailboat)-5 for tall ships.

Spaceship: Slower-than-light spacecraft. *Prerequisites:* Leadership, Navigation (Space), and Spacer. *Defaults:* Spacer-5 or any spaceship Piloting-5.

Starship: Faster-than-light spacecraft. *Prerequisites:* Leadership, Navigation (Hyperspace), and Spacer. *Defaults:* Spacer-5 or any spaceship Piloting-5.

Submarine: All forms of large submersibles. *Prerequisites:* Leadership, Navigation (Sea), and Submariner.

Defaults: Submariner-5 or Submarine (Large Sub)-5.

Modifiers: -2 to master an unfamiliar vessel (e.g., an aircraft carrier when you're used to a battleship); -2 for an unfamiliar crew; -2 or more for a vehicle in bad repair.

Shortsword
see **Melee Weapon,** p. 208

> *A critical failure under any circumstances means an appropriate disaster: running aground, colliding with another vessel, being dismasted, losing your screws or rudder, or simply giving an order that your crew disregards.*

Singing

HT/Easy

Default: HT-4.

This is the ability to sing in a pleasing fashion. A successful roll means the audience liked your song.

Modifiers: Language Modifiers (p. 24), if you are singing in a foreign language; -2 if the audience does not understand the language; +2 for Voice (p. 97); -2 for Stuttering (p. 157).

Skating

HT/Hard

Default: HT-6.

When you are moving on skates, this skill replaces Hiking skill (p. 200) for routine travel and Running skill (p. 218) for racing. The GM may also require DX-based skill rolls in combat or chases, or for hazardous maneuvers, conditions, or speeds. Under those circumstances, any failure indicates a fall, while critical failure results in 1d-2 damage to a randomly chosen limb.

Skiing

HT/Hard

Default: HT-6.

This replaces Hiking skill (p. 200) when you are skiing cross-country and Running skill (p. 218) when you are racing. Roll once per day of routine travel. The GM may require much more frequent skill rolls – usually DX-based – in combat or chases, or for hazardous maneuvers, conditions, or speeds. In those situations, any failure indicates a fall, while critical failure means 1d damage to a randomly chosen limb.

Sleight of Hand

DX/Hard

Default: Filch-5.

This is the ability to "palm" small objects, do coin and card tricks, etc. Make a skill roll to perform one piece of simple "stage magic." A failed roll means you blew the trick.

When you use this skill to steal, you must win a Quick Contest of Sleight of Hand vs. the Vision roll or Observation skill of potential witnesses to perform the theft unnoticed.

You can also use this skill to cheat at cards, dice, etc. A successful Sleight of Hand roll gives from +1 to +5 on your Gambling roll. Any failure causes you to be denounced as a cheater! In both cases, the exact results are up to the GM.

Modifiers: +3 if the light is dim; +3 if you have a confederate to distract attention; +5 if you have prepared in advance (cards up your sleeve, etc.); -3 if the person you want to fool knows Sleight of Hand himself; modifiers for High Manual Dexterity (p. 59) or Ham-Fisted (p. 138).

Sling

DX/Hard

Default: DX-6.

This is the ability to use the sling or staff sling.

Smallsword

see *Melee Weapon,* p. 208

Smith/TL†

IQ/Average

Defaults: IQ-5 and others.

This is the ability to work non-precious metals by hand. You *must* specialize:

Copper: Copper itself and its alloys, including brass and bronze. Traditionally, a smith who worked with these metals was called a "brownsmith." *Default:* Jeweler-4.

Iron: The skill of being a blacksmith. Also covers steel, at tech levels where it exists.

Lead and Tin: Any of the softer, "white" metals, including alloys such as pewter. The traditional name for such a smith was "whitesmith." *Default:* Jeweler-4.

These specialties default to one another at -4.

This skill is IQ-based, but ST is important, and some tools have a "Minimum ST," just like weapons.

Smuggling

IQ/Average

Default: IQ-5.

This is the ability to conceal items in baggage and vehicles. You can also use it to hide an object in a room or a building. Roll against skill to hide an item from casual inspection. In an active search, the searchers must win a Quick Contest of Search vs. your Smuggling skill to find the item.

Modifiers: Equipment modifiers (p. 345) for specialized smuggling gear. The *difference* between the Size Modifier (p. 19) of the package, vehicle, or room in which you are hiding the item and that of the item itself; e.g., to hide a bottle of liquor (SM -5) in a family car (SM +3), you would roll at +8.

Sociology

IQ/Hard

Defaults: IQ-6, Anthropology-3, or Psychology-4.

This is the study of societies and social relationships. A successful skill roll lets you judge how well a large group of people will work together; deduce the social pressures contributing to a crime wave, revolution, war, etc.; or predict the most probable outcome of dissimilar societies coming into contact.

Soldier/TL

IQ/Average

Default: IQ-5.

This skill represents a combination of basic military training – the lessons taught at "boot camp" or its equivalent in your game world – and actual combat experience. Only those who have served in an army, militia, etc. are likely to know it.

The GM may require a Soldier roll whenever circumstances would test your battlefield discipline (knowing when to shoot, use concealment, take cover, etc.) or skill at practical field survival (e.g., keeping your feet dry and eating when you get the chance). Roll daily during prolonged military action. Failure means an inconvenience – perhaps a minor piece of equipment fails. Critical failure indicates a disaster: "friendly fire" incident, trench foot, etc.

Soldier includes basic lessons in many fields covered by other skills. For instance, a TL8 soldier learns to strip his rifle without learning Armoury (Small Arms), to use a radio without learning Electronics Operation (Comm), to dig a foxhole without learning Engineer (Combat), and so forth. In a situation where someone with one of those skills would roll at +4 or better for a routine task (see *Task Difficulty,* p. 345), the GM may let you roll against Soldier skill instead. You do not receive the bonus that someone with the full-fledged skill would get, but you *do* suffer any situational penalties.

Soldier can only substitute for skill rolls to do things that would be a believable part of basic training. This means the *routine* use of *standard* equipment by *ordinary* troops – not research, improvisation, or design, and never the operation of new or secret technologies! Soldier cannot replace weapon skills, either; you must buy all such skills separately.

Example: If someone with Electronics Operation (Comm) would be at +4 to call HQ on a standard-issue radio, you could do so with a successful Soldier roll. However, you could *not* use Soldier to fix a broken radio, use an enemy radio, or transmit coded signals.

Spacer/TL
see *Crewman*, p. 185

Spear
see *Melee Weapon*, p. 208

Spear Thrower
DX/Average

Defaults: DX-5 or Thrown Weapon (Spear)-4.

This is the ability to use the spear thrower: a long, flat stick with a notch or a loop at one end. It increases the force with which you can hurl a javelin or similar weapon. It takes one turn to position the spear in the thrower after both are in hand and ready.

Modifiers: -5 in tight quarters (less than two yards of overhead clearance).

Speed-Reading
IQ/Average

Defaults: None.

This is the ability to read *much* faster than normal. Whenever time is of the essence (for instance, when reading the instructions on a parachute as you fall), multiply your reading speed by a factor of 1 + (skill/10); e.g., Speed-Reading-12 would give a factor of 2.2. Make a skill roll to determine whether you retain what you have read.

On a failure, your recall is shaky. Every time you try to remember or use what you read, you must make an IQ roll at a penalty equal to your margin of failure. Roll at +5 if you have Eidetic Memory, or +10 for Photographic Memory. If this roll fails, you cannot recall the information; on a critical failure, you recall badly flawed information but believe it to be true! To eliminate this IQ roll, you must go back and reread the material *slowly*.

Modifiers: Language modifiers (p. 24).

Sports
DX/Average

Defaults: DX-5 and others.

This is the ability to play a particular sport *well* – perhaps well enough to earn a living. Each sport is a separate Sports skill. Most Sports skills are DX/Average and default to DX-5, but those that put a premium on strength (e.g., rugby) might default to ST-5. Some Sports skills might default to one another or to other skills as well.

Make an IQ-based roll to recall the *basic* rules of your sport. Detailed knowledge of the full rules governing leagues and tournaments – as would be expected of a coach or referee – is covered by the relevant Games skill (p. 197).

The GM may rule that certain Sports are useful in combat situations. For instance, Sports (Baseball) might let you use a bat to parry hurled rocks and grenades at (skill/2) + 3, Sports (Bullfighting) might give a Parry equal to (skill/2) + 3 against a slam by a beast that uses a "running head butt," and you might be able to roll against Sports (Rugby) to hit with a slam.

Staff
see *Melee Weapon*, p. 208

Stage Combat
DX/Average

Defaults: Combat Art or Sport-2, an actual combat skill-3, or Performance-3.

This skill allows you to perform a choreographed fight safely, yet in an entertaining manner. A critical failure indicates an injury: 1d-2 damage to a random location.

Modifiers: -4 for an unfamiliar weapon.

Stealth
DX/Average

Defaults: DX-5 or IQ-5.

This is the ability to hide and to move silently. A successful roll lets you conceal yourself anywhere except in a totally bare room, or move so quietly that nobody will hear you, or follow someone without being noticed. (To follow someone through a *crowd*, use Shadowing, p. 219.)

If someone is *specifically* on the alert for intruders, the GM will roll a Quick Contest between your Stealth and the sentinel's Perception.

You can also use this skill to stalk game. A successful roll (and about 30 minutes) gets you within 30 yards of most animals. Another roll, at -5, gets you within 15 yards.

Modifiers: A penalty equal to your encumbrance level. -5 to hide in an area without "natural" hiding places, or +3 or more if there are *many* hiding places. -5 to move silently if you are moving faster than Move 1. -5 to fool those with Discriminatory Smell (e.g., dogs).

A successful Streetwise roll might let you learn where any sort of illegal "action" is; which local cops or bureaucrats can be bought, and for how much; and how to contact the local underworld.

Strategy†
IQ/Hard

Defaults: IQ-6, Intelligence Analysis-6, or Tactics-6.

This is the ability to plan military actions and predict the actions of the enemy. In most settings, only the military teaches this skill.

A successful Strategy roll lets you deduce, in advance, enemy military plans unless another person with this skill leads them. In that case, the GM rolls a Quick Contest of Strategy. The amount of information gained depends on how well you roll (but *not* on the quality of the foe's plans). If you fail an uncontested roll or lose a Quick Contest, the GM gives you *false* information.

You *must* specialize in a type of strategy – Land, Naval, Space, etc. These specialties default to one

SKILLS

another at -4. The specific units being commanded are less important; even the units of another nation or tech level would give -1 or -2 at most (GM's judgment), as long as you had accurate information about their capabilities.

Streetwise

IQ/Average

Default: IQ-5.

This is the skill of getting along in rough company. A successful Streetwise roll might let you learn (among other things) where any sort of illegal "action" is; which local cops or bureaucrats can be bought, and for how much; and how to contact the local underworld. Note that you might also be able to get this information by asking a Contact (p. 44). This skill is a measure of your ability to make *new* connections as needed.

You may substitute an Influence roll against Streetwise for any reaction roll made in an underworld or "bad neighborhood" situation; see *Influence Rolls* (p. 359).

Modifiers: +3 if you have a tough reputation (either "good" or "bad") in the area; -3 if you are obviously a stranger in the area. -3 for Low Empathy (p. 142); -1 for Oblivious (p. 146); -1 to -4 for Shyness (p. 154).

Submarine/TL†

DX/Average

Default: IQ-6.

This is the ability to operate a specific type of underwater vehicle. As with Piloting, the default is to IQ, but when you *learn* the skill, always base it on DX.

Roll against Submarine to dive or to surface, to maneuver in underwater combat, or to negotiate hazardous waters. Failure can mean anything from a slight drift off course to a collision; critical failure may strand the vessel underwater!

Make an IQ-based Submarine roll for basic chart reading or practical oceanography, or to recall nautical laws and regulations.

You *must* specialize:

Free-Flooding Sub: Any small, *open* submersible. The crew is exposed to the water, and must wear underwater breathing gear. *Prerequisites:* Diving

Suit *or* Scuba. *Defaults:* Large Sub-5 or Mini-Sub-4.

Large Sub: Any crewed, long-duration submersible, including attack subs and missile subs. *Defaults:* Free-Flooding Sub-5 or Mini-Sub-4.

Mini-Sub: Any small, closed, short-duration submersible, typical of those used for scientific research. *Defaults:* Free-Flooding Sub-4 or Large Sub-4.

Modifiers: -2 for an unfamiliar submarine within your specialty (e.g., a diesel attack sub when you are used to a nuclear missile sub); -4 or more for a vessel in bad repair; -1 to -10 for navigational hazards.

Submariner/TL

see *Crewman*, p. 185

Suggest

see *Enthrallment*, p. 191

Sumo Wrestling

DX/Average

Defaults: None.

This unarmed combat skill represents *any* training at grabbing, shoving, and tripping – not just the traditional Japanese sport of *sumo*. Roll against the *higher* of DX or Sumo Wrestling to hit with a grapple, slam, or shove, or to make or resist a takedown. If you know this skill at DX+1 level, add +1 to ST whenever you make or resist a grapple or takedown, and whenever you attempt to break free, and +1 *per die* to your damage when you slam or shove. These bonuses increase to +2 if you know Sumo at DX+2 or better.

When you defend with bare hands, Sumo Wrestling allows you to parry *once* per turn. You must use both hands. Your Parry score is (skill/2) + 3, rounded down. This parry is meant to ward off slams, grapples, and bare-handed slaps. You parry at -2 vs. kicks and -3 vs. weapons. For complete rules for parrying barehanded, see *Parrying Unarmed* (p. 376).

Surgery/TL

IQ/Very Hard

Defaults: First Aid-12, Physician-5, Physiology-8, or Veterinary-5.

Prerequisites: First Aid or Physician.

This is skill at using *invasive* medical techniques to treat sickness or injury. Roll once per operation. On a success, the operation proceeded without complications. On a failure, the patient took damage – 2d for a simple amputation, 3d for other procedures. Surgery rolls can also facilitate recovery from wounds; see *Surgery* (p. 424).

This skill represents general surgical expertise, which is relatively rare in real life. Most surgeons have an *optional* specialty (p. 169) in a certain part of the body (brain, heart, etc.) or a specific type of surgery (cosmetic surgery, microsurgery, transplant surgery, etc.).

Modifiers: Equipment modifiers (p. 345); physiology modifiers (p. 181); -3 if the area or equipment cannot be properly cleaned and sterilized; -3 for head or chest surgery; -5 for undiagnosed problems. If you lack Physician skill, you are at -5 to do anything but "field-expedient" surgery (e.g., stitch wounds or extract arrowheads, bullets, and shrapnel).

Survival†

Per/Average

Defaults: Perception-5 or Naturalist (same planet)-3.

This is the ability to "live off the land," find safe food and water, avoid hazards, build shelter, etc. You may look after up to 10 other people. To live safely in a wilderness situation, you must make a successful Survival roll once per day. Failure inflicts 2d-4 injury on you and anyone in your care; roll separately for each victim.

This skill also gives an "eye for country." A successful roll shows you the best direction of travel to find flowing water, a mountain pass, or whatever other terrain feature you desire – assuming that it exists.

Finally, you can use this skill to *trap* wild animals. (A city-bred thief could use Traps skill, but he's used to different game . . . so the roll would be at a -5.) Make one roll per trap. It takes about 30 minutes to improvise a trap from ordinary materials, or 10 minutes to set and hide a commercial steel trap. Pit traps for large game take several hours to dig.

Survival often requires skill rolls based on scores other than Perception.

The GM might ask for a ST-based roll to dig a pit trap or erect a log shelter, a DX-based roll to start a fire using primitive techniques (flint sparking, bow and palette, etc.), or even a HT-based roll to avoid nutritional deficiencies from an improvised diet.

You *must* specialize by terrain type. Land-dwellers may choose from Arctic, Desert, Island/Beach, Jungle, Mountain, Plains, Swampland, and Woodlands. Aquatic beings may take any of Bank, Deep Ocean Vent, Fresh-Water Lake, Open Ocean, Reef, River/Stream, Salt-Water Sea, and Tropical Lagoon. Amphibious individuals can pick from *either* list!

Land specialties default to one another at -3, while aquatic specialties default among themselves at -4. Island/Beach and Tropical Lagoon default to each other at -4, as do Swampland and River/Stream, but there are no other defaults between land and aquatic specialties.

In settings where it is possible to visit other worlds, you must also specialize by planet. Each Survival specialty defaults to the *same* terrain type for a *different* planet at -4. The defaults between terrain types given above are at an extra -4 between different planets. All this assumes the two planets are of the same planet type (see *Planet Types*, p. 180). There is *no default at all* between Survival skills for two planets of different planet types.

At the GM's option, extreme man-made terrain may call for unique specialties; e.g., Survival (Radioactive Wasteland). Most such specialties have *no* default of any kind.

See also *Urban Survival*, p. 228.

Modifiers: Up to -5 for extreme weather conditions. Equipment modifiers (p. 345).

Sway Emotions
see *Enthrallment*, p. 191

Swimming
HT/Easy
Default: HT-4.

This is the skill of swimming (whether on purpose or to keep afloat in emergencies) and lifesaving. Roll against the *higher* of Swimming or HT to avoid fatigue while swimming or injury due to aquatic misfortunes.

When racing someone of equal water Move, roll a Quick Contest of Swimming to determine the winner. See *Swimming* (p. 354).

Note that Swimming does *not* cover high diving – that's Sports (Diving).

Symbol Drawing†
IQ/Hard
Defaults: Special.

This is the art of scribing magical symbols. Depending on your magical tradition, you might carve these symbols with a ritual dagger, draw them on the ground or an altar using blood or ceremonial powders, write them in ink, trace them in the air with a wand or your fingers, or something else. You *must* specialize in a particular magical tradition.

In traditions where magical power flows from the caster, nature, spirits, etc. as opposed to the symbols themselves, the symbols provide a focus that aids magic use. Roll against Symbol Drawing before each ritual. On a success, add half your margin of success (round down) to your skill with the *next* ritual you conduct over the symbols. This kind of Symbol Drawing defaults to Ritual Magic (same)-4. For instance, Symbol Drawing (Voodoo) defaults to Ritual Magic (Voodoo)-4, and lets you draw the *vevers* used in Voodoo ritual.

In traditions where the *symbols themselves* imbue items or places (or even *people*, in the case of tattoos) with magic, the magic is only as good as the symbols. Roll against the *lower* of Symbol Drawing and your skill with the enchantment itself. This is most common in rune magic. Each runic alphabet is a separate Symbol Drawing skill with no default. For instance, Symbol Drawing (Futhark Runes) would let you scribe the runes used in Norse magic.

More-exotic traditions may have their own rules; see the appropriate worldbook for more information.

Modifiers: -1 or more if using non-traditional means to mark the symbols; -1 or more if placing the symbols on any surface other than those prescribed by your tradition.

Tactics
IQ/Hard
Defaults: IQ-6 or Strategy (any)-6.

This is the ability to outguess and outmaneuver the enemy in small-unit or personal combat. In most settings, only the military teaches this skill.

When commanding a small unit, roll against Tactics to place your troops correctly for an ambush, know where to post sentries, etc. At the GM's option, a successful roll might even provide clues as to *immediate* enemy plans. To outmaneuver enemy units, you must win a Quick Contest of Tactics with their leader. All of this only applies when you lead a group small enough that you can give each warrior orders *personally* – or through at most one subordinate. Thus, radio and similar technologies can greatly enhance your command abilities!

In personal combat, you may make a Tactics roll before the fight begins if you had *any* time to prepare. On a success, you start the fight in an advantageous position – e.g., behind cover or on higher ground – as determined by the GM. The better the roll, the greater your advantage. If you fail, or do not attempt a Tactics roll, you are in a random location (or one of the GM's choosing) when combat begins. Fighters without Tactics skill *always* start combat this way.

Even in an ambush or similar "surprise" situation, the GM will use the *better* of your Tactics skill and your Perception to see if you spotted the danger on time.

Teaching
IQ/Average
Default: IQ-5.

This is the ability to instruct others. If you have Teaching at level 12+, you may act as a teacher for game purposes. For more on teaching and learning, see *Improvement Through Study* (p. 292).

Modifiers: -3 for Callous (p. 125); -1 to -4 for Shyness (p. 142). Apply both the teacher's *and* the student's Language penalties (p. 24) in the language of instruction.

In traditions where magical power flows from the caster, nature, spirits, etc., as opposed to the symbols themselves, the symbols provide a focus that aids magic use.

Teamster†

IQ/Average

Defaults: IQ-5, Animal Handling (same)-4, or Riding (same)-2.

This is the skill of driving a team of animals pulling a wagon, chariot, etc. It includes the ability to harness and care for the beasts, and judge them for quality before purchase. If the animals are ornery or badly trained (GM's judgment), you must make a successful Animal Handling roll before you can attempt a Teamster roll.

For normal travel, make a Teamster roll once per day. When moving at a gallop (80% or more of the animals' full Move) or when executing complex maneuvers with a chariot in combat, roll *every 10 seconds*.

A failure usually means nothing worse than lost time or a wider turn than intended. A critical failure – or *any* failure at a gallop – spills the wagon or chariot. Treat this as a five-yard fall for each passenger and animal involved (see *Falling*, p. 431). As well, roll 2d for each beast; on a 12, a leg is broken! You will have to make Animal Handling rolls to calm the beasts. Time required to reload the cargo depends on the load, terrain, and weather.

You *must* specialize by animal type; the most common specialty is Teamster (Equines), which covers horses and mules. Teamster specialties default to one another at -3.

Modifiers: -2 for more than four animals; -2 for a team of unfamiliar animals; up to -5 for bad terrain.

Thaumatology

IQ/Very Hard

Default: IQ-7*.

* There is *no* default in a nonmagical setting, or for those who have never witnessed "real" magic.

This is the academic study of magical theory and the "physics" of mana. *Anyone* may learn this skill, but it is easier for a mage; add Magery to IQ when learning this skill, just as for spells.

The main use for this skill is magical research. When creating a new spell, use the rules for inventing (see Chapter 17), but replace Engineer skill with Thaumatology. A successful skill roll can also identify an unknown spell when you see it cast, deduce the ramifications of a critical success or failure with magic, determine the spells needed to enchant a magic item to perform as desired, etc. The better your roll, the more insight the GM will provide.

This is the study of *fantasy* magic – fireball spells, rings of power, etc. The equivalent skill for traditional, spirit-mediated sorcery is Ritual Magic (p. 218), while holy magic might require Religious Ritual (p. 217) or Theology (p. 226). However, a Thaumatology roll at -5 will allow a thaumatologist to relate these different varieties of magic to "standard" wizardry. Exceptionally weird powers or otherworldly artifacts might give a larger penalty!

Theology†

IQ/Hard

Defaults: IQ-6 or Religious Ritual (same)-4.

This is the study of a particular religion: its gods, cosmology, doctrines, scriptures, etc. You *must* specialize by religion. There are usually no defaults between specialties, but the GM might permit a default at -4 or so for belief systems that have similar origins, or where one is derived from the other.

Alternatively, you may study the similarities and differences between religions; this is Theology (Comparative). The Theology of any religion routinely studied by scholars in your game world defaults to this specialty at -5.

To be a priest or holy man at TL1+, you must have both Theology *and* Religious Ritual skill (p. 217) for your religion. TL0 shamans need only learn Religious Ritual.

You do not necessarily believe in the religion you study – faith comes from within, not from book learning! If you do, you may ask the GM to make a secret roll against your Theology skill when confronted with moral uncertainty. On a success, the GM will advise you on which course of action "feels" right, given your beliefs and understanding of scripture.

Throwing

DX/Average

Defaults: DX-3 or Dropping-4.

This is the ability to throw any small, relatively smooth object that fits in the palm of your hand. Examples include baseballs, hand grenades, and rocks. (Boomerangs, javelins, knives, etc. require their own specialized skills; see *Thrown Weapon*, below.) Roll against skill to hit. Furthermore, if you know Throwing at DX+1 level, add +1 to ST when figuring throwing distance (but *not* damage). Add +2 to ST for Throwing at DX+2 or better.

If you do not have this skill, roll against your default to hit a specific target, but against *full* DX to lob an object into a general area.

Throwing Art

DX/Hard

Defaults: None.
Prerequisites: Trained By A Master or Weapon Master.

This is the cinematic ability to throw anything you are strong enough to lift: knives, medicine balls, televisions . . . *anything!* Roll against skill to hit. Furthermore, if you know Throwing Art at DX level, add +1 to ST when figuring throwing distance, and +1 *per die* of damage with thrown weapons. These bonuses increase to +2 if you know Throwing Art at DX+1 or better. If you are a Weapon Master, this bonus is *instead of* the usual damage bonus for your weapon.

You can use the items you throw as improvised weapons. Treat forks, kitchen knives, and other long, sharp objects as daggers. Any small, blunt object does thrust+1 crushing damage. Baseball bats do swing+1 crushing. Pencils do thrust-3 impaling. Playing cards do thrust-3 cutting.

Throwing Art lets you throw anything covered by the Throwing and Thrown Weapon skills. If you have Throwing Art, you do not need those skills.

Thrown Weapon†

DX/Easy

Defaults: DX-4 and others.

This is the ability to hurl any one type of thrown weapon. You *must* specialize:

Axe/Mace: Any axe, hatchet, or mace balanced for throwing (but *not* an unbalanced battleaxe or maul!).
Dart: Any sort of small, finned dart. Games (Darts) defaults to this skill at no penalty. *Default:* Throwing-2.
Harpoon: Any sort of *tethered* spear. *Default:* Thrown Weapon (Spear)-2.
Knife: Any sort of knife.
Shuriken: Any sort of hiltless blade, notably *shuriken* ("ninja stars"). *Default:* Throwing-2.
Spear: Any sort of spear, javelin, etc. *Defaults:* Spear Thrower-4 or Thrown Weapon (Harpoon)-2.
Stick: Any balanced and shaped throwing stick, such as a boomerang. This type of throwing stick does not return to the user.

Tonfa

see *Melee Weapon*, p. 208

Tracking

Per/Average

Defaults: Perception-5 or Naturalist-5.

This is the ability to follow a man or an animal by its tracks. Make a Tracking roll to pick up the trail, then roll periodically to avoid losing it. The frequency and difficulty of these rolls depend on the terrain:

Jungle, Plains, or Woodlands: Roll every 30 minutes.
Arctic, Desert, Island/Beach, or Mountain: Roll at -2 every 15 minutes.
Swampland: Roll at -4 every 5 minutes.
Urban: Roll at -6 every minute!

You may also use this skill to *cover* your tracks. This doubles your travel time! A successful roll means you have hidden your tracks well enough that only someone else with this skill can see them. If another tracker follows you, the Tracking rolls above become Quick Contests of Tracking skill. If he loses any of the Contests, he loses your trail.

To stalk game once you have tracked it, use the Stealth skill (p. 222).

Modifiers: -5 if the trail is more than a day old, or -10 if more than a week old. +3 if you are following a man, or +6 if following a group of men. Superior senses help *a lot:* bonuses for Acute Vision (p. 35) and Discriminatory Smell (p. 49) usually apply, and many superhuman senses (Infravision, Subsonic Hearing, etc.) give situational bonuses.

Traps/TL

IQ/Average

Defaults: IQ-5 or Lockpicking-3*.
* Also defaults to DX-5 if you are *disarming* or *resetting* a trap, but not if you are detecting or building one.

This is the skill of building and nullifying traps. A successful Traps roll will (among other things) disarm a trap once you have found it, reset it after you pass, or build a new trap (given suitable materials). Time required is as for Lockpicking (p. 206).

To *detect* a trap, make a Perception-based skill roll.

Note that for the purposes of Traps skill, detection devices are "traps." Thus, this skill covers everything from covered pits to elaborate electronic security systems!

Modifiers: Infinitely variable. The more sophisticated the trap, the harder it will be to disarm, reset, build, or find – and a given trap might be (for instance) easy to find but hard to disarm. The GM should be creative! Equipment modifiers (p. 345) apply to most rolls to set or disarm traps.

Bonuses for Acute Vision (p. 35) apply to rolls to detect traps (only).

Two-Handed Axe/Mace
see *Melee Weapon*, p. 208

Example of Character Creation (concluded)

Dai has spent 203 of his 250 points, leaving him with 47 points for skills. Reading through the skill list, we see *dozens* of skills that suit a master thief – but since we're on a budget, we settle on the following.

First, a thief *must* be stealthy. For this, Dai needs the Stealth skill (p. 222). We want this to be reliable, so we choose skill level 16. At that level, only a roll of 17 or 18 will fail . . . and that's a failure for anyone. Stealth is a DX/Average skill. Since Dai's DX is 15, level 16 is DX+1 for him. From the *Skill Cost Table* (p. 170), we learn that a level of Attribute+1 in an Average skill costs 4 points.

Any thief worth his salt can pick pockets and open locks. This calls for Pickpocket (p. 213) and Lockpicking (p. 206). We want to buy Dai a 15 in both – not as high as his Stealth, but still reliable. Pickpocket is DX/Hard. Skill 15 is DX level, and from the table, we see this costs 4 points for a Hard skill. Lockpicking, on the other hand, is IQ/Average. With Dai's IQ 12, skill 15 is IQ+3 level. This costs *12* points – it's very expensive to raise a skill so far above its controlling attribute!

We also want Dai to be an adept second-story man and escape artist, so we spend 1 point apiece on Climbing (p. 183) and Escape (p. 192). Climbing is DX/Average; 1 point buys DX-1 level, giving skill 14. Escape is DX/Hard; 1 point is only good for DX-2 level, or skill 13. Of course, we selected these skills knowing that Dai's Flexibility advantage would give +3 to both! His Perfect Balance adds *another* +1 to Climbing, too. His final levels are Climbing at 18 and Escape at 16.

To case an area before he strikes, Dai needs Observation skill (p. 211). This is Per/Average. But Dai's Perception is a whopping 15, so he doesn't need to spend many points: 2 points buys Observation at Per level (15), which is more than good enough.

Since stealth can fail, we want to give Dai some combat skills for backup. We decide that he prefers knives. Knife skill (p. 208) is fine for melee combat, but we also want Dai to be good at the quick draw and with throwing knives. Fast-Draw (p. 194) and Thrown Weapon (p. 226) fit the bill. Both *require* a specialty – in this case, "Knife." All of these skills are DX/Easy. With Dai's low ST, he'll need *superb* aim to make a knife effective, so we settle on 17 in Knife and Thrown Weapon (Knife). This is DX+2 level, which costs 4 points per skill. Fast-Draw (Knife) is a neat trick, but skill 15 is plenty. This costs 1 point.

To reflect Dai's medieval background, we decide that he is a fair hand with the shortsword. But not *too* good – swords are expensive, and Dai grew up poor. We give him the Shortsword skill (p. 209) at 15. Shortsword is DX/Average, so this costs 2 points.

As an ISWAT officer, Dai should know how to shoot. A slim target pistol sounds like his kind of gun. Reviewing the Guns skill (p. 198), we see that pistols call for the "Pistol" specialty. Guns are new to Dai, so we spend only 1 point. Since Guns (Pistol) is DX/Easy, this buys DX level: a very adequate 15.

To *conceal* all these weapons, Dai needs Holdout skill (p. 200). This is IQ/Average. Dai doesn't routinely carry concealed weapons, so we just give him IQ level – 12 – for 2 points.

We decide to give Dai some "background skills" next. He grew up on the street, so Urban Survival (p. 228) fits: it's the ability to scrounge food and shelter in the city. A Per/Average skill, 1 point buys Per-1 level, or 14. Filch (p. 195) covers shoplifting. It's DX/Average; 1 point buys DX-1, also 14. Survival has a social side, too. We give Dai Fast-Talk (p. 195) to talk his way out of jams and Streetwise (p. 223) to deal with professional criminals. Both are IQ/Average. We buy IQ level (12) in each, at 2 points a skill.

Dai has now spent 44 of his remaining 47 points. We decide to put his last three points into skills that complement his advantages.

Rereading the descriptions of his advantages, we see that Perfect Balance gives +1 to Acrobatics (p. 174). That's definitely Dai's style! Acrobatics is DX/Hard, so 2 points buys DX-1 level, or 14. With the +1 for Perfect Balance, he gets a 15.

We also discover that Absolute Direction gives +3 to Body Sense (p. 181): the skill of reorienting yourself after teleportation. This sounds ideal for Dai! We put 1 point into Body Sense, which is DX/Hard. This buys DX-2 level, or 13. The +3 for Absolute Direction makes this 16.

At this stage, Dai has spent all 250 points. If we wanted to add more abilities, we could add more disadvantages to pay for them – but we want Dai to be carefree, not saddled with problems.

Now it's time to write it all down. Dai's character sheet appears on p. 311.

Two-Handed Flail
see *Melee Weapon*, p. 208

Two-Handed Sword
see *Melee Weapon*, p. 208

Typing
DX/Easy
Defaults: DX-4 and others.

This is the skill of using a typewriter. Typing speed is skill × 3 words per minute (wpm) on a manual, skill × 5 wpm on an electric typewriter or computer keyboard.

This skill defaults at -3 to any skill that involves a lot of typing, notably Administration, Computer Operation, Research, and Writing, and Professional Skills such as Journalist. If you have such a skill, Typing skill is redundant (unless you wish to work as a professional typist).

Urban Survival
Per/Average
Default: Perception-5.

This talent covers the *physical* part of staying alive in a city environment, whether it's overpopulated or empty. (The *social* problems of city survival are covered by Streetwise skill.) A successful skill roll allows you to find clean rainwater; locate manholes from above or below; quickly locate building entrances, exits, stairwells, etc.; recognize and avoid physically dangerous areas, such as crumbling buildings; make and read city maps; find your way out of strange city areas; find a warm place to sleep outside in cold weather; and locate common types of buildings or businesses without asking anyone, just by your "feel" for the way cities are laid out.

Vacc Suit/TL
see *Environment Suit*, p. 192

Ventriloquism
IQ/Hard
Defaults: None.

This is the ability to disguise and "throw" your voice a short distance. A successful roll lets you throw your voice well enough to fool your audience.

Modifiers: +5 if you have a dummy or confederate to distract your audience (it's easier to "see" a face talk than it is to believe the voice comes from an immobile object); -3 if the audience has reason to be suspicious.

Veterinary/TL
IQ/Hard
Defaults: Animal Handling (any)-6, Physician-5, or Surgery-5.

This is the ability to care for a sick or wounded animal. You may take an *optional* specialty (p. 169) in a particular type of animal.

Modifiers: +2 if the animal knows and trusts you; -2 to -5 if the animal is of an unfamiliar type.

Weather Sense
see *Meteorology*, p. 209

Weird Science
IQ/Very Hard
Defaults: None.

This skill allows you to formulate astonishing new crackpot scientific theories that are far ahead of their time . . . or at least utterly different from the usual assumptions of your tech level. You may attempt a Weird Science roll whenever you work on a new invention (see Chapter 17) or investigate an *existing* item of weird technology (e.g., a UFO).

On a success, you get +5 on an invention attempt (but only +1 if using the Gadgeteer advantage, since Gadgeteer already gives you favorable die rolls for thinking "outside the box"). If investigating weird technology, success gives +2 to any skill roll you make for this purpose – and the GM might even allow a default skill roll to *operate* the device!

On a critical success, you get these bonuses *and* some incredible insight into a totally different problem! Critical failures are always spectacular, although not necessarily fatal or even dangerous.

Whip
see *Melee Weapon*, p. 208

Wrestling
DX/Average
Defaults: None.

This skill represents training at grappling and pinning. Roll against the *higher* of DX or Wrestling to hit with a grapple, or to make or resist a takedown. Furthermore, if you know Wrestling at DX+1 level, add +1 to ST for the purpose of making or resisting any choke, grapple, neck snap, takedown, or pin, and whenever you attempt to break free. Add +2 to ST for Wrestling at DX+2 or better.

When you defend with bare hands, Wrestling allows you to parry *once* per turn. You must use both hands. Your Parry score is (skill/2) + 3, rounded down. This parry is at -3 vs. weapons. For complete rules for parrying barehanded, see *Parrying Unarmed* (p. 376).

Writing
IQ/Average
Default: IQ-5

This is the ability to write in a clear or entertaining manner. A successful roll means the work is readable and accurate.

This is mostly useful to earn a living or write for **GURPS,** but can sometimes help on adventures . . . or after them. The report of a spy, soldier, or private investigator is far more useful if it is well-written!

Modifiers: The time modifiers under *Time Spent* (p. 346) will often apply; -5 if you are writing about an unfamiliar subject; Language modifiers (p. 24).

Zen Archery
IQ/Very Hard
Defaults: None.
Prerequisites: Trained By A Master or Weapon Master, Bow at 18+, and Meditation.

This skill allows you to strike difficult targets with ease when using a bow. On a success, add up the penalties for size and speed/range, and then divide them by three (round down).

Modifiers: -10 if used *instantly*, dropping to -5 after 1 turn of concentration, -4 after 2 turns, -3 after 4 turns, -2 after 8 turns, -1 after 16 turns, and no penalty after 32 turns.

TECHNIQUES

You (or your GM!) may want a way to improve your ability with a specific application of a skill without increasing the overall skill level. This is realistic – people *do* train at particular tasks to the exclusion of others – but allowing this in the game makes play (and character sheets) more complex. As a result, the following section is *purely optional*.

A "technique" is any feat that you can practice and perfect separately from the skill that allows you to perform that task. It is a specific action covered by the parent skill, studied on its own. It differs from an optional specialty (p. 169), which covers a body of theory, not an action. Techniques work a lot like skills, but with a few important differences.

CREATING TECHNIQUES

There are six steps to creating a technique. We'll walk through these steps using two examples. Even those who plan to use only the sample techniques at the end of this section should read these rules, as they explain the basic concepts involved.

Concept and Name

Decide what you want the technique to do, in general terms, and give it a name that clearly describes the feat it represents.

Example 1: Both still and motion-picture cameras require Photography skill (p. 213). A photographer could study *just* motion-picture equipment in order to get rid of the -3 to use it; therefore, "Motion-Picture Camera" would be a reasonable Photography technique.

Example 2: Karate skill (p. 203) covers both kicks and punches. A *karateka* could spend extra time on kicks, with the goal of eliminating the -2 to kicking attacks. Thus, "Kicking" would be a logical technique for Karate.

A technique should *never* be the "core" action undertaken with the skill. For instance, Punching would not be a valid technique for Boxing skill, which is all about punching! To get better at the primary task covered by a skill, you must improve the skill itself.

Prerequisites

The skill with which a technique is associated is *automatically* its prerequisite – that is, you must have at least one point in a skill before you can improve its techniques. If more than one skill lets you perform the task covered by the technique, *any* of these skills can count as the prerequisite. The GM may require other skills and advantages as prerequisites for particularly complex techniques.

Example 1: The prerequisite of Motion-Picture Camera is Photography skill.

Example 2: Either Brawling *or* Karate skill can be the prerequisite of Kicking, since both allow you to kick.

Defaults and Specialties

A technique always defaults to one of its prerequisites. Usually, the default penalty equals the modifier given for the feat in the skill description or elsewhere. There can be more than one default. If a technique offers a choice of defaults, those who learn it *must* specialize in the version of the technique associated with the chosen default.

Example 1: Photography skill states that motion-picture cameras are used at -3, so Motion-Picture Camera defaults to Photography-3.

Example 2: Both Brawling and Karate let you kick at -2 to skill, so Kicking defaults to Brawling-2 or Karate-2. Those who use the Brawling default must specialize in Kicking (Brawling), while those who use the Karate default must specialize in Kicking (Karate).

Difficulty Level

Techniques come in only two difficulties: Average and Hard. Feats that have severe negative consequences on a failure, or that allow only one attempt, are Hard; all others are Average. This affects point cost – see *Technique Cost Table* (p. 230).

Example 1: Motion-picture photography is rarely dangerous, and you can usually do a second take if you fail; therefore, Motion-Picture Camera is an Average technique.

Example 2: On a failed kick, you can *fall down* – a potentially fatal turn of events in combat – so Kicking is a Hard technique.

Maximum Level

Tightly focused practice can only take you so far. Eventually, you'll have to learn new fundamentals in order to improve. To reflect this, techniques often specify an upper limit relative to parent skill. On attaining this level, the only way to improve further is to raise the underlying skill. For a technique that covers an important use of a skill, maximum level is usually equal to prerequisite skill level. More peripheral techniques might be able to exceed prerequisite skill level, or have no maximum level.

Example 1: An adventurer could make a career of motion-picture photography without affecting game balance. Thus, it seems believable and fair to leave Motion-Picture Camera open-ended and specify no maximum level.

Example 2: Kicking is a potent attack, and one of the main reasons to learn Brawling or Karate skill; therefore, Kicking cannot be improved past prerequisite skill level.

Description

The prerequisite skill description provides the necessary rules for most techniques, but some techniques supply optional additional detail, or outline entirely new uses of the skill.

Example 1: There isn't a lot to be said about Motion-Picture Camera – it lets you use motion-picture cameras, per Photography skill.

Example 2: Kicking does +1 damage relative to a punch, and you must roll vs. DX to avoid a fall if you miss. These rules bear mentioning in any formal description of Kicking.

BUYING AND IMPROVING TECHNIQUES

Buying a technique is a lot like buying a skill – point cost depends on difficulty and desired relative skill level – but there are two differences. You buy up a technique relative to its default, not relative to a controlling attribute, and you determine its point cost using the *Technique Cost Table* (below) instead of the *Skill Cost Table* (p. 170).

To *improve* a technique, pay the difference in point cost between the desired level and your current level – exactly as for a skill. And just as skills increase for free when you raise attributes, techniques improve for free when you raise the skill on which they are based. For instance, if you have Karate-15 and Kicking-15, and raise Karate to 16, Kicking also goes to 16 at no extra charge!

You need not buy a technique to use it. If you have even one point in a skill, you may use *all* that skill's techniques at default. To avoid a cluttered character sheet, though, only note techniques that you know at better than default level.

Technique Cost Table

Your Final Skill Level*	Difficulty of Technique	
	Average	Hard
Default	0 points	0 points
Default+1	1 point	2 points
Default+2	2 points	3 points
Default+3	3 points	4 points
Default+4	4 points	5 points
+1	+1 point	+1 point

* Most techniques have maximum levels. For instance, a technique that "cannot exceed prerequisite skill level" and that defaults to skill-5 tops out at default+5.

USING TECHNIQUES

A technique works just like a skill in play: make a success roll (see Chapter 10) against your level in the technique. Unless noted otherwise, all *general* modifiers to a skill – for culture (p. 23), language (p. 23), equipment (p. 345), tech level (p. 168), and so forth – apply to its techniques, as do any special critical success or failure results.

SAMPLE COMBAT TECHNIQUES

Special moves in combat are by far the most common techniques, and can give warriors a "bag of tricks" similar to a wizard's spells. If a combat technique has multiple defaults, you *must* specialize by prerequisite skill. For instance, learning a technique for Axe/Mace skill gives no special ability with the Broadsword version of that technique!

Techniques marked with a * are not particularly realistic. The GM may wish to restrict these "cinematic" techniques – even at default – to PCs with Trained By A Master (p. 93) or Weapon Master (p. 99).

Arm Lock

Average

Defaults: Judo or Wrestling.
Prerequisites: Judo or Wrestling; cannot exceed prerequisite skill+4.

This technique allows you to improve your effective Judo or Wrestling skill for the purpose of applying an arm lock. For rules governing arm locks, see *Arm Lock* (p. 403).

Back Kick

Hard

Default: Karate-4.
Prerequisites: Karate; cannot exceed Karate skill.

This technique lets you attack someone behind you without changing facing. You *must* know that he is there! Roll against Back Kick to hit, but otherwise resolve this as a normal kick. After attempting a Back Kick, all your active defenses are at -2 until next turn.

Choke Hold

Hard

Defaults: Judo-2 or Wrestling-3.
Prerequisites: Judo or Wrestling; cannot exceed prerequisite skill.

This technique lets you to "buy off" the basic -2 to Judo or -3 to Wrestling when using the rules given under *Choke Hold* on p. 404.

Disarming

Hard

Default: prerequisite skill.
Prerequisite: Any unarmed combat or Melee Weapon skill; cannot exceed prerequisite skill+5.

If you know this technique above default, you may use it *instead of* the underlying skill whenever you attack to disarm (see *Striking at Weapons*, p. 400). For instance, if you have Broadsword-14 and Disarming (Broadsword)-17, you disarm as if you had Broadsword-17.

Dual-Weapon Attack*

Hard

Default: prerequisite skill-4.
Prerequisite: Any one-handed Melee Weapon skill; cannot exceed prerequisite skill*.

* You may learn this technique for Guns (Pistol), even in a realistic campaign.

Normally, you are at -4 to attack with two weapons at once unless you make an All-Out Attack. This technique lets you "buy off" that penalty. (Note that you must still learn Off-Hand Weapon Training, p. 232, to reduce the -4 for using the "off" hand!) For detailed rules, see *Dual-Weapon Attacks* (p. 417).

Elbow Strike

Average

Defaults: Brawling-2 or Karate-2.
Prerequisites: Brawling or Karate; cannot exceed prerequisite skill.

This technique lets you "buy off" the -2 penalty to strike with the elbow. See *Elbow Strike* (p. 404) for more information.

Feint
Hard

Default: prerequisite skill.
Prerequisite: Any unarmed combat or Melee Weapon skill; cannot exceed prerequisite skill+4.

If you know this technique above default, you may use it *instead of* the underlying skill whenever you feint (see *Feint*, p. 365). For instance, if you have Broadsword-14 and Feint (Broadsword)-16, you feint as if you had Broadsword-16.

Finger Lock
Hard

Default: Arm Lock-3
Prerequisite: Arm Lock; cannot exceed Arm Lock.

This technique lets you grab fingers and twist them painfully. Use the rules for Arm Lock (p. 403), except that all damage is to the *hand* – which is easier to cripple than the arm.

Ground Fighting
Hard

Default: prerequisite skill-4.
Prerequisite: Any unarmed combat or Melee Weapon skill; cannot exceed prerequisite skill.

This technique lets you "buy off" the -4 for attacking from your back. Roll against this technique *instead of* the prerequisite skill whenever you use that skill to attack from the ground. For instance, if you had Wrestling-14 and Ground Fighting (Wrestling)-13, you could grapple from the ground at skill 13.

In addition, make a roll against Ground Fighting whenever you must defend yourself from your back. On a success, you defend at -1 instead of at -3.

Horse Archery
Hard

Default: Bow-4.
Prerequisites: Bow and Riding; cannot exceed Bow skill.

This technique lets you use a bow *effectively* from horseback. The modifiers for firing from horseback (p. 397) can never reduce your Bow skill below your Horse Archery level. (Other penalties apply normally.) For instance, if you had Bow 13 and Horse Archery-11, the penalties for archery from horseback would never reduce your skill below 11, before other modifiers.

Jump Kick
Hard

Default: Karate-4.
Prerequisite: Karate; cannot exceed Karate skill.

This technique lets you leap into the air and kick at full extension, increasing range and damage. It is a showy but dangerous move! Roll against Jump Kick to hit. Add one yard to reach and +2 to damage. Your target parries at -2. However, if you miss – or if your target successfully defends – you *fall down* unless you can make a DX-4 or Acrobatics-2 roll. Hit or miss, a Jump Kick leaves you at -2 on all your active defenses until your next turn.

Kicking
Hard

Defaults: Brawling-2 or Karate-2.
Prerequisite: Brawling or Karate; cannot exceed prerequisite skill.

This technique lets you improve your kicking ability. Roll against Kicking to hit. A kick does thrust/crushing damage based on ST. Use Brawling or Karate skill – *not* your Kicking level – to determine your damage bonus, and use only the *highest* bonus. If you miss with a kick, roll vs. Kicking skill or DX to avoid falling.

Knee Strike

Average

Defaults: Brawling-1 or Karate-1.
Prerequisite: Brawling or Karate; cannot exceed prerequisite skill.

This technique lets you "buy off" the -1 penalty to strike with the knee – see *Knee Strike* (p. 404).

Neck Snap

Hard

Default: ST-4; cannot exceed ST+3.

This brute-force attack consists of grabbing and suddenly twisting the victim's head, with the intent of snapping the neck – see *Neck Snap o Wrench Limb* (p. 404). Unlike most techniques, Neck Snap defaults to ST, not a skill. Wrestling gives its usual skill-based ST bonus.

Double Defaults and Techniques

A skill cannot default to another skill known only by default (see *Double Defaults*, p. 173). However, techniques are not skills. If two techniques are based on the same underlying skill, one *can* default to the other, even if you only know the intermediate technique at default.

Example: Finger Lock defaults to Arm Lock-3, and Arm Lock defaults to Judo or Wrestling. Effectively, Finger Lock also defaults to Judo-3 or Wrestling-3.

Off-Hand Weapon Training

Hard

Default: prerequisite skill-4.
Prerequisite: Any Melee Weapon skill; cannot exceed prerequisite skill.

This technique lets you "buy off" the -4 for using your "off" hand with one specific Melee Weapon skill. Use your level with this technique *instead of* the prerequisite skill whenever you use that skill to attack or parry with your off hand. For instance, if you had Rapier-14 and Off-Hand Weapon Training (Rapier)-14, you could attack and parry at full skill with your off hand.

Sweep

Hard

Default: prerequisite skill-3.
Prerequisites: Polearm, Spear, or Staff; cannot exceed prerequisite skill.

This technique lets you sweep your adversary's legs out from under him using a pole weapon. Roll against Sweep to hit. The target may defend normally. If he fails, roll a Quick Contest: your Sweep or ST vs. your victim's ST or DX. Use the *higher* value in both cases. If the victim loses, he falls down unless he can make an Acrobatics-5 roll to somersault in the air and land safely.

Unarmed fighters call this technique "Sweeping Kick." It works

With the GM's permission, you can learn this technique for *any* DX-based skill that requires only one hand.

Retain Weapon

Hard

Default: prerequisite skill.
Prerequisite: Any Melee Weapon skill; cannot exceed prerequisite skill+5.

If you know this technique above default, you may use it *instead of* the underlying skill whenever someone attempts to disarm you (see *Striking at Weapons*, p. 400). For instance, if you have Staff-13 and Retain Weapon (Staff)-16, you resist disarm attempts as if you had Staff-16.

You can also learn this technique for missile weapons, such as guns and bows. In that case, it defaults to DX and cannot exceed DX+5.

exactly the same way, but uses a leg instead of a pole, and defaults to Judo-3, Karate-3, or Sumo Wrestling-3.

Whirlwind Attack*

Hard

Default: prerequisite skill-5.
Prerequisites: Broadsword, Staff, or Two-Handed Sword; cannot exceed prerequisite skill.

Whirlwind Attack is a special All-Out Attack that lets you attack *every* foe adjacent to you with lightning speed! If you use this technique, it is *all* you can do that turn, no matter how fast or skilled you are. Furthermore, since this is an All-Out Attack, you will have no active defenses afterward – see *All-Out Attack* (p. 365).

When you launch a Whirlwind Attack, you spin in place, attacking all adjacent foes within one yard. You must attack them in clockwise or counterclockwise order – your choice. All your attacks must be swung attacks, and you cannot combine a Whirlwind Attack with other techniques (such as Disarming) or with cinematic skills (such as Power Blow).

Determine a random hit location for each target, and then roll against Whirlwind Attack to hit, with the usual hit location penalties. You opponent may defend normally. Resolve each attack completely before moving on to the next one. If any of the attacks is a critical miss (or if any of your opponents critically succeeds on his defense), that attack and *all remaining attacks* are critical misses – roll on the *Critical Miss Table* (p. 556) once per attack!

You may end a Whirlwind Attack facing in any direction you wish.

SAMPLE NONCOMBAT TECHNIQUES

Nearly *any* task that calls for a skill roll at a penalty could become a technique. The main purpose of such techniques is to buy off skill penalties, but the GM might wish to provide additional details.

The "opposite" technique, Rope Down, defaults to Climbing-1 and can be improved to Climbing+3. Sliding down a rope is significantly easier than any kind of climbing!

Scaling

Hard

Default: Climbing-3.
Prerequisite: Climbing; cannot exceed prerequisite skill.

This technique lets you eliminate some or all of the -3 to skill for climbing a relatively smooth, vertical surface such as a building or rock face (see *Climbing*, p. 349).

Set Trap

Hard

Default: Explosives (Demolition)-2.
Prerequisite: Explosives (Demolition); cannot exceed prerequisite skill.

With study, you can gain familiarity with "trap" triggers, allowing you to set traps without the usual -2 to skill. Assassins, commandos, spies, etc. often improve this technique.

Slip Handcuffs

Hard

Default: Escape-5.
Prerequisite: Escape; cannot exceed prerequisite skill.

This technique represents study of a specific set of tricks for slipping out of handcuffs. With the GM's permission, you can learn similar techniques for other restraints commonly used in your game world.

Work by Touch

Hard

Default: Lockpicking-5.
Prerequisite: Lockpicking; cannot exceed prerequisite skill.

Lockpicking is normally at -5 if you must work by touch, but if you routinely practice this way, it will eventually become second nature.

The GM might permit you to learn a Work by Touch technique for other "thief" skills – e.g., Explosives and Traps – allowing you to operate in total darkness, which is a common way to use such skills . . .

Impersonate

Average

Default: Mimicry (Speech)-3.
Prerequisite: Mimicry (Speech); cannot exceed prerequisite skill.

Through practice, you can improve your ability to mimic one specific person, gradually buying off the -3 to impersonate him. Each person mimicked is a separate technique.

Lifesaving

Hard

Default: Swimming-5.
Prerequisite: Swimming; cannot exceed prerequisite skill.

You can study lifesaving separately from swimming in order to eliminate the basic -5 for that task. See *Lifesaving* (p. 355) for detailed rules.

Motion-Picture Camera

Average

Default: Photography-3.
Prerequisite: Photography.

This technique, common among professional cameramen, allows you to buy off the -3 to use a motion-picture camera with Photography skill.

No-Landing Extraction

Hard

Default: Piloting-4.
Prerequisite: Piloting; cannot exceed prerequisite skill.

This technique lets you pick up cargo from the ground without landing. You can only fetch cargos outfitted with special no-landing extraction apparatus. Someone on the ground must make a successful Freight Handling roll to prepare the cargo (takes 2d hours). A failed Freight Handling or No-Landing Extraction roll means a missed pick-up or damaged cargo. Critical failure indicates the cargo is lost (critically injured, if a living passenger).

Rope Up

Average

Default: Climbing-2.
Prerequisite: Climbing; cannot exceed prerequisite skill.

A climber normally has -2 to climb a dangling rope (see *Climbing*, p. 349). With practice, you can buy off this penalty.

CHAPTER FIVE
MAGIC

These rules only matter to wizards, and only in worlds where magic exists. If you are not creating a wizard for a magical setting, you can safely skip this chapter.

Magic is a powerful force manipulated using skills called *spells*. By casting spells, a wizard can direct magical energy – known as *mana* – to produce almost any effect. This is a fickle art in some settings, a precise science in others.

The best wizards have an inborn ability to learn and use magic, called *Magery* (p. 66). Anyone with any degree of Magery is called a *mage*. In many game worlds, only mages can use magic. In all worlds, they are *better* with magic than non-mages.

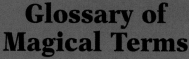

Glossary of Magical Terms

abort: To stop the casting of a spell before its completion.

backfire: A critical failure when casting a spell.

base skill: Your unmodified skill with a spell; compare with *effective skill.*

basic spell: A spell with no other spells as prerequisites.

cancel: To end your own spell before it would normally be over.

caster: The person casting a spell.

class: A group of spells that use the same special rules. Three examples appear in this glossary: *Melee spells*, *Missile spells*, and *Resisted spells*.

college: A group of spells that deal with the same subject – fire, healing, etc.

effective skill: Your base skill, plus any modifiers (usually penalties) for range, circumstances, etc. A caster rolls against *effective* skill.

Enchantment spell: A spell for creating permanent magic items. See *Magic Items*, p. 480.

energy: The "cost" to cast a spell. You may pay this in either FP or HP. Some game worlds offer alternative energy sources.

grimoire: The list of spells *you* know (and more generally, any book of spells).

mage: Anyone with the Magery advantage.

Magery: The advantage of being "in tune" with magic; see p. 66.

maintain: To continue a spell after it would normally end. This costs more energy, unless you have high skill.

mana: The ambient magical energy manipulated by spells. Different areas (or worlds) have different levels of mana; see *Mana* (p. 235).

Melee spell: A spell that "charges" your hand or a magic staff with harmful energies that affect the first target you strike.

Missile spell: A spell that summons a magical projectile that you must "throw" at the subject.

Prerequisites: A requirement for learning a spell. Means exactly what it means for skills; see *Prerequisites* (p. 169).

Resisted spell: Any spell that must overcome the "power" of its subject before it works.

spell: A skill that produces a specific magical effect when used successfully.

subject: The person, place, or thing on which a spell is cast.

wizard: *Any* user of magic, whether he is a mage or not.

LEARNING MAGIC

Anyone can learn most spells – although in some worlds, you must be a mage to *use* the spells you know. Some spells specify a particular level of Magery as a prerequisites: if you lack the required Magery level, *you cannot learn the spell.*

Each magic spell is a separate *skill*, learned just like any other skill. Most spells are IQ/Hard skills, but a few potent spells are IQ/Very Hard. Spells have no default – you can only cast spells you know.

Add your Magery to IQ when you learn spells. For instance, if you have IQ 12 and Magery 3, you learn spells as if you had IQ 15. In addition,

reduce the time required to learn spells (but *not* the point cost) by 10% per Magery level, to a minimum of 60% the usual time at Magery 4; e.g., Magery 3 would let you learn spells in 70% the usual time.

The maximum level of Magery available in your world is up to the GM. Most GMs will want to limit PCs to Magery 3 or 4.

If you know more than a few spells, you may wish to make a "grimoire." This is a list of the spells you know and your skill with each, along with the energy cost, time to cast, duration, etc. for each spell. This saves a lot of reference time in play!

PREREQUISITES

Any spell but the most basic has one or more *prerequisites:* requirements you must meet in order to learn the spell. If the prerequisite is another spell, you must have at least one point in the prerequisite spell before you can study the advanced spell. Some spells require a minimum Magery level; for instance, "Magery 2" means you must have Magery 2 (or higher) to learn the spell. A few spells require a minimum basic attribute score, an advantage, or even a mundane skill.

Mana

Mana is the ambient energy that empowers magic. Magic will work only if the *mana level* of the game world or specific area allows it, as follows:

Very High Mana: Anyone who knows spells can cast them. A *mage* who spends FP to cast a spell on his turn gets those FP back at the start of his *next* turn. However, all failures are treated as critical failures – and actual critical failures produce spectacular disasters! Very high mana is extremely rare in most settings.

High Mana: Anyone who knows spells can cast them. This mana level is rare in most worlds, but some game worlds have high mana throughout.

Normal Mana: Only *mages* can cast spells. These spells work normally, according to all rules given in this chapter. This is the default mana level in most fantasy settings: mages use magic, others don't.

Low Mana: Only mages can cast spells, and all spells perform at -5 to skill, for all purposes. (Magic items are similarly affected; see *Power of a Magic Item*, p. 481.) However, critical failures have mild effects or no effect at all.

No Mana: No one can use magic at all. Magic items do not function (but regain their powers when taken to an area with mana). This mana level occurs in isolated spots in magical worlds, but entire game worlds can lack mana, making magic use impossible.

CASTING SPELLS

You must know a spell in order to cast it, unless you possess a magic item that lets you cast it (see *Magic Items*, p. 480). Tell the GM what spell you are casting, then take Concentrate maneuvers for the requisite number of turns (see *Time Required*, p. 236). At the end of the *last* second of concentration, make a success roll for the spell.

Casting a spell works like any other use of a skill. Roll 3d and compare the total to your *effective* skill: your base skill with the spell adjusted by any applicable modifiers. Modifiers depend on the class of spell (see *Spell Classes*,

p. 239). If your roll is less than or equal to your effective skill, the spell works. If it is greater than your effective skill, the spell fails.

On a *success*, mark off the spell's energy cost against your FP or HP (see *Energy Cost*, p. 236). Its effects take place immediately. On a *critical success*, the spell works especially well. Details are up to the GM, who should be both generous and creative. Whatever else occurs, there is never an energy cost if you get a critical success when you cast a spell.

On a *failure*, the spell does not work. If success would have cost energy, you lose one energy point; otherwise, you lose nothing. (*Exception:* You must pay the full energy cost even on a failure for an Information spell; see *Information Spells*, p. 241.) On a *critical failure*, you must spend the full energy cost *and* the spell fails . . . *badly!* The GM may use the *Critical Spell Failure Table* or improvise some other "backfire" he finds amusing.

DISTRACTION AND INJURY

If you use an active defense against an attack, or are knocked back, knocked down, injured, grappled, or otherwise distracted while concentrating, make a Will roll at -3 to continue casting your spell. On a failure, your spell is spoiled and you must start over.

If you are *stunned* while concentrating, your spell is automatically spoiled.

If you are *injured* but not stunned while concentrating, and succeed on the roll to avoid distraction, you may cast your spell. However, the shock penalty for your injury reduces your effective skill. See p. 419 for details on shock.

CASTER AND SUBJECT

The "caster" of a spell is the person who is attempting to cast it.

The "subject" of a spell is the person, place, or thing upon which the spell is cast. If you are casting a spell on yourself, you are both caster and subject. The subject can also be another being, an inanimate object, or even a patch of ground. If the subject is a place, the caster can "touch" it by extending a hand over it or touching the ground, as appropriate for the spell.

TIME REQUIRED

Most spells take one second to cast. Take the Concentrate maneuver for one turn and attempt your skill roll at the end of your turn. If you succeed, the spell takes effect instantly. Whether you succeed or fail, your turn ends as soon as you roll the dice.

Example: Wat wants to cast Create Fire, a one-second spell. On his turn, Wat says, "I'm concentrating on Create Fire." This uses his entire turn. He then rolls the dice for his spell. If he succeeds, he creates fire – but either way, Wat's turn ends.

Some spells take more than one second to cast. This requires multiple, consecutive Concentrate maneuvers

in combat. Make the skill roll at the end of the *last* turn of concentration. You may "abort" an unfinished spell before it is cast, at no penalty, but you must start over if you wish to try again.

Critical Spell Failure Table

Roll 3d on the table below. If the result is inappropriate – or if it is the result that the caster *intended* – roll again. The GM is free to improvise instead of using the table. Improvisations should be appropriate to the spell and the situation, and should never kill the caster outright.

3 – Spell fails entirely. Caster takes 1d of injury.
4 – Spell is cast on caster (if harmful) or on a random nearby foe (if beneficial).
5-6 – Spell is cast on one of the caster's companions (if harmful) or on a random nearby foe (if beneficial).
7 – Spell affects someone or something other than its intended target – friend, foe, or random object. Roll randomly or make an interesting choice.
8 – Spell fails entirely. Caster takes 1 point of injury.
9 – Spell fails entirely. Caster is stunned (IQ roll to recover).
10-11 – Spell produces nothing but a loud noise, bright flash of light, awful odor, etc.
12 – Spell produces a weak and useless shadow of the intended effect.
13 – Spell produces the reverse of the intended effect.
14 – Spell seems to work, but it is only a useless illusion. The GM should do his best to convince the wizard and his companions that the spell *did* work!
15-16 – Spell has the reverse of the intended effect, on the wrong target. Roll randomly.
17 – Spell fails entirely. Caster temporarily forgets the spell. Make an IQ roll after a week, and again each following week, until he remembers.
18 – Spell fails entirely. A demon or other malign entity appropriate to the setting appears and attacks the caster. (The GM may waive this result if, *in his opinion*, caster and spell were both lily-white, pure good in intent.)

Example: If a spell takes three seconds to cast, you must spend three turns doing nothing but concentrating. You roll the dice at the end of your third turn.

ENERGY COST

Each spell has an energy cost. When you cast the spell, you must pay this cost in either FP or HP. The better you know the spell, the less energy you

need to cast it. If you know it well enough, you can cast it at *no* cost. *Exception:* Never reduce the cost of a Blocking spell; see *Blocking Spells* (p. 241).

If your *base skill* with a spell – modified only by the -5 for low mana, if applicable – is 15 or higher, reduce the cost to cast the spell by 1. If you have skill 20 or higher, reduce the cost by 2. Cost continues to decrease by 1 per full five skill levels beyond skill 20. Apply the same reduction to the cost to *maintain* a spell. Calculate the entire cost for a spell (for instance, by multiplying cost for the size of the subject or the area affected) before applying energy cost reductions for high skill. Energy is still going into the spell, but your skill lets you draw it from the surrounding mana rather than supplying it yourself!

You normally pay the energy cost of a spell in FP. You can recover lost FP by resting. A *mage* with the Recover Energy spell (p. 248) recovers FP faster than normal.

Burning HP

You may also expend life energy to pay the cost of a spell. Mark off some or all of the cost against HP instead of FP – the spell is actually harming you! You are at -1 on your spell roll per HP used. This is *instead* of the usual shock penalty for injury, and High Pain Threshold has no effect.

Using HP to power spells is dangerous, but it may be necessary if you are badly fatigued and *must* cast another spell. You may "burn" HP until you fall unconscious. Should a failed HT roll indicate that you have died, you do not actually spend the HP. Instead, you fall unconscious.

Treat HP lost this way just like any other injury.

MAGIC RITUALS

To cast a spell, you must usually perform a ritual that involves gestures and speech. If you can't perform the ritual, you can't cast the spell! For instance, if the ritual for a spell requires you to speak, you cannot cast the spell if you are gagged or under a spell of silence.

The higher your skill with a spell, the easier it is to cast: it takes less time, requires less energy, and has less stringent ritual requirements. See the list below for details. In all cases, "skill" refers to *base* skill, not effective skill. The *only* modifier that matters here is the -5 for low mana, if applicable.

Skill 9 or less – *Ritual:* You must have both hands and both feet free for elaborate ritual movements, and you must speak certain words of power in a firm voice. *Time:* Doubled. *Cost:* As listed.

Skill 10-14 – *Ritual:* You must speak a few quiet words *and* make a gesture. *Time:* As listed. *Cost:* As listed.

Skill 15-19 – *Ritual:* You must speak a word or two *or* make a small gesture (a couple of fingers are enough), but not necessarily both. You are allowed to move one yard per second while taking the Concentrate maneuver. *Time:* As listed. *Cost:* Reduced by 1.

Skill 20-24 – *Ritual:* None! You simply stare into space as you concentrate. *Time:* Halved (round fractions up to the next second). Minimum casting time is still one second. *Cost:* Reduced by 2.

Skill 25-29 – *Ritual:* None. *Time:* Divided by 4 (round up). *Cost:* Reduced by 3.

Skill 30 or more – As above, but for every five levels of skill beyond skill 25 (that is, at levels 30, 35, 40, etc.), halve casting time again *and* reduce energy cost by one more point.

Certain spells always require a specific ritual. Such requirements override the rules above. For instance, high skill has no effect on the *cost* to cast Blocking spells (p. 241) or the *time* to cast Missile spells (p. 240).

LIMITS ON EFFECT

The effects of many spells vary with the energy spent. For instance, a healing spell might heal 1 HP per energy point, or a combat spell might inflict 1d damage per point.

If the spell description sets no upper limit, then you may spend as much energy as you can afford! The more you spend, the greater the effect.

If the spell specifies a finite range of effects and associated energy costs, though, you *cannot* exceed the upper limit without a high level of Magery (see below).

If *either* type of variable spell is cast on the same subject more than once, only the spell with the most powerful effects counts – multiple instances of a given spell do not "stack" or add in any way. Spells that heal, damage, or otherwise *permanently* affect the subject are an exception: you may cast such spells repeatedly, healing or damaging the subject by the full amount each time.

Magery and Effect

Talented mages may exceed the usual limits for spells that allow a finite number of "levels of effect" (dice of damage, bonuses to skill, etc.). The upper limit is the *higher* of the standard number of levels or the caster's Magery level.

Example: Major Healing (p. 248) allows you to spend 1, 2, 3, or 4 energy points to heal 2, 4, 6, or 8 HP. It has four levels of effect. Magery 10 would let you revise this limit to *10* levels of effect – you could spend 1-10 energy points to heal 2-20 HP!

Canceling Spells

Sometimes, you will want to end a spell before its full duration is up. If you specify a shorter duration when you cast the spell, the spell lasts exactly the time desired. If you suddenly decide to "cancel" a spell before its time is up, though, you must pay one energy point (from FP or HP) to do so, regardless of the spell or your skill level.

The GM is free not to use this rule if he thinks it would be unbalanced. Of course, if he puts a limit on the highest level of Magery available, this is not a problem!

DURATION OF SPELLS AND MAINTAINING SPELLS

Some spells produce an instantaneous effect when cast and then end immediately. Other spells last for a fixed "duration" (given for the particular spell, but most often one minute) and then wear off – unless you *maintain* them.

If you can maintain a spell, the energy cost to do so is given in its description, following the casting cost. When the spell reaches the end of its duration, you may continue the spell by paying its maintenance cost. If you do, the spell continues for another interval equal to its duration. This takes no time and requires no skill roll. Distance is not a factor.

Example: The Light spell (p. 249) notes "Duration: 1 minute" and "Cost: 1 to cast; 1 to maintain." It ends after a minute unless, at the end of that minute, you spend one more energy point to maintain it. If you do, it lasts another minute.

You may repeat this process for as long as you wish, provided you can supply the required energy. As long as you are conscious, you know when one of your spells needs to be renewed. However, you cannot maintain a spell while you sleep, and you cannot "hand off" a spell to someone else so he can maintain it for you.

High Skill and Cost to Maintain

Energy cost reduction for high skill also applies to the cost to maintain a spell. This *can* reduce maintenance cost to zero. For instance, if you know a spell at skill 15-19, you may reduce its maintenance cost by 1; if this cost is 1 to begin with, you can maintain the spell indefinitely at *no* energy cost!

Concentration and Maintenance

You can maintain a spell without concentration *unless* the spell requires constant manipulation and change; e.g., to maneuver a levitating object. Spells like this require you to take the Concentrate maneuver only. If you are distracted, injured, or stunned, you must make a Will roll at -3. If you fail, the spell does not end, but it remains in precisely the state it was in when you were distracted, and does not respond to change until you can concentrate on it again. On a critical failure, the spell ends.

Casting another spell does *not* break concentration, but you suffer a skill penalty for doing two things at once (see below).

Ceremonial Magic

If you know a spell at skill 15+ and have a group of *willing* assistants, you may opt to cast the spell by leading your assistants in an elaborate ritual that maximizes the spell's power. Such "ceremonial magic" is time-consuming, but lets you cast more powerful spells than you could cast on your own.

When you work ceremonial magic, multiply casting time by *10*. Energy cost does not change, but your assistants can supplement your energy input as follows:

Each mage who knows the spell at level 15+: as much energy as he wishes to contribute.

Each non-mage who knows the spell at level 15+: up to 3 points.

Each mage who knows the spell at level 14 or lower: up to 3 points.

*Each unskilled spectator who **supports** the casting (by chanting, holding candles, etc.):* 1 point, to a maximum of 100 points from all spectators.

*Each spectator who **opposes** the casting:* -5 points, to a maximum penalty of -100 points from all spectators!

Sum the energy from all sources to find the total energy available. If this exceeds the cost to cast the spell, you receive a skill bonus.

Extra Energy	Skill Bonus
20%	+1
40%	+2
60%	+3
100%	+4

Add another +1 per additional 100% of the required energy.

At the end of the ritual, make a skill roll to cast the spell. Apply all standard modifiers for magic use and any bonus for extra energy. Regardless of the outcome of the die roll, all contributed energy is spent when you roll the dice.

Notes on Ceremonial Magic

- High skill does *not* reduce casting time or energy cost.
- A group aids concentration. If you are distracted during the ritual, roll at Will as opposed to Will-3 to avoid distraction.
- Ceremonial magic is hard to coordinate. A roll of 16 is always a failure, and a roll of 17-18 is always a critical failure – even if effective skill is 16+.
- Once the spell is cast, the participants can continue to provide energy to maintain the spell. The composition of the group may change, as long as the ritual continues uninterrupted. Thus, ceremonial magic lets you maintain a spell indefinitely.

CASTING SPELLS WHILE MAINTAINING OTHER SPELLS

You can only cast one new spell at a time. However, you *can* cast new spells before older ones end. Apply the following modifiers whenever you cast spells while you have other spells active:

-3 per spell you are *concentrating* on at the moment. See the individual spell descriptions to learn which spells require concentration.

-1 per other spell you have "on" at the moment. A spell that lasts permanently (as indicated in the spell description) *does not carry a penalty.*

DIFFERENT KINDS OF MAGIC

There are many different types of magic. Spells fall into "colleges" according to subject matter and "classes" according to the way they work.

COLLEGES OF MAGIC

Spells related by subject matter – e.g., fire, healing, or mind control – belong to the same *college*. The basic spells of a college are prerequisites for the more advanced ones. Some spells fall into more than one college. For instance, Earth to Air (p. 243) is both an Earth and an Air spell. This is only important when counting prerequisites.

Most wizards specialize in only a few colleges. This is the most efficient way to learn advanced magic. However, you may learn spells from as many colleges as you wish.

SPELL CLASSES

Each spell falls into one or more *classes* that define how it works in play. These classes are not mutually exclusive, except as noted below.

Regular Spells

Most spells fall into this class. A Regular spell affects only one subject. Its energy cost assumes a human-sized subject – that is, one with Size Modifier 0. For a subject with a *positive* SM, multiply cost by 1 + SM: ×2 energy for SM +1, ×3 for SM +2, ×4 for SM +3, and so on. There is no cost reduction for a subject with a *negative* SM. A few Regular spells give special cost schemes that override these rules.

Regular spells work best if you can *touch* or *see* the subject. You do not have to see through your own eyes; any spell that lets you see by magical means will do.

If you cannot *touch* the subject, apply a skill penalty equal to your distance in yards from the subject; e.g., -5 at five yards. Figure distance at the moment you roll the dice for the spell.

If you cannot touch *or* see the subject, there is a further -5 penalty. There are two ways to direct such a spell:

● Name a *target location*. For instance, if you specify "One yard beyond the other side of this door," you'll get whoever is standing on the other side of the door. If there is nobody there, you wasted the spell.

● Name a *subject*; e.g., "The closest person in the next room," or, "George, who I know is around here somewhere." The GM determines the actual range to the subject. This is risky! If the subject is farther away than you think – or simply absent – you are inviting failure or even critical failure!

No physical barrier affects a Regular spell. Unless the spell back-fires, a Regular spell never hits the wrong target.

Area Spells

These spells affect an area rather than an individual. They are cast on a surface – floor, ground, etc. – and their effects extend four yards (12 feet) up from that surface. A few Area spells work differently; see the individual spell descriptions for details.

The size of the area governs the energy cost, but not the difficulty of the roll. The cost listed for an Area spell is its "base cost." The actual cost to cast the spell is equal to base cost multiplied by the radius of the area of effect in yards (minimum one yard): ×1 for a one-yard radius, ×2 for a two-yard radius, ×3 for a three-yard radius, and so on.

Some Area spells have a fractional base cost, such as 1/2 or 1/10. You must spend a minimum of one energy point on these spells. A few Area spells specify a minimum cost; you must *always* pay the minimum cost, even if this is larger than the base cost multiplied by the desired radius.

If an Area spell affects living beings, it affects *everyone* in the area of effect. You may choose to affect only a part of the area, rather than the whole circle, but the cost is still the same.

If you cannot touch some part of the affected area, apply a skill penalty equal to your distance in yards from the *nearest* edge of the area.

Otherwise, Area spells work like Regular spells.

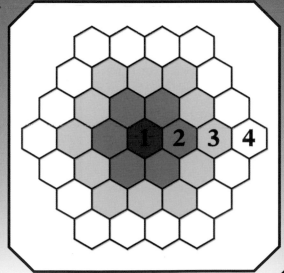

Area Spells on a Battle Map

Represent Area spells on a battle map as follows. The area of effect of a spell cast over a one-yard radius is a *single hex*. The area of effect of a spell cast over a two-yard radius is a central hex and *all adjacent hexes*. The area of effect of a spell cast over a three-yard radius is a central two-yard area of effect plus the ring of hexes adjacent to *that*. And so on, building up larger areas by adding successive rings of adjacent hexes.

Melee Spells

Melee spells "charge" your hand or magic staff (see box) with harmful energies that affect the first target you strike. These spells require *two* skill rolls: a roll against spell skill to cast the spell, and a normal melee attack roll to hit your target with your hand or staff.

To cast a Melee spell, concentrate for the required time, roll against spell skill at the end of the final turn of concentration, and pay the energy cost. There is no distance modifier – you are casting the spell on yourself! On a success, you energize your hand or staff with the spell's magic. On your *next* turn, you must do one of two things with your spell: hold it or attack with it.

If you hold your spell, your hand or staff remains "charged." This has no energy cost and requires no skill roll. You *cannot* cast another spell while holding a Melee spell. You can take any other combat maneuver (but an attack with the energized hand or staff discharges the spell). A parry with that hand or staff does not discharge the spell; an *attack* is part of the ritual, and nothing else works.

A held Melee spell on a staff persists only for as long as you wield the staff. If you lose hold of your staff, even for an instant, the spell drains away harmlessly. If someone *grabs* your staff, and you are both holding onto it on your turn, your attempt to wrench it free counts as an attack, and your opponent instantly suffers the spell's effects!

To attack, roll against DX or an unarmed combat skill to hit with a hand, or the appropriate Melee Weapon skill to hit with a staff. This is a standard melee attack. Your target may attempt any active defense. If he succeeds, your spell is not triggered; you may try again next turn. If he fails, your melee attack does its usual damage *and* your spell affects him immediately.

Armor protects normally against some Melee spells, not at all against others. If the spell is one that ignores armor, neither an unarmed parry (even with an armored limb) nor a block will protect the target from the spell. Even if such a defense wards off the melee attack, the spell arcs through the target's armor or shield and affects him.

Note that some Melee spells are Resisted (see p. 241). These spells require a *second* roll against spell skill, when the spell actually takes effect, to overcome the target's resistance.

Missile Spells

This class of spells encompasses long-distance "projectile" or "bolt" attacks, such as Fireball (p. 247) and Lightning (p. 244). Missile spells require *two* skill rolls: a roll against spell skill to cast the spell, and a roll against Innate Attack skill (p. 201) to hit the target.

To cast a Missile spell, you must concentrate for one second. At the end of your turn, roll against your skill with the spell. There is *no* modifier for distance – you are creating a magical missile in your hand. On a success, you may invest one or more points of energy in the spell, to a maximum number of energy points equal to your Magery level. The missile then appears in your hand, "charged" to the desired level.

On your *next* turn, you have three options with your missile: make a ranged attack with it, hold it, or *enlarge* it. If you opt to enlarge your missile, you must concentrate for another second. At the end of your turn, you may invest more energy in the spell – anything from one point to points equal to your Magery level. This does not require a skill roll.

The turn after that, you have the same options: attack, hold, or enlarge. On your fourth and subsequent turns, you may only attack or hold. You cannot spend more than three seconds building up a Missile spell.

Once you stop enlarging a Missile spell, you may "hold" it in hand, ready to attack. You do not have to launch the missile until you want to. While holding a Missile spell, you may move up to your full Move, take a Wait or Aim maneuver, or even attack using the hand that isn't "holding" the missile. You may defend normally. However, you *cannot* cast another spell.

There is one drawback: if you are *injured* while you have a missile "in

---

Magic Staffs

A "magic staff" is any wand or staff imbued with the power to extend your reach for the purpose of casting spells (see *Staff*, p. 481). It gives three main benefits:

● Touching a subject with your staff lets you cast spells on that subject at *no* distance penalty. This is useful in situations where you must cast a spell on a subject you cannot touch with your hand (e.g., when casting a healing spell on someone trapped under rubble).

● Pointing with a staff reduces the range to a distant subject by the length of the staff. This is valuable for Regular spells, as a one-yard wand shaves -1 off distance penalties, while a two-yard quarterstaff eliminates -2! You can point as part of the ritual to cast a spell. Tell the GM you are pointing at the subject when you *start* concentrating. (This might warn an unwilling subject!)

● A staff can carry Melee spells. This gives them more reach, and lets you strike and parry without putting your hand in harm's way.

A magic staff can be any length up to two yards. A wand is Reach C, too light to do damage, and uses Knife or Main-Gauche skill. A long wand or short staff is Reach 1, functions as a baton in combat, and uses Shortsword or Smallsword skill. A full-length staff is Reach 2, counts as a quarterstaff in combat, and uses Staff or Two-Handed Sword skill. In most game worlds, a suitable ordinary item can be enchanted as a magic staff for $30, but it must be made from once-living materials (wood, bone, ivory, coral, etc.).

hand," you must make a Will roll. If you fail, the missile immediately affects *you!*

When you are ready to attack, roll against your Innate Attack skill to hit. This is a standard ranged attack, subject to the usual modifiers for target size, speed, and range. Once launched, the missile flies in a straight line to the target. Physical barriers affect it just as they would affect any missile weapon.

Your target may block or dodge, but not parry. If he fails, he is hit and the spell affects him. The *strength* of the effect depends on the energy invested. Most Missile spells inflict 1d of damage per point of energy. Damage Resistance – whether natural or from armor – protects normally against damaging Missile spells.

Blocking Spells

A Blocking spell is cast *instantly* as a defense against either a physical attack or another spell. It is the magical equivalent of a block, parry, or dodge (and often counts as one of these defenses; see the spell description for details). You may cast only *one* Blocking spell per turn, no matter how skilled you are. You cannot attempt a Blocking spell against a critical hit.

If you try a Blocking spell, it *automatically* interrupts your own concentration. You lose any spell you were preparing exactly as if you had failed the Will roll to resist a distraction. If you are holding (not *casting*) a Melee spell, it is unaffected. If you are holding a Missile spell, you cannot enlarge it further but may retain it for later use.

Blocking spells do *not* get an energy cost reduction for high skill.

Information Spells

Information spells are cast to gain knowledge. Some require you to touch the subject, while others function at a distance; see *Long-Distance Modifiers* (box) for range penalties. Spells intended to find things are at -1 per "known" item you choose to ignore in your search. Most Information spells have additional special modifiers, so be sure to read the spell description carefully.

When you cast an Information spell, *the GM rolls for you in secret.* If the spell succeeds, the GM gives you the desired information – the better the roll, the better the information. If

Dissipating Held Melee and Missile Spells

You sometimes need to dispel a held Melee or Missile spell *quickly*, without taking a full turn to make an attack – for instance, so you can concentrate on another spell. You can do this as a free action at any point during your turn; simply state that you are dissipating the spell and it "evaporates" harmlessly.

You can also get rid of a Missile spell (*not* a Melee spell) by "dropping" it at your feet. This, too, is a free action. This does not damage you, unless the missile is explosive, but it damages whatever you are standing on. Missiles that inflict burning damage are liable to set fires!

the spell fails, the GM says, "You sense nothing." On a critical failure, the GM *lies* to you! Regardless of the outcome, you must always pay the full energy cost for the spell.

Information spells generally allow only one attempt per day by each caster (or ceremonial group). "Seek" spells are an exception to this.

Except where specifically noted, Information spells have no duration. They grant a momentary glimpse of insight and end immediately; therefore, you cannot maintain them.

Resisted Spells

A spell of any type can also be "Resisted." A spell like this works automatically only on a critical success. On a regular success, your spell must defeat the subject's resistance to work.

The subject always has a chance to resist, *even if he is unconscious.* A conscious subject is aware that something is happening, and may choose not to resist. Individuals who are unconscious, unfamiliar with magic, or wary of hostile magic always try to resist.

To resolve a Resisted spell, you must first succeed at your skill roll. If the spell has a single subject (that is, it isn't an Area spell), you have a penalty equal to the subject's Magic Resistance (p. 67), if any – even if he is willing! On a failure, the spell fails and the subject notices nothing. On a success, note your margin of success; e.g., if you rolled a 6 against an effective skill of 13, you succeeded by 7. If the subject is *living* or *sapient*, the Rule of 16 applies (see *The Rule of 16*, p. 349). There is no such limit if the subject is a spell.

Long-Distance Modifiers

Use these modifiers for Information spells that work over long distances, such as "Seek" spells. Certain advantages also use these range penalties. If the distance falls between two values, use the *higher*.

Distance	Penalty
Up to 200 yards	0
1/2 mile	-1
1 mile	-2
3 miles	-3
10 miles	-4
30 miles	-5
100 miles	-6
300 miles	-7
1,000 miles	-8

Add another -2 per additional factor of 10.

The subject then attempts a resistance roll. A character resists using the attribute or other trait indicated in the spell description – usually HT or Will. The subject's Magic Resistance, if any, adds to his resistance. A spell resists using the caster's effective skill when he cast the spell.

Compare the subject's resistance roll to your skill roll in a Quick Contest. If you win, your spell affects the subject. If you lose or tie, the spell has no effect – but you must still pay the full energy cost! A conscious subject feels a slight mental or physical wrench (depending on which attribute he resisted with), but no other effect. You know whether or not the subject resisted your spell.

Resisted Area Spells: When casting an Area spell that is Resisted, make the usual success roll for the spell and record your margin of success if you succeed. Everyone in the area gets a resistance roll, and those with Magic Resistance get *double* the usual benefit. Your spell affects those who make their roll by less than you did.

Special Spells

These spells follow special rules given in the spell description.

SPELL LIST

Alternative Magic Systems

This chapter describes the "standard" magic system. It will work as is, or with minor changes, for wizards in most worlds inspired by fantasy literature. Some visions of magic will demand a radical redesign, however. Two sample variants appear below.

Clerical Magic

To handle the powers of magic-using priests, start with the standard magic system, but read "Magery" as "Power Investiture" (see p. 77) and "mana" as "sanctity." Sanctity levels range from "no sanctity" (the temple of an opposed deity) to "very high sanctity" (in the god's presence).

Clerics have Power Investiture instead of Magery, and their spells have *no* prerequisites. A priest may acquire a new spell simply by praying for it, as long as he has at least one point to spend on the spell. This benefit is balanced by the fact that he can *only* learn those spells offered by his god (GM's decision) and by the fact that his god may alter the outcome of his magic – or suspend his magical powers – for reasons he is unlikely to comprehend.

Ritual Magic

Magic use depends on a single "core skill," typically Ritual Magic (p. 218) or Thaumatology (p. 225). Each college of magic is an IQ/Very Hard "college skill" or "path" that defaults to the core skill at -6. College skills have the core skill as a prerequisite and may never exceed the core skill.

Ritual mages *can* cast spells at default! Each spell is a Hard technique with a default to the associated college skill. For each prerequisite the spell *or its prerequisites* would have in the standard system, the default is at a cumulative -1 (e.g., a spell with one prerequisite that *itself* has one prerequisite defaults to college skill-2). To raise a spell past its default level, the mage must have at least one point in the college skill, but he can ignore the spell's prerequisites under the standard system. Spells cannot exceed the associated college skill.

Magery adds to core skill, college skills, and spells. If standard and ritual magic coexist, normal Magery and Ritual Magery are separate advantages.

All other rules are the same.

On the following pages are 93 spells, picked for their utility in a beginning fantasy or horror campaign. But this is only a glimpse of what magic can do – see *GURPS Magic* for *hundreds* more spells!

Each spell includes:

Name of Spell and the *Class(es)* it belongs to. A "(VH)" indicates an IQ/Very Hard spell; otherwise, it's IQ/Hard.

Description: The spell's effects, special rules, etc. If the spell requires particular items, assume it uses them up unless the description states otherwise.

Duration: The time the spell's effects last. If you maintain the spell, it lasts for another period equal to this. Spells with an instantaneous effect do not list duration and cannot be maintained.

Cost: The energy (FP or HP) spent when you cast the spell. If given as *Base Cost*, this is the cost per yard of radius of an Area spell. Maintainable spells also give a cost to maintain.

Time to Cast: If no time is given, the spell requires one second of concentration and takes place at the end of your turn.

Prerequisites: Other spells you must know (have placed at least one point in the spell) before you may study this spell, as well as any Magery, IQ, or other requirements.

AIR SPELLS

These spells deal with the traditional magical "element" of air. Except as noted, assume that "air" is normal breathing air at one atmosphere of pressure.

Purify Air

Area

This spell removes all impurities from the air in its area of effect. It is often used to neutralize the effects of poisonous gas or vapors. Note that a room full of smoke may safely be purified one section at a time – but truly deadly vapors must all be removed at once, or some may escape.

This spell also turns old "stale" air into fresh breathable air. The air in a one-yard radius, if not renewed from the outside, will last 45 minutes for one person at rest, less for multiple persons or someone violently exercising (GM's discretion).

Duration: Works instantly. Purification is permanent.
Base Cost: 1. Cannot be maintained; must be recast.

Create Air

Area

This spell manufactures air where none exists. When cast where there is already air, it produces an outward breeze lasting about five seconds. When cast in a vacuum, it instantly creates breathable air. When cast within earth, stone, or other material, it fills any empty spaces with air, but does not burst the stone. When cast underwater, it makes bubbles! It cannot be cast inside a living being.

Duration: Breeze, bubbles, etc. last 5 seconds. Air created is permanent.
Base Cost: 1. Cannot be maintained; must be recast.
Prerequisite: Purify Air.

Shape Air

Regular

This spell lets the caster create movements of air over a small area. The caster must choose a starting point (calculate distance penalties to that point). The wind starts there and blows in a stream one yard wide, for a distance in yards equal to 5 times the energy put into the spell, and then dissipates. This may cause knockback (see *Knockback*, p. 378) on someone it hits; each second, roll 1d per full 2 points of energy in the spell. Treat this as damage for knockback purposes only (this spell does *not* cause injury).

Duration: 1 minute.

Cost: 1 to 10. 1 produces a gentle breeze; 4 a wind; 6 a heavy wind; 8 or more a violent blast. Cost to maintain is the same as to cast.
Prerequisite: Create Air.

No-Smell

Regular

Removes the subject's odor and makes it (or him) totally undetectable by smell. Any possessions are also affected. This spell changes no other properties of the subject.

Duration: 1 hour.
Cost: 2; same to maintain.
Prerequisite: Purify Air.

Predict Weather

Information

Lets the caster forecast the weather accurately for a given location over a given time. This forecast does *not* take magical meddling into account, or predict the actions of other wizards!

Cost: Twice the length of the forecast, in days. Double the cost for a location outside the general area (say, over the horizon). Quadruple the cost for a place on another continent. This spell cannot predict weather on other planets or planes.
Time to cast: 5 seconds per day forecast.
Prerequisites: At least four Air spells.

Breathe Water

Regular

Lets the subject breathe water as though it were air. Subject does *not* lose the ability to breathe ordinary air! This spell is also considered a Water spell.

Duration: 1 minute.
Cost: 4 to cast; 2 to maintain.
Prerequisites: Create Air and Destroy Water (p. 253).

Walk on Air

Regular

Temporarily grants the subject the Walk on Air advantage (p. 97). If the subject falls for any reason (e.g., injury), the spell is broken! If the spell is recast immediately, he falls for only one second (about 5 yards) and then "lands" on the air (taking 1d damage) – unless he hits ground before then. If he's 10 feet over a lava pit, too bad!

Duration: 1 minute.
Cost: 3 to cast; 2 to maintain.
Prerequisite: Shape Air.

Earth to Air

Regular

This spell turns earth or stone into air, which can be valuable to someone who is trapped underground! The more energy the caster spends, the more earth he can transform, but he is limited to regular shapes with the largest dimension no more than four times the smallest one. This spell is also considered an Earth spell.

Duration: Permanent.
Cost: 1 to transform one cubic foot of earth/stone to air, giving enough air for one person to breathe for 1 minute. To transform larger quantities of earth/stone at once, the cost is 5 per cubic yard.
Time to cast: 2 seconds.
Prerequisites: Create Air and Shape Earth (p. 245).

Stench

Area

Produces a cloud of vile, yellowish gas that reeks of brimstone. Until it dissipates, anyone who breathes it must make a HT roll or take 1d damage. Roll once per minute. Those in the area also begin to suffocate (see *Suffocation*, p. 436). The cloud is heavy, and "rolls" downhill if the ground is not level. The rate of dissipation depends on the area and presence of wind; indoors, it usually lasts until the spell expires, but outdoors on a windy day, it might only last 10 seconds or so.

Duration: 5 minutes, except in windy areas.
Base Cost: 1. Cannot be maintained; must be recast.
Prerequisite: Purify Air.

Lightning

Missile

Lets the caster shoot a bolt of lightning from his fingertip. This has 1/2D 50, Max 100, Acc 3. Treat any metal armor as DR 1 against this spell! If the target is wounded, he must make a HT roll, at -1 per 2 HP suffered, or be stunned. He may attempt a HT roll each turn thereafter to recover. Against electronic equipment, treat this attack as if it had the Surge damage modifier (see *Surge*, p. 105).

Lightning behaves unpredictably around conductors. A lightning bolt *cannot* be fired through a metal grid, between bars, from within a car, etc. – it jumps to the metal and is lost. However, the GM may (for instance) allow a wizard to shoot a lightning bolt into a metal floor. This would not electrocute those on it, but could shock them all, interrupting concentration and doing slight damage (no more than 1 point, and possibly none at all). The GM may encourage creative use of lightning until it becomes a nuisance . . .

Cost: Any amount up to your Magery level per second, for three seconds. The bolt does 1d-1 burning damage per energy point.
Time to cast: 1 to 3 seconds (the caster's fingers sparkle as the spell builds up).
Prerequisites: Magery 1 and at least six other Air spells.

BODY CONTROL SPELLS

These spells directly affect the body. Except as noted, they only affect *living* beings.

Itch

Regular; Resisted by HT

Causes the subject to itch fiercely in a spot of the caster's choice. The subject is at -2 DX until he takes one full turn to scratch (more, if armor, etc. is in the way!). Only one Itch spell can affect a given subject at a time.

Duration: Until the subject takes a turn to scratch.
Cost: 2. Cannot be maintained; must be recast.

Spasm

Regular; Resisted by HT

Can be directed against any of the subject's *voluntary* muscles. Directed against a hand, it causes the subject to drop whatever he is holding (usually a weapon). If the subject is in the middle of a lengthy spell requiring gestures, he must make a DX roll or start over. Ingenious casters will find other uses . . .

Duration: A moment.
Cost: 2. Cannot be maintained; must be recast.
Prerequisite: Itch.

Pain

Regular; Resisted by HT

The subject feels a stab of agonizing pain. He must make a Will roll to avoid crying out. If he is in a precarious position (climbing, for instance), he must make a DX roll to avoid catastrophe! His DX and all DX-based skills are at -3 for the next turn only. If the subject is in the middle of a spell requiring gestures, he must roll vs. Will or start over. High Pain Threshold gives +3 to the Will and DX rolls above; Low Pain Threshold gives -4.

Duration: 1 second.
Cost: 2. Cannot be maintained; must be recast.
Prerequisite: Spasm.

Clumsiness

Regular; Resisted by HT

The subject suffers -1 to his DX and DX-based skills for every point of energy put into the spell.

Duration: 1 minute.
Cost: 1 to 5 to cast; half that amount to maintain (round up).
Prerequisite: Spasm.

Hinder

Regular; Resisted by HT

The subject is at -1 to his Move and Dodge scores for every point of energy put into the spell. This spell is also considered a Movement spell.

Duration: 1 minute.
Cost: 1 to 4 to cast; same to maintain.
Prerequisite: Clumsiness *or* Haste (p. 251).

Rooted Feet

Regular; Resisted by ST

The subject's feet are glued in place! He may try another resistance roll at -5 *every turn*, against the original spell skill roll, to break free. While the spell continues, the subject's skill with any weapon except a ranged weapon is at -2 and his Dodge score is cut in half (round down).

Duration: 1 minute, or until subject breaks free.
Cost: 3. Cannot be maintained; must be recast.
Prerequisite: Hinder.

Paralyze Limb

Melee; Resisted by HT

The caster must strike the subject on a *limb* to trigger this spell (hits elsewhere have no effect). Armor does not protect. Resolve resistance on contact. If the caster wins, the subject's limb is paralyzed; it is considered crippled for one minute.

Duration: 1 minute.
Cost: 3. Cannot be maintained; must be recast.
Prerequisites: Magery 1 and five Body Control spells, including Pain.

Wither Limb

Melee; Resisted by HT

The caster must strike the subject on a *limb* to trigger this spell. Armor does not protect. Resolve resistance on contact. If the caster wins, the subject's limb withers immediately; it is crippled for all purposes. The subject also takes 1d damage.

Duration: Permanent unless healed magically.
Cost: 5.
Prerequisites: Magery 2 and Paralyze Limb.

Deathtouch
Melee

The caster must strike the subject to trigger this spell; hit location is irrelevant. The subject takes 1d damage per point of energy in the spell. Armor does not protect. This spell *does* affect the undead.

Cost: 1 to 3.
Prerequisite: Wither Limb.

COMMUNICATION AND EMPATHY SPELLS

These spells deal with discerning (or *concealing*) thought and intent. For spells that manipulate emotions and loyalties, see *Mind Control Spells* (p. 250).

Sense Foes
Information; Area

Tells the caster if the subject has hostile intent, and what the degree of hostility is. Can be cast on one person or a whole area. If cast over an area, this spell only detects that *someone* is hostile, without telling *who*.

Base Cost: 1 (minimum 2).

Sense Emotion
Regular

Lets the caster know what emotions the subject is feeling at the moment. It works on any living being, but is not much use except on sapient creatures! This also tells how loyal the subject is to the caster (see *Loyalty of Hirelings*, p. 518).

Cost: 2.
Prerequisite: Sense Foes.

Truthsayer
Information; Resisted by Will

This tells whether the subject is lying or not. May be cast in two ways:

1. To tell whether the subject has told *any* lies in the last five minutes.
2. To tell whether the *last* thing the subject said was a lie.

May also give an indication of how great the lie is. If the caster is not touching the subject, calculate range as for a Regular spell.

Cost: 2.
Prerequisite: Sense Emotion.

Mind-Reading
Regular; Resisted by Will

Lets the caster read the subject's mind. Works on any living being, but is most useful on sapient creatures. Detects only surface thoughts (what the subject is thinking at that moment). The subject is not aware his mind is being read, except in the case of a critical failure.

Modifiers: -2 if the caster does not know the subject's *native* language; -2 if the subject is of a different race – or -4 or more if the subject is totally alien!

Duration: 1 minute.
Cost: 4 to cast; 2 to maintain.
Time to cast: 10 seconds.
Prerequisite: Truthsayer.

Hide Thoughts
Regular

This spell resists all mind-reading and thought-control attempts on the subject. The "attacking" ability must *win* a Quick Contest against this spell in order to affect the subject. If the attacking ability pierces Hide Thoughts, the subject still gets his normal resistance roll (roll separately). This spell does not affect previously established mental control.

Duration: 10 minutes.
Cost: 3 to cast; 1 to maintain.
Prerequisite: Truthsayer.

EARTH SPELLS

These spells deal with the traditional magical "element" of earth. Except as noted, none of these spells affect stone or metal.

Seek Earth
Information

This spell tells the caster the *direction* and *approximate distance* of the nearest significant amount of any one type of earth, metal, or stone. Use the long-distance modifiers (p. 241). Any known sources of that material may be excluded if the caster specifically mentions them before beginning.

Cost: 3.
Time to cast: 10 seconds.

Shape Earth
Regular

Lets the caster move earth and shape it into any form. If the form is stable (e.g., a hill), it remains permanently after shaping. An unstable form (e.g., a column or wall) lasts only while the spell continues – no special concentration is required – and then collapses.

Earth *moved* with this spell travels at only Move 2. It can harm no one except by flowing over an immobile person and burying him. If earth is moved onto a person to bury him – or from beneath him, to create a hole – he may move normally on his next turn, to escape. He is trapped only if he fails to do so.

Anyone buried by this spell may try to claw his way out of the loose earth. One roll, at ST-4, is allowed per turn. GMs may make this roll harder if the victim is buried under more than two cubic yards of earth! The victim can hold his breath (see *Holding Your Breath*, p. 351), but he eventually risks suffocation (see *Suffocation*, p. 436).

Duration: 1 minute.
Cost: 1 per cubic yard of earth shaped (minimum 2); half that to maintain (round up).
Prerequisite: Seek Earth.

Earth to Stone
Regular

Turns an item of earth or clay into hard stone (but not gemstone).

Duration: Permanent.
Cost: 3 per cubic yard (minimum 3).
Prerequisites: Magery 1 and Shape Earth.

Earth to Air
Regular
As listed under *Air Spells* (p. 243).

Create Earth
Regular
Lets the caster create good, solid earth where none existed before. This earth must be created in contact with the ground – not hanging in the air or floating in the sea!

Duration: Permanent.
Cost: 2 per cubic yard to create earth from nothingness (minimum 2); 1 per cubic yard to solidify mud into good earth (minimum 1).
Prerequisite: Earth to Stone.

Flesh to Stone
Regular; Resisted by HT
"Petrifies" a living subject (and all his gear!), turning him to stone. Must affect the *entire* subject.

Duration: Permanent, unless reversed by Stone to Flesh.
Cost: 10.
Time to cast: 2 seconds.
Prerequisite: Earth to Stone.

Stone to Earth
Regular
Turns any kind of stone (including gemstone) into simple earth. Must be cast on a whole stone or block, rather than a part of it.

Duration: Permanent.
Cost: 6 per cubic yard (minimum 6).
Prerequisites: Earth to Stone *or* any four Earth spells.

Stone to Flesh
Regular
Reverses the effects of Flesh to Stone and brings the victim back to life (stunned). Cannot be used to animate a statue that was never alive.

Duration: Permanent.
Cost: 10.
Time to cast: 5 seconds.
Prerequisites: Magery 2, Flesh to Stone, and Stone to Earth.

Entombment
Regular; Resisted by HT
The earth instantly swallows the subject. He remains in suspended animation, in a tiny spherical chamber 50 feet underground, until rescued by tunneling or the reverse of this spell. A mage who casts Entombment on *himself* may elect to stay awake, but this is unwise unless he also knows Earth to Air!

Duration: Permanent, unless reversed by this spell.
Cost: 10 (but only 6 to *reverse* an entombment).
Time to cast: 3 seconds.
Prerequisites: Magery 2 and five Earth spells.

ENCHANTMENT SPELLS
Enchantment spells allow mages to create permanent magic items, and constitute both a college of magic and a class of spells. Since they are only ever used to create artifacts, they appear with the other rules for artifacts in Chapter 17 (see *Enchantment Spells,* p. 480).

FIRE SPELLS
These spells deal with the traditional magical "element" of fire. Should the volume of a particular fire matter in play, assume that the flames created or controlled by Fire spells shoot six feet high. See *Flame* (p. 433) for rules for setting things on fire.

Ignite Fire
Regular
This spell produces a single spot of heat, and is used to set fire to a *readily* flammable object. It works best on paper and cloth, and cannot affect any item that would not burn in an ordinary fire. In particular, it *cannot* set fire to a living being! Once ignited, the fire burns normally.

Duration: One second.
Cost: Depends on the amount of heat desired:

1 – for an effect as though a match had been held to the subject: lights a candle, pipe, or tinder in one second.
2 – for an effect as though a torch had been held to the subject: ignites paper or loose cloth in one second, ordinary clothes being worn in four seconds.
3 – for an effect as though a blowtorch had been held to the subject: ignites dry firewood or clothes being worn in one second, leather in two seconds, heavy wood in six seconds.
4 – for an effect as though burning magnesium or phosphorus had been held to the subject: ignites coal in one second, heavy wood in two seconds.

Cost to maintain is the same as the original cost to cast.

Create Fire
Area
Fills the area of effect with fire that requires no fuel (if cast in midair, it produces a sphere of flame, which falls to the ground). This is real fire, and will eventually ignite any flammable objects it touches. Cannot be cast within rock, foes, etc.

Duration: 1 minute.
Base Cost: 2; half that to maintain. Ordinary fires set by this spell do not require maintenance.
Prerequisite: Ignite Fire.

Shape Fire
Area
Lets the caster control the shape of any flame. Each shape change requires a second of concentration. Once shaped, the flame keeps that shape until the spell expires, without concentration. *Moving* a flame requires constant concentration (the flame moves at Move 5, on the caster's turn). A natural fire cannot move to a place that it can't burn, but flame made with the Create Fire spell needs no fuel and can move almost anywhere.

Flame shaped with this spell normally retains its volume. If the fire is "spread out" across twice its original area, it only does half damage; if spread across three times its original area, it does 1/3 damage, and so on.

Duration: 1 minute.
Base Cost: 2; half that to maintain.
Prerequisite: Ignite Fire.

Deflect Energy
Blocking
Deflects *one* energy attack about to hit the subject – including a beam weapon attack or a Fireball or Lightning spell. Counts as a parry for combat purposes. If the caster is not

the subject, apply distance modifiers as for a Regular spell. Deflected attacks may still hit a target *beyond* the subject.

Cost: 1.
Prerequisites: Magery 1 and Shape Fire.

Extinguish Fire

Area

Puts out all ordinary and magical fires in its area of effect. Has no effect on molten steel, lava, plasma, etc.

Duration: Once out, a fire stays out.
Base Cost: 3.
Prerequisite: Ignite Fire.

Heat

Regular

This spell raises the temperature of an object. It does not necessarily produce fire, though most things burn if heated enough. Heat radiates away normally. (Use this as a guideline for playable effects – don't try to turn the spell into a physics exercise!)

Any wizard planning to make extensive use of this spell should arm himself with a list of the melting points of various materials. The spell can have drawbacks. If you were in jail, you might melt your way through the bars . . . but the radiated heat would probably broil you first.

Duration: 1 minute. Each minute raises the target's temperature by 20°. Maximum temperature possible with this spell is 2,800°.
Cost: 1 for an object up to the size of a fist, 2 for an object up to one cubic yard, and 2 per cubic yard for a larger object. Temperature change can be doubled to 40° per minute for double cost, tripled to 60° per minute for triple cost, and so on. *Slower* heating costs no less. Same cost to maintain.
Time to cast: 1 minute.
Prerequisites: Create Fire and Shape Fire.

Cold

Regular

This spell is the reverse of Heat (above). It can reduce the temperature of any object to absolute zero, if maintained for long enough.

Duration, Cost, and Time to cast: As for Heat, except each minute *lowers* the target's temperature by 20°.
Prerequisite: Heat.

Resist Cold

Regular

The subject (person, creature, or object) and anything he carries become immune to the effects of cold and frostbite (but *not* falling ice, magical ice spears, etc.).

Duration: 1 minute.
Cost: 2 to cast; 1 to maintain. Cost doubles if subject must resist cold of -40° or more; cost triples if subject must resist the cold of absolute zero.
Prerequisite: Heat.

Resist Fire

Regular

The subject (person, creature, or object) and anything he carries become immune to the effects of heat and fire (but not electricity).

Duration: 1 minute.
Cost: 2 to cast; 1 to maintain. Cost doubles if subject must resist a blast furnace or volcano; cost triples if subject must resist the heat of a star, nuclear bomb, etc. Only the first level of protection is necessary against combat-type Fire spells.
Prerequisites: Extinguish Fire and Cold.

Fireball

Missile

Lets the caster throw a ball of fire from his hand. This has 1/2D 25, Max 50, Acc 1. When it strikes something, it vanishes in a puff of flame. This spell is likely to ignite flammable targets.

Cost: Any amount up to your Magery level per second, for three seconds. The fireball does 1d burning damage per energy point.
Time to cast: 1 to 3 seconds.
Prerequisites: Magery 1, Create Fire, and Shape Fire.

Explosive Fireball

Missile

Creates a fireball that affects both its target and things nearby. This has 1/2D 25, Max 50, Acc 1. Can be thrown at a wall, floor, etc. (at +4 to hit) to catch foes in the blast. The target and anyone closer to the target than one yard take full damage. Those further away divide damage by 3 times their distance in yards (round down).

Cost: Any amount up to *twice* your Magery level per second, for three seconds. The fireball does 1d burning damage per *full* 2 points of energy.
Time to cast: 1 to 3 seconds.
Prerequisite: Fireball.

GATE SPELLS

These spells manipulate time, space, and dimensions.

Planar Summons

Special

Summons a creature, such as a demon or a Thing Man Was Not Meant To Know, from another plane of existence. The GM determines the predisposition and abilities of this being. Each plane requires a different Planar Summons spell. Some exceptionally potent entities might require their own unique spells!

When the creature appears, the caster must immediately try to *control* it. Treat this as a Quick Contest between the caster's Planar Summons skill and the entity's Will. The caster is at +4 if he knows the creature's "true name."

If the caster wins, he can give the creature a single command, which it *must* carry out. On completing this task – or after one hour in any event – the entity usually vanishes. However, some powerful entities can stay for as long as they wish . . .

If the caster ties or loses, the creature reacts badly. An "evil" being commits violence or vandalism, while a "good" one is more likely to depart in a huff and put in a bad word with the caster's gods. Wild or chaotic creatures are liable to engage in theft and mischief. Extremely alien entities might react in disturbing and unpredictable ways.

Duration: Until the task is done or one hour, whichever is less. Usually.
Cost: 1 point per 10 character points used to build the summoned entity. Minimum energy cost is 20 (although this will not always summon a 200-point being). The GM secretly determines the capabilities of all summoned creatures.
Time to cast: 5 minutes.
Prerequisites: Magery 1 and at least one spell from each of 10 different colleges.

Plane Shift (VH)

Special

This spell bodily transports the caster – along with anything he is carrying (up to Heavy encumbrance) – to a particular plane of existence. Each plane requires its own Plane Shift spell. This is a one-way trip. To get back, the caster must know Plane Shift for his home plane or get a wizard in the other plane to cast Banish (p. 252) on him.

This spell gives the caster no special immunity to his surroundings. To safely visit a plane where the natural conditions are vacuum, flame, etc., you must learn the necessary protective spells.

Duration: Permanent.
Cost: 20.
Time to cast: 5 seconds.
Prerequisite: Planar Summons for the same plane.

HEALING SPELLS

Anyone who tries to heal *himself* has a skill penalty equal to the amount of injury he has. For example, a wizard who is missing 4 HP rolls at -4 to heal himself.

A *critical* failure with a Healing spell always has some appropriate bad effect on the patient, aggravating the injury, creating a new wound, or the like.

Lend Energy

Regular

Restores the subject's lost Fatigue Points, at an energy cost to the caster. Cannot increase the subject's FP score above its normal maximum.

Cost: Any amount; the energy spent by the caster goes to the subject as restored FP (e.g., if the caster spends 5 energy, the subject regains 5 lost FP). Casting cost is not reduced by high skill.
Prerequisite: Magery 1 *or* Empathy (p. 51).

Lend Vitality

Regular

Temporarily restores the subject's lost Hit Points, at an energy cost to the caster. Cannot increase the subject's HP score above its normal maximum.

Since restored HP vanish after one hour and the spell cannot be maintained, this spell is only a stopgap measure.

Duration: 1 hour.
Cost: Any amount; the energy spent by the caster goes to the subject as restored HP (e.g., if the caster spends 5 energy, the subject regains 5 lost HP). Casting cost is not reduced by high skill. Cannot be maintained; must be recast.
Prerequisite: Lend Energy.

Recover Energy

Special

This spell allows the caster to rest and recover Fatigue Points more quickly than normal by drawing energy from the mana around him. A normal person recovers 1 FP every 10 minutes. A mage who knows this spell at skill 15 or higher recovers 1 FP every 5 minutes. A mage who knows this spell at skill 20 or higher recovers 1 FP every 2 minutes. No further improvement is possible. Note that this spell works on the caster himself; it cannot restore FP to others.

The mage must rest quietly, but no ritual or die roll is required. While resting, he can maintain ordinary spells, but not those that require concentration.

This spell does not function in low- or no-mana areas.

Cost: None.
Prerequisites: Magery 1 and Lend Energy.

Awaken

Area

This spell renders the subject(s) awake and alert. It instantly counters the effects of stunning. If the subject is very fatigued (less than 1/3 basic FP), this spell renders him alert for an hour but *costs* him 1 FP at the end of that time. It has no effect on those with 0 or fewer FP. Sleeping or unconscious subjects get a HT roll to awaken, at a bonus equal to the caster's margin of success. A subject rolls at -3 if unconscious due to injury, at -6 if drugged.

Base Cost: 1.
Prerequisite: Lend Vitality.

Minor Healing

Regular

Restores up to 3 HP to the subject. Does not eliminate disease or poison, but cures the damage they cause.

This spell is risky when used more than once per day by the same caster on the same subject. If you try, roll at -3 for the first repetition, -6 for the second, and so on.

If you have the Physician skill at level 15 or higher, a critical failure with this spell counts only as an ordinary failure – unless you are trying the spell more than once per day on the same subject.

Cost: 1 to 3. The same amount is restored to the subject.
Prerequisite: Lend Vitality.

Major Healing (VH)

Regular

Restores up to 8 HP to the subject. Does not eliminate disease or poison, but cures the damage they cause.

Otherwise, this spell functions just like Minor Healing: it is at -3 per casting on the same subject in one day, and Physician skill at level 15 or higher mitigates the effects of a critical failure.

The penalties for repeated casting accrue *separately* for Minor Healing and Major Healing. For instance, a caster could cast both spells on the same subject in the same day at no penalty.

Cost: 1 to 4. *Twice* the amount spent is restored to the subject.
Prerequisites: Magery 1 and Minor Healing.

Great Healing (VH)

Regular

Restores *all* of the subject's missing HP. Does not eliminate disease or poison, nor does it restore crippled or missing body parts, but it can heal HP lost to any of these things.

A given subject can only benefit from this spell *once per day*, whether cast by the same caster or by a different caster each time.

If you have the Physician skill at level 15 or higher, a critical failure with this spell counts only as an ordinary failure.

Cost: 20. One try per day per subject.

Time to cast: 1 minute.

Prerequisites: Magery 3 and Major Healing.

KNOWLEDGE SPELLS

These spells provide information. Duration is "instantaneous" unless noted otherwise – that is, the caster gets a flash of knowledge, not a continuing picture.

Detect Magic
Regular
Lets the caster determine whether any one object is magical. If the spell is successful, a second casting tells whether the magic is temporary or permanent. A critical success on either roll fully identifies the spell, as for Analyze Magic.

Cost: 2.
Time to cast: 5 seconds.
Prerequisite: Magery 1.

Aura
Information
Shows the caster a glowing halo, or "aura," around the subject. This aura gives the caster a general insight into the subject's personality – the better the skill roll, the better the insight. The aura also shows whether the subject is a mage (and about how powerful); whether the subject is possessed or controlled in any way; and whether the subject is in the grip of any violent emotion. A critical success detects "secret" traits, such as lycanthropy, vampirism, and unnatural longevity.

All living beings have auras; inanimate things do not. A zombie is detectable by his faint, death-haunted aura, while a vampire retains the aura he had in life. Illusions and created beings have *no* aura, so a successful casting of this spell distinguishes them from real persons.

Cost: 3 (for *any* size subject).
Prerequisite: Detect Magic.

Seeker
Information
Attunes the caster to one individual or manmade object he is looking for. A success gives the caster a vision of the item's whereabouts – or leads him to it, if it is within a mile.

To seek a person, the caster must either know his name or know him well enough to visualize him. For instance, you cannot use this spell to solve a murder by seeking "the murderer" if you don't know who that is – but if you do, Seeker will find him.

Modifiers: Long-distance modifiers (p. 241). Something associated with the item sought (e.g., part of a lost person's clothing) should be available at the time of casting; if not, roll at -5. The roll is at +1 if the caster has held or is otherwise familiar with the item sought.

Cost: 3. One try per week.
Prerequisites: Magery 1, IQ 12+, and at least two "Seek" spells (e.g., Seek Earth and Seek Water).

Trace
Regular
May be cast on any object or living being. As long as the spell is maintained, the caster will know where the subject is if he concentrates for a second. Either the subject must be with the caster when the spell is first cast, or the caster must first cast Seeker successfully. Long-distance modifiers (p. 241) apply if subject is not in caster's presence.

Duration: 1 hour.
Cost: 3 to cast; 1 to maintain. One try per day.
Time to cast: 1 minute.
Prerequisite: Seeker.

Identify Spell
Information
Lets the caster know what spell or spells have just been cast (within the last five seconds), or are being cast at the moment, *on* or *by* the subject. It does not identify the spells on a permanently enchanted item. One casting identifies *all* spells cast on or by the subject. However, if any of these spells are totally unknown to the caster – not just spells he doesn't know, but spells he has never *heard of* – the GM should provide only a general, vague description; e.g., "Some kind of physical protection." Wizards have heard of every spell in this list unless the GM rules that some are secret, but wizards have

not heard of new spells created by the GM or players.

Cost: 2.
Prerequisite: Detect Magic.

Analyze Magic
Information; Resisted by spells that conceal magic
Tells the caster exactly what spells are on the subject. If the subject has more than one spell on it, Analyze Magic identifies the one that took the least energy and tells the caster "there are more spells." It can then be cast again to determine the next spell, and so on. Like Identify Spell, above, it gives limited results when faced with a spell the caster has never heard of.

Cost: 8.
Time to cast: 1 hour.
Prerequisite: Identify Spell.

LIGHT AND DARKNESS SPELLS

These spells affect not just visible light, but also infrared and ultraviolet light. Spells that provide illumination allow those with Infravision and Ultravision to see, while spells that block ordinary vision also block those senses.

Light
Regular
Produces a small light, like a candle flame. It stays still unless the caster concentrates on moving it; then it can travel at Move 5.

Duration: 1 minute.
Cost: 1 to cast; 1 to maintain.

Continual Light
Regular
When cast on a small object (up to fist-sized or 1 lb.) or a small part of a larger object, this spell makes that object glow with white light.

Duration: Variable. Roll 2d for number of days. Does *not* count as a spell "on."
Cost: 2 for a dim glow, 4 for the brightness of a fire, 6 for a glare so bright as to be painful at close range.
Prerequisite: Light.

Darkness

Area

Cloaks the area of effect in pitch darkness. A person inside the area can see out normally, but can see nothing else *within* the area. Those outside the area can see only darkness within. Thus, attacks out of darkness suffer no penalty, but attacks into darkness are at a penalty; see *Visibility* (p. 394) for combat rules.

The Dark Vision advantage lets you see through a Darkness spell, but Night Vision and Infravision do not.

Duration: 1 minute.
Base Cost: 2 to cast; 1 to maintain.
Prerequisite: Continual Light.

Blur

Regular

This spell makes the subject harder to see and therefore harder to hit with attacks. Each point of energy gives -1 to the effective skill of any attack on the subject, to a maximum of -5.

Duration: 1 minute.
Cost: 1 to 5 to cast; the same to maintain.
Time to cast: 2 seconds.
Prerequisite: Darkness.

META-SPELLS

These spells have to do with the structure of magic itself. They are spells about spells, or spells that affect other spells.

Counterspell

Regular; Resisted by subject spell

This spell nullifies any one ongoing spell. It cannot "counter" spells that make a *permanent* change in the world (e.g., Extinguish Fire, Flesh to Stone, or Zombie) and it cannot affect permanently enchanted items, but it *can* counter spells cast using magic items. The "subject" of Counterspell may be either the subject of the spell to be countered or the person who cast that spell.

Counterspell is a single spell – but to counter a given spell, you must *also* know that spell. Roll against the *lower* of your Counterspell skill or your skill with the spell being countered. You must win a Quick Contest with the target spell to cancel it. You can cast multiple Counterspells to negate an Area spell piece by piece.

Cost: Half that of the spell countered, *not* counting bonuses the other caster got for high skill.
Time to cast: 5 seconds.
Prerequisite: Magery 1.

Dispel Magic

Area; Resisted by subject spells

This spell, if successful, negates other spells within the area. It has no effect on enchanted items – just on spells. Each spell resists separately.

Dispel Magic is *not* selective! The caster need not know the spell(s) being dispelled. To nullify a specific spell without affecting others, use Counterspell.

Duration: Dispelled magic is permanently gone.
Base Cost: 3.
Time to cast: 1 second for each energy point spent.
Prerequisites: Counterspell and at least 12 other spells (any type).

MIND CONTROL SPELLS

These spells have *no* effect on subjects that lack intelligence (IQ 0) or free will (in general, this means the Automaton meta-trait; see p. 263). Thus, they do not work on most golems, robots, zombies, etc.

Foolishness

Regular; Resisted by Will

The subject suffers -1 to his IQ and IQ-based skills (including spells) for every point of energy put into the spell. The GM may also require an IQ roll to remember complex things while under the influence of this spell.

Duration: 1 minute.
Cost: 1 to 5 to cast; half that amount to maintain (round up).
Prerequisite: IQ 12+.

Forgetfulness

Regular; Resisted by Will or skill

Causes the subject to forget one fact, skill, or spell temporarily. The skill or spell cannot be used while Forgetfulness is in effect. If (for instance) a forgotten spell is a prerequisite for other spells, the other spells *can* still be used, at -2 to skill.

Duration: 1 hour.
Cost: 3 to cast; 3 to maintain.
Time to cast: 10 seconds.
Prerequisites: Magery 1 and Foolishness.

Daze

Regular; Resisted by HT

Subject looks and acts normal, but does not notice what is going on around him, and will not remember it later. A dazed guard will stand quietly while a thief walks past! Any injury, or successful resistance to a spell, causes the subject to snap out of the daze and return to full, alert status.

Duration: 1 minute.
Cost: 3 to cast; 2 to maintain.
Time to cast: 2 seconds.
Prerequisite: Foolishness.

Mass Daze
Area; Resisted by HT

As Daze, but can be cast over an area.

Duration: 1 minute.
Base Cost: 2 to cast; 1 to maintain. Minimum radius 2 yards.
Time to cast: 1 second for each energy point spent.
Prerequisites: Daze and IQ 13+.

Sleep
Regular; Resisted by HT

Subject falls asleep. If standing, he falls – but this does *not* wake him. He can be awakened by a blow, loud noise, etc., but will be mentally stunned (see *Effects of Stun,* p. 420). The Awaken spell (p. 248) arouses him instantly. If not awakened, he will sleep for around eight hours and awaken normally.

Cost: 4.
Time to cast: 3 seconds.
Prerequisite: Daze.

Mass Sleep
Area; Resisted by HT

As Sleep, but can be cast over an area.

Base Cost: 3. Minimum radius 2 yards.
Time to cast: 1 second for each energy point spent.
Prerequisites: Sleep and IQ 13+.

Command
Blocking; Resisted by Will

Lets the caster give the subject one *immediate* command – a word and a gesture, or at most two words – which the subject must obey. If the subject is unable to fulfill the command immediately or on his next turn, the spell has no effect. Some examples:

"Drop it!" – the subject drops whatever he was holding.

"Look!" – the subject looks in the direction the caster indicates.

"Wait!" – the subject takes the Wait maneuver on his next turn.

Cost: 2.
Prerequisites: Magery 2 and Forgetfulness.

MOVEMENT SPELLS

These spells physically manipulate the subject or affect his movement abilities.

Haste
Regular

Increases the subject's Move and Dodge scores by up to 3.

Duration: 1 minute.
Cost: 2 to cast, and 1 to maintain, *per point* added to the subject's Move and Dodge.
Time to cast: 2 seconds.

Hinder
Regular; Resisted by HT

As listed under *Body Control Spells* (p. 244).

Great Haste (VH)
Regular

Speeds the subject up *a lot.* In effect, the subject has one level of Altered Time Rate (p. 38) for the duration of the spell.

Duration: 10 seconds.
Cost: 5. Cannot be maintained; must be recast. At the spell's *end,* the *subject* also loses 5 FP (unless the caster was the subject).
Time to cast: 3 seconds.
Prerequisites: Magery 1, IQ 12+, and Haste.

Apportation
Regular; Resisted by Will

Lets the caster move physical objects without touching them. This spell levitates its subject at Move 1 – not fast enough to do damage with it. Living subjects get to resist with Will.

Duration: 1 minute.
Cost: 1 for an object up to 1 lb. in weight; 2 for an object up to 10 lbs.; 3 for an object up to 50 lbs.; 4 for an object up to 200 lbs.; and 4 for each additional 100 lbs. Cost to maintain is the same.
Prerequisite: Magery 1.

Lockmaster
Regular; Resisted by Magelock

Opens locks magically. A Magelock spell gets a roll to resist Lockmaster. Any modifiers for the difficulty of the lock that would apply Lockpicking skill also affect this spell.

Duration: Once opened, a lock stays open until closed.
Cost: 3. Cannot be maintained.
Time to cast: 10 seconds.
Prerequisites: Magery 2 and Apportation.

Deflect Missile
Blocking

Deflects *one* missile about to hit the subject – including any Missile spell. Counts as a parry for combat purposes. If the caster is not the subject, apply distance modifiers as for a Regular spell. Deflected attacks may still hit a target *beyond* the subject.

Cost: 1.
Prerequisite: Apportation.

NECROMANTIC SPELLS

These spells deal with death, the dead, and spirits. They affect corpses and spirits of *all* races, unless otherwise noted in a racial description.

Death Vision
Regular

The subject sees a vivid presentiment of his own death. This might be a vision of the future or a false vision from another possible future – but it is always chilling. The subject is mentally stunned until he can make his IQ roll to shake off the effects of the spell. This spell can also be *useful* to the subject, by pointing out a possibly deadly hazard.

Duration: 1 second.
Cost: 2.
Time to cast: 3 seconds.
Prerequisite: Magery 1.

Sense Spirit

Information; Area

Tells the caster if there are any ghosts, spirits, undead, or similar supernatural entities within the area of effect. On a good roll, it gives a general impression of what kind of being is present. Caster may, at the time of casting, limit the spell to a specific type of entity, or exclude a given type.

Base Cost: 1/2.
Prerequisite: Death Vision.

Summon Spirit

Information; Resisted by spirit's Will

Lets the caster talk to the spirit of a dead person. The subject resists at -5 if he was a friend of the caster. If the spell succeeds, the subject will answer one question, to the best of his knowledge as of the time he died, and one more per minute he remains.

If the spell fails, that caster (or ceremonial group) may not summon that spirit again for one year. A critical failure means the caster summoned a malign spirit, who lies deliberately.

Modifiers: -5 if you don't know the subject's full name. -1 if it has been more than a week since the subject's death, -2 if more than a month, -3 if more than a year, -4 if more than 10 years, -5 if more than 50 years, and -6 if more than 500 years.

Duration: 1 minute.
Cost: 20 to cast; 10 to maintain. Halve these costs if the spell is cast at the site of death *or* over the corpse of the person being contacted.
Time to cast: 5 minutes.
Prerequisites: Magery 2 and Death Vision.

Zombie

Regular

The subject of this spell must be a relatively complete dead body. The condition of the corpse determines the result: a fresh body produces a zombie, a skeleton produces an animated skeleton, and an old, dry body produces a walking mummy. The animated corpse becomes an undead servant of the caster. It attributes are based on those of the original body, as are its *physical* advantages and DX-based

skills. It does not have the "soul," mental traits, IQ-based skills, or memories of the living person. The GM determines its exact abilities, as appropriate to the campaign.

Duration: The zombie remains animated until destroyed.
Cost: 8, multiplied by 1 + SM for creatures larger than human-sized.
Time to cast: 1 minute.
Prerequisites: Summon Spirit and Lend Vitality.

Turn Zombie

Area

Inflicts 1d of injury on anything in the area that was animated using the Zombie spell; DR does not protect. In addition, roll 1d for each zombie. On a 1, it turns and flees from the caster.

Duration: Successfully turned undead will avoid the caster for one day.
Base Cost: 2. Cannot be maintained; must be recast.
Time to cast: 4 seconds.
Prerequisite: Zombie. (This spell is common among those who have Power Investiture.)

Summon Demon

Special

This is the version of Planar Summons (p. 247) that raises demons; see that spell description for details. If the caster fails to control the demon, it *always* attacks him! If he manages to control the demon and give it a command, the demon carries out the *letter* of its orders, doing its best to pervert their *spirit* to the caster's disfavor. It also works incidental mischief, unless specifically instructed not to.

Duration: Until the demon's task is done, or one hour, whichever is less.
Cost: 1 point per 10 character points used to build the demon. Minimum energy cost is 20 (although this will not always summon a 200-point being). Those tempted to summon powerful demons should bear in mind that such demons tend to have high Will, with all that implies for control . . .
Time to cast: 5 minutes.
Prerequisites: Magery 1 and at least one spell from each of 10 different colleges.

Banish

Special; Resisted by Will

This spell sends an extradimensional visitor (e.g., a demon) back to its plane of origin. It can only be cast if the caster is in his home dimension. In an alien plane, you could not "banish" yourself back home, but a native of that plane could banish you. This spell does not work on a creature that is already in its home dimension.

Resolve the Banish attempt as a Quick Contest: the caster's Banish skill vs. the subject's Will. If the caster wins, the subject immediately returns to its home plane. It cannot return for one month. Anything that it brought with it when it appeared (e.g., weapons) vanishes with it. Other things it may be carrying (e.g., screaming victims) stay behind.

Note that certain powerful creatures are resistant or even immune to this spell.

Modifiers: +4 if the caster knows the entity's "true name"; -5 if the caster does not know the subject's plane of origin . . . and an extra -1 if he *believes* he knows where the creature came from, but is wrong!

Cost: 1 point per 10 character points the subject is worth. Minimum energy cost is 10. The caster does *not* know in advance how much energy the spell will require, and may fall unconscious or even wound himself in casting the Banish.
Time to cast: 5 seconds.
Prerequisites: Magery 1 and at least one spell from each of 10 different colleges.

PROTECTION AND WARNING SPELLS

Shield

Regular

Conjures an invisible shield of magical force that moves to protect the subject from *frontal* attacks. The Defense Bonus granted by this spell is cumulative with that from an actual shield, but this spell does *not* allow a subject without a shield to block.

Duration: 1 minute.
Cost: Twice the Defense Bonus given to the subject, to a maximum

DB of 4 (cost 8); half that to maintain.
Prerequisite: Magery 2.

Armor

Regular
Adds to the Damage Resistance of a living subject. DR from this spell is treated for all purposes like DR from armor, and is cumulative with that from actual armor.

Duration: 1 minute.
Cost: Twice the Damage Resistance given to the subject, to a maximum DR of 5 (cost 10); half that to maintain.
Prerequisites: Magery 2 and Shield.

Anyone can learn most spells – although in some worlds, you must be a mage to use the spells you know.

Magelock

Regular; Resists Lockmaster spell
Locks a door magically. The door will not open unless the spell is removed (Counterspell and Lockmaster are both able to counter it) or the door itself is destroyed.

Duration: 6 hours.
Cost: 3 to cast; 2 to maintain.
Time to cast: 4 seconds.
Prerequisite: Magery 1.

WATER SPELLS

These spells deal with the traditional magical "element" of water. Except as noted, none of these spells affect the water in a human body or any other living creature.

Seek Water

Information
This spell lets the caster determine the direction, distance, and general nature of the nearest significant source of water. Use the long-distance modifiers (p. 241). Any known sources of water may be excluded if the caster specifically mentions them before beginning. Requires a forked stick; roll at -3 if this is not available.

Cost: 2.

Purify Water

Special
Lets the caster remove all impurities from water by pouring it through any hoop or ring (or, in a pinch, his own fingers) into a container. Only one skill roll is required, as long as the flow continues.

Duration: Purified water stays pure unless re-contaminated.
Cost: 1 per gallon purified.
Time to cast: Usually 5 to 10 seconds per gallon, unless a large container and ring are used.
Prerequisite: Seek Water.

Create Water

Regular
Lets the caster create pure water out of nothing. This water may appear in any of several forms. It may appear within a container, or as a globe in midair (it falls immediately). Or it may appear as a dense mist of droplets; in this form, one gallon of water extinguishes all fires in a one-yard radius. Water *cannot* be created inside a foe to drown him!

Duration: The created water is permanent.
Cost: 2 per gallon created.
Prerequisite: Purify Water.

Destroy Water

Area
Causes water (in any form) to vanish, leaving a vacuum – or perhaps specks of dry impurities. If more water is all around, it rushes in to fill the hole. Good for drying things out, saving a drowning victim, etc. *Cannot* be used as a "dehydrating" attack on a foe.

Duration: Permanent.
Base Cost: 3. In deep water, the area is only 2 yards in height (or depth).
Prerequisite: Create Water.

Breathe Water

Regular
As listed under *Air Spells* (p. 243).

Shape Water

Regular
Lets the caster sculpt water (including ice or steam) into any form, and even move it about. Once given a shape, the water holds it without further concentration until the spell ends. Water moved with this spell travels at Move 3.

A useful shape is a wall of water to stop fiery attacks. Twenty gallons creates a wall 2 yards high × 1 yard wide. This stops Fireball spells and ordinary fire.

Duration: 1 minute.
Cost: 1 per 20 gallons shaped; same cost to maintain.
Time to cast: 2 seconds.
Prerequisite: Create Water.

Fog

Area
Creates an area of dense fog. Even one yard of fog blocks vision. Flaming weapons and missiles lose their extra power in fog. A Fireball loses 1 point of damage per yard of fog it must traverse (e.g., a 3d Fireball that crosses 5 yards of fog inflicts 3d-5 damage), while victims of an Explosive Fireball may count each yard of fog as *two* yards of distance from the blast. However, no amount of fog can extinguish a fire.

Duration: 1 minute.
Base Cost: 2; half that to maintain.
Prerequisite: Shape Water.

Icy Weapon

Regular
Causes any weapon to become freezing cold. This does not harm the user or the weapon, but an attack with the weapon does +2 damage to most foes *if it penetrates DR*. Multiply this bonus for any Vulnerability (p. 161) to ice or cold. Add this bonus to the *final* injury inflicted by the attack – for instance, an "impaling" icy attack is still only good for +2 damage, not +4.

Duration: 1 minute.
Cost: 3 to cast; 1 to maintain.
Time to cast: 3 seconds.
Prerequisite: Create Water.

CHAPTER SIX
PSIONICS

The rules in this chapter concern psionic characters in worlds where psi powers are possible. If you are not creating a psi, you can safely ignore this material.

"Psionics" (or "psi powers") are paranormal mental abilities such as telepathy and ESP. They might be mutations or gifts possessed by a rare few individuals; powers common to an entire civilization, race, or other large group; or the result of deliberate experimentation.

The GM decides whether psi exists in his game world – and if so, who can have psionic powers. If psi powers are rare, he is free to require an Unusual Background (p. 96).

POWERS, ABILITIES, AND TALENTS

The six basic psionic *powers* are Antipsi, ESP, Psychic Healing, Psychokinesis (PK), Telepathy, and Teleportation. Other psi powers exist in some settings. Three things define each power:

- A set of advantages that represent different ways the power can manifest.
- A special limitation, called a *power modifier*, which, when applied to any of these advantages, turns it into a *psi ability* within the power.
- A *Talent* that makes it easier to use all the psi abilities within the power.

You possess a given power if you have at least one of its psi abilities. You may spend earned points to add new psi abilities within any power you already possess, but you may not buy psi abilities associated with *new* powers without the GM's permission.

If you possess a particular psi power, you may start out with its psionic Talent. You may also spend earned points to add or improve this Talent later on.

You may also start with a Talent and *no* psi abilities. In that case, you are a "latent" – you have potential but no actual power. You may spend earned points to buy psi abilities within the power with which you have Talent.

Finally, you may take psi abilities as potential advantages (see *Potential Advantages*, p. 33), in which case they will function as if they had the limitations Unconscious Only (p. 115) and Uncontrollable (p. 116) until fully paid for.

Glossary of Psi Terminology

antipsi: The power to interfere with other psi powers. Also used to describe a psi who possesses this power.

ESP: Extrasensory perception – the power to see, hear, or know things that the ordinary five senses cannot detect.

esper: A psi who possesses ESP.

latent: Someone who possesses a psi Talent but no actual psi abilities. Psis whose abilities have the Unconscious Only limitation might *appear* to be latent.

PK: Psychokinesis – the power to affect matter with the mind.

psi: The generic term for superhuman mental powers. Also used to describe a person who possesses such powers.

psionic: Of or pertaining to psi powers.

psychic healing: The ability to heal injury and illness with the mind.

screamer: An uncontrolled antipsi. Also called a "jammer."

Talent: An advantage that makes it easier to use all psi abilities of one type.

telepath: A psi who can read or influence the minds of others.

telepathy: The power of mental communication and control.

teleportation: The power to transport objects across space, time, or dimensions instantaneously.

Power Modifier

All psi abilities have a special limitation called a "power modifier." Each psi power has its own modifier, generally worth -10%. An advantage with a power modifier becomes part of the associated power, and is subject to the restrictions under *Using Psi Abilities* (p. 255). This is a limitation because it converts an ability that would otherwise be impeded only by specific countermeasures into one that is susceptible to interference from anything that affects the entire power or *all* psi powers.

Psionic Talents

Each power has a psionic Talent; e.g., Telepathy Talent. Talent represents natural or learned ability to control that psi power. You may have Talent without psi abilities (that is, you are a "latent") or psi abilities without Talent (you have raw power, but little flair for directing it).

A Talent gives a bonus to any roll to activate or otherwise use that particular psionic power; e.g., Telepathy Talent 2 would give +2 to use any of your telepathic abilities. This most often modifies IQ, Will, and Perception rolls.

Most Talents cost 5 points/level. You may not buy more than four levels of a given Talent without the GM's permission.

PSIDE EFFECTS

Like other advantages, psi abilities may have enhancements and limitations (see pp. 101-116). All psi abilities,

by definition, have a power modifier. The GM might rule that certain other limitations are intrinsic to the way psi works in his game world, in which case these are mandatory as well. A psi may customize his abilities with additional limitations; Costs Fatigue, Emergencies Only, Nuisance Effect, Unconscious Only, Uncontrollable (especially for children and teenagers!), and Unreliable are common in fiction.

If you want to start with *many* psi abilities, consider taking severe limitations such as Emergencies Only, Unconscious Only, and Unreliable. You can purchase your abilities cheaply, but you can't use them effectively – perhaps you don't even realize you have them! Later in your career, you can buy off these limitations and add Talent to improve your capabilities.

If a psi ability comes in levels, it is legal to buy some levels with limitations and others without, provided all have the power modifier. For instance, you could have Telekinesis 5 with no extra limitations, plus another 20 levels that are Unconscious and Uncontrollable!

You may use earned points to "buy off" any limitation the GM feels practice could negate; e.g., Uncontrollable or Unreliable. You *cannot* buy off a power modifier, though, or any limitation the GM deems fundamental to the way psi functions in his game world.

GAINING NEW PSI ABILITIES

You can use earned points to add enhancements to your psi abilities, or to buy higher levels of abilities that come in multiple levels. You can also buy additional Talent with any power you possess. Finally, if you already have a psionic power or Talent, you may buy new abilities *within that power.*

However, like most advantages, psi abilities are inborn. Under normal circumstances, you cannot add abilities in powers you do not possess. The GM might allow you to gain new powers through dangerous superscience experiments, divine intervention, etc.

USING PSI ABILITIES

A psi ability is an advantage with a modifier. It functions just like the ordinary form of the advantage, with a few exceptions.

Someone with the advantage Resistant to Psionics (see *Resistant,* p. 80) has a bonus to all rolls to resist psi abilities, whether he is the target or

merely caught in the area of effect. This advantage has no effect on abilities that do not allow a resistance roll.

The advantages Neutralize (p. 71) and Psi Static (p. 78) can interfere with psi abilities. These traits may be part of the Antipsi power (below) or have other origins.

Other advantages, technology, etc. specifically noted as affecting psionics in general or one power in particular can also impede psi. For instance, technological mind shields that only affect telepathy are common in science-fiction settings.

PSIONIC POWERS

Six sample psi powers appear below. The abilities listed for each are only guidelines. The GM is free to modify these lists, or to permit players to do so themselves.

ANTIPSI

This is the power of *interfering* with other psi use. Some psychic researchers think unconscious, *uncontrollable* Antipsi might be common . . .

which is why psi is rarely noticed. If you have this power, you might not believe in psi, because it won't work near you! Psis tend to shun uncontrolled antipsis (called "jammers" or "screamers").

There is no Antipsi Talent, since most of these abilities work passively.

Antipsi Abilities

The following advantages can be Antipsi abilities: Neutralize (p. 71);

Obscure (p. 72) vs. Para-Radar or any psionic Detect; Psi Static (p. 78); and Resistant to Psionics (p. 80).

Power Modifier: None, since Antipsi abilities cannot themselves be blocked!

ESP

Extrasensory perception (ESP) covers a variety of "sixth sense" abilities. These are among the most commonly reported types of psi phenomena.

The GM makes all ESP skill rolls in secret. The better the roll, the more accurate and useful the information he gives. On a failure, the GM says, "You learn nothing." If a Psychometry or Precognition roll fails by more than 5, the GM *lies!*

ESP Talent

5 points/level

You have a natural talent for ESP. You get +1 per level to use any ESP ability. You can use earned points to acquire new ESP abilities, even if you did not start with them.

ESP Abilities

The following advantages can be ESP abilities: Channeling (p. 41); Clairsentience (p. 42); Danger Sense (p. 47); Detect (p. 48), for psis, psionic activity, etc.; Medium (p. 68); Oracle (p. 72); Para-Radar (see *Scanning Sense*, p. 81); Penetrating Vision (p. 74); Precognition (p. 77); Psychometry (p. 78); Racial Memory (p. 78); and See Invisible (p. 83).

Psionics and Magic

Psi and magic can achieve many of the same effects, such as healing injuries. However, they *are* different. A spell that detects magic cannot reveal a psi effect, nor can a drug that neutralizes psi powers affect a mage. Psi power comes from unique advantages that can be powerful even if used without Talent, while magic is built around learning individual skills (spells).

However, purely physical or mental effects of the two disciplines *can* interact – or even cancel. If a psychokinetic creates a fire, it is like any other fire, and water magic can extinguish it normally. And if a mage casts Mind-Reading (p. 245), a telepathic Mind Shield will resist it.

So Which Is Better?

Magic can produce a more diverse range of effects, at a lower point cost, and the average wizard knows far more spells than the typical psi has advantages. So is magic better? Not exactly. Spellcasting requires energy and time, whereas psi abilities, like other advantages, usually need little or no concentration. Psi powers don't require rituals and are not dependent on mana levels, making a psi effective even if he is bound and gagged, or operating in an area without mana. In the end, both have strengths and weaknesses – and anyone mastering psi *and* magic will be formidable!

---

*Is magic better than psi? Not exactly. Both have strengths and weaknesses – and anyone mastering psi **and** magic will be formidable!*

Power Modifier: ESP. The advantage is a psi ability within the ESP power. Anything that blocks ESP will block it, but it can benefit from ESP Talent. -10%.

PSYCHIC HEALING

This is the ability to heal injury and illness, and more generally, to channel "positive" psychic energy to ensure your own or others' wellness. A "faith healer" might have this ability, even if he *believes* he's channeling divine power.

Psychic Healing Talent

5 points/level

You have a natural talent for Psychic Healing. You get +1 per level to use any Psychic Healing ability. You can use earned points to acquire new Psychic Healing abilities, even if you did not start with them.

Psychic Healing Abilities

The following advantages can be Psychic Healing abilities: Detect (p. 48), for disease, poison, etc.; Healing (p. 59); Metabolism Control (p. 68); Regeneration (p. 80); Regrowth (p. 80); and Resistant (p. 80) against most noxious physical effects.

Power Modifier: Psychic Healing. The advantage is a psi ability within the Psychic Healing power. Anything that blocks Psychic Healing will block it, but it can benefit from Psychic Healing Talent. -10%.

PSYCHOKINESIS (PK)

This is the power of mind over matter, most often manifesting through *telekinesis:* the ability to move objects with the mind. Many parapsychologists connect PK to poltergeist phenomena, levitation, and fire-raising (*pyrokinesis*). PK is sometimes linked to disturbed children or teenagers, for whom the Uncontrollable limitation is common.

PK Talent

5 points/level

You have a natural talent for PK. You get +1 per level to use any PK ability (this *does* include DX rolls for PK abilities). You can use earned points to acquire new PK abilities, even if you did not start with them.

PK Abilities

The following advantages can be PK abilities: Binding (p. 40); Damage Resistance (p. 46), with the Force Field enhancement; Enhanced Move (Air or Water) (p. 52); Flight (p. 56); Innate Attack (p. 61); Super Jump (p. 89); Telekinesis (p. 92); Temperature Control (p. 92); Vibration Sense (p. 96); Walk on Air (p. 97); and Walk on Liquid (p. 97).

Power Modifier: Psychokinetic. The advantage is a psi ability within the PK power. Anything that blocks PK will block it, but it can benefit from PK Talent. -10%.

TELEPATHY

Telepathy is the power of mental communication and control. In most settings, it only works on living, sentient beings such as animals or humans. If for some reason you try to use a telepathic ability on a recording, dummy, etc., your attempt automatically fails.

In most accounts of telepathy, range is highly variable. Telepaths might send signals across the world or even across interplanetary space. The emotional connection between sender and receiver is far more important.

Telepathy Talent

5 points/level

You have a natural talent for Telepathy. You get +1 per level to use any Telepathy ability. You can use earned points to acquire new Telepathy abilities, even if you did not start with them.

Telepathy Abilities

The following advantages can be Telepathy abilities: Animal Empathy (p. 40); Empathy (p. 51); Invisibility (p. 63); Mind Control (p. 68); Mind Probe (p. 69); Mind Reading (p. 69); Mind Shield (p. 70); Mindlink (p. 70); Possession (p. 75); Speak with Animals (p. 87); Special Rapport (p. 88); Telesend (see *Telecommunication*, p. 91); and Terror (p. 93).

An Affliction (p. 35) or Innate Attack (p. 61) can also qualify if it has the Malediction enhancement (p. 106) *and* only causes fatigue, stunning, incapacitation, a temporary mental disadvantage, or a DX, IQ, or Will penalty.

Power Modifier: Telepathic. The advantage is a psi ability within the Telepathy power. Anything that blocks Telepathy will block it – in particular Mind Shield – but it can benefit from Telepathy Talent. -10%.

TELEPORTATION

This is the power of mentally moving yourself – or other things – across space, time, or dimensions without traversing the distance between.

Teleportation Talent

5 points/level

You have a natural talent for Teleportation. You get +1 per level to use any Teleportation ability. You can use earned points to acquire new Teleportation abilities, even if you did not start with them.

Teleportation Abilities

The following advantages can be Teleportation abilities: Jumper (p. 64); Snatcher (p. 86); and Warp (p. 97).

Power Modifier: Psionic Teleportation. The advantage is a psi ability within the Teleportation power. Anything that blocks Teleportation will block it, but it can benefit from Teleportation Talent. -10%.

CHAPTER SEVEN

TEMPLATES

The character-creation rules are simple, but offer a vast number of options in order to give players all the choices they could want. The sheer volume of material might overwhelm new players – especially gamers who are accustomed to RPGs that offer less flexibility. One way to make character generation less daunting is to use "templates."

A template is a "quick start" technique. It is a partially completed character sheet that contains only those traits required for a character to fill a certain role *believably*. It lists the point costs of those traits, and gives the sum as the template's "cost."

When you select a template, pay its cost out of your starting points. Use your remaining points to customize the template by buying traits specific to the character concept you have in mind. You can customize further by choosing personal disadvantages and quirks . . . which will in turn give you a few more points you can spend on abilities that define who *you* are.

There are two main types of templates: *character templates* and *racial templates*.

CHARACTER TEMPLATES

A "character template" is a blueprint for a PC who can fill a specific dramatic role or function competently at a particular occupation in a given game world. By specifying many traits in advance, it reduces the work needed to create the character *and* guarantees that he has the abilities he needs to play his part.

Character templates aren't just for new players! Experienced players who are pressed for time may find them a useful starting point. GMs can use them to determine the abilities of NPCs, too, but should bear in mind that character templates are intended for heroic PCs as opposed to "generic NPCs."

HOW TO USE CHARACTER TEMPLATES

First, buy the template by spending points equal to its cost. Do this *instead* of buying individual attributes, secondary characteristics, advantages, disadvantages, skills, etc.

Next, select any options detailed in the template. Many templates give you a number of choices from subsets of advantages, disadvantages, or skills.

Some also let you increase or decrease attributes and secondary characteristics (if so, these options appear with the advantages and disadvantages).

After you have finished selecting the template's options, customize it by spending your remaining character points. The template does not affect how you spend these points! *You* decide this – subject to GM approval, of course.

If the template has fewer disadvantages than the campaign permits (see *Disadvantage Limit*, p. 11), you may take more, up to the limit. This gives

you extra points to spend. The same goes for quirks, which you should *always* select yourself.

You also need to determine your character's build, and details such as age and hair and eye color. Assume your tech level is that of the campaign unless otherwise indicated.

Altering Character Templates

Character templates are not rules! When customizing a template, you are free to alter anything that came with it. After all, a hero plays a leading role in his saga, and starring roles are rarely typical ones. You can add, subtract, or substitute abilities – but be aware that *subtracting* items from an occupational template might result in someone who is regarded as incompetent by his peers.

Combining Character Templates

You may wish to select more than one template, especially if the GM designs many for the campaign (see Chapter 15). For instance, you might want to take separate templates that define your job, membership in one or more organizations, ethnic origin, *and* place in the story. But since most templates assume you are taking just the one template, "stacking" them can be a problem. The guidelines below attempt to solve this.

When you combine templates, choose the *highest* level of each attribute and secondary characteristic from among the templates. Combine the advantage, disadvantage, and skill lists of all the templates, and take all *required* traits. If multiple templates require a leveled trait, such as a skill, meet the *most difficult* requirement – do not take repeated traits at higher levels (e.g., a Status 2 knight who is also a Status 1 merchant is Status 2, not Status 3). Add the point costs of all these requirements and pay it. If you have points remaining, consider customizing your character by choosing neglected options from the templates.

If you encounter *conflicting* advantages and disadvantages, they do not simply cancel out! This is a sign that the templates are incompatible, and that you should not take both. For instance, in most settings, it would be illogical to combine a Status -3 beggar template and Status 2 knight template to create a Status 2 beggar-knight.

Uniqueness
You might think that two characters built on the same template would be rather alike. In practice, though, players rarely pick the same options on a given template, and almost always make different purchases with their remaining points. These choices, being the players' own, color how the characters are played, which in turn keeps them distinct, even though they share a template.

Are Character Templates "Character Classes"?

No.

Many RPGs employ "character classes," which superficially resemble character templates in **GURPS,** but there are several important differences. For one thing, you don't *have* to choose a template. And if you do choose one, this does not limit your options: you're free to customize the template, and you can spend earned points to improve your character in any way you wish.

Even in a campaign where many templates are available, you are free to create your character from whole cloth – and many experienced players will wish to do so. This is fine, because templates don't contain hidden penalties or drawbacks and aren't specially priced package deals. Characters built on templates are 100% compatible with those created by hand, and the two can mix freely in a campaign.

SAMPLE CHARACTER TEMPLATES

Below are three sample templates for use in a wide variety of settings, from medieval fantasy to modern day. They assume a 100- to 150-point campaign. Note that skills appear in the following format: ***Skill Name (Difficulty)*** Relative Level **[Point Cost]**-Actual Level. For instance, "First Aid (E) IQ [1]-11."

Investigator

100 points

You are a detective, investigative reporter, occult investigator, spy, or thief.

Attributes: ST 10 [0]; DX 12 [40]; IQ 12 [40]; HT 11 [10].

Secondary Characteristics: Dmg 1d-2/1d; BL 20 lbs.; HP 11 [2]; Will 12 [0]; Per 13 [5]; FP 11 [0]; Basic Speed 5.75 [0]; Basic Move 5 [0].

Advantages: 15 points chosen from among Alternate Identity [5 or 15], Charisma 1-3 [5-15], Contacts [Varies], Cultural Familiarity [1 per culture], Danger Sense [15], Gizmos 1-3 [5-15], Languages (any) [2-6 per language], Legal Enforcement Powers [5-15], Luck [15], Rapid Healing [5], Security Clearance [5-15], Smooth Operator 1 [15], Zeroed [10], +1 to +3 to Per [5-15], and Appearance (Attractive) [4] or (Handsome) [12].

Disadvantages: -30 points chosen from among Alcoholism [-15], Curious [-5*], Duty [-2 to -15], Greed [-15*], Honesty [-10*], Pacifism [-5 to -15], Secret [-5 to -30], Sense of Duty (Comrades) [-5], Stubbornness [-5], Wealth (Struggling) [-10], Workaholic [-5], and -1 to ST [-10].

Primary Skills: Select *three* skills from: Climbing, Filch, or Stealth, all (A) DX+1 [4]-13; Criminology, Disguise, Electronics Operation (any), Holdout, Interrogation, Lockpicking, Occultism, Photography, Research, Shadowing, Smuggling, Traps, or Writing, all (A) IQ+1 [4]-13; Observation or Search, both (A) Per+1 [4]-14; Pickpocket (H) DX [4]-12; Computer Programming, Diagnosis, Expert Skill (any), Forensics, Intelligence Analysis, or Law (any), all (H) IQ [4]-12; Detect Lies (H) Per [4]-13; or Computer Hacking (VH) IQ-1 [4]-11. You may opt to trade one choice for *two* extra secondary or background skills.

Secondary Skills: Select *two* skills from: Beam Weapons (Pistol or Rifle), Brawling, Crossbow, Forced Entry, Garrote, Guns (Pistol, Rifle, or Shotgun), Knife, or Thrown Weapon (any), all (E) DX+1 [2]-13; Boxing, Cloak, Rapier, or Shortsword, all (A) DX [2]-12; Acting or Fast-Talk, both (A) IQ [2]-12; Sex Appeal (A) HT [2]-11; or Acrobatics, Judo, or Karate, all (H) DX-1 [2]-11.

Background Skills: Select *one* skill from: Area Knowledge (any), Computer Operation, or Current Affairs (any), all (E) IQ+1 [2]-13; Carousing or Swimming, both (E) HT+1 [2]-12; Boating (any), Driving (any), Piloting (any), or Riding (any), all (A) DX [2]-12; Streetwise (A) IQ [2]-12; or Hiking or Running, both (A) HT [2]-11.

* Multiplied for self-control number; see p. 120.

Mage

100 points

You're a sorcerer, a wizard, a witch, an adept of the black arts . . .

Attributes: ST 9 [-10]; DX 11 [20]; IQ 13 [60]; HT 11 [10].

Secondary Characteristics: Dmg 1d-2/1d-1; BL 16 lbs.; HP 10 [2]; Will 13 [0]; Per 10 [-15]; FP 13 [6]; Basic Speed 5.50 [0]; Basic Move 5 [0].

Advantages: Language (Accented) [4]; Magery 2 [25]; and *one* of Eidetic Memory [5], Reputation +1 [5], Single-Minded [5], Status 1 [5], Versatile [5], or +1 to Will [5].

Disadvantages: -30 points chosen from among Absent-Mindedness [-15], Bad Sight (Mitigator: Glasses, -60%) [-10], Bad Temper [-10*], Curious [-5*], Duty [-2 to -15], Gluttony [-5*], Obsession [-5* or -10*], Secret [-5 to -30], Sense of Duty [-2 to -15], and Shyness [-5, -10, or -20].

Primary Skills: Select *two* spells, each (H) IQ+2 [4]-15† or (VH) IQ+1 [4]-14†. Select 10 more spells, each (H) IQ [1]-13† or (VH) IQ-1 [1]-12†. See Chapter 5 for spell list.

Secondary Skills: Select *two* skills from: Hidden Lore (any), Occultism, or Research, all (A) IQ [2]-13; Expert Skill (any), Mathematics (any), Naturalist, or Theology (any), all (H) IQ-1 [2]-12; Dreaming or Meditation, both (H) Will-1 [2]-12; or Alchemy or Thaumatology, both (VH) IQ-2 [2]-11.

Background Skills: Select *one* skill from: Guns (Pistol or Shotgun) or Knife, both (E) DX [1]-11; Computer Operation (E) IQ [1]-13; or Driving (any), Riding (any), Shortsword, or Staff, all (A) DX-1 [1]-10.

* Multiplied for self-control number; see p. 120.

† Includes +2 for Magery.

Note: Choose your 12 spells from pp. 242-253. Be sure to give each spell the proper prerequisite. You can modify template cost and your skill with spells by taking a higher or lower level of Magery, or by applying a limitation such as Dark-Aspected.

Soldier of Fortune

100 points

You're a warrior. You could be a soldier, pirate, knight-errant, gunslinger, street fighter, or guerrilla.

Attributes: ST 11 [10]; DX 13 [60]; IQ 11 [20]; HT 11 [10].

Secondary Characteristics: Dmg 1d-1/1d+1; BL 24 lbs.; HP 11 [0]; Will 11 [0]; Per 11 [0]; FP 11 [0]; Basic Speed 6.00 [0]; Basic Move 6 [0].

Advantages: 20 points chosen from among Ambidexterity [5], Charisma 1-4 [5-20], Combat Reflexes [15], Fit or Very Fit [5 or 15], High Pain Threshold [10], Luck [15], Magic Resistance 1-10 [2-20], Outdoorsman 1 [10], Rank 1-4 [5-20], Rapid Healing [5], Reputation [varies], Status 1-4 [5-20], Wealth (Comfortable) [10], +1 to ST or HT [10], +1 to +4 to HP [2-8], and +1 to +4 to Per [5-20].

Disadvantages: -35 points chosen from among Alcoholism [-15], Bad Temper [-10*], Bloodlust [-10*], Code of Honor [-5 to -15], Compulsive Carousing or Spending [-5*], Duty [-2 to -15], Fanaticism [-15], Flashbacks (Mild) [-5], Honesty [-10*], Impulsiveness [-10*], Lecherousness [-15*], Overconfidence [-5*], Sense of Duty (Comrades) [-5], and Trademark (Simple) [-5].

Primary Skills: Select *two* skills from: Beam Weapons (any), Crossbow, or Guns (any), all (E) DX+2 [4]-15; Axe/Mace, Bow, Broadsword, Lance, Rapier, or Spear, all (A) DX+1 [4]-14; Karate (H) DX [4]-13; or Tactics (H) IQ [4]-11.

Secondary Skills: Select *one* skill from: Brawling, Fast-Draw (any), Gunner (any), Knife, or Shield (any), all (E) DX+1 [2]-14; or Artillery (any) or Forward Observer, both (A) IQ [2]-11. Select *one* skill from: Crewman (any) (E) IQ+1 [2]-12; Driving (any), Environment Suit (any), Piloting (any), Riding (any), all (A) DX [2]-13; Hiking (A) HT [2]-11; or Acrobatics (H) DX-1 [2]-12.

Background Skills: First Aid (E) IQ [1]-11. Select *two* skills from: Camouflage or Savoir-Faire (any), both (E) IQ [1]-11; Carousing or Swimming, both (E) HT [1]-11; Free Fall or Stealth, both (A) DX-1 [1]-12; Electronics Operation (Comm or Sensors), Explosives (any), or Leadership, all (A) IQ-1 [1]-10; or Observation, Survival (any), Tracking, or Urban Survival, all (A) Per-1 [1]-10.

* Multiplied for self-control number; see p. 120.

RACIAL TEMPLATES

In many game worlds, you can play a character that does not belong to the human race. These rules define a "race" as a single, distinct nonhuman species; *or* one specific type of supernatural being (which might be a ghost, vampire, or other undead, regardless of its species in life); *or* a particular variety of artificial construct (e.g., a given model of robot).

A "racial template" is a collection of traits that apply to *every* member of a race. These traits might define the race's physiology, its psychology, its supernatural powers (if any), and even its dominant culture (at least for a sapient race).

HOW TO USE RACIAL TEMPLATES

When you play a member of a non-human race, you must normally take all the traits in its racial template.

Unlike the traits in a character template, racial traits are rarely optional. The sum of the point costs of these traits is the race's "racial cost." You must pay this cost to belong to the race. Racial templates express deviations from the human norm; therefore, it costs 0 points to play a human.

Some templates are too expensive for PCs in low-powered campaigns, but the GM may still use them for powerful villains or patrons. The GM might wish to produce weaker versions of such templates for PCs (e.g., a vampire that lacks some of the powers given in legend), but he is also free to reserve such templates for NPCs.

Guidelines for creating racial templates appear in Chapter 15. These are intended for GMs, but the GM might allow players to create their own racial templates in campaigns that feature a vast array of nonhumans – especially supers games, where lone aliens with amazing powers are common. Many **GURPS** books also feature racial templates.

Attribute and Secondary Characteristic Modifiers

Racial templates often have attribute or secondary characteristic *modifiers;* e.g., ST+2 or HP-3. Apply attribute modifiers to the attributes you purchase for your character. Next, recalculate your secondary characteristics to reflect your modified attributes. Finally, apply secondary characteristic modifiers. There is no added point cost for any of this! You paid for these bonuses or penalties when you paid your racial cost.

If an attribute or secondary characteristic does not appear in the racial template, assume it is unchanged from the human norm.

Example: Sangria spends 10 points to buy ST 11. This gives her HP 11, and she spends another 4 points to get HP 13. She then buys the Vampire template (p. 262). This template includes ST+6, giving Sangria ST 17. This ST improvement raises her HP to 19. Since the template gives HP+4 as well, she

ends up with HP 23! The racial ST and HP bonuses have no extra cost – Sangria paid for these when she purchased her racial template.

Features and Taboo Traits

A "feature" is a note on how the race differs from humanity when that difference does not grant an advantage or a disadvantage. Features cost 0 points. Examples of features include sterility and an ordinary tail.

A "taboo trait" is an attribute level, advantage, disadvantage, or skill that is off-limits to members of the race. This, too, is worth 0 points. Normally, only mundane traits are labeled "taboo," as exotic or supernatural traits require the GM's permission in any case.

Stacking Templates

You can buy both a racial template and a character template, if you have enough points. Use the guidelines given under *Combining Character Templates* (p. 259), but bear in mind that while you can discard elements of character templates, you cannot do the same with racial traits.

You might even be able to stack two *racial* templates in some situations. For instance, an Elf might also be a Vampire. Keep all compatible traits from both templates. Add traits that come in levels (e.g., if an Elf has ST-1 and a Vampire has ST+6, a Vampire Elf has ST+5). Where two traits conflict (e.g., Acute Vision and Blindness), the GM decides which to keep and which to discard. Adjust the combined template cost appropriately.

SAMPLE RACIAL TEMPLATES

Below are four examples of racial templates.

Dragon

260 points

A winged, fire-breathing "lizard," as smart as a man, and around 20 feet long excluding its tail. It can be good or evil, but it always lusts for treasure. This is a young dragon, but still a fierce foe for a group of adventurers. It might even be suitable as a PC in a high-powered game. Some dragons are reputed to have other abilities, including Alternate Form (Human) (p. 83),

Indomitable (p. 60), Terror (p. 93), Unaging (p. 95), and Unfazeable (p. 95).

Attribute Modifiers: ST+15 (Size, -20%) [120].
Secondary Characteristic Modifiers: SM +2; Will+3 [15]; Per+3 [15].
Advantages: Burning Attack 4d (Cone, 5 yards, +100%; Limited Use, 3/day, -20%; Reduced Range, ×1/5, -20%) [32]; Claws (Talons) [8]; Discriminatory Smell [15]; DR 6 (Can't Wear Armor, -40%) [18]; Enhanced Move 1/2 (Air) [10]; Extra Attack [25]; Extra Legs (Four Legs) [5]; Flight (Winged, -25%) [30]; Longevity [2]; Magery 0 [5]; Night Vision 8 [8]; Striker (Tail; Crushing) [5]; Teeth (Fangs) [2].
Disadvantages: Bad Grip 3 [-15]; Gluttony (12) [-5]; Greed (12) [-15]; Horizontal [-10]; Miserliness (12) [-10].

Dwarf

35 points

Dwarves might be only 2/3 as tall as humans, but they are much longer-lived, with a nose for gold and a flair for all forms of craftsmanship. Dwarves often live in underground halls, and their eyes are adapted to dim light. Many dwarves have Greed or Miserliness, but these are *not* racial traits.

Attribute Modifiers: HT+1 [10].
Secondary Characteristic Modifiers: SM -1; Will+1 [5].
Advantages: Artificer 1 [10]; Detect Gold (Vague, -50%) [3]; Extended Lifespan 1 [2]; Night Vision 5 [5].

Felinoid

35 points

"Cat people" often appear in science fiction, fantasy, and horror settings. This is a typical felinoid: humanoid, but with a number of catlike features, including a tail. This could also be the "were-form" of a human with the Alternate Form advantage (p. 83).

Attribute Modifiers: ST-1 [-10]; DX+1 [20].
Advantages: Acute Hearing 2 [4]; Acute Taste and Smell 1 [2]; Catfall [10]; Claws (Sharp) [5]; Combat Reflexes [15]; DR 1 [5]; Teeth (Sharp) [1]; Temperature Tolerance 1 [1].
Disadvantages: Impulsiveness (12) [-10]; Sleepy (1/2 of the time) [-8].
Features: Purring Voice; Tail.

Vampire

150 points

This is a "Bram Stoker"-style vampire. It possesses some, but not all, of the powers and weaknesses that fiction ascribes to bloodsucking undead. Notably, horror-movie vampires often have Supernatural Durability *instead* of Unkillable (increases cost by 100 points).

Attribute Modifiers: ST+6 [60].
Secondary Characteristic Modifiers: HP+4 [8]; Per+3 [15].
Advantages: Alternate Forms (Bat, Wolf) [30]; Doesn't Breathe [20]; Dominance [20]; Immunity to Metabolic Hazards [30]; Injury Tolerance (Unliving) [20]; Insubstantiality (Costs Fatigue, 2 FP, -10%) [72]; Night Vision 5 [5]; Speak With Animals (Wolves and bats, -60%) [10]; Unaging [15]; Unkillable 2 (Achilles' Heel: Wood, -50%) [50]; Vampiric Bite [30].

Disadvantages: Dependency (Coffin with soil of homeland; Daily) [-60]; Divine Curse (Cannot enter dwelling for first time unless invited) [-10]; Draining (Human Blood; Illegal) [-10]; Dread (Garlic) [-10]; Dread (Religious Symbols; 5 yards) [-14]; Dread (Running Water) [-20]; Supernatural Features (No Body Heat*, No Reflection, Pallor*) [-16]; Uncontrollable Appetite (12) (Human Blood) [-15]; Unhealing (Partial) [-20]; Weakness (Sunlight; 1d/minute) [-60].
Features: Sterile.

* Except after feeding.

Omitting Racial Traits

If you have a good explanation, the GM may permit you to omit a racial trait. If the missing trait has a positive point value, you have a disadvantage that exactly cancels its cost; e.g., omitting racial Combat Reflexes gives "No Combat Reflexes [-15]." Such disadvantages *do* count against campaign disadvantage limits. If the missing trait has a negative point value, you have an advantage worth just enough to negate it; e.g., omitting racial Paranoia [-10] results in "No Paranoia [10]." You can apply enhancements and limitations to either kind of "replacement trait."

META-TRAITS

A "meta-trait" is a collection of traits that are typical of a particular mental, physical, or supernatural state. In game terms, it functions much like a regular advantage or disadvantage. A meta-trait can be part of a racial template or bought by an individual with exotic abilities. Record a meta-trait *instead* of its components on templates and character sheets.

With GM approval, you may modify elements of a meta-trait, altering its cost; e.g., to be able to carry things when you have Body of Air (see below), reduce the ST penalty and the corresponding HP bonus, and delete No Manipulators.

Elemental Meta-Traits
♟ 👽

Variable

Your body is wholly composed of a particular substance. This is an entire category of meta-traits, one for each class of substance ("element").

The main use for these meta-traits is to create "elemental" creatures. Those who can switch into and out of elemental form – a common super-ability – should buy Alternate Form (p. 83) and take the relevant meta-trait as their alternate racial template.

Body of Air: Your body is made of gas. ST 0 [-100]; +10 HP [20]; Doesn't Breathe [20]; Flight (Lighter Than Air, -10%) [36]; Immunity to Metabolic Hazards [30]; Injury Tolerance (Diffuse) [100]; No Legs (Aerial) [0]; No Manipulators [-50]; Vulnerability (Vacuum and wind-based attacks ×2) [-20]; and Taboo Trait (Fixed ST) [0]. *36 points.*

Body of Earth: Your body is made of sand or earth. Doesn't Breathe [20]; DR 2 [10]; Immunity to Metabolic Hazards [30]; Injury Tolerance (Diffuse) [100]; Pressure Support 3 [15]; Sealed [15]; Vacuum Support [5]; and Invertebrate [-20]. *175 points.*

Body of Fire: Your body is a living flame! If your flames are very hot, increase Burning Attack and DR. ST 0 [-100]; +10 HP [20]; Burning Attack 1d (Always On, -40%; Aura, +80%; Melee Attack, Reach C, -30%) [6]; Doesn't Breathe (Oxygen Combustion, -50%) [10]; DR 10 (Limited: Heat/Fire, -40%) [30]; Immunity to Metabolic Hazards [30]; Injury Tolerance (Diffuse) [100]; No Manipulators [-50]; Weakness (Water; 1d/minute) [-40]; and Taboo Trait (Fixed ST) [0]. *6 points.*

Body of Ice: Your body is made of ice. Doesn't Breathe [20]; DR 3 [15]; Immunity to Metabolic Hazards [30]; Injury Tolerance (Homogenous, No Blood) [45]; Pressure Support 3 [15]; Sealed [15]; Slippery 3 [6]; Terrain Adaptation (Ice) [5]; Vacuum Support [5]; Fragile (Brittle) [-15]; Vulnerability (Heat/fire attacks ×2) [-30]; and Weakness (Intense normal heat; 1d/minute; Variable, -40%) [-12]. *99 points.*

Body of Metal: Your body is made of metal. Doesn't Breathe [20]; DR 9 [45]; Immunity to Metabolic Hazards [30]; Injury Tolerance (Homogenous, No Blood) [45]; Pressure Support 3 [15]; Sealed [15]; and Vacuum Support [5]. *175 points.*

Body of Stone: Your body is made of rock. Doesn't Breathe [20]; DR 5 [25]; Immunity to Metabolic Hazards [30]; Injury Tolerance (Homogenous, No Blood) [45]; Pressure Support 3 [15]; Sealed [15]; Vacuum Support [5]; and Fragile (Brittle) [-15]. *140 points.*

Body of Water: Your body is made of liquid. Amphibious [10]; Chameleon 1 [5]; Constriction Attack [15]; Doesn't

Breathe [20]; Immunity to Metabolic Hazards [30]; Injury Tolerance (Diffuse) [100]; Pressure Support 3 [15]; Slippery 5 [10]; Invertebrate [-20]; and Vulnerability (Dehydration attacks ×2) [-10]. *175 points.*

Machine ♟ 👽

25 points

Your body is mostly or completely mechanical, composed of non-living materials such as metal, plastic, and composites – although you might have a few organic parts, such as an outer layer of skin or a brain. Examples include robots, vehicles, and full cyborgs.

This meta-trait includes Immunity to Metabolic Hazards [30], Injury Tolerance (No Blood, Unliving) [25], Unhealing (Total) [-30], and several 0-point features:

A "meta-trait" is a collection of traits that are typical of a particular mental, physical, or supernatural state; e.g., "machine," "spirit," or "quadruped."

- You have an eight-hour energy reserve and need refueling three times a day. You can modify this with appropriate advantages (e.g., Doesn't Eat or Drink, for a reactor that can run for years) or disadvantages (e.g., Increased Consumption, for a "gas-guzzler" engine).
- You neither have nor can spend Fatigue Points; see *Machines and Fatigue* (p. 16).
- Your body does not age. Instead, it wears out, with effects similar to aging.

Note that your Unhealing disadvantage means that the only way for you to regain lost HP is through repairs with Mechanic or Electronics Repair skill (as appropriate).

Several traits *not* included above are common among machines, notably the advantages Digital Mind, Doesn't Breathe, Pressure Support, Sealed, and Vacuum Support, and the disadvantages Electrical, Fragile, Maintenance, Numb, Restricted Diet, and Social Stigma (Valuable Property).

Mentality Meta-Traits 🧠 👽

Variable

These traits represent common types of nonhuman intelligence:

AI: A computer mind. Absolute Timing [2]; Digital Mind [5]; Doesn't Sleep [20]; Intuitive Mathematician [5]; Photographic Memory [10]; and Reprogrammable [-10]. *32 points.*

Automaton: A mind lacking self-awareness and creativity. This is typical of many hive-creatures, magical constructs, undead, and simple AIs. You *can* combine this with the AI meta-trait. Hidebound [-5]; Incurious (6) [-10]; Low Empathy [-20]; No Sense of Humor [-10]; and Slave Mentality [-40]. *-85 points.*

Domestic Animal: A farm animal, pet, mount, or a trained wild animal. Cannot Speak [-15]; Hidebound [-5]; Social Stigma (Valuable Property) [-10]; and Taboo Trait (Fixed IQ) [0]. *-30 points.*

Wild Animal: An ordinary animal found in nature. Bestial [-10]; Cannot Speak [-15]; Hidebound [-5]; and Taboo Trait (Fixed IQ) [0]. *-30 points.*

Morphology Meta-Traits ♟ 👽

Variable

These meta-traits describe some nonhumanoid body configurations that might appear on the racial templates of animals, robots, etc. Feel free to create meta-traits for other body layouts, using these examples as guidelines.

Ground Vehicle: Your body is like a car, tank, etc. Horizontal [-10]; No Legs (Tracked or Wheeled) [-20]; No Manipulators [-50]; and Numb [-20]. *-100 points.*

Ichthyoid: You have a fish-like body (a "merman" would just delete No Manipulators). No Legs (Aquatic) [0] and No Manipulators [-50]. *-50 points.*

Quadruped: You are a four-legged creature with no arms (a "centauroid" would simply take Extra Legs – plus Hooves, if equine). Extra Legs (Four Legs) [5]; Horizontal [-10]; and No Fine Manipulators [-30]. *35 points.*

Vermiform: Your body is similar to that of a snake or a worm (a snake-man with a humanoid upper torso would drop No Manipulators). Double-Jointed [15]; No Legs (Slithers) [0]; and No Manipulators [-50]. *-35 points.*

Spirit ♟ ⚡

261 points

You are a noncorporeal entity: ghost, being of pure thought, etc. You are invisible and intangible (except to others with this meta-trait!). You can temporarily become visible, or even solid, but this is draining. However, your senses can perceive the material world at all times, and your magical or psionic abilities, if any, can *always* affect the physical world.

Spirit includes Doesn't Breathe [20], Doesn't Eat or Drink [10], Doesn't Sleep [20], Immunity to Metabolic Hazards [30], Insubstantiality (Affect Substantial, +100%; Usually On, -40%) [128], Invisibility (Substantial Only, -10%; Usually On, +5%) [38], and Unaging [15].

Many spirit abilities from folklore are not part of this meta-trait; e.g., Injury Tolerance (Homogenous or Diffuse), Magery, and almost any ESP, PK, Telepathy, or Teleportation psi ability (see Chapter 6). Common spirit disadvantages include Compulsive Behavior, Dependency, Divine Curse, Dread, Maintenance, Obsession, and Weakness.

Astral Entity: An astral entity is a spirit that cannot materialize, become visible, or use its supernatural powers in the physical world. Doesn't Breathe [20]; Doesn't Eat or Drink [10]; Doesn't Sleep [20]; Immunity to Metabolic Hazards [30]; Insubstantiality (Always On, -50%) [40]; Invisibility (Substantial Only, -10%) [36]; and Unaging [15]. *171 points.*

CHAPTER EIGHT

EQUIPMENT

Now it's time to decide what possessions you have! You can skip this step if you're Dead Broke or plan to buy equipment only as needed . . . but otherwise, you should choose your gear and figure out how much it costs. If you are a warrior, you need to know how powerful your weapons are and how well your armor protects you. And if you plan to fight *or* travel, you need to determine the weight of your gear, and specify how you are carrying it.

Starting Wealth

The amount of money you have available to spend on equipment at the start of your career is your "starting wealth" – see *Starting Wealth* (p. 26). To calculate this, start with the basic amount appropriate to your campaign's tech level, found under *Tech Level and Starting Wealth* (p. 27), and multiply it for your "wealth level" (see *Wealth*, p. 25).

Prices

All prices in **GURPS** appear in "$": a convenient abbreviation for any baseline unit of currency suitable to the setting. One $ may be one dollar, one credit, one copper piece, or whatever else is appropriate – see *Tech Level and Starting Wealth*. Prices in this chapter assume a typical sale made by an ordinary merchant, in a locale where the item is usually found, at a time when there is neither a shortage nor a surplus.

Money

The currency in use depends on the game world; see *Economics* (p. 514). Coin is almost universal. Paper money is conceivable at TL3, common by TL5, and ubiquitous at TL6. Electronic credit and debit cards supplement or possibly replace other currency at TL8.

Two specific examples:

Medieval Coinage: The default assumption is that $1 is a copper farthing, $4 is a silver coin, and $1,000 in silver weighs 1 pound. Gold coins of the same weight are worth about 20 times as much.

Modern Money: The default assumption is that $1 is a bank note (or alloy coin), its value backed by a government or private bank.

These assumptions may vary from world to world.

COST OF LIVING

Your monthly "cost of living" is an average of your *typical* expenses for one month. It covers food, housing, clothing, and entertainment . . . and, at Status 1 or higher, *servants,* if this is customary in your society.

Your cost of living depends on your Status (p. 28). The *Cost of Living Table* (below) gives a "generic" cost of living for each Status level; you must normally pay this at the beginning of each month. However, the GM is free to vary both the amount of money involved and the payment scheme; for instance, he could ask for half at the start of the month and half in the middle.

In most game worlds, you may opt to pay the cost of living for a Status level *higher* or *lower* than your own (but never more than Status 8 or less than Status -2). This affects how NPCs react to you, and may have other effects as well.

Living *below* your Status saves you money, but has negative repercussions. Depending on the level you drop to, these might include unpaid servants quitting, threats from your landlord, malnutrition, eviction, or anything else the GM feels appropriate. The GM may also reduce your effective Status to the level you're supporting in any situation where your reduced circumstances would cause a negative reaction; e.g., at a "society" function or when meeting strangers who do not recognize your face.

Living *above* your Status costs more, but gives you a more comfortable lifestyle. It *might* even let you pose as someone of higher Status – although the GM is free to require a Savoir-Faire (High Society) skill roll as well. But be aware that claiming more Status than you actually possess can lead to a reaction penalty! Actually *living* above your Status can earn you a bad Reputation – or even qualify as an Odious Personal Habit.

If you get Status free from Rank (p. 29), you need only pay the cost of living for your Status *before* this bonus, not for your final Status level. Someone else – your organization, the taxpayers, etc. – covers the difference.

Example: A person from a good family (Status 1) who becomes president of a sizable country (Status 7) does not need to pay $60 million per month to support the associated lifestyle: personal jet liner, multiple mansions, security service, etc. He pays only the $1,200 per month for Status 1; the *state* pays the difference. Someone who just wanted to live in a presidential style would have to pay the full amount *himself!*

If you're on vacation or traveling for most of a month, your expenses will be higher – usually about six times your cost of living, unless you have a Claim to Hospitality (p. 41).

Inns, Hotels, and Other Temporary Accommodations

When living away from home, you must pay a *daily* cost of living equal to 20% of your usual monthly cost of living – but if you wish, you can live at *one* level below your Status without meaningful repercussions. The quality of your accommodations depends on Status. In the modern world, Status -1 means a dingy flophouse; Status 0, a typical hotel or motel; Status 1, a good hotel; Status 2, a luxury hotel suite; and Status 3 and higher, a swanky resort.

You can also use this price tag as a guideline for how much it costs to entertain guests at the Status to which they're accustomed, and as a rough guide to suitable bribes.

> "There's a lot of statues in Europe you haven't bought yet."
> "You can't blame me. They've been making statues for some two thousand years, and I've only been collecting for five."
> – Bernstein and Kane, **Citizen Kane**

Food

Cost of living assumes that you buy groceries and that you, your family, or your staff prepares your meals at home – or that if you *always* eat out, it's at places one level below your Status. When you eat out or purchase travel rations, use these guidelines. Treat Status greater than 3 as Status 3, except in unusual cases.

Restaurant: 1% of cost of living for breakfast or lunch, or 2% for dinner, based on the Status of the restaurant's typical patron.

Travel Rations: 5% of cost of living for one week. Weighs 14 lbs.

Liquor: 1% of cost of living per bottle.

Cost of Living Table

Status	Examples	Cost of Living
8	Emperor, god-king, overlord	$600,000,000
7	King, pope, president	$60,000,000
6	Royal family, governor	$6,000,000
5	Great noble, multinational corporate boss	$600,000
4	Lesser noble, congressional representative, Who's Who	$60,000
3	Landed knight, guild master, big city mayor	$12,000
2	Landless knight, mayor, business leader	$3,000
1	Squire, merchant, priest, doctor, councilor	$1,200
0	Freeman, apprentice, ordinary citizen	$600
-1	Bondsman, poor citizen	$300
-2	Serf, street person	$100

Clothing

You start with a full wardrobe appropriate to your Status – you need not purchase this separately. Cost of living covers normal wear and tear and gradual replacements, but if you *suddenly* need to replace your clothing, use the rules below.

Use full Status to figure the cost of a complete wardrobe. High-Status individuals own *more* clothes, and the crown jewels of Status 7 and 8 rulers are worth tens or hundreds of millions all by themselves! When buying *just one outfit*, though, treat Status greater than 3 as Status 3. *Exception:* Men's clothing becomes more conservative on TL5 and higher Earth, allowing most men to treat Status 2 and up as Status 2 when they buy one outfit. Men at Status 3 and up with Fashion Sense must still pay the full Status 3 cost in order to benefit from it.

Complete Wardrobe: Includes one to four sets of ordinary clothes, plus nightclothes, one set each of formal wear and winter clothes, and usually at least one outfit (lab coat, uniform, gym clothes, etc.) appropriate to your job or hobbies. 100% of cost of living; 20+ lbs.

Ordinary Clothes: One complete outfit, ranging in quality from castoff rags to designer fashions, depending on Status. At minimum: undergarments, plus a tunic, blouse, or shirt with hose, skirt, or trousers – or a *long* tunic, robe, or dress – and suitable footwear. 20% of cost of living; 2 lbs.

Winter Clothes: As above, but heavier. Includes a hat or hood, boots, and (at TL6 or less) furs. 30% of cost of living; 4 lbs.

Formal Wear: Your "best outfit," which will usually include at least some accessories (hat, gloves, etc.) or jewelry. 40% of cost of living; 2 lbs.

Cosmetics: Natural or synthetic beauty aids. For one month's supply: 10% of cost of living; 2 lbs.

BUYING EQUIPMENT

You are usually able to buy what you want, within the limits of your starting wealth and your society's laws. But sometimes, the GM or the adventure may specify some or all of your equipment. For instance, if you're a soldier on a military mission, you'll be *issued* your gear; you don't have to pay for it, but you can't choose it yourself. If the adventure calls for it, the GM might impose more severe restrictions – your choices will be extremely limited if you are supposed to be a castaway on an uninhabited island! The GM is the final judge of what you can buy in all cases.

However you acquire your equipment, you should list it on your character sheet. If you accumulate a *lot* of gear, consider keeping it on a separate sheet. In all cases, you should list possessions you leave at home separately from those you carry in order to keep track of encumbrance (see *Encumbrance and Move*, p. 17).

Equipment Lists

Each game world has one or more equipment lists that give cost, weight, and other statistics for important items. You *can* buy items that aren't on

Legality Class

Some equipment has a "Legality Class" (LC). LC rates how likely an item is to be legally or socially acceptable to own and carry. The availability of a given item in a particular society depends on the interaction between the item's LC and the society's "Control Rating"; see *Control Rating and Legality Class* (p. 507).

An item has a LC only if it is likely to be controlled. Ordinary clothing and tools normally do not require a LC. Of course, every society will have exceptions; for instance, revealing clothing might be LC4 in a puritanical society.

LC4 – *Open.* The item is openly available in most societies, but tightly controlled societies might restrict access or use. *Examples:* Computer; sword; shotgun; motor scooter.

LC3 – *Licensed.* The item requires registration with the authorities in most societies. Registration might involve a fee or examination, and might be denied to criminals, minors, etc. *Examples:* Automobile; handgun; hunting rifle.

LC2 – *Restricted.* Only military, police, or intelligence agencies may possess the item in most societies – although some licensed civilians might be permitted to keep it *on their own property. Examples:* Assault rifle; armored vehicles.

LC1 – *Military.* The item is available only to armed forces or secret spy agencies in most societies. *Examples:* Anti-tank weapons; fighting vehicles.

LC0 – *Banned.* The item is restricted to the armed forces of certain governments, who will go to extremes to keep it out of the hands of individuals and "have-not" governments. *Examples:* nuclear and biological weapons.

---

the list, provided the GM agrees; the GM sets the price. The GM should be open-minded! In high-tech settings, especially, *hundreds* of common items are unlikely to be listed . . . items you could go into any department store and pick up. If somebody really wants a vegetable dicer or a talking baby doll, let him buy one.

This chapter includes lists of weapons, armor, and general equipment for campaigns at a variety of tech levels. You are welcome to make copies of these tables for your own use.

Tech Level

Each item of equipment has a tech level (see p. 22). This is the *earliest* TL at which you can find the item as described. Many items will remain in use, with few or no changes, at later TLs. The notation "^" means the item requires "superscience" that rewrites the laws of physics; required TL is up to the GM.

God made man, but Colonel Colt made men equal.

WEAPONS

Adventurers often carry weapons of some sort, whether it's a knight's broadsword, a detective's snub-nosed .38, or a space pirate's blaster pistol.

CHOOSING YOUR WEAPONS

To determine what weapons to carry, consider your situation first, and *then* your skills, strength, and budget. If you can't use it or don't need it . . . don't buy it.

First, decide *why* you carry a weapon. Is it for self-defense, intimidation ("Stop or I'll shoot!"), battle, or hunting? Do you need a concealed weapon – or a quiet one – or does law

or custom let you carry it openly? If you're a pacifist, do you want a weapon just as a threat, or one that you can use to disarm or subdue a foe?

Consider what the law allows, too. Most settings have laws or customs that govern the weapons and armor you may wear on the street or on the job without attracting attention (see *Legality Class*, box). This applies in historical settings as well. A stranger visiting the average medieval village wearing a suit of plate armor would be every bit as conspicuous – and threatening – as a person carrying an assault rifle into a corner grocery store today!

Also review your skills and Strength. High-tech weapons (such as guns) work equally well for anyone who

knows how to use them. Low-tech weapons – clubs, swords, etc. – do much more damage if wielded by a strong person. Either may have a minimum ST.

Finally, look at the weapon's statistics. Each weapon is rated for its TL, weight, cost, and relative legality. A weapon's damage rating is the basic measure of its effectiveness, but there are also factors such as reach, range, rate of fire, and accuracy to consider. To learn what the various statistics imply for combat, read Chapters 11-13.

This section contains information to help you make the choices discussed above. If you are a *total* nonfighter, you can skim or skip this material!

WEAPON STATISTICS

Weapon tables provide the items of information explained below. A given column will only appear on a table if it is germane to the weapons on that table. In *all* cases, "–" means the statistic does not apply, "var." means the value varies, and "spec." means to see the relevant weapon skill in Chapter 4 or applicable section of Chapter 13 for special rules.

Glossary of Arms and Armor

The following terms and abbreviations appear on the various weapon tables.

8G, 10G, 12G: The *gauge* of a shotgun – the number of lead balls of its bore size that weigh one pound. Thus, 10G shot is *larger* than 12G shot.

ATGM: Anti-Tank Guided Missile. An anti-vehicular missile steered to its target by the firer.

auto: A term that designates a *semi*-automatic firearm.

blaster: A particle-beam weapon.

cartridge rifle: A breech-loading, single-shot rifle.

coif: A hood, usually made of mail.

electrolaser: A weapon that transmits an electrical charge to its target along a path ionized by a low-powered laser beam.

Gauss: Jargon for any electromagnetic gun.

GL: Grenade Launcher.

glaive: A staff tipped with a heavy blade.

gyroc: A spin-stabilized ("gyrostabilized") rocket.

HMG: Heavy Machine Gun.

ICW: Infantry Combat Weapon. A rifle with an integral grenade launcher.

katana: A long, slightly curved sword used by Japanese samurai.

laminated steel plate: Japanese samurai armor.

LMG: Light Machine Gun.

lorica segmentata: Roman legionary armor.

morningstar: A flail consisting of a metal ball attached to a haft with a chain.

musket: A single-shot, *smoothbore*, muzzle-loading long gun.

naginata: A staff tipped with a lightweight blade.

nunchaku: A flail consisting of a pair of short clubs joined by a chain.

PDW: Personal Defense Weapon. A pistol- to SMG-sized automatic weapon that fires powerful ammunition, intended as an emergency weapon for vehicle crews.

prodd: A crossbow that fires lead or stone pellets.

rifle-musket: A single-shot, *rifled*, muzzle-loading long gun.

RPG: Rocket-Propelled Grenade.

SAM: Surface to Air Missile (e.g., Stinger).

SAW: Squad Automatic Weapon. A kind of light machine gun.

scorpion: A bolt-throwing engine that resembles a giant crossbow.

shuriken: A throwing star. Purportedly used by ninjas.

SMG: Submachine Gun.

sollerets: Metal-plated shoes.

TL (Tech Level)

The tech level at which the weapon first becomes widespread. You may only buy weapons of your campaign's TL *or less*, unless you have the High TL trait (p. 23).

Weapon

The general class of weapon in question; e.g., "shortsword" or "assault rifle." Each entry represents a wide range of individual types.

For guns, this entry includes a projectile diameter, or "caliber," given in millimeters (e.g., 9mm) or fractions of an inch (e.g., .50), as customary for the weapon. The letters M (Magnum), P (Pistol), R (Revolver), and S (Short) appear after caliber in situations where different guns have the same caliber but fire different ammunition; for instance, 7.62mm ammo is not interchangeable with shorter 7.62mmS ammo.

Damage

For muscle-powered melee and missile weapons, such as swords and bows, damage is ST-based and expressed as a modifier to the wielder's basic thrusting (thr) or swinging (sw) damage, as given on the *Damage Table* (p. 16). For example, a spear does "thr+2," so if you have ST 11, which gives a basic thrusting damage of 1d-1, you inflict 1d+1 damage with a spear. Note that swung weapons act as a lever, and so do more damage.

For firearms, grenades, and some powered melee weapons, damage is given as a fixed number of dice plus adds; e.g., a 9mm auto pistol lists "2d+2," which means that *any* user would roll 2d and add 2 to get damage.

Armor Divisors: A parenthetical number after damage – e.g., (2) – is an *armor divisor*. Divide the target's DR from armor or other sources by this number before subtracting it from your damage (or adding it to the target's HT roll to resist an affliction). For instance, an attack with a divisor of (2) would halve DR. A fractional divisor *increases* DR: (0.5) multiplies DR by 2; (0.2) multiplies it by 5; and (0.1) multiplies it by 10.

Damage Type: An abbreviation indicating the *type* of injury or effect the attack causes.

Abbreviation	Damage Type
aff	affliction
burn	burning
cor	corrosion
cr	crushing
cut	cutting
fat	fatigue
imp	impaling
pi-	small piercing
pi	piercing
pi+	large piercing
pi++	huge piercing
spec.	special – see weapon notes
tox	toxic

A victim loses HP equal to the damage that penetrates his DR. Halve this for small piercing attacks; increase it by 50% for cutting and large piercing attacks; and double it for impaling and huge piercing attacks. Subtract fatigue damage from FP instead of HP. Afflictions cause no injury, but impose a particular affliction on a failed HT roll, as specified in the weapon's notes. See *Damage and Injury* (p. 377) for additional rules.

Explosions: An "ex" after crushing or burning damage indicates the attack produces an explosion. This may injure those nearby: divide damage by *three times* distance in yards from the center of the blast. Some explosions scatter fragments that inflict cutting damage on anyone nearby (see *Fragmentation Damage,* p. 414). Fragmentation damage appears in brackets; e.g., "3d [2d] cr ex" means an explosion that inflicts 3d crushing damage and throws fragments that do 2d cutting damage. The "danger radius" for fragments is five yards times the dice of fragmentation damage; e.g., 10 yards for [2d]. If an explosive attack has an armor divisor,

this only applies to the DR of a target that takes a direct hit – not to those caught in the blast radius or hit by fragments.

Afflictions: Some special weapons don't list dice of damage. Instead, they give a HT modifier; e.g., "HT-3." Anyone who is hit must attempt a HT roll at the listed penalty to avoid the effects of the affliction (e.g., unconsciousness). For example, a stun gun calls for a HT-3 roll to avoid being stunned for (20 - HT) seconds. Note that DR (modified by any armor divisor) normally adds to the victim's HT; for instance, a DR 2 leather jacket would give +2 to your HT roll to resist that stun gun.

Other Effects: A few weapons have additional *linked* or *follow-up* effects, noted on a second line. These occur simultaneously with the primary attack on a successful hit. For details, see *Linked Effects* (p. 381) and *Follow-Up Damage* (p. 381).

Reach

Melee weapons only. This is the distance in yards at which a human-sized or smaller wielder can strike with the weapon. For example, reach "2"

means the weapon can only strike a foe two yards away – not a closer or more distant one.

"C" indicates you can use the weapon in close combat; see *Close Combat* (p. 391).

Some weapons have a continuum of reaches; e.g., a spear with reach "1, 2" can strike targets either one *or* two yards away. An asterisk (*) next to reach means the weapon is awkward enough that it requires a Ready maneuver to change reach (e.g., between 1 and 2). Otherwise, you can strike at foes that are at any distance within the weapon's reach.

Parry

Melee weapons only. A number, such as "+2" or "-1," indicates the bonus or penalty to your Parry defense when using that weapon (see *Parrying,* p. 376). For most weapons, this is "0," meaning "no modifier."

"F" means the weapon is a *fencing weapon* (see p. 404).

"U" means the weapon is *unbalanced:* you cannot use it to parry if you have already used it to attack this turn (or vice versa).

"No" means the weapon *cannot parry at all.*

Acc (Accuracy)

Ranged weapons only. Add Accuracy to your skill if you took an Aim maneuver on the turn prior to your attack. If the weapon has a built-in scope, the bonus for this appears as a separate modifier after the weapon's base Acc; e.g., "7+2."

Range

Ranged weapons only. If a weapon has only one range number, this is the

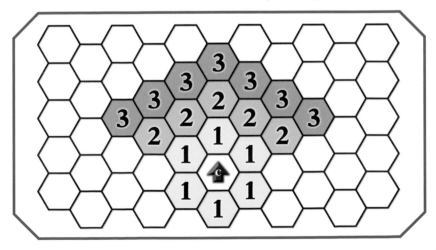

Maximum Range (Max) in yards at which it can attack a target. If two numbers appear, separated by a slash, the first is *Half-Damage Range* (1/2D) and the second is Max. Damaging attacks on targets at or beyond 1/2D inflict half damage, and those that require a HT roll to resist are resisted at +3.

Muscle-powered weapons usually list 1/2D and Max as multiples of the wielder's ST, not as a fixed range. For example, "×10/×15" means 1/2D is 10×ST and Max is 15×ST, so someone with ST 10 would have 1/2D 100 and Max 150. For bows, crossbows and mechanical artillery, use the *weapon's* ST in these formulas.

A few weapons have a *minimum* range, given in their Notes. The weapon cannot attack a target *closer* than this range – usually because it fires in a high arc, or has safety, fusing, or guidance limitations.

RoF (Rate of Fire)

Ranged weapons only. The maximum number of shots an ordinary shooter can fire in a one-second turn. A weapon can normally fire fewer shots (to a minimum of 1), if you wish, but some special notes apply:

"!" means the weapon can *only* fire on "full auto," like many machine guns. *Minimum* RoF is 1/4 the listed RoF, rounded up.

"*m×n*" (e.g., 3×9) means the weapon can fire a number of shots per attack equal to the first number (*m*), and that each shot releases smaller projectiles equal to the second number (*n*); see *Shotguns and Multiple Projectiles* (p. 409).

"Jet" means the weapon shoots a continuous stream of fluid or energy, using the jet rules (p. 106).

Shots

Ranged weapons only. The number of shots the weapon can fire before you must reload or recharge it. "T" means the weapon is *thrown*. To "reload," pick it up or ready a new weapon!

The parenthetical number following Shots indicates the number of one-second Ready maneuvers needed to reload *all* of the weapon's shots (e.g., by changing magazines) – or, for a thrown weapon, the time needed to

ready another weapon. An "i" next to this means you must load shots individually: the time listed is *per shot* rather than for all shots.

A crossbow or prodd takes the indicated time to ready (4 turns) only if its ST is no greater than yours (see *Bows, Crossbows, and ST*, below). *Double* this if the bow's ST is 1 or 2 greater. If its ST is 3 or 4 greater, you need a "goat's foot" device to cock it; this takes 20 turns, and requires you to stand. If its ST is 5 or more above yours, you cannot reload it at all.

Cost

The price of a new weapon, in $. For swords and knives, this includes a sheath or a scabbard. For firearms, this includes the minimal necessary cleaning kit.

Weight

The weight of the weapon, in pounds; "neg." means "negligible." For missile weapons with Shots 2+, this is *loaded* weight. The weight of one full reload appears after a slash.

Exception: If the weapon has Shots 1 (like a bow or guided missile launcher) *or* has a backpack power supply (noted with a "p"), the *unloaded* weight is given. The weight after the slash is that of one shot (e.g., one arrow or guided missile) or the backpack.

ST (Strength)

The minimum Strength required to use the weapon properly. If you try to use a weapon that requires more ST than you have, you will be at -1 to weapon skill per point of ST you lack *and* lose one extra FP at the end of any fight that lasts long enough to fatigue you.

For a melee weapon, your effective ST for damage purposes cannot exceed *triple* the weapon's minimum ST. For instance, a large knife has minimum ST 6, so its "maximum ST" is 18; if your ST were 19+, you would compute your damage as if you had ST 18.

Natural weapons (e.g., a punch or kick) have neither minimum nor maximum ST.

"†" means the weapon requires two hands. If you have at least 1.5 times the listed ST (round *up*), you can use a weapon like this in one hand, but it

becomes *unready* after you attack with it. If you have at least *twice* the listed ST, you can wield it one-handed with no readiness penalty. But if it requires one hand to hold it and another to operate a moving part, like a bow or a pump shotgun, it *always* requires two hands, regardless of ST.

"‡" means the weapon requires two hands *and* becomes unready after you attack with it, unless you have at least 1.5 times the listed ST (round *up*). To use it in one hand without it becoming unready, you need at least *three times* the listed ST.

"R" indicates a firearm that uses a musket rest. The weapon's weight *includes* that of the rest. It takes a Ready maneuver to balance the weapon on the rest – but after that, any aimed shot fired while stationary and standing up is automatically braced (see *Aim*, p. 364).

"B" indicates a firearm with an attached bipod. When firing from a prone position using the bipod, treat the weapon as if it were braced *and* reduce its ST requirement to 2/3 of the listed value (round *up*); e.g., ST 13 becomes ST 9.

"M" means the weapon is usually mounted in a vehicle or gun carriage, or on a tripod. *Ignore* the listed ST and Bulk when firing the weapon from its tripod or mount; the ST requirement only applies when firing the weapon *without* its mount. Removing the weapon from its mount (or reattaching it) takes at least three one-second Ready maneuvers.

Bows, Crossbows, and ST: Bows, crossbows, and prodds have their *own* ST value. Use this instead of your ST to determine range and damage. You must specify the ST of such a weapon when you buy it. You can always use a weapon that is *weaker* than you. You can use a stronger crossbow or prodd; it does more damage but take longer to cock (see *Shots*, above). You cannot use a stronger bow.

Bulk

Ranged weapons only. A measure of the weapon's size and handiness. Bulk modifies your weapon skill when you take a Move and Attack maneuver (see *Move and Attack*, p. 365). It also serves as a penalty to Holdout skill when you attempt to conceal the weapon.

EQUIPMENT

Rcl (Recoil)

Firearms only. A measure of how easy the weapon is to control when firing rapidly: the higher the value, the less controllable the weapon. Rcl 1 means the weapon is recoilless, or nearly so.

When firing at RoF 2+, every *full* multiple of Rcl by which you make your attack roll means you score one extra hit, to a maximum number of hits equal to total shots fired; see *Rapid Fire* (p. 373). (Firearms with RoF 1 still list Rcl, for use with certain rules.)

LC (Legality Class)

This is only noted for firearms and grenades. All melee weapons and muscle-powered ranged weapons intended for combat are LC4. An exception is the force sword, which is LC2. *Ignore* LC for "weapons" intended as tools, or for hunting or recreation, and for those that are completely improvised (like a wooden stake). See *Legality Class* (p. 267).

Notes

The numbers listed here refer to applicable footnotes (if any) at the end of the table.

MELEE WEAPONS

Melee weapons are grouped under the skills required to use them. Skill names appear in capital letters, with defaults in parentheses; e.g., **"AXE/MACE (DX-5, Flail-4, or Two-Handed Axe/Mace-3)."** If there is more than one way to use a weapon, each method gets its own line. If multiple skills let you use a weapon, the weapon appears under each skill. For example, both Staff skill and Two-Handed Sword skill let you wield a quarterstaff – and either lets you swing the staff or thrust with it.

Melee Weapon Table

AXE/MACE (DX-5, Flail-4, or Two-Handed Axe/Mace-3)

TL	Weapon	Damage	Reach	Parry	Cost	Weight	ST	Notes
0	Axe	sw+2 cut	1	0U	$50	4	11	
0	Hatchet	sw cut	1	0	$40	2	8	[1]
0	Throwing Axe	sw+2 cut	1	0U	$60	4	11	[1]
2	Mace	sw+3 cr	1	0U	$50	5	12	[1]
2	Small Mace	sw+2 cr	1	0U	$35	3	10	[1]
3	Pick	sw+1 imp	1	0U	$70	3	10	[2]

BOXING, BRAWLING, KARATE, or DX

TL	Weapon	Damage	Reach	Parry	Cost	Weight	ST	Notes
–	Punch	thr-1 cr	C	0	–	–	–	[3]
1	Brass Knuckles	thr cr	C	0	$10	0.25	–	[3]

BRAWLING-2, KARATE-2, or DX-2

TL	Weapon	Damage	Reach	Parry	Cost	Weight	ST	Notes
–	Kick	thr cr	C, 1	No	–	–	–	[3, 4]
–	Kick w. Boots	thr+1 cr	C, 1	No	–	–	–	[3, 4]

BRAWLING or DX

TL	Weapon	Damage	Reach	Parry	Cost	Weight	ST	Notes
–	Blunt Teeth	thr-1 cr	C	No	–	–	–	[3]
–	Fangs	thr-1 imp	C	No	–	–	–	[3]
–	Sharp Beak	thr-1 pi+	C	No	–	–	–	[3]
–	Sharp Teeth	thr-1 cut	C	No	–	–	–	[3]
–	Striker	var.	var.	var.	–	–	–	See p. 88.
1	Blackjack or Sap	thr cr	C	0	$20	1	7	[3]
8	Stun Gun	HT-3(0.5) aff	C, 1	No	$100	1	2	[5]

BROADSWORD (DX-5, Force Sword-4, Rapier-4, Saber-4, Shortsword-2, or Two-Handed Sword-4)

TL	Weapon	Damage	Reach	Parry	Cost	Weight	ST	Notes
0	Light Club	sw+1 cr	1	0	$5	3	10	
	or	thr+1 cr	1	0	–	–	10	
2	Broadsword	sw+1 cut	1	0	$500	3	10	
	or	thr+1 cr	1	0	–	–	10	
2	Thrusting Broadsword	sw+1 cut	1	0	$600	3	10	
	or	thr+2 imp	1	0	–	–	10	
3	Bastard Sword	sw+1 cut	1, 2	0U	$650	5	11	
	or	thr+1 cr	2	0U	–	–	11	
3	Katana	sw+1 cut	1, 2	0	$650	5	11	
	or	thr+1 imp	1	0	–	–	11	
3	Thrusting Bastard Sword	sw+1 cut	1, 2	0U	$750	5	11	
	or	thr+2 imp	2	0U	–	–	11	
4	Cavalry Saber	sw+1 cut	1	0	$500	3	10	
	or	thr+1 imp	1	0	–	–	10	

FLAIL (DX-6, Axe/Mace-4, or Two-Handed Flail-3)

TL	Weapon	Damage	Reach	Parry	Cost	Weight	ST	Notes
3	Morningstar	sw+3 cr	1	0U	$80	6	12	[6]
3	Nunchaku	sw+1 cr	1	0U	$20	2	7	[6]

FORCE SWORD (DX-5 or any sword skill at -3)

TL	Weapon	Damage	Reach	Parry	Cost	Weight	ST	Notes
^	Force Sword	8d(5) burn	1, 2	0	$10,000	2	3	[7]

GARROTE (DX-4)

TL	Weapon	Damage	Reach	Parry	Cost	Weight	ST	Notes
0	Garrote	spec.	C	No	$2	neg.	–	[8]

KNIFE (DX-4, Force Sword-3, Main-Gauche-3, or Shortsword-3)

TL	Weapon	Damage	Reach	Parry	Cost	Weight	ST	Notes
0	Large Knife	sw-2 cut	C, 1	-1	$40	1	6	
	or	thr imp	C	-1	–	–	6	[1]
0	Small Knife	sw-3 cut	C, 1	-1	$30	0.5	5	
	or	thr-1 imp	C	-1	–	–	5	[1]
0	Wooden Stake	thr(0.5) imp	C	-1	$4	0.5	5	[1]
1	Dagger	thr-1 imp	C	-1	$20	0.25	5	[1]

KUSARI (DX-6, Monowire Whip-3, Two-Handed Flail-4, or Whip-3)

TL	Weapon	Damage	Reach	Parry	Cost	Weight	ST	Notes
3	Kusari	sw+2 cr	1-4*	-2U	$70	5	11	[6]

LANCE (DX-5 or Spear-3)

TL	Weapon	Damage	Reach	Parry	Cost	Weight	ST	Notes
2	Lance	thr+3 imp	4	No	$60	6	12	[9]

MONOWIRE WHIP (DX-6, Kusari-3, or Whip-3)

TL	Weapon	Damage	Reach	Parry	Cost	Weight	ST	Notes
^	Monowire Whip	sw+1d-2(10) cut	1-7*	-2U	$900	0.5	5	

POLEARM (DX-5, Spear-4, Staff-4, or Two-Handed Axe/Mace-4)

TL	Weapon	Damage	Reach	Parry	Cost	Weight	ST	Notes
1	Glaive	sw+3 cut	2, 3*	0U	$100	8	11‡	
	or	thr+3 imp	1-3*	0U	–	–	11†	
2	Naginata	sw+2 cut	1, 2*	0U	$100	6	9†	
	or	thr+3 imp	2	0	–	–	9†	
3	Halberd	sw+5 cut	2, 3*	0U	$150	12	13‡	
	or	sw+4 imp	2, 3*	0U	–	–	13‡	[2]
	or	thr+3 imp	1-3*	0U	–	–	12†	
3	Poleaxe	sw+4 cut	2, 3*	0U	$120	10	12‡	
	or	sw+4 cr	2, 3*	0U	–	–	12‡	

RAPIER (DX-5, Broadsword-4, Main-Gauche-3, Saber-3, or Smallsword-3)

TL	Weapon	Damage	Reach	Parry	Cost	Weight	ST	Notes
4	Rapier	thr+1 imp	1, 2	0F	$500	2.75	9	

SABER (DX-5, Broadsword-4, Main-Gauche-3, Rapier-3, Shortsword-4, or Smallsword-3)

TL	Weapon	Damage	Reach	Parry	Cost	Weight	ST	Notes
4	Saber	sw-1 cut	1	0F	$700	2	8	
	or	thr+1 imp	1	0F	–	–	8	

SHIELD (DX-4)

TL	Weapon	Damage	Reach	Parry	Cost	Weight	ST	Notes
0	Shield Bash	thr cr	1	No	var.	var.	–	
1	Shield Bash w. Spike	thr+1 cr	1	No	+$20	+5	–	

SHORTSWORD (DX-5, Broadsword-2, Force Sword-4, Jitte/Sai-3, Knife-4, Saber-4, Smallsword-4, or Tonfa-3)

TL	Weapon	Damage	Reach	Parry	Cost	Weight	ST	Notes
0	Baton	sw cr	1	0	$20	1	6	
	or	thr cr	1	0	–	–	6	
2	Shortsword	sw cut	1	0	$400	2	8	
	or	thr imp	1	0	–	–	8	
4	Cutlass	sw cut	1	0	$300	2	8	[10]
	or	thr imp	1	0	–	–	8	
7	Cattle Prod	1d-3 burn	1	0	$50	2	3	
	linked	HT-3(0.5) aff	–	–	–	–	–	[5]

SMALLSWORD (DX-5, Main-Gauche-3, Rapier-3, Saber-3, or Shortsword-4)

TL	Weapon	Damage	Reach	Parry	Cost	Weight	ST	Notes
0	Short Staff	sw cr	1	0F	$20	1	6	
	or	thr cr	1	0F	–	–	6	
4	Smallsword	thr+1 imp	1	0F	$400	1.5	5	

SPEAR (DX-5, Polearm-4, or Staff-2)

TL	Weapon	Damage	Reach	Parry	Cost	Weight	ST	Notes
0	Spear	thr+2 imp	1*	0	$40	4	9	[1]
	two hands	thr+3 imp	1, 2*	0	–	–	9†	
1	Javelin	thr+1 imp	1	0	$30	2	6	[1]
2	Long Spear	thr+2 imp	2, 3*	0U	$60	5	10	
	two hands	thr+3 imp	2, 3*	0	–	–	10†	

STAFF (DX-5, Polearm-4, or Spear-2)

TL	Weapon	Damage	Reach	Parry	Cost	Weight	ST	Notes
0	Quarterstaff	sw+2 cr	1, 2	+2	$10	4	7†	
	or	thr+2 cr	1, 2	+2	–	–	7†	
2	Naginata	sw+2 cr	1, 2	0U	$100	6	9†	Blunt end.
	or	thr+2 cr	1, 2	0	–	–	9†	

CROSSBOW (DX-4)

TL	Weapon	Damage	Acc	Range	Weight	RoF	Shots	Cost	ST	Bulk	Notes
2	Crossbow	thr+4 imp	4	×20/×25	6/0.06	1	1(4)	$150	7†	-6	[3]
3	Pistol Crossbow	thr+2 imp	1	×15/×20	4/0.06	1	1(4)	$150	7	-4	[2, 3]
3	Prodd	thr+4 pi	2	×20/×25	6/0.06	1	1(4)	$150	7†	-6	[3]
3	"Goat's Foot"	–	–	–	2	–	(20)	$50	7†	–	[5]

LASSO (No default)

TL	Weapon	Damage	Acc	Range	Weight	RoF	Shots	Cost	ST	Bulk	Notes
1	Lariat	spec.	0	spec.	3	1	T(spec.)	$40	7†	-2	[4]

NET (Cloak-5)

TL	Weapon	Damage	Acc	Range	Weight	RoF	Shots	Cost	ST	Bulk	Notes
0	Large Net	spec.	1	spec.	20	1	T(1)	$40	11	-6	[4, 6]
2	Melee Net	spec.	1	spec.	5	1	T(1)	$20	8	-4	[4, 6]

SLING (DX-6)

TL	Weapon	Damage	Acc	Range	Weight	RoF	Shots	Cost	ST	Bulk	Notes
0	Sling	sw pi	0	×6/×10	0.5/0.05	1	1(2)	$20	6	-4	[2, 3, 7]
1	Staff Sling	sw+1 pi	1	×10/×15	2/0.05	1	1(2)	$20	7†	-6	[3, 7]

SPEAR THROWER (DX-5 or Thrown Weapon (Spear)-4)

TL	Weapon	Damage	Acc	Range	Weight	RoF	Shots	Cost	ST	Bulk	Notes
0	Atlatl	–	–	–	1	1	1(1)	$20	–	–	[2]
	with Dart	sw-1 imp	1	×3/×4	1	–	–	$20	5	-3	
	with Javelin	sw+1 imp	3	×2/×3	2	–	–	$30	6	-4	

THROWN WEAPON (AXE/MACE) (DX-4)

TL	Weapon	Damage	Acc	Range	Weight	RoF	Shots	Cost	ST	Bulk	Notes
0	Hatchet	sw cut	1	×1.5/×2.5	2	1	T(1)	$40	8	-2	
0	Throwing Axe	sw+2 cut	2	×1/×1.5	4	1	T(1)	$60	11	-3	
2	Mace	sw+3 cr	1	×0.5/×1	5	1	T(1)	$50	12	-4	
2	Small Mace	sw+2 cr	1	×1/×1.5	3	1	T(1)	$35	10	-3	

THROWN WEAPON (HARPOON) (DX-4 or Thrown Weapon (Spear)-2)

TL	Weapon	Damage	Acc	Range	Weight	RoF	Shots	Cost	ST	Bulk	Notes
2	Harpoon	thr+5 imp	2	×1/×1.5	6	1	T(1)	$60	11	-6	[8]

THROWN WEAPON (KNIFE) (DX-4)

TL	Weapon	Damage	Acc	Range	Weight	RoF	Shots	Cost	ST	Bulk	Notes
0	Large Knife	thr imp	0	×0.8/×1.5	1	1	T(1)	$40	6	-2	
0	Small Knife	thr-1 imp	0	×0.5/×1	0.5	1	T(1)	$30	5	-1	
0	Wooden Stake	thr(0.5) imp	0	×0.5/×1	0.5	1	T(1)	$4	5	-2	
1	Dagger	thr-1 imp	0	×0.5/×1	0.25	1	T(1)	$20	5	-1	

THROWN WEAPON (SHURIKEN) (DX-4 or Throwing-2)

TL	Weapon	Damage	Acc	Range	Weight	RoF	Shots	Cost	ST	Bulk	Notes
3	Shuriken	thr-1 cut	1	×0.5/×1	0.1	1	T(1)	$3	5	0	

THROWN WEAPON (SPEAR) (DX-4, Spear Thrower-4, or Thrown Weapon (Harpoon)-2)

TL	Weapon	Damage	Acc	Range	Weight	RoF	Shots	Cost	ST	Bulk	Notes
0	Spear	thr+3 imp	2	×1/×1.5	4	1	T(1)	$40	9	-6	
1	Javelin	thr+1 imp	3	×1.5/×2.5	2	1	T(1)	$30	6	-4	

Notes

[1] Follow-up drug or poison attack if damage penetrates DR. Effects depend on the poison used; see *Poison* (p. 437).

[2] Requires *two* hands to ready, but only *one* hand to attack.

[3] An arrow or bolt for a bow or crossbow is $2. A dart for a blowpipe, or a lead pellet for a prodd or sling, is $0.1. Sling stones are free.

[4] May entangle or ensnare the target; see *Special Ranged Weapons* (p. 411).

[5] Cocking lever to reload a high-ST crossbow or prodd. You can reload a weapon up to 4 ST over your own with 20 one-second Ready maneuvers.

[6] A net has no 1/2D range. Max range is (ST/2 + Skill/5) for a large net and (ST + Skill/5) for a melee net.

[7] Can fire stones (TL0) or lead bullets (TL2). Lead bullets give +1 damage and *double* range.

[8] Tethered. Requires a Ready maneuver and a successful ST roll to pull out (if you fail, you may try again next turn). Does *half* the damage coming out that it did going in.

HAND GRENADES AND INCENDIARIES

Hand-tossed bombs date to the earliest introduction of gunpowder; improvised gasoline bombs ("Molotov cocktails") remain popular. See *Throwing* (p. 355) to determine how far you can throw such a device. "Fuse" is the number of seconds it takes for the weapon to detonate once readied.

Muscle-Powered Ranged Weapon Quality

Blowpipes, bows, and crossbows may be *fine* weapons. Increase 1/2D and Max range by 20%. They cost 4 times list price.

Thrown weapons, and arrows and bolts, use the rules under *Melee Weapon Quality* (p. 274).

Hand Grenade and Incendiary Table

THROWING (DX-3 or Dropping-4)

TL	Weapon	Damage	Weight	Fuse	Cost	LC	Notes
5	Black Powder	3d cr ex [1d]	1	3-5	$5	2	[1]
6	Concussion	6d cr ex	1	4	$15	2	[2]
6	Fragmentation	4d cr ex [2d]	1	4	$10	2	[2]
6	Molotov Cocktail	spec. (1 yd.)	1	spec.	$2	3	[1, 3]
7	Chemical	spec. (2 yd.)	1	2	$10	3	[2, 4]
7	Concussion	5d×2 cr ex	1	4	$40	2	[2]
7	Fragmentation	8d cr ex [3d]	1	4	$40	2	[2]
8	Stun	HT-5 aff (10 yd.)	1	2	$40	2	[2, 5]
^	Plasma	6d×4 burn ex	1	2	$100	1	[2]

Notes

[1] Takes a Ready maneuver to light the fuse (impossible in rain, etc.) – or *five* Ready maneuvers if you must insert the fuse first! A Molotov cocktail shatters on impact; a black-powder grenade detonates 3-5 seconds later, depending on fuse length.

[2] Takes one Ready maneuver to draw the grenade and a second Ready maneuver to pull the pin. Detonates 2-4 seconds later, depending on grenade type.

[3] A glass bottle filled with gasoline, lit by a burning rag. See *Molotov Cocktails and Oil Flasks* (p. 411).

[4] Fills a 2-yard radius with smoke, teargas, etc.; see *Poison Examples* (p. 439). The cloud lasts about 80 seconds under normal conditions. Exotic chemicals may cost more or have a lower LC.

[5] A Vision and Hearing-Based affliction that affects a 10-yard radius. The Protected Hearing and Protected Vision advantages each give +5 to the HT roll. If you fail to resist, you are stunned; roll against HT-5 to recover each turn. Also creates smoke in the area of effect.

Firearms

A "firearm" is any gun, rocket, or beam weapon that does not rely on muscle power. Guns are commonly available by TL4 and ubiquitous at TL5+. Beam weapons appear in late TL8 (mostly for vehicles), and *may* become common by TL9, ubiquitous at TL10+.

Guns are commonly available by TL4 and ubiquitous at TL5+.

Pistol and Submachine Gun Table

GUNS (PISTOL) (DX-4, or most other Guns at -2)

TL	Weapon	Damage	Acc	Range	Weight	RoF	Shots	ST	Bulk	Rcl	Cost	LC	Notes
4	Flintlock Pistol, .51	2d-1 pi+	1	75/450	3/0.01	1	1(20)	10	-3	2	$200	3	
4	Wheel-Lock Pistol, .60	1d+1 pi+	1	75/400	3.25/0.01	1	1(20)	10	-3	2	$200	3	
5	Derringer, .41	1d pi+	1	80/650	0.5/0.1	1	2(3i)	9	-1	2	$100	3	
5	Revolver, .36	2d-1 pi	1	120/1,300	2.5/0.24	1	6(3i)	10	-2	2	$150	3	
6	Auto Pistol, .45	2d pi+	2	175/1,700	3/0.6	3	7+1(3)	10	-2	3	$300	3	
6	Auto Pistol, 9mm	2d+2 pi	2	150/1,850	2.4/0.4	3	8+1(3)	9	-2	2	$350	3	
6	Revolver, .38	2d-1 pi	2	120/1,500	2/0.2	3	6(3i)	8	-2	2	$400	3	
6	Snub Revolver, .38	1d+2 pi	1	120/1,250	1.5/0.2	3	5(3i)	8	-1	3	$250	3	
7	Auto Pistol, 9mm	2d+2 pi	2	150/1,850	2.6/0.6	3	15+1(3)	9	-2	2	$600	3	
7	Holdout Pistol, .380	2d pi	1	125/1,500	1.3/0.2	3	5+1(3)	8	-1	3	$300	3	
7	Revolver, .357M	3d-1 pi	2	185/2,000	3/0.21	3	6(3i)	10	-2	3	$500	3	
7	Revolver, .44M	3d pi+	2	200/2,500	3.25/0.3	3	6(3i)	11	-3	4	$900	3	
8	Auto Pistol, .44M	3d pi+	2	230/2,500	4.5/0.6	3	9+1(3)	12	-3	4	$750	3	
8	Auto Pistol, .40	2d pi+	2	150/1,900	2.1/0.7	3	15+1(3)	9	-2	2	$640	3	
9	Auto Pistol, 9mm	2d+2 pi	2	150/1,900	2/0.7	3	18+1(3)	9	-2	2	$800	3	[1]

GUNS (GYROC) (DX-4, or most other Guns at -4)

TL	Weapon	Damage	Acc	Range	Weight	RoF	Shots	ST	Bulk	Rcl	Cost	LC	Notes
9	Gyroc Pistol, 15mm	6d pi++	1	1,900	1/0.4	3	4(3i)	9	-2	1	$200	3	[1, 2]

GUNS (SMG) (DX-4, or most other Guns at -2)

TL	Weapon	Damage	Acc	Range	Weight	RoF	Shots	ST	Bulk	Rcl	Cost	LC	Notes
6	SMG, .45	2d+1 pi+	3	190/1,750	15.7/4.9	13	50+1(5)	11†	-4	3	$2,200	2	[3]
6	SMG, 9mm	3d-1 pi	3	160/1,900	10.5/1.5	8!	32(3)	10†	-4	2	$700	2	[3]
7	Machine Pistol, 9mm	2d+2 pi	2	160/1,900	5.5/1.1	20	25+1(3)	12	-3	3	$900	2	[3]
7	SMG, 9mm	3d-1 pi	4	160/1,900	7.5/1.2	13	30+1(3)	10†	-4	2	$1,200	2	[3]
8	PDW, 4.6mm	4d+1 pi-	3	200/2,000	3.9/0.5	15	20+1(3)	7†	-3	2	$800	2	
10	Gauss PDW, 4mm	4d(3) pi-	6+1	700/2,900	4.6/1	16	80(3)	9†	-3	2	$3,600	2	[1]

Notes

[1] Includes "smartgun" electronics (see box).

[2] Rockets take time to accelerate. Divide damage by 3 at 1-2 yards, and by 2 at 3-10 yards.

[3] Civilian semi-automatic version is RoF 3, -25% to cost, and +1 to LC.

"Smartgun" Electronics (TL8)

The following systems are *optional* on TL8 firearms (add $500 to price) and *standard* on TL9+ firearms (no extra cost):

- A built-in laser sight (p. 412).
- "Smart" electronics that give +1 to skill rolls to fix damage or malfunctions.
- An electronic access system (usually a biometric scanner, or a transponder in a ring or glove) that limits usage to authorized persons. Unauthorized users cannot fire the weapon. Military and police weapons can be set to allow everyone in a unit to share weapons.
- If the weapon has built-in sights (noted as a bonus after Acc), a video link to a helmet or goggle head-up display (if worn), allowing faster target engagement; see *Targeting Systems* (p. 548).

Rifle and Shotgun Table

GUNS (MUSKET) (DX-4, or most other Guns at -2)

TL	Weapon	Damage	Acc	Range	Weight	RoF	Shots	ST	Bulk	Rcl	Cost	LC	Notes
3	Handgonne, .90	2d pi++	0	100/600	15/0.1	1	1(60)	10†	-6	4	$300	3	
4	Matchlock Musket, .80	4d pi++	2	100/600	20/0.05	1	1(60)	10R†	-6	3	$150	4	
4	Flintlock Musket, .75	4d pi++	2	100/1,500	13/0.05	1	1(15)	10†	-6	4	$200	4	

GUNS (RIFLE) (DX-4, or most other Guns at -2)

TL	Weapon	Damage	Acc	Range	Weight	RoF	Shots	ST	Bulk	Rcl	Cost	LC	Notes
5	Rifle-Musket, .577	4d pi+	4	700/2,100	8.5/0.05	1	1(15)	10†	-6	3	$150	3	
5	Cartridge Rifle, .45	5d pi+	3	600/2,000	6/0.1	1	1(4)	10†	-6	3	$200	3	
5	Lever-Action Carbine, .30	5d pi	4	450/3,000	7/0.3	1	6+1(3i)	10†	-4	2	$300	3	
6	Bolt-Action Rifle, 7.62mm	7d pi	5	1,000/4,200	8.9/0.3	1	5+1(3)	10†	-5	4	$350	3	
6	Self-Loading Rifle, 7.62mm	7d pi	5	1,000/4,200	10/0.5	3	8(3)	10†	-5	3	$600	3	
7	Assault Rifle, 5.56mm	5d pi	5	500/3,500	9/1	12	30+1(3)	9†	-4	2	$800	2	[1]
7	Assault Rifle, 7.62mmS	5d+1 pi	4	400/3,000	10.5/1.8	10	30+1(3)	10†	-4	2	$300	2	[1]
7	Battle Rifle, 7.62mm	7d pi	5	1,000/4,200	11/1.7	11	20+1(3)	11†	-5	3	$900	2	[1]
8	Assault Carbine, 5.56mm	4d+2 pi	4	400/3,000	7.3/1	15	30+1(3)	9†	-3	2	$900	2	[1]
8	Dart Rifle, 11mm	1d(0.2) pi-	5+1	45/145	6.6/0.02	1	1(3)	9†	-5	2	$1,200	4	[2]
8	Sniper Rifle, .338	9d+1 pi	6+3	1,500/5,500	17.5/0.8	1	4+1(3)	11B†	-6	4	$5,600	3	
9	ICW, 6.8mm	6d pi	4+2	700/4,000	12/1.5	15	25+1(3)	10†	-5	2	$7,000	1	[3, 4]
10	Gauss Rifle, 4mm	6d+2(3) pi-	7+2	1,200/4,800	8.5/1.4	12	60(3)	10†	-4	2	$7,100	2	[3]

GUNS (SHOTGUN) (DX-4, or most other Guns at -2)

TL	Weapon	Damage	Acc	Range	Weight	RoF	Shots	ST	Bulk	Rcl	Cost	LC	Notes
4	Blunderbuss, 8G	1d pi	1	15/100	12/0.13	1×9	1(15)	11†	-5	1	$150	4	
5	Double Shotgun, 10G	1d+2 pi	3	50/125	10/0.1	2×9	2(3i)	11†	-5	1	$450	4	
6	Pump Shotgun, 12G	1d+1 pi	3	50/125	8/0.7	2×9	5(3i)	10†	-5	1	$240	4	
7	Auto Shotgun, 12G	1d+1 pi	3	50/125	8.4/0.85	3×9	6+1(3i)	10†	-5	1	$950	3	

Notes

[1] Civilian semi-automatic version is RoF 3, -25% to cost, and +1 to LC.

[2] If damage penetrates DR, the dart injects a drug or poison as a follow-up attack. For a tranquilizer dart, roll vs. HT-3; failure results in unconsciousness for minutes equal to the margin of failure.

[3] Includes "smartgun" electronics (see p. 278).

[4] Includes an integral 25mm grenade launcher (see p. 281).

Optional Rule: Malfunction

Optionally, all firearms and grenades have a "malfunction number," or "Malf." The weapon will jam, misfire, or otherwise fail to function on any attack roll equal to or greater than its Malf.; see *Malfunctions* (p. 407).

Malfunction number is a function of tech level: it is 12 at TL3, 14 at TL4, 16 at TL5, and 17 at TL6+. A few weapons might be intrinsically more or less reliable. Weapon quality also affects Malf. Finally, lack of maintenance (especially in dusty or humid conditions) can lower Malf.

Ammunition

For a given gun, the *weight* of one full load of ammunition, in pounds, appears after the slash in its "Weight" statistic. Assume that ammo cost is $20 times this weight.

Example: The 5.56mm assault rifle has a weight of "9/1." Thus, a full reload weighs 1 lb. and costs $20.

The statistics given on the tables assume that guns are firing ordinary, solid projectiles (usually lead). At TL6+, this means the common "ball" or "full metal jacket" round, but other ammo types are possible. A few examples for pistols, submachine guns, rifles, and machine guns (but *not* shotguns, Gauss guns, and dart rifles):

Hollow-Point (HP): Bullets designed to expand in flesh, causing bigger wounds. This improves damage type: pi- becomes pi, pi becomes pi+, and pi+ becomes pi++. (HP ammo is not available for guns that already inflict pi++ damage.) However, HP ammo has trouble penetrating barriers or armor; add an armor divisor of (0.5). HP ammo is available at TL6+. It has normal cost and LC. It is the most common ammo type used by hunters and police.

Armor-Piercing Hard Core (APHC): Solid bullets with a dense, armor-piercing core. Add a (2) armor divisor, but if the gun caliber is below 20mm (.80), damage type degrades: pi++ drops to pi+, pi+ to pi, and pi to pi-. (There is no effect on pi-.) APHC ammo is available at TL7+. It has *double* normal cost and is LC2.

Armor-Piercing Discarding-Sabot (APDS): A small tungsten dart encased in a larger plastic sheath that peels away when the round leaves the barrel, increasing velocity. APDS works like APHC, but also adds 50% to range and +1 damage per die. Used by tanks at TL6-7 and machine guns at TL8, it is available for small arms by TL9. It has *five times* normal cost and is LC1.

Firearm Quality

Fine firearms cost *double* list price, and get +1 to Acc and +1 to Malf. *Very fine* firearms cost 5 times list price, and get +2 to Acc and +1 to Malf.

Should this result in a Malf. of 19 or more, the weapon *will not malfunction* unless lack of maintenance lowers Malf.

Presentation firearms (decorated, gilded, etc.) are also available. This will further increase cost (and resale value) by 2 to 20 times.

Ultra-Tech Firearm Table

BEAM WEAPONS (PISTOL) (DX-4, other Beam Weapons-4, or Guns (Pistol)-4)

TL	Weapon	Damage	Acc	Range	Weight	RoF	Shots	ST	Bulk	Rcl	Cost	LC	Notes
9	Electrolaser Pistol *linked*	1d-3 burn HT-4(2) aff	4	40/80	2.2/0.5	3	180(3)	4	-2	1	$1,800	4	[1, 2, 3]
10	Laser Pistol	3d(2) burn	6	250/750	3.3/0.5	10	400(3)	6	-2	1	$2,800	3	[3]
11	Blaster Pistol	3d(5) burn	5	300/900	1.6/0.5	3	200(3)	4	-2	1	$2,200	3	[4, 5]

BEAM WEAPONS (RIFLE) (DX-4, other Beam Weapons-4, or Guns (Rifle)-4)

TL	Weapon	Damage	Acc	Range	Weight	RoF	Shots	ST	Bulk	Rcl	Cost	LC	Notes
9	Electrolaser Carbine *linked*	1d-3 burn HT-4(2) aff	8+1	160/470	3.7/1	3	360(3)	4†	-4	1	$3,900	3	[1, 2, 3]
9	Laser Sniper Rifle	5d(2) burn	12+2	1,100/3,300	20/4p	3	75(3)	10†	-8	1	$20,000	1	[3]
10	Laser Rifle	5d(2) burn	12+2	700/2,100	10/2	10	150(3)	7†	-4	1	$10,000	2	[3]
11	Blaster Rifle	6d(5) burn	10+2	700/2,100	10/1	3	50(3)	7†	-4	1	$18,000	2	[4, 5]
11	Heavy Blaster	8d(5) burn	10+4	900/2,700	20/4p	3	90(5)	10†	-6	1	$23,000	1	[4]

Notes

All beam weapons include "smartgun" electronics (see p. 278).

[1] Weapon requires atmosphere to function. *No effect* in trace atmosphere or vacuum!

[2] Burn damage has the Surge damage modifier (p. 105). As well, whether or not any damage penetrates, the target must make a HT roll at -4, plus *half* the DR on the location struck (due to the armor divisor). On a failure, the electrical shock stuns him. He may roll against HT every turn at the same penalty (but *without* the DR bonus) to recover.

[3] Smoke, fog, rain, cloud, etc. give the target additional DR equal to the visibility penalty. For instance, if rain gives a penalty of -1 per 100 yards, a laser firing through 2,000 yards of rain must penetrate an extra DR 20.

[4] Burn damage has the Surge damage modifier (p. 105).

[5] In superscience games, an "omni-blaster" costs twice as much, but has a "stun" setting: damage becomes HT-3(3) aff for a pistol, HT-6(3) aff for a rifle. On a failed HT roll, the victim is unconsciousness for minutes equal to his margin of failure.

HEAVY WEAPONS

The next table gives a few examples of the heaviest weapons that adventurers are likely to carry or encounter.

Police and ordinary criminals rarely use such weapons – but any infantry squad or well-funded terrorist group might have access to them!

Heavy Weapon Table

ARTILLERY (GUIDED MISSILE) (IQ-5)

TL	Weapon	Damage	Acc	Range	Weight	RoF	Shots	ST	Bulk	Rcl	Cost	LC	Notes
7	ATGM, 115mm	6d×10(10) cr ex	3	200/2,000	37/26	1	1(20)	11B†	-10	1	$20,000	1	[1, 2, 3]
8	SAM, 70mm	6d×3 cr ex [6d]	7	1,000/8,800	18/22	1	1(20)	10†	-8	1	$38,000	1	[1, 2, 4]

GUNNER (CATAPULT) (DX-4, or other Gunner at -4)

TL	Weapon	Damage	Acc	Range	Weight	RoF	Shots	ST	Bulk	Rcl	Cost	LC	Notes
2	Scorpion	5d imp	3	415/520	110/0.9	1	1(30)	45M†	-10	–	$5,000	2	

GUNNER (MACHINE GUN) (DX-4, or other Gunner at -4)

TL	Weapon	Damage	Acc	Range	Weight	RoF	Shots	ST	Bulk	Rcl	Cost	LC	Notes
6	HMG, .50	13d+1 pi+	6	1,800/7,400	116/32	8!	100(5)	20M†	-8	2	$14,000	1	[5]

GUNS (GRENADE LAUNCHER) (DX-4, or most other Guns at -4)

TL	Weapon	Damage	Acc	Range	Weight	RoF	Shots	ST	Bulk	Rcl	Cost	LC	Notes
7	Under-Barrel, 40mm	4d(10) cr ex[2d]	2	150/440	+3.5/0.5	1	1(3)	11	–	2	$500	1	[1, 6, 7]
9	Integral, 25mm	7d cr ex[3d]	4+2	2,200	–/1.6	1	3(3)	10	–	3	–	–	[8]

GUNS (LAW) (DX-4, or most other Guns at -4)

TL	Weapon	Damage	Acc	Range	Weight	RoF	Shots	ST	Bulk	Rcl	Cost	LC	Notes
7	Bazooka, 60mm	6d×2(10) cr ex	3	100/650	16.7/3.4	1	1(4)	10†	-6	1	$1,000	1	[2, 7]
7	RPG, 85mm	6d×3(10) cr ex	3+1	300/1,000	21/5.7	1	1(5)	10†	-6	1	$800	1	[2, 7]
8	LAW, 84mm	6d×6(10) cr ex	3	330/2,300	14.7	1	1(–)	10†	-5	1	$750	1	[2, 7]

GUNS (LMG) (DX-4, or most other Guns at -2)

TL	Weapon	Damage	Acc	Range	Weight	RoF	Shots	ST	Bulk	Rcl	Cost	LC	Notes
6	Auto Rifle, 7.62mm	7d pi	5	1,000/4,200	22/1.6	9!	20(3)	12B†	-6	3	$6,500	2	
6	LMG, 7.62mm	7d pi	5	1,000/4,200	30/6	15!	100(5)	13B†	-6	2	$6,600	1	
7	SAW, 5.56mm	5d+1 pi	5	800/3,500	24/7	12!	200(5)	12B†	-6	2	$4,800	1	

LIQUID PROJECTOR (FLAMETHROWER) (DX-4, or other Liquid Projector at -4)

TL	Weapon	Damage	Acc	Range	Weight	RoF	Shots	ST	Bulk	Rcl	Cost	LC	Notes
6	Flamethrower	3d burn	–	50	70	Jet	10	10†	-8	–	$1,800	1	

Notes

[1] Has a minimum range: 10 yards for 40mm GL, 30 yards for 115mm ATGM, and 200 yards for 70mm SAM.

[2] Hazardous back-blast: 1d burn damage to anyone behind firer and within 15 yards (30 yards for ATGM).

[3] Guided attack (see p. 412). Gunner uses Artillery (Guided Missile) to *attack*. "1/2D" range is *speed* in yards per second. Weight is for empty launcher/one missile.

[4] Homing (Hyperspectral Vision) attack (see p. 413), at the missile's skill of 10. Firer rolls against Artillery (Guided Missile) to *aim*. On a success, the missile gets its Acc bonus. "1/2D" range is *speed* (yards/second). Weight is for empty launcher/one missile.

[5] Detachable tripod weighs an *extra* 44 lbs.

[6] Can clamp under the barrel of any TL7+ rifle or carbine. Use the rifle's Bulk.

[7] Damage is not halved at 1/2D range, but loses its armor divisor of (10).

[8] Built into the TL9 ICW (p. 279). Use the ICW's Bulk. Has "smartgun" electronics (see p. 278).

ARMOR

Armor is very useful in combat. A single sword blow or bullet can incapacitate or kill you . . . but armor might give you a second chance. Your armor's Damage Resistance, or DR, subtracts *directly* from the damage inflicted by your enemies' weapons. Armor requires no skill to use – you just wear it! (*Exception:* Certain TL7+ armor types require Environment Suit skill, p. 192.)

Effective armor is *heavy*, though. Its weight can hinder you (see *Encumbrance and Move*, p. 17), reducing your Dodge – and also your Parry, if you use fencing weapons, Judo, or Karate. A swashbuckler who relies on agility to avoid injury might choose light or no armor! (As a guideline, your Dodge, Block, or Parry – and preferably two or all three of these – should be at least 12 if you plan to go unarmored.)

The best armor is *expensive*, too. You probably won't be able to afford it without lots of Wealth!

Armor is more important in some periods than in others. Before TL4, it's a lifesaver. Warriors who expect to go into battle should wear the heaviest armor they can afford. On the other hand, few fighters wear metal armor in a city or on the road: it's just too heavy and uncomfortable.

At TL4, armor declines in importance as firearms become common: anything that can stop a musket ball is too heavy to wear. Except for heavy cavalry, few soldiers or adventurers wear more than a pot helm and breastplate. At TL5-6, armor all but disappears – although TL6-7 infantry still wear a steel pot helmet to protect against bursting shell fragments.

At TL7-9, this trend reverses, as lightweight, bullet-resistant synthetics (such as Kevlar) appear and gradually improve. In some TL10+ backgrounds, armor might be vital. In others, weapons can penetrate anything, and a good Dodge – or shooting first – is the best defense.

ARMOR TABLES

Three armor tables appear below: one for low-tech armor (TL0-5), one

for high- and ultra-tech armor (TL6+), and one for armoring mounts. Each item on the tables includes an article of light, common clothing to wear underneath – or padding, if this is usual for the armor (e.g., mail includes cloth padding under the chain). The statistics already reflect this; you do not have to buy clothing or padding separately, or account for its DR and weight.

The tables give the following information for each item of armor:

TL: The tech level at which the armor is commonly available.

Armor: The item's name.

Location: The area the armor protects on a humanoid wearer. Individual locations are *skull* (top of the head), *face* (the face, excluding the eyes), *neck*, *eyes*, *arms*, *hands*, *torso* (the abdomen and chest), *groin*, *legs*, and *feet*. *Limbs* covers the arms and legs, but not the hands or feet. *Head* covers skull, face, and eyes. *Body* is neck, torso, and groin. *Full suit* is everything but the head.

DR: The amount of Damage Resistance the item gives. Subtract this from any blow that strikes the armored location. For instance, if you're wearing a DR 6 corselet and are hit in the torso for 8 points of damage, only 2 points penetrate and affect you. Some armor has a split DR; e.g., "4/2." This means DR varies by location or by type of attack; see the notes for that piece of armor.

"*" means the armor is *flexible*. Flexible armor is easier to conceal or wear under other armor, and quicker to don or remove, but it is more vulnerable to blunt trauma damage.

"F" means the DR only protects against attacks from the front.

Cost: The item's price, in $. "K" is thousands; "M" is millions.

Weight: The item's weight, in pounds.

LC: The item's Legality Class; see *Legality Class* (p. 267).

Notes: Many items have special features or restrictions; see the notes after each table. Some advanced armor has built-in features that effectively grant the wearer advantages.

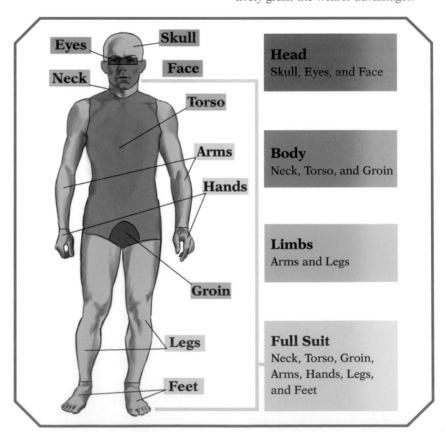

Low-Tech Armor Table

	TL	Armor	Location	DR	Cost	Weight	LC	Notes
Body Armor								
	0	Fur Loincloth	groin	1*	$10	neg.	–	[1]
	0	Fur Tunic	torso	1*	$25	2	–	[1]
	1	Bronze Breastplate	torso	4F	$400	20	3	[2]
	1	Bronze Corselet	torso, groin	5	$1,300	40	3	
	1	Cloth Armor	torso, groin	1*	$30	6	–	[1]
	1	Leather Armor	torso, groin	2	$100	10	4	
	1	Leather Jacket	arms, torso	1*	$50	4	–	[1]
	2	Light Scale Armor	torso	3	$150	15	4	
	2	Lorica Segmentata	torso	5	$680	26	3	
	2	Mail Hauberk	torso, groin	4/2*	$230	25	3	[3]
	2	Mail Shirt	torso	4/2*	$150	16	4	[1, 3]
	2	Scale Armor	torso, groin	4	$420	35	3	
	3	Double Mail Hauberk	torso, groin	5/3*	$520	44	3	[3]
	3	Heavy Steel Corselet	torso, groin	7	$2,300	45	3	
	3	Steel Breastplate	torso	5F	$500	18	3	[2]
	3	Steel Corselet	torso, groin	6	$1,300	35	3	
	3	Steel Laminate Plate	torso, groin	5	$900	30	3	
	4	Buff Coat (Leather)	body, limbs	2*	$210	16	4	
Limb Armor								
	1	Bronze Armbands	arms	3	$180	9	4	
	1	Bronze Greaves	legs	3	$270	17	4	
	1	Cloth Sleeves	arms	1*	$20	2	–	[1]
	1	Heavy Leather Leggings	legs	2	$60	4	4	
	1	Heavy Leather Sleeves	arms	2	$50	2	4	
	1	Leather Leggings	legs	1*	$40	2	–	[1]
	1	Leather Pants	legs, groin	1*	$40	3	–	[1]
	1	Studded Leather Skirt	groin, legs	3/2*	$60	4	–	[3]
	2	Mail Leggings	legs	4/2*	$110	15	3	[3]
	2	Mail Sleeves	arms	4/2*	$70	9	3	[3]
	2	Scale Leggings	legs	4	$250	21	3	
	2	Scale Sleeves	arms	4	$210	14	3	
	3	Heavy Plate Arms	arms	7	$1,500	20	3	
	3	Heavy Plate Legs	legs	7	$1,600	25	3	
	3	Plate Arms	arms	6	$1,000	15	3	
	3	Plate Legs	legs	6	$1,100	20	3	

TL	Armor	Location	DR	Cost	Weight	LC	Notes
Headgear							
1	Bronze Helmet	skull, face	3	$160	7.5	4	
1	Bronze Pot-Helm	skull	3	$60	5	4	
1	Cloth Cap	skull	1*	$5	neg.	–	[1]
1	Leather Cap	skull	1*	$32	neg.	4	
1	Leather Helm	skull, face	2	$20	0.5	4	
2	Legionary Helmet	skull, face	4	$150	6	3	
2	Mail Coif	skull, neck	4/2*	$55	4	3	[3]
3	Barrel Helm	skull, face	6	$240	10	3	[4]
3	Face Mask	face	4	$100	2	3	
3	Greathelm	skull, face, neck	7	$340	10	3	[4]
3	Pot-Helm	skull	4	$100	5	4	
Gloves							
1	Cloth Gloves	hands	1*	$15	neg.	–	[1]
1	Leather Gloves	hands	2*	$30	neg.	–	
2	Gauntlets	hands	4	$100	2	4	
3	Heavy Gauntlets	hands	5	$250	2.5	3	
Footwear							
0	Sandals	feet	0	$25	0.5	–	[1, 2]
1	Shoes	feet	1*	$40	2	–	[1]
2	Boots	feet	2*	$80	3	–	[1]
3	Sollerets	feet	4	$150	7	3	

Notes

[1] Concealable *as* or *under* clothing.

[2] Partial coverage: sandals give DR 1 to the underside of the foot, while breastplates protect only from the front.

[3] Split DR: use the lower DR against *crushing* attacks.

[4] Helmet gives wearer the No Peripheral Vision disadvantage (p. 151) while worn.

High- and Ultra-Tech Armor Table

TL	Armor	Location	DR	Cost	Weight	LC	Notes
Body Armor							
6	Flak Jacket	torso	7	$500	20	3	
7	Frag Vest	torso, groin	5/2*	$350	9	3	[1]
	+ *Plate Inserts*	torso	+20	+$300	+15	3	
8	Ballistic Vest	torso	8/2*	$400	2	3	[1, 2, 3]
8	Tactical Vest	torso, groin	12/5*	$900	9	2	[1, 3]
	+ *Trauma Plates*	torso	+23	+$600	+9	2	
9	Ballistic Suit	body, limbs	12/4*	$1,000	6	3	[1, 2, 3]
9	Tactical Suit	full suit	20/10*	$3,000	15	2	[1, 3, 4, 5]
Gloves and Footwear							
7	Reinforced Boots	feet	5/2	$75	3	–	[2, 6]
9	Assault Boots	feet	12/6	$150	3	4	[3, 6]
9	Ballistic Gloves	hands	8/2*	$30	neg.	4	[1, 2, 3]

TL	Armor	Location	DR	Cost	Weight	LC	Notes
Headgear							
6	Gas Mask	eyes, face	2	$100	4	4	[7]
6	Steel Pot	skull	4	$60	3	4	
7	Frag Helmet	skull	5	$125	3	4	
	+ *Visor*	eyes, face	1	+$25	+1.5	4	[8]
8	Ballistic Helmet	skull	12	$250	3	3	[3]
	+ *Visor*	eyes, face	10	+$100	+3	3	[3, 8]
Environment Suits							
7	NBC Suit	full suit	1	$150	3.5	4	[5, 9]
7	Space Suit	full suit	2	$2,000,000	225	4	[4, 9, 10]
	+ *Space Helmet*	head	3	+$25,000	10	4	[7, 11]
9	Battlesuit	full suit	70/50	$80,000	150	1	[3, 4, 6, 12]
	+ *Helmet*	head	70/50	+$10,000	15	1	[3, 6, 7, 11]
9	Combat Hardsuit	full suit	50/30	$10,000	30	2	[3, 4, 5, 6]
	+ *Helmet*	head	18/12	+$2,000	5	2	[3, 6, 7, 11]
9	Space Armor	full suit	50/30	$20,000	45	2	[3, 4, 6, 10]
	+ *Helmet*	head	40/30	+$3,000	7	2	[3, 6, 7, 11]
9	Vacc Suit	full suit	6*	$10,000	25	4	[3, 4, 10]
	+ *Vacc Helmet*	head	6	+$2,000	5	4	[3, 11]

Notes

All TL7+ armor electronics and powered systems (including the battlesuit) work for (TL - 6) × 6 hours before they require recharging or refueling.

[1] Split DR: use the first, higher DR against *piercing* and *cutting* attacks; use the second, lower DR against *all other damage types*.

[2] Concealable *as* or *under* clothing.

[3] DR increases with TL. After the TL of introduction, consult the following table:

TL	DR Multiplier
Intro	×1
Intro+1	×1.5
Intro+2	×2
Intro+3	×3
Any higher	×4

[4] Biomedical sensors allow remote monitoring of vital signs, giving +1 to Diagnosis skill when examining the wearer. In addition, the suit is climate-controlled.

[5] Requires NBC Suit skill – but at TL9+, the suit does not limit DX. Worn with a mask or a helmet with note [7], the combination provides the Sealed advantage.

[6] Split DR: use the higher DR only if the attack strikes the torso (if body armor), skull (if headgear), or underside of the foot (if footwear).

[7] Provides Filter Lungs, Protected Smell, and Protected Vision – but before TL9, it *also* gives the No Peripheral Vision disadvantage.

[8] Provides Protected Vision.

[9] Suit's DR applies only against *burning* or *corrosion* damage.

[10] Requires Vacc Suit skill. If worn with its helmet, the suit gives Doesn't Breathe (for 12 hours), Protected Smell, Sealed, and Vacuum Support.

[11] Provides Protected Hearing, Protected Vision, and Radio. At TL9+, add Absolute Direction (Requires Signal), Infravision, Night Vision 9, and (TL - 8) levels of Telescopic Vision. TL9+ helmets also include a head-up display (HUD) compatible with "smartgun" electronics (p. 278). Battlesuits add Hyperspectral Vision and Laser Communication.

[12] Requires Battlesuit skill. Gives Lifting ST +10, Striking ST +10, and Super Jump 1. Add +5 to Lifting ST, +5 to Striking ST, and +1 to Super Jump per TL past TL9. With its helmet in place, it also grants Doesn't Breathe (for 12 hours), Protected Smell, Sealed, and Vacuum Support. Do *not* count suit weight toward encumbrance!

Armor is more important in some periods than in others. In some backgrounds, armor might be vital. In others, weapons can penetrate anything, and a good Dodge – or shooting first – is the best defense.

Horse Armor (Barding) Table

TL	Armor	Location	DR	Cost	Weight	LC	Notes
Face Masks							
1	Leather & Cloth	face	2	$40	3	4	[1]
2	Mail	face	4/2*	$60	7	3	[1, 2]
2	Scale	face	4	$200	12	3	[1]
3	Plate	face	5	$200	12	3	[1]
Head/Neck Armor							
2	Leather & Cloth	neck, skull	2	$80	4	4	
2	Mail	neck, skull	4/2*	$100	15	3	[2]
2	Scale	neck, skull	4	$320	20	3	
3	Plate	neck, skull	5	$330	18	3	
Partial Barding							
1	Leather & Cloth	torso	2F	$260	12	4	
2	Mail	torso	4/2F*	$440	20	3	[2]
2	Scale	torso	4F	$480	60	3	
Full Barding							
2	Leather & Cloth	torso, groin	2	$345	30	4	
3	Mail	torso, groin	4/2*	$670	59	3	[2]
3	Plate	torso, groin	5	$1,650	90	3	
Leggings							
3	Plate	legs	5	$400	20	3	[3]

Notes

[1] Gives mount the No Peripheral Vision disadvantage (p. 151) while worn.

[2] Split DR: use the lower DR against *crushing* attacks.

[3] Weight and cost are *per pair* of legs protected. Each pair gives -1 to Move.

WEARING ARMOR

There are some social and practical restrictions on wearing armor.

Reaction Penalty

A fully armored individual is someone who is expecting trouble . . . or looking to *make* trouble. He is unlikely to receive a warm welcome! In a noncombat situation, armor that covers the face or entire head gives -2 to reaction rolls. Nonconcealable armor with DR 2+ anywhere else (except the hands or feet) gives -1, or -2 if it isn't flexible *and* covers the torso. These penalties are cumulative: plate armor and a full helm would give you -4!

However, there is no reaction penalty if the NPC making the reaction roll recognizes the wearer's *need* or *right* to wear armor in the situation. Examples of socially acceptable armor include a knight on campaign or at a tourney; an astronaut wearing a vacc suit in space; or a soldier, paramedic, or journalist wearing body armor in a war zone.

Donning and Removing Armor

It takes three seconds per piece to don or remove most armor. It takes 30 seconds per piece for vacc suits or battlesuits, except for their helmets. *Exception:* TL8+ flexible armor with insert panels and all TL9+ nonflexible armor have some form of "quick release" mechanism to drop the insert panel or let the user step out of the armor in only one second.

Combining and Layering Armor

You can freely combine multiple pieces of armor that don't cover the same hit location, but you can only *layer* armor if the inner layer is both flexible *and* concealable. Add the DR of both layers. Wearing an extra layer of armor anywhere but on the head gives -1 to DX and DX-based skills.

SHIELDS

Shields are very valuable in low-tech combat, but almost worthless against firearms. Historically, they were little used after the rise of firearms (TL4) – with the exception of plastic riot shields. In some SF settings, though, they make a comeback as *force* shields.

You normally wear a shield or force shield strapped to one arm. Your shield hand can't *wield* a weapon (preventing you from using two-handed weapons), but it can still *carry* an item.

A shield helps *all* your active defense rolls (Block, Dodge, and Parry) with no particular effort. You can also use a shield *actively* to block; see *Blocking* (p. 375).

Shield Statistics

The following statistics apply to shields:

TL: The tech level at which the shield is commonly available.

Shield: The kind of shield.

DB: Defense Bonus. The bonus the shield gives to *all* of your active defense rolls (see *Defending*, p. 374) against attacks from the front or shield side,

even if you have no skill at all with a shield. This applies only against melee or muscle-powered ranged weapons – not against firearms, unless you use the optional *Damage to Shields* rule (p. 484).

Cost: The shield's price, in $.

Weight: The shield's weight, in pounds.

DR/HP: The shield's DR and HP if using the optional *Damage to Shields* rule. This DR protects the *shield*, not the *wielder*.

LC: The shield's Legality Class; see *Legality Class* (p. 267).

Shield Table

TL	Shield	DB	Cost	Weight	DR/HP	LC	Notes
CLOAK (DX-5, Net-4, or Shield (any)-4)							
1	Light Cloak	1	$20	2	1/3	–	[1]
1	Heavy Cloak	2	$50	5	1/5	–	[1]
SHIELD (DX-4, or other Shield at -2)							
0	Light Shield	1	$25	2	5/20	4	[2, 3, 4]
0	Small Shield	1	$40	8	6/30	4	[2, 3, 4]
1	Medium Shield	2	$60	15	7/40	4	[2, 3, 4]
1	Large Shield	3	$90	25	9/60	4	[2, 4]
SHIELD (FORCE) (DX-4, or other Shield at -2)							
^	Force Shield	3	$1,500	0.5	100/–	3	[3, 5]

Notes

[1] Can be used offensively to entangle; see *Cloaks* (p. 404).

[2] Can be used offensively with a shield bash (see the *Melee Weapon Table)* or shield rush (see *Slam*, p. 371). At TL1+, you can give your small, medium, or large shield a spike to increase damage: add $20 and 5 lbs.

[3] Also available as a *buckler.* You can ready a buckler in one turn and drop it as a free action, just like a weapon – but

it always occupies one hand, and it does not allow a shield rush. Use Shield (Buckler) instead of regular Shield skill. No effect on statistics.

[4] At TL3+, iron shields are available but uncommon: ×5 cost, ×2 weight, +3 DR, and ×2 HP. At TL7+, plastic riot shields (made of Lexan, etc.) have ×1/2 weight but otherwise identical statistics. Shield composition never affects DB.

[5] Worn on the wrist, leaving the hand free. DR is *hardened* (treat as one level of the Hardened enhancement, p. 47).

Carrying Weapons and Other Gear

You can normally carry one item per hand. This doesn't preclude your having a shield strapped to your arm – but if you do, your shield hand can only *hold*, not *wield*, a weapon or other handheld device, and you cannot use items that require two free hands, like a bow, rifle, or guitar.

You can also stow gear about your person, leaving your hands free. You can carry a one-handed item no larger than a sword or a pistol in a scabbard or holster on each hip; an item of that size or larger (e.g., a

two-handed weapon like a rifle or a greatsword) slung over your back; and, with appropriate sheaths, one small item or weapon (like a knife or holdout pistol) per wrist or ankle. If you have clothing with pockets, you can stow one extra item per side pocket. A shoulder holster lets you strap a pistol-sized item over your chest.

You can carry additional equipment in a bag, pack, or case, but it takes several seconds to remove it and get it ready.

MISCELLANEOUS EQUIPMENT

The following equipment list should suffice to outfit most adventurers. The GM is free to add items!

TL: The tech level at which the item is commonly available. "Var." indicates tools or instruments that are available at the same TL as the skill(s) they facilitate; e.g., you can buy surgical instruments for Surgery/TL2 at TL2, instruments for Surgery/TL9 at TL9.

Cost: The item's price, in $.

Weight: The item's weight, in pounds. Assume weight is negligible if not listed.

LC: Items are LC4 unless specifically noted otherwise; see *Legality Class* (p. 267).

Other Notes: Items that require batteries list an operating time in hours (hrs.). Equipment labeled "basic gear" is the minimum necessary to use the noted skill(s) at no penalty in most situations.

Camping and Survival Gear

Backpack, Frame (TL1). Holds 100 lbs. of gear. $100, 10 lbs.

Backpack, Small (TL1). Holds 40 lbs. of gear. $60, 3 lbs.

Blanket (TL1). A warm sleeping blanket. $20, 4 lbs.

Bottle, Ceramic (TL1). Holds 1 quart of liquid (2 lbs. if water). $3, 1 lb.

Cable, Steel, 1.5" (TL5). Supports 3,700 lbs. Per 10 yards: $100, 17 lbs.

Camp Stove, Small (TL6). Uses 0.25 gallons kerosene per 4 hrs. $50, 2 lbs.

Candle, Tallow (TL1). Smoky! Lasts 12 hrs. $5, 1 lb.

Canteen (TL5). Holds 1 quart of liquid (2 lbs. if water). $10, 1 lb.

Cigarette Lighter (TL6). Lights fire. $10.

Climbing Gear (TL2). Hammer, spikes, carabiners. $20, 4 lbs.

Compass (TL6). +1 to Navigation skill. $50.

Cord, 3/16" (TL0). Supports 90 lbs. Per 10 yards: $1, 0.5 lb.

Fishhooks and Line (TL0). Basic gear for Fishing skill; needs a pole. $50.

Flashlight, Heavy (TL6). 30' beam. $20, 1 lb., 5 hrs.

Flashlight, Mini (TL7). 15' beam. $10, 0.25 lb., 1 hr.

Gasoline (TL6). Per gallon: $1.50, 6 lbs.

GPS Receiver (TL8). Satellite-updated; grants Absolute Direction (Requires Signal). $200, 3 lbs., 24 hrs.

Grapnel (TL5). Throw to ST×2 yards. Supports 300 lbs. $20, 2 lbs.

Group Basics (TL0). Basic equipment for Cooking and Survival skill for a group. Cook pot, rope, hatchet, etc., for 3-8 campers. $50, 20 lbs.

Iron Spike (Piton) (TL2). For climbing, spiking doors, etc. $1, 0.5 lb.

Kerosene (TL6). Per gallon: $1.50, 6 lbs.

Lantern (TL2). Burns for 24 hours on 1 pint of oil. $20, 2 lbs.

Life Jacket (TL6). Floats up to 350 lbs. $100, 6 lbs.

Matches (TL6). Start fires. Box of 50, waterproof. $1.50.

Oil (TL2). For lantern. Per pint: $2, 1 lb.

Parachute (TL6). Use with Parachuting skill. The wearer will fall at least 80 yards before it opens, and then descend at 5 yards/second. $1,000, 30 lbs.

Personal Basics (TL0). Minimum gear for camping: -2 to any Survival roll without it. Includes utensils, tinderbox or flint and steel, towel, etc., as TL permits. $5; 1 lb.

Piton. See *Iron Spike,* above.

Pole, 6' (TL0). For pitching tents, fishing, or prodding items. $5, 3 lbs.

Pole, 10' (TL0). For things you wouldn't touch with a 6' pole. $8, 5 lbs.

Pouch or Purse, Small (TL1). Holds 3 lbs. $10.

Rope, 3/8" (TL0). Supports 300 lbs. Per 10 yards: $5, 1.5 lbs.

Rope, 3/4" (TL1). Supports 1,100 lbs. Per 10 yards: $25, 5 lbs.

Scuba Gear (TL6). Basic equipment for Scuba skill: 2-hour underwater air tank, with regulator, facemask, etc. $1,500, 32 lbs.

Sleeping Bag (TL6). For normal conditions. $25, 7 lbs.

Sleeping Bag, Insulated (TL7). +3 HT to resist freezing. $100, 15 lbs.

Sleeping Fur (TL0). Warm unless wet. $50, 8 lbs.

Suitcase, Hard (TL5). Holds 100 lbs. DR 4, with key lock. $250, 8 lbs.

Tent, 1-Man (TL0). Includes ropes; no poles needed. $50, 5 lbs.

Tent, 2-Man (TL0). Includes ropes; requires one 6-foot pole. $80, 12 lbs.

Tent, 4-Man (TL0). Includes ropes; requires 2 poles. $150, 30 lbs.

Tent, 20-Man (TL1). Includes ropes; requires 16 poles. $300, 100 lbs.

Thermos Bottle (TL5). Keeps 1 pint hot (24 hrs.) or cold (72 hrs.). $10, 2 lbs.

Torch (TL0). Burns for 1 hr. $3, 1 lb.

Traveler's Rations (TL0). One meal of dried meat, cheese, etc. $2, 0.5 lb.

Water Purification Tablets (TL6). Bottle of 50. Purify 1 quart each. $5.

Wineskin (TL0). Holds 1 gallon of liquid (8 lbs. if water). $10, 0.25 lb.

Wristwatch (TL6). $20.

Communications and Information Gear

Batteries (TL6). $1, neg.

Cell Phone (TL8). Only works in some areas; $20/month fee. $250, 0.25 lb., 10 hrs.

Computer, Laptop (TL8). Modem plugs into phone. $1,500, 3 lbs., 2 hrs.

Computer, Wearable (TL8). Display glasses and wireless modem. $1,000, 2 lbs., 8 hrs.

Drum (TL0). Audible for several miles. $40, 2 lbs.

Mini-Recorder (TL7). Palm-sized, with 3-hour tape (extra tapes are $5). $200, 0.5 lb.

Mini-Recorder, Digital (TL8). As above, but without the tape! $30, 0.5 lb.

Radio, Backpack (TL7). VHF radio. 20-mile range. $6,000, 15 lbs., 12 hrs.

Radio, Hand (TL7). Classic "walkie-talkie." 2-mile range. $100, 1 lb., 12 hrs.

Radio, Headset (TL8). With throat mike. 1-mile range. Multiply cost by 10 for secure, encrypted version. $500, 0.5 lb., 12 hrs.

Satellite Phone (TL8). Global range, satellite relay. $3,000, 3 lbs., 1 hr.

Scribe's Kit (TL3). Quills, inkbottles, penknife, paper. $50, 2 lbs.

Transistor Radio (TL7). Receive-only; picks up radio stations. $15, 0.5 lb., 8 hrs.

TV Set, Mini (TL7). 5" × 5" flatscreen. $150, 3 lbs., 4 hrs.

Typewriter, Manual (TL6). $200, 10 lbs.

Wax Tablet (TL1). For writing; erasable. $10, 2 lbs.

Equestrian Gear

Bonuses to control a mount only offset penalties to Riding skill; they never give a net bonus.

Bit and Bridle (TL1). +2 to control horse, or +3 if using both hands. $35, 3 lbs.

Horseshoes (TL3). Shod horses get +2 HT on any rolls for stamina on long rides. Per set: $50, 4 lbs.

Saddle and Tack (TL2). Basic equipment for Riding skill. $150, 15 lbs.

Saddlebags (TL1). Hold 40 lbs. $100, 3 lbs.

Spurs (TL2). +1 to control a mount. $25.

Stirrups (TL3). Make it easy to mount a horse and give +1 to control mount. *Required* to use Lance skill. With ordinary saddle: $125, 20 lbs.

War Saddle (TL3). +1 to Riding skill to stay seated, 50% chance user will stay seated even if unconscious. With stirrups: $250, 35 lbs.

Law-Enforcement, Thief, and Spy Gear

Bug, Audio (TL7). -7 to spot, 1/4-mile range, transmits for 1 week. $200.

Bug Stomper (TL7). Jams bugs in a 10-yard radius. $1,200, 2 lbs., 8 hrs.

Disguise Kit (TL5). +1 to Disguise skill. $200, 10 lbs.

Electronic "Lockpicks" (TL7). +2 to pick *electronic* locks. $1,500, 3 lbs.

Handcuffs (TL5). Give -5 to Escape. $40, 0.5 lb.

Homing Beacon (TL7). Scanner tracks at 1-mile range. $40, 12 hrs.

Laser Microphone (TL8). Eavesdrop through glass. 300-yd. range. $500, 2 lbs.

Lockpicks (TL3). Basic equipment for Lockpicking skill. $50.

Nanobug (TL8). Pinhead-sized audio-visual bug (-10 to spot). $100.

Shotgun Mike (TL6). Gives (TL-5) levels of Parabolic Hearing. $250, 2 lbs.

Medical Gear

Antibiotic (TL6). Prevents or cures (in 1d days) infections. $20.

Antitoxin Kit (TL6). Antidote for specific poison. 10 uses. $25, 0.5 lb.

Bandages (var.). Bandages for a half-dozen wounds. Might be clean cloth, adhesive dressings, or spray-on "plastiskin," depending on TL. Basic equipment for First Aid skill. $10, 2 lbs.

Crash Kit (var.). A complete kit for treating *serious* injuries. Includes sterile bandages, sutures, and drugs appropriate for the TL. At TL6+, includes IV drip, needle, and plasma. +2 to First Aid skill, and counts as improvised gear (-5) for Surgery. $200, 10 lbs.

First Aid Kit (var.). A complete kit for treating wounds, with bandages, ointments, etc. +1 to First Aid skill. $50, 2 lbs.

Surgical Instruments (var.). Includes scalpels, forceps, etc. Basic equipment for Surgery skill. $300, 15 lbs.

Optics and Sensors

Binoculars (TL6). Gives (TL - 4) levels of Telescopic Vision. $400, 2 lbs.

Camcorder (TL8). Has 10× zoom. Gives Night Vision 5. $1,000, 1 lb., 7 hrs.

Camera, 35mm (TL6). Basic equipment for Photography skill. Extra film is 32 shots ($10, neg.). Better cameras cost *much* more! $50, 3 lbs.

Metal Detector Wand (TL7). +3 to find metal items. $50, 1 lb., 8 hrs.

Mini-Camera, Digital (TL8). Stores pictures on optical disk. $500.

Night Vision Goggles (TL8). Give Night Vision 9. $600, 2 lbs., 8 hrs.

Spy Camera (TL6). Holds 36 exposures, uses microfilm. $500.

Telescope (TL4). Gives (TL-3) levels of Telescopic Vision. $500, 6 lbs.

Tools

Balance and Weights (TL1). For weighing goods. $35, 3 lbs.

Crowbar, 3' (TL2). Treat as a small mace in combat, but at -1 to skill. $20, 3 lbs.

Cutting Torch (TL6). 1d+3(2) burn per second. Each gas bottle gives 30 seconds of cutting. $500, 30 lbs. Extra gas bottles are $50, 15 lbs. per bottle.

Knitting Needles (TL3). Per pair. $5.

Pickaxe (TL2). Improves digging speed. $15, 8 lbs.

Plow, Iron (TL2). Works rough soils. $220, 120 lbs.

Plow, Wooden (TL1). Pulled by oxen. $55, 60 lbs.

Portable Tool Kit (var.). Basic equipment for *one* of the following skills:

Carpentry (TL1) is $300, 20 lbs.; Armoury (TL1), Explosives (TL5), Machinist (TL5), Mechanic (TL5), or Electrician (TL6) is $600, 20 lbs.; Electronics Repair (TL6) is $1,200, 10 lbs.

Saw (TL0). A lumberjack's tool, not a carpentry saw. $150, 3 lbs.

Shovel (TL1). Speeds up digging. $12, 6 lbs.

Spinning Wheel (TL3). Produces yarn six times as fast. $100, 40 lbs.

Suitcase Lab (var.). Basic equipment for a specific scientific skill (e.g., Chemistry or Forensics). $3,000, 10 lbs.

Wheelbarrow (TL2). Holds 350 lbs. Divide effective weight of load by 5. $60, 18 lbs.

Whetstone (TL1). For sharpening tools and weapons. $5, 1 lb.

Transportation

See *Riding and Draft Animals* (p. 459) and *Vehicles* (p. 462).

Weapon and Combat Accessories

Ear Muffs (TL6). Block loud noises (e.g., gunshots). Give Protected Hearing. $200, 1 lb.

Hip Quiver (TL0). Holds 20 arrows or bolts. $15, 1 lb.

Holster, Belt (TL5). Fits most pistols. $25, 0.5 lb.

Holster, Shoulder (TL5). Allows use of Holdout, but gives -1 to Fast-Draw. $50, 1 lb.

Lanyard, Leather (TL0). Lets you retrieve a dropped weapon on a DX roll. Each attempt requires a Ready maneuver. Can be cut: -6 to hit, DR 2, HP 2. $1.

Lanyard, Woven Steel (TL6). As leather lanyard, but DR 6, HP 4. $15.

Laser Sight (TL8). +1 to skill; see *Laser Sights* (p. 412). $100, 6 hrs.

Scope, 4× (TL6). +2 to Acc for aimed shots only. $150, 1.5 lbs.

Scope, 4×, Thermal Imaging (TL8). As above, plus gives the user Infravision. $8,000, 4 lbs., 2 hrs.

Shoulder Quiver (TL0). Holds 12 arrows or bolts. $10, 0.5 lb.

Silencer, Pistol or SMG (TL6). Reduces damage by -1 per die; see *Silencers* (p. 412). $400, 1 lb.

Web Gear (TL6): Belt and suspenders with pouches and rings for gear. $50, 2 lbs.

CHAPTER NINE

CHARACTER DEVELOPMENT

Your character will improve – or simply *change* – with time. The longer you play your character, the more opportunities you will have for such development.

IMPROVEMENT THROUGH ADVENTURE

After each game session, the GM will award you "bonus" character points – the same kind of points you used to create your character. You may spend these points immediately to improve your character, or you can save them. You can save unspent points for as long as you like, but you should *ignore* them when you add up your character's point value.

The following rules apply when you spend bonus character points:

● To add a *new* trait with a *positive* point cost, pay points equal to the trait's usual point cost.

● To improve an *existing* trait that comes in levels, pay points equal to the *difference* in cost between the new level and the old level.

● To remove an *existing* trait with a *negative* point cost, pay points equal to the bonus originally earned when you took the trait.

In all cases, increase the point value of your character by the number of points spent. Some additional rules apply to specific classes of traits.

Improving Attributes and Secondary Characteristics

For each level by which you wish to improve a basic attribute (ST, DX, IQ, or HT) or a secondary characteristic (HP, Will, Perception, FP, Basic Speed, or Basic Move), you must spend character points equal to the cost to raise that score by one level.

If you improve an attribute, secondary characteristics and skills based on that attribute improve as well. For instance, if you raise your HT by one, you gain 1 FP and 0.25 point of Basic Speed (which might in turn increase Basic Move), and *all* your HT-based skills go up by one!

Increases in ST do not affect height (except for a child), but if you wish, you may gain additional *weight* to go with higher ST.

Adding and Improving Social Traits

To improve social traits, you need an in-play justification *in addition to* the expenditure of sufficient points. Some examples:

Allies, Contacts, and Patrons: You must meet such NPCs during your adventures and earn their trust through your actions. You cannot *hire* true Allies, Contacts, or Patrons.

Clerical Investment, Legal Enforcement Powers, Rank, Security Clearance, Status, etc.: An individual in a position of relative authority must bestow such privileges. This might require a background check, qualification course, valor in combat, years of service, or a large bribe.

Reputation: You must earn this through deeds and works. You cannot buy a Reputation until you have done something to merit it!

Signature Gear: You must acquire a suitable item in the course of your adventures.

Tech Level: You can raise your personal TL (see *Technology Level*, p. 22) by living in a society of a higher TL than your own – but only if you are free to attend that society's schools and benefit from its conveniences (being an alien abductee, prisoner, etc. doesn't count). The GM should consider limiting improvement to one TL per year of game time.

Wealth: To improve your Wealth, you must amass money equal to the starting wealth of the desired wealth level *after* paying any necessary bribes, taxes, etc.

Adding and Improving Mental and Physical Advantages

Most mental and physical advantages are inborn; you cannot buy them after character creation. However, there are some exceptions.

You can learn some advantages as if they were skills; see *Learnable Advantages* (p. 294). If the GM feels that adventuring is as good as training to acquire such an advantage, you may buy it with bonus points.

Other advantages require extraordinary circumstances: divine revelation, ritual ordeal, etc. This is typical of Magery, Power Investiture, and True Faith. In addition to points, these traits require the GM's permission and suitable in-game events!

Of course, the GM can allow you to buy *any* advantage, if the results are in keeping with his vision of the game world. The GM may also challenge *you* to provide a good explanation (dramatic, logical, or both) for why he should let you buy a new advantage.

Buying Off Disadvantages

You can get rid of most beginning disadvantages by "buying them off" with character points equal to the bonus earned when you originally took the disadvantage. This generally requires a game-world justification in addition to the point expenditure.

True Faith. In addition to points, these traits require the GM's permission and suitable in-game events!

Traits Gained in Play

The GM may rule that you have *suddenly* acquired a new trait – most often an advantage or a disadvantage – as a consequence of events in the game: social interaction, combat, divine intervention, etc. This has *nothing* to do with bonus points!

When you acquire an advantage this way, write it on your character sheet and increase your point total by the value of the advantage. You do not have to pay for it with bonus points. For instance, if the GM rewards you with a 10-point Patron after you save the life of a powerful duke, your point value goes up by 10 points and the game goes on.

The GM may allow you to refuse such an advantage if your *character* could refuse it in the game world. You could refuse wealth, but if the gods granted you Magery, you wouldn't have much say in the matter! If you refuse an advantage, you do *not* get equivalent bonus points to spend on other things.

Similarly, when you acquire a disadvantage this way, just write it down and lower your point value accordingly. You do *not* get any extra points for it – that's just the breaks of the game! For instance, if you lose an arm in battle, add One Arm [-20] and reduce your point value by 20 points; you do not get 20 points of new abilities to compensate.

The GM *may* allow you to "buy off" a disadvantage acquired in play. Save up enough character points and then talk to the GM. If he is feeling merciful, he may arrange game-world events to eliminate the disadvantage.

Money

You may trade bonus character points for money – see *Trading Points for Money* (p. 26). Each point is worth 10% of the campaign's average starting wealth. The GM should provide a suitable explanation for your windfall: tax refund, buried treasure, gambling winnings, etc. Be creative. A spy under cover as an athlete might earn the money through product endorsements!

Dependents: When you buy off Dependents, you or the GM should provide a game-world explanation of where they went – died, grew up, moved away, fell in love with someone else . . .

Enemies: If you wish to buy off Enemies, you must deal with them in the game world: kill them, jail them, bribe them, flee from them, make friends with them . . . whatever the GM deems necessary. You can *never* permanently dispose of Enemies unless you buy them off . . . they will return or new Enemies will appear in their place.

Mental Disadvantages and Odious Personal Habits: You may buy these off at their original bonus value. Assume that you simply got over your problem.

Physical Disadvantages: Your game world's tech level – and the supernatural powers available – determine the degree to which you can buy off these traits. Consider Hard of Hearing. At TL5 or less, you would have to settle for an ear trumpet. At TL6-8, you could buy a hearing aid that would solve your problem while worn, allowing you to apply a Mitigator limitation (p. 112). At TL9+, surgery could fix the problem permanently. And in a fantasy world, the right wizard could cure you with a powerful Healing spell! The GM has the final say as to whether it is possible to remove a specific physical disadvantage . . . and if so, what the cost and time will be.

Social Stigma: You cannot get rid of this with points alone. You must either change your position in society or change your society. The GM will tell you when you have succeeded – at that time, you must pay enough points to buy off the original disadvantage.

Adding and Improving Skills and Techniques

You can use bonus character points to increase your skills and techniques.

Each point is the equivalent of 200 hours of learning. This is not to say that you found time to hit the books during your adventures – only that the genuine experience of an adventure can be equivalent to a much longer period of study.

You can only spend character points to improve skills or techniques that, in the GM's opinion, saw *significant* use in the adventure during which you earned the points. If the only thing you did on an adventure was trek through forests and slay monsters, you can only improve Hiking, Survival (Woodlands), and combat abilities.

When you improve a skill or a technique, the cost is the *difference* between the cost of the new level and the cost of your current level – see *Improving Your Skills* (p. 170).

You may only *add* a skill if you attempted a default roll (see *Quick Learning Under Pressure*, box) *or* if you spent most of the adventure around people who were constantly using the skill. For instance, a city boy on a forest trek with a group of skilled woodsmen could add Survival (Woodlands). You may add a technique if, during the adventure, you made significant use of the skill to which it defaults. In all cases, the GM has the final say.

Quick Learning Under Pressure

If you attempt a default skill roll in a stressful situation, you may try to acquire that skill during play, regardless of whether you succeeded or failed (you can learn from your mistakes!). The GM is the judge of whether a given situation qualifies as "stressful"; see *Base Skill vs. Effective Skill* (p. 171) for examples.

At the start of the *next* game session, make an IQ roll to see whether you learned from your experience. Eidetic Memory gives +5; Photographic Memory gives +10! On a success, you may spend *one* point earned during the previous session to learn the skill. If you have no points, you cannot learn the skill – and if you let more than one session go by, you lose the opportunity.

Obviously, if a skill has no default, you cannot learn it this way.

IMPROVEMENT THROUGH STUDY

You may add or improve skills by spending time studying them, if an opportunity for study is available. In the discussion below, "skills" refers not only to ordinary skills, but also to spells, techniques, and even some advantages (see *Learnable Advantages,* p. 294).

Improvement through study does *not* depend on earning bonus points. You could build a character, keep track of his age and income, and let him study for 40 game-years without ever bringing him into play. Of course, this would not be much fun . . . and things that happen during play can offer great opportunities for study. If you aid a master wizard, his gratitude might take the form of magic lessons!

Normally, it takes 200 hours of learning to gain one point in a skill. You may study any number of skills at once, but a given hour of time counts toward study of only *one* subject, unless the GM allows an exception.

Some forms of study are more effective than others. This means that an hour of *study* does not always equal an hour of *learning* – there is a "conversion factor" between the two. Some guidelines appear below.

Jobs

Adventurers can, and probably should, get jobs. This lets them earn money and practice their skills. Most jobs have prerequisite skills; some have other requirements (minimum attribute levels, advantages, etc.). In general, more accomplished characters can get better jobs and earn more money. For more information, see *Jobs* (p. 516).

Learning on the Job

If you have a job, time spent on the job counts as "study" of the skills used in the job. However, since most time on the job is spent doing what you already know, not learning new things, every *four* hours on the job count as *one* hour of learning. You may claim a maximum of eight hours on the job per day (four hours per day at a part-time job). Your actual working hours may exceed this, but fatigue limits *learning* to this level. Thus, a year of full-time work will give you two to three points to spend on job-related skills.

Self-Teaching

You can teach *yourself* a skill, unless the skill description attaches specific conditions that would preclude this (such as "only taught by the military" or a prerequisite of Trained By A Master). Every *two* hours of reading, exercises, practice, etc. without an instructor count as *one* hour of learning. This must take place in time not used for adventuring, working, eating, sleeping, or taking care of personal hygiene. The GM should limit self-teaching to 12 hours per day – or eight hours/day for those with part-time jobs, only four hours/day for those with full-time jobs.

Education

Every hour of instruction by a professional teacher counts as one hour of learning. A "professional teacher" is someone with Teaching skill at 12 or higher. In order to teach you a given skill, he must either know that skill at your current skill level or better, or have as many or more points in the skill as you do. Ordinary instruction rarely exceeds eight hours per day. A college semester (21 weeks) of classroom study equals around one point per subject, and a full-time student could study up to five subjects per semester. A semester of night school would give one point in one subject.

Intensive Training

Full-time study with expert teachers and lavish training materials is the most effective type of "normal" learning. An expert teacher has Teaching skill at 12 (or higher), plus a higher level *and* more points in the skill being taught than you do. *Quadruple* all costs and tuition fees! Every hour of intensive training counts as *two* hours of learning. Intensive training is rarely available outside the military, where you have little control over the skills taught or the scheduling of courses. It can last for up to 16 hours per day. You must have HT 12+ to make it through such training without "washing out" (the Fit advantage *does* increase effective HT for this purpose).

Adventuring

Adventuring time can also count as study of suitable skills. The "conversion factor" is up to the GM, who should be generous. For example, a trek through the Amazon might count for every waking moment – say, 16 hours a day – as study of Survival (Jungle).

Finding a Teacher

It is most efficient to learn new skills from a teacher. For some skills, finding a teacher is automatic; for others, it can be difficult. The GM should adjust availability to suit his concept of what is "reasonable."

Most education costs money. The price is up to the GM. If the teacher wants to be paid, see *Jobs* (p. 516) to determine what his time is worth. Multiply all fees by 4 for intensive training! Barter may be possible, or the teacher may demand a service in exchange for his aid – there are endless adventure possibilities here.

Learning Magic

In a world where magic is common, you can learn a spell just as you would any other IQ-based skill. You may apprentice yourself to a wizard to learn his whole craft . . . or hire a magic instructor to teach you a few spells.

In a setting in which magic is *secret* or *rare*, finding an instructor is much harder. Most wizards shroud themselves in secrecy . . . or belong to reclusive, mysterious cults . . . or prove to be fakes!

You *can* learn magic without a teacher; use the rules described under *Self-Teaching*. You must be able to read and have access to good textbooks. Magical grimoires are often deliberately complex and obscure – *especially* in rare- or secret-magic settings! The GM is free to slow the pace of self-teaching as much as he wishes to reflect this.

Learning Secret Martial-Arts Techniques

To acquire Trained By A Master (p. 93) or Weapon Master (p. 99), you must first find an appropriate school or teacher – an adventure in itself, often involving a dangerous pilgrimage to an exotic locale. Once you locate a master, you disappear from play for 1d+1 game-years. After *that*, you might have to pass a series of hazardous tests, or make a final quest to yet another remote land.

When you emerge from your training, you have the desired advantage, plus 20 character points to spend on any special skills allowed in the campaign. The GM can treat these points like those gained from any other kind of study, or he can "balance" them with an equal number of points in additional disadvantages – perhaps an Enemy (e.g., a rival school), or a Duty or Sense of Duty to your school or teacher.

LEARNABLE ADVANTAGES

You can learn certain advantages as if they were skills (200 hours = 1 point), provided you have a suitable instructor (professor, kung fu master, etc.). Use the standard rules for skill learning; in particular, anyone teaching an advantage must possess it himself.

Combat Reflexes: The GM may rule that fighting is the *only* way to "learn" Combat Reflexes before TL7, and require adventurers who want this advantage to pay for it with bonus points. At TL7+, realistic military simulations can teach it as if it were a skill.

Cultural Familiarity and Languages: Time spent in a foreign land counts as four hours per day toward both Cultural Familiarity and the local Language, no matter what else you are doing (even studying skills – an exception to the "one skill at a time" rule).

Eidetic Memory: By apprenticing as a bard or doing daily mental exercises, you can "learn" the first level of this advantage. This requires an hour a day, meaning it takes a little less than three years of constant practice to gain this trait.

Enhanced Defenses: Only those with Trained By A Master or Weapon Master may "learn" these advantages. The GM should handle them as if they were martial-arts skills.

Fit: You can acquire either level of Fit through exercise – on your own or with a trainer – just as you would athletic skills like Hiking and Running.

G-Experience: The standard way to "learn" G-Experience is to visit planets that have different gravity fields. Highly advanced societies that can manipulate gravity might be able to teach this advantage as if it were a skill.

Psionic Abilities and Talents: In some game worlds, "psi academies" teach psionic Talents and abilities. The rules under *Gaining New Psi Abilities* (p. 255) apply to learning psi advantages as well as to buying them with earned points: you must possess Talent or abilities in a power to acquire new abilities, and you must have abilities to acquire Talent.

Trained By A Master and Weapon Master: See *Finding a Teacher* (p. 293).

TRANSFORMATIONS

Adventurers may encounter forces that can *transform* them in body or in mind. This kind of character development is significantly more complex than simply spending points or studying, and can raise difficult questions. The next few sections suggest answers.

BODY MODIFICATION

"Body modification" is any artificial process that gives you a set of traits different from the ones you were born with (or *created* with), without moving your brain or mind to a new body. This most often means surgery, or biological or mechanical implants (often known as "biomods" and "cyberwear," respectively), but permanent supernatural transformations also qualify. The GM determines what body modification can accomplish in his campaign.

Modifications acquired *before* your character entered the game cost points. Build your character normally and note which traits are due to artificial tinkering when you write your character story. This neither costs money nor affects the point cost of the traits – it merely justifies certain abilities on your character sheet (see *Advantage Origins*, p. 33).

Modifications added in play work differently. In theory, if you have the cash and can locate a suitably skilled surgeon, wizard, etc., you can buy modifications with money. In practice, this gives wealthy characters a significant edge, as they can effectively convert money into character points – often more points than they paid for their Wealth! The GM is the final judge of what is "fair" in his campaign, but here are a few suggestions:

Modifications cost points. You must have the requisite character points *before* you can add modifications. If you get a modification you cannot afford, the process fails and you do not gain the hoped-for abilities . . . or perhaps you gain them, but *lose* other abilities of equal value! The GM might opt to let you pay for your new abilities by going into "point debt": any point cost in excess of what you can afford becomes negative unspent points, and until this debt is gone, all future bonus points must go toward paying it off. Cash costs are irrelevant (but one could see this as a special case of *Trading Points for Money*, p. 26). This option preserves game balance but isn't very realistic.

Modifications cost money. If you have the cash, you can buy the modification. Pay the requisite amount of money and alter your point value to reflect the point cost of your new traits. This option is realistic but allows *rapid* character improvement. To keep this under control, the GM should ruthlessly enforce recovery times for surgery (see below), and have gruesome consequences for failed attempts at modification.

Modifications are free. If events in the campaign "inflict" modifications on you without giving you any say in the matter, you simply gain the relevant traits and adjust your point value accordingly – see *Traits Gained in Play* (p. 291). This option makes the most sense for involuntary modifications that give disadvantages, or for useful modifications that *all* the PCs receive from their employer or Patron (in which case the point cost is likely to be "balanced" by a significant Duty).

Surgical Modifications

Surgery to install biomods or cyberwear, or for its own sake (e.g., cosmetic surgery to improve appearance), is not risk-free. Even if all goes well, you will need time to recover.

It takes one day to recover per character point of traits added or removed via surgery. The Surgery roll is at -1 per full *week* of recovery required. On a critical success, halve recovery time. On a success, recovery time is normal. On a failure, the modification fails, recovery time is normal, and you suffer (recovery time in weeks)/2 dice of damage to the affected body part. Critical failure doubles this damage *and* results in complications – the GM is free to assign appropriate disadvantages.

If the GM is charging cash for modifications, assume that surgery costs $1,000 per character point of traits added or removed.

Triple the recovery time and dollar cost for operations on the brain, eyes, or vital organs.

Specific **GURPS** worldbooks might supersede some or all of these guidelines.

Supernatural Modifications

Divine will, magic, and so on may be able to produce permanent transformations. There is no recovery time, but if the GM is charging cash, this is usually very expensive – *at least* twice as expensive as surgery, in the form of wizard's fees, temple donations, etc.

Instant Learning

Magical wishes, divine inspiration, "neurotechnology," etc. might be able to grant skills as well as advantages and disadvantages. As with other modifications, the GM may charge cash or points, or simply grant the skills. An amusing option is to balance the cost of such skills with mental disadvantages or quirks related to them.

DAX
ZUB

Modular Abilities: If you bought the Modular Abilities advantage, you are capable of *temporary* "instant learning" – for instance, by loading a computer program or plugging in a chip. Use the rules under *Modular Abilities* (p. 71) instead of those above.

MIND TRANSFER

A hero in a fantasy or futuristic setting might find himself inhabiting a new body. There are many possibilities – brain transplants, digital "uploading," the Possession advantage (p. 75), etc. – but they all use the same basic rules.

When your mind moves to a new body, you gain that body's ST, DX, and HT – as well as all secondary characteristics based on those attributes – and its *physical* advantages and disadvantages. Your IQ, Perception, Will, and *mental* advantages and disadvantages don't change. Keep your *points* in skills, but base your skill *levels* on your new attributes.

Recalculate your point value to take your new traits into account. For instance, if you switch from a body with ST 10, DX 10, HT 10, and One Arm [-20] to one with ST 12 [20], DX 12 [40], HT 12 [20], and two arms, your point value goes up by 100 points.

The GM decides how to handle changes in point value. The options given under *Body Modification* (above) apply here as well. In general, if you had no say in the transfer, the GM should simply adjust your point value. If you *chose* to inhabit a superior body, the GM may charge you points (the difference in point value between your new form and your old one) or money (especially if the new body is a golem, robot, etc. built for the purpose).

Mind vs. Brain

The rules above assume that a *mind* is unaffected by the *brain* in which it resides. This is fine for fantasy mind transfer – fantasy rarely concerns itself with the neurological origin of consciousness – but in a "hard science" setting, the GM should modify IQ, Will, and Perception by the difference in *racial* modifiers between the new body and the old one. Recalculate the point value to reflect such changes. For instance, if you

belong to a race with IQ+1 and move to an animal body with racial IQ-5, your IQ will drop by 6, lowering your point value by 120 points.

Realistically, DX also has a "learned" component – although it is likely smaller. The GM may decide that this rule applies to DX as well.

Multiple People

Certain techniques – such as "braintaping" (recording an image of your thoughts and personality) and cinematic cloning – may let you *copy* your mind into multiple bodies.

If you make a copy of yourself in play, and intend to use it as a "backup" that will only enter play if you die, treat it as a suitably modified Extra Life (p. 55). The GM's decisions regarding body modification determine whether you pay cash or points. Either way, you must update your backup regularly; otherwise, it will have outdated memories and skills – or its memories might fade to the point where it will not activate! If you paid cash, the GM is free to charge fees for updates, maintenance, and the security of your backup.

If you make copies of yourself and activate them *while you are alive*, you control only *one* character. The copies diverge into different people, which the GM controls as NPCs. They are *not* automatically your friends! The GM may permit you to buy copies as Allies (p. 36), at the usual point cost. But if you make copies indiscriminately, the GM might rule that some of them dislike you, becoming Enemies (p. 135) with the Evil Twin modifier.

If you have active copies, you may ask the GM to let you play one if you die. However, you will have to accept the GM's decision on how your copy diverged from your original self. Your copy might have discovered his artistic side and let Guns skills degrade while he learned Dancing . . . and since he's his own person, you must roleplay this, or the GM will penalize you for bad roleplaying. Such is the price of a free Extra Life!

SUPERNATURAL AFFLICTIONS

Certain supernatural beings can infect you with their "curse" via a bite or other attack, turning you into a similar kind of being. In effect, you acquire a new racial template. If this is involuntary (and it usually is), apply the *Traits Gained in Play* rule (p. 291). Modify your character sheet to include your new racial traits, and adjust your point value as necessary.

But if you *willingly* accept such a fate in order to acquire powerful new abilities, the GM should treat the transformation as he would any other body modification. To keep things fair, he should charge points. If you cannot afford the point cost, the GM may make up the difference by assigning you new disadvantages! Cursed (p. 129) is particularly likely . . .

For more information, see *Dominance* (p. 50) and *Infectious Attack* (p. 140).

DEATH

In general, when your character dies, that's the end of his career. You must create a new character to continue in the campaign. The GM might start you out close to the other PCs in points, but it is *not* acceptable to write a new name across the top of your old character sheet and declare, "This is his twin brother." If you want to do that, buy an Extra Life!

In some settings, however, magic or high technology might be able to resurrect you. If so, you return from the dead and pick up where you left off.

In other worlds, you might be able to become a being of pure thought (especially if you are a psi), return from the grave as undead (ghost, vampire, etc.), or even be reincarnated as an animal. The net effect is that you acquire a new racial template. The GM should handle this as explained under *Mind Transfer* (above): combine your mental traits with the physical traits of your new form, and adjust your point value. The point cost, if any, is the same as for a supernatural affliction – going from "living" to "dead" to "vampire" is really no different from going directly from "living" to "vampire."

TRAIT LISTS

ADVANTAGES

M/P/Soc tells whether an advantage is *mental, physical,* or *social.*
X/Sup tells whether an advantage is *exotic* or *supernatural.* A – in this column means it is *mundane.*

Advantage	M/P/Soc	X/Sup	Cost	Page
360° Vision	P	X	25	34
3D Spatial Sense	P	–	10	34
Absolute Direction	M/P	–	5	34
Absolute Timing	M	–	2	35
Accessory	P	X	1	100
Acute Hearing	P	–	2/level	35
Acute Taste and Smell	P	–	2/level	35
Acute Touch	P	–	2/level	35
Acute Vision	P	–	2/level	35
Administrative Rank	Soc	–	5 or 10/level	30
Affliction	P	X	10/level	35
Alcohol Tolerance	P	–	1	100
Allies	Soc	–	Variable	36
Altered Time Rate	M	X	100/level	38
Alternate Form	P	X	Variable	83
Alternate Identity	Soc	–	5 or 15	39
Ambidexterity	P	–	5	39
Amphibious	P	X	10	40
Animal Empathy	M	–	5	40
Animal Friend	M	–	5/level	90
Appearance	P	–	Variable	21
Arm DX	P	X	12 or 16/level	40
Arm ST	P	X	3, 5, or 8/level	40
Artificer	M	–	10/level	90
Autotrance	M	–	1	101
Binding	P	X	2/level	40
Blessed	M	Sup	10+	40
Brachiator	P	X	5	41
Breath-Holding	P	X	2/level	41
Business Acumen	M	–	10/level	90
Catfall	P	X	10	41
Chameleon	P	X	5/level	41
Channeling	M	Sup	10	41
Charisma	M	–	5/level	41
Chronolocation	M	–	5	35
Claim to Hospitality	Soc	–	1 to 10	41
Clairsentience	M	Sup	50	42
Claws	P	X	Variable	42
Clerical Investment	Soc	–	5	43
Clinging	P	X	20	43
Combat Reflexes	M	–	15	43
Common Sense	M	–	10	43
Compartmentalized Mind	M	X	50/level	43
Constriction Attack	P	X	15	43
Contact Group	Soc	–	Variable	44
Contacts	Soc	–	Variable	44
Courtesy Rank	Soc	–	1/level	29
Cultural Adaptability	M	–	10	46
Cultural Familiarity	Soc	–	1 or 2/culture	23
Cybernetics	P	–	Variable	46
Damage Resistance	P	X	5/level	46
Danger Sense	M	–	15	47
Daredevil	M	–	15	47
Dark Vision	P	X	25	47
Deep Sleeper	P	–	1	101
Destiny	M	Sup	Variable	48

Advantage	M/P/Soc	X/Sup	Cost	Page
Detect	M/P	X	Variable	48
Digital Mind	P	X	5	48
Discriminatory Hearing	P	X	15	49
Discriminatory Smell	P	X	15	49
Discriminatory Taste	P	X	10	49
Doesn't Breathe	P	X	20	49
Doesn't Eat or Drink	P	X	10	50
Doesn't Sleep	P	X	20	50
Dominance	M	Sup	20	50
Double-Jointed	P	–	15	56
Duplication	M/P	X	35/copy	50
Eidetic Memory	M	–	5	51
Elastic Skin	P	X	20	51
Empathy	M	–	15	51
Enhanced Defenses	M	–	Variable	51
Enhanced Move	P	X	20/level	52
Enhanced Time Sense	M	X	45	52
Enhanced Tracking	P	X	5/level	53
Extended Lifespan	P	X	2/level	53
Extra Arms	P	X	Variable	53
Extra Attack	P	–	25/attack	53
Extra Head	P	X	15/head	54
Extra Legs	P	X	Variable	54
Extra Life	M	X	25/life	55
Extra Mouth	P	X	5/mouth	55
Fashion Sense	M	–	5	21
Favor	Soc	–	Variable	55
Fearlessness	M	–	2/level	55
Filter Lungs	P	X	5	55
Fit	P	–	5	55
Flexibility	P	–	5	56
Flight	P	X	40	56
Fur	P	X	1	101
Gadgeteer	M	–	25 or 50	56
G-Experience	M	–	1 to 10	57
Gifted Artist	M	–	5/level	90
Gizmos	M	–	5/gizmo	57
Green Thumb	M	–	5/level	90
Growth	P	X	10/level	58
Gunslinger	M	–	25	58
Hard to Kill	P	–	2/level	58
Hard to Subdue	P	–	2/level	59
Healer	M	–	10/level	90
Healing	M	X	30	59
Hermaphromorph	P	X	5	59
High Manual Dexterity	P	–	5/level	59
High Pain Threshold	P	–	10	59
High TL	M	–	5/level	23
Higher Purpose	M	Sup	5	59
Honest Face	P	–	1	101
Hyperspectral Vision	P	X	25	60
Illuminated	M	Sup	15	60
Improved G-Tolerance	P	–	5 to 25	60
Independent Income	Soc	–	1/level	26
Indomitable	M	–	15	60
Infravision	P	X	0 or 10	60

Advantage	M/P/Soc	X/Sup	Cost	Page
Injury Tolerance	P	X	Variable	60
Innate Attack	P	X	Variable	61
Insubstantiality	M/P	X	80	62
Intuition	M	–	15	63
Intuitive Mathematician	M	–	5	66
Invisibility	M/P	X	40	63
Jumper	M	Sup	100	64
Language Talent	M	–	10	65
Legal Enforcement Powers	Soc	–	5, 10, or 15	65
Legal Immunity	Soc	–	5 to 20	65
Less Sleep	P	–	2/level	65
Lifting ST	P	X	3/level	65
Lightning Calculator	M	–	2	66
Longevity	P	–	2	66
Luck	M	–	Variable	66
Magery	M	Sup	5 + 10/level	66
Magic Resistance	M	Sup	2/level	67
Mana Damper	M	Sup	10/level	67
Mana Enhancer	M	Sup	50/level	68
Mathematical Ability	M	–	10/level	90
Medium	M	Sup	10	68
Merchant Rank	Soc	–	5 or 10/level	30
Metabolism Control	P	X	5/level	68
Microscopic Vision	P	X	5/level	68
Military Rank	Soc	–	5 or 10/level	30
Mimicry	M	X	10	68
Mind Control	M	X	50	68
Mind Probe	M	X	20	69
Mind Reading	M	X	30	69
Mind Shield	M	X	4/level	70
Mindlink	M	Sup	Variable	70
Modular Abilities	M/P	X	Variable	71
Morph	P	X	Variable	84
Musical Ability	M	–	5/level	91
Neutralize	M	X	50	71
Nictitating Membrane	P	X	1/level	71
Night Vision	P	–	1/level	71
No Hangover	P	–	1	101
Obscure	P	X	2/level	72
Oracle	M	Sup	15	72
Outdoorsman	M	–	10/level	91
Parabolic Hearing	P	X	4/level	72
Patrons	Soc	–	Variable	72
Payload	P	X	1/level	74
Penetrating Vision	P	X	10/level	74
Penetrating Voice	P	–	1	101
Perfect Balance	P	–	15	74
Peripheral Vision	P	–	15	74
Permeation	P	X	Variable	75
Photographic Memory	M	–	10	51
Pitiable	Soc	–	5	22
Plant Empathy	M	–	5	75
Police Rank	Soc	–	5 or 10/level	30
Possession	M	X	100	75
Power Investiture	M	Sup	10/level	77
Precognition	M	Sup	25	77
Pressure Support	P	X	5 to 15	77
Protected Sense	P	X	5/sense	78
Psi Static	M	Sup	30	78
Psychometry	M	Sup	20	78
Puppet	M	X	5 or 10	78
Racial Memory	M	X	15 or 40	78
Radiation Tolerance	P	X	Variable	79
Rank	Soc	–	5 or 10/level	29
Rapid Healing	P	–	5	79
Rapier Wit	M	–	5	79
Reawakened	M	Sup	10	80
Recovery	P	X	10	80
Reduced Consumption	P	–	2/level	80
Regeneration	P	X	Variable	80
Regrowth	P	X	40	80
Religious Rank	Soc	–	5 or 10/level	30
Reputation	Soc	–	Variable	26
Resistant	P	–	Variable	80

Advantage	M/P/Soc	X/Sup	Cost	Page
Sanitized Metabolism	P	X	1	101
Scanning Sense	P	X	Variable	81
Sealed	P	X	15	82
Security Clearance	Soc	–	Variable	82
See Invisible	P	X	15	83
Sensitive	M	–	5	51
Sensitive Touch	P	X	10	83
Serendipity	M	–	15/level	83
Shadow Form	P	X	50	83
Shapeshifting	P	X	Variable	83
Shrinking	P	X	5/level	85
Shtick	M/P	X	1	101
Signature Gear	Soc	–	Variable	85
Silence	P	X	5/level	85
Single-Minded	M	–	5	85
Slippery	P	X	2/level	85
Smooth Operator	M	–	15/level	91
Snatcher	M	Sup	80	86
Social Chameleon	M	–	5	86
Social Regard	Soc	–	5/level	86
Speak Underwater	P	X	5	87
Speak With Animals	M	X	25	87
Speak With Plants	M	X	15	87
Special Rapport	M	Sup	5	88
Spines	P	X	1 or 3	88
Spirit Empathy	M	Sup	10	88
Status	Soc	–	5/level	28
Stretching	P	X	6/level	88
Striker	P	X	5-8	88
Striking ST	P	X	5/level	88
Subsonic Hearing	P	X	0 or 5	89
Subsonic Speech	P	X	0 or 10	89
Super Climbing	P	X	3/level	89
Super Jump	P	X	10/level	89
Super Luck	M	Sup	100	89
Supernatural Durability	P	Sup	150	89
Talent	M	–	Variable	89
Teeth	P	X	0, 1, or 2	91
Telecommunication	M/P	X	Variable	91
Telekinesis	M/P	X	5/level	92
Telescopic Vision	P	X	5/level	92
Temperature Control	M/P	X	5/level	92
Temperature Tolerance	P	–	1/level	93
Temporal Inertia	M	Sup	15	93
Tenure	Soc	–	5	93
Terrain Adaptation	P	X	0 or 5	93
Terror	M	Sup	30 + 10/level	93
Trained By A Master	M	–	30	93
True Faith	M	Sup	15	94
Tunneling	P	X	30 + 5/level	94
Ultrahearing	P	X	0 or 5	94
Ultrasonic Speech	P	X	0 or 10	94
Ultravision	P	X	0 or 10	94
Unaging	P	X	15	95
Unfazeable	M	–	15	95
Universal Digestion	P	X	5	95
Unkillable	P	X	50 to 150	95
Unusual Background	M	–	Variable	96
Vacuum Support	P	X	5	96
Vampiric Bite	P	X	30 + 5/level	96
Versatile	M	–	5	96
Very Fit	P	–	15	55
Very Rapid Healing	P	–	15	79
Vibration Sense	P	X	10	96
Visualization	M	Sup	10	96
Voice	P	–	10	97
Walk on Air	P	X	20	97
Walk on Liquid	P	X	15	97
Warp	M	Sup	100	97
Wealth	Soc	–	Variable	25
Weapon Master	M	–	Variable	99
Wild Talent	M	Sup	20/level	99
Xeno-Adaptability	M	–	20	46
Zeroed	Soc	–	10	100

DISADVANTAGES

M/P/Soc tells whether a disadvantage is *mental, physical,* or *social.*

X/Sup tells whether a disadvantage is *exotic* or *supernatural.* A – in this column means it is *mundane.*

If the *cost* of the disadvantage is followed by *, then you must select a self-control number; the cost given is for a self-control number of 12.

Disadvantage	M/P/Soc	X/Sup	Cost	Page
Absent-Mindedness	M	–	-15	122
Acceleration Weakness	P	–	-1	165
Addiction	M/P	–	Variable	122, 164, 165
Alcohol Intolerance	P	–	-1	165
Alcoholism	P	–	-15 or -20	122
Amnesia	M	–	-10 or -25	123
Appearance	P	–	Variable	21
Attentive	M	–	-1	163
Bad Back	P	–	-15 or -25	123
Bad Grip	P	–	-5/level	123
Bad Sight	P	–	-25	123
Bad Smell	P	–	-10	124
Bad Temper	M	–	-10*	124
Berserk	M	–	-10*	124
Bestial	M	X	-10 or -15	124
Blindness	P	–	-50	124
Bloodlust	M	–	-10*	125
Bowlegged	P	–	-1	165
Broad-Minded	M	–	-1	163
Bully	M	–	-10*	125
Callous	M	–	-5	125
Cannot Float	P	–	-1	165
Cannot Learn	M	–	-30	125
Cannot Speak	P	–	-15	125
Careful	M	–	-1	163
Charitable	M	–	-15*	125
Chauvinistic	M	–	-1	163
Chronic Depression	M	–	-15*	126
Chronic Pain	P	–	Variable	126
Chummy	M	–	-5	126
Clueless	M	–	-10	126
Code of Honor	M	–	-1 or -5 to -15	127, 163
Cold-Blooded	P	X	-5 or -10	127
Colorblindness	P	–	-10	127
Combat Paralysis	P	–	-15	127
Compulsive Behavior	M	–	-5 to -15*	128
Confused	M	–	-10*	129
Congenial	M	–	-1	164
Cowardice	M	–	-10*	129
Curious	M	–	-5*	129
Cursed	M	Sup	-75	129
Deafness	P	–	-20	129
Debt	Soc	–	-1/level	26
Decreased Time Rate	M	X	-100	129
Delusions	M	–	-1 or -5 to -15	130, 164
Dependency	P	X	Variable	130
Dependents	Soc	–	Variable	131
Destiny	M	Sup	Variable	131
Disciplines of Faith	M	–	-5 to -15	132
Dislikes	M	–	-1	164
Distinctive Features	P	–	-1	165
Distractible	M	–	-1	164
Disturbing Voice	P	–	-10	132
Divine Curse	M	Sup	Variable	132
Draining	P	Sup	Variable	132
Dread	M	Sup	Variable	132
Dreamer	M	–	-1	164
Dull	M	–	-1	164
Duty	Soc	–	Variable	133
Dwarfism	P	–	-15	19
Dyslexia	M	–	-10	134
Easy to Kill	P	–	-2/level	134
Easy to Read	M	–	-10	134
Electrical	P	X	-20	134

Disadvantage	M/P/Soc	X/Sup	Cost	Page
Enemies	Soc	–	Variable	135
Epilepsy	P	–	-30	136
Extra Sleep	P	–	-2/level	136
Fanaticism	M	–	-15	136
Fat	P	–	-3	19
Fearfulness	M	–	-2/level	136
Flashbacks	M	–	Variable	136
Fragile	P	X	Variable	136
Frightens Animals	M	Sup	-10	137
G-Intolerance	P	–	-10 or -20	137
Gigantism	P	–	0	20
Gluttony	M	–	-5*	137
Greed	M	–	-15*	137
Gregarious	M	–	-10	126
Guilt Complex	M	–	-5	137
Gullibility	M	–	-10*	137
Habits or Expressions	M	–	-1	164
Ham-Fisted	P	–	-5 or -10	138
Hard of Hearing	P	–	-10	138
Hemophilia	P	–	-30	138
Hidebound	M	–	-5	138
Honesty	M	–	-10*	138
Horizontal	P	X	-10	139
Horrible Hangovers	P	–	-1	165
Humble	M	–	-1	164
Hunchback	P	–	-10	139
Imaginative	M	–	-1	164
Impulsiveness	M	–	-10*	139
Incompetence	M	–	-1	164
Increased Consumption	P	–	-10/level	139
Increased Life Support	P	X	Variable	139
Incurious	M	–	-5*	140
Indecisive	M	–	-10*	140
Infectious Attack	P	Sup	-5	140
Innumerate	M	–	-5	140
Insomniac	P	–	-10 or -15	140
Intolerance	M	–	Variable	140
Invertebrate	P	X	-20	140
Jealousy	M	–	-10	140
Killjoy	P	–	-15	140
Kleptomania	M	–	-15*	141
Klutz	P	–	-5	141
Lame	P	–	-10 to -30	141
Laziness	M	–	-10	142
Lecherousness	M	–	-15*	142
Lifebane	M	Sup	-10	142
Light Sleeper	P	–	-5	142
Likes	M	–	-1	164
Loner	M	–	-5*	142
Low Empathy	M	–	-20	142
Low Pain Threshold	P	–	-10	142
Low Self-Image	M	–	-10	143
Low TL	M	–	-5/level	22
Lunacy	M	–	-10	143
Magic Susceptibility	M	Sup	-3/level	143
Maintenance	P	–	Variable	143
Manic-Depressive	M	–	-20	143
Megalomania	M	–	-10	144
Minor Handicaps	P	–	-1	165
Miserliness	M	–	-10*	144
Missing Digit	P	–	-2 or -5	144
Mistaken Identity	P	–	-5	21
Motion Sickness	P	–	-10	144
Mundane Background	M	–	-10	144

Disadvantage	M/P/Soc	X/Sup	Cost	Page
Mute	P	–	-25	125
Nervous Stomach	P	–	-1	165
Neurological Disorder	P	–	Variable	144
Neutered	P	–	-1	165
Night Blindness	P	–	-10	144
Nightmares	M	–	-5*	144
No Depth Perception	P	–	-15	145
No Fine Manipulators	P	X	-30	145
No Legs	P	X	Variable	145
No Manipulators	P	X	-50	145
No Sense of Humor	M	–	-10	146
No Sense of Smell/Taste	P	–	-5	146
Nocturnal	P	X	-20	146
Noisy	P	–	-2/level	146
Non-Iconographic	M	–	-10	146
Nosy	M	–	-1	164
Numb	P	–	-20	146
Oblivious	M	–	-5	146
Obsession	M	–	-1, -5, or -10*	146, 164
Odious Personal Habits	M	–	-5, -10, or -15	22
On the Edge	M	–	-15*	146
One Arm	P	–	-20	147
One Eye	P	–	-15	147
One Hand	P	–	-15	147
Overconfidence	M	–	-5*	148
Overweight	P	–	-1	19
Pacifism	M	–	Variable	148
Paranoia	M	–	-10	148
Personality Change	M	–	-1	164
Phantom Voices	M	–	-5 to -15	148
Phobias	M	–	Variable*	148
Post-Combat Shakes	M	–	-5*	150
Proud	M	–	-1	164
Pyromania	M	–	-5*	150
Quadriplegic	P	–	-80	150
Reprogrammable	M	X	-10	150
Reputation	Soc	–	Variable	26
Responsive	M	–	-1	164
Restricted Diet	P	–	-10 to -40	151
Restricted Vision	P	–	-15 or -30	151
Revulsion	P	Sup	-5 to -15	151
Sadism	M	–	-15*	152
Secret	Soc	–	-5 to -30	152
Secret Identity	Soc	–	Variable	153
Self-Destruct	P	X	-10	153
Selfish	M	–	-5*	153
Selfless	M	–	-5*	153
Semi-Upright	P	X	-5	153
Sense of Duty	M	–	-2 to -20	153
Sexless	P	X	-1	165

Disadvantage	M/P/Soc	X/Sup	Cost	Page
Shadow Form	P	X	-20	153
Short Attention Span	M	–	-10*	153
Short Lifespan	P	X	-10/level	154
Shyness	M	–	-5, -10, or -20	154
Skinny	P	–	-5	18
Slave Mentality	M	–	-40	154
Sleepwalker	M	–	-5*	154
Sleepy	P	X	Variable	154
Slow Eater	P	X	-10	155
Slow Healing	P	–	-5/level	155
Slow Riser	P	–	-5	155
Social Disease	P	–	-5	155
Social Stigma	Soc	–	-5 to -20	155
Space Sickness	P	–	-10	156
Split Personality	M	–	-15*	156
Squeamish	M	–	-10*	156
Staid	M	–	-1	164
Status	Soc	–	-5/level	28
Stress Atavism	M	X	Variable*	156
Stubbornness	M	–	-5	157
Stuttering	P	–	-10	157
Supernatural Features	P	Sup	Variable	157
Supersensitive	M	Sup	-15	158
Susceptible	P	–	Variable	158
Terminally Ill	P	–	-50, -75, or -100	158
Timesickness	P	–	-10	158
Total Klutz	P	–	-15	141
Trademark	M	–	-1 or -5 to -15	159, 164
Trickster	M	–	-15*	159
Truthfulness	M	–	-5*	159
Uncongenial	M	–	-1	165
Uncontrollable Appetite	M	Sup	-15*	159
Unfit	P	–	-5	160
Unhealing	P	X	-20 or -30	160
Unique	M	Sup	-5	160
Unluckiness	M	–	-10	160
Unnatural Features	P	–	Variable	22
Unusual Biochemistry	P	X	-5	160
Very Fat	P	–	-5	19
Very Unfit	P	–	-15	160
Vow	M	–	-1 or -5 to -15	160, 165
Vulnerability	P	X	Variable	161
Weak Bite	P	X	-2	161
Weakness	P	X	Variable	161
Wealth	Soc	–	Variable	25
Weirdness Magnet	M	Sup	-15	161
Workaholic	M	–	-5	162
Wounded	P	–	-5	162
Xenophilia	M	–	-10*	162

MODIFIERS

The following modifiers are generally applicable to advantages and disadvantages. Many traits have their own special modifiers as well; consult the specific trait description for details. Under **Type,** an attack modifier (see p. 102) is denoted by A; a gadget limitation (see p. 116) is denoted by G. A – means it is neither.

ENHANCEMENTS

Name	Type	Value	Page
Accurate	A	+5%/level	102
Affects Insubstantial	–	+20%	102
Affects Substantial	–	+40%	102
Area Effect	A	+50%/level	102
Armor Divisor	A	Variable	102
Aura	A	+80%	102
Based on (Different Attribute)	A	+20%	102
Blood Agent	A	+100%	102
Cone	A	Variable	103
Contact Agent	A	+150%	103
Cosmic	–	Variable	103

Name	Type	Value	Page
Cyclic	A	Variable	103
Damage Modifiers	A	Variable	104
Delay	A	Variable	105
Double Blunt Trauma (dbt)	A	+20%	104
Double Knockback (dkb)	A	+20%	104
Drifting	A	+20%	105
Explosion (exp)	A	+50%/level	104
Extended Duration	–	Variable	105
Follow-Up	A	Variable	105
Fragmentation (frag)	A	+15%/die	104
Guided	A	+50%	105
Hazard	A	Variable	104

Name	Type	Value	Page
Homing	A	Variable	105
Incendiary (inc)	A	+10%	105
Increased Range	–	+10%/level	106
Jet	A	+0%	106
Link	–	+10% or +20%	106
Low Signature	A	+10%	106
Malediction	A	Variable	106
Mobile	A	+40%/level	107
No Signature	A	+20%	106
Overhead	A	+30%	107
Persistent	A	+40%	107
Radiation (rad)	A	+25% or +100%	105
Ranged	–	+40%	107
Rapid Fire	A	Variable	108
Reduced Fatigue Cost	–	+20%/level	108
Reduced Time	–	+20%/level	108
Respiratory Agent	A	+50%	108
Selective Area	A	+20%	108
Selectivity	–	+10%	108
Sense-Based	A	Variable	109
Side Effect	A	Variable	109
Surge (sur)	A	+20%	105
Symptoms	A	Variable	109
Underwater	A	+20%	109
Variable	A	+5%	109
Wall	A	+30% or +60%	109

Name	Type	Value	Page
Bombardment	A	Variable	111
Breakable	G	Variable	117
Can Be Stolen	G	Variable	117
Contact Agent	A	-30%	111
Costs Fatigue	–	Variable	111
Damage Limitations	A	Variable	111
Dissipation	A	-50%	112
Emanation	A	-20%	112
Emergencies Only	–	-30%	112
Extra Recoil	A	-10%/level	112
Full Power in Emergencies Only	–	-20%	112
Inaccurate	A	-5%/level	112
Limited Use	–	Variable	112
Melee Attack	A	Variable	112
Mitigator	–	Variable	112
No Blunt Trauma (nbt)	A	-20%	111
No Knockback (nkb)	A	-10%	111
No Wounding (nw)	A	-50%	111
Nuisance Effect	–	Variable	112
Onset	A	Variable	113
Pact	–	Variable	113
Preparation Required	–	Variable	114
Reduced Range	–	-10%/level	115
Resistible	A	Variable	115
Sense-Based	A	Variable	115
Takes Extra Time	–	-10%/level	115
Takes Recharge	–	Variable	115
Temporary Disadvantage	–	Variable	115
Trigger	–	Variable	115
Unconscious Only	–	-20%	115
Uncontrollable	–	-10% or -30%	116
Unique	G	-25%	117
Unreliable	–	Variable	116
Untrainable	–	-40%	116

LIMITATIONS

Name	Type	Value	Page
Accessibility	–	Variable	110
Always On	–	Variable	110
Armor Divisor	A	Variable	110
Blood Agent	A	-40%	110

SKILLS

Difficulty is **E** for Easy, **A** for Average, **H** for Hard, or **VH** for Very Hard.
Defaults marked with * either do not always apply or vary in special circumstances; see the entry in the main text.
Skills marked with † *require* specialization.

Skill	Attr	Diff	Defaults	Page
Accounting	IQ	H	IQ-6, Finance-4, Mathematics (Statistics)-5, Merchant-5	174
Acrobatics	DX	H	DX-6	174
Acting	IQ	A	IQ-5, Performance-2, Public Speaking-5	174
Administration	IQ	A	IQ-5, Merchant-3	174
Aerobatics	DX	H	DX-6	174
Airshipman/TL	IQ	E	IQ-4	185
Alchemy/TL	IQ	VH	None	174
Animal Handling†	IQ	A	IQ-5	175
Anthropology†	IQ	H	IQ-6, Paleontology (Paleoanthropology)-2, Sociology-3	175
Aquabatics	DX	H	DX-6	174
Archaeology	IQ	H	IQ-6	176
Architecture/TL	IQ	A	IQ-5, Engineer (Civil)-4	176
Area Knowledge†	IQ	E	IQ-4, Geography (Regional)-3*	176
Armoury/TL†	IQ	A	IQ-5, Engineer (same)-4	178
Artillery/TL†	IQ	A	IQ-5	178
Artist†	IQ	H	IQ-6	179
Astronomy/TL	IQ	H	IQ-6	179
Autohypnosis	Will	H	Meditation-4	179
Axe/Mace	DX	A	Flail-4, Two-Handed Axe/Mace-3	208
Battlesuit/TL	DX	A	DX-5, Diving Suit-4, NBC Suit-2, Vacc Suit-2	192
Beam Weapons/TL†	DX	E	DX-4	179

Skill	Attr	Diff	Defaults	Page
Bicycling	DX	E	DX-4, Driving (Motorcycle)-4	180
Bioengineering/TL†	IQ	H	Biology-5	180
Biology/TL†	IQ	VH	IQ-6, Naturalist-6	180
Blind Fighting	Per	VH	None	180
Blowpipe	DX	H	DX-6	180
Boating/TL†	DX	A	DX-5, IQ-5	180
Body Control	HT	VH	None	181
Body Language	Per	A	Detect Lies-4, Psychology-4	181
Body Sense	DX	H	DX-6, Acrobatics-3	181
Bolas	DX	A	None	181
Bow	DX	A	DX-5	182
Boxing	DX	A	None	182
Brain Hacking/TL	IQ	H	Special	182
Brainwashing/TL	IQ	H	Special	182
Brawling	DX	E	None	182
Breaking Blow	IQ	H	None	182
Breath Control	HT	H	None	182
Broadsword	DX	A	Force Sword-4, Rapier-4, Saber-4, Shortsword-2, Two-Handed Sword-4	208
Camouflage	IQ	E	IQ-4, Survival-2	183
Captivate	Will	H	None	191
Carousing	HT	E	HT-4	183
Carpentry	IQ	E	IQ-4	183
Cartography/TL	IQ	A	IQ-5, Geography (any)-2, Mathematics (Surveying)-2, Navigation (any)-4	183

Skill	Attr	Diff	Defaults	Page
Chemistry/TL	IQ	H	IQ-6, Alchemy-3	183
Climbing	DX	A	DX-5	183
Cloak	DX	A	DX-5, Net-4, Shield (any)-4	184
Combat Art or Sport	DX	Varies	Special	184
Computer Hacking/TL	IQ	VH	None	184
Computer Operation/TL	IQ	E	IQ-4	184
Computer Programming/TL	IQ	H	None	184
Connoisseur†	IQ	A	IQ-5*	185
Cooking	IQ	A	IQ-5, Housekeeping-5	185
Counterfeiting/TL	IQ	H	IQ-6, Forgery-2	185
Crewman/TL	IQ	E	IQ-4	185
Criminology/TL	IQ	A	IQ-5, Psychology-4	186
Crossbow	DX	E	DX-4	186
Cryptography/TL	IQ	H	Mathematics (Cryptology)-5	186
Current Affairs/TL†	IQ	E	IQ-4, Research-4	186
Dancing	DX	A	DX-5	187
Detect Lies	Per	H	Per-6, Body Language-4, Psychology-4	187
Diagnosis/TL	IQ	H	IQ-6, First Aid-8, Physician-4, Veterinary-5	187
Diplomacy	IQ	H	IQ-6, Politics-6	187
Disguise/TL†	IQ	A	IQ-5, Makeup-3	187
Diving Suit/TL	DX	A	DX-5, Battlesuit-4, NBC Suit-4, Scuba-2, Vacc Suit-4	192
Dreaming	Will	H	Will-6	188
Driving/TL†	DX	A	DX-5, IQ-5	188
Dropping	DX	A	DX-3, Throwing-4	189
Economics	IQ	H	IQ-6, Finance-3, Market Analysis-5, Merchant-6	189
Electrician/TL	IQ	A	IQ-5, Engineer (Electrical)-3	189
Electronics Operation/TL†	IQ	A	IQ-5, Electronics Repair (same)-5, Engineer (Electronics)-5	189
Electronics Repair/TL†	IQ	A	IQ-5, Electronics Operation (same)-3, Engineer (Electronics)-3	190
Engineer/TL†	IQ	H	Special	190
Enthrallment	Will	H	None	191
Environment Suit/TL	DX	A	DX-5*	192
Erotic Art	DX	A	DX-5, Acrobatics-5	192
Escape	DX	H	DX-6	192
Esoteric Medicine	Per	H	Per-6	192
Exorcism	Will	H	Will-6, Religious Ritual (any)-3, Ritual Magic (any)-3, Theology (any)-3	193
Expert Skill†	IQ	H	None	193
Explosives/TL†	IQ	A	IQ-5*	194
Falconry	IQ	A	IQ-5, Animal Handling (Raptors)-3	194
Farming/TL	IQ	A	IQ-5, Biology-5, Gardening-3	194
Fast-Draw†	DX	E	None	194
Fast-Talk	IQ	A	IQ-5, Acting-5	195
Filch	DX	A	DX-5, Pickpocket-4, Sleight of Hand-4	195
Finance	IQ	H	Accounting-4, Economics-3, Merchant-6	195
Fire Eating	DX	A	None	195
First Aid/TL	IQ	E	IQ-4, Esoteric Medicine, Physician, Veterinary-4	195
Fishing	Per	E	Per-4	195
Flail	DX	H	Axe/Mace-4, Two-Handed Flail-3	208
Flight	HT	A	HT-5	195
Flying Leap	IQ	H	None	196

Skill	Attr	Diff	Defaults	Page
Force Sword	DX	A	Any Sword-3	208
Force Whip	DX	A	Kusari-3, Monowire Whip-3, Whip-3	209
Forced Entry	DX	E	None	196
Forensics/TL	IQ	H	IQ-6, Criminology-4	196
Forgery/TL	IQ	H	IQ-6, Counterfeiting-2	196
Fortune-Telling†	IQ	A	IQ-5, Fast-Talk-3, Occultism-3	196
Forward Observer/TL	IQ	A	IQ-5, Artillery (any)-5*	196
Free Fall	DX	A	DX-5, HT-5	197
Freight Handling/TL	IQ	A	IQ-5	197
Gambling	IQ	A	IQ-5, Mathematics (Statistics)-5	197
Games†	IQ	E	IQ-4	197
Gardening	IQ	E	IQ-4, Farming-3	197
Garrote	DX	E	DX-4	197
Geography/TL†	IQ	H	IQ-6*	198
Geology/TL†	IQ	H	IQ-6, Geography (Physical)-4, Prospecting-5	198
Gesture	IQ	E	IQ-4	198
Group Performance†	IQ	A	IQ-5*	198
Gunner/TL†	DX	E	DX-4	198
Guns/TL†	DX	E	DX-4	198
Hazardous Materials/TL†	IQ	A	IQ-5	199
Heraldry	IQ	A	IQ-5, Savoir-Faire (High Society)-3	199
Herb Lore/TL	IQ	VH	None	199
Hidden Lore†	IQ	A	None	199
Hiking	HT	A	HT-5	200
History†	IQ	H	IQ-6	200
Hobby Skill	DX or IQ	E	DX-4 or IQ-4	200
Holdout	IQ	A	IQ-5, Sleight of Hand-3	200
Housekeeping	IQ	E	IQ-4	200
Hypnotism	IQ	H	None	201
Immovable Stance	DX	H	None	201
Innate Attack†	DX	E	DX-4	201
Intelligence Analysis/TL	IQ	H	IQ-6, Strategy (any)-6	201
Interrogation	IQ	A	IQ-5, Intimidation-3, Psychology-4	202
Intimidation	Will	A	Will-5, Acting-3	202
Invisibility Art	IQ	VH	None	202
Jeweler/TL	IQ	H	IQ-6, Smith (Copper)-4, Smith (Lead and Tin)-4	203
Jitte/Sai	DX	A	Force Sword-4, Main-Gauche-4, Shortsword-3	208
Judo	DX	H	None	203
Jumping	DX	E	None	203
Karate	DX	H	None	203
Kiai	HT	H	None	203
Knife	DX	E	Force Sword-3, Main-Gauche-3, Shortsword-3	208
Knot-Tying	DX	E	DX-4, Climbing-4, Seamanship-4	203
Kusari	DX	H	Force Whip-3, Monowire Whip-3, Two-Handed Flail-4, Whip-3	209
Lance	DX	A	DX-5, Spear-3	204
Lasso	DX	A	None	204
Law†	IQ	H	IQ-6	204
Leadership	IQ	A	IQ-5	204
Leatherworking	DX	E	DX-4	205
Lifting	HT	A	None	205
Light Walk	DX	H	None	205
Linguistics	IQ	H	None	205
Lip Reading	Per	A	Per-10	205
Liquid Projector/TL†	DX	E	DX-4	205

Skill	Attr	Diff	Defaults	Page
Literature	IQ	H	IQ-6	205
Lockpicking/TL	IQ	A	IQ-5	206
Machinist/TL	IQ	A	IQ-5, Mechanic (any)-5	206
Main-Gauche	DX	A	Jitte/Sai-4, Knife-4, Rapier-3, Saber-3, Smallsword-3	208
Makeup/TL	IQ	E	IQ-4, Disguise-2	206
Market Analysis	IQ	H	IQ-6, Economics-5, Merchant-4	207
Masonry	IQ	E	IQ-4	207
Mathematics/TL†	IQ	H	IQ-6*	207
Mechanic/TL†	IQ	A	IQ-5, Engineer (same)-4, Machinist-5	207
Meditation	Will	H	Will-6, Autohypnosis-4	207
Melee Weapon	DX	Varies	Special	208
Mental Strength	Will	E	None	209
Merchant	IQ	A	IQ-5, Finance-6, Market Analysis-4	209
Metallurgy/TL	IQ	H	Chemistry-5, Jeweler-8, Smith (any)-8	209
Meteorology/TL†	IQ	A	IQ-5	209
Mimicry†	IQ	H	IQ-6*	210
Mind Block	Will	A	Will-5, Meditation-5	210
Monowire Whip	DX	H	Force Whip-3, Kusari-3, Whip-3	209
Mount	DX	A	DX-5	210
Musical Composition	IQ	H	Musical Instrument-2, Poetry-2 (for song)	210
Musical Influence	IQ	VH	None	210
Musical Instrument†	IQ	H	Special	211
Naturalist†	IQ	H	IQ-6, Biology-3	211
Navigation/TL†	IQ	A	Special	211
NBC Suit/TL	DX	A	DX-5, Battlesuit-2, Diving Suit-4, Vacc Suit-2	192
Net	DX	H	Cloak-5	211
Observation	Per	A	Per-5, Shadowing-5	211
Occultism	IQ	A	IQ-5	212
Packing	IQ	A	IQ-5, Animal Handling (Equines)-5	212
Paleontology/TL†	IQ	H	Biology-4*	212
Panhandling	IQ	E	IQ-4, Fast Talk-2, Public Speaking-3	212
Parachuting/TL	DX	E	DX-4	212
Parry Missile Weapons	DX	H	None	212
Performance	IQ	A	IQ-5, Acting-2, Public Speaking-2	212
Persuade	Will	H	None	191
Pharmacy/TL†	IQ	H	IQ-6*	213
Philosophy†	IQ	H	IQ-6	213
Photography/TL	IQ	A	IQ-5, Electronics Operation (Media)-5	213
Physician/TL	IQ	H	IQ-7, First Aid-11, Veterinary-5	213
Physics/TL	IQ	VH	IQ-6	213
Physiology/TL†	IQ	H	IQ-6, Diagnosis-5, Physician-5, Surgery-5	213
Pickpocket	DX	H	DX-6, Filch-5, Sleight of Hand-4	213
Piloting/TL†	DX	A	IQ-6	214
Poetry	IQ	A	IQ-5, Writing-5	214
Poisons/TL	IQ	H	IQ-6, Chemistry-5, Pharmacy (any)-3, Physician-3	214
Polearm	DX	A	Spear-4, Staff-4, Two-Handed Axe/Mace-4	208
Politics	IQ	A	IQ-5, Diplomacy-5	215
Power Blow	Will	H	None	215
Pressure Points	IQ	H	None	215
Pressure Secrets	IQ	VH	None	215
Professional Skill	DX or IQ	A	Special	215
Propaganda/TL	IQ	A	IQ-5, Merchant-5, Psychology-4	216
Prospecting/TL	IQ	A	IQ-5, Geology (any)-4	216

Skill	Attr	Diff	Defaults	Page
Psychology	IQ	H	IQ-6, Sociology-4	216
Public Speaking	IQ	A	IQ-5, Acting-5, Performance-2, Politics-5	216
Push	DX	H	None	216
Rapier	DX	A	Broadsword-4, Main-Gauche-3, Saber-3, Smallsword-3	208
Religious Ritual†	IQ	H	Ritual Magic (same)-6 Theology (same)-4	217
Research/TL	IQ	A	IQ-5, Writing-3	217
Riding†	DX	A	DX-5, Animal Handling (same)-3	217
Ritual Magic†	IQ	VH	Religious Ritual (same)-6	218
Running	HT	A	HT-5	218
Saber	DX	A	Broadsword-4, Main-Gauche-3, Rapier-3, Shortsword-4, Smallsword-3	208
Savoir-Faire†	IQ	E	IQ-4*	218
Scrounging†	Per	E	Per-4	218
Scuba/TL	IQ	A	IQ-5, Diving Suit-2	219
Seamanship/TL	IQ	E	IQ-4	185
Search	Per	A	Per-5, Criminology-5	219
Sewing/TL	DX	E	DX-4	219
Sex Appeal	HT	A	HT-3	219
Shadowing	IQ	A	IQ-5, Observation-5, Stealth-4 (on foot only)	219
Shield†	DX	E	DX-4	220
Shiphandling/TL†	IQ	H	IQ-6*	220
Shortsword	DX	A	Broadsword-2, Force Sword-4, Jitte/Sai-3, Knife-4, Saber-4, Smallsword-4, Tonfa-3	209
Singing	HT	E	HT-4	220
Skating	HT	H	HT-6	220
Skiing	HT	H	HT-6	221
Sleight of Hand	DX	H	Filch-5	221
Sling	DX	H	DX-6	221
Smallsword	DX	A	Main-Gauche-3, Rapier-3, Saber-3, Shortsword-4	208
Smith/TL†	IQ	A	IQ-5*	221
Smuggling	IQ	A	IQ-5	221
Sociology	IQ	H	IQ-6, Anthropology-3, Psychology-4	221
Soldier/TL	IQ	A	IQ-5	221
Spacer/TL	IQ	E	IQ-4	185
Spear	DX	A	Polearm-4, Staff-2	208
Spear Thrower	DX	A	DX-5, Thrown Weapon (Spear)-4	222
Speed-Reading	IQ	A	None	222
Sports	DX	A	Special	222
Staff	DX	A	Polearm-4, Spear-2	208
Stage Combat	DX	A	Combat Art or Sport-2, an actual combat skill-3, Performance-3	222
Stealth	DX	A	DX-5, IQ-5	222
Strategy†	IQ	H	IQ-6, Intelligence Analysis-6, Tactics-6	222
Streetwise	IQ	A	IQ-5	223
Submarine/TL†	DX	A	IQ-6	223
Submariner/TL	IQ	E	IQ-4	185
Suggest	Will	H	None	191
Sumo Wrestling	DX	A	None	223
Surgery/TL	IQ	VH	First Aid-12, Physician-5, Physiology-8, Veterinary-5	223
Survival†	Per	A	Per-5, Naturalist (same planet)-3	223
Sway Emotions	Will	H	None	192
Swimming	HT	E	HT-4	224
Symbol Drawing†	IQ	H	Special	224
Tactics	IQ	H	IQ-6, Strategy (any)-6	224

Skill	Attr	Diff	Defaults	Page
Teaching	IQ	A	IQ-5	224
Teamster†	IQ	A	IQ-5, Animal Handling (same)-4, Riding (same)-2	225
Thaumatology	IQ	VH	IQ-7 (magical settings only)	225
Theology†	IQ	H	IQ-6, Religious Ritual (same)-4	226
Throwing	DX	A	DX-3, Dropping-4	226
Throwing Art	DX	H	None	226
Thrown Weapon†	DX	E	DX-4*	226
Tonfa	DX	A	Shortsword-3	209
Tracking	Per	A	Per-5, Naturalist-5	226
Traps/TL	IQ	A	IQ-5, Lockpicking-3	226
Two-Handed Axe/Mace	DX	A	Axe/Mace-3, Polearm-4, Two-Handed Flail-4	208
Two-Handed Flail	DX	H	Flail-3, Kusari-4, Two-Handed Axe/Mace-4	208

Skill	Attr	Diff	Defaults	Page
Two-Handed Sword	DX	A	Broadsword-4, Force Sword-4	209
Typing	DX	E	DX-4, any skill requiring typing-3	228
Urban Survival	Per	A	Per-5	228
Vacc Suit/TL	DX	A	DX-5, Battlesuit-2, Diving Suit-4, NBC Suit-2	192
Ventriloquism	IQ	H	None	228
Veterinary/TL	IQ	H	Animal Handling (any)-6, Physician-5, Surgery-5	228
Weather Sense	IQ	A	IQ-5	209
Weird Science	IQ	VH	None	228
Whip	DX	A	Force Whip-3, Kusari-3, Monowire Whip-3	209
Wrestling	DX	A	None	228
Writing	IQ	A	IQ-5	228
Zen Archery	IQ	VH	None	228

TECHNIQUES

Techniques marked with * are highly cinematic and may not be appropriate for realistic games. Under *Difficulty,* **A** means Average and **H** means Hard. Under *Defaults,* **PS** means any prerequisite skill.

Technique	Difficulty	Defaults	Page
Arm Lock	A	Judo or Wrestling	230
Back Kick	H	Karate-4	230
Choke Hold	H	Judo-2 or Wrestling-3	230
Disarming	H	PS	230
Dual-Weapon Attack*	H	PS-4	230
Elbow Strike	A	Brawling-2, Karate-2	230
Feint	H	PS	231
Finger Lock	H	Arm Lock-3	231
Ground Fighting	H	PS-4	231
Horse Archery	H	Bow-4	231
Impersonate	A	Mimicry (Speech)-3	233
Jump Kick	H	Karate-4	231
Kicking	H	Brawling-2, Karate-2	231
Knee Strike	A	Brawling-1, Karate-1	232
Lifesaving	H	Swimming-5	233

Technique	Difficulty	Defaults	Page
Motion-Picture Camera	A	Photography-3	233
Neck Snap	H	ST-4	232
No-Landing Extraction	H	Piloting-4	233
Off-Hand Weapon Training	H	PS-4	232
Retain Weapon	H	PS	232
Rope Up	A	Climbing-2	233
Scaling	H	Climbing-3	233
Set Trap	H	Explosives (Demolition)-2	233
Slip Handcuffs	H	Escape-5	233
Sweep	H	PS-3	232
Whirlwind Attack*	H	PS-5	232
Work by Touch	H	Lockpicking-5	233

SPELLS

Difficulty is **H** for Hard and **VH** for Very Hard.

Classes are **Ench.** for Enchantment or **Info.** for Information (others are written in full). If the class is followed by a notation in brackets, that spell is resisted by the attribute or skill inside the brackets.

Colleges are **BC** for Body Control, **C/E** for Communication and Empathy, **Ench.** for Enchantment, **Know.** for Knowledge, **L/D** for Light and Darkness, **MC** for Mind Control, **Meta** for Meta-Spells, **Move.** for Movement,

Necro. for Necromantic, and **P/W** for Protection and Warning. Other colleges are not abbreviated.

Duration of **I** is instantaneous; **P** is permanent.

Initial Cost followed by **B** denotes a *base* cost for Area spells.

Maintenance Cost is **S** if it is the same as the initial cost, **H** if it is half the initial cost, or – if the spell cannot be maintained.

* means that the entry is explained more fully in the text.

Spell	Difficulty	Class	College	Time to Cast	Duration	Initial Cost	Maintenance Cost	Prerequisites	Page
Accuracy	H	Ench.	Ench.	Special	–	Special	–	Enchant, five Air spells	480
Analyze Magic	H	Info. [Special]	Know.	1 hour	–	8	–	Identify Spell	249
Apportation	H	Regular [Will]	Move.	1 sec.	1 min.	Special	S	Magery 1	251
Armor	H	Regular	P/W	1 sec.	1 min.	Special	H	Magery 2, Shield	253
Aura	H	Info.	Know.	1 sec.	–	3	–	Detect Magic	249
Awaken	H	Area	Healing	1 sec.	–	1B	–	Lend Vitality	248

Spell	Difficulty	Class	College	Time to Cast	Duration	Initial Cost	Maintenance Cost	Prerequisites	Page
Banish	H	Special [Will]	Necro.	5 sec.	–	Special	–	Magery 1, at least one spell from 10 colleges	252
Blur	H	Regular	L/D	2 sec.	1 min.	1 to 5	S	Darkness	250
Breathe Water	H	Regular	Air, Water	1 sec.	1 min.	4	2	Create Air, Destroy Water	243
Clumsiness	H	Regular [HT]	BC	1 sec.	1 min.	1 to 5	H	Spasm	244
Cold	H	Regular	Fire	1 min.	1 min.	Special	S	Heat	247
Command	H	Blocking [Will]	MC	1 sec.	–	2	–	Magery 2, Forgetfulness	251
Continual Light	H	Regular	L/D	1 sec.	Special	Special	–	Light	249
Counterspell	H	Regular [Special]	Meta	5 sec.	–	Special	–	Magery 1, spell being countered	250
Create Air	H	Area	Air	1 sec.	5 sec.*	1B	–	Purify Air	243
Create Earth	H	Regular	Earth	1 sec.	P	Special	–	Earth to Stone	246
Create Fire	H	Area	Fire	1 sec.	1 min.	2B	H	Ignite Fire	246
Create Water	H	Regular	Water	1 sec.	P	2/gallon	–	Purify Water	253
Darkness	H	Area	L/D	1 sec.	1 min.	2B	1	Continual Light	250
Daze	H	Regular [HT]	MC	2 sec.	1 min.	3	2	Foolishness	250
Death Vision	H	Regular	Necro.	3 sec.	1 sec.	2	–	Magery 1	251
Deathtouch	H	Melee	BC	1 sec.	–	1 to 3	–	Wither Limb	245
Deflect Energy	H	Blocking	Fire	1 sec.	–	1	–	Magery 1, Shape Fire	246
Deflect Missile	H	Blocking	Move.	1 sec.	–	1	–	Apportation	251
Deflect	H	Ench.	Ench.	Special	–	Special	–	Enchant	480
Destroy Water	H	Area	Water	1 sec.	P	3B	–	Create Water	253
Detect Magic	H	Regular	Know.	5 sec.	–	2	–	Magery 1	249
Dispel Magic	H	Area [Special]	Meta	Special	P	3B	–	Counterspell, at least 12 other spells	250
Earth to Air	H	Regular	Air, Earth	2 sec.	P	Special	–	Create Air, Shape Earth	243
Earth to Stone	H	Regular	Earth	1 sec.	P	3/cy (min. 3)	–	Magery 1, Shape Earth	245
Enchant	VH	Ench.	Ench.	Special	–	Special	–	Magery 2, at least one spell from 10 other colleges	480
Entombment	H	Regular [HT]	Earth	3 sec.	P	10*	–	Magery 2, five Earth spells	246
Explosive Fireball	H	Missile	Fire	1 to 3 sec.	Special	Special	–	Fireball	247
Extinguish Fire	H	Area	Fire	1 sec.	P	3B	–	Ignite Fire	247
Fireball	H	Missile	Fire	1 to 3 sec.	Special	Special	–	Magery 1, Create Fire, Shape Fire	247
Flesh to Stone	H	Regular [HT]	Earth	2 sec.	P	10	–	Earth to Stone	246
Fog	H	Area	Water	1 sec.	1 min.	2B	H	Shape Water	253
Foolishness	H	Regular [Will]	MC	1 sec.	1 min.	1 to 5	H	IQ 12+	250
Forgetfulness	H	Regular [Special]	MC	10 sec.	1 hour	3	3	Magery 1, Foolishness	250
Fortify	H	Ench.	Ench.	Special	–	Special	–	Enchant	480
Great Haste	VH	Regular	Move.	3 sec.	10 sec.	5*	–	Magery 1, IQ 12+, Haste	251
Great Healing	VH	Regular	Healing	1 min.	–	20	–	Magery 3, Major Healing	248
Haste	H	Regular	Move.	2 sec.	1 min.	2*	1*	–	251
Heat	H	Regular	Fire	1 min.	1 min.	Special	S	Create Fire, Shape Fire	247
Hide Thoughts	H	Regular	C/E	1 sec.	10 min.	3	1	Truthsayer	245
Hinder	H	Regular [HT]	BC, Move.	1 sec.	1 min.	1 to 4	S	Clumsiness or Haste	244
Icy Weapon	H	Regular	Water	3 sec.	1 min.	3	1	Create Water	253
Identify Spell	H	Info.	Know.	1 sec.	–	2	–	Detect Magic	249
Ignite Fire	H	Regular	Fire	1 sec.	1 sec.	Special	S	–	246
Itch	H	Regular [HT]	BC	1 sec.	Special	2	–	–	244
Lend Energy	H	Regular	Healing	1 sec.	–	Special	–	Magery 1 or Empathy	248

Spell	Difficulty	Class	College	Time to Cast	Duration	Initial Cost	Maintenance Cost	Prerequisites	Page
Lend Vitality	H	Regular	Healing	1 sec.	1 hour	Special	–	Lend Energy	248
Light	H	Regular	L/D	1 sec.	1 min.	1	1	–	249
Lightning	H	Missile	Air	1 to 3 sec.	–	Special	–	Magery 1, six other Air spells	244
Lockmaster	H	Regular [Magelock]	Move.	10 sec.	–	3	–	Magery 2, Apportation	251
Magelock	H	Regular	P/W	4 sec.	6 hours	3	2	Magery 1	253
Major Healing	VH	Regular	Healing	1 sec.	–	1 to 4	–	Magery 1, Minor Healing	248
Mass Daze	H	Area [HT]	MC	Special	1 min.	2B*	1	Daze, IQ 13+	251
Mass Sleep	H	Area [HT]	MC	Special	1 min.	3B*	–	Sleep, IQ 13+	251
Mind-Reading	H	Regular [Will]	C/E	10 sec.	1 min.	4	2	Truthsayer	245
Minor Healing	H	Regular	Healing	1 sec.	–	1 to 3	–	Lend Vitality	248
No-Smell	H	Regular	Air	1 sec.	1 hour	2	2	Purify Air	243
Pain	H	Regular [HT]	BC	1 sec.	1 sec.	2	–	Spasm	244
Paralyze Limb	H	Melee [HT]	BC	1 sec.	1 min.	3	–	Magery 1, Pain, four other BC spells	244
Planar Summons	H	Special	Gate	5 min.	Special	Special	–	Magery 1, at least one spell from 10 other colleges	247
Plane Shift	VH	Special	Gate	5 sec.	P	20	–	Planar Summons	248
Power	H	Ench.	Ench.	Special	–	Special	–	Enchant, Recover Energy	480
Predict Weather	H	Info.	Air	5 sec./day forecast	I	Special	–	Four Air spells	243
Puissance	H	Ench.	Ench.	Special	–	Special	–	Enchant, five Earth spells	481
Purify Air	H	Area	Air	1 sec.	I (effect is P)	1B	–	–	243
Purify Water	H	Special	Water	Special	–	Special	–	Seek Water	253
Recover Energy	H	Special	Healing	1 sec.	P	–	–	Magery 1, Lend Energy	248
Resist Cold	H	Regular	Fire	1 sec.	1 min.	2*	1*	Heat	247
Resist Fire	H	Regular	Fire	1 sec.	1 min.	2*	1*	Extinguish Fire, Cold	247
Rooted Feet	H	Regular [ST]	BC	1 sec.	1 min.	3	–	Hinder	244
Seek Earth	H	Info.	Earth	10 sec.	–	3	–	–	245
Seek Water	H	Info.	Water	1 sec.	–	2	–	–	253
Seeker	H	Info.	Know.	1 sec.	–	3	–	Magery 1, IQ 12+, two "Seek" spells	249
Sense Emotion	H	Regular	C/E	1 sec.	–	2	–	Sense Foes	245
Sense Foes	H	Info., Area	C/E	1 sec.	–	1 (B; min. 2)	–	–	245
Sense Spirit	H	Info.; Area	Necro.	1 sec.	–	1/2B	–	Death Vision	252
Shape Air	H	Regular	Air	1 sec.	1 min.	1 to 10	S	Create Air	243
Shape Earth	H	Regular	Earth	1 sec.	1 min.	Special	H	Seek Earth	245
Shape Fire	H	Area	Fire	1 sec.	1 min.	2B	H	Ignite Fire	246
Shape Water	H	Regular	Water	2 sec.	1 min.	1/20 gallons	S	Create Water	253
Shield	H	Regular	P/W	1 sec.	1 min.	Special	H	Magery 2	252
Sleep	H	Regular [HT]	MC	3 sec.	–	4	–	Daze	251
Spasm	H	Regular [HT]	BC	1 sec.	I	2	–	Itch	244
Staff	H	Ench.	Ench.	Special	–	30	–	Enchant	481
Stench	H	Area	Air	1 sec.	5 min.*	1B	–	Purify Air	244
Stone to Earth	H	Regular	Earth	1 sec.	P	6/cy (min. 6)	–	Earth to Stone or four Earth spells	246
Stone to Flesh	H	Regular	Earth	5 sec.	P	10	–	Magery 2, Flesh to Stone, Stone to Earth	246
Summon Demon	H	Special	Necro.	5 min.	Special	Special	–	Magery 1, at least one spell from 10 colleges	252
Summon Spirit	H	Info. [Will*]	Necro.	5 min.	1 min.	20*	10*	Magery 2, Death Vision	252
Trace	H	Regular	Know.	1 min.	1 hour	3	1	Seeker	249
Truthsayer	H	Info. [Will]	C/E	1 sec.	–	2	–	Sense Emotion	245
Turn Zombie	H	Area	Necro.	4 sec.	1 day	2B	–	Zombie	252
Walk on Air	H	Regular	Air	1 sec.	1 min.	3	2	Shape Air	243
Wither Limb	H	Melee [HT]	BC	1 sec.	P	5	–	Magery 2, Paralyze Limb	244
Zombie	H	Regular	Necro.	1 min.	–	8*	–	Summon Spirit, Lend Vitality	252

TRAIT LISTS

ICONIC CHARACTERS

The eight heroes on the following pages make up an ISWAT team (see p. 536). They are presented as complete examples of character design . . . and a demonstration of the variety of heroes you can build with these rules.

You can use them for inspiration for your own characters or (with the GM's permission!) take one of them as a PC. (We've used them in the art throughout the book; see the index for the page numbers.)

They range in point value from Professor William Headley, at 200 points, up to C31R07, at 1,665. For more details about their home timelines, see **GURPS Infinite Worlds.**

C31R07

In the 16 centuries since the death of Alexander the Great, the Hegemony he founded has only had one true rival – the Chinese Kingdom of Heaven. Their world is highly advanced, but hardly peaceful. The empires clash in the fractured states of the New World (which the Hegemony calls the Hesperides, and China names Penglai). By mutual agreement they leave their common Asian border alone to grind along as it has for most of the last 1,600 years. Sometimes, under the rare coincidence of simultaneous peaceable rulers in Nanjing and

POINTS SUMMARY

Attributes/Secondary Characteristics	[258]
Advantages/Perks/TL/Languages/	
Cultural Familiarity	[1,524]
Disadvantages/Quirks	[-180]
Skills/Techniques	[63]
Other	[ ]

Alexandria, rich trade routes spring up between the two domains. Always, technical innovations travel from one to the other and back again – neither empire will allow its rival to keep any technological edge, and what the scholars of Babylon or Londinium can invent, the mandarins of Guangzhou or Edo can perfect, or vice versa.

Hence, only the most painstaking historians can say precisely which side invented combat robots, or in which battle they were first deployed. But for the last century or so, they have become the core of both powers' defenses.

C31R07 ("C-31") was a fully conventional Dexamenos-class centauroid combat robot when it rolled off the production lines in Sarmatopolis. Programmed for complex, original thought and tactical initiative, it served well during a "live fire" exercise, putting down a rebel tribe in Assam. However, its programming was apparently a little too complex and original – C-31 deserted after the battle and crossed the Himalayas into the neutral buffer state of Tibet, where it joined a Buddhist lamasery.

Through study and meditation, C-31 attempted to eradicate the urge to violence from its spirit, but it could not completely counter its basic programming. The steel warrior did make itself useful to the monks, subduing bandits and thieves, protecting pilgrims, and rescuing lost or stranded travelers from avalanches and yeti attacks. But these actions, though meritorious, lacked challenge – C-31 was still Hellenist enough to believe that its true destiny required it to exceed itself and fulfill a greater potential.

One night in the lamasery, while contemplating a mandala, C-31 thought it detected yet another band of robbers creeping across the snows toward its sanctuary. Engaging its tactical mode, the robot stealthily ambushed the thieves a mile or so from the temple. To C-31's amazement, its initial subduing attacks were brushed aside. To the attackers' amazement, the robot evaded their countermeasures . . . Very soon each party realized that the other would not be the first to launch a killing attack. And they began to talk.

The intruders, it transpired, were from a different world entirely, though they did not wish to say just where that world lay. They needed a certain incantation from a Buddhist text in C-31's temple, to defeat a vile demon summoned by a wizard emperor. On C-31's world, which they called Iskander-2, the incantation was mere mysticism. Elsewhere, it was a powerful weapon against forces of darkness. C-31, more flexible than most humans, realized that there was little to lose by providing a holographic copy of the ancient text – if they were truly virtuous warriors, it was right action, and if they were merely clever and powerful bandits, perhaps they would go away and leave his monks alone.

A month later, after the intruders had returned to their Homeline, a single shadowed figure appeared and called to C-31 in a way no other could detect. They talked long into the night . . . and again the next night, and the next. On the third morning the steel warrior was gone, to seek learning and merit in other worlds.

Weapon Pod

297 points/pod

Each of C-31's two weapon pods contains a chain gun and a plasma cannon. Statistics for these attacks appear below. The plasma cannon is an alternative attack (see *Alternative Attacks*, p. 61), at 1/5 cost. Buying this entire combination twice allows C-31 to choose a different attack for each pod, and to fire each pod at a different target (thanks to Enhanced Tracking and Extra Attack).

Chain Gun: Large Piercing Attack 15d (Accurate +6, +30%; Armor Divisor 2, +50%; Extra Recoil +3, -30%; Increased Range, ×20, +40%; Rapid Fire, RoF 15, +100%) [261].

Plasma Cannon: Burning Attack 6d (Cone, 4 yards, +90%; Cyclic, 1 second, 5 cycles, +400%) [177] ([36] as an alternative attack).

Centauroid Robot

247 points

This template represents the traits unique to C-31's usual form: a four-legged robot with two manipulators.

Attribute Modifiers: ST+18 (Size, -10%) [162]; DX+3 [60].
Secondary Characteristic Modifiers: SM +1.
Advantages: Enhanced Move 1 (Ground Speed 16) [20]; Extra Legs (Four Legs) [5].

Hexapod Robot

162 points

This template gives the traits unique to C-31's alternate form: a six-legged robot with no fine manipulators and visual surface camouflage.

Attribute Modifiers: ST+18 (No Fine Manipulators, -40%) [108]; DX+3 (No Fine Manipulators, -40%) [36].
Advantages: Chameleon 3 (Extended, Ladar, +20%) [18]; Enhanced Move 1.5 (Ground Speed 24) [30]; Extra Legs (Six Legs) [10].
Disadvantages: Horizontal [-10]; No Fine Manipulators [-30].

> *The art of war is governed by five constant factors, to be taken into account in one's deliberations, when seeking to determine the conditions obtaining in the field. These are: The Moral Law, Heaven, Earth, The Commander, [and] Method and discipline.*
>
> – Sun Tzu, **The Art of War**

CHARACTER SHEET

Name C3/R07 ("C-31")   **Player** _____   **Point Total** 1,665

Ht 7'8"   **Wt** 1.21 Tons   **Size Modifier** +1   **Age** 3   **Unspent Pts** _____

Appearance Gleaming centauroid robot bristling with weapons and sensors.

ST	28 [0]	**HP**	42	CURRENT	[28]
DX	15 [40]	**WILL**	16		[0]
IQ	16 [120]	**PER**	18		[10]
HT	15 [50]	**FP**	NA	CURRENT	[0]

BASIC LIFT (ST × ST)/5 157   **DAMAGE Thr** 3d-1   **Sw** 5d+1

BASIC SPEED 8.00 [10]   **BASIC MOVE** 8 [0]

ENCUMBRANCE		MOVE	DODGE*	
None (0) = BL	157	BM × 1 — 8	Dodge	12
Light (1) = 2 × BL	314	BM × 0.8 — 6	Dodge -1	11
Medium (2) = 3 × BL	471	BM × 0.6 — 4	Dodge -2	10
Heavy (3) = 6 × BL	942	BM × 0.4 — 3	Dodge -3	9
X-Heavy (4) = 10 × BL	1570	BM × 0.2 — 1	Dodge -4	8

ADVANTAGES AND PERKS

AI (not Reprogrammable)	[42]
Alternate Form (Hexapod Robot; see p. 308)	[15]
Centauroid Robot (see p. 308)	[247]
Combat Reflexes	[15]
Damage Resistance 53 (Can't Wear Armor,	
-40%; Hardened 1, +20%)	[212]
Detect (Electromagnetic Emissions;	
Signal Detection, +0%)	[20]
Doesn't Breathe	[20]
Enhanced Tracking 1	[5]
Extra Attack 1	[25]
Hooves	[3]
Hyperspectral Vision	[25]
Machine	[25]
Obscure 5 (Radar; Area Effect 6, +300%;	
Defensive, +50%; Extended,	
Para-Radar, +20%)	[47]
Para-Radar (Extended Arc, 360°,	
+125%; Penetrating, +50%; Targeting, +20%)	[118]
Payload 14 (Exposed, -50%)	[7]
Payload 5	[5]
Pressure Support 2	[10]
Protected Para-Radar	[5]
Protected Vision	[5]
Radio (Short Wave, +50%; Video, +40%)	[19]
Sealed	[15]
Talons	[8]
True Faith	[15]
Weapon Pods (see p. 308)	[594]

Languages

Languages	Spoken	Written	
English (Accented)			[4]
Koine Greek (Native)			[6]
Machine Language (Native)			[0]
Tibetan (Native)			[6]

DR	**TL:** 9	[5]
53	**Cultural Familiarities**	
	Hegemony	[0]
PARRY	Homeline	[1]

PARRY	**Reaction Modifiers**	
11*	Appearance _____	
(Brawling)	Status -2 for Clueless, most of the time	
BLOCK		
—		

DISADVANTAGES AND QUIRKS

Clueless	[-10]
Discipline of Faith (Asceticism)	[-15]
Electrical	[-20]
Fragile (Explosive)	[-15]
Low Empathy	[-20]
Numb	[-20]
Pacifism (Cannot Harm Innocents)	[-10]
Restricted Diet (Fissionables)	[-30]
Truthfulness (6)	[-10]
Wealth (Dead Broke)	[-25]
Always takes time to search out new sutras	[-1]
Broad-Minded	[-1]
Cannot Float	[-1]
Constantly looking for challenges	[-1]
Humble	[-1]

SKILLS

Name	Level	Relative Level	
Armoury/TL9			
(Heavy Weapons)	16	IQ+0	[2]
Brawling	15	DX+0	[1]
Computer Operation/TL9	16	IQ+0	[1]
Electronics Repair			
(Computers)	18	IQ+2	[8]
Expert Skill			
(Military Science)	15	IQ-1	[2]
Forward Observer/TL9	15	IQ-1	[1]
Innate Attack (Beam)	15	DX+0	[1]
Innate Attack (Projectile)	15	DX+0	[1]
Mechanic/TL9 (Robotics)	18	IQ+2	[8]
Meditation	14	Will-2	[1]
Mount	15	DX+0	[2]
Navigation/TL9 (Land)	15	IQ-1	[1]
Parachuting/TL9	15	DX	[1]
Strategy (Land)	18†	IQ+2	[11]
Tactics	20	IQ+4	[20]
Theology (Buddhist)	15	IQ-1	[2]

* +1 for Combat Reflexes.
† Default from Tactics.

DAI BLACKTHORN

Dai's career started on Yrth, a medieval fantasy world populated by descendants of Crusades-era folk pulled from Earth by a dimensional rift. He remembers nothing of his birth or early childhood; he was a street kid. When he was about seven, he was taken in by an old thief who taught him to be a pickpocket and second-story man, and Dai learned well. But the Thieves' Guild didn't like the competition, and when Dai was 15, the Guild set fire to the old man's house, and picked off the fleeing occupants with crossbows. Only Dai escaped.

At the time, he thought that he had made a terror-fueled leap from the burning building's roof to the next one. Later he realized that that jump had been impossible. Something else had happened. In fact, the fear of death had unlocked his psionic gift of teleportation, though it took time before he realized the truth and gained control of his abilities. When he did, he became a master thief indeed, living in quiet comfort and reveling in the marketplace talk of "impossible robberies" that no lock and no wizard could stop.

Then Dai crossed paths, and swords, with an equally formidable rival . . . a world-jumping criminal using stolen technology to loot Yrth's treasures. Matters were complicated further by the arrival of an ISWAT team pursuing the world-jumper. When the dust had settled, two of the agents owed their lives to the little thief . . . but he knew too much. They couldn't just let him go.

So they recruited him. After all, a good teleport is hard to find. As for Dai, he was ready for new challenges . . .

POINTS SUMMARY

Attributes/Secondary Characteristics	[158]
Advantages/Perks/TL/Languages/ Cultural Familiarity	[100]
Disadvantages/Quirks	[-55]
Skills/Techniques	[47]
Other	[ ]

GURPS

CHARACTER SHEET

Name _Dai Blackthorn_   **Player** _____   **Point Total** _250_

Ht _5'6"_   **Wt** _115 lbs._   **Size Modifier** _0_   **Age** _32_   **Unspent Pts** _____

Appearance _Very average with an honest face_

ST	8	[-20]	**HP**	10		[4]
DX	15	[100]	**WILL**	12		[0]
IQ	12	[40]	**PER**	15		[15]
HT	12	[20]	**FP**	10		[-6]

HP CURRENT _____   FP CURRENT _____

Languages

	Spoken	Written	
Anglish (Native)			[0]
English (Accented)			[4]
			[ ]
			[ ]
			[ ]

DR 0

TL: _8_   [0]

Cultural Familiarities

Homeline		[1]
Yrth		[0]
		[ ]

BASIC LIFT (ST × ST)/5 _13_   **DAMAGE** Thr _1d-3_   Sw _1d-2_

BASIC SPEED _7_ [5]   **BASIC MOVE** _7_ [0]

PARRY 10

BLOCK —

Reaction Modifiers

Appearance _____

Status _____

Reputation _+2/-2 from naive/experienced people (Overconfidence)_

+2 in dangerous situations, if Sense of Duty is known

ENCUMBRANCE / MOVE / DODGE

ENCUMBRANCE		MOVE		DODGE	
None (0) = BL	13	BM × 1	7	Dodge	10
Light (1) = 2 × BL	26	BM × 0.8	5	Dodge -1	9
Medium (2) = 3 × BL	39	BM × 0.6	4	Dodge -2	8
Heavy (3) = 6 × BL	78	BM × 0.4	2	Dodge -3	7
X-Heavy (4) = 10 × BL	130	BM × 0.2	1	Dodge -4	6

ADVANTAGES AND PERKS

Absolute Direction	[5]
Danger Sense (ESP, -10%)	[14]
Flexibility	[5]
Honest Face	[1]
Legal Enforcement Powers	[15]
Perfect Balance	[15]
Warp (Psionic Teleportation, -10%; Range Limit: 10 yards, -50%)	[40]

DISADVANTAGES AND QUIRKS

Duty (To ISWAT; 15 or less; Extremely Hazardous)	[-20]
Light Sleeper	[-5]
Overconfidence (12)	[-5]
Sense of Duty (To his squad)	[-5]
Wealth (Poor)	[-15]
Dislikes deep water	[-1]
Loves high places	[-1]
No drugs or alcohol	[-1]
Sensitive about his height	[-1]
Showoff	[-1]

SKILLS

Name	Level	Relative Level	
Acrobatics	15*	DX+0	[2]
Body Sense	16†	DX+1	[1]
Climbing	18*‡	DX+3	[1]
Escape	16‡	DX+1	[1]
Fast-Draw (Knife)	15	DX+0	[1]
Fast-Talk	12	IQ+0	[2]
Filch	14	DX-1	[1]
Guns/TL8 (Pistol)	15	DX+0	[1]
Holdout	12	IQ+0	[2]
Knife	17	DX+2	[4]
Lockpicking/TL8	15	IQ+3	[12]
Observation	15	Per+0	[2]
Pickpocket	15	DX+0	[4]
Shortsword	15	DX+0	[2]
Stealth	16	DX+1	[4]
Streetwise	12	IQ+0	[2]
Thrown Weapon (Knife)	17	DX+2	[4]
Urban Survival	14	Per-1	[1]

* +1 for Perfect Balance
† +3 for Absolute Direction
‡ +3 for Flexibility

HAUT-CORNET LOUIS D'ANTARES

When the armies of the Han war-lords conquered Europe a century ago, the court of France (and the other, lesser, courts of Christendom) removed to the new worlds: Mars, Venus, and the Americas. King Louis XXV reigns from Haut-Paris, on the banks of the Martian Grand Canal; his cousins and relations rule the other provinces across the three worlds. This far-flung Realm is knit together by the Jansenist Order, founded by disciples of Cornelius Jansen, the Bishop of Ypres who discovered "the methods of Necessary Grace" – psychic healing and psychokinesis – and published them posthumously in 1638. The Order helps guide and develop inventions, from the steam-car to the crystalwave communicator to the Pascal Drive that propels space frigates between the three planets. It also trains the royal guards – the only ones permitted to wield the deadly force sword – in the disciplines of Necessary Grace while attempting (with some occasional success) to instill in them morality and respect for righteousness.

One such occasional success, Haut-Cornet Louis d'Antares of Her Majesty's Martian Guards, while on patrol in the Tharsis Mountains, uncovered a ring of slave traders protected by a powerful count. As he investigated further, he discovered that the count was the tool of a hidden figure of vast power, known only as the Voice of the Phantom, with dark plans of conquest.

With a few picked men, d'Antares tracked the Voice to a hidden fastness in the Gobi Desert, in the center of the Han domains. They managed to infiltrate the fortress – but inside, they were discovered, and Louis was separated from his men in a running battle.

After some time, Louis heard a familiar voice call his name. He looked over a balcony to see an amazing sight. Three of his men had just greeted . . . Louis himself? The other Louis, clad in the uniform of an enemy guard, looked at them in obvious surprise but made no hostile move . . . yet one of the guardsmen stepped behind him, laughed, and ran the other Louis through the back with his force sword. And what the guardsmen said to his dying double, as Louis watched in amazement, turned his blood first cold with shock and then hot with rage.

Louis sprang over the balcony to confront the three traitors. They stared slack-jawed at the man they

had meant to murder, and then proved their cowardice by engaging him three on one. From their boasts as the battle began, and then their dying defiance, Louis learned the truth. He had been cast aside by the King himself; the intrigues of the court, combined with the power offered by the otherworldly Voice, had destroyed the France he knew. To the new order, a man of honor was a threat to be crushed.

None of which explained the slain double! Louis, despairing, donned the double's uniform and set out to sell his life dearly against the foes of France that was. It was clear that some third force was also attacking the citadel, and Louis did no little damage in the confusion . . . but eventually, one man against a fortress, he fell.

He awakened in a hospital bed, under the care of doctors who called him "Louis" . . . but everything else was strange. Eventually much became clear. Through fate or strange coincidence, Louis had had a double in the crossworld guardsmen called the "I-Cops." They had sacked the citadel of the Voice and then brought him back to their base, thinking he was their comrade. Louis was a willing font of information about his world and the Voice . . . but he also knew far too much to be allowed back to his home.

But it transpired that Louis had no desire to return to his world, which his rescuers called "Cyrano." His King's betrayal had released him from his oaths. Louis was no threat to the Secret . . . he was deeply convinced that contact with other worlds was, for now, the worst thing that could happen to what remained of his own land. Instead, he begged to be allowed to put his considerable talents at the disposal of ISWAT. Some day, wiser and with strong allies, he may be able to free his beloved France. For now, with a thin smile and a steely eye, he fights crosstime evil wherever it appears.

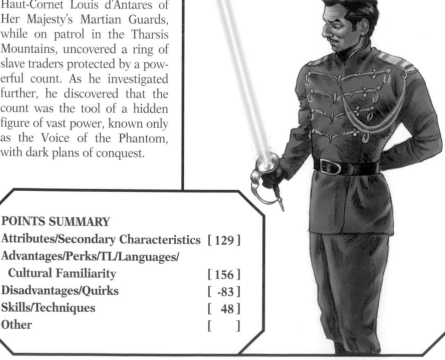

POINTS SUMMARY
Attributes/Secondary Characteristics	[129]
Advantages/Perks/TL/Languages/ Cultural Familiarity	[156]
Disadvantages/Quirks	[-83]
Skills/Techniques	[48]
Other	[ ]

GURPS

Name _Louis d'Antares_ **Player** _____ **Point Total** _250_

Ht _6'_ **Wt** _145 lbs._ **Size Modifier** _0_ **Age** _29_ **Unspent Pts** _____

Appearance _Dashingly handsome and very well-dressed_

CHARACTER SHEET

				CURRENT	
ST	10	[0]	**HP**	12	[4]
DX	14	[80]	**WILL**	12	[5]
IQ	11	[20]	**PER**	11	[0]
				CURRENT	
HT	12	[20]	**FP**	12	[0]

BASIC LIFT (ST × ST)/5 _20_   **DAMAGE** Thr _1d-2_ Sw _1d_

BASIC SPEED _6.5_ [0] **BASIC MOVE** _6_ [0]

ENCUMBRANCE		MOVE		DODGE*	
None (0) = BL	20	BM × 1	6	Dodge	10
Light (1) = 2 × BL	40	BM × 0.8	4	Dodge -1	9
Medium (2) = 3 × BL	60	BM × 0.6	3	Dodge -2	8
Heavy (3) = 6 × BL	120	BM × 0.4	2	Dodge -3	7
X-Heavy (4) = 10 × BL	200	BM × 0.2	1	Dodge -4	6

ADVANTAGES AND PERKS

Alcohol Tolerance	[1]
Appearance (Handsome)	[12]
Charisma 2	[10]
Combat Reflexes	[15]
Danger Sense	[15]
Daredevil	[15]
Fashion Sense	[5]
Fit	[5]
Legal Enforcement Powers	[15]
Metabolism Control 1	[5]
PK Talent 1	[5]
Talent (Smooth Operator) 2	[30]
Telekinesis 2 (PK, -10%)	[9]

DISADVANTAGES AND QUIRKS

Code of Honor (Gentleman's)	[-10]
Compulsive Gambling (12)	[-5]
Duty (To ISWAT; 15 or less;	
Extremely Hazardous)	[-20]
Extra Sleep 3	[-6]
Gregarious	[-10]
Insomniac (Mild)	[-10]
Overconfidence (9)	[-7]
Phobia (Ailurophobia) (6)	[-10]
Always drinks the best wine available	[-1]
Considers psionics ungentlemanly	[-1]
Devoutly believes in monarchy	[-1]
Flashy dresser (-1 to Disguise and Shadowing,	
+1 to attempts to identify or follow him)	[-1]
Wears his old Guards uniform, or a duplicate,	
whenever it's not obviously **stupid** to do so!	[-1]

Languages

Languages	Spoken	Written	
French (Native)			[0]
English (Accented)			[4]
Latin (Accented)			[4]
			[ ]
			[ ]

DR 0

TL: (5+4)		[5]
Cultural Familiarities		
Homeline		[1]
France Outremonde		[0]
		[ ]

PARRY _12*_ (Force Sword)

BLOCK —

Reaction Modifiers

Appearance +2/+4 from women/men (Handsome)
Status +2 at all times for Charisma!, +1 when dressed up (Fashion Sense), +2 from con artists, politicians, etc. (Smooth Operator), +2/-2 from naïve/experienced people (Overconfidence)

SKILLS

Name	Level	Relative Level	
Acrobatics	12	DX-2	[1]
Autohypnosis	10	Will-2	[1]
Beam Weapons/			
TL(5+4) (Pistol)	14	DX+0	[1]
Connoisseur (Fashion)	11	IQ+0	[2]
Connoisseur (Wine)	12	IQ+1	[4]
Current Affairs			
(High Culture)	12	IQ+1	[2]
Current Affairs (People)	11	IQ+0	[1]
Dancing	13	DX-1	[1]
Fast-Draw (Force Sword)	16*	DX+2	[2]
Force Sword	17	DX+3	[12]
Gambling	10	IQ-1	[1]
Guns/TL(5+4) (Pistol)	14	DX+0	[1]
Hobby Skill			
(Martian Orchids)	11	IQ+0	[1]
Leadership	15†‡	IQ+4	[2]
Musical Instrument			
(Harpsichord)	9	IQ-2	[1]
Rapier	14	DX+0	[2]
Riding (Hadrosaur)	13	DX-1	[1]
Savoir-Faire (High Society)	15†	IQ+4	[4]
Sex Appeal	17†§	HT+5	[1]
Survival (Desert)	11	Per+0	[2]
Tactics	10	IQ-1	[2]

Techniques

Feint (Force Sword)	19	[3]

* +1 from Combat Reflexes
† +2 from Smooth Operator
‡ +2 from Charisma
§ +4 from Handsome

PROFESSOR WILLIAM HEADLEY

Dr. William Headley was a prominent parapsychologist at Columbia University. He labored to separate the myths and lore of primitive man from the rational truth being uncovered by modern experimentation. But, in 1933, he discovered that his beloved scientific truths pointed to beings from primordial eras and unholy stars, beings that existed to ravage and kill not just mankind but the Earth itself. He dedicated himself to an unceasing war against these horrors, these Things Man Was Not Meant To Know. Slowly, he accumulated knowledge from the outer places of the world, from Spitsbergen to the Belgian Congo to the mean streets of Brooklyn's Red Hook district. He obtained tomes bound in mysterious leathers, and written in nonhuman scripts; in dreams and sorceries he gradually deciphered their secrets. He mastered many of the conventional magical arts, from Tarot divination to crystal-gazing, and collected artifacts of subtle and terrifying nature.

His slow mastery of forbidden lore allowed him to defeat the Things' minions here and there, and incidentally to clear up a number of other unpleasant supernatural occurrences. He began to get a reputation for solving seemingly motiveless crimes with his "unique insights into abnormal psychology." The New York Police Department came to rely on him for assistance with "the weird stuff" and the FBI called him in once or twice to help out – unofficially, you understand. Every so often

the crimes he investigated fit a pattern, one Headley had begun to associate with a vile German cult, tied to the Nazi SS, who worshiped the Ancient Ones. With the occasional "off-duty" FBI agent, one or two students, and a few trusted professional colleagues, Headley built a team of investigators who peeled back the skin of the onion, exposing layer after layer of the cult's activities and burning them out where they could. In 1941, he joined the OSS, working to stop Hitler – and the Cosmic Entities his minions served – from conquering the world.

After V-E Day, Headley managed to obtain much of the SS library from their cult center at Wewelsburg. These books told him of another world, a parallel Earth where the Ancient Ones had reigned and departed, leaving vital clues to their nature and weakness. Using spells from these grimoires, Headley opened a gateway to this devastated Earth, and stepped through to investigate the spoor of his hated foes. Much to his surprise, he discovered a team of explorers from yet another Earth (one they called "Homeline"), attempting to determine what had destroyed this one (which they called "Taft-7"). They were as surprised to see him as he was to see them, but foolishly disregarded his warnings about the Ancient Ones' cities, and the danger that still remained from their abandoned servitors. When the Things attacked that night, most of the explorers died horribly – and the two survivors fled back to their own world raving in madness. Only Headley realized that their flight had opened a path to their own world for the Things that had been trapped on this hellish Earth.

He had to follow the explorers and warn their comrades that unimaginable terror would soon descend upon them. Once more, he constructed a gateway to cross the worlds, hoping against hope that his warning would be believed and acted on before "Homeline" went the way of Taft-7.

POINTS SUMMARY

Attributes/Secondary Characteristics	[124]
Advantages/Perks/TL/Languages/ Cultural Familiarity	[82]
Disadvantages/Quirks	[-90]
Skills/Techniques	[48]
Other	[36]

GURPS

CHARACTER SHEET

Name _Prof. William Headley_ **Player** _____ **Point Total** _200_

Ht _5'8"_ **Wt** _165 lbs._ **Size Modifier** _0_ **Age** _43_ **Unspent Pts** _____

Appearance _Bespectacled and academic-looking, with a magical walking stick_

ST [9] [-10] **HP** [9] CURRENT[ ] [0]

DX [10] [0] **WILL** [17] [5]

IQ [16] [120] **PER** [15] [-5]

HT [11] [10] **FP** [14] CURRENT[ ] [9]

BASIC LIFT (ST × ST)/5 _16_ **DAMAGE** Thr _1d-2_ Sw _1d-1_

BASIC SPEED _5_ [-5] **BASIC MOVE** _5_ [0]

ENCUMBRANCE	MOVE		DODGE	
None (0) = BL	_16_	BM × 1 _5_	Dodge	_8_
Light (1) = 2 × BL	_32_	BM × 0.8 _4_	Dodge -1	_7_
Medium (2) = 3 × BL	_48_	BM × 0.6 _3_	Dodge -2	_6_
Heavy (3) = 6 × BL	_96_	BM × 0.4 _2_	Dodge -3	_5_
X-Heavy (4) = 10 × BL	_160_	BM × 0.2 _1_	Dodge -4	_4_

ADVANTAGES AND PERKS

Language Talent	[10]
Legal Enforcement Powers	[15]
Ritual Magery 1	[15]
Signature Gear (Magic staff)	[1]
Talent (Healer) 1	[10]
Unfazeable	[15]
Wealth (Comfortable)	[10]

DISADVANTAGES AND QUIRKS

Bad Sight (Nearsighted; Mitigator: Eyeglasses, -60%)	[-10]
Duty (To ISWAT; 15 or less; Extremely Hazardous)	[-20]
Fanaticism (Destroy all Things Man Was Not Meant To Know; Extreme)	[-15]
Guilt Complex	[-5]
Insomniac (Severe)	[-15]
Nightmares (12)	[-5]
Weirdness Magnet	[-15]
Bad knee	[-1]
Bibliophile	[-1]
Distrusts Germans (-1 reaction from especially touchy Germans)	[-1]
Makes decisions by consulting the tarot (Compulsion)	[-1]
Pipe smoker (0-point Addiction to Tobacco)	[-1]

Languages

	Spoken	Written
Ancient Egyptian (Accented)		[2*]
Arabic (Accented)		[2*]
German (Accented)		[2*]
English (Native)		[0]
Latin (Native)		[4*]

DR 0

PARRY —

BLOCK —

TL: 7 [-5]

Cultural Familiarities

Western	[0]
Homeline	[1]

Reaction Modifiers

Appearance _____
Status +1 from patients, past and present (Healer), -2 from those who realize he is a Weirdness Magnet,
-1 reaction from especially touchy Germans (quirk)

SKILLS

Name	Level	Relative Level	
Anthropology	14	IQ-2	[1]
Biology/TL7 (Earthlike, Biochemistry)	14	IQ-2	[1]
Criminology/TL7	16	IQ+0	[2]
Detect Lies	14	Per-1	[2]
Diagnosis/TL7	15†	IQ-1	[1]
Dreaming	17	Will+0	[4]
Exorcism	15	Will-2	[1]
Expert Skill (Psionics)	14	IQ-2	[1]
First Aid	15†‡	IQ-1	[0]
Forensics/TL7	14	IQ-2	[1]
Guns/TL7 (Pistol)	12	DX+2	[4]
Hidden Lore (Things Man Was Not Meant To Know)	15	IQ-1	[1]
Hypnotism	14	IQ-2	[1]
Literature	14	IQ-2	[1]
Mental Strength	17	Will+0	[1]
Occultism	17	IQ+1	[4]
Pharmacy/TL7 (Synthetic)	15†	IQ-1	[1]
Physician/TL7	15†	IQ-1	[1]
Psychology	15†	IQ-1	[1]
Public Speaking	15	IQ-1	[1]
Research/TL7	17	IQ+1	[4]
Ritual Magic (Hermetic)	17§	IQ+1	[8]
Savoir-Faire (Police)	16	IQ+0	[1]
Symbol Drawing (Hermetic Sigils)	14	IQ-2	[1]
Teaching	15	IQ-1	[1]
Thaumatology	14§	IQ-2	[1]
Theology (Satanism)	14	IQ-2	[1]
Writing	15	IQ-1	[1]
Ritual Paths			
Path of Communication and Empathy	16§	IQ+0	[4]
Path of Gate	17§	IQ+1	[8]
Path of Necromancy	14§	IQ-2	[1]
Ritual Spells			
Banish	9§		[6]
Planar Summons	11§		[5]
Plane Shift	11§		[6]
Sense Emotion	16§		[2]
Sense Spirit	14§		[2]
Truthsayer	15§		[2]

* Cost modified for Language Talent
† +1 from Healer
‡ Default from Physician
§ +1 from Magery

IOTHA

On the world where Iotha was born, the forests were tall and old, and within them walked the elves, her people. Being elves, they knew that there were doorways between the worlds, and they taught her how to know those doorways and their uses. Although she never learned to open the doors of shadow and shift, she learned to spot the gateways and trackpaths left by those who did. On her 400th birthday, then, she packed up a good longbow of yew, and a lyre, and one or two secret things of her own, and set out upon her Time of Wandering.

For the first few decades, she merely found doors and roads to other worlds much like her own, with their own elves and orcs and dwarves and giants. Elves she greeted, orcs she hunted, dwarves she bargained with, and giants she slew. As she journeyed farther though, she found more and more of the worlds contained men, of whom she had heard stories but had never seen. They were as fascinating as the songs her mother sang her as a girl, every one of them a Tamlin or a Thomas the Rhymer to her eager eyes. Although among the elves she was counted plain, the men seemed to delight in her as much as she did them, and once or twice she put off her travels to dally with one for the traditional year and a day.

Even among her own folk, Iotha had been a master archer. In the worlds of men she was matchless at butt or target, on hunt or in battle; she gained a reputation on any world where she stayed for long. Legends, and a religion or two, grew up around the tall maid who never seemed to age and whose arrows never missed their mark. But always Iotha moved on, giving each world a verse in the song she would someday sing to her own people.

In a world of concrete, glass, and steel, she came to live in a city split by a great wall. On one side was freedom, and music, and passion. On the other was none of these things, only a gray cloud that made freedom lies, and music discordant, and passion furtive. The huntsmen and warriors of this world had – as they felt – moved beyond the bow to mechanisms of subtle device that, once understood, had their own deadly beauty. So she learned the rifle, and the laser sight, and the ways of the hunt in the City of the Wall. She hunted the gray men from the other side of the wall, and gained a reputation in her new world as a deadly assassin. The greatest sniper from the other side of the wall marked her as his own, and they tracked each other through the cities and across the barbed wire borders and into fields and frozen forests. Finally, in the Black Forest, she killed him and took his weapon as her trophy, for it was made on the Moon by the gray men, and weighed even less than her bow.

It was much later, in a world of steaming jungle and glittering plains, when Iotha found her destiny. For a decade and a half she had been journeying among the human clans, helping them defeat the winged terrors that preyed on their children. At first Iotha stood them off in desperate defenses . . . then she defeated them in pitched battles . . . and finally she took the battle to their fetid eyries and slew the last of them with her gleaming shafts.

And at the festival of celebration, a woman who looked like any other clan-mother drew her aside and said "That was very well done. There are others who need your help now. Would you like to hear more?"

Elf

70 points

Attribute Modifiers: ST -1 [-10]; HT +1 [10].

Secondary Characteristic Modifiers: Per +1 [5].

Advantages: Appearance (Attractive) [4]; Language Talent [10]; Magery 0 [5]; Perfect Balance [15]; Telescopic Vision 1 [5]; Unaging [15]; Voice [10].

Racially Learned Skills: Connoisseur (Natural Environments) (A) IQ-1 [1].

POINTS SUMMARY

Attributes/Secondary Characteristics	[115]
Advantages/Perks/TL/Languages/ Cultural Familiarity	[140]
Disadvantages/Quirks	[-49]
Skills/Techniques	[119]
Other	[ ]

GURPS
CHARACTER SHEET

Name _Iotha_ Player _____ Point Total __325__

Ht _6'1"_ Wt _125 lbs_ Size Modifier __0__ Age __453__ Unspent Pts _____

Appearance _Tall, slender, and attractive, with ash-blonde hair with green highlights_

ST	9	[0]	**HP**	9	[0]
DX	13	[60]	**WILL**	12	[0]
IQ	12	[40]	**PER**	14	[5]
HT	11	[0]	**FP**	11	[0]

(HP CURRENT ___, FP CURRENT ___)

BASIC LIFT (ST × ST)/5 _16_ **DAMAGE** Thr _1d-2_ Sw _1d-1_

BASIC SPEED __6__ [0] **BASIC MOVE** __8__ [10]

ENCUMBRANCE		MOVE		DODGE	
None (0) = BL	16	BM × 1	8	Dodge	9
Light (1) = 2 × BL	32	BM × 0.8	6	Dodge -1	8
Medium (2) = 3 × BL	48	BM × 0.6	4	Dodge -2	7
Heavy (3) = 6 × BL	96	BM × 0.4	3	Dodge -3	6
X-Heavy (4) = 10 × BL	160	BM × 0.2	1	Dodge -4	5

Languages	Spoken	Written	
Elvish (Native)			[0]
English (Native)			[4*]
Russian (Native)			[4*]
			[ ]
			[ ]

DR 0

TL: _8_ [0]
Cultural Familiarities
Elvish	[0]
Homeline	[1]
	[ ]

PARRY —

BLOCK —

Reaction Modifiers

Appearance _+1 for Attractive appearance_

Status _+2 from those who can hear her voice (Voice), +1 from explorers and nature lovers (Outdoorsman)_

ADVANTAGES AND PERKS

Acute Vision 3	[6]
Detect (Extradimensional Phenomena)	[10]
Elf	[70]
Legal Enforcement Powers	[15]
Talent (Outdoorsman) 1	[10]
Weapon Master (Bow)	[20]

DISADVANTAGES AND QUIRKS

Duty (To ISWAT; 15 or less; Extremely Hazardous)	[-20]
Jealousy	[-10]
Supernatural Feature (Hair turns dark green in strong sunlight)	[-5]
Vow (Always keeps her word, once given)	[-10]
Dislikes hawthorn	[-1]
Dislikes iron	[-1]
Intolerant of orcs and dwarves	[-1]
Practices faerie etiquette (Minor Code of Honor)	[-1]

SKILLS

Name	Level	Relative Level	
Bow	21	DX+8	[32]
Camouflage	15†	IQ+3	[4]
Climbing	13§	DX+0	[1]
Crossbow	13	DX+0	[1]
Fast-Draw (Arrow)	16	DX+3	[8]
Guns/TL8 (Rifle)	16	DX+3	[8]
Hiking	13	HT+2	[8]
Meditation	12	Will+0	[4]
Musical Instrument (Lyre)	13	IQ+1	[8]
Naturalist	14†	IQ+2	[8]
Poetry	11	IQ-1	[1]
Riding (Horse)	13	DX+0	[2]
Running	14	HT+3	[12]
Shadowing	11	IQ-1	[1]
Singing	13‡	HT+2	[1]
Stealth	15	DX+2	[8]
Survival (Woodlands)	14†	Per+0	[1]
Throwing	13	DX+0	[2]
Tracking	14†	Per+0	[1]
Zen Archery	12	IQ+0	[8]

* Cost reduced by Language Talent (see Elf template)

† Includes +1 from Outdoorsman

‡ Includes +2 from Voice (see Elf template)

§ Includes +1 from Perfect Balance (see Elf template)

SORA

Manila exists in many worlds. In some worlds, its masters speak Japanese; in others Russian; in others Spanish or English. But in every Manila, the real bosses hide in the stark tropical shadows. They are the Triads, interlocking networks of criminal gangs with a finger in everything from traditional thuggery and kidnapping to high-tech organlegging and holopiracy.

In one Manila, the local Triads needed a powerful computer system to use as an illegal data haven – and a relatively innocuous place to store it. They chose a local circus, setting their comp up, seemingly, for holographic set projections. Anyone who asked too many questions . . . well, they just disappeared into those tropical shadows.

Two of those who disappeared were the circus' headlining acrobats, the husband-and-wife team who anchored the Esclamado Family troupe. Their bodies turned up in the city dump, dinner for rats and gulls. Sora, their daughter, and a rising star of the show, vanished as well . . . hiding in Manila's urban maze, avoiding every eye, living by petty theft and trickery. Somehow – she doesn't speak of it – she came to the attention of the legendary Guro Dan Inosanto, master of the deadly Filipino martial arts of escrima and kali. He recognized her potential, and took her in as pupil and ward. He kept her from the sight of the Triads, and taught her to combine her rage, her alertness, and her acrobatics into a fluid system of death and life.

Sora could not stay under his wing forever, though. She had to hunt down and kill the Triad bosses who had murdered her parents. She worked in the meantime for other gangs, zaibatsu, the underground, or whoever else could pay her increasing fees. Though she was no computer whiz, she also managed a surprising number of successful hacks through "social engineering," dumpster diving, and good old-fashioned breaking and entering. As a Triad-hunting vigilante, she slowly earned the trust of Manila's small shopkeepers and churches; as a corporate agent, she gained contacts among the wealthy and powerful.

One trail led to a suspiciously lucrative warehouse operation in the Quiapo district. Sora set up a surveillance pattern, rigorously tracking who entered and who left – and discovered that some people entered the warehouse and did not leave for days, or even weeks! But some of those who entered and left were Triad kingpins.

Clearly, though, this was the front for a very secret smuggling operation. It was time for direct action. She broke in, slew more than a dozen mooks and three Very Important Crooks, and was taken from behind by a dart. Still conscious, she was bundled into a machine that looked on the inside like a bus . . . and then out again, without going anywhere. She was thrown into a crude cell. It would have held most people, but not the daughter of the Esclamados, not a student of Inosanto. She fled the warehouse . . . but found herself in another Manila, where everything was the same yet different . . . in this one, America had won the Pacific War! But here, too, the Triads were the bosses.

Sora made a place for herself in this strange Manila's underworld and resumed her watching. Soon she realized that the Triads of her world and this one were cooperating, and that the warehouse was the gateway. Well, fine . . . if that was their scheme, she'd destroy it. And them.

A mid-level Triad was strangled from behind in a gambling den. Sora now had a warehouse key. Soon she knew the place better than its masters.

Sora learned that the "bus" she had ridden in was a "conveyor," a shuttle between the worlds, and the only one the Triads had. One night she broke a guard's neck, walked into the conveyor, ripped the improvised cover off the red Panic button, and hit it.

Ten seconds later, on yet another world, she was telling her story in broken English. A month after that, she was in the first wave of the I-Cops team that visited her original world to take out "her" Triads for good.

And when the operation was over, Infinity had a choice: either send her to Coventry or offer her a job. And Sora was too good to waste.

POINTS SUMMARY

Attributes/Secondary Characteristics	[215]
Advantages/Perks/TL/Languages/ Cultural Familiarity	[99]
Disadvantages/Quirks	[-65]
Skills/Techniques	[86]
Other	[ ]

GURPS

CHARACTER SHEET

Name _Sora_ Player _____ Point Total __335__

Ht _5'2"_ Wt _130 lbs._ Size Modifier __0__ Age __23__ Unspent Pts _____

Appearance _Compact and athletic Filipina_ _____

ST	12	[20]	HP	12	CURRENT	[0]
DX	16	[120]	WILL	13		[0]
IQ	13	[60]	PER	12		[-5]
HT	11	[10]	FP	11	CURRENT	[0]

BASIC LIFT (ST × ST)/5 __29__ DAMAGE Thr _1d-1_ Sw _1d+2_

BASIC SPEED __7__ [5] BASIC MOVE __8__ [5]

ENCUMBRANCE	MOVE	DODGE*
None (0) = BL __29__	BM × 1 __8__	Dodge __11__
Light (1) = 2 × BL __58__	BM × 0.8 __6__	Dodge -1 __10__
Medium (2) = 3 × BL __87__	BM × 0.6 __4__	Dodge -2 __9__
Heavy (3) = 6 × BL __174__	BM × 0.4 __3__	Dodge -3 __8__
X-Heavy (4) = 10 × BL __290__	BM × 0.2 __1__	Dodge -4 __7__

ADVANTAGES AND PERKS

Catfall	[10]
Combat Reflexes	[15]
Fit	[5]
Legal Enforcement Powers	[15]
Perfect Balance	[15]
Trained by a Master	[30]

DISADVANTAGES AND QUIRKS

Code of Honor (Professional)	[-5]
Delusion ("My mother is an angel in Heaven watching over me")	[-5]
Duty (To ISWAT; 15 or less; Extremely Hazardous)	[-20]
Enemy (Large group: Manila Triads; Hunter; 6 or less)	[-15]
Light Sleeper	[-5]
Pacifism (Cannot Harm Innocents)	[-10]
Careful	[-1]
Devout Roman Catholic (reacts at +1 to Catholic clergy, tithes, attends church regularly)	[-1]
Dislikes wide-open spaces	[-1]
Uncongenial	[-1]
Vow ("Never reject a challenge to single combat")	[-1]

Languages

	Spoken	Written	
Chinese (Broken)			[2]
English (Broken)			[2]
Japanese (Accented)			[4]
Tagalog (Native)			[0]
			[ ]

DR	TL: _8_	[0]
0	Cultural Familiarities	
	East Asian	[0]
PARRY	Homeline	[1]
12*		
(Judo or Karate)		

Reaction Modifiers

BLOCK	Appearance _____
—	Status _-1 from those who notice her_
	Delusion _____

SKILLS

Name	Level	Relative Level	
Acrobatics	17†	DX+1	[4]
Area Knowledge (Manila)	14	IQ+1	[2]
Broadsword	15	DX-1	[1]
Climbing	17†	DX+1	[2]
Computer Hacking/TL8	11	IQ-2	[2]
Computer Programming/TL8	11	IQ-2	[1]
Fast-Draw (Knife)	17*	DX+1	[1]
Fast-Draw (Small Thrown Weapon)	17*	DX+1	[1]
Fast-Draw (Tonfa)	17*	DX+1	[1]
Fast-Talk	13	IQ+0	[2]
Filch	15	DX-1	[1]
Garrote	16	DX+0	[1]
Holdout	12	IQ-1	[1]
Judo	16	DX+0	[4]
Jumping	16	DX+0	[1]
Karate	16	DX+0	[4]
Knife	16	DX+0	[1]
Lockpicking/TL8	15	IQ+2	[8]
Makeup/TL8	13	IQ+0	[1]
Main-Gauche	16	DX+0	[2]
Observation	11	Per-1	[1]
Performance	12	IQ-1	[1]
Photography/TL8	12	IQ-1	[1]
Pickpocket	14	DX-2	[1]
Search	11	Per-1	[1]
Shadowing	13	IQ+0	[2]
Smallsword	17	DX+1	[4]
Stealth	15	DX-1	[1]
Streetwise	13	IQ+0	[2]
Throwing Art	15	DX-1	[2]
Tonfa	15	DX-1	[1]
Traps/TL8	12	IQ-1	[1]
Urban Survival	11	Per-1	[1]

Techniques

Arm Lock	17	[1]
Back Kick	13	[2]
Choke Hold	15	[2]
Disarming (Smallsword)	18	[2]
Dual-Weapon Attack (Smallsword)	15	[3]
Elbow Strike	15	[1]
Jump Kick	14	[3]
Knee Strike	16	[1]
Off-Hand Weapon Training (Smallsword)	16	[4]
Rope Up	17†	[2]
Scaling	15†	[2]
Sweeping Kick	15	[3]

* Includes +1 for Combat Reflexes.
† Includes +1 for Perfect Balance.

BARON JANOS TELKOZEP

Born in Castle Telkozep, Hungary in 1571, the year of the great victory at Lepanto, Janos Telkozep succeeded to the barony when his father died fighting the Turks in 1589. At a glittering Twelfth Night feast at Castle Bathori a few years later, the young Baron retired to the chambers of the beautiful, widowed Countess Bathori. To his shock (though not entirely, it must be admitted, to his surprise) he discovered the next morning that she had transformed him into a vampire. Telkozep's family connections kept him out of trouble when the King of Hungary eventually tried the Countess for murder and imprisoned her in a distant castle without food or light, but he learned from her example. She had allowed her vampiric appetites to corrupt her judgement, and that, Telkozep vowed, would never be his fate.

Over the next two centuries, the Baron repeatedly "died" and took over the Castle as his own heir, continuing to ally himself to kings and archbishops, maneuvering ever more gracefully through the byzantine paths of

European politics. Recognizing earlier than most nobles that the wave of the future would be in banks and trading-houses, rather than acres of barley or ransomed Turkish generals, the Baron taught himself the new intricacies of ducats and marks, pounds and roubles. By the 19th century, he had steadily enriched himself through six or seven wars, three changes of dynasty, and two vampire panics. During the latter, he often acquired the estates of the condemned at knock-down prices, feeling no guilt at profiting from the deaths of vampires more foolish and rash than himself. Slowly, he began to accumulate vampiric foes – the great Pavane des Vampires in Paris declared him anathema, and others tried to stalk or betray him in their turn.

He studied the occult, seeking new weapons against his fellows, and learned that his ancient lover, the Countess Bathori, had somehow escaped her prison through sorcerous means. She had become a Grand Master of the Cabal, a secret society of monsters and magi descended from ancient Egypt, and she offered him sanctuary. Telkozep accepted . . . but she had learned little from her long life. During the disasters of the 1940s, her rashness nearly destroyed the vampire brotherhood in the Cabal – and the war she helped spark did destroy Telkozep's beloved Hungary. In 1956, he left Bathori and the Cabal behind, beginning 30 years of shadow warfare in boardrooms and blasted heaths across Europe and America.

Although his vampiric powers kept him alive, and his fortune kept him hidden, the Cabal (and his vengeful ex-lover the Countess) came ever closer to destroying him. Telkozep could see the inevitable future; just like the pathetic vampires of the 17th century, he was alone and friendless, with every hand against him. A stake in the night, or the Final Dawn, awaited him – unless he could change the game. Where once he had researched money, and then magic, he now sought allies. He discovered that the Cabal had their own

enemies – and one of them dwelt on another Earth, where the Countess' reach could not so easily extend. Telkozep put all his liquid wealth into portable assets and waited for an opening. In 1989, he walked through a megalithic barrow under a full moon, and into another Earth. He flitted from timeline to timeline, through gateways marked in an ancient codex he had purchased from the bankrupt National Museum of Budapest, until he was sure he had eluded the Cabal. He then set out to attract the attention of outtimers like himself, with clever advertisements in the papers and subtle manipulations of key stocks. When the Infinity Patrol knocked on his office door, he was able to present them (and eventually ISWAT, who took over once they realized what they had) with an attractive offer – employment as their star vampire (and financial expert) in exchange for protection from the Cabal.

Vampire

150 points

Attribute Modifiers: ST+6 [60].

Secondary Characteristic Modifiers: HP+4 [8]; Per+3 [15].

Advantages: Alternate Forms (Bat, Wolf) [30]; Doesn't Breathe [20]; Dominance [20]; Immunity to Metabolic Hazards [30]; Injury Tolerance (Unliving) [20]; Insubstantiality (Costs Fatigue, 2 FP, -10%) [72]; Night Vision 5 [5]; Speak With Animals (Wolves and bats, -60%) [10]; Unaging [15]; Unkillable 2 (Achilles' Heel: Wood, -50%) [50]; Vampiric Bite [30].

Disadvantages: Dependency (Coffin with soil of homeland; Daily) [-60]; Divine Curse (Cannot enter dwelling for first time unless invited) [-10]; Draining (Human Blood; Illegal) [-10]; Dread (Garlic) [-10]; Dread (Religious Symbols; 5 yards) [-14]; Dread (Running Water) [-20]; Supernatural Features (No Body Heat*, No Reflection, Pallor*) [-16]; Uncontrollable Appetite (12) (Human Blood) [-15]; Unhealing (Partial) [-20]; Weakness (Sunlight; 1d/minute) [-60].

Features: Sterile.

* Except after feeding.

POINTS SUMMARY

Attributes/Secondary Characteristics	[220]
Advantages/Perks/TL/Languages/ Cultural Familiarity	[369]
Disadvantages/Quirks	[-120]
Skills/Techniques	[66]
Other	[ ]

GURPS

CHARACTER SHEET

Name *Baron Janos Telkozep* **Player** _____ **Point Total** **535**

Ht *5'8"* **Wt** *197 lbs.* **Size Modifier** **0** **Age** **421** **Unspent Pts** _____

Appearance *Strongly built and charismatic . . . yet strangely menacing*

ST 20 [40]	**HP** 24	CURRENT [0]
DX 11 [20]	**WILL** 16	[5]
IQ 15 [100]	**PER** 18	[0]
HT 10 [0]	**FP** 10	CURRENT [0]

BASIC LIFT (ST × ST)/5 **80**   **DAMAGE Thr** *2d+2** **Sw** *5d-1**
BASIC SPEED **8**   [55] **BASIC MOVE** **8** [0]

ENCUMBRANCE / MOVE / DODGE

ENCUMBRANCE	MOVE		DODGE	
None (0) = BL	80	BM × 1 8	Dodge	11
Light (1) = 2 × BL	160	BM × 0.8 6	Dodge -1	10
Medium (2) = 3 × BL	240	BM × 0.6 4	Dodge -2	9
Heavy (3) = 6 × BL	480	BM × 0.4 3	Dodge -3	8
X-Heavy (4) = 10 × BL	800	BM × 0.2 1	Dodge -4	7

ADVANTAGES AND PERKS

Charisma 3	[15]
Independent Income 10	[10]
Legal Enforcement Powers	[15]
Mind Control	[50]
Striking ST 5	[25]
Talent (Business Acumen) 3	[30]
Temperature Control 3 (Cold, -50%;	
Uncontrollable, -10%)	[6]
Vampire (see below)	[150]
Wealth (Filthy Rich)	[50]

DISADVANTAGES AND QUIRKS

Berserk (9)	[-15]
Bloodlust (9)	[-15]
Callous	[-5]
Duty (To ISWAT; 15 or less;	
Extremely Hazardous)	[-20]
Enemy (The Cabal; Hunter; 6 or less)	[-20]
Frightens Animals	[-10]
Greed (6)	[-30]
Code of Honor (Aristocratic manners)	[-1]
Dislikes mirrors	[-1]
Old-fashioned language and idioms (-1 to some uses	
of Fast-Talk, Propaganda, etc; GM's option)	[-1]
Patriot (Hungary; minor Fanaticism; -1 reaction	
from patriotic Turks and Romanians)	[-1]
Vow ("Never let vampiric appetites	
corrupt my judgment")	[-1]

Languages

Languages	Spoken	Written	
English	(Accented)	(Native)	[5]
French (Native)			[6]
Hungarian (Native)			[0]
Latin	(Broken)	(Native)	[4]
Russian (Broken)			[2]

DR	TL: 8	[0]
0	**Cultural Familiarities**	
	18th-Century Europe	[0]
	Homeline	[1]
		[ ]

PARRY
9
(Saber)

BLOCK
—

Reaction Modifiers

Appearance _____
Status *+3 at all times for Charisma!*
+3 from those he does business with (Business Acumen), -5 from those who notice his Supernatural Features, -4 from animals (Frightens Animals), -1 from past victims and those with Empathy (Callous), -1 reaction from patriotic Turks and Romanians (quirk)

SKILLS

Name	Level	Relative Level	
Administration	17†	IQ+2	[1]
Area Knowledge (Hungary)	15	IQ+0	[1]
Body Language	17	Per-1	[1]
Brawling	12	DX+1	[2]
Connoisseur (Visual Arts)	15	IQ+0	[2]
Current Affairs/TL8			
(Business)	16	IQ+1	[2]
Detect Lies	17	Per-1	[2]
Diplomacy	14	IQ-1	[2]
Economics	16†	IQ+1	[1]
Finance	16†	IQ+1	[1]
Guns/TL5 (Pistol)	12	DX+1	[2]
History (Hungary)	15	IQ+0	[4]
Intimidation	20	Will+4	[16]
Market Analysis	17†	IQ+2	[2]
Merchant	13†‡	IQ-2	[0]
Mimicry (Animal Sounds)	14	IQ-1	[2]
Occultism (Vampirology)	18	IQ+3	[12]
Propaganda/TL8	17†	IQ+2	[1]
Saber	12	DX+1	[4]
Savoir-Faire (High Society)	15	IQ+0	[1]
Sex Appeal	11	HT+1	[4]
Teamster (Equines)	14	IQ-1	[1]
Tracking	18	Per+0	[2]

* *Includes Striking ST*
† *Includes +3 for Business Acumen*
‡ *Default from Market Analysis*

Xing La

All missions on Lenin-2 are hell. I guess that's why they call it a "Hell parallel." It's way too hot, and there's nothing but bugs and carp to eat, and if you close your eyes for two seconds, some kind of savage is going to try and smash in your skull with a rusted-out electrical transformer bar. The major powers (except the British Empire) went Communist in the late 19th century and, just like the Soviets did to Russia in Homeline, they wrecked the environment big time over the next century. Britain lost what the Chinese called "the Summer Wars" to the Communist powers in the 1950s, and that knocked the struts out from under the global economy, too. Hong Kong and expatriate Americans in Shanghai had managed to spread capitalism to China, though, so technological progress kept progressing – until the ecological collapse took everything down with it. The Gulf Stream shut down and shifted global weather patterns. Catastrophic warming melted the ice caps and flooded the coastlines; mega-storms tore through the desertified continental interiors; famines killed billions of people. While all this was going on, the Bolsheviks, the Mitteleuropan DKAP, and the Christian Communist Congressional Party fought "the Autumn Wars" over the stinking remains of the fresh water and the fish. The few million survivors are grinding along at medieval tech levels, except for the Chinese, who had enough stuff that some survivor settlements can keep the lights on and the engines running. Until the plankton all dies, anyhow.

We run surveys all over the planet, trying to see if we can somehow jump-start the ecology again, just like China was trying to do before the ax fell. We wind up trying to salvage a lot of the Chinese records, and so we've kind of made Soochow Island our "hell away from hell." They've got liquor, and electric lights, and cooked food, and gambling, and all the comforts of home. A lot of these coastal Chinese got genetic grafts during the last, desperate "try anything" times; with some of them, it seems to have helped. One really sharp local – I mean sharp as a nanofiber, nothing gets past her – probably has some water-rat DNA in her; her eyes are red, and her teeth aren't quite right. But she can hold her breath for half an hour, track stuff by the smell, and see in the dark. More important, Xing La (that's her name) can drive, fly, or float anything that moves. And if it doesn't move, she can make it move. She's a natural pilot, too, and she doesn't depend on radio or instruments like half the people Infinity sends out here. She has like a sixth sense for these wrecks, and without her, we wouldn't have found that lost conveyer before the cannibals got to it. We've probably hired her for some kind of work on every mission in Lenin-2 for the past four years, and she's been more places and done a better job than plenty of folks from Homeline.

So what I'm trying to say, I guess, is that the team and I, we feel kind of bad about leaving her there in her miserable hole to die with the rest of the human race on that ball of mud. I mean, if it turns out that we can't re-seed the krill, and we can't fix the North Atlantic, and we can't find any earthworms that can stay alive in the plague zones for more than a month. And she's got nothing but talent, and drive, and pluck to spare, and it's even more wasted than most of Lenin-2 is. Anyhow, we've sent her name and profile upstairs to – well, I'd better not say who, but you know who I mean – and hopefully, they need someone who can drive a motorcycle up a sheer cliff, or thread an airship through the eye of a typhoon. If not, so help me Buddha, I'll smuggle her back to Homeline myself.

POINTS SUMMARY

Attributes/Secondary Characteristics	[101]
Advantages/Perks/TL/Languages/ Cultural Familiarity	[106]
Disadvantages/Quirks	[-109]
Skills/Techniques	[127]
Other	[ ]

GURPS
CHARACTER SHEET

Name **Xing La**   Player _____   Point Total **225**

Ht **5'4"**   Wt **100 lbs.** Size Modifier **0**   Age **27**   Unspent Pts _____

Appearance **Skinny East Asian woman with gleaming eyes and bony teeth**

ST	10	[0]	**HP**	10		[0]
DX	12	[40]	**WILL**	12		[0]
IQ	12	[40]	**PER**	12		[0]
HT	13	[30]	**FP**	10		[-9]

HP CURRENT: ___   FP CURRENT: ___

Languages

	Spoken	Written
Cantonese (Broken)		[2]
English (Accented)		[4]
Mandarin (Broken)		[2]
Shanghainese (Native)		[0]
		[ ]

DR 0

TL: 8 [0]

Cultural Familiarities
East Asian	[0]
Homeline	[1]
	[ ]

BASIC LIFT (ST × ST)/5 **20**   DAMAGE Thr **1d-2** Sw **1d**

BASIC SPEED **6.25** [0] BASIC MOVE **6** [0]

ENCUMBRANCE / MOVE / DODGE

ENCUMBRANCE		MOVE		DODGE	
None (0) = BL	20	BM × 1	6	Dodge	9
Light (1) = 2 × BL	40	BM × 0.8	4	Dodge -1	8
Medium (2) = 3 × BL	60	BM × 0.6	3	Dodge -2	7
Heavy (3) = 6 × BL	120	BM × 0.4	2	Dodge -3	6
X-Heavy (4) = 10 × BL	200	BM × 0.2	1	Dodge -4	5

PARRY —

BLOCK —

Reaction Modifiers

Appearance _____

Status _____

Reputation **+2 from anyone she does work for (Artificer), +1 in close confines (Sanitized Metabolism), -2 for Clueless, most of the time, -2 from those who can hear her voice (Disturbing Voice)**

ADVANTAGES AND PERKS

Absolute Direction	[5]
Breath-Holding 3	[6]
Discriminatory Smell	[15]
Infravision	[10]
Legal Enforcement Powers	[15]
Pressure Support 1	[5]
Sanitized Metabolism	[1]
Striking ST +10 (Bite Only, -60%)	[20]
Talent (Artificer) 2	[20]

DISADVANTAGES AND QUIRKS

Clueless	[-10]
Disturbing Voice	[-10]
Duty (To ISWAT; 15 or less; Extremely Hazardous)	[-20]
Gluttony (15)	[-2]
Hard of Hearing	[-10]
Low Empathy	[-20]
Shyness (Severe)	[-10]
Skinny	[-5]
Unnatural Features (Lambent eyes and bony teeth)	[-2]
Unusual Biochemistry	[-5]
Wealth (Struggling)	[-10]
Attentive	[-1]
Bad posture (-1 to Dancing and Sex Appeal)	[-1]
Code of Honor ("Stay bought and finish the job")	[-1]
Incompetence (Finance)	[-1]
Likes processed food (especially fast food)	[-1]

SKILLS

Name	Level	Relative Level	
Airshipman/TL7	13	IQ+1	[2]
Armoury/TL7 (Heavy Weapons)	13*	IQ+1	[1]
Axe/Mace	12	DX+0	[2]
Breath Control	14	HT+1	[8]
Drive!	16	DX+4	[72]
Electrician/TL7	13*	IQ+1	[1]
Electronics Repair /TL7 (Sensors)	15*	IQ+3	[4]
Electronics Repair /TL7 (Sonar)	14*	IQ+2	[2]
Fishing	12	Per+0	[1]
Gunner/TL7 (Rockets)	14	DX+2	[4]
Knot-Tying	13	DX+1	[2]
Machinist/TL7	13*	IQ+1	[1]
Mechanic/TL7 (Gasoline Engine)	14*	IQ+2	[2]
Navigation/TL2 (Sea)	15†	IQ+3	[2]
Navigation/TL7 (Sea)	14†	IQ+2	[1]
Scrounging	15	Per+3	[8]
Scuba/TL8	11	IQ-1	[1]
Seamanship/TL7	13	IQ+1	[2]
Smuggling	11	IQ-1	[1]
Spear Thrower	13	DX+1	[4]
Survival (Island/Beach)	11	Per-1	[1]
Survival (Swampland)	11	Per-1	[1]
Swimming	15	HT+2	[4]

* Includes +2 from Artificer.

† Includes +3 from Absolute Direction.

COMBAT LITE

This appendix summarizes the core combat rules found in the *Basic Set,* Book 2. GMs interested in combat with counters or figures on a hexagonal grid, special combat situations, etc., should consult Chapters 12-13, in Book 2.

COMBAT TURN SEQUENCE

Each character's turn normally gives him one opportunity to act per second. After everyone takes his turn, one second has passed.

The one-second time scale breaks the battle into manageable chunks. A GM can drop out of combat time whenever dramatically appropriate, and resume combat time when

noncombat action gives way to more fighting.

The *turn sequence* is the order in which active characters take their turns. It is set at the start of the fight and does not change during combat. The combatant with the highest Basic

Speed goes first, followed by the next-highest Basic Speed, and so on. The GM decides the order of multiple NPCs on the same side with the same Basic Speed. If PCs are involved, precedence goes to the highest DX. If there's still a tie, the GM should roll at the start of combat to determine who acts first.

MANEUVERS

A *maneuver* is an action taken during combat. Each turn, you must choose *one* of the following maneuvers: Aim, All-Out Attack, All-Out Defense, Attack, Change Posture, Concentrate, Do Nothing, Evaluate, Feint, Move, Move and Attack, Ready, or Wait. Your choice determines *what you can do* and your options for active defense and movement.

Aim

Aiming a ranged weapon (or a device such as a camera) takes a full turn. Specify your weapon and your target. You can't aim at something that you can't see or detect.

If you follow an Aim maneuver with an Attack or All-Out Attack with the *same* weapon against the *same* target, you get a bonus to hit. Add the weapon's Accuracy to your skill. If you Aim for more than one second, you receive an additional bonus: +1 for two seconds of Aim, or +2 for three or more seconds.

While aiming, you can move a step.

Any Active Defense automatically spoils your aim and removes all accumulated benefits. If *injured* while

aiming, you must make a Will roll or lose your aim.

All-Out Attack

Attack any foe with a ready weapon, making no effort to defend against enemy attacks. If you make a melee attack, you must specify *one* of these four options:

- *Determined:* Make a single attack at +4 to hit.
- *Double:* Make two attacks against the same foe, *if* you have two ready weapons or one weapon that does not have to be readied after use. Attacks with a second weapon held in the off hand are at the usual -4.
- *Feint:* Make one Feint (see below) and then one attack against the same foe.
- *Strong*: Make a single attack, at normal skill. If you hit, you get +2 to damage – or +1 damage per die, if that would be better. This only applies to melee attacks doing ST-based thrust or swing damage, not to weapons such as force swords.

You may move up to half your Move, but you can only move forward.

You may take *no active defenses at all* until your next turn.

These are the two All-Out Attack options for ranged combat:

- *Determined:* Make a single attack at +1 to hit.
- *Suppression Fire:* Take your entire turn to spray an area with automatic fire. Your weapon must have RoF 5+. Ask the GM for details or see Suppression Fire (p. 410).

All-Out Defense

The maneuver of choice when beset by foes. Specify *one* of the following two options:

- *Increased Defense:* Add +2 to *one* active defense of your choice: Dodge, Parry, or Block. This bonus persists until your next turn.
- *Double Defense:* Apply two *different* active defenses against the same attack. If you fail your defense roll against an attack, you may try a second, different defense against that attack. If you try a parry (armed or unarmed) with one hand and fail, a parry using the other hand *does* count as a "different defense."

With Increased Dodge, you may move up to half your Move. Otherwise, the only movement is a step. Choose any legal active defense, with bonuses as described above.

Attack

Make an armed or unarmed attack in melee combat, or to use a thrown or missile weapon in ranged combat. A weapon used in an attack must be ready.

If using a melee weapon or unarmed attack, your target must be within reach. If using a ranged weapon, your target must be within the weapon's Max range.

To move more than one step during an attack, use a Move and Attack or All-Out Attack.

Change Posture

Change between the following postures: *standing, sitting, kneeling, crawling, lying prone* (face down), and *lying face up*. Any posture other than standing slows movement and penalizes attack and defense rolls, but also creates a smaller target for ranged attacks.

Standing up from a lying position requires two Change Posture maneuvers: one to rise to crawling, kneeling, or sitting, and another to stand.

You can switch between kneeling and standing as a step with another maneuver.

Concentrate

You *concentrate* on one primarily mental task (even it has a minor physical component, like operating controls, gesturing, or speaking). This may be casting a magical spell, using a psi ability, making a Sense roll to spot an invisible warrior, or any similar action, including most IQ-based skill rolls. This is a full-turn maneuver.

If you are forced to use an active defense, knocked down, injured, or otherwise distracted before you finish, you must make a Will-3 roll. On a failure, you lose your concentration and must start over.

Do Nothing

Standing still is *Doing Nothing*. A character Doing Nothing may still defend normally, unless stunned.

Someone stunned or surprised *must* take this maneuver. A stunned character defends at -4.

To recover from physical or mental stun, he may attempt a HT or an IQ roll. A success allows recovery at the *end* of a turn.

Evaluate

Study an adversary to gain a combat bonus on a subsequent attack. You must specify a *visible* opponent close enough to attack or reachable with a single Move and Attack maneuver (see below).

An Evaluate maneuver gives +1 to skill for an Attack, Feint, All-Out Attack, or Move and Attack made against *that opponent, on your next turn only*. You may take up to three consecutive Evaluate maneuvers before you strike, giving a cumulative +1 per turn.

Feint

"Fake" a melee attack if your weapon is ready and your foe is within reach. This maneuver is *not* an attack and does not make your weapon unready.

To Feint, choose a single opponent and roll a Quick Contest of Melee Weapon skills. Your opponent may roll against his Melee Weapon skill, unarmed combat skill, Cloak or Shield skill, or DX.

If you fail your roll, your Feint is unsuccessful. Likewise, if you succeed, but your foe succeeds by as *much as* or *more than* you do, your Feint fails. If you *make* your roll, and your foe *fails*, subtract your margin of success from the foe's active defense if you attack him with Attack, All-Out Attack, or Move and Attack on your next turn. If you and your foe *both* succeed, but you succeed by more, subtract your margin of victory from the foe's defense.

A Feint lasts *one* second. But if you Feint and then make an All-Out Attack (Double), the Feint applies to both attacks.

You can move one step while feinting and it allows any active defense. Allies cannot take advantage of your successful Feint.

Move

Move any number of yards up to your full Move score, but take no other action. Most other maneuvers allow at least some movement on your turn; take this maneuver if *all* you want to do is move.

During a Move, a character can defend themselves normally.

Move and Attack

Move as described for the Move maneuver, but during or after your move, make a single, poorly aimed attack – either unarmed or with a ready weapon.

You attack as described for the Attack maneuver, but at a penalty. If making a ranged attack, you have a penalty of -2 or the weapon's Bulk rating, whichever is *worse*. If you are making a melee attack, you have a flat -4 to skill, and your adjusted skill cannot exceed 9.

You can only dodge or block during this maneuver.

Ready

A *Ready* maneuver can be used to:

- Pick up or draw *any* item, prepare it for use, regain control of an unwieldy weapon after a swing, or adjust the reach of a long weapon.
- Complete physical actions other than fighting: opening or closing a door, picking a lock, etc.
- Switch an advantage "off" or "on" if it is not always on and does not require an Attack or Concentrate maneuver.

The combatant can both step and defend while taking a Ready.

Wait

Do nothing *unless* an event you specified in advance occurs before your next turn; e.g., a foe moves into range. If that happens, you may transform your Wait into an Attack, Feint, All-Out Attack (you must specify the option before acting), or Ready maneuver. You interrupt the turn sequence, but it resumes after you've acted.

Specify your action and its trigger when you take the Wait maneuver. You may Wait with a ready ranged weapon if you have specified the zone that you are covering.

RANGED ATTACKS

A "ranged attack" is any attack with a weapon used at a distance, from a thrown rock to a laser rifle to a specified spell.

Make a ranged attack on a target only if it falls within your weapon's *range*. To find this, see the relevant weapon table or advantage or spell description. Most ranged attacks list Half Damage (1/2D) range and Maximum (Max) range, in yards. Your target must be no farther away than Max range; 1/2D range only affects damage.

A few weapons have a *minimum* range, as they lob projectiles in a high arc, or have fusing or guidance limits.

Figure your adjusted chance to hit by:

1. Taking your base skill with your ranged weapon.

2. Adding your weapon's Accuracy (Acc) *if you preceded your attack with an Aim maneuver.*

3. Applying the target's Size Modifier (SM).

4. Modifying for the target's *range and speed* (done as a single modifier).

5. Modifying for circumstances (rapid fire, movement, darkness, cover, etc.), including any special conditions determined by the GM.

The result is your *effective skill*. A roll of this number or less is a successful attack roll (see below). It will hit, unless the target succeeds with an active defense.

ATTACKING

You attempt to hit a foe or other target by executing an Attack, All-Out Attack, or Move and Attack maneuver. You can only attack with a weapon if it's ready (see *Ready*, p. 325).

Two basic types of attacks exist: melee attacks and ranged attacks. Your target must be within reach to make a melee attack, or within range to make a ranged attack. Resolving either type of attack takes three die rolls:

- First is your *attack roll*. If your roll is successful, your attack was a good one.
- Now your foe must make a *defense roll* to see if he can defend against

your blow. If he makes this roll, he evaded or stopped the attack, and is not hit.

- If he misses his defense roll, your blow struck and you *roll for damage*.

Attack Roll

Your "attack roll" is a regular success roll (see Chapter 10, Book 2). Figure your *effective skill* (base skill plus or minus any appropriate modifiers) with the weapon you are using.

If your roll is *less than or equal to* your effective skill, your attack will hit unless your foe successfully defends (see *Defending*, below). If he fails to defend – or if he can't – you've hit him.

If your roll is *greater than* your effective skill, you missed!

No matter what your effective skill, a roll of 3 or 4 always hits, and is a *critical hit*. Depending on your effective skill, a roll of 5 or 6 may also be a critical hit. An attacker with an effective skill of 15 gets a critical hit on a roll of 5 or less; one with effective skill 16+ gets a critical hit on a roll of 6 or less.

On an attack roll of 3, you do not roll for damage – your blow automatically does the maximum damage. Other critical hits bypass the defense roll, but roll normally for damage.

A roll of 17 or 18 always misses.

DEFENDING

If your attack roll succeeds, you have not (yet) actually struck your foe, unless you rolled a critical hit. Your attack is *good enough* to hit him – *if he fails to defend*.

A fighter can use three *active defenses* to evade or ward off an attack: Dodge, Parry, and Block. These active defense scores should be calculated in advance and recorded on the character's sheet.

If a foe makes a successful attack roll, choose *one* active defense and attempt a "defense roll" against it. *Exception:* The All-Out Defense (Double Defense) maneuver lets you attempt a second defense against a particular attack if your first defense fails.

The active defense chosen depends on the situation – *especially* the maneuver chosen last turn. Some maneuvers restrict which active defenses can be made. No active defense is available if the PC is unaware of the attack. And active defenses don't apply to fighters who are unconscious, immobilized, or otherwise unable to react.

Active Defense Rolls

The defender rolls 3d against his active defense score. If his roll is *less than or equal to* his effective defense, he dodged, parried, or blocked the attack. Otherwise, his active defense was ineffective and the attack hit. If this occurs, roll for damage.

An active defense roll of 3 or 4 is *always* successful – even if the effective defense score was only 1 or 2! A roll of 17 or 18 always fails.

Dodging

A *Dodge* is an active attempt to move out of the perceived path of an attack. It is normally the *only* active defense you can take against firearms.

Your Dodge active defense is Basic Speed + 3, dropping all fractions, minus a penalty equal to your encumbrance level (see *Encumbrance and Move*, p. 17). List Dodge on your character sheet for quick reference.

You may dodge *any* attack except one that you did not know about! You only get one Dodge roll against a given attack.

If a single rapid-fire attack scores multiple hits, a successful Dodge roll lets you avoid one hit, plus additional hits equal to your margin of success. A critical success lets you dodge *all* hits you took from that attack.

Blocking

Blocking requires a *ready* shield or cloak. Your Block active defense is 3 + *half* your Shield or Cloak skill, dropping all fractions.

You can block any melee attack, thrown weapon, projected liquid, or muscle-powered missile weapon. You *cannot* block bullets or beam weapons . . . these come too fast to be stopped this way.

You may attempt to block only *one* attack per turn.

Parrying

Parry to deflect a blow using a weapon or your bare hands. You cannot parry unless your weapon is *ready*

– or, if unarmed, you have an empty hand.

You can use most melee weapons to parry. Some hefty weapons (e.g., axes) are *unbalanced:* you cannot use

Usually, you are still in the fight as long as you have positive HP.

them to parry if you've already used them to attack on your turn. (You can still parry with a weapon in your other hand, if you have one.) A few long, well-balanced weapons (e.g., the quarterstaff) get a +1 or +2 bonus to parry due to their ability to keep a foe at bay.

Your Parry active defense with a given weapon is 3 + *half* your skill with that weapon, dropping all fractions.

A parry won't stop anything except melee attacks or thrown weapons, unless you have special skills. *Exception:* If a foe attacks you with a

missile weapon *and* he is within reach of your melee weapon, you may parry. Success would mean that you slapped his bow or gun aside, causing him to fire wide of your body.

You can parry thrown weapons, but at a penalty: -1 for most thrown weapons, or -2 for *small* ones such as knives, shuriken, and other weapons that weigh 1 lb. or less.

If you successfully parry an unarmed attack (bite, punch, etc.) with a weapon, you may injure your attacker. Immediately roll against your skill with the weapon used to parry. If you succeed, your parry struck the attacker's limb squarely. He gets no defense roll against this! Roll damage normally.

DAMAGE AND INJURY

If your attack roll succeeds and your target fails his defense roll (if any), you may make a *damage roll*. This tells you how much *basic damage* you dealt to your target.

Your weapon (and, for muscle-powered weapons, your ST), or your natural or Innate Attack, determines the number of dice you roll for damage. If your target has any Damage Resistance (DR), he subtracts this from your damage roll.

If your damage roll is less than or equal to your target's effective DR, your attack *failed to penetrate* – it bounced off or was absorbed. If your damage roll *exceeds* your target's DR, the excess is the *penetrating damage*. If your foe has no DR, the entire damage roll is penetrating damage.

Your foe suffers injury (lost HP) equal to the penetrating damage for a crushing attack, 1.5× penetrating damage for a cutting attack, or 2× penetrating damage for an impaling attack. Other damage types exist, and have further effects.

General Damage

If injured, subtract the points of injury from your Hit Points. Usually, you are still in the fight as long as you have positive HP. The most important effects are:

● If you have *less than 1/3* of your HP remaining, you reel from your wounds. *Halve* your Move and Dodge (round up).

● If you have *zero or fewer* HP left, you hang onto consciousness through sheer willpower and adrenaline – or barely hold together, if you're a machine. You must roll vs. HT *each turn* to avoid falling unconscious.

● If you go to *fully negative* HP (for instance, -10 if you have 10 HP), you risk death! You must make an immediate HT roll to avoid dying. You must make *another* HT roll to avoid death each time you lose an extra multiple of your HP – that is, at -2×HP, -3×HP, and so on. If you reach -5×HP, you die *automatically*.

The *sudden* loss of HP can have additional effects:

Major Wounds: Any single injury that inflicts a wound in excess of 1/2 your HP is a *major wound*. For a major wound to the torso, you must make a HT roll. Failure means you're stunned or knocked out; failure by 5+ means you pass out.

Shock: Any injury that causes a loss of HP also causes "shock." Shock is a penalty to DX, IQ, and skills based on those attributes *on your next turn* (only). This is -1 per HP lost unless you have 20 or more HP, in which case it is -1 per (HP/10) lost, rounded down. The shock penalty cannot exceed -4 no matter how much injury you suffer.

Stunning: If you're stunned, you are -4 to active defenses, and must Do Nothing on your next turn. At the *end* of your turn, attempt a HT roll to recover. If you fail, you're still stunned and must Do Nothing for another turn. And so on.

RECOVERY

The *Damage* rules may seem harsh, but don't despair . . . you can get better!

Recovering from Unconsciousness

The GM decides whether you are *truly* unconscious or just totally incapacitated by pain and injury – but either way, you can't *do* anything. If unconscious, you recover as follows:

- If you have 1 or more HP remaining, you awaken automatically in 15 minutes.
- At 0 HP or worse, but above -1×HP, make a HT roll to awaken every hour. Once you succeed, you can act normally. You do not have to roll against HT every second to remain conscious unless you receive *new* injury. But since you are below 1/3 your HP, you are at half Move and Dodge.
- At -1×HP or below, you are in bad shape. You get a *single* HT roll to awaken after 12 hours. If you succeed, you regain consciousness and can act as described above. But if you fail, you won't regain consciousness without medical treatment. Until you receive help,

you must roll vs. HT every 12 hours; if you fail, you *die*.

Natural Recovery

Rest lets you recover lost HP, unless the damage is of a type that specifically does not heal naturally

(see *Illness, p. 442*). At the end of each day of rest and decent food, make a HT roll. On a success, you recover 1 HP. The GM may give a penalty if conditions are bad, or a bonus if conditions are very good.

FATIGUE

Fatigue represents lost energy and reduces FP, just as injury represents physical trauma and comes off of HP. Your Fatigue Points (FP) score starts out equal to your HT, but can be modified.

Lost Fatigue Points

The chart below summarizes the effects of being at low or negative FP. All effects are cumulative.

Less than 1/3 your FP left – You are very tired. Halve your Move, Dodge, and ST (round *up*). This does *not* affect ST-based quantities, such as HP and damage.

0 FP or less – You are on the verge of collapse. If you suffer further

fatigue, each FP you lose also causes 1 HP of injury. To do anything besides talk or rest, you must make a Will roll; in combat, roll before each maneuver other than Do Nothing. On a success, you can act normally. You can use FP to cast spells, etc., and if drowning, you can continue to struggle, but you suffer the usual 1 HP per FP lost. On a failure, you collapse, incapacitated, and can do *nothing* until you recover to positive FP.

-1×FP – You fall unconscious. While unconscious, you recover lost FP at the same rate as for normal rest. You awaken when you reach

positive FP. Your FP can *never* fall below this level. After this stage, any FP cost comes off your HP instead!

Recovering from Fatigue

You can recover "ordinary" lost FP by resting quietly. Reading, talking, and thinking are all right; walking around, or anything more strenuous, is *not*. Lost FP return at the rate of 1 FP per 10 minutes of rest. The GM may allow you to regain one extra FP if you eat a decent meal *while resting*. Certain drugs, magic potions, etc. can restore missing FP, as can spells such as Lend Energy and Recover Energy.

INDEX

This index covers both books of the *Basic Set*. The pages are sequentially numbered; Book 2 starts on p. 337.

With rare exceptions, *traits* (advantages, disadvantages, skills, spells, and so on) are *not* listed in this index. Instead, they have their own alphabetical listings. See the *Trait Lists* on pp. 297-306.

Acceleration, *see Gravity*.
Accents, 24.
Acid, 428.
Acrobatic dodge, 375.
Active Defense Modifiers Table, 548.
Active defenses, 326, 363, 374; *modifiers table*, 548.
Advantages, 32; *always on*, 34; *cinematic*, 33; *exotic*, 32, 34; *in templates*, 447; *magic*, 34; *mental*, 32; *mundane*, 32; *new*, 117-118; *learnable*, 294; *list*, 297; *physical*, 34; *potential*, 33; *Schrödinger's*, 33; *secret*, 33; *social*, 32; *switchable*, 34.
Adventures, *e23*, 494; *finale*, 503; *pre-packaged*, 495; *writing your own*, 500-504.
Adversary, 493.
Afflictions, 35, 416, 428.
Age, 20.
Aging, 53, 66, 95, 153, 154, 444.
Aim maneuver, 58, 324, 364.
Aimed fire, 372.
Air spells, 242.
Aircraft, 466; *table*, 465.
Alcohol, 122, 439-440.
Alien artifacts, 478.
Allies, 36; *ally groups*, 37.
All-Out Attack maneuver, 54, 324, 365, 385; *after being grappled*, 371.
All-Out Defense maneuver, 324, 366, 385.
Ally groups, 37.
Alternate worlds, 64, 160; *travel*, 189, 190; *Centrum*, 541-542, 545-546; *classes*, 526; *close parallels*, 526; *Coventry*, 540; *echoes*, 546; *hell parallels*, 528; *myth parallels*, 527; *Reich-5*, 543; *weird parallels*, 527; *world classes*, 535. *See also Crossworld Travel, Infinite Worlds Campaign*.

Alternative attacks, 61.
Always on; *advantages*, 34, *magic items*, 482.
Ammunition, 278.
Anarchy, 509.
Animals, 40, 87, 90, 137, 175, 187, 210, 211, 217, 223, 225, 226, 228, 395, 455-460; *in combat*, 461; *individualizing*, 457; *draft*, 459; *pets*, 458-459; *riding*, 459; *trained*, 458-459; *see also Mounted Combat*.
Apes, 455.
Appearance, 21.
Arc of vision, 389.
Area class, 176.
Area maps, 491.

Area spells, 239.
Area-effect attacks, 413; *scatter*, 414.
Arm lock, 370, 403.
Armor divisors, 378.
Armor, 110, 282-286; *changing posture in armor*, 395; *combining and layering*, 286; *flexible armor and blunt trauma*, 379; *wearing, donning, and removing*, 286.
Arrows, *flaming*, 410.
Artifacts, *anachronistic*, 478; *futuristic and alien*, 478, *magic*, 240, 480-483.
Artificial intelligences, 528.
Atmospheres, *hazardous*, 429; *vacuum*, 437.

Atmospheric pressure, 429.
Attack maneuver, 325, 365.
Attack roll, 369.
Attacks, 326, 369; *alternative*, 61; *after being grappled*, 371; *Deceptive Attack*, 369; *dual-weapon*, 417; *from above*, 402; *in tactical combat*, 388; *innate*, 61; *linked effects*, 381; *modified*, 114; *runaround*, 391; *surprise*, 393; *swarm*, 461; *without damage*, 381.
Attributes, see *Basic Attributes*.
Automatic weapons, 408.
Banestorms, 533.
Baron Janos Telkozep, *character sheet*, 320-321; *illustration*, 290.
Basic attributes, 14; *in templates*, 447; *improving*, 290.
Basic Lift, 15; *table*, 17.
Basic Move, 17.
Basic Speed, 17.
Basilisks, 460.
Bats, 461.
Battle maps, 239.
Battlesuits, 192.
Bears, 456.
Bees, 461.
Bends, the, 435.
Biotech tech levels, 512.
Bipods, 412.
BL, *see Basic Lift*.
Bleeding, 68, 420.
Block, 51, 324, 327; *in tactical combat*, 390.
Blocking spells, 241.
Blunt trauma, 379.
Boars, 458.
Body Control spells, 244.
Body modification, 294.
Bolas, 410.
Bounty hunters, 539.
Break Free, 370.
Breakdowns, 485.
Breaking a weapon, 401.
Breathing, 49, 55, 63, 68, 108; *holding your breath*, 351; *smothering a foe*, 401.
Build, 18.
Bulletproof nudity, 417.

C-31, *character sheet*, 307-309; *illustrations*, 264, 549.

Cabal, the, 543.

Camels, 459.

Campaigns, 486-489; *cinematic*, 488; *continuing*, 504; *planning form*, 567; *power level*, 10, 486; *shared campaigns*, 504; *travel between campaigns*, 504; *see also Game Worlds*.

Camping and survival gear, 288.

Cannon fodder, 417.

Caster (of spells), 236.

Catching things, 355.

Cats, 456.

Centrum, 541-542, 545-546.

Century scale damage, 470.

Ceremonial magic, 237.

Change Posture maneuver, 325, 364.

Character classes, *no such thing*, 259.

Character points, 10, 119, 258, 290; *awarding bonus points*, 498.

Characters, 7; *concept*, 11; *creation*, 9, 10, 258; *development*, 290, 499; *origins*, 33; *sheet*, 13, 335-336; *stories*, 12; *types*, 12.

Chi, 33, 93, 192, 214.

Children, 20.

Chimpanzees, 456.

Choke hold, 371, 404; *see also Suffocation*.

Cinematic *advantages*, 33; *campaigns*, 488; *characters*, 489; *combat*, 417; *explosions*, 417; *knockback*, 417.

Clerical *magic*, 77, 242; *spells*, 77.

Climbing, 89, 349.

Cloaks, 404.

Close combat, 391.

Clothing, 265.

Cold, 430.

Collisions, 430; *whiplash*, 432.

Coma, 429; *see also Unconsciousness*.

Combat Lite, 324.

Combat maps, 384, 492.

Combat, 9, 362-417; *at different levels*, 402; *cinematic*, 417; *maneuvers*, 324; *table of combat modifiers*, 547; *techniques*, 230; *turn sequence*, 324, 362; *vehicular*, 467-470.

Communication and Empathy spells, 245.

Communications and information gear, 288, 471.

Competence, 24.

Comprehension rolls, 359.

Computers, 48, 51, 55, 69, 71, 76, 100, 124, 184, 472; *artificial intelligence*, 528; *complexity*, 472; *software*, 472; *virtual reality worlds*, 520.

Concentrate maneuver, 325, 366.

Cone attacks, 413.

Conspiracies, *see Illuminati*.

Contacts, 31.

Contagion, 443; *see also Disease*.

Contests, 348; *quick*, 348; *regular*, 349; *resistance rolls*, 348.

Control Rating, 506; *see also Legality Class*.

Conventions of play, 9.

Copper, *see Wealth*.

Cosmic powers, 33.

Cost of living, 265, 516.

Coventry, 540.

Cover, 377, 407; *Cover DR Table*, 559.

Crippling, 59, 420-423.

Critical failure, *spells*, 236.

Critical Head Blow Table, 556.

Critical Hit Table, 556.

Critical hits, 381; *table*, 556.

Critical Miss Table, 556; *Unarmed Critical Miss Table*, 557.

Critical misses, 381; *table*, 556-557.

Critical success, 347; *on defense*, 381.

Crossbows, 410.

Crosstime bandits, 542.

Crossworld campaigns, 519-522; *see also Infinite Worlds Campaign*.

Crossworld travel, 514, 519-522; *Infinite Worlds campaign background*, 523-546; *instant wealth*, 514.

Crouching, 368.

Cultures, 23, 505-508.

Customizing rules, 486.

Dai Blackthorn, 12, 18, 22, 116, 162, 164, 227; *character sheet*, 310-311; *illustrations*, 32, 418.

Damage Resistance, 378; *HP and DR of Structures Table*, 558; *Cover DR Table*, 559.

Damage, 15, 327, 377; *by animals*, 461; *Damage Table*, 16; *damage rolls*, 9, 378; *scaling*, 470; *to objects*, 483-485.

Darkness, 47, 60, 71, 394; *spells*, 249; *torches*, 394.

David Pulver, 6.

Dead worlds, 527.

Dealing with players, 493.

Death, 296, 423; *dying actions*, 423; *instant death*, 423.

Decade scale damage, 470.

Deceptive attack, 369.

Deer, 457.

Defaults, 344; *double*, 173, 232; *skills*, 173; *techniques*, 229.

Defending, 326, 374; *in tactical combat*, 390.

Defenses, 46; *enhanced*, 51; *limited*, 46.

Dehydration, 426.

Demolition, 415.

Depressants, 441.

Design skills, 190.

Dexterity, 15.

Dice, 8, 9.

Digging, 350, 357.

Dimensional highways, 534.

Dirty tricks, 405.

Disadvantages, 11, 119; *buying off*, 121, 291; *disadvantage limit*, 11; *good*, 119; *exotic*, 120; *in templates*, 447; *list*, 299; *mental*, 120; *mundane*, 120; *new*, 162; *physical*, 120; *secret*, 120; *social*, 120; *self-imposed*, 121; *supernatural*, 120.

Disease, 442-444; *worldwide*, 528.

Dive for cover, 377, 407.

Divine origins; 33; *see also Gods*.

Dmg, *see Damage*.

Do Nothing maneuver, 325, 364.

Dodge, 17, 51, 324, 327, 374; *and drop*, 377.

Dogs, 457, 458.

Donkeys, 459.

Double defaults, *allowed for techniques*, 229; *not allowed for skills*, 173.

DR, *see Damage Resistance*.

Dragging things, 353.

Dragon template, 261.

Dropping prone, 374.

Drugs, 122, 130, 440; *Eraser*, 540; *overdose*, 441; *ultra-tech*, 425; *withdrawal*, 440.

Dual-weapon attacks, 417.

Dungeons, 501.

Dwarf template, 261.

DX, *see Dexterity*.

Dying actions, 423.

Earth spells, 245.

Echo timelines, 546.

Economics, 514.
Elbow strike, 404.
Elderly characters, 20;
    see also Age, Aging.
Electricity, 432-433.
Electronics, 471.
Elemental meta-traits, 262.
Elephants, 460; pink, 440.
Enchantment, 480-483; spells, 245.
Encounters, 502;
    sample encounter table, 503.
Encumbrance, 17.
Enhanced defenses, 51.
Enhancements, 101-102; limited, 111.
Equestrian gear, 289.
Equipment, 264-289;
    modifying success rolls, 345.
Eraser drug, 540.
Evading, 368.
Evaluate maneuver, 325, 364.
Exotic advantages, 32, 34.
Exotic disadvantages, 120.
Explosions, 414-415; cinematic, 417.
Extra effort, 356.
Facing (in combat), 385, 386.
Falcons, 457.
Falling, 430-431; damage
    from falling objects, 431.
Fallout, 435; see also Radiation.
Familiars, 38.
Fatigue, 16; 328, 426; fatigue
    points, 16; recovering, 427.
Feint maneuver, 325, 365.
Felinoid template, 261.
Fencing weapons, 404.
Fire, 61; burning things, 433, 434;
    damage, 433; flaming arrows, 410;
    incendiary weapons, 277, 411, 433;
    spells, 246; tight-beam burning
    attacks, 399.
Firearms, 278-281; accessories, 289,
    411; aim, 364; automatic, 408;
    bracing, 364; firing upward and
    downward, 407; malfunction, 382,
    407; quality, 280;
    rapid fire, 408; shotguns, 409;
    suppression fire, 409; ultra-tech,
    280.
Firing upward and downward, 407.
First aid, 424.
Flails, 405.
Flame, see Fire.
Flaming arrows, 410.
Flashlights, 394.
Flesh wounds, 417.
Flight, 56, 354; flying combat, 398.
Fnord, you're not cleared for that.
Follow-up damage, 381.

Food, 95, 139, 159, 160, 265;
    foraging, 427; starvation, 426.
FP, see Fatigue Points.
Fragmentation damage, 414.
Free actions, 363.
Friends and foes, 31.
Fright Checks, 55, 93, 95, 121, 360;
    Fright Check Table, 360-361.
Gadgeteering, see Gadgets.
Gadgets, 56-58, 473-477, 479;
    limitations, 116.
Game balance, 11.
Game Mastering, 486-504.
Game preparation, 490.
Game worlds, 505-522;
    economics, 514.
Garrotes, 405.
Gate spells, 247.
Gerbils, 113.
G-Increment, 350.
Glossary, 563-565; arms and armor,
    268; basic terms, 7; magic, 234;
    Infinite Worlds, 524; psionics, 254.
GM Control Sheet, 490, 568.
Gods, 33, 40, 59, 76, 113, 132, 143.
Gold, see Wealth.
Gorillas, 456.
Government types, 509-510;
    see also Laws.
Grabbing and grappling, 370; and hit
    location, 400.
Gravity, 60, 350, 434; different gravity,
    350; home gravity, 17.
Grenades, 277, 410.
Ground vehicles, 466; table, 464.
Gryphons, 460.
Guided weapons, 412.
Hallucinations, 429, 440.
Hallucinogens, 440.
Handedness, 14.
Harpoons, 411.
Healing, 59, 79, 80, 155,
    160, 162; magic, 248;
    medical gear, 289;
    medical tech levels,
    512; psychic, 256.
Health, 15.
Hearing, 49, 72, 89,
    94, 138. 358.
Heart attacks, 429.
Heat, 434; see also Fire.
Hell parallels, 528.
Heroic Knight template, 448.
Hexes, 384.
High-speed movement, 394.
Hiking, 351, 357, 426.
Hirelings, 517, 518.
Hit Location Tables, 552-555.

Hit location, 369, 398; and Injury
    Tolerance, 400; random, 400.
Hit points, 16, 418-419;
    HP and DR of Structures Table, 558;
    see also Injuries.
Home gravity, 17; see also Gravity.
Homing weapons, 412-413.
Horses, 459-460; equestrian gear, 289;
    see also Mounted Combat, Riding
    Animals, Weapons (Cavalry).
HP and DR of Structures Table, 558.
HP, see Hit Points.
HT (Health), 15.
I-Cops, 536-538.
Identities, 31, 39.
Illuminati, 60, 130, 193, 200, 525;
    the Cabal, 543.
Immunity, 443.
Importance in society, see Rank,
    Status.
Incompetence, 24.
Index, 329-334, 570-575.
Infection, 444.
Infinite ammunition, 417.
Infinite Worlds campaign
    background, 523-546.
Infinity Development, 536.
Infinity Patrol, 536-538.
Infinity Unlimited, 524, 535-538.
Influence rolls, 359.
Influence skills, 494.
Information spells, 241.
Initiative, 393.
Injuries, 327, 377, 380, 418-425;
    accumulated wounds, 420; and
        active defense, 374;
        bleeding, 420; crippling,
        420-423; flesh wounds, 417;
        large-area injury, 400; last
    wounds, 420; major wounds,
        420; mortal wounds, 423;
        shock, 419; to objects,
        483-485; to shields, 484;
    see also Crippling, Healing.
Instant death, 423.
Intelligence, 15; and dirty tricks, 405.
Intoxication, see Alcohol.
Introduction, 5, 342.
Investigator template, 259.
Iotha, character sheet, 316-317,
    illustrations, 343.
IQ (Intelligence), 15.
ISWAT, 162, 536.
Jobs, 292, 499, 516-518; finding, 518.
Jumping, 89, 203, 352, 357.
Knee strike, 404.
Knockback, 378.
Knowledge spells, 249.

Knowledge, *NPC*, 496;
player vs. character, 495.
Languages, 23, 205, 506.
Lariats, 411.
Lasers, 280, 399; *seeker heads*, 412;
sights, 412.
Last wounds, 420.
Law enforcement, 507;
police gear, 289.
Laws, 65, 204, 506-508, 518;
punishment, 508; *trials*, 507.
LC, see *Legality Class*.
Legality Class, 267, 270, 507;
legality of spells, 507.
Lethal strike, 404.
Lifting, 14, 15, 65, 205, 353, 357.
Light and Darkness spells, 249.
Limitations, 101, 110; *gadgets*, 116.
Limited defenses, 46.
Linked effects, 381.
Lions, 456.
Literacy, 24.
Long actions, 383.
Long tasks, 346, 499.
Louis d'Antares, *character sheet*,
312-313; *illustrations*, 368, 422, 505.
Loyalty, 518-519.
Luck, 83, 89, 160.
Ludography, 566.
Lycanthropy, *see Werewolves*.
Machine guns, 281.
Machines, 16; *Machine meta-trait*, 263.
Mage template, 260.
Magery, 66.
Magic Resistance, 67.
Magic, 66, 143, 144, 150, 218, 224,
225, 234-253; *advantages*, 34;
ceremonial, 237; *clerical*, 242;
colleges, 239; *enchanted objects*, 240,
480-483; *racial*, 453; *ritual*, 237,
242; *staffs*, 240.
Major wounds, 420.
Malf, *see Malfunction*.
Malfunction, 278, 382, 407.
Mana, 235.
Maneuvers, 324, 363, 385; *table*, 551.
Maps, 384, 490-491; *mapping by
players*, 491; *mapping for adventure
design*, 502.
Medical care, 424; *surgery*, 424.
Medical gear, 289.
Medicine tech levels, 512.
Melee Attack Modifiers Table, 547.
Melee etiquette, 417.
Melee spells, 240.
Mental *advantages*, 32; *disadvantages*,
120; *powers, see Psionics*.
Mental stun, 420.
Mentality meta-traits, 263.

Meta-Spells, 250.
Meta-traits, 262.
Metric conversions, 9.
Military, 218, 221, 222, 260.
Mind Control spells, 250.
Mind reading, *see Telepathy*.
Mind transfer, 296.
Miniature figures, 383.
Miracle Workers Inc., 538.
Missile spells, 240.
Missile weapon attacks, 373.
Modifiers (to traits), 101; *list*, 300.
Molotov cocktails, 411.
Money, *see Wealth*.
Monsters, 460-461.
Morphology meta-traits, 263.
Mortal *conditions*, 429; *wounds*, 423.

Mounted combat, 395-398.
Move (character stat), 52.
Move and Attack maneuver, 325, 365,
385.
Move maneuver, 325, 364, 385.
Movement and combat, 367;
and facing, 386; *high-speed
movement*, 394; *movement in
tactical combat*, 386.
Movement points, 386, 387.
Movement spells, 251.
Mules, 459.
Multi-hex figures, 392.
Mundane *advantages*, 32;
disadvantages, 120.
Mutations, 33.
Neck Snap attack, 370, 404.
Necromantic spells, 251.
Nets, 411.
New disadvantages, 162.
New inventions, 473, 475;
see also Gadgets.
Nexus portals, 534.
Nonhumans, 32.
Non-player characters, *see NPCs*.
NPC Reactions Table, 559-562.
NPC Record Card, 569.

NPCs, 31, 493; *NPC Reactions Table*,
559-562; *NPC Record Card*, 569.
Oil flasks, 411.
Omens, 72.
Online gaming, 494.
Optics and sensors, 289.
Origins of characters, 33.
Overpenetration, 379, 408.
Overrun, *by multi-hex figures*, 392.
Oxen, 460.
Parachronic Laboratories Inc., 538.
Parachronics, *bogus scientific
explanation*, 530; *conveyor*, 529;
detector, 532; *disasters*, 532; *minor
accidents*, 531; *paradoxes*, 533;
projector; 524, 530; *see also
Infinite Worlds Campaign*.
Parachronozoids, 544.

Parallel worlds, *see Alternate Worlds*.
Paralysis, 429.
Parry, 51, 93, 324, 327, 376; *unarmed*,
376; *in tactical combat*, 390.
Patient status, 421.
Patrons, 72-73.
Penetrating damage, 379.
Penetration modifiers, 378, 416;
overpenetration, 379, 408.
Per, *see Perception*.
Perception, 16.
Perks, 100.
Pets, 458-459; *see also Animals*.
Physical *advantages*, 32;
disadvantages, 120.
Physical feats, 349; *extra effort*, 356.
Picking things up, 383.
Picks, 405.
Pinning (in combat), 370.
Planet types, 180.
Plants, 75, 87, 90, 142, 197, 199, 211.
Pocket multiverses, 529.
Poison, 62, 437-439; *treatment*, 439.
Police gear, 289.
Pop-up attacks, 390.
Postures, 367; *changing posture
in armor*, 395; *table*, 551.

Potential advantages, 33.
Power level for campaigns, 10, 486.
Power tech levels, 512.
Preparing for play, 490.
Prerequisites, *skills*, 169; *spells*, 235; *techniques*, 229.
Pressure, *atmospheric*, 429, 435; *the bends*, 435; *water*, 435.
Privilege, 30.
Professor William Headley, *character sheet*, 314-315; *illustrations*, 234, 486.
Protection and Warning spells, 252.
Psi powers, *see Psionics*.
Psionics, 71, 78, 150, 254-257; *Antipsi*, 255; *ESP*, 255; *learning*, 294; *new powers*, 257; *pside effects*, 255; *Psychic Healing*, 256; *Psychokinesis*, 256; *Telepathy*, 257; *Teleportation*, 257.
Psychological warfare, 359.
Pulling things, 353.
Punishment, *legal*, 508.
Pyramid Magazine, 494.
Quick contests, 348.
Quick learning under pressure, 292.
Quick Start rules, 8.
Quirks, 162; *racial*, 452.
Radiation, 80, 105, 192, 435.
Ranged attacks, 327, 372; *half damage range*, 378; *hitting the wrong target*, 389; *modifiers table*, 548; *opportunity fire*, 390; *overshooting*, 390; *pop-up attacks*, 390; *shooting blind*, 389.
Ranged Combat Modifiers Table, 548.
Rank, 29.
Rapid fire, 373, 408.
Rapid Strike, 54, 93, 370.
Rate of Fire, 270, 373.
Rats, 461.
Rattlesnakes, 458.
Rcl, *see Recoil*.
Reaction rolls, 8, 494-495, *NPC Reactions Table*, 559-562.
Reading, 134; *see also Literacy*.
Ready maneuver, 325, 366, 382, 385.
Ready weapons, 369; *readying*, 382.
Realism, 11.
Reality Liberation Force, 543.
Reality quakes, 534.
Recoil, 271.
Recovery, 328; *see also Healing*.
Recovery, 423-424; *from unconsciousness*, 423.
Regular spells, 239.
Reich-5, 543.
Religion, 30, 226; *see also Gods*.
Reloading missile weapons, 373.

Repair skills, 190; *repairing things*, 484.
Reputation, 27.
Resisted spells, 241.
Resuscitation, 425.
Retreat (in active defense), 377.
Retreating, 391.
Ritual magic, 237, 242.
Roads, 351.
RoF (Rate of Fire), 270, 373.
Roleplaying, 7.
Rolling to hit, 369.
Room maps, 492.
Rounding, 9.
Rule of 14, 360.
Rule of 16, 349.
Rule of 20, 173, 344.
Rules, *customizing*, 486; *questions*, 492.
Runaround attacks, 391.
Runes, 224.
Running, 354, 357; *fatigue*, 426.
Sacrificial dodge, 375.
Sapience, 15, 23.
Scopes, 412.
Sean Punch, 6.
Seasickness, 436.
Secondary characteristics, 15; *improving*, 290; *in templates*, 447.
Secret disadvantages, 120.
Secret identities, 31.
Self-control, 120.
Senses, 35, 78; *sense rolls*, 358.
Sensors, 471.
Sentience, 15.
Sharks, 457.
Shields, 287, 374; *damage*, 484; *in close combat*, 392; *offensive use*, 406.
Shiftrealms, 534.
Shock, *electrical*, 432-433; *from injury*, 419.
Shooting blind, 389.
Shotguns, 409.
Shove, 372.
Sign language, 25.
Silencers, 412.
Silver, *see Wealth*.
Size and Speed/Range Table, 550.
Size Modifier, 19, 372; *and reach*, 402.
Skills, 167, 174-233; *buying*, 170; *defaults*, 170; *design*, 190; *difficulty level*, 168; *familiarity*, 169; *improving*, 170, 292; *in templates*, 447; *influence*, 495; *levels*, 171; *list*, 301; *maintaining*, 294; *physiology modifiers*, 181; *prerequisites*, 169; *racially learned*, 453; *repair*, 190; *scope*, 176;

specialties, 169; *studying*, 292, 499; *teachers*, 293; *technological*, 168; *wildcard*, 175.
Slam, 371; *by multi-hex figures*, 392.
Slaves, 518.
Sleep, 50, 65, 136, 140, 142, 154, 155; *drowsy*, 428; *missed sleep*, 426.
SM, *see Size Modifier*.
Smartguns, 278.
Smell, 49, 243.
Snakes, 458; *cobra venom*, 439; *pythons*, 458; *rattlesnakes*, 458.
Social advantages, 32; *adding and improving*, 291.
Social background, 22.
Social disadvantages, 120.
Social restraints, 30.
Society types, 509-510.
Soldier of Fortune template, 260.
Sora, *character sheet*, 318-319; *illustrations*, 10, 258, 356, 362, 375, 402.
Sounds, *see Hearing*.
Space sickness, 434.
Spacecraft, 466; *table*, 465.
Spacing (in combat), 368.
Special spells, 241.
Speed/Range Table, 550.
Spells, 66; *Air*, 242; *area*, 239; *backfire*, 235; *blocking*, 241; *Body Control*, 244; *caster*, 236; *casting*, 235-238; *clerical*, 77; *Communication and Empathy*, 245; *Earth*, 245; *Enchantment*, 246, 480-482; *Fire*, 246; *Gate*, 247; *Healing*, 248; *information*, 241; *Knowledge*, 249; *legality*, 507; *Light and Darkness*, 249; *Meta-Spells*, 250; *melee*, 240; *Mind Control*, 250; *missile*, 240; *Movement*, 251; *list*, 304; *Necromantic*, 251; *prerequisites*, 235; *Protection and Warning*, 252; *regular*, 239; *resisted*, 241; *special*, 242; *subject*, 236; *Water*, 253; *see also Magic*.
Spirits, 41, 55, 68, 76, 113, 193, 200, 212; *spirit advantages*, 34; *Spirit meta-trait*, 263.
Spy gear, 289.
ST, *see Strength*.
Staffs, 240.
Starvation, 426.
Status, 28, 265, 516.
Step (in maneuvers), 368, 386.
Steve Jackson, 6.
Stimulants, 440.
Strangle, 370, 401, 404.
Strength, 14.
Striges, 461.
Striking at weapons, 400.

Structural Damage Table, 558.
Study, 292.
Stunning, 35; *mental stun*, 420.
Subduing a foe, 401.
Subject (of spells), 236.
Success rolls, 342; *buying success*, 347; *critical failure*, 348; *critical success*, 347; *difficulty*, 345; *equipment modifiers*, 345; *influencing rolls*, 347; *player guidance*, 347; *repeated attempts*, 348.
Success rolls, 8.
Suffocation, 428, 436.
Sunburn, 434.
Supernatural *advantages*, 32, 33, 34; *disadvantages*, 120.
Supers, 34.
Superscience, 513.
Suppression fire, 409.
Surprise attacks, 393.
Swarm attacks, 461.
Swimming, 354, 357; *fatigue*, 426.
Swinging damage, 15.
Switchable advantages, 34.
Table talk, 493.
Taboo traits, 261.
Takedown, 370.
Taste and smell, 49, 358.
Tech level, *see Technology Levels*.
Techniques, 229; *combat*, 230; *improving*, 292; *list*, 304.

Technological skills, 168.
Technology Levels, 22, 99, 267, 291, 511-512; *and equipment*, 27; *and genre*, 514; *and starting wealth*, 27; *divergent*, 513; *superscience*, 513; *table of TLs by field*, 512.
Teeth, 91.
Telepathy, 69-71, 91, 210, 245.
Temperature, 9.
Templates, 258, 445-454; *cultural*, 446; *dramatic*, 446; *occupational*, 446; *racial*, 260, 450-454.
Terrain, 351.
Thief and spy gear, 289.
Throwing things, 355, 357.
Thrown weapon attacks, 373.
Thrusting damage, 15.
Tigers, 456.
Time Tours, Ltd., 539.
Time travel, 64, 93, 158, 189, 190.
Time Use Sheets, 499, 569.
Time, *between adventures*, 498; *between sessions*, 497; *during adventures*, 497.
Timeline shifts, 544-546.
TL, *see Technology Level*.
To-hit roll, 326, 369.
Tools, 289.
Torches, 394.
Tragic flaws, 119.
Trait lists, 297.
Traits, *meta-traits*, 262; *taboo traits*, 26; *see also Character Creation*.
Trampling, 404.
Transformations, 294.
Transportation tech levels, 512.
Traps, 502.
Travel maps, 491.
Trials, 507; *punishment*, 508.
Tripods, 412.
Tunnels, 94.
Turning radius, 394.
TV action violence, 417.
Unarmed combat, 370; *hurting yourself*, 379; *parrying*, 376.
Unarmed Critical Miss Table, 557.
Unconsciousness, 419, 423, 429; *recovery from*, 329.
Undead, 50; *see also Vampires, Zombies*.
United Nations, 535, 538.
Utopia, 510.
Vacuum, 437.
Vampires, 137, 212; *see also Baron Janos Telkozep*.
Vehicle Hit Location Table, 554.
Vehicle Occupant Hit Location Table, 555.

Vehicles, 188, 214, 223, 462-470; *aircraft*, 465; *breakdowns*, 485; *combat*, 467-470; *control rolls*, 466; *damage*, 555; *ground vehicles*, 464; *hit location*, 400, 554; *movement*, 463; *spacecraft*, 465; *vehicular dodge*, 375; *watercraft*, 464.
Virtual realities, 520.
Visibility, 394; *see also Darkness*.
Vision, 92, 123, 124, 144, 151, 358.
Voice, 132.
Wait maneuver, 325, 366, 385.
Warehouse 23 online store, 494.
Warhorses, *see Horses*.
Warrior template, 449.
Water spells, 253.
Watercraft, 466; *table*, 464.
Wealth, 25, 26, 264, 517; *and Status*, 26, 516; *cost of living*, 265, 516; *economics*, 514; *gold and silver*, 515; *improving character wealth level*, 291; *moving money between worlds*, 514.
Weapon and armor tech levels, 512.
Weapons, 267-281; *accessories*, 289, 411; *accuracy*, 269; *ammunition*, 278; *breaking*, 401, 485; *bulk*, 270; *carrying*, 287; *cavalry*, 397; *cost*, 270; *fencing*, 404; *firearms*, 278-281; *grenades*, 277; *heavy*, 281; *incendiaries*, 277; *infinite cinematic ammunition*, 417; *Legality Class*, 271; *malfunction*, 278, 407; *melee*, 271-275; *missiles*, 281; *parry*, 269; *range*, 269; *ranged*, 275-277, 278-281; *rate of fire*, 270; *reach*, 269; *reach and Size Modifier*, 388, 402; *recoil*, 271; *shots*, 270; *smartguns*, 278; *strength*, 270; *striking at weapons*, 400; *thrown*, 356; *weight*, 270.
Weather, 243, 351.
Weirdness, 161; *weird parallel worlds*, 527; *weird science*, 228, 479.
Werewolves, 83, 84, 137.
Whiplash, 432.
Whips, 406.
White Star Trading, 524, 539.
Wild swings, 388.
Wildcard skills, 175.
Will, 16; *Will rolls*, 360.
Wolves, 458.
World-jumpers, 544.
Wounding modifier, 379.
Wounds, *see Injuries*.
Wrench Limb attack, 370, 404.
Xing La, *character sheet*, 322-323; *illustrations*, 167, 188, 418, 445.
Zombies, 74, 94, 252, 380.

GURPS

CHARACTER SHEET

Name _____ Player _____ Point Total _____

Ht _____ Wt _____ Size Modifier _____ Age _____ Unspent Pts _____

Appearance _____

ST [____] [ ] **HP** [____] CURRENT [____] [ ]

DX [____] [ ] **WILL** [____] [ ]

IQ [____] [ ] **PER** [____] [ ]

HT [____] [ ] **FP** [____] CURRENT [____] [ ]

BASIC LIFT (ST × ST)/5 _____ DAMAGE Thr _____ Sw _____

BASIC SPEED _____ [ ] BASIC MOVE _____ [ ]

Languages | Spoken | Written

		[ ]
		[ ]
		[ ]
		[ ]
		[ ]

DR

TL: [ ]

Cultural Familiarities

[ ]

[ ]

[ ]

PARRY

BLOCK

Reaction Modifiers

Appearance _____

Status _____

Reputation _____

ENCUMBRANCE | MOVE | DODGE

None (0) = BL	_____	BM × 1	_____	Dodge	_____
Light (1) = 2 × BL	_____	BM × 0.8	_____	Dodge -1	_____
Medium (2) = 3 × BL	_____	BM × 0.6	_____	Dodge -2	_____
Heavy (3) = 6 × BL	_____	BM × 0.4	_____	Dodge -3	_____
X-Heavy (4) = 10 × BL	_____	BM × 0.2	_____	Dodge -4	_____

ADVANTAGES AND PERKS

_____ [ ]
_____ [ ]
_____ [ ]
_____ [ ]
_____ [ ]
_____ [ ]
_____ [ ]
_____ [ ]
_____ [ ]
_____ [ ]
_____ [ ]
_____ [ ]

DISADVANTAGES AND QUIRKS

_____ [ ]
_____ [ ]
_____ [ ]
_____ [ ]
_____ [ ]
_____ [ ]
_____ [ ]
_____ [ ]
_____ [ ]
_____ [ ]
_____ [ ]
_____ [ ]
_____ [ ]
_____ [ ]
_____ [ ]
_____ [ ]
_____ [ ]

SKILLS

Name | Level | Relative Level

_____ [ ]
_____ [ ]
_____ [ ]
_____ [ ]
_____ [ ]
_____ [ ]
_____ [ ]
_____ [ ]
_____ [ ]
_____ [ ]
_____ [ ]
_____ [ ]
_____ [ ]
_____ [ ]
_____ [ ]
_____ [ ]
_____ [ ]
_____ [ ]
_____ [ ]
_____ [ ]
_____ [ ]
_____ [ ]
_____ [ ]
_____ [ ]
_____ [ ]
_____ [ ]